FOOD MARKETING

AN INTERNATIONAL PERSPECTIVE

FOOD MARKETING

AN INTERNATIONAL PERSPECTIVE

David J. Schaffner
California Polytechnic State University

William R. Schroder
Monash University, Australia

Mary D. Earle
Massey University, New Zealand

Boston, Massachusetts   Burr Ridge, Illinois   Dubuque, Iowa
Madison, Wisconsin   New York, New York   San Francisco, California   St. Louis, Missouri

WCB/McGraw-Hill

*A Division of The **McGraw·Hill** Companies*

Sponsoring Editors: *Anne Duffy* and *Lynne Meyers.*
Cover Designer: *Chris Brady.*
Design Manager: *Joan O'Connor.*
Production supervisor: *Kathryn Porzio.*
Compositor: *Graphic World Incorporated.*
Project supervision: *Tage Publishing Service, Inc.*
Printer: *R. R. Donnelley & Sons Company.*

FOOD MARKETING

An International Perspective

1 2 3 4 5 6 7 8 9 0   DOC DOC   9 0 9 8 7

ISBN 0-07-057206-2

http://www.mhhe.com

ABOUT THE AUTHORS

David J. Schaffner is a professor in the Agribusiness Department, California Polytechnic State University, San Luis Obispo. In the past twenty-five years, he has taught agricultural and food marketing courses to over 5,000 students, in both the undergraduate and Agribusiness MBA programs. He has also been a visiting professor at the Institute of Agribusiness, Santa Clara University, and at Massey University, New Zealand.

Within the marketing area, Professor Schaffner specializes in futures, options, and their use in price risk management. He has taught executive short courses on the futures market in Australia and serves as an arbitrator for the National Futures Association. Also interested in agricultural cooperatives, he has authored publications for the Center for Cooperatives, University of California, Davis.

William R. Schroder is Head of the David Syme School of Business—Peninsula, Monash University, Melbourne, Australia. His Ph.D. is from Purdue University. He has taught and conducted research in agribusiness and food marketing since 1980, before which he worked for a major agribusiness company in New Zealand.

Dr. Schroder has over 70 publications relating to agribusiness and food marketing. His current research interests are in the areas of business-to-business linkages in food marketing and government/agribusiness relationships. Dr. Schroder was the Foundation Co-Editor of the *Australasian Agribusiness Review* and is co-editor of a recent book on food industry/government relationships.

Mary D. Earle is Professor Emeritus of the Faculty of Technology, at Massey University, Palmerston North, New Zealand. At Massey University, she introduced courses in food marketing and product development in the food technology degree and eventually organized the first four-year degree in product development in New Zealand. She also helped to introduce food technology and product development degrees in five universities in Thailand.

Professor Earle was a pioneer in product development, in both university and industry. Over the last thirty years, she has organized many workshops and seminars on food marketing and product development in New Zealand, Australia, Southeast Asia, Canada, and Denmark. Her involvement with the New Zealand food industry has included over three hundred student product development projects with many different companies, food industry consultancies, and the development of the Food Technology Research Centre, which aids the food companies' product development projects.

CONTENTS
IN BRIEF

CONTENTS

PREFACE

Food is eaten daily by everyone in the world. Food marketing is the system by which foods reach individuals—attractive, safe, and nutritional products that meet their needs.

Food products are biological materials from the land and sea and are needed for the nutrition and health of consumers. From initial production to final consumption, the food system is a biological system. However, consumers need food products not only for their nutritional benefits, but also for the enjoyment and pleasure such products give. Therefore, there are two important parts of food marketing—the food system and the consumer.

THE CONSUMER

Food Marketing: An International Perspective focuses on the consumer as the driving force of the food marketing system. People's eating habits and preferences vary from country to country, culture to culture, and social group to social group. Individuals' eating habits and preferences are influenced by age, sex, education, economic status, health, and psychological needs. But food-consumption patterns in different countries are becoming more similar, and some food products are marketed in many countries. Gradually, food products from ethnic groups are being adapted to gain global appeal; also, new products are designed to be acceptable to many different groups of consumers.

In this book, consumers and their needs, attitudes, and behavior toward foods are studied in some detail. It is the increasingly sophisticated and internationally oriented consumer who is the ultimate arbiter of every facet of the food system, from the design of a genetically engineered tomato to the layout of a supermarket.

THE FOOD SYSTEM

Food production has evolved from primitive subsistence activity to the complex global industry we enjoy today. Consumers still may raise their own food or purchase directly from the grower. However, for most foods the process of transforming raw materials into consumer products, available when and where they are wanted by buyers, is more complex. It has become important for food manufacturers and distributors to control aspects of agricultural production in order to provide food products of the right quality, at the right time, place, and price.

Management of the food system from farm or sea to consumer is essential to food marketing, because if the product does not move through the system efficiently, the end result may be a product that is of poor quality, too expensive, or too late. Food products are biological and change through natural biological processes. Perishable products must be moved quickly or preserved to maintain safety and prevent deterioration. The market system, particularly storage and physical distribution, has to be organized around these characteristics.

Coordination of food marketing activities can be through the "invisible hand" of the market or by one organization that controls several stages of the food system. Large food companies now have greater control over agricultural production, either through contracts or by actual ownership. For example, tomatoes and potatoes are grown to processor specifications through contracts. In the poultry industry, almost all eggs and meat are produced either on company-owned farms or on contract with producers. These companies recognize that although price is a primary consumer consideration, product variety and quality have become increasingly important. Along with satisfying quality and value needs, today's food system must respond to consumers' environmental and social concerns.

The main organizations and companies in the food marketing system are agricultural and marine producers, primary and secondary processors, food manufacturers, and wholesalers-retailers. Related organizations, such as packaging companies, chemical companies, agents, merchants, and transport and storage companies also help move products through the system. Marketing occurs at every stage as food products are processed and manufactured, until the products reach the final consumer. Commodity marketing is concerned with the agricultural products that are the raw materials of the food system; industrial marketing involves tailoring agricultural products and other ingredients to the requirements of food manufacturers and the food service industry; reseller marketing focuses on selling to wholesalers and retailers; and consumer marketing is concerned with marketing branded food products to end consumers.

Food marketers deal with ingredients that may be gathered from and processed in several countries, with final products sold in local or export markets, or both. The multiplicity of paths taken by different food products makes food marketing both international and complex.

PHILOSOPHY OF THIS BOOK

Food Marketing: An International Perspective differs from most textbooks in agricultural marketing because it emphasizes the consumer, recognizes the different approaches to marketing at different stages in the food system, and reflects the system's trend toward globalization. This text's international scope encourages students to look beyond their national boundaries. As well as applying economic and functional concepts to the study of the food system as a whole, *Food Marketing: An International Perspective* emphasizes the management of food marketing and distribution. It is designed to allow students to approach food marketing from a managerial perspective early in their education.

This text also differs from most general marketing books in that food marketing requires technical knowledge of the food system, as well as in-depth knowledge of the consumer-product relationship. In *Food Marketing: An International Perspective,* the connection between the technical and marketing activities of the food industry is stressed. It applies marketing management concepts to each stage of the food system—agricultural and marine production, first-stage processing, food manufacturing, food distribution, and the food service industry. The environments in which the food system works—physical, economic, social, ethical, and legal—are also addressed.

Food Marketing: An International Perspective aims to develop:

- an understanding of the food consumers' needs (nutrition, safety, sensory, and social needs) in different cultures and societies
- the ability to analyze the complex system required to supply food products to the final consumer
- knowledge of the economic, political, social, and environmental factors that affect the food system
- an understanding of food marketing systems from a global perspective, recognizing the importance of issues such as trade policy, food security, nutrition, and environmental issues
- a focus on food marketing from a managerial viewpoint, whereby all members of the food system recognize that they are not only dealing with their immediate customers; they also need to understand the management decisions facing their customers' customers, down to the final consumer.

The textbook material is divided into five parts:

  I. Introduction to the Food System
 II. Consumers
III. The Food System
IV. Commodity Marketing Management
 V. Branded Product Marketing Management

Parts I, II, and III are concerned with the basic components of food marketing—the consumer and the system, whereas Parts IV and V address the management of the two main groups of products—commodities and branded products. The marketing of industrial food products, those partly processed raw materials that are used by food manufacturers, is specifically addressed in Part III, Chapter 7. Branded-product marketing management theory and techniques also apply to the marketing of industrial food products, an important but often neglected sector of the food system.

To encourage student interaction, "Think Breaks" scattered throughout the chapters ask the readers to stop and use their new knowledge. Information for the Think Breaks comes from the text itself and from observation of food marketing activities in places as diverse as the futures-market pit and the supermarket shelf. The instructor could encourage students to take part in the Think Breaks by using them as in-class discussions or as assignments. Food marketing is ever-changing and these Think Breaks can show the students the changes taking place.

An introductory level text, this book is written for sophomore or junior students in agricultural business, agricultural economics, food engineering, food science, and general business. It is preferable, but not essential that students have completed a course in agricultural economics, or another microeconomics course, and an introductory course in general marketing. Although primarily a textbook, *Food Marketing: An International Perspective* is also a useful reference for people in industry who are moving into food marketing from technical positions or from other product marketing sectors.

ACKNOWLEDGMENTS

Food Marketing: An International Perspective began its journey in July 1993, when the authors met at Monash University, Australia, to discuss the idea of writing such a book, and its enveloping philosophy, direction, and content. Since that initial meeting, this book has undergone many revisions, and we have incorporated suggestions from the following reviewers, to whom we are grateful: Peter Barry, University of Illinois; Juan Batista, Mississippi State University; Cynda Clary, New Mexico State University; James Epperson, University of Georgia; Gary Fairchild, University of Florida; Charles Hall, Texas A&M; Arne Hallam, Iowa State University; Kevin McNew, University of Maryland; Joe Outlaw, Texas A&M; Nigel Poole, University of London; Wayne Purcell, Virginia Tech; Steve Turner, University of Georgia; and C. Thomas Worley, Washington State University.

Mary Earle would like to acknowledge the cooperation of Dr. Allan Anderson and of Dr. Juliet Wiseman in the course on food marketing at Massey University, on which the consumer material is based. Bill Schroder appreciates the contributions of two research assistants, Nicole Isaac-Griggs and Amelia Kelly; David Schaffner thanks research assistant Cindy Gray.

Throughout the writing of the book, Anne Duffy, Agricultural Editor at McGraw-Hill, has been most supportive and helpful in taking the authors' vision to reality. A special mention and thanks must be given to Paula Schaffner, who provided the word processing and "in-house" editing expertise in preparing the manuscript. It is fair to say that *Food Marketing: An International Perspective* would not have been completed without her tireless efforts. As for errors and omissions, the authors take responsibility for them, individually and collectively; it is hoped that they are few in number.

David J. Schaffner

William R. Schroder

Mary D. Earle

FOOD
MARKETING
AN INTERNATIONAL
PERSPECTIVE

INTRODUCTION TO
THE FOOD SYSTEM

An overview of the Food System and the types of food marketing—commodity, industrial, and consumer

| **CHAPTER 1** Dimensions of Food Marketing |
| **CHAPTER 2** Economics of the Food System |

The modern Food System is complex, dynamic, and international. The Marketing Concept states that what the customer wants influences every aspect of the Food System. Food marketing is a fascinating activity, moving food materials and food products throughout the world to the final consumer. We hope you will enjoy studying it.

Chapter 1 describes the global food industry and the food marketing activities in it, as well as the different ways food marketing can be studied. Chapter 2 studies the economic interplay between supply and demand in the Food System. Consumers' demand for food depends on their needs, preferences, and income. Supply from the farm and the sea is affected by many factors, including the weather. In market economies, prices respond to both supply and demand.

1

1

DIMENSIONS OF FOOD MARKETING

CHAPTER OUTLINE

LEARNING OBJECTIVES

After reading this chapter and answering the questions in the Think Breaks and at the end of the chapter, you should be able to:

- Understand that there is a total food system from farm/sea to the consumer's plate, and see the place of food marketing in this system.
- Appreciate the increasingly global nature of the food system.
- Understand how food marketing is similar to but has different features from marketing in general.
- Relate the Marketing Concept to your own experiences as a consumer.
- Recognize why acceptance of the Marketing Concept by companies and organizations is necessary for food marketing success.
- Place the food system in its historical context, appreciating that what exists today has its roots in early civilization but is constantly changing.
- Be able to differentiate the four methods of studying marketing: Institutional, Functional, Types of Customer and Product, and Marketing Management.
- Understand that although production agriculture, fishing, and primary processing are a smaller part of the total economy than they were 100 years ago, employment and career opportunities in the food system are growing.

INTRODUCTION

The following news items may not make front-page headlines, but they are important to decision makers in the world of food. Such news is not out of the ordinary, because the food system is dynamic and changing:

- Budweiser, one of America's most popular beers, is also the second most popular beer in Ireland. It's most popular with younger drinkers, who prefer a milder flavor than their elders do.

- In 1994, in response to frosts in Brazil that sharply reduce production, coffee prices skyrocket from 85 cents a pound to $2.35, and then, in 1995, fall to $1.35.
- Salsa replaces catsup as America's number-one condiment. Campbell Soup Co. pays $1.1 billion for Pace, the leading producer of Mexican sauces.
- India's Godrej Foods discusses alliances with three food giants: ConAgra, H. J. Heinz, and Grand Metropolitan, PLC (U.K.). The company's chairman, Mr. Adi B. Godrej, remarks: "We must have an international tie-up because we won't be able to compete in the market without it."[1]
- J. R. Simplot, the Idaho-based potato and vegetable processor, buys the Australian Edgell-Birds Eye canned and frozen food operations as "a base for expansion into Asia, focusing on China, Malaysia, Japan, and South Korea."[2]

These news items underscore four important themes in food marketing—the effect of raw-materials supply on prices and, therefore, on demand for final products; the importance of the consumer in food marketing; the food system's complexity, and its global nature. Setting the foundation for all discussions of marketing are the economic principles underlying marketing activities, briefly explained in Chapter 2 of **Part One, Introduction to the Food System.**

A major theme is that the food system is consumer driven, even in the sale of a bulk raw material (commodity), such as wheat or soybeans. Thus, the study of consumer needs, attitudes, behavior, and concerns is positioned early in the book, in **Part Two, Consumers.**

Part Three, Food Marketing System, describes the many participants in the food system: producers, processors, manufacturers, distributors, and retailers. Recognizing the various ways in which these participants are linked and the issues which arise as these linkages cross national boundaries is vital to an understanding of the food marketing system.

Commodity raw materials for the food system are subject to tremendous fluctuations in price, as demonstrated by coffee's threefold price increase in 1994. How producers, processors, exporters, and other handlers of commodities deal with this price risk is discussed in **Part Four, Commodity Marketing Management,** along with other commodity marketing issues.

Finally, **Part Five, Branded Product Marketing Management,** describes the functions and strategies used to market branded products, thousands of which are introduced into the food system each year.

All parts of *Food Marketing: An International Perspective* approach the theory and practice of marketing from the viewpoint that the world, if not borderless to the food marketer, is moving toward that condition.

THE FOOD SYSTEM IN THE GLOBAL ENVIRONMENT

The global *food system* can be thought of as consisting of three dimensions, as illustrated by Figure 1-1. The vertical dimension represents stages in the food

---

[1]"India's Godrej Foods Discussing Alliances with 3 Big Companies," *Wall Street Journal,* December 2, 1994: A7E.
[2]"Pacific Dunlop Sells Majority of Food Unit," *Wall Street Journal,* August 4, 1995: B5A.

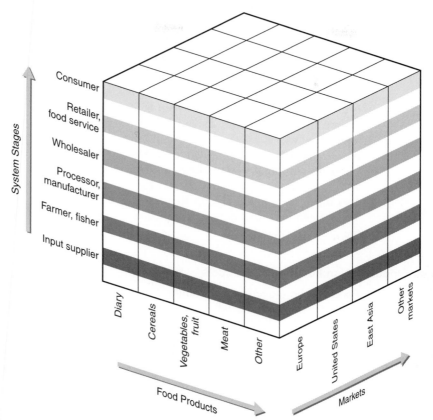

FIGURE 1-1   The international food system. (*Adapted from* The International Food Industry (Amsterdam: Rabobank Nederland, 1995), *p. 6. Reprinted with permission of Rabobank International.*)

system, from the suppliers of farm inputs through to the end consumer. The horizontal dimension shows that all the different food products follow these steps, and depth is provided by the international dimension. Internationally, as illustrated by the news items mentioned earlier, the food system has become much more complex than it was 100 years ago. Any single box can be further subdivided, which indicates the size and complexity of the food system. For example, the box, "retailer of dairy products in Europe," can be divided into types of retailers, types of products, and different countries.

The world food and beverage market is enormous, having an estimated value of over $2.7 trillion in retail sales. Spending in North America comes to $650 billion, in Europe to $750 billion, and in the growth market of East Asia to over $500 billion. These three regions account for over two-thirds of the value of world food sales. Markets of particular importance are Southeast Asia (Malaysia, Singapore, Thailand, Indonesia, the Philippines) and Far East Asia (China, Japan, South

Korea, Taiwan), consisting of 2.7 billion consumers. Although income levels in most of these countries are much lower than those in developed Western countries, over 50 percent of income is spent on food. Therefore, a large percentage of economic growth in these countries goes toward food, and the East Asian food market is estimated to grow at 5 to 7 percent annually, as compared with 0 to 1.5 percent in developed countries. Having doubled in size betwen 1980 and 1995, this market is expected to treble in size between 1995 and 2010.

In China, for example, the number of consumers with an income of over $1,000 annually—which allows for the purchase of products having higher quality and more value added—is expected to exceed 200 million by the year 2000. Brand consciousness is rapidly increasing in China, and well-known brands are associated with a certain lifestyle. Not only has Kentucky Fried Chicken arrived in China, but also other brands that signify the "good life" of American and Western cultures. The tremendous market potential of these markets makes them a logical focus for the global food industry.[3]

Commodity, Industrial, and Consumer Products

Food can be moved across country boundaries at any stage of the food marketing system. For example, wheat after primary cleaning and grading is moved from Canada to the Middle East countries, crude sugar crystals are moved from the West Indies to North America and Europe, and palm oil from Malaysia to the United States. Standardized agricultural products that have had little or no processing and are often raw materials for further processing, such as raw sugar, wheat, and oils, are referred to as *commodities.* Other characteristics of commodity products are that they are unbranded and that they can experience considerable price fluctuations, over which the marketer has no control.

Industrial food products are partly processed raw materials. Increasing amounts of such products are moved across national boundaries. For example, dairy proteins travel from New Zealand to the United States and Asian countries, soy proteins from the United States to Australia, vegetable fat fractions from Malaysia to Europe, and cornstarch products from the United States to Europe. A food manufacturer may combine in one consumer product raw materials from four or five countries, or even more, if you include the many spices and flavors used. Industrial products are designed for specific processes and are sold to specification; as such, they are differentiated from other industrial products by their qualities and, increasingly, by brands.

Branded consumer products are also differentiated from competing products. Using advertising and public relations campaigns, products such as Coca-Cola and Pepsi-Cola, McDonald's hamburgers, and Kentucky Fried Chicken have developed markets in many countries. These foods are based on technology—both technical and marketing—and on a good understanding of the consumer. For example, Pepsi-Cola's initial success in the Philippines was based on the introduction of an

[3]*The International Food Industry* (Amsterdam: Rabobank Nederland, 1995): 18–22.

excellent distribution system, and also of refrigerators, to the small sari-sari stores throughout the islands.

The internationalization of companies within their own operations or through alliances around the world is more the norm than the exception. H. J. Heinz has processing operations in over 30 countries. General Mills and Nestlé have joined in an alliance to produce and market cereals in Europe. General Mills has the technology and product, Nestlé, the European marketing and distribution network. Figure 1-2 shows that on the cereal shelf of a London supermarket, the major brands are Sainsbury's own brand, Kellogg's, and Nestlé-General Mills.

Internationalization of Food Products

An important change during the last 40 years has been the internationalization of food products. Before, the acceptability of foods in a community was related to the food raw materials available, the climate, the cultural and social effects on food eating, religious beliefs, and history. Therefore different countries and even different districts had their own cooking and eating habits and preferences for certain food products. Some peoples, such as the British, preferred bland foods; Indians and Thais liked "hot" foods. The basic carbohydrate food varied by culture: potatoes—Scots and Irish; rice—Chinese; bread—French; tortillas—Mexicans.

Increasing efficiency in physical distribution of foods and very rapid communication among countries have encouraged changes in food menus to include inter-

FIGURE 1-2   Cereal shelf at a London J. Sainsbury's supermarket. *(Source: David J. Schaffner.)*

national foods, either by adapting a traditional food or by designing a widely acceptable new food. For instance, the food industry has taken pasta and pizza from Italy, conducted consumer research to learn how to make them acceptable to the new communities, and developed technology to make them in large quantities.

Many technologies can be moved easily from country to country, so that flour mills and bakeries are built in Singapore and Malaysia, and canning and freezing plants for fruits and fish in Thailand. Sometimes these new technologies are introduced to produce export products—for example, freezing was brought to Thailand to produce export frozen prawns, and canning to produce canned pineapple—but usually the technology is also extended to produce food for the local market. Products such as bread and breakfast cereals are produced for the English and Americans living and traveling in foreign countries, but often the use of these products expands into the local population, who have seen them on television.

This internationalization of foods will continue rapidly over the coming years. Modern technology in food processing and marketing can easily be transferred from country to country. Consumers can move, and have moved, quickly from their traditional foods to these new foods. In the global food marketing system, consumer marketing has become the main driving force; the agricultural producer, the fishing company, and the processors who follow them through the food system ignore the consumer at their peril.

BOX 1-1

THE SNAP, CRACKLE, POP HEARD AROUND THE WORLD

Kellogg Co. makes seven of the ten top-selling cold cereals in the world. As Arnold G. Langbo, chairman and chief executive officer, says, "Our opportunity to grow this business is truly global and giant." Kellogg's holds a world-wide market share of 43 percent by volume and a 37 percent share of the US cereal market.

To capitalize on this opportunity, Kellogg is expanding its overseas manufacturing capability. An Argentine plant is being enlarged to serve the rapidly-growing Latin American market. A new factory is being built in Riga, Latvia, to serve the Baltic states, Byelorussia, and parts of the Russian republic, including St Petersburg.

Kellogg, based in Battle Creek, Michigan, is also building a cereal making facility in Bombay, India, due to open in mid-1994, and it recently broke ground on a plant in Canton, China. By 2000, Kellogg expects to be reaching one billion potential new customers world-wide, stated Mr. Langbo.

Competition for Kellogg comes from archrival General Mills, Inc. and their overseas joint venture with Nestlé SA, called Cereal Partners Worldwide (CPW). Kellogg admits that CPW hurt them in Mexico, Kellogg's biggest Latin American market, but feels that CPW was suffering some share loss in Europe after initial successes, Kellogg puts CPW's global share at about 17 percent.

The world's biggest cereal-eating countries are led by Ireland, with per-capita consumption of 17.2 pounds a year, followed by the United Kingdom at 13.6. Australia is third at 13 pounds, followed by New Zealand and Canada. The US is sixth at 10.1 pounds, which Mr. Langbo believes can be raised to 15 pounds a person.

FOOD MARKETING

Food Marketing Activities

At the core of marketing is *exchange:* someone or some organization has something of value to another. Marketing is then all the activities that go into the process of making this exchange. As Figure 1-3 emphasizes, the essential idea of an exchange is that of giving something of value in return for something of value. Of course, exchanges occur not only at the consumer level, but between producer and processor, processor and manufacturer,[4] manufacturer and distributor, and at other points in the marketing system. Customer needs vary at each level, but the exchange process is still a central activity.

Food marketing can be defined as "the activities needed at all stages in the food system to facilitate the exchange of food products and services which satisfy the needs and wants of individual consumers and organizations." How does food marketing differ from marketing in general? First, all the world's 5.4 billion people are involved in these exchanges, which are greater in number than for any other product or service category. The other major characteristic of food marketing is that the product are often perishable and are purchased on a continuous basis, requiring special handling and a rapid inventory turnover.

The following conditions are necessary for a successful exchange to occur:

- At least two parties must be involved.
- Each party must have something that interests the other party.
- Each party must be able to communicate and deliver.

[4]The term *processor* generally refers to a company that converts raw materials into ingredients: a soybean processor extracts oil from beans for use as an ingredient. A food *manufacturer* combines various ingredients into final consumer products. However, these terms are sometimes used interchangeably—for example, fruit and vegetable canners are usually referred to as processors, even though they often manufacture.

FIGURE 1-3   The consumer exchange process.

Cash, barter, time, behavior

THE EXCHANGE PROCESS:

In the exchange process, marketers offer elements of value, in exchange for cash or other items of value

MARKETER:
Goods and Services
The benefits provided by ideas, people, and places

CUSTOMER:
Needs
And
Wants

Health, safety, sensory enjoyment, social exchange

- Each party must be free to accept or reject any offer from the other party.
- Each party must consider it desirable, or at least acceptable, to deal with the other party.[5]

The words "Needs and Wants" in Figure 1-3 have importance to the marketer. *Needs* are "differences between customers' actual conditions and their desired condition"—they are really the driving force behind all purchases. Say it is 11 p.m. as you are reading this in your dorm or hostel room, and your stomach is giving you signs that you are hungry—your choices are to finish off the bag of chips that has been kicking around your room for the past week, run downstairs to the common room and see what the vending machine has to offer, go to a nearby convenience store, or try the new restaurant that just opened up. You need food; you want either pasta with shrimp, a convenience-store microwavable hamburger, a vending-machine granola bar, or the stale chips (after all, they are cheap and fast!). *Wants* are, then, the particular choices (including the type of product and specific brands) that people make to satisfy their needs. Satisfying consumer needs gives rise to *demand,* a measure of the desire that potential customers have for a product and their ability and willingness to pay for it.[6]

Think Break

Remember a situation where you had a Need but it was not converted into a Want and Demand in the marketplace. What factor or factors resulted in this lack of demand on your part?

Food Marketing Philosophy

To be successful in today's highly competitive marketing arena, the farmer, manufacturer, and retailer must all embrace the *Marketing Concept.* The Marketing Concept is defined as "the philosophy of the company to satisfy consumer needs at a profit." This basic view that the company takes of itself is in sharp contrast to an inwardly focused or production-focused view that producers and food marketers often held in the past. An example of the old production-oriented company is Pillsbury, as it described itself in earlier days:

We are professional flour millers. Blessed with a supply of the finest North American wheat, plenty of water power, and excellent milling machinery, we produce flour of the highest quality. Our basic function is to mill high-quality flour, and of course (and almost incidentally), we must hire salesmen to sell it, just as we hire accountants to keep our books.[7]

---

[5]Franklin S. Houston and Jule B. Gassenheimer, "Marketing and Exchange," *Journal of Marketing.* 51 (October 1987): 3–18.

[6]Adapted from Courtland L. Bovée, Michael J. Houston, and John V. Thill, *Marketing,* 2d ed. (New York: McGraw-Hill, 1995): 8.

[7]As cited in Robert J. Keith, "The Marketing Revolution," *Journal of Marketing* 24 (January 1960): 36.

With this view it is not hard to imagine that a company might miss out on changes and opportunities in the marketplace that could mean greatly improved sales and profits, or, in some instances, the survival or failure of the organization. In the Pillsbury example, what if they were selling flour only in 100-pound (45.4-kg) sacks and had the attitude that "any size sack is O.K. as long as it is a 100-pound sack?" In other words, Pillsbury would be saying, "Here is our product, the best. Come and get it." Obviously there is a problem with this approach. What if lifestyles have changed and consumers now shop weekly and do not bake as much, and therefore want to buy flour in five- or ten-pound bags?

If the company is to adopt the Marketing Concept, a necessary first step is to carry out a continuing program of market research. The company must find out what consumers like and dislike and how their attitudes and lifestyles are changing. It is impossible to be consumer oriented unless one understands consumer behavior and motives. Peter Drucker, noted business management writer and scholar, says this regarding the marketer's knowledge of his customers,

> To satisfy the customer is the mission and purpose of every business. . . . What a company's different customers consider value is so complicated that it can be answered only by the customers themselves. Management should not even try to guess at the answers— it should always go to the customers in a systematic quest for them.[8]

Understanding customers is particularly important in international marketing. Suppose a cereal-manufacturing company is launching its range of products in India and Latvia. What if people in India believe that the company is bad to do business with because of the fact or rumors that they made fun of the strictures of the Hindu religion? Or, what if in Latvia the company attempts to market only presweetened cereals that jar the taste buds of Latvians and Russians who are used to a slice of bread and meat for breakfast?

THE FOOD SYSTEM

History

A brief sketch of the historical context of the food system helps to put food marketing into perspective. In the development of early agrarian societies, after the stage of hunting and gathering for the family or the group, more settled agricultural production was established. Food marketing began when improving technology enabled farmers to grow and fishermen to catch in excess of their requirements. Even in those early days, there were movements of food products, usually ingredients, between districts; gradually they were moved over long distances. China was an early example of this food marketing, moving foods over the great distances within the boundaries of today's China. International marketing of food is not new; it has been going on for many centuries.

[8]Peter Drucker, *Management: Tasks, Responsibilities, Practices* (New York: Harper & Row, 1974): 79, 86.

The domestication of horses, oxen, and camels as transport made international food marketing easier; and then sailing ships, steamships, railways, motor transport, and finally airplanes made it all much speedier. Satisfying consumers' wants for a variety of foods by obtaining them from other districts and other countries is still the driving force, but modern communication allows this to occur not only more quickly and more easily, but also more cheaply. One can see this transition condensed into a short period in the primitive civilization of Papua New Guinea, which has developed during only 30 years from a country eating basic foods to one wanting the variety of international foods.

In the nineteenth and early twentieth centuries, not only were greater quantities of food crops being grown on the known land in Europe, but also there was a search for new lands in America, Australasia, Southern South America, and East Africa—where there were similar climates and a great deal of land. These countries became the offshore farms for Europe, shipping "bulky" basic foods, such as wheat, corn, frozen meat, and cured meat. In the tropical countries, the Europeans also developed plantations for basic food raw materials.

FIGURE 1-4   Improvements in technology. Grain harvesting from the early to late twentieth century. Mechanization is one reason fewer farmers can feed more people than ever before. *(Source: U.S. Department of Agriculture.)*

Agricultural Production and Marine Resources

Agricultural technology has developed in three ways—increased quantity per acre or hectare, and improved quality, and a greater variety of foods produced. A dramatic change in the last century has been in the mechanization of agricultural production. The harnessing first of animal power and then of mechanical energy led to the ability to produce in large quantities. Figure 1-4 illustrates the application of mechanization to harvesting, improving both speed and labor efficiency.

Improved quality has resulted from genetic improvement in plants and animals, as well as technologies that have improved the storage and handling of products, particularly perishables. These technologies have opened up new markets, whether it be a United States market for New Zealand apple producers or a Japanese market for Washington State apple producers. Varieties have proliferated with better technology and the exchange of genetic material. There is no monopoly on technology: drip irrigation technology developed in Israel finds its way to the desert valleys of California, and mechanized harvesters that automatically color-sort tomatoes for processing, developed in California, are found in Italian and Australian fields.

Of course, the above developments are not found in every country. The countries that were under the control of the former Soviet Union are struggling to improve agricultural production, as are many developing countries. In developed countries, major issues have been overproduction and the controls that have been put into

FIGURE 1-4   *Continued*

place to restrict production and trade, which in turn have distorted the global food production and trading system.

Marine resources have served largely as a hunting reserve, and only in the last twenty years has there been significant growth in fish farming. Fish farming is not new—the Chinese have been doing this for many centuries; but it was thought easier to allow the seas and rivers to produce fish naturally and for people to go out to hunt them.

Technological developments in fish production improved the type of boat, the method of propulsion, and the method of catching. There were advances from the small rowing boat to the sailing ship to steam trawlers, finally to the large motorized trawlers of today. The small net and the line gave way to large seine nets, trawl nets, and long nets. Yield and cost control were again the aims—catch as many fish as possible with as few people as possible. In recent years, the seas and rivers have not kept up with this rate of catching, and today many fishing areas are depleted of fish. The use of wild fish in large quantities as food is not possible any more, because the present methods of fishing cannot keep up with demand—now it is necessary to farm the oceans and rivers.

Food Processing and Manufacture

The basic purpose of food processing has remained unchanged over the centuries—to transform animal, plant, and marine raw materials from relatively bulky, perishable commodities into foods that are more palatable, nutritionally dense, stable, and portable. At one time, foods and often food raw materials had very short lives; this is still a restriction in many countries. It has been estimated that India loses 30 percent of the food it produces because of deterioration and attack by rodents and insects.

There were three early methods of preservation—drying, salting and pickling. Many centuries ago people found that the sun or a fire could dry out meat, for example, and this meat could be stored for a later meal when fresh meat was sparse. After salt was found, they discovered that if they rubbed salt onto the meat, the final texture was much better than that of dried meat—it was a more attractive product. Both the dried meat and the salted meat could be stored throughout the winter. Meat drying was known to the North American Indians, fish drying to the prehistoric peoples of Japan, and egg drying to the prehistoric Chinese.

Fermentation was also developed in the early years, when it was discovered that if some foods were allowed to ferment, they would then keep. This led to yogurt and pickled vegetables, as well as wine and beer. Home brewing is not a craft recently developed by college students in their dormitory clothes closets but was practiced in Europe by 6000 B.C.; the addition of hops for flavor and preservation was discovered about 1000 B.C.

Today, most methods of preservation available are essentially variations of heat sterilization and pasteurization or of chilling and freezing. Heat sterilization by canning was first developed in the early 1800s, and the use of ice began to be technologically improved when Clarence Birdseye discovered quick freezing in the 1920s.

The old methods of drying, salting, and pickling, and fermentation come and go in popularity. Drying is widely used in the food-ingredient industry with products such as dried milk, potatoes, onions, and garlic, which are used in other value-added products.[9]

Milling and baking started with the grinding of grains between stones to produce flour for making a porridge, but the discovery of yeast led to bread and other fermented products which were much more edible. Today, wheat flour is used as a basic ingredient in a variety of products, and in recent years it has been developed into specialized starch and protein components. This is one example of the sophisticated technology that has been developed to purify and treat starches, proteins, and fats from many different raw materials, and to design specific ingredients for a wide variety of food processes and products. Food science is now the basis for a technological industry, with the knowledge and ability to prepare suitable ingredients and to restructure them into attractive foods, such as ice cream, pizzas, and frozen meals.

[9]Many of the historical examples of food-processing techniques were drawn from various articles in the *Encyclopedia Britannica.*

BOX 1-2

THE FRENCH OILS AND FATS INDUSTRY: A SUCCESS STORY

Oils and fats science and technology have played an important role in the history of French industry. This history has been marked by the contributions of several well-known scientists:

- Chevreul discovered the triglyceride structure of fats.
- Mege-Mouries patented the formulation and preparation of margarine.
- Sabatier and Sanderens showed hydrogenation changed oils into solid fats.
- Bouveault and Blanc discovered the conversion of fatty esters into fatty alcohols.
- Deiss patented the solvent-based extraction of oil from oilseed cakes.
- Bataille was the first to refine edible oils as it is done today.

After the Second World War, two important industrial breakthroughs were the use of plastic bottles for packaging edible vegetable oils and the physical refinement of edible oil.

Two important incidents struck Western Europe during the 1970s: the U.S. government's embargo on soybean exports, and the petroleum crisis which jeopardized the industry. France was dependent on imports in several cases—peanuts from Western Africa; palm oil, kernels, and copra from Southeast Asia and Africa; soybeans and products, mainly meals, from the United States. The French government and the vegetable-oil industry launched the "French Protein Plan" to reduce French dependence on imported products and to minimize the balance-of-payments deficit. The Protein Plan worked simultaneously on oilseeds, including rapeseeds, sunflower seeds, and soybeans, and on protein-rich crops including peas and fava beans. Research programs concentrated on the selection of new varieties, not only of high productivity and resistance to disease, but also of increased suitability to consumer needs. Pilot plants were built to study the whole oil-processing system. Oil consumption from 1975 to 1986 increased; the spectacular change was that sunflower oil became the leader in 1980. Since that date the market share has increased regularly, at the expense of peanut oil, and now has a 50 percent market share.

Source: Aldo Uzzan, "The French Oils and Fats Industry: a Success Story," *Chemistry & Industry* 19 (October 2, 1989): 623–629. Reprinted with permission.

Retailing

The wholesale/retail part of food marketing has also changed dramatically—from the stall in the marketplace to the "mega" formats, such as warehouse clubs and hypermarkets found in the United States and in Europe. Temporary stalls in the marketplace, usually selling specialized foods, developed into the small specialist shops—grocer, greengrocer, butcher, baker; these were very important in the nineteenth century and survived until the 1950s and '60s in Western countries. They still survive in some countries, such as France. In the late nineteenth and twentieth centuries, chains of small grocers' shops were developed by entrepreneurs such as Sainsbury in Britain and Hartford and Gilman, who started the Great Atlantic and Pacific Tea Company, in the United States. These shops offered a very small range of processed food products which had a reasonable shelf life or a fast turnover—products like bacon, butter, flour, bread, jam, coffee, tea, salt, and sugar. Even in New York City, as illustrated in Figure 1-5, food sellers were specialized and numerous.

The introduction of self-service stores and then supermarkets has changed the whole retailing system; the number of wholesalers has decreased, and of course, small retailers have just about disappeared in Western countries. Large

FIGURE 1-5 Food retailing in New York City before supermarkets. *(Source: U.S. Department of Agriculture.)*

supermarkets require a wide variety of food products and have spurred a tremendous surge in product development—now thousands of food products are born and die regularly.

Internationally, all types of retailers can be found, from simple open-air markets, small specialty shops, and convenience stores to self-service stores, supermarkets, and megamarkets. In international marketing, it is important to identify the most desirable retail outlet for a product and to develop a marketing plan to reach that market.

APPROACHES TO STUDYING FOOD MARKETING

The ultimate objective of all activities in the food system is to satisfy the needs of the final consumer. Even for an unprocessed product such as lettuce there is a complex sequence of activities and changes of ownership between the farm and the consumer. In cases where food marketing spans several countries and several stages of processing, the system becomes even more complex. How can we make sense of all this and study the food marketing taking place in the system?

There are several approaches to analyzing the activities in the food system. The different categories of business in the food chain—brokers, agents, merchants, processors, and retailers—are studied in the *institutional approach*. Along with understanding the various types of institutions, we can analyze the structure of the food system. Why do some distribution channels have many intermediaries and others have few? Why in some cases are buyers and sellers bound by a detailed contract, while in others they have no direct contact, operating through some type of anonymous market? And how competitive are the various sections of the food system? What are the actual costs in the system, and does the consumer pay a "fair" price? These questions about the institutions and structure are referred to as industrial organization issues.

The food system may also be viewed in terms of the activities carried out—processing, transport, finance, etc. This is called the *functional approach*. The functional approach allows us to analyze the activities in terms of their cost and effectiveness in meeting customer needs and wants.

The *types of customer and product* provide another framework for the study of food marketing. Commodity marketing is often a topic of its own because of its unique characteristics: commodities involve price risk and are generally low-value, bulky products that necessitate low-cost logistics for transportation and storage. Industrial marketing of ingredients to food processors is unique in terms of buyer behavior and channels of distribution and can be a subject by itself. Wholesalers and retailers, who play a crucial role in distribution, have books and courses organized around their management.

The one type of customer not mentioned above, the consumer, is better studied under the micro or *marketing management approach*.

Where the above three approaches are used to examine and understand marketing tasks, institutions, and systems, the marketing management approach defines *marketing* as "the process of planning and executing the conception, pricing, promotion, and distribution of ideas, goods, and services to create exchanges that satisfy individual and organizational objectives."[10]

Think Break _____

Compare the above definition of food marketing to the definition found on page 9 and list the differences. How would each definition affect the study of food marketing?

_____

Sometimes marketing is confused with selling. While selling is part of the marketing process and is included under promotion, there is much more to marketing, as seen in the above definition and in the chapters that follow. Another misconception is that marketing is essentially coercion, convincing the buyer, through clever advertising or persuasive salesmanship, to purchase that pizza or 2-liter bottle of cola. But successful marketers understand that they need to develop a long-term relationship with the buyer.

Food Marketing Institutions

The following are the major types of institutions found in the food marketing system:

• Agricultural and marine producers, processors, and manufacturers combine inputs to create products in a form that is significantly different from the raw materials used in their production. An introduction to industrial food marketing and the concerns of food manufacturers as customers is the main topic of Chapter 7.

• Merchant middlemen take title to a product. Merchants do not usually change the form of a product, but they provide storage and build assortments of products for the convenience of their customers. Merchant middlemen are of two types: those who operate on margins that are established at the time of purchase, discussed in Chapter 8; and those who are price takers in commodity markets, described in Chapter 10.

• Agent middlemen, also referred to as brokers, do not take title and therefore avoid the risk of holding stocks. Agents act on behalf of principals, who may be either buyers or sellers. Income is based on commission, which is usually a percentage of selling price.

• Facilitative organizations assist in the value-adding process but are not directly involved as manufacturers, processors, merchants, retailers, or agents. Examples of businesses that are facilitative to the marketing task are banks, transportation, freight forwarders, and providers of market information.

• Regulatory agencies are concerned with, for example, food quality, food labeling, managing international trade, and promoting effective competition.

[10]"AMA Board Approves New Marketing Definition," *Marketing News,* March 1, 1985: 1.

Any one company may carry out the functions of more than one type of intermediary. In fact, it is difficult to find participants in the food system that fit neatly into any one of the categories discussed above.

Functions of the Food System

Food marketing can also be thought of as providing economic utility, which is the product's inherent ability to satisfy a customer's needs. There are four types of utility: time, form, place, and possession. These utilities are created by the various marketing functions:

Physical functions:	Manufacturing, processing, and packaging
	Transportation
	Storage
Exchange functions:	Buying and selling
	Price determination
	Risk bearing
Facilitating functions:	Standardization, grading
	Financing
	Market intelligence
	Communication, advertising, promotion, public relations

Physical functions   Agricultural products are often produced seasonally, but demand either tends to be relatively constant over time or to follow a different seasonal pattern than that of production. Therefore, such products must be stored—the creation of *time utility.* Even for nonseasonal products, storage is required to act as buffer between day-to-day variations in supply and demand and to facilitate production scheduling. Because production and consumption do not occur simultaneously, financing of stock holding is required at all levels in the system. Risks arise because food products may deteriorate or be lost/damaged by fire, theft, or accident. Sellers may not realize an expected price; buyers may pay higher prices than predicted.

We do not usually consume agricultural products in the form in which they leave the farm. They are processed to a greater or lesser degree—the creation of *form utility.* Furthermore, consumption does not usually occur at the point of production; agricultural products must be transported—the creation of *place utility.* The form of the product and the place where it can be bought are important for all buyers, from the raw materials processor to the final customer.

Exchange functions   Companies that provide information about alternative buyers and suppliers, such as brokers and agents, facilitate the creation of *possession utility.* Exchange is a fundamental component of any marketing transaction. It involves establishing the price and transferring title from seller to buyer. Buyers may default on credit transactions. International transactions may be complicated by additional laws, regulations, and monetary exchange rates. All these are marketing risks, and assuming these risks is the risk-bearing function.

Facilitating function   The facilitating function of grading allows the exchange and physical functions to operate smoothly. Grading methods seek to sort heterogeneous raw materials into categories that meet the needs of buyers. Specifications and quality assurance methods, which ensure that quality meets acceptable tolerance limits, are also discussed in Chapters 7 and 11. The facilitating functions may include a number of merchandising and promotional activities. For an exchange to occur, information is required—prices, product information, credit terms, etc. The provision of such information is the market intelligence function.

Marketing by Type of Customer and Product

While the consumer is the most important customer of the food system, intermediaries are also customers. The basic concepts are the same for marketing to both groups, but the details of implementation are certainly different. We can identify at least four different marketing situations classified by product and customer characteristics:

- Supplying consumers, generally with branded products—consumer marketing.
- Supplying differentiated ingredients to processors and manufacturers—industrial marketing.
- Supplying undifferentiated raw materials—commodity marketing.
- Supplying merchant intermediaries—reseller marketing.

The basic principle for all four approaches is the same: the marketing concept says that suppliers should identify the needs of the buyers and tailor their marketing activities toward meeting these needs. The complex needs and wants of food consumers are discussed in Chapters 3 and 4. Food processors and manufacturers need to be able to process economically and to produce a quality product. Industrial marketing, which responds to their particular needs, is discussed in Chapter 7.

Marketing Management of Branded Products

The term *market* is often used without considering what the requirements are for people or organizations to really be a market; do they have needs to satisfy, money to spend, and the authority and willingness to spend it? A *target market* consists of a group of customers (people or organizations) at whom the seller directs a marketing program.

A company may have a single target market; for example, a grower of certified organically grown produce has defined a target market. More likely, a company will have multiple target markets. Kellogg's has identified several target markets in developing their portfolio of brands. Target-market selection requires market research and market segmentation (Chapter 12) to analyze market opportunities. Once target markets have been selected, the company can move to the next step in marketing planning, which is developing a market strategy and designing a marketing mix. Chapters 6, 13, 14, and 15 discuss the place, product, price, and promotion of the marketing mix. Marketing strategy and planning is appropriately discussed in the last chapter, Chapter 16, because in order to develop a successful plan, the marketing manager must first understand the marketing system, target markets, and the elements of the marketing mix.

The combination of the four primary elements that comprise a company's marketing program is termed the *marketing mix*. The marketer uses the marketing mix to successfully implement the idea of the marketing concept in satisfying consumer needs and achieving profits for the company.[11]

The four elements of the marketing mix are:

• Product—Managing the product mix includes planning and developing the right products to be marketed by the company. Decisions also must be made regarding branding, packaging, and various other product features. The process of developing new products is particularly important to the survival of food companies, where thousands of new products are introduced each year. Product issues are discussed in Chapter 13.

• Promotion—This encompasses a wide variety of techniques for communication with a target market. The main categories of promotion are advertising, personal selling, public relations, and sales promotion. As discussed further in Chapter 14, in recent years the food industry has changed its emphasis in the promotional mix, spending relatively more dollars on personal selling and sales promotional efforts to obtain the support of distributors, and less on direct advertising to consumers.

• Price—Setting prices is one of the most difficult tasks facing the marketing professional and is the topic of Chapter 15. Costs of raw materials and production must be considered, as well as consumer demand and the actions of competitors in the marketplace.

• Distribution—Even though marketing intermediaries, primarily wholesalers and retailers, are not under the direct control of manufacturers, this element of the marketing mix can often be the most creative and can provide the greatest competitive advantage for the marketer. Alliances, such as the Nestlé/General Mills example, and other methods of managing distribution channels can provide the astute marketer significant advantages in the marketplace. A good understanding of marketing intermediaries and channel organization and control, discussed in Chapters 5 and 6, is essential to developing successful distribution strategies.

Think Break

Choose from the food system a favorite product that you either consume or are interested in as a marketer. What would you need to know about this product in order to market it, and what approach(es) would best help you achieve this marketing knowledge?

---

[11]Adapted from William J. Stanton, Michael J. Etzel, and Bruce J. Walker, *Fundamentals of Marketing,* 9th ed. (New York: McGraw-Hill, 1991): 11–13.

THE FOOD INDUSTRY AS AN EMPLOYER

While the agricultural production (farming) sector of most developed economies has declined in importance as to employment and contribution to the Gross National Product, the food system remains a vibrant part of the economy and offers diverse opportunities in food-related industries for university graduates.

Whereas a farmer in the United States once fed 10 other people, today one farmer feeds over 100 other people. The result has been a dramatic transformation in production agriculture; by 1995, the number of farms in the United States had declined to less than 2 million, about the same number that existed at the time of the Civil War. One of the results of this trend toward fewer and larger farms is that employment in farming has fallen by more than half in the past 50 years. However, that decline has been more than offset by increases in food service and food retailing employment (Figure 1-6).

Today, the food system in its entirety (inputs to agriculture, production, transportation, manufacturing, wholesaling, food service, retailing, and other ancillary industries) constitutes 16 percent of the United States gross national product and employs 21 million people—more than the health care industry employs. It is estimated that through the 1990s more than 48,000 annual openings will be available in the United States food system alone for those with undergraduate degrees. Of these positions, approximately one-third, or 16,000, are projected in the area of marketing, merchandising, and sales representatives. Almost an equal number of positions will be available in the scientific and technical areas, such as food process engineering, reproductive physiology, and environmental sciences.[12]

[12]"Employment Opportunities for College Graduates in the Food and Agricultural Sciences" (Washington, D.C.: Cooperative State Research Service, USDA, December 1990): 10–16.

FIGURE 1-6   Employment trends in the US Food System, Percent of Jobs in 1950 and 1995. *(Source: Adapted from Bureau of the Census (1977d) and Bureau of Labor Statistics (1995).)*

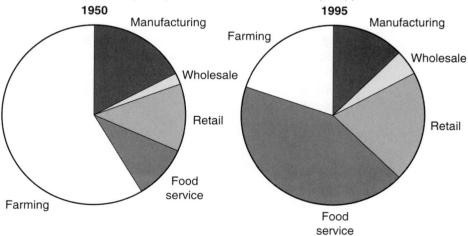

Many of these careers result in opportunities for international travel and living, of which the following are samples: A General Mills food processing engineer, a graduate of a United States midwestern university, is in Britain, assigned to the start-up of a manufacturing plant for the Nestlé/General Mills joint venture; a New Zealander works in California with H. J. Heinz's tomato processing operation; and an agribusiness graduate from a California university travels to Australia each year to supervise vegetable-seed production operations.

Think Break

Where might a person with a Bachelor's degree in your area of study find employment in the food system? Have you explored the employment trends and the projections for opportunities in the future for graduates in your major?

SUMMARY

The international food system has three important dimensions: breadth—products; height—stages in the system; and depth—countries and regions. In the breadth dimension are a wide variety of food products, taken from farm/sea and moved through the stages of production, processing, and retailing. Country boundaries are crossed by trade in raw materials and consumer products, or by companies forming international alliances. The greatest potential for market growth in the food system lies outside the developed countries. In particular, the Asian market will be the focus of marketing activity for many food-system participants.

Behind all marketing activities is the idea of exchange. Marketing "bridges the gaps between producer and consumer." Implicit in this thought is that specialization of production occurs when one group—company, village, region, country—develops low-cost, efficient production and wants to share the products with other people. Marketing accomplishes this bridge between the producer and consumer, but there must be a demand for a product—potential customers who have both the need for a product and the ability and willingness to pay for it.

The marketing concept states that the purpose of the company is to satisfy consumer desires and wants. Successful marketers constantly keep in touch with demographic trends (age, income, ethnicity) in the marketplace, as well as with how consumer lifestyles and attitudes are changing. Market research is critical to understanding the dynamics of the marketplace, ferreting out opportunities, and reacting in a timely manner to factors that are threats to a product or industry.

There is no single approach to studying the food system. Two classic approaches are institutional and functional. Their names are fairly self-explanatory: the institutional approach explores the different types of companies and organizations—comparing agent (broker) to merchant wholesaler in distribution, for example; the functional approach examines the functions that are carried out in bridging the gap between producer and consumer. These functions can best be thought of in terms of the economic utilities that the marketing system provides: time, form, place (location), and possession.

Two other approaches are the study of "types of customer and product" and marketing management. In the food system, marketing to particular customer types is a useful way of studying marketing. A supplier of ingredients to an ice cream manufacturer has a different marketing task than does Nestlé in marketing milk products to consumers. The characteristics of undifferentiated raw materials and products lead to the study of commodity marketing, which centers on the issues of price-risk management, grades and grading systems, and efficient logistics. The marketing management approach emphasizes differentiated, branded-product marketing as practiced by all the major food and beverage manufacturers—for example, Kellogg, Heinz, Nestlé, Pepsi, and Budweiser. A marketing plan is developed through target-market identification and creative application of the marketing mix: price, product, channels of distribution (place), and promotion.

Although farm employment has been shrinking over the past 50 years, new opportunities for growth in other sectors of the food system have more than made up for the decline in production agriculture. Many of the new professional opportunities require college degrees in agribusiness, agricultural economics, and the agricultural and food sciences. About one-third of the available positions are in marketing and sales, and about an equal number are in the technical areas that serve the food system, from farm production through retail and food service. Careers are available as technical sales representative, food broker, grain merchandiser, food scientist, food technologist and engineer, quality assurance specialist, and nutritionist; the list continually changes and expands.

IMPORTANT TERMS AND CONCEPTS

branded consumer products 6	marketing 17
branded products 20	marketing concept 10
commodity 6	marketing management approach 17
demand 10	marketing mix 21
exchange 9	needs 10
exchange functions 19	physical functions 19
facilitating functions 20	place utility 19
food system 4	possession utility 19
form utility 19	target market 20
functional approach 17	time utility 19
industrial food products 6	type of customer and product
institutional approach 17	approach 17
market 20	wants 10

QUESTIONS

1 What should be the major objective of participants in the food system?
2 One of your friends, an engineering major, asks you what this course is all about, and you reply, "Food-system marketing." She then asks, "What is the food system?" What is your response?
3 Explain what food marketing is and what the prerequisites are for marketing to occur.
4 Differentiate between consumer Needs and Wants.
5 Peter Drucker says, "What people in business think they know about their customers and the market is more likely to be wrong than right." If Drucker is correct in this assessment, what must a marketer do to be successful?
6 Identify the different types of institutions that make up the food marketing system.
7 What is a commodity, and what characteristics of a commodity make for a different marketing situation than that of branded products?
8 You have just been appointed marketing manager of a small start-up food manufacturer of specialty condiments (relishes, mustards, salad dressings). The company president has asked you to develop a strategic marketing plan for these products. What two key elements are you going to use to organize your plan?
9 What are the similarities and differences between the food marketing system of 100 years ago and that of today?
10 What was the major sector for employment in the food system 50 years ago? What is the major sector today? Critique the statement, "Today there are fewer farms than at any time since the Civil War; therefore, job opportunities in the food system are few and becoming fewer all the time."

REFERENCES AND RESOURCES

"AMA Board Approves New Marketing Definition." *Marketing News.* March 1, 1985: 1.

Bovée, C. L., M. J. Houston, and J. V. Thill. *Marketing.* 2d ed. New York: McGraw-Hill, 1995.

Drucker, Peter. *Management: Tasks, Responsibilities, Practices.* New York: Harper & Row, 1974.

Goldberg, R. A. "New International Linkages Shaping the Food System." *Food and Agricultural Markets: The Quiet Revolution.* Ed. L. P. Schertz and L. M. Daft. Washington, D.C.: Economic Research Service, U.S. Department of Agriculture, 1994.

Haas, R. W. "Chapter 1: The Business Marketing System." *Business Marketing, A Managerial Approach.* 6th ed. Cincinnati, OH: South-Western College Pub., 1995.

Henderson, D. R., and C. R. Handy. "International Dimensions of the Food System." *Food and Agricultural Markets: The Quiet Revolution.* Ed. L. P. Schertz and L. M. Daft. Washington, D.C.: Economic Research Service, U.S. Department of Agriculture, 1994.

Houston, F. S., and J. B. Gassenheimer. "Marketing and Exchange." *Journal of Marketing* 51 (October 1987): 3–18.

Keith, R. J. "The Marketing Revolution." *Journal of Marketing* 24 (January, 1960): 36.

Lee, J. E. "Trends in Agriculture and Trade in High-Value Products." *Food Technology* 42.9 (1988): 119–127.

Stanton, W. J., M. J. Etzel, and J. Walker. *Fundamentals of Marketing.* 10th ed. New York: McGraw-Hill, 1994.

2

ECONOMICS OF THE FOOD SYSTEM

CHAPTER OUTLINE

LEARNING OBJECTIVES

After reading this chapter and answering the questions in the Think Breaks and at the end of the chapter, you should be able to:

- Understand how the demand for a food product is determined by the product's price, the price of substitute products, income, tastes and preferences, and marketing activity.
- Define elasticity of demand.
- Explain how elasticity of demand is influenced by the availability of substitute products, income, time, degree of aggregation, and marketing activity.
- Define price flexibility and explain the factors influencing it.
- Understand how the supply of a food product is determined by the product's price, the price of alternative enterprises available to the supplier, time, perishability/storability, excess capacity, industry structure and organization, and technological change.
- Show how price is established at the intersection of the supply and demand curves.
- Understand how prices change in response to shifts of the supply and demand curves.
- Explain the concept of derived demand and the nature of the marketing margin.

INTRODUCTION

In Chapter 1, the food marketing system was described as a sequence of activities from the supply of raw materials (agricultural products, packaging supplies, and so on) through processing and distribution, to purchase by the final consumer. This sequence forms the food value-adding channel, to be discussed further in Chapters 5 and 6. This chapter applies basic economic concepts to explain how prices are established between suppliers of raw materials and food processors, between food processors and distributors, and between retailers and final consumers. The marketers in Figure 2-1 would benefit from reading the following sections on supply and demand.

Consumer demand derives from consumers' needs and wants, as explained in the previous chapter. The demand for farm products and other raw materials derives from consumer demand, but consumer demand is not the only determinant of "farm-gate" demand; the price received by agricultural producers is also influenced by the structure and organization of the processing and distribution sectors. Economic concepts provide a useful framework for studying these linkages.

THE DEMAND FOR FOOD PRODUCTS

The economic model of demand states that the quantity of any food product demanded by consumers is determined by:

- The product's price
- The price of other products competing for the consumer's dollar
- Consumers' incomes
- Consumers' tastes and preferences.

This relationship is stated algebraically as:

$$QD = f(PO,PS,I,T),$$

where QD = quantity demanded
  PO = the product's price
  PS = the price of substitute products
  I = income
  T = tastes (equivalent to needs and wants)
  f = function.

Each of these variables will be considered in turn.

FIGURE 2-1   Unclear on the concept. *(©1993, Washington Post Writers Group. Reprinted with permission.)*

The Relationship between Quantity Demanded and the Product's Price

The *law of demand* states that, other things being equal, quantity demanded falls as price increases.[1] The *demand curve* graphs the schedule of quantities sold at various prices (Figure 2-2).

Figure 2-2 shows two demand curves of different slopes. In Figure 2-2A, a price increase from P_1 to P_2 causes the quantity sold to fall from Q_1 to Q_2. In Figure 2-2B, the same price increase causes a fall in consumption of Q_3–Q_4, greater than Q_1–Q_2. This is because the demand curve in Figure 2-2B is flatter than that in Figure 2-2A.

The economic measure of the sensitivity of quantity sold to price changes is called *price elasticity of demand* (PED). Price elasticity is the proportional change in quantity for a specified proportional change in price. That is:

$$PED = \frac{\Delta Q/Q}{\Delta P/P}$$

The most straightforward definition is to express PED as the percentage change in quantity in response to a 1 percent change in price. For example, in Figure 2-2A, suppose $P_1 = 100$, $P_2 = 110$, $Q_1 = 1{,}000$, and $Q_2 = 950$. The percentage change in price is 10 percent and the percentage change in quantity is 5 percent. Therefore, PED = 0.5. If PED is greater than 1, demand is said to be *elastic;* if it is less than 1, demand is *inelastic.*

[1]It is possible to find cases that apparently do not conform to this law. That is, the quantity sold increases as the price increases. This can happen for luxury products such as diamonds or, possibly, food products such as caviar. In such cases, however, it could be argued that the "other things being equal" assumption may not hold. If buyers associate price with quality, the higher-priced brand is, in the mind of the consumer, a different product than the lower-priced version.

FIGURE 2-2   Two demand curves for a food product.

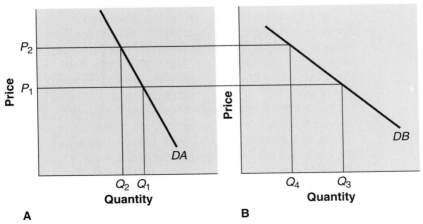

A   B

Availability of Substitutes and Price Elasticity

The main factor influencing price elasticity of demand is the existence of *substitutes*. If a product B is seen to be a close substitute for product A in the minds of buyers, they will be able to switch easily to product B in response to an increase in the price of product A. Note the phrase, "in the minds of buyers"; it is the consumer's perception of the degree of closeness that is important, not the supplier's. In Chapter 12 the idea of positioning, which is a measure of the "closeness" of products to each other in the minds of consumers, is discussed. What buyers see as close substitutes may not be obvious; for example, the nearest substitute for a meal at an expensive restaurant (a food event) may be an evening at the theater (nothing to do with food)—both are "big-ticket" recreational events.

Necessities, such as maize in many African countries, have no real substitutes and therefore have an inelastic demand. The demand for luxuries is more elastic, because buyers will postpone expenditure in response to a price increase.

Income can affect elasticity. Rich consumers are likely to be less responsive to price increases, especially for products that represent a small proportion of the household budget.

Time is important. Given enough time, buyers will be able to locate substitutes (and competing suppliers will enter the market), and the buyers' demand for existing products will therefore be more elastic. On the other hand, buyers may react quickly to a price increase but revert to established purchasing patterns after the market settles down.

The degree of aggregation in the definition of the "product" influences substitutability. For example, a supermarket manager, reflecting the requirements of her customers, recognizes that there are no close substitutes for the aggregate product category "milk." Different brands of milk of the same type, however, are close substitutes and therefore close competitors for the retailer's scarce shelf space.

Related to the previous point is the idea that branding represents marketers' efforts to distance their products from substitutes, effectively making the demand for their brand less elastic. For food products, the familiarity and security of a well-known brand is often its main differentiating factor.

Farm products usually sit at the other end of the differentiation spectrum. Farmer A's wheat is 100 percent substitutable for Farmer B's, and the elasticity of demand facing an individual farmer is infinite—a flat demand curve. Such products are called commodities. The farmer can sell all he can produce at the market price and will sell none at all at any price above this. The farmer is therefore a "price taker."

Any barrier to the supply of substitute products will make the demand for established products more inelastic. Until recently, there was an almost 100 percent barrier to imported rice in Japan. Japanese suppliers were able to increase their price without substantially affecting quantity sold; that is, the demand for locally produced rice was inelastic. There are other reasons for this inelasticity. Japanese buyers really do believe local rice is different, although this would be difficult to show by any objective measure. In general, trade barriers for food and agricultural products are falling (Chapter 9), and the demand for the product of any individual supplier country should therefore be more elastic. Within a country, any barrier to entry to an industry reduces the availability of substitute products, making the demand for existing products more inelastic.

The demand for raw materials in the production of agricultural products and in food processing is influenced more by technical factors. For example, an animal feed mill will substitute soybean meal for other sources of plant protein, depending on the amino acid mix required for the particular ration being produced as well as on relative prices.

Think Break

In each of the examples below, which product would you expect to have the more elastic demand:

Milk or beef in Japan
Milk in Zimbabwe, East Africa, or milk in Sweden
Milk as a generic product or a particular brand of milk
Wheat as a generic product or the wheat supplied by an individual farmer.

Price Flexibility

For most agricultural and marine products, price changes occur mainly in response to changes in supply, demand being both relatively stable and inelastic. This is because of the biological nature and structure of agricultural production. The quantity harvested by farmers today is not influenced by today's price. It is determined by farmers' price expectations at the time of planting and variables such as weather and disease between planting and harvest. Depending on the product, there is a substantial lead time between the decision to plant (or breed, in the case of animals) and when the product is sold. In any case, individual producers know that they cannot control or influence the selling price because they have a very small share of a commodity market.

In this situation, it is more interesting to note how prices change in response to a change in quantity supplied than how quantity supplied changes in response to price. This is measured by *price flexibility* (FP), which is the inverse of price elasticity and is defined as:

$$FP = \frac{\Delta P}{\Delta Q} \times \frac{Q}{P}.$$

The greater the elasticity of demand, the smaller the price flexibility, and vice versa. Figure 2-3 illustrates price flexibilities for several agricultural products.

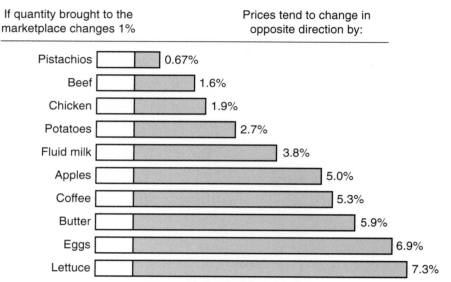

If quantity brought to the marketplace changes 1%	Prices tend to change in opposite direction by:

Pistachios — 0.67%
Beef — 1.6%
Chicken — 1.9%
Potatoes — 2.7%
Fluid milk — 3.8%
Apples — 5.0%
Coffee — 5.3%
Butter — 5.9%
Eggs — 6.9%
Lettuce — 7.3%

FIGURE 2-3   How change in supply affects price received by farmers. (*Sources: K.S. Huang, USDA, ERS Tech. Bulletin 1714, 1985, and California Pistachio Commission.*)

Think Break ———————————————————————————

Which product in Figure 2-3 is the most responsive to a change in quantity? Which is the least? Why? If the farm-gate price of beef is 60 cents a pound, what will the price be if the quantity supplied increases by 10 percent?

Demand and the Price of Substitute Products

As discussed earlier, the availability of substitute products is the main factor influencing own-price elasticity of demand. If product B is a close substitute for product A, changes in its price would be expected to affect sales of product A. The impact of a change in the price of one product on sales of another is measured by the *cross-price elasticity of demand* (XED) and is defined as the percentage change in the quantity of product A demanded resulting from a 1 percent change in the price of product B. Or:

$$XED = \frac{\Delta Q_a / Q_a}{\Delta P_b / P_b},$$

where $\Delta P_b / P_b$ is a 1 percent change.

Some examples of own- and cross-price elasticities are given in Table 2-1.

In Table 2-1, the diagonal elements are own-price elasticities. The cross-price elasticities are the percentage changes in quantity of the items in the rows demanded in response to a 1 percent change in the price of the column items. For example, a 1 percent increase in the price of beef and veal causes consumption of pork to increase by 0.19 percent. All except one of the cross-price elasticities are positive, indicating substitute products. A negative cross-price elasticity indicates that the products are *complements;* that is, the demand for product A increases as the price of product B increases. Complements are products that "go together"—for example, cranberry sauce and turkey at Thanksgiving in the United States. Complements are unlikely to be found at the level of product aggregation in Table 2-1.

Think Break

What products appear to be the closest substitutes in Table 2-1? The impact of a 1 percent increase in the price of beef and veal on the quantity of eggs demanded is greater than the impact of a 1 percent increase in the price of eggs on the demand for beef and veal (1993 figures). Why? Generally, both own-price and cross-price elasticities have fallen between 1971 and 1993. Why?

TABLE 2-1   ELASTICITIES (PED) AND CROSS-PRICE ELASTICITIES (XED) FOR SELECTED FOOD PRODUCTS IN THE UNITED STATES

Demand for		Beef & veal	Pork	Chicken	Eggs	Cheese	Non-food
		para					
Beef & Veal (Note 1)	1993	−0.62	0.11	0.02	0.02	−0.03	NA
	1971	−0.64	0.08	0.07	*	*	0.10
Pork	1993	0.19	−0.73	0.01	*	0.01	NA
	1971	0.07	−0.41	0.03	*	*	0.05
Chicken	1993	0.10	0.05	−0.37	0.08	0.04	NA
	1971	0.20	0.12	−0.78	*	*	0.06
Eggs	1993	0.09	0.01	0.06	−0.11	0.01	NA
	1971	0.01	0.01	*	−0.32	0.01	0.02
Cheese	1993	0.09	0.01	0.06	0.11	−0.25	NA
	1971	*	*	*	0.01	−0.66	0.09
Nonfood	1993	NA	NA	NA	NA	NA	−0.98
	1971	0.02	0.03	0.01	0.01	0.01	−1.02

Percentage change in row item in response to a 1% change in column item

*<0.01.
NA = Not available.
Note 1: 1993—beef & veal; 1971—beef only.
Note 2: □ signifies PED; the other data are XED.
Sources: P. S. George and G. A. King, "Consumer Demand for Food Commodities in the United States with Projections for 1980," *Giannini Foundation Monograph 26,* California Agricultural Experiment Station, 1971; and Juo S. Huang, "A Complete System of US Demand for Food," *USDA, ERS, Technical Bulletin 1821,* 1993.

The answer to the second question in the Think Break may not be all that obvious. The asymmetry of cross-price elasticities relates to the proportion of the food budget that each item represents. Beef and veal have a higher share of the food budget than eggs, and changes in their price would be expected to have a bigger impact on the sales of eggs, rather than the other way around.

The Effects of Consumer Income on Demand

Not only does income affect own- and cross-price elasticity of demand; income also affects consumption directly. Over 100 years ago a German statistician, Engel, identified the relationship between the quantity of food consumed and income shown in Figure 2-4.

More recent studies show that this relationship continues to exist—between income groups within a country, between countries, and over time. The measure of responsiveness of quantity demanded to changes in income is given by the *income elasticity of demand,* defined in the same way as price elasticity. That is: Income elasticity of demand (IED) is the percentage change in quantity demanded in response to a 1 percent change in household income. Or:

$$IED = \frac{\Delta Q/Q}{\Delta I/I},$$

where *I* is household income and $\Delta I/I = 1$ percent.

In Zone A of Figure 2-4, IED is positive and greater than 1; that is, a 1 percent increase in income results in an increase in quantity demanded of greater than

FIGURE 2-4   Relationship between food consumption and income.

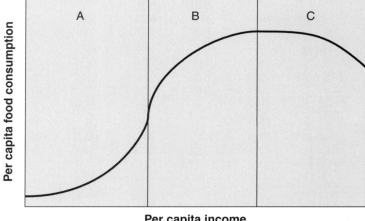

Per capita income

TABLE 2-2 INCOME ELASTICITIES FOR SELECTED FOOD PRODUCTS IN SELECTED COUNTRIES

	United States	Australia	Brazil	Indonesia
Wheat	−0.3	−0.1	0.4	1.0
Fruit	0.2	0.7	0.5	0.8
Meat	0.2	0.1	0.5	1.3
Milk	−0.5	0	0.6	2.0

Source: Christopher Ritson, *Agricultural Economics: Principles and Policy* (London: Granada Publishing, 1978): 34.

1 percent. In Zone B, IED is positive but less than 1. In Zone C, IED is negative—an increase in income is associated with a fall in consumption.

Some income elasticities for food products in various countries are given in Table 2-2. The United States and Australia are relatively rich countries and, in general, income elasticities for the selected food products are around zero or negative. Indonesia, on the other hand, is a relatively poor developing country with much higher income elasticities. Brazil lies between the United States and Indonesia.

Data on income elasticities, per capita incomes, and population growth can be combined to develop forecasts of growth in food consumption. This is done in Table 2-3.

The rapidly growing economies of Asia are in the "medium income" category in Table 2-3, showing high rates of population and income growth, as well as a fast rate of increase in the demand for food. This situation can be expected to continue. For most of these countries, demand for food will outstrip their ability to produce it, with the result that there will be a sharp increase in their requirements for imported food. However, some countries with low incomes, such as Bangladesh, have little growth and are not good prospects for food exporters from other countries, except as recipients of food aid.

TABLE 2-3 COMPARISON OF GROWTH OF DEMAND FOR AGRICULTURAL PRODUCTS AT DIFFERENT STAGES OF DEVELOPMENT, HYPOTHETICAL CASES

Levels of development	Population in agriculture, %	Population growth rate, %	Per capita income growth rate, %	Income elasticity of demand	Rate of growth of food demand, %
Very low income	70	2.5	0.5	1.0	3.0
Low income	60	3.0	1.0	0.9	3.9
Medium income	50	2.5	4.0	0.7	5.1
High income	30	2.0	4.0	0.5	4.0
Very high income	10	1.0	3.0	0.1	1.3

Source: Reprinted from *Food Policy,* Vol. 11, J. W. Mellor and R. H. Adams, "The New Political Economy of Food and Agricultural Development," page 290, Copyright 1986, with kind permission from Elsevier Science Ltd, The Boulevard, Langford Lane, Kidlington OX5 1GB, UK.

Think Break

You are given the following information for a certain developing country:

Population: 50 million
Per capita fresh milk consumption: 10 liters per year
Population growth rate: 3 percent per year
Per capita income growth rate: 5 percent per year
Income elasticity of demand for fresh milk: 2.0

What is your best estimate of total milk consumption in 5 years time. What other information would you need to provide a more reliable forecast?

Tastes and Preferences

The last variable in the demand model is consumer tastes and preferences. To an economist, these represent anything that cannot be explained by prices and incomes. This rather cavalier treatment of tastes contrasts with the attention paid to them by marketers. Of course, food consumption is influenced by more than economic variables. A myriad of cultural, social, and psychological variables affect the way people eat (see Chapters 3 and 4). For example, consumers' health concerns have resulted in increased sales of nutritionally improved foods.

From an economic perspective the objective of marketing activity is a) to move the demand curve to the right, and/or b) to make it more inelastic, as shown in Figure 2-5.

FIGURE 2-5   Impact of marketing activity on demand.

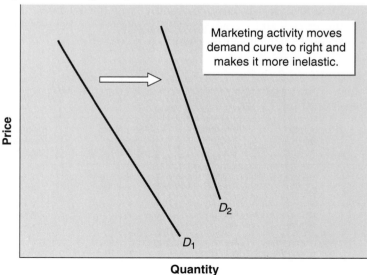

Marketing activity moves demand curve to right and makes it more inelastic.

THE SUPPLY OF FOOD PRODUCTS

The economic model of supply states that the supply of any food product is determined by:

- The product's price
- The prices of alternative products that compete for the resources of the producing company
- The prices of inputs used in the production process
- The changes in technology in the production process.

Impact of Changes in Price on Quantity Supplied

In Figure 2-6A, an increase in price from P_1 to P_2 results in an increase in the quantity supplied from Q_1 to Q_2. In Figure 2-6B, the increase in quantity supplied for the same price increase is greater, indicating a more elastic supply.

Elasticity of supply is defined in the same way as all the previous measures of elasticity: ES = percentage change in quantity supplied resulting from a 1 percent change in price. Or:

$$ES = \frac{\Delta Q/Q}{\Delta P/P},$$

where $\Delta P/P = 1$ percent.

The *supply curve* normally slopes upward, although, like demand, in rare cases it does not.

Several factors influence the elasticity of supply:

Availability of Alternative Enterprises   The more alternatives available to the farmer, processor, or distributor, the more flexible they will be in switching supply

FIGURE 2-6   Two supply curves.

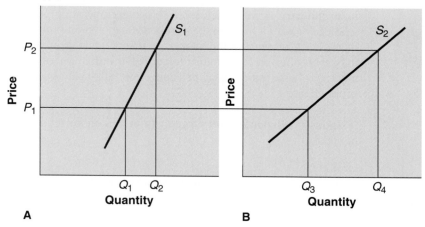

A   B

activities and the greater the elasticity of supply will be for all the products they are able to produce. For crop producers, production flexibility is determined mainly by soil quality and climatic factors. For food processors, the ability to switch depends mainly on the extent to which their equipment is specialized for the production of a particular product line, shut-down and set-up costs, and whether there is excess capacity available. Retailers are assortment builders for food shoppers and will respond quickly to changes in shopper preferences. A supermarket's supply of a particular product line is highly elastic; shelf space is a very flexible input.

Time Supply is generally more elastic in the long term than in the short, because suppliers can make changes more easily if they have more time. In the very short run, supply tends to be inelastic. An agricultural producer, being committed to a particular production enterprise, is likely to complete the production cycle and market the product, irrespective of the current price.[2] On the other hand, in the very long run, all costs become variable. New factories and warehouses can be built, and more land can be brought into production. Supply becomes highly elastic.

Perishability/Storability The supply of perishable products tends to be inelastic, because suppliers have no choice but to move their products to market. Storability, on the other hand, allows suppliers to delay, making short-term supply more elastic.

Think Break

To supply the Japanese market for pumpkins during their winter, pumpkins are grown in Tonga, a South Sea island, for the early market and in New Zealand for the later market. If the Tongan crop failed, what would happen to the price and quantity sold of the New Zealand crop?

Excess Capacity Supply becomes more elastic where there is excess capacity in an industry. A manufacturer with a plant operating at 50 percent capacity or a wholesaler with a half-empty warehouse can respond immediately to a small price increase by increasing the supply of manufacturing or warehouse capacity. They may even offer price discounts to get better utilization of their facilities. In this situation, volume increases as per-unit price falls—an apparently downward-sloping supply curve.

Industry Structure and Organization Economists describe industry structure in terms of:

---

[2]The rational producer will supply the product as long as the variable costs associated with completing the production and marketing cycle are less than the market price. For example, if a crop is ready for harvest, a rational supplier will calculate harvesting and transport costs and, if these are less than the prevailing price, the producer will harvest and market the crop. All other costs are, at this stage, bygone and irrelevant to the decision on whether or not to harvest.

- The number and size distribution of suppliers
- Barriers to entry of new suppliers
- The extent to which suppliers act independently of each other in establishing prices and other terms of sale
- Product homogeneity/differentiation between suppliers
- The availability of alternative products from related industries.

As discussed above, the supply of agricultural products is generally inelastic in the short term. In the long term, the competitive structure of the agricultural production sector ensures that the supply of agricultural products is highly elastic: existing producers act independently to increase production (they know that their individual actions will not affect the market price), new producers can enter the industry, and there is no product differentiation between suppliers.

Impact of Changes in the Prices of Alternative Products

If a farmer, processor, or distributor has many production alternatives and low switching costs, supply would be expected to be elastic, with respect both to changes in the product's own price and to changes in the price of alternative products. Supply changes in response to changes in the product's own price are shown by movements along the supply curve; supply changes in response to changes in the price of alternative products are shown by shifts in the supply curve. An increase in the price of an alternative product causes the supply curve to shift to the left; a decrease causes it to shift to the right (Figure 2-7).

Impact of Changes in Input Prices

Other things being equal, an increase in the price of an input will result in decreased output; that is, the supply curve shifts to the left (Figure 2-7). For example, if the price of fertilizer increases, less wheat will be produced. This is true in theory, but for most inputs the price change would have to be substantial to affect output very much. This is because the loss in production is likely to be worth more than the increased input cost.

Of course, an increase in the price of an input will result in the producer substituting other inputs to the extent to that this is technically possible. The demand for inputs becomes more elastic in the longer term when producers have more time to change their management practices. For example, a food processor can respond to an increase in the price of cans by substituting another packaging material, but this can happen only after major changes to the production line have been made. The implication of input substitution is that the long-term impact of an input price change is likely to be greater than the short-term.

Impact of Changes in Technology

Broadly defined, technology is the conversion relationship between inputs and outputs. A technological advance occurs where more output is produced from the same

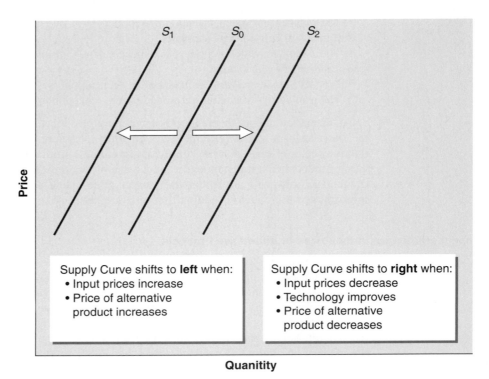

FIGURE 2-7   Supply curve shifters.

input mix or less inputs are required for the same output. For example, the "green revolution" of the 1950s and '60s resulted in significant increases in yield per acre for staple crops such as wheat and rice. The impact of a technological advance is to move the supply curve to the right.

EFFECTS OF SUPPLY AND DEMAND CHANGES ON PRICE

Price is established at the intersection of the supply and demand curves. Prices change because the supply and/or the demand curve shifts.

Figure 2-8A shows the effect of shift in the supply curve (from S_1 to S_2). Any of the supply-curve shifters discussed above may cause this to happen. The initial price P_1 is established at the intersection of the supply curve S_1, and both the elastic demand curve D_e and the inelastic demand curve D_i (the intersection of D_e and D_i at this point is only to keep things simple—it gives us the same starting price, P_1). The impact of a shift in the supply curve to S_2 is to depress the price to P_2 for the elastic demand curve, D_e, and to P_2' for the inelastic demand curve, D_i. Recalling the earlier discussion on price flexibility, we can now state an important

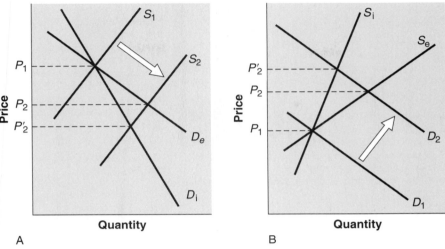

FIGURE 2-8   Supply and demand curve shifters.

conclusion: The impact of a shift in the supply curve on price depends on the elasticity of demand—the less elastic, the greater the impact.

Figure 2-8B shows the same idea but in terms of a shift in demand from D_1 to D_2. This causes the price to increase to P_2 for the elastic supply S_e, and to P'_2 for the inelastic supply, S_i. That is: The impact of a shift in the demand curve on price depends on the elasticity of supply—the less elastic, the greater the impact. For most basic food raw materials, demand is both relatively stable and inelastic. Price instability is caused mainly by unpredictable changes in supply, often due to weather.

Prices for agricultural products can change sharply from year to year, and even from month to month. The basic cause of price instability is that both supply and demand at the farm gate tend to be inelastic, with the result that relatively small shifts in demand and supply can have a significant effect on price. To appreciate how this works for a specific product requires an understanding of the product's seasonal and geographic patterns of supply and demand and awareness of substitute products, as well as supply and demand elasticities. For example, until the 1960s, the United States was the only significant producer of soybeans, most of which were used by United States processors. Demand, driven by the United States requirements for animal feed, was both relatively stable and quite inelastic. In this environment, price changes from year to year were mainly the result of changes in United States plantings, yields, and production, and price changes within a season were driven by supply shifts as the result of weather in the Midwest. This simple model was complicated by Brazil's becoming a major soybean producer and by increased demand from other countries, such as Japan, for United States soybeans.

Southern Hemisphere producers of horticultural products, such as New Zealand and Chile, find profitable seasonal opportunities in the "off season" for Northern

BOX 2-1

WHEAT PRICES: THE STORY BEHIND THE LINE

An analysis of the peaks and valleys of U.S. wheat prices from 1989 through 1996 demonstrates supply and demand in action.

A Big U.S. winter wheat crop is expected along with larger foreign crops. U.S. crop of 2.730 billion bushels. Stocks at end of crop year increase by 62%.
B Small 1991 wheat crop of only 1.981 billion bushels.
C Increased export demand.
D Winter wheat production up 13%; yield is second

highest on record. Total wheat supplies are largest since 1990/91.
E China's wheat imports in 1995/96 are projected to rise to 12 million tons, a 20% increase.
F Because of adverse weather, U.S. wheat production is projected to fall for third consecutive year.
G Southern Plains wheat crop is down 30% from 1995, owing to dry weather. Total supplies of wheat are 9% lower.

Source: USDA, *Agricultural Outlook*, various issues, 1990–96.

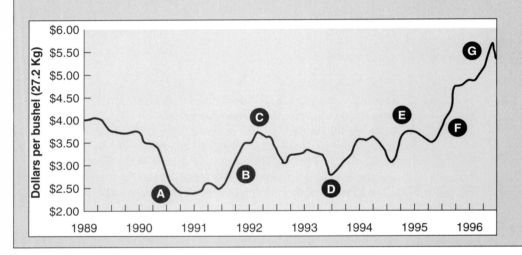

Hemisphere producers, the result of which is that Northern Hemisphere prices are more stable than they would have been without these alternative sources of supply.

Industry Structure

Both demand and supply elasticity are determined mainly by the availability of substitutes, either within the industry (one soybean producer versus another) or from alternative products (soybean meal versus meat meal). The possibility of substitutes depends on how the industry is organized—what economists call its structure. The main variables influencing *industry structure* are discussed above.

There are two extremes on the industry structure continuum:

Perfect Competition. Many suppliers, all producing the same product and acting independently of each other; no barriers to entry for new suppliers.

Monopoly. One supplier; complete barriers to entry for both potential alternative products and new companies.

It is, in fact, difficult to find industries that meet the requirement of being either perfectly competitive or a monopoly, although agricultural production in many parts of the world approaches the perfect-competition model. The reality is that most industries lie somewhere between the two extremes. Economists have a variety of words for such industries: *duopoly*—two suppliers; *oligopoly*—a "small number" of suppliers; and *monopolistic competition*—a relatively large number of producers, relative freedom of entry and exit, but each supplier sells a product that is somewhat different from that of competing suppliers (this differentiation often being achieved by branding). These terms refer to an industry as a supplier; similar terms are also used to describe an industry as a buyer: monopsony—one buyer; or oligopsony—a small number of buyers.

While it is difficult to establish a clear relationship between structure and performance for anything but the two (theoretical) ends of the continuum, it is certainly useful to recognize that monopoly and monopsony power are important issues in the food system. It should also be recognized that structure at one level in the system should not be considered independently of structure at other levels. For example, the structure of food manufacturing tends to be much more concentrated, with higher barriers to entry than agricultural production, implying that processors have some power in their relationship with farmers. On the other hand, in some countries (for example, England and Australia), food retailing is becoming more concentrated than many food manufacturing sectors, suggesting increasing retailer power relative to their suppliers. These issues will be discussed in more detail in Chapter 6.

DERIVED DEMAND

The demand for food products at retail is the *primary demand* in the food system. This primary demand translates into *derived demand* at various stages in the food system. For example, the derived demand for any quantity of a food product at the factory door is retail demand less the retailer's and wholesaler's margins. Consumers' primary demand for pasta, Figure 2-9, governs derived demand for durum wheat.

Three levels of demand in a simplified food system are shown in Figure 2-10. M_1 is the retailer's margin, M_2 is the processor's margin, and M_3 is the total marketing margin, farm gate to retail.

The processing and retail margins are constant in this example, and the three demand curves are therefore parallel. What does a constant margin mean? The *margin* can be thought of as the price of providing processing and retailing services. The relationship between the margin and quantity is therefore the supply curve for processing or distribution services. In the example shown in Figure 2-10, the margins do not change with volume, implying a flat supply curve—that is, an infinitely elastic supply of both processing and retailing services. This situation is illustrated in Figure 2-11.

FIGURE 2-9   The derived demand for durum wheat. Farmers grow durum wheat specially for pasta making, a specific process, and perhaps for a specific miller of semolina (durum wheat flour). The demand for durum wheat is derived from consumer demand for pasta. *(Courtesy of R. Lamberts, New Zealand Institute of Crop and Food Research.)*

FIGURE 2-10   Derived demand in the food system.

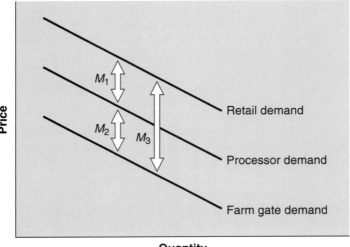

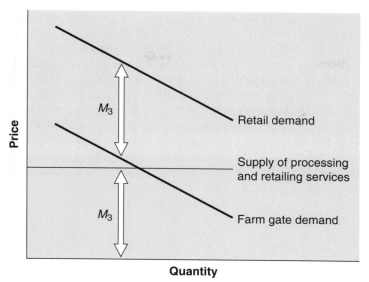

FIGURE 2-11   The marketing margin and the supply of marketing services.

In Figure 2-11, the supplies of processing and retailing services are added together.

The total margin, farm gate to retail, is M_3. This is also the supply curve for processing and retailing services. An upward-sloping supply curve (the usual situation) implies a margin structure as shown in Figure 2-12A. Margins of the percentage mark-up type, commonly observed in wholesaling and retailing, imply a derived

FIGURE 2-12   Derived demand: marketing margins change with quantity sold.

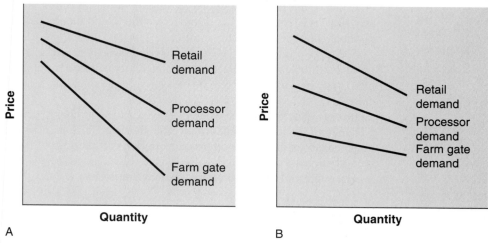

demand structure as shown in Figure 2-12B—a downward-sloping supply curve for distribution services.

In the short term at least, a downward-sloping supply of marketing services is quite common in food processing and distribution. In the discussion on elasticity of supply, it was suggested that a warehouse operator might offer a quantity discount in marketing storage. This is most likely to happen when a) there is excess capacity and b) a high proportion of the supplier's costs are fixed.

The previous section discussed how industry structure affects elasticity of supply. The supply of agricultural products is highly elastic in the long term, because the agricultural production sector is one with many suppliers, low barriers to entry, and little product differentiation. In general, the structure of the processing and distribution stages of the food system is less than perfectly competitive, and the supply of processing and distribution services is correspondingly less elastic.

SUMMARY

The demand for a food product or raw material at any stage of the food system derives from consumer demand. This chapter introduces economic concepts of the relationship between prices, demand, and supply.

The economic model of demand states that the quantity of any food product demanded by consumers is determined by:

- The product's price
- The price of other products competing for the consumer's dollar
- Consumers' incomes
- Consumers' tastes and preferences.

Elasticity of demand measures the change in quantity purchased in response to a change in price. Generally, demand is more elastic when the product has close substitutes and is not a necessity. The marketing activity of food manufacturers uses branding to distance products from substitutes, making demand less elastic. On the other hand, the product supplied by an individual producer of a commodity (such as wheat) is identical to that of other suppliers, and the demand facing such an individual supplier is infinitely elastic.

For farm products, price changes occur in response to changes in supply, and price flexibility, which measures the sensitivity of price to changes in quantity supplied, may be a more appropriate measure of price/quantity sensitivity than demand elasticity.

Income elasticity is a measure of how quantity purchased changes in response to a change in income. In general, income elasticity falls as income rises and can become negative for basic food products in rich communities; that is, demand falls as income increases.

The supply of any food product is determined by:

- The product's price
- The prices of products that compete for the resources of the producing company

- The prices of inputs used in the production process
- The technical relationships in the production process.

Elasticity of Supply is a measure of the sensitivity of quantity supplied to changes in price and is influenced by the availability of alternative production enterprises, time (the longer suppliers have to adjust, the more elastic the supply), perishability/storability, and industry structure and organization.

The price is established at the intersection of the supply and demand curves. Price changes are caused by either the supply or demand curve shifting and will be highest when demand and supply are inelastic.

Retail demand is the primary demand in the food system. Demand at earlier stages is derived from this primary demand. For example, ex-plant demand for a food manufacturer is retail demand less the retailer's margin. Margin is the price of providing retailing services, and the relationship between it and the volume of product traded is the supply of retailing services.

IMPORTANT TERMS AND CONCEPTS

complement products 33	monopolistic competition 43
cross-price elasticity of demand 32	monopoly 43
demand curve 29	oligopoly 43
derived demand 43	perfect competition 42
elastic 29	price elasticity of demand 29
income elasticity of demand 34	price flexibility 31
industry structure 42	primary demand 43
inelastic 29	substitute products 30
law of demand 29	supply curve 37
margin 43	

QUESTIONS

1 What is the law of demand? Under what situations might this law not hold true?

2 The price of a package of a certain brand of cereal is reduced from $2.00 to $1.90. Sales increase from 1,000 to 1,100 packages. What is the apparent elasticity of demand for this brand?

3 List the main factors affecting elasticity of demand. For each of the following pairs of products, which would you expect to have the most elastic demand?
   a Potatoes and avocados.
   b Unbranded fresh market potatoes and "X" brand frozen french fries.
   c Milk in China and milk in Germany.
   d Australian soft winter wheat and soft winter wheat produced by farmer Alan Smith in New South Wales, Australia.

4 Define price flexibility. If world wheat production increases by 20 percent and the wheat price falls by 80 percent, what is the apparent price flexibility? What is the apparent elasticity of demand for wheat? Australian wheat production increases by 20 percent and the wheat price falls by 5 percent; what is the apparent price flexibility for Australian wheat? Why is this less than the price flexibility for wheat as a whole?

5 Define cross-price elasticity. The price of eggs falls by 10 percent and chicken consumption increases by 1 percent. What is the cross-price elasticity? On the other hand, if the price of chicken increases by 10 percent, egg consumption falls by 2 percent. What is the cross-price elasticity?

   Why the difference between the two elasticities? In general, would you expect cross-price elasticities between different food products to be higher or lower in a wealthy country, such as Sweden, compared with a developing country, such as Zimbabwe?

6 What are the determinants of the supply of a food product or value-adding activity?

7 Define elasticity of supply. List factors influencing elasticity of supply. In each of the following cases, which product or service would you expect to have the most elastic supply?

   a Wheat produced in the Canadian Prairies/wheat produced in East Anglia (a fertile crop producing area in southeast England).

   b Broilers/milk (over the next year).

   c Lettuce at harvest/wheat at harvest.

   d Broilers where all broiler sheds are being used to maximum capacity/broilers where there is excess broiler production capacity.

   e Dairy cabinet space in the supermarket/branded dairy products supplied to the supermarket.

8 "Farm-gate demand is generally less elastic than demand at retail." Do you agree with this statement? Give reasons for your answer.

REFERENCES AND RESOURCES

George, P. S., and G. A. King. "Consumer Demand for Food Commodities in the United States With Projections for 1980." *Giannini Foundation Monograph 26,* California Agricultural Experiment Station, 1971.

Huang, Kuo S. "A Complete System of US Demand for Food." *USDA, ERS, Technical Bulletin 1821,* 1993.

Mellor, J. W., and R. H. Adams. "The New Political Economy of Food and Agricultural Development." *Food Policy,* November 1986.

Ritson, Christopher. *Agricultural Economics: Principles and Policy.* London: Granada Publishing, 1978.

Seitz, Wesley D., Gerald C. Nelson, and Harold G. Halcrow. *Economics of Resources, Agriculture, and Food.* New York: McGraw-Hill, 1994.

Tomek, William G., and Kenneth L. Robinson. *Agricultural Product Prices.* 3d ed. Cornell: University Press, 1990.

Internet Sources

United States Department of Agriculture's Economic Research Service. Home page: www.econ.ag.gov/

USDA Agricultural Statistics: www.usda.gov/nass/

PART TWO

CONSUMERS

A study of consumers' basic need for food, their concerns about food, and how they buy and use food products

In Part One you learned about the Food System and the strong influence of the consumer on food marketing throughout the system. Therefore, it is important that you have knowledge of the consumers' needs, attitudes, and behavior toward foods, before studying how to organize food marketing.

Consumers have basic nutritional needs, but many other factors also affect their buying behavior, such as their culture, society, education, and income. These, and a model of food-buying behavior, are the subjects of Chapter 3. Because foods are part of their daily lives and affect their health, consumers have safety, environmental, and other concerns about foods which food marketers need to understand. Chapter 4 describes some of these concerns and their current and future effects on food marketing.

3

FOOD CONSUMPTION AND BUYING BEHAVIOR

CHAPTER OUTLINE

LEARNING OBJECTIVES

After reading this chapter and answering the questions in the Think Breaks and at the end of the chapter, you should be able to:

- Compare nutritional food consumption in different countries.
- Compare the consumption of the basic food groups in different countries.
- Recognize changes in food consumption that occur with improvement in economic conditions.
- Recognize changes in consumers' food behavior processes in affluent societies.
- Identify consumers' sources of knowledge on foods.
- Appreciate the increasing acceptance, around the world, of foods foreign to the tastes and cultures of a given country or region.
- Analyze the effect of the consumers' environment on their food behavior.
- Understand consumer food behavior and the Food-Buying Decision Process.

INTRODUCTION

Food consumption can be studied at the overall level of a country and at the level of an individual consumer or group of consumers. The general food consumption in a country is important because it indicates both the nutritional standard of the country and the amounts consumed of different food groups—cereals, meat, vegetables, fruit, and dairy products. This "macro" information is useful when identifying overseas markets for future development and for studying trends in eating patterns. The study of individual consumers or groups of consumers is the basis of food marketing; it is at this micro level that market research can identify the consumer behaviors which can be related to product strategy, promotion and advertising, market-channel organization, and pricing strategy.

This chapter compares the consumption of foods in different countries and how it is affected by the economic status of the people in these countries. It discusses how the types of foods eaten change as the economic status rises and the food-production and food-processing industries become more technologically advanced. In particular, it shows the food changes which occur when a country becomes more affluent (see Figure 3-1).

Many factors affect consumer food behavior, from physiological hunger pangs to culture and nationality. The wider aspects of the environment that affect consumer food behavior include nationality, culture, social groups, technology, and food availability. Companies exporting foods to other countries need to understand the environment of the consumers in those countries.

Consumer food behavior can be divided into four parts—buying; carrying home; preparing, cooking, and serving; and eating. All need to be considered in food marketing. Although the main emphasis in food marketing is on the buying behavior, as this is the ultimate acceptance or rejection of the food product, buying behavior is based on consumer acceptance/rejection during the entire Food-Buying Decision Process. In marketing food products, it is important to consider every behavioral step in product development, promotion, and distribution.

FIGURE 3-1   How are food-buying choices made? The typical grocery basket differs from country to country, region to region, and year to year, reflecting the varying lifestyles and tastes of consumers. *(Source: U.S. Department of Agriculture.)*

FOOD CONSUMPTION

Aggregate food consumption can be studied on two bases—the average *nutritional intake per capita* and the quantities of the different basic food groups eaten per capita. Nutritional intake was used in the past mainly in comparison with national or international standards for nutritional needs to develop national health policies. Today, the food industry is interested in this information because of consumers' increasing awareness of the food industry's responsibility for health. The quantities of different basic foods eaten also provides a great deal of information on the size of different food markets. More importantly, food marketers must watch for any long-term changes that are occurring, as these changes indicate opportunities for new markets and new products.

Nutritional Food Consumption

Nutritional food consumption is usually reported on the basic nutritional components of foods—calories, protein, fat, and carbohydrates—but vitamins and minerals may also be included. The *Recommended Dietary Allowance* (RDA), the recommended nutritional intake, is set internationally by the Food and Agriculture Organization (FAO), but many countries set their own RDA. Countries can be divided into three broad groups—below, around, and above the international recommended nutritional standard. Examples of representative countries are shown in Table 3-1.

In countries of lower nutritional intakes, the calories are mainly from plant products, but in an affluent country like the United States, one-third of calories are from animal products. Some countries with acceptable nutritional intakes have crops as

TABLE 3-1   QUANTITIES AVAILABLE FOR NUTRITIONAL INTAKE IN DIFFERENT COUNTRIES

		Ghana	Peru	Malaysia	United States	International standard Men	International standard Women
Total	Calories[1]	1733	2192	2723	3642	2900	2200
	Protein[2]	38	79	62	107	63	50
	Fat[3]	31	40	74	164	97	73
Animal	Calories	90	274	434	1228	—	—
	Protein	12	31	32	71	—	—
	Fat	4	13	47	93	—	—
Crop	Calories	1643	1918	2289	2414	—	—
	Protein	26	48	30	36	—	—
	Fat	27	27	27	71	—	—

[1]Calories/capita/day (1 calorie = 4.2 joules).
[2]Grams/capita/day.
[3]Grams/capita/day.
Source: FAO Production Year Book, Vol. 42, 1988, for 1984–86.

the major sources of calories and proteins, and, as a result, they often have low fat intakes. The United States has much higher protein and fat intakes than many countries. Not only are these country comparisons important, but the different markets within a country can be studied in the same way to give basic marketing information. For example, in poor districts the emphasis is on high-calorie, bulky staple foods; in the more affluent areas, low-calorie or reduced-calorie foods in great variety and small quantities are emphasized. As discussed in Chapter 2, the income elasticity of demand in developed countries for many food products is near zero or negative, with the result that changing incomes do not really result in much, if any, increase in consumption.

The daily intake of nutrients and the RDA vary for different age groups. When studying food marketing at the consumer level, it is important to recognize these differences. For example, in the United States in 1985, the total calories available daily per capita were 3,500 (14,700 joules),[1] but according to diet surveys the average intake for adult women was 1,517 calories, for adult men, 2,558 calories, and for children, 1,440 calories. The recommended energy intakes are, for adult women 1,900–2,200; for adult men, 2,300–3,000; and for children, 1,300–2,000 calories/capita/day, depending on age, weight, and height.[2]

Think Break

In two different districts in your town/city—one a poor district and one an affluent district—what are the retail facilities, and what appear to be the most important food-product types sold in each?

Consumption of Basic Food Groups

The consumption of *basic food groups* can also be compared in different countries. The proportion of these foods—cereals, legumes, fruit and vegetables, meat, and dairy products—is affected not only by economics but also by culture, general availability of foods, the technology of agricultural production, and food processing. In Table 3-2 the foods eaten in four economic regions of the world are compared.

Table 3-2 shows how drastically the consumption of the food groups shifts as nations develop. Note that cereal consumption in the Asian developing region is almost twice that in the United States and Canada, which in turn consume over twelve times as much meat and poultry as the least-developed countries of the world. Interestingly, in comparing the United States and Canada and the European

---

[1] Joules are the metric measure of energy: 1 calorie = 4.2 joules.

[2] Detailed information on food consumption in the United States can be found in B. Senauer, E. Asp, and J. Kinsey, *Food Trends and the Changing Consumer* (St. Paul, MN: Eagan Press, 1991). Many countries have similar reviews of changing food consumption, e.g., R. Bailey and M.D. Earle, *Home Cooking and Take-aways: A History of 100 Years of Food Consumption in New Zealand* (Wellington, New Zealand: SIR Publishing, 1993).

TABLE 3-2   CONSUMPTION OF BASIC FOOD GROUPS IN FOUR REGIONS, 1990–92

	Pounds*/per capita/per year			
	United States & Canada	European Union[1]	Developing[2]	Least developed[3]
Cereals	243	242	438	329
Starchy roots and pulses	141	188	99	221
Fruits and vegetables	572	524	231	132
Sugar and sweeteners	142	85	34	16
Meat and poultry	253	192	37	20
Milk and other dairy	565	523	69	51
Fish and seafood	49	54	22	15
Vegetable oils	53	53	18	12
Animal fats[4]	21	24	3	1

*One pound = 0.454 kg.
[1]Belgium, Luxembourg, Denmark, France, Germany, Greece, Ireland, Italy, The Netherlands, Portugal, Spain, and United Kingdom.
[2]Such as Iran, Iraq, Turkey, India, China, Korean Republic, Malaysia, the Philippines, Thailand, and Vietnam.
[3]Such as Botswana, Chad, Ethiopia, Rwanda, Somalia, Uganda, Afghanistan, Bangladesh, Cambodia, Haiti, Samoa, and Solomon Islands.
[4]Includes butter, lard, fish oils, and edible tallow.
Source: Selected commodities from FAO Agrostat database, as cited in "World Food Consumption Up, But Not Everywhere," *Food Review* 18:2 (May–August 1995): 50–51.

Union (E.U.), the consumption figures are remarkably similar, except for the United States and Canada's higher consumption of meat and poultry and 67 percent greater sugar and sweetener consumption.

CHANGES IN FOOD CONSUMPTION

There are two main causes of change in food consumption: rise in economic status and, in affluent societies, the variety of foods produced by highly technological agricultural production and food processing.

Changes in Food Consumption as a Country Develops

Food marketing is dependent on a country's economic level of development, as discussed in Chapter 2 (see Table 2-3). Through the interaction of social and cultural values with government policies, development determines the level and type of food marketing activity. There are different ways of describing the stages of a country's development; Table 3-3 offers a useful description for food marketing.

Some of the changes that occur in human food consumption as a country develops from stage to stage are:

• A smaller percentage of consumer income is spent on food. At the base level, a high percentage of income (or physical effort) is spent on food—about 80 percent. As the country moves to higher stages, this percentage gradually decreases until, in the affluent society, it is less than 20 percent.

TABLE 3-3   STAGES OF A COUNTRY'S FOOD-RELATED DEVELOPMENT

Stage 1: The base society	Primitive agriculture Food prepared by householders Primitive technology Low level of literacy
Stage 2: Preconditions for take-off	Simple agricultural technology Craftspeople in food processing Modern science and technology being introduced Development of education Development of power, transport, and communications
Stage 3: The take-off	Modern technology in agriculture Small/medium-sized food factories Science and technology education Development of industry, human resources, and financial systems Commodity marketing to overseas markets
Stage 4 The drive to maturity	Modern technology applied to all sectors Large agricultural and food processing organizations/companies High level of education Development of complex infrastructure and large-scale industry Industrial product marketing to overseas markets
Stage 5: The affluent society	Agriculture and food processing employ decreasing numbers of people Continuous food processing High level of research and technical development Economic affluence Multinational food companies

• The number of calories eaten increases gradually from about 1,500 per capita per day in the basic society to about 2,500 in the middle stages, to 3,000–3,500 in the last two stages. It stays around this level for some time but may gradually decrease.

• Protein in the diet increases from approximately 40 g/capita/day to about 85–90 g/capita/day. This happens at a slightly slower rate than the calories increase, and the rate is dependent on the source of protein. That is, protein levels rise faster when the source is legume and cereal proteins than when it is animal protein. This is mainly the effect of cost of production.

• There is also a change in types of food eaten, principally a decrease in the basic carbohydrate—bread in the European countries and rice in Asian countries. For example, Turkey and Yugoslavia have higher intakes of bread than the United States and the Netherlands.

• Usually consumption of meat and dairy products increases, but this depends on availability and cost.

Think Break

How would consumption of cereal products change as a family's income increases in your country? In New Zealand, as family income increases, the family purchases smaller quantities of plain products, such as flour and porridge oats, and more white bread, cracker biscuits, and sweet biscuits, gradually adding more expensive and fancy foods—whole-grain breads, chocolate biscuits, and breakfast cereals such as muesli, Honey Puffs, and Coco-Pops.

How do you expect your food choice to change as you move from a student income to a high salary?

Changes in an Affluent Society's Food Consumption

The rising affluence in the United States, then in Europe, and now in Asian countries has resulted in major changes in food eating habits. Table 3-4 illustrates in detail the dramatic changes that occurred in the diet of the Japanese people as their economy grew from being one of the poorest to one of the richest in the world. Note how the basic energy food, rice, has decreased, and meat, eggs, and dairy products have increased.

TABLE 3-4   JAPANESE FOOD CONSUMPTION FROM 1955 TO 1990

	Pounds per capita per year			
Food	1955	1970	1990	% Increase/decrease 1955–1990
Cereals	344	283	228	−34
Rice	244	210	154	−37
Wheat	55	68	70	27
Other cereals	45	5	4	−91
Meats	7	30	63	800
Beef and veal	2	5	13	550
Pork	2	12	25	1,150
Poultry	1	8	23	2,200
Whale	2	3	<1	−95
Other meats	<1	2	2	275
Fish and shellfish	58	70	82	41
Eggs	8	33	36	350
Milk and dairy products	27	111	183	578
Fruit	27	83	82	204
Vegetables	182	255	236	30
Potatoes	102	36	45	−56
Starches	10	18	35	250
Pulses	21	22	21	0
Sugar	27	59	46	70
Fats and oils	6	20	32	433

Source: Japan's Statistical Yearbook of the Ministry of Agriculture, Forestry, and Fisheries, 1990–91 and previous issues.

Increasing affluence has resulted in two trends in food consumption: *converging food preferences* and a *greater diversity of foods eaten.* Food preferences in different cultures may vary widely, but as consumers grow more affluent, their preferences become more similar and converge. The food markets in the United States, Europe, and Australasia have expanded to include a large number of ethnic foods: Italian, Chinese, Mexican, Greek, Indian, Thai, and now Celtic! These ethnic foods are nearly always adapted to produce a more generally acceptable flavor and texture. Any extremes of, for example, "hotness" or "bitterness" are reduced, and any unacceptable raw material is removed or disguised. These internationally acceptable foods are then introduced in the other countries, usually to the middle classes. Thus, one discovers that lasagna, in a form slightly different than the Italian original, is now readily available in many European and Asian countries.

The affluent society is also affected by the development of new food industries, importation of foods from many countries, and consumers' increasing knowledge about foods. This is graphically demonstrated in the United States by the decreased use of animal fats, including butter, and the increased use of vegetable oils (see Figure 3-2.)

Animal fats were made by simple methods which were large-scale versions of what was done on the farm or in the home, such as butter churning, but the vegetable-oil industry has been built on the new technology of chemical engineering. Also, people started to realize from the media that animal fats could be related to heart diseases.

FIGURE 3-2   Consumption of oils and fats in the United States, 1940–1995. *(Source: USDA, Agricultural Outlook, June 1996.)*

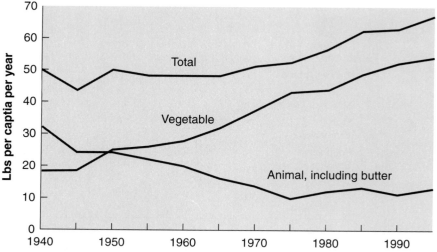

THE EFFECTS OF CULTURE, SOCIETY, EDUCATION, AND FOOD AVAILABILITY ON CONSUMER FOOD BEHAVIOR

The greatest influence on a consumer's choice of food products is nationality or race. Within a race or nationality, differences of choices result from the various factors shown in Figure 3-3.

Individuals—Age, Sex, Education, and Standard of Living

Although individuals' choices of food are affected by their age and sex, their education, their standard of living, and the family or group in which they live, their choices are ultimately governed by their own psychological and physiological make-up.

Consumer's individual characteristics may be considered in two areas:

Psychological make-up: Personality, fears, pride
Physiological make-up: Sensory abilities, hunger, nutritional needs

Individuals have their own sets of preferences which, to greater or lesser extent, override preferences defined by culture or religion. The consumer may eat to overcome loneliness, to feel happiness, or to gain prestige. Each individual has physiological needs for energy, protein tissue building, vitamins, and minerals. Some may need high calorie intake, some low calorie intake. There are also differences among individuals in their sensory reactions to foods. Blue-vein cheese, from Denmark, or durian fruit, from Malaysia, may be liked by some and loathed by others.

Age influences not only the quantities of food eaten, but also the types of food and the eating place. Eating changes as the person develops from baby to child to teenager to adult, and finally to elderly. There are different foods for different age groups: baby foods, children's biscuits and cereals, teenagers' snacks, diet foods for young women,

FIGURE 3-3   The factors affecting consumer choice of foods.

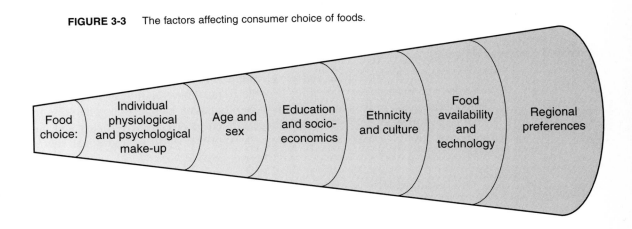

low-fat and salt-free products for the elderly.[3] Increasing life expectancies are resulting in the graying of America; by the year 2000, 50 percent of the elderly will live to age 80. This growing market segment is different in their food-buying profile: they spend less on food-away-from-home and eat less than the average amount of red meat and dairy products. Designing, packaging, and delivering food to this group will provide opportunities as well as challenges to the food system.[4]

The difference in eating habits between the sexes is not marked in Western cultures except for quantity and caloric intake, but it still exists in many other cultures. Generally women eat less than men and, in a family, may have the poorer food. In some cultures, women may not eat with men and they have different foods. In the United States, women are decreasing their caloric intake faster than men; usually they are more nutrition conscious. Most diet foods are designed for women.

Think Break

How has your food behavior changed from child to teenager to adult? What types of food did you eat at each age? What foods do you expect to eat in the future?

Higher education normally tends to lead to more varied eating habits, because more information about foods is available, foods are not as subject to taboos and customs, and people travel more and try other ethnic foods. Better education also leads to more knowledge of nutrition, and the nutritional attributes of the products become important.

The higher the standard of living, the greater will be people's ability to change their eating habits, as they can buy a variety of foods. Also, there will be a tendency to travel more, to see more advertising, and to have refrigerators, freezers, microwave ovens, and cars, which will change their whole food behavior. Generally the basic simple foods are replaced by more sophisticated and complex foods in a wider selection. Usually consumption of the staple carbohydrate (energy) food decreases, and consumption of protein foods, such as meat and dairy products, increases. People with high incomes also eat out more in restaurants.

Household Composition and Social Groups

Family or household behavior still has an important effect on food marketing. How and what the parent feeds the child lays the foundations for future eating habits. Hence there tends to be a continuation of family eating habits from generation to generation, unless there are strong outside influences. Today, advertising and the media are strong forces, causing changes around the world in traditional eating habits.

[3]C. O'Donnell, "Food Products for Different Age Groups: Formulating for the Ages," *Prepared Foods* (April 1994): 39–44.
[4]Jean Kinsey, "Changes in Food Consumption from Mass Market to Niche Markets," *Food and Agricultural Markets,* ed. Schertz and Daft (Washington, D.C.: National Planning Assn., 1994): 30.

Households of single people and single heads of households have increased, and today more than half of all households in the United States have only one or two inhabitants. These households tend to eat more food-away-from-home, purchase more convenience-type items, and as a result spend more per capita on food. Other Western countries and some parts of East Asia are also tending toward small households.

At the same time, the upward trend of increasing employment of women outside the home has continued. Today in the United States, almost 70 percent of married women in child-bearing years are now in the labor force. Studies have shown that the time devoted to household work is decreasing. In households, capital (microwave ovens) and purchased services (convenience food and food-away-from-home) are being substituted for household labor. Usually one person is responsible for buying the family's food; employed women still do 86 percent of the cooking, and 91 percent do most of the shopping. Though they may be accompanied by children or another adult who may influence the food purchased, they are looking for ways to feed the family quickly. Most spend less than 30 minutes preparing an evening meal, and 20 percent spend less than 15 minutes. The conclusion from all of this is, as Kinsey puts it, ". . . the demand for value-added food products is not about to end."[5]

Of course the "American experience" described above is not true around the world. In many countries, eating is still essentially a family affair, with mother doing the shopping and cooking. Men never buy food except when eating outside the house. The effect of the family on food eating is dependent on culture, education, standard of living, and of course, the individuals themselves. It is usually greater in cultures where the family eats together at least once a day.

The social group also affects the food eaten. Social groups can be social classes, sports groups, work groups, entertainment groups, and so on. Social classes are easy to identify and are often used to compare food behavior, but in some countries they are not important. However, in Britain and the United States there can be differences not only in the foods eaten but also in the brand bought by the lower and upper social classes. Cooper's marmalade would indicate an upper-class household in Britain and HP sauce a lower-class household. There is a difference between tennis and football clubs in Australia and New Zealand in the brands and types of beer drunk: light lagers in tennis clubs, heavy dark beer in football clubs.

Ethnicity, Culture, and Regional Preferences

Food in Cultures around the World   Around the world various *cultures* have different behavior toward foods and different eating habits and food symbols. Food has different prestige and emotionally satisfying properties. The French, for instance, hold food in high regard and are famous for their cuisine. The Italians take great pleasure in eating and in family meals, while the Thais and the Japanese present food with an attractive, even artistic, appearance.

[5]Kinsey, p. 33.

Meal patterns vary with the culture in the number of meals in a day, the way food is eaten, where it is eaten, and what utensils are used. In Western cultures, there are generally three meals per day: light breakfast, light-medium lunch, and heavy dinner, but now there is a tendency to have more snacks throughout the day. This snacking pattern is very similar to that in some Asian countries, where six or seven small meals may be taken each day.

The way food is bought and prepared also varies a great deal. While the French prefer fresh ingredients and buy small quantities often, Americans want to shop as seldom as possible and either buy frozen food or freeze fresh food when they arrive home. In many Western countries convenience is very important, so people want to prepare, cook, and serve food as quickly as possible, preferably in 30 minutes, but in other cultures preparation, cooking, and serving give great pleasure and can take several hours.

The food chosen may also have traditional significance. For example, turkey at Thanksgiving, a family event in the United States, originated from the use of wild turkeys by the Pilgrims in Massachusetts as their best source of meat. Certain foods become associated with special times of the year and often are not eaten outside of this time. Hot cross buns and Easter eggs are enjoyed at Easter, a Christian celebration. For the New Year, the Chinese eat special buns, while the Scots prepare shortbread and black buns.

Food preferences are often related to culture. There may be religious taboos, prohibiting pork for Jews or beef for Hindus, for instance; or there may be ritual methods of preparing foods: Kosher (Jewish) and Halal (Muslim) killing of animals.[6] There may also be nonreligious taboos, such as rejection by many Westerners of animal offal, which Thais and Chinese value highly. Thus a culture often divides foods into two groups—foods we eat and foods they eat. There are also status foods in a culture, which are usually presented to the higher or older members on a special occasion or are used to show the status of an individual. Culture affects all aspects of food behavior, but, except for strongly held taboos and preferences, culturally based food behavior can and does change with time.

Ethnicity and Culture in the United States   The United States continues to undergo changes in the composition of its population. While the white population increased at a rate of 0.5 percent in 1990, the African American population grew three times as fast, and the Hispanics and other races increased at six times that rate. By the end of the century, one-fourth of the population will be Hispanic and African American, with Hispanics being the single largest ethnic group.

This transformation in the ethnic composition of America has affected consumption patterns of different food types (see Figure 3-4). Ethnic minorities consume fewer fruits and vegetables, but more dark green vegetables, less milk and beef, and fewer desserts. They are more likely to eat rice, legumes, pork, fish,

---

[6]To study the effects of Kosher needs on foods and food processing, read J. M. Regenstein and C. E. Regenstein, "The Kosher Dietary Laws and Their Implementation in the Food Industry," *Food Technology* 42 (1988): 86–94.

FIGURE 3-4 Ethnic diversity presents opportunities, as well as challenges, for marketers. *(Source: U.S. Department of Agriculture.)*

poultry and eggs, and sweet beverages. With movement from low- to high-income groups, African Americans increase expenditures on beef and poultry by only about 5 percent, while Hispanics increase expenditures for beef by 37 percent and for poultry by 116 percent. Thus, increasing Hispanic incomes would contribute to higher meat consumption and be a positive factor in the demand for meat products. Higher-income ethnic groups spend about 20 percent less on milk products.[7]

Marketers are looking at the opportunities that *ethnic diversity* creates. Examples: one group of Hispanics in New York City proved to be a niche market for extra-high-fat milk.[8] It is reported that half of Quaker Oats' corn products are sold to ethnic minorities. One of their vice-presidents was quoted as saying, "We want ethnic marketing deeply embedded in every business manager in this company."[9] Salsa's replacing catsup as the most favored condiment, a marker of change in American eating habits, gives a strong warning to the astute, progressive marketer to pay attention to demographic trends. For example, Americans consider horsemeat as not for human consumption, but Box 3-1 indicates that not all cultures and eras agree.

[7]Kinsey, 24–27.
[8]Senauer, Asp, and Kinsey, 74–76.
[9]Leon E. Wynter, "People Patterns," *Wall Street Journal,* November 16, 1992: B1.

BOX 3-1

HORSEMEAT ANYONE?

The eating of horsemeat goes back tens of thousands of years and has continued down to historic times in the immense region stretching from Eastern Europe to Mongolia. These pastoral economies have been centered around the horse; it was used for transporting humans and cargo, the hide went into various manufactured items, the meat was eaten, and the milk was fermented into a liquor known as *kumiss.*

The practice of eating horseflesh spread from central Eurasia to many parts of the continent. It was favored in the court of Emperor Tamerlane at Samarkand and was once widespread among the Germanic tribes of Northern Europe. Sooner or later, the major religions turned against the practice. The Jews declared the horse to be an abomination because it did not satisfy the requirements of chewing the cud and being cloven hoofed; the Buddha specifically prohibited eating horseflesh; and the prophet Mohammed personally avoided horseflesh, although he did not forbid it to others. With the spread of Christianity, an attack was launched upon the consumption of horseflesh, ostensibly because of its association with the worship of the pagan deities; in A.D. 732 the practice was finally forbidden to Christians by Pope Gregory III. Being forced to give up hippophagy made pagans such as those of Iceland reluctant to convert.

The prohibitions against horseflesh consequently became ingrained as a repugnance in much of Europe and in some other parts of the world influenced by the colonial powers.

Hippophagy nevertheless persisted, and indeed horses were prized for food in places in Europe where forage was available. In Switzerland, monks were eating horseflesh in the eleventh century, despite the ban imposed on it four centuries earlier. Toward the end of the nineteenth century, its sale was legalized in France, Germany, Austria, and Scandinavia. The siege of Paris by German forces in 1870–71, during which time Parisians consumed at least 70,000 horses, had much to do with overcoming the prejudice against it. In France, around 1960 as many as 3,500 butcher shops were specializing in horsemeat.

Since then consumption of horsemeat has once again declined rapidly throughout Western Europe. A new wave of revulsion against it has been blamed on an outbreak of salmonella in 1967, but much more probably the decline has to do with ecology and economics. When, over the past few decades, armies stopped purchasing horses for cavalry and transport, they did away with a major incentive for the raising of horses, which were already becoming a luxury with the mechanization of farms. Most of the horsemeat eaten in Western Europe in the past few decades has therefore had to be imported; but transportation and related costs have raised the price to about that of beef and veal, further discouraging a horse food industry. Because horses compete for grass and grain with other herbivores, which are superior to them in fertility, tractability, and the amount of meat produced per pound of animal, horsemeat will probably not again become an important food in Western Europe.

Source: Peter Farb and George Armelagos, *Consuming Passions: An Anthropology of Eating* (Boston: Houghton Mifflin Co., 1980): 169–71.

Regional Preferences   Regional preferences tend to be especially evident in larger countries where there are difficulties in communication and transport, areas of different geography, or areas which have been settled by people from different areas of the world.

Even in a country the size of Britain, preferred foods and flavors differ by region: sweet sauces in southeast England, hot sauces in northern England; tripe (beef stomach) is enjoyed in the north, disliked in the south. In a large country like the United States the effect of local ethnic communities can be very marked: Mexican food is a favorite in California, Jewish food in New York, English food in the Northeast. The provinces in China not only have different foods but different styles of cooking, such as Cantonese or Schzechuan.

So many factors affect consumers' food behavior that it may seem too difficult to consider them all in building up a market strategy. It is important to identify which are most important to the consumer/product relationship for a specific product and a specific consumer group. Market segmentation, discussed in Chapter 12, is a means of identifying the consumer group for a particular product.

Food Availability and Technology

A country's geography affects its eating habits. The soils and climate determine what types of crops can be grown and therefore what is eaten. Although the inhabitants of Puerto Rico and Hawaii come from entirely different ethnic backgrounds, there is a great similarity in the tropical fruits eaten in each of these countries. In Southeast Asia, where rice flourishes, the people are rice eaters. In temperate climates, wheat, rye, and oats are the traditional carbohydrate sources. The introduction of maize into areas of Africa and of potatoes into Europe, where the climates favor these crops, changed the basic carbohydrate foods.

Modern agriculture now allows crops to be grown in a wide variety of countries, and modern transport eases movement of agricultural products from country to country, so the effect of geography on the foods eaten in a specific country is lessening.

Technological development is one of the strongest forces in causing changes in food eating habits. The introduction of new processing techniques—freezing, canning, and freeze-drying—made foods from far-away places more readily available. More rapid and efficient transport systems throughout the world have brought new foods to countries where they had not been seen; tropical fruit came to Britain, ocean fish to the midwestern United States. Also, certain foods can be eaten fresh for longer periods, through year-round production in Northern and Southern Hemisphere countries: strawberries and tomatoes are no longer eaten just in summer, or apples in autumn. Various vegetables and fruits can be eaten all year round in many countries, because they can be brought from countries with alternate seasons.

International Acceptance of Foods

Although all the above factors still have a very important effect on food behavior, the amazing change has been the international acceptance of foods. This has been encouraged by the development of foods such as Coca-Cola, hamburgers, and Kentucky Fried Chicken from the United States; yogurt and croissants from France; meat pies from Australia; rice noodles from China; and kiwifruit from New Zealand. These foods can be accompanied by heavy branding and promotions or can be sold as a "generic" product, as is kiwifruit.

Even international food products are not always identical throughout the world. International differences in food preferences can be analyzed in terms of the four basic tastes in food—sweetness, saltiness, sourness, and bitterness. Different cultures or social groups identify the levels of these basic tastes acceptable to them. These preferences can be quite basic and difficult to change. A food company can change these basic tastes in their product from country to country; for example, soft drink companies change the sugar and acid levels but keep the main flavor the same in all countries. Or a company can decide to design the product with a bland level acceptable in all countries but not necessarily the highest preference for each country. Over time, the consumers in all countries can accept these generalized sensory properties, and an international food preference develops.

However, this is not necessarily achievable in all cases. For example, in Thailand, instant noodles were introduced with flavors identical to those offered in Europe. They were a failure, but when a packet of a hot Thai sauce was added to the package, they were an instant success. In this case, the bland international flavor was not acceptable in the Thai market.

International food marketers need to *either:*

- identify the types of new imported foods which are being accepted by the middle class of a country

or:

- study the changes occurring in food eating habits in a country,
- study the basic tastes acceptable in these foods, and
- identify the aromas and flavors acceptable in foods.

Then they must either adapt their present products to the preference of the new consumers or design a new product which would be acceptable not only in their home market but in other countries as well. Box 3-2 illustrates the efforts of marketers to adapt Thai food flavors to mainstream U.S. consumer preferences.

Usually an innovative product can become international more quickly, as there are no basic cultural norms for the product, provided the innovation is not too great a change in food eating habits for the consumers to accept.[10]

FOOD-BUYER BEHAVIOR

Not only the overall food consumption, but also the food-buying behavior of individuals or groups of people should be studied. This is the basis for food marketing strategies. Consumers do not come to the buying situation with a complete blank page; they are bringing buying habits, attitudes, motives, and knowledge that they have built up through the years. Because food has to be bought regularly and prepared, food habits are developed which may change slowly. Many food-buying habits have developed from consumers' early years and change with time, so that food marketers have to research continually to recognize changes and take advantage of them.

Consumers' Attitudes, Motives, and Knowledge

Consumers have *attitudes* toward foods and motives for buying foods which always have to be recognized in food marketing. Attitudes are one of many psychological

---

[10]For predictions about the consumer in the twenty-first century, read G. M. Piggot, "Who Is the 21st Century Consumer?" *Infofish International,* January 1994: 12–20.

BOX 3-2

THAI MARKETERS DISH UP YUPPIE, GOURMET TASTES

A Thai food purist would sniff at the Thai offerings making their way into supermarkets, but that hasn't stopped food marketers, who are entering the ethnic foods arena with Thai seasonings for everyday food.

There isn't a strong market in U.S. grocery stores for authentic Thai foods, says Frank Laundry, president of Andre Prost, Inc., importer of A Taste of Thai seasonings sauce and mixes. But he thinks Americans will be looking to spice up their mainstream fare with the new taste of the Orient. "We're targeting the health conscious, round eye yuppie, who is desperately looking for a new way to serve chicken," Mr. Laundry says. San-J international is using a similar strategy for its San-J Thai Peanut Sauce. The sauce is recommended for stir-fry, pastas, and salads.

Other marketers are appealing to the more sophisticated gourmet cook. Restaurateur Tommy Tang, who owns popular Thai restaurants in New York and Los Angeles, relies on recipe cards, a home video, and a cookbook to promote his seasoning line.

Thai is one type of Oriental food that's pushing the category to new growth. Oriental food sales at retail grew for the second consecutive year in 1991, up 5.5% to $991 million. Thai food's ultimate success at the grocery store will depend on how well it complements cuisine Americans already eat, says Harry Balzer, VP of NPD Group, a food service consultancy. "If it revolutionizes the way we eat, it doesn't have a chance," he says. "Mexican food would not have taken off if it had not been a new way to cook ground beef." Thai food's potential lies in what it can do for foods Americans already consume—chicken, pasta, noodle dishes.

Mr. Balzer doesn't consider the U.S.'s growing Asian population a factor in Thai foods' success in the supermarket. "Immigration by the Hispanic and Asian populations may have introduced those foods to this country, but clearly their success has been due to their adoption by non-Hispanics and non-Asians."

Adapted from the article, "Thai Marketers Dish Up Yuppie, Gourmet Tastes," *Advertising Age,* April 27, 1992: S-12. Reprinted with permission from *Advertising Age.*

influences operating within individuals that determine people's general behavior and thus influence their behavior as consumers. Attitudes are people's favorable or unfavorable evaluations, emotional feelings, and tendencies in regard to a product. Do they regard hot oatmeal as children's food, as old people's food, as a breakfast food, or as food for horses? Do they buy ice cream for children because of the good milk protein and the calories, or to keep them quiet, or to make them happy?

A *motive* is an internal factor that activates and directs behavior toward some goal.[11] Sometimes motives are subconscious, and it takes skilled research to uncover them. In-depth interviews are used to discover, for example, why people eat yogurt and other fermented milk products (which also have a medicinal effect). Their sensory attitudes and motives are easy to discover, but often medicinal or health motives are based on deep fears.

Finally, consumers have *knowledge* about foods. This knowledge will come from their first days to the present time; some knowledge may be lost, but some early food experiences last a lifetime. The knowledge may come from the family, peer groups, education, society, the media, and advertising. It may not be correct or true knowledge always, but it is their knowledge. Factors influencing learning, attitudes, and motives are shown in Figure 3-5.

[11]Courtland L. Bovée, Michael J. Houston, and John V. Thill, *Marketing,* 2d ed. (New York: McGraw-Hill, 1992): 115–123.

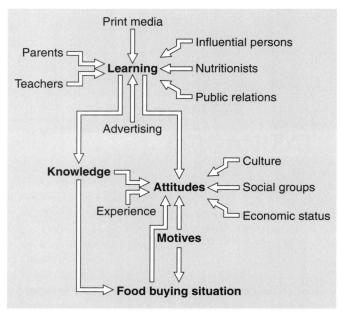

FIGURE 3-5   Psychological influences on food-buyer behavior.

The Food-Buying Decision Process

There are two important facets of consumer food behavior that need to be studied—the *Food-Buying Decision Process* and the relationships between the food and the consumer at each stage of this process. It can be divided into six broad stages: preaction, search action, buying action, preparation action, eating action, and postaction. It is important to remember that either an individual or a group of people may take part in each stage, and although only one person may actually be buying, there can be a strong influence by the group. So in the preaction it is not just the knowledge, motives, and attitudes of buyers that are present, but also those of the group, sometimes even when buyers are purchasing only for their own use.

When people are faced with a food, they perceive its physical and social attributes through the sensory perceptors. These perceptors in turn arouse the central control unit (the brain) to make a comparison between the perceived sensory properties and the acceptable criteria for the food, based on personal preferences and past experience. The result of this comparison is acceptance or rejection of the product. This can occur at any stage of the Food-Buying Decision Process. The product may be rejected at the preaction stage, because it does not fit the cultural pattern, or someone in the household dislikes it, or it does not suit the eating occasion. It can be rejected at the buying action stage, because the package is a revolting pink color, or it does not have nutritional labeling, or it looks off-color or has an unpleasant odor.

Similar judgments will take place throughout the preparation, cooking, and eating stages. Basically there is an important relationship between the consumer and the food throughout the Food-Buying Decision Process; both the food and the consumer have attributes, and it is the compatibility of these attributes which determines acceptance or rejection of a food product.

The Food-Buying Decision Process varies a great deal, depending on both the type of product and the consumer, but generally follows the path shown in Figure 3-6. The food marketer has to identify the needs of the consumers for the food

FIGURE 3-6 The food-buying decision process.

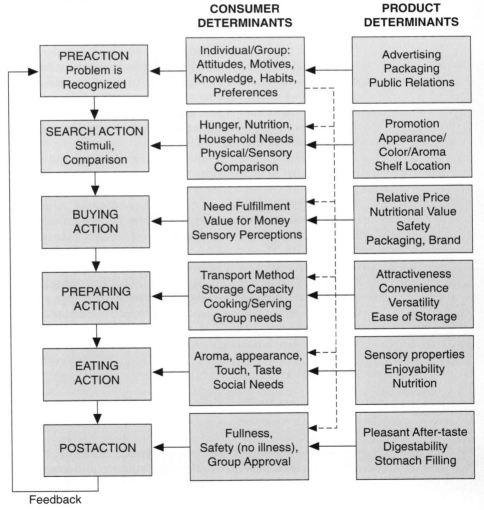

product. This may prove difficult, as different target markets may be using a product to fulfill different needs. For example, a can of condensed milk may be needed for baking by an American, to make a mayonnaise by a New Zealander, and to sweeten coffee by a Malaysian. The product has to be able to cope with all these different needs, or three different products must be marketed.

The choice of brand is mainly based on brand recognition and on the buyer's knowledge of and attitude toward the brand, and not on actual comparison of the quality or value of the two products. Many companies have tested their product against the competitors' products in unidentified sensory testing, and it has come out as the preferred product. If tested against the same products with brands identified, their product may score at the bottom—hence the "strength" of a brand. The brand symbol may also have cultural or societal significance; for example, a crowing rooster may signify power in a culture, giving power to the brand.

The consumers' use of food is basic to food marketing. Every stage of the use of a food to its final eating, even the disposal of waste materials and packaging, should be considered in food marketing. Consumers' major concerns in transporting and storing food need to be considered. Study of the transport of yogurt and beer from store to home led to the "six-pack." A study of the thawing of frozen foods being carried home might lead to a new packaging method. Obviously the spacing of shelves in storage cupboards and refrigerators enters into the design of food product sizes, but in some countries it is more important to study methods of protection from insects and rodents.

The amount of time and work needed to prepare and cook food has been a major concern of food marketers in Western countries over the past thirty years. Many of the new food products have been developed to reduce the time taken to clean and cut vegetables, to slice/mince meat, and to collect raw materials for cakes and sauces, until finally the whole meal may be bought prepared on a plate for microwave heating. In some countries, where the prestige of women is based on their culinary skills, these products may not be accepted for a very long time.

The act of eating a food needs to be pleasant to the individual. The reaction to food is immediate and may have long-term effects on attitudes toward this product or that brand. Because consumers can easily correct an unpleasant experience by asking for or buying an alternative product, food marketers may not soon know about it unless they are doing continuous consumer research on their present products. Only an eventual decrease in sales will tell them.

Think Break _____

Consider the following buying and eating situations:

- *A **staple food**, such as a loaf of bread. This could be purchased fresh daily or weekly and kept in the freezer. There need not be much daily thought, but more a general consideration, and then a buying habit develops. The habit may change as other factors are considered in the future, such as the need for bran in bread.*

Families with teenagers will want bulk and economy and may buy daily from a local store.

How would an elderly person, health conscious, living alone, buy bread?

- An **impulse food,** *such as an ice cream cone, purchased by a teenager. The stimulus could be the weather (hot!), a friend, the sign outside the shop, some consideration of price and size of cone. Final selection would be based on flavor preference, previous knowledge, and appearance of the ice cream.*

   What would a person doing the household's weekly shopping consider when buying the specially priced chocolate cookies on display at the supermarket entrance?

- A **luxury food,** *such as a box of chocolates purchased for a birthday present. Bought to show affection, this food has to be attractive, have prestige, and be high class—both in the packaging and the product. It is purchased after careful analysis of how the item "lives up" to the characteristics wanted in the product. The box of chocolates will be wrapped attractively before the final presentation.*

   How would a company manager select a restaurant and the food for an overseas buyer who might give the company a long-term order for their products?

SUMMARY

Food consumption can be studied at country level and at the level of an individual consumer or group of consumers. In countries of lower nutritional intakes, the calories are mainly from plant products, but in an affluent country such as the United States, one-third of calories come from animal products. As a country develops, the following occur: the quantities of food, calories, and protein content increase, with greater consumption of meat and dairy products. Two major trends accompany growing affluence: converging food preferences and a greater diversity of foods eaten.

Many factors affect a consumer's choice of foods: age, socioeconomic status, ethnicity, and regional preferences. America's population is growing older, its ethnic diversity is increasing, and the number of single-adult, single parent and two-job households is on the rise. These trends also exist, to a greater or lesser extent, in many European and East Asian countries. All of these situations provide opportunities, but also pitfalls, for the food marketer.

Different foods, from soft drinks to fried chicken, have found a broad-based acceptance across country borders. However, often international food products are not identical throughout the world. For example, sugar and acid levels may be changed in soft drinks, but the main flavor is kept the same in all countries. Or marketers can design a product using measures of sweetness, saltiness, sourness, and bitterness that are not the highest preference in any particular country, but are acceptable in many countries.

In studying food-buying behavior, it is important to recognize that it is shaped not only by the demographic/social influences, but also by psychological factors, such as attitudes, motives, habits, and knowledge that are specific to the consumer.

The food-buying decision is a process that has several stages. All of the stages have importance in determining whether consumer satisfaction will result and re-purchase will occur. Judgments do not end at the store, but continue to take place throughout the preparation, cooking, and eating stages. The consumer and the product each have attributes, and it is the compatibility of these attributes which determines acceptance or rejection of a food.

It also must be remembered that the environment—including competing products, media, politics, economics, society, culture, ethics, environmental concerns, technology, and even the weather—also affects the consumer/food relationship. The marketing company may work to influence the consumer/food relationship in one direction, but the marketing environment, aspects of which are discussed in Chapter 4, may exert an opposite influence.

IMPORTANT TERMS AND CONCEPTS

attitudes   66
basic food groups   54
converging food preferences   58
cultures   61
ethnic diversity   63
Food Buying Decision Process   68

greater diversity of foods eaten   58
knowledge   67
motives   67
nutritional intake per capita   53
recommended dietary allowance   53

QUESTIONS

1 Many people do not eat certain foods because of religious taboos or because of social restrictions or family training. Discuss these restrictions in your own food behavior and how they might be overcome in food marketing.
2 Discuss the sources used by your peer group to acquire knowledge on food products and the stimuli which encourage them to buy particular products.
3 How can the food marketer use advertising and promotions to increase the consumers' knowledge and also stimulate them to buy particular products?
4 Describe how you would organize a consumer survey to study the consumption of bread in your town, including types available, places bought, and how the bread is used, relating the results to different types of households.
5 Contrast the buying and eating behavior of consumers as related to the following products: fresh hens' eggs and chocolate Easter eggs; rice and puffed rice cereals.
6 Discuss how habit and problem solving can both be strong influences on food-buying behavior, giving examples of your own buying of foods.

REFERENCES AND RESOURCES

Assael, H. *Consumer Behavior and Marketing Action.* 4th ed. Boston: PSW-KENT, 1992.

Bovée, Courtland L., Michael J. Houston, and John V. Thill. *Marketing.* 2d ed. New York: McGraw-Hill, 1992.

Engel J. F., R. D. Blackwell, and P. W. Miniard. *Consumer Behavior.* 7th ed. New York: Dryden, 1993.

Fieldhouse, P. *Food and Nutrition: Customs and Culture,* London: Mackays of Chatham, 1988.

Hawkins, D. I., R. J. Best, and K. A. Coney. *Consumer Behavior: Implications for Marketing Strategy.* 5th ed. Boston: Von Hoffmann, 1992.

Kinsey, Jean. "Changes in Food Consumption from Mass Market to Niche Markets." *Food and Agricultural Markets.* Lyle P. Schertz and Lynn M. Daft, eds. Washington, D.C.: National Planning Assn., 1994.

Kotler, P., and G. Armstrong. *Principles of Marketing.* 7th ed. Englewood Cliffs, NJ: Prentice-Hall, 1996.

Mowen, J. C. *Consumer Behavior.* 2d ed. New York: Macmillan, 1990.

O'Donnell, C. "Food Products for Different Age Groups: Formulating for the Ages." *Prepared Foods* (April 1994): 39–44.

Senauer, B., E. Asp, and J. Kinsey. *Food Trends and the Changing Consumer.* 2d ed. St. Paul, MN: Eagan, 1993.

Solomon, Michael R. *Consumer Behavior.* 3d ed. Brookvale, NSW, Australia: Prentice-Hall, 1996.

Wynter, Leon E. "People Patterns." *Wall Street Journal* (November 16, 1992): B1.

4

CONSUMER CONCERNS ABOUT FOOD PRODUCTS

CHAPTER OUTLINE

LEARNING OBJECTIVES

After reading this chapter and answering the questions in the Think Breaks and at the end of the chapter, you should be able to:

- Understand the nutritional needs and concerns of consumers.
- Plan product development and promotion based on nutrition.
- Identify food safety concerns and how they can be met.
- Discuss the place of food safety in food marketing.
- Understand the control of the life of food products and the use of date marking.
- Recognize the environmental and animal-welfare concerns of consumers.
- Be aware of potential use of biotechnology in food marketing.
- Know the place of legislation and ethics in taking care of consumer concerns.
- Relate nutritional, food safety, and environmental concerns to the other consumer concerns of value for money/price, convenience, and attractive eating qualities.

INTRODUCTION

Consumers develop attitudes toward foods and food eating which are the basis for their motives in buying food. These attitudes lead to acceptance/rejection of foods and to preference ratings between foods. Throughout the centuries, there have been basic attitudes toward food and health, food and safety, food and work, food and value for money, and food and enjoyment. This chapter considers food and health, food and safety, and also the social and environmental concerns important to consumers when selecting food for themselves or for a group.

There has always been the hope that if one ate some type of food, one would be healthy or would even be cured of an illness. In the past, magic potions had reputations for miracle working, but these have been replaced by nutritional ingredients, such as vitamins, fiber, or minerals, in efforts to produce an active, healthy person. The miracle worker of the past has been replaced by the nutritionist, with the media's help and, indeed, often with the food company's advertising. At the beginning of this chapter, the basic nutritional needs and concerns of different consumers are discussed and related to food choice and food marketing.

People have always had fears that certain foods are unsafe and could harm them. Many surveys have shown that consumers are concerned about chemicals in foods—for example, pesticides, new food chemicals, or additives. The experts tend to worry more about microbiological food poisoning and the natural biological toxins which can be present in foods, because the ill effects are immediate and can cause death or at least serious illness. In recent years, the food industry has felt an increasing need to develop controls to reduce the risks of any significant outbreak of food poisoning because it could destroy a company, a brand, or even an industry.

Some of the other concerns of consumers today are the poorer qualities which they identify with processed foods, the quality of foods in storage, and the freshness or age of foods. These product qualities are important for the continuing acceptability of branded products and even of types of food products.

Two other consumer concerns are the environment and animal welfare. Groups trying to maintain the land for future generations exert pressure to establish sustainable agricultural systems and to reduce intensive farming which causes air, water, and soil pollution. Other environmental concerns are the use and disposal of packaging and the control of wastes from food factories. Intensive farming and some production practices give rise to concerns about animal welfare.

A major cause for consumer concern this decade is the development of new plants and animals based on recombinant DNA technology, variously called *biotechnology,* molecular biology, or genetic engineering. The first plant product was introduced into the market in 1994 in the United States, and molecular biology may be the basis for product development in the future, if consumer concerns are answered. Consumers in affluent countries are also concerned with sociological aspects of the food industry—are poor people being exploited in the production and processing of foods; are the pollution effects being exported to underdeveloped countries; are virgin forests in these countries being exploited; are fishing methods putting the fish and mammals in the sea under stress?

Finally, the food marketer has to decide how to deal with these issues—should there be ethical standards, or does one wait for legislators to set the standards? This is a difficult question, but one that must be addressed. In the past, the food industry has tended to wait for the legislation, but this has led to the image of the food industry as untrustworthy.

The other problem for the food marketer is to balance the importance of these consumer concerns with the other factors that are considered in buying food—convenience, changing needs and activities of the individual, family, or group, and the need for variety and attractive sensory properties.

NUTRITION

Consumers are increasingly aware of the relationships between health and nutrition. They know that they have to consume certain nutrients for health and that in excess these nutrients can cause problems. Very often, consumers have little idea of the role of each nutrient and how much to consume, but their fear of poor nutrition is valid.

Nutritional Needs of Consumers

Nutrition means receiving nutrients, substances which are contained in foods and which are necessary for health, growth, and development. Good nutrition means getting enough (but not too much) of all nutrients. The *essential nutrients* and their functions are:

Carbohydrates	Provide energy
Fats	Provide energy and some essential fatty acids
Proteins	Provide essential amino acids for growth and repair and limited amounts of energy
Vitamins—organic compounds which cannot be synthesized in the body	Perform various functions, including the release of energy from fats and carbohydrates
Minerals—inorganic elements essential in the diet	Help structure, i.e., calcium in the bone; and other functions—for instance, iron forms a part of hemoglobin and is responsible for oxygen transport around the body.

Poor nutrition or *malnutrition* means not getting enough of all essential nutrients or getting too much of some nutrients. Starving or poorly fed people lack all essential nutrients; they fail to grow through lack of energy and protein, and they have multiple vitamin and mineral deficiencies. More common in developed countries is malnutrition associated with overweight and problems caused by eating too much energy-containing foods, mainly fats. Some nutritional diseases and illnesses are shown in Table 4-1.

These nutritional diseases can be prevented by eating sufficient but not excessive calories and ensuring that the required amounts of the other nutrients, usually available in a balanced diet of the different food groups, are consumed.

Think Break

A confectionary advertisement said: **"Growing children need lots of energy—give them a Chocolate Bar—full of energy needed for active kids."** *Discuss this advertisement from the standpoint of the nutritional needs of a child.*

TABLE 4-1   EXAMPLES OF MALNUTRITION

Caused by insufficient nutrients	Caused by excess or imbalance of nutrients
Starvation—lack of energy-providing nutrients	Obesity—excess of energy-providing nutrients
Anemia—lack of iron and some B group vitamins	Diabetes—poor blood glucose control, not caused by sugar
Scurvy—lack of vitamin C	Coronary heart disease—overconsumption of fat and saturated fat
Beri-beri—lack of vitamin B1	
Osteoporosis—lack of calcium	Cancers—possible link with overconsumption of fat and energy
Goiter—lack of iodine	Hypertension—possible link with overconsumption of salt
Rickets—lack of vitamin D	
	Constipation, diverticulitis—due to lack of fiber
	Cancer of colon—possibly due to lack of fiber

Nutritional Concerns

What are consumers' main concerns about nutrition? Consumers wish to remain healthy for as long as possible, and they also wish their bodies to be attractive for a long time. They want their children to grow into healthy adults and to develop mentally as well as physically. However, consumers' specific concerns evolve in response to new scientific theories and research findings.

In recent years, Western countries have experienced a succession of specific concerns regarding heart disease, strokes, and cancer. These have become major causes of death, not that infectious diseases related to malnutrition have disappeared. Recently, consumers have been concerned about refined white sugar, unsaturated and saturated fats, cholesterol, calories, fiber, salt, calcium, fish oils, and polyunsaturated omega-3 fatty acids. Other major nutritional concerns include "junk" foods and nutrient-empty foods, such as soft drinks, and that baby formula and infant foods are replacing breast milk.

Fat, cholesterol, fiber, and calcium are now thought of as traditional nutritional issues and are leveling off as consumer concerns. A new area for growth is self-medication, which is related to the development of nutraceuticals—substances that are a food or a part of a food and provide medical and health benefits. Consumers believe they need special foods and vitamins as a means of protection against disease and for reduction of stress, the problem of the '90s.[1] This attitude will encourage development of proprietary foods, protected by patents. If this product group grows, the food industry will move closer to the pharmaceutical industry, because all claims will have to be clinically proven.[2]

[1]L. J. Machlin and H. E. Sauberlich, "New Views on the Function and Health Effects of Vitamins," *Nutrition Today* (January/February 1994): 25–29.

[2]S. L. DeFelice, "The Nutraceutical Revolution: Its Impact on the Food Industry R&D," *Trends in Food Science and Technology* 6.2 (1995): 59–61.

Nutrition and Food Choice

Most food choices are made for reasons other than nutrition. Even if the choice is based on nutrition—for example, to use diet colas or low-calorie margarine—other factors may influence the decision, particularly sensory and psychological factors. Diet Coke has excitement and a sophisticated image, as well as fewer calories. Low-calorie margarine may sound like you are doing something for your health—better for you than butter and ordinary margarine—but is it? Are you cutting down fat in your diet; are you sure that the low-calorie margarine contains less saturated fat than butter? In a recent study in Britain on consumers' attitudes on the consumption of olive oil, the attributes most strongly correlated with the intention to use olive oil were "improves the taste of salads and of cooking"; health considerations were a secondary factor.[3]

Nutritional choice is influenced by the media and by advertising, but nutritionists exert the stronger influence if they use the media to reach their audience. Food companies are well aware of this and often use nutritionists to promote their products. It is evident that people are more concerned about nutrition these days and more aware of nutrition issues. Almost every woman's magazine or sports magazine will contain nutrition articles or dietary advice. Although the issues of popular concern are not always those of most interest in public health terms, they have been and will continue to be the basis for new product development and advertising in food marketing.

Think Break

> *How important is nutritional value to you when you choose foods? What aspect is important—calories, fat content, vitamin content?*
> *How do you judge whether a food is nutritionally good or not?*

Nutrition and Food Marketing

Nutrition has been used for over 100 years in food-product development and advertising—since the beginning of modern food processing. Food manufacturers have developed new or *nutritionally modified foods* in line with consumers' nutritional concerns. They have also used nutritional claims in promotion, advertising, and public relations, sometimes helping to educate the consumer and improve the national diet, but at other times probably causing confusion and misleading people.

Development of Nutritionally Modified Foods   Modifying foods nutritionally can be very beneficial, but care must be taken in product development to see that the change is significant in the diet and that the change does not have a deleterious effect on another type of consumer of the food product. The total nutritional

[3]K. E. Thompson, N. Haziris, and P. J. Alekos, "Attitudes and Food Choice Behavior," *British Food Journal* 96.11 (1994): 9–13.

composition of the food should be considered when designing products, particularly formulated products but also fresh foods which are being developed by plant breeding and molecular biology. Nutritional composition must always be one of the factors—not just yield, appearance, or other sensory properties.

To be useful in improving the diet, a product needs to be eaten regularly, be a significant change from previously available products, and not be much more expensive. Some products which make a significant difference to the diet are meat trimmed of fat (trim beef, lamb, pork) when eaten in place of fatty meats, and low-fat milks, when substituted for whole milk by people who drink reasonable quantities of milk.

Examples of food which do not help to improve the diet are biscuits with added fiber but still high in fat content, yogurts which claim to be low in fat but are only fractionally lower than any other yogurt, and dairy products which claim to be low in cholesterol but are still high in saturated fat. Any infrequently eaten luxury item, such as a birthday cake, does not make a significant impact on the whole diet. Therefore, choosing a "healthier" version will make no difference. Any improved food which is so much more expensive that people cannot afford to eat it regularly will not help most people to improve their diet.

In the cereal industry, nutrition has been important for over a hundred years. Cold breakfast cereals were introduced as a cheap, high-energy breakfast; then they were fortified with vitamins and trace minerals. Now cereals are designed to provide sustained energy for athletes, high fiber for those concerned about constipation, low salt/low sugar for those afraid of high quantities of these, and low fat, although many cereals are naturally low in fat.

When consumers are asked to reduce fat in their diet, they usually replace it with something else, or the food processor does it for them. For example, to produce low-fat foods, processors replace the fat with carbohydrate, protein, or water; to reduce calories in a soft drink, processors replace sugar with water and a small amount of another sweetener. These changes may cause the overall nutritional value of the diet to change, not just the calories. Box 4-1 provides a detailed discussion of fat replacement technology.

Changing the fat content of foods is particularly dangerous where a complete food is replaced; for instance, removal of whole milk from the diet reduces the fat content and calories in the diet, but also reduces the calcium below recommended levels. Introduction of low-fat milk, sometimes with added protein and minerals, reduces the calories but retains calcium and protein levels. The total nutritional picture must be considered when introducing new products, not just one aspect.

Think Break _____

> *Choose one or two food-product groups in your supermarket, such as processed meat or ice cream, and identify the products which have been developed for a particular nutritional need or concern.*

BOX 4-1

OLESTRA GETS THE FAT OUT OF FOOD

On January 24, 1996, the U.S. Food and Drug Administration (FDA) approved the use of olestra as a direct food additive in salted snacks and crackers. Heralded as a major development in fat replacement, olestra not only has the properties of fat while adding no calories or fats to food—because it passes through the body undigested, but it is the first fat replacer that can withstand the high temperatures of baking and frying.

Fats are not all bad, nutritionally: they are high sources of energy, supply essential fatty acids, and carry fat soluble vitamins. When in the 1980s nutritionists in Western countries noted that fat intakes, averaging 40 percent of calories, were too high, the food industry responded by developing low-fat foods. However, fats are often important to the sensory properties of foods, affecting their appearance, texture, and flavor.

Five methods of fat reduction have been discovered:

- breeding and production of animals with low fat
- reducing fat absorption during processing
- direct removal of fat
- replacement of fat with other ingredients
- development of low-fat products that match the sensory qualities of the original fatty food.

Direct removal of fat is the most common method of producing low-fat products. For example, low-fat milk and yogurt are produced by centrifuging whole milk, and lean cuts of meat are obtained by hand-trimming of external fat. In formulated products, such as margarine and ice cream, fat may be replaced by carbohydrates, protein, or water. The proportion of the other nutrients in the formula changes as the fat decreases: polyunsaturated margarine may have 15 percent water and 82 percent fat, while reduced fat margarine has 52 percent water and 46 percent fat. Because very often the texture and flavor of low-fat foods are not as attractive as those of the original foods, recently researchers have concentrated on developing new ingredients which mimic fat in foods but do not add calories to the food.

Fat replacers include starch products, seaweed extracts, gums, celluloses, proteins, and emulsifiers. Simplese, by Nutrasweet, is protein based; Pfizer's Dairylight is a whey protein concentrate; N-Oil is National Starch and Chemical Company's tapioca dextrin fat replacer; and Trim Choice, by Con-Agra, is an enzyme modified oat material.

Olestra, the latest fat replacer, has sucrose polyesters, which are synthesized by reacting fatty acids with the eight hydroxyl groups of sucrose in the presence of catalysts. This large number of fatty acid molecules prevents the digestive enzymes from getting to the sucrose backbone in the time the food takes to move down the digestive tract, so the fatty acids are not absorbed into the body. Products made with olestra can have the same flavor, texture, and feel in the mouth as the original foods. Similar to the effect of using noncaloric sweeteners in sugar-based products, olestra will allow consumers to reduce their fat intake without altering their eating habits.

Source: Adapted from James Giese, "Olestra: Properties, Regulatory Concerns, and Applications," *Food Technology* 50:3 (March 1996): 130–131.

- *Look at the nutritional labels and determine the nutritional differences between nutritionally designed products and unmodified products.*
- *Look at the ingredient labels and see how the manufacturers have achieved the nutritional standards for those products, compared with the unmodified products.*

Nutritional Claims in Advertising and Promotion   Food manufacturers should be aware of the dangers and benefits of using nutrition in advertising. The use of nutritional claims is a pitfall for food manufacturers—dishonesty or haziness in claims makes not only government food regulators but also consumers suspicious. Many of the claims used in food marketing are what is known as "negative claims." They may be confusing to consumers and can be used inappropriately. "No added sugar," often seen on foods such as fruit juices, is misleading. These foods are high in sugars which are naturally present, and these sugars are no better for you than any other type of sugars. Another example is the use of "cholesterol free" on jelly, a food which would never contain cholesterol, as it is only present in foods of animal origin. When such a claim appears on one brand of jelly, it leads the buyer to think that other brands of jelly *do* contain cholesterol. "Only 5% fat" on a breakfast cereal, when most cereals are low in fat, is another misleading statement.

This type of promotion and advertising has given the food industry a poor reputation; now regulatory bodies are more tightly controlling nutritional claims. For example, in the United States, the Nutrition Labeling and Education Act of 1990 controls the nutritional labeling of food and also the nutritional claims about foods, requiring food manufacturers to disclose what is in their products in a uniform manner. In several countries, in order for a food to be described as "low-fat," it must meet certain criteria; for example, its fat level must be at least one-third less in comparison with a standard product. In the United States, the following are the per-serving requirements:

Calorie free	Fewer than 5 calories
Low calorie	40 calories or less
Light or lite	Less than 0.5 gram fat
Low fat	3 grams or less fat
Cholesterol free	Less than 2 milligrams cholesterol and 2 g or less saturated fat
Low cholesterol	200 milligrams or less cholesterol and 2 g or less saturated fat
Sodium free	Less than 5 milligrams sodium
Low sodium	140 milligrams or less sodium.

The label must include any nutrient for which a claim is made.[4] As part of their marketing strategy, some producers of health-related products, such as breakfast cereals, have chosen to give information over and above what is required, either on the package or in leaflets.

If food manufacturers are to use nutrition in their marketing, they must become knowledgeable about products, use this knowledge in product design, and impart this information to the consumers through promotion and media advertising. They need to be aware of:

- Recommended Daily Allowances (RDA) of nutrients for different individuals
- Dietary goals and guidelines
- The nutritional composition of their products
- The place of their products in the diet.

[4]R. Gibson, "Label Laws Stir up Food Companies," *The Wall Street Journal* (June 2, 1993): B1.

This is very easy to write but not so easy to practice. RDAs for different countries and for different types of people in the country may vary. So which RDA does the manufacturer select? Today, there is a great deal of information on the composition of food products, but the food manufacturer has two problems: the data is only for a small sample, and the data may not be true for the company's product. Nutritional composition analysis is costly and time consuming but is the only means to obtain true information. However, if raw materials are changed, the information will no longer be accurate. To understand the place of the product in the diet, data is needed from nutritional surveys, which again may not be available.

The food manufacturer must recognize that nutrition is an inexact science which has to be translated into reasonably definite recommendations by health authorities. These recommendations must then be used by the manufacturer in an honest way. Future strategies of the food industry should include:

- Providing clear nutritional labeling
- Developing foods which are consistent with food and nutrition guidelines
- Controlling nutrient losses during processing and storage
- Increasing nutritional education
- Ensuring that all products make a useful contribution to the diet.

FOOD SAFETY

Food safety has always been important to consumers—they do not want to be sick or die after eating food. The materials that may cause ill effects can be broadly divided into microbiological, chemical, added, and natural materials. These toxins can exist in the original plant, animal, or fish, be added during production, develop during storage of raw materials, be added during processing or manufacture, or develop during storage of the product. In order to control toxins, quality assurance systems from the farm to the consumer's plate are being developed; in turn, changes in farming and manufacturing practices may be required. Some of the pressure for these changes has developed from consumer concerns, but much of it has been fueled by the disastrous consequences to a company or an industry of any food-poisoning outbreak.

Microbiological Food Safety

Microbiological food poisoning has been recognized for nearly two hundred years as a cause of illness and death, but because the traditional forms had been brought under control with only sporadic outbreaks, consumers were not concerned. Significant food-poisoning outbreaks in recent times have caused increasing concern over microbial and viral infections in food, particularly in Great Britian and Europe. This concern will most likely grow in the future and will lead to more regulations on food hygiene and limits on microbial counts in food.

Some major international *food-borne disease* outbreaks during recent years are shown in Table 4-2.

TABLE 4-2   SOME MAJOR INTERNATIONAL FOOD BORNE OUTBREAKS

Year	Location	Food vehicle	Etiological agent	Number of people affected
1985	United States	Pasteurized milk	Salmonella	16,000
1985	United States	Cheese	Listeria	142
1985	United States	Chocolate milk	*Staphylococcus aureus*	860
1985–87	Britain	Cooked salmon	*Clostridium perfringens*	500
1988	China	Shellfish	Viral hepatitis	400,000
1988	Malta	Mayonnaise	Salmonella	322
1989	Britain	Paté	Listeria	355
1989	Britain	Yogurt	Botulism	27
1989	Britain	Cooked meats	Salmonella	545
1989	Japan	Vegetables in peanut butter	Small round structured viruses	3,353
1990	Australia	Oysters	Norwalk virus	752
1991	Airline (ex Australia)	Orange juice	Norwalk virus	3,000
1992	Airline (ex Peru)	Seafood salad	*Vibrio cholerae*	100
1992	France	Pork tongue	Listeria	279
1992–93	United States	Hamburgers	*Escherichia coli*	583
1996	Japan	School meals	*Escherichia coli*	9,000

Source: J. C. M. Sharp and W. J. Reilly, "Recent Trends in Foodborne Infections in Europe and North America," *British Food Journal* 96.7 (1994): 25–34, and *Wall Street Journal* (August 8, 1996): 1.

These, of course, are just some major outbreaks, but they show the variety of foods affected and the organisms involved. Poultry meat, cooked meats, eggs, mayonnaise, dairy and bakery products, shellfish, and rice dishes are common sources of food poisons. The outbreaks in the table of *Escherichia coli* O157:H7 are indicative of a food-borne pathogen which has rapidly spread since it emerged in 1982; in the United States, up to 20,000 cases and 250 deaths per year are thought to result from this infection. It is difficult to identify in food, and the only effective way to control it is by careful processing. Every food company needs, in addition to processing procedures that seek to prevent all types of food poisoning, an emergency plan to control any outbreak that may occur.[5]

Think Break

Have you ever felt ill after having a meal at a restaurant? What did you do—report it to the health authorities, complain to the restaurant manager, never go to the restaurant again, or just ignore it? Why did you take this action?

Chemical and Physical Food Safety

In earlier times, toxic chemical substances were added to foods, such as alum in bread and boric acid in bacon. Food regulations introduced in many European

[5]For further perspectives on this issue, see Sean F. Alterkruse and D. L. Swerdlow, "The Future of Food Borne Diseases," *Chemistry and Industry* (February 19, 1996): 132–35.

countries and in the United States at the beginning of this century were designed to prevent the presence of harmful chemicals in foods. These food regulations have been changed several times over the last 90 years to accommodate new compounds added to foods and also to restrict many compounds formerly allowed.

Sources of harmful chemicals in foods, discussed in detail below, have been summarized by Farrer.[6]

Normal constituents of food plants and animals
Substances absorbed from the environment
Residues of agricultural chemicals
Metabolites of preprocessing microbial growth
Substances formed, absorbed, or added during cooking or processing
Migrant substances from packaging.

Natural toxicants and food contaminants from farm to plate   Toxins can be present naturally in food raw materials, or foods can be contaminated in their growing environment by natural materials, by man-made agricultural practices, or by pollution. For example cassava/manioc and some types of beans contain natural toxins—cyanides and alkaloids—which have to be removed by washing. There are also a number of fish and shellfish which contain toxins; the Japanese have a very expensive fish delicacy which has to be cooked properly to destroy the toxin or it will cause death. Industrial pollution can cause contamination of food; for example, mercury waste in Japan contaminated fish, and the radioactive materials from the Chernobyl disaster contaminated meat not only in the surrounding area but also across Northern Europe.

During storage, microbiological activity, often of fungi, can produce toxins. A well-known example of this is alfatoxins in peanuts; the toxins are often present in noncooked or lightly cooked foods and animal feeds made from peanuts or other nuts and legumes which are stored under conditions of high humidity/temperature.

Harmful substances can be added during processing. Heat processing can produce carcinogens, and foods can also be contaminated by zinc, copper, or other material from equipment. Finally, contamination can come from packaging, through migration of the packaging materials into the food.

Food additives   Concern about additives began in the 1980s, when it became a legal requirement in some countries to name the additives on food products. This led to greater awareness of additives and some concern about the amount of unknown chemicals in foods. These chemicals have been accused of causing a range of health problems, including migraine headaches, hyperactivity, allergies, and cancers. Some accusations made about additives are only partly true. Additives are used in foods for many purposes—for example, acidulants, antioxidants, colors, emulsifiers, gums and stabilizers, and fat replacers.

The use of additives has increased markedly during the last forty years, as chemical companies have designed many new products for use in food. These additives

---

[6]K. T. H. Farrer, "Are We Designed for What We Eat?" *Food Science and Technology Today*, 8.3 (1994): 130–135.

have often improved the color and eating qualities and extended the life of products. However, some additives have been shown to cause cancer or trigger asthma, leading to reactions throughout the food system: consumer fears regarding all additives, the increased use of the terms "natural" or "preservative free" in food advertisements, regulations on the use of all additives and labeling, and more organic and health food products.

Pesticides, insecticides, fertilizers The agricultural industry has been controlling pests and improving yields by using synthetic compounds since the 1950s. Pesticide application, by land or air, has become an accepted process in the cultivation of many food products (see Figure 4-1). When consumers became concerned about residues of these compounds left in food, strict regulations were written; the market share of "organic" foods has also expanded. Consumers are still concerned about pesticides, even though efforts have been made to change farming practices and reduce the cause for concern. Today, pesticides and herbicides are used in much lower dosages, are less toxic and more specific in their activity, and are less persistent in the environment. Regulators are also strict regarding the residues left in the food, and these have been decreasing as more accurate methods of measuring them have been found.

Consumers in one survey wanted all produce clearly labeled to disclose pesticides used, so that they could make more informed purchasing decisions; this

FIGURE 4-1 Spraying fungicide on a Florida orange grove. Pesticide use is at or near the top of the list of consumer concerns about food safety. *(Source: U.S. Department of Agriculture.)*

desire for information may be shared by a majority of consumers. Some produce is sold as organic or pesticide residue free (PRF). PRF produce is grown conventionally, then tested and certified as free of pesticide residues.

Animal remedies and hormonal treatments   Animal remedies that may contaminate animals grown for consumption include veterinary medicines, animal vaccines, animal parasiticides (to control worms, fleas, lice, blowflies), and animal growth promotants. These have caused just as much consumer concern as the plant pesticides. Consumers have feared that animal vaccines might affect their reactions to antibiotics. Animal growth promotants have caused controversy in some countries, particularly in Europe. It has taken some time for them to be allowed to be used, and in some countries they are still not allowed.

Physical contaminants   There can also be physical contaminants in food: nuts and bolts from machinery, pieces of wire from electrical repairs, finger bandages, or glass from broken bottles. Agricultural production may also leave physical contaminants: stones and even coins and jewelry have been found. Food raw materials need careful cleaning and sometimes hand inspection on reaching the plant. Today, there is also the problem of physical tampering with packages—placing toxic substances or other materials such as glass into them in supermarkets or in the plant.

Identification of contaminants in a package by a consumer or the supermarket staff can cause a complete recall of all products with the same code numbers—a very extensive and expensive exercise. If a consumer is hurt, courts can assess large damages.

Think Break

Suppose you heard on the news that in a supermarket some of your favorite ice cream novelties had been found to be contaminated with glass—what would you do? If you were the marketing manager of the ice cream company, what steps would you take to overcome this disastrous contamination, which could have occurred in the factory or in the supermarket?

CONSUMERS' PRODUCT CONCERNS: SAFETY, QUALITY, AND SHELF LIFE

Consumers expect products they purchase not only to be safe and nutritional, but also to retain that quality and safety for a reasonable time period. Their buying decisions include considerations of safety, quality, and shelf life, and they will not repurchase a product that fails to meet their standards in any one of these areas.

Food Safety Concerns

The dramatic consumer concern when a food-poisoning or food-contamination incident occurs usually galvanizes the company and the health authorities into action.

The costs of a food-poisoning incident to a company can be very high because of reduced demand for the products, product recall costs, fines, investigation costs, clean-up costs, plant downtime, liability suits, and possibly food-handler illness. The company has to have in place an emergency system to organize the product recall and the public relations in order to react very quickly if food poisoning is recognized.

What are consumers' basic reactions to food safety? Their concerns vary with the product and the time; today they assume that the government agencies and the companies are controlling the older *food-contamination* problems, and their own fears are usually related to what they regard as "unknown" food-poisoning contaminants, which they cannot easily recognize and which regulatory organizations do not appear to control. For example, they have fears of food additives, pesticides, and listeria, but not of botulism, salmonella, and metals.

Consumers want to control their acceptance of food safety measures themselves, judging on the basis of cleanliness, appearance, odor, texture, and past experience. Having had some bad experiences or gained unfavorable knowledge of the food companies and the regulatory authorities, they may not accept the procedures in place. They can exercise their own concern for food safety by never buying certain products which they recognize as potential carriers, such as shellfish, by never buying certain brands, by always cooking food well, by never visiting certain restaurants or fast-food stores, or by never buying certain products at a specific supermarket.

Effects of Food Safety Concerns On Food Marketing

Consumer food safety concerns are very real, but how are they related to food marketing? First, food marketers must follow the government and international regulations which have grown from these concerns. Second, food companies need to find methods of marketing food safety.

Food regulations Every country has food regulations, both for the internal market and for foods imported into the market. Unfortunately, these regulations vary from country to country. The U.N. Food and Agricultural Organization, in cooperation with the World Health Organization, has attempted to develop international standards. The Codex Alimentarius is often used as the basis for national regulations, but it is not a set of international regulations accepted by all countries. This often makes food marketing difficult, as a product accepted in one country may not be accepted in another.

Food regulations may have the political intent of protecting local farmers or local industry. This is a controversial area under the new GATT agreement (Chapter 9). Countries have often used food safety measures to control imports, and there is some speculation that this will increase under GATT. Although there have been attempts for many years to develop international food regulations, this seems to be an area of international discussion fraught with bureaucratic difficulties. However, in time, international regulations to which all countries agree may be developed.

The new GATT agreement provides a framework for distinguishing protectionist regulations from legitimate sanitary and phytosanitary (SPS) regulations. In order to promote harmonization, three organizations are recognized—Codex Alimentarius Commission, the International Office of Epizootics, and the International Plant Protection Convention, which develop standards for foods, animal health, and plant health, respectively. "E" numbers, showing the additives in the food, used first in Europe and now spreading to other countries, are having a strong effect on food marketing, as are new labeling regulations, including nutritional labeling.[7]

Think Break

What are the regulations in your state or country regarding colors and microbiological standards? Are these controlled very strictly, or can you see products in your supermarket which do not comply with the regulations? Are these products local or imported?

Marketing food safety In communities such as the E.U., where food safety is well controlled and all companies have similar food safety standards, it appears difficult to use food safety as a marketing tool. But in countries where food regulations are not strongly enforced, food safety can be very important in marketing foods. Certainly, in many countries one of the recommendations for Coca-Cola is that it is safe to drink when the water supply is unsafe; also, the hygiene practices of McDonald's encourage people to eat there.

Caswell, Roberts, and Jordan stated that, "Success in capitalizing on these opportunities will rely on identifying important food safety attributes, developing vertical control systems to address these attributes, and credibly communicating quality assurance programs to consumers."[8] An adaptation of their safety product development program is shown in Figure 4-2.

Hazard analysis critical control points Significant in recent years has been the introduction of HACCP (Hazard Analysis Critical Control Points) systems, which are now expanding to take in the whole channel, from farm or fishnet to the consumer's plate. Although this system was orginally developed to control microbial food poisoning, it has expanded to include all aspects of food safety and now quality, as well.

HACCP is a preventive system to eliminate or minimize potential biological, chemical, and physical hazards to the safety and quality of foods. Critical points in each part of the food system are identified, and then a method of control at each point must be developed. To apply HACCP to each food safety and food quality

---

[7]L. Unnevehr, L. Deaton, and C. Kramer, "International Trade Agreement Provides New Framework for Food Safety Regulation," *Food Review* 17.3 (September/December 1994): 2–6.

[8]J. Caswell, T. Roberts, and C. T. Jordan Lin, "Opportunities to Market Food Safety," *Food and Agricultural Markets: The Quiet Revolution,* ed. L. P. Schertz and L. M. Daft (Washington, D.C.: Economic Research Service, U.S. Department of Agriculture, 1994): 229–48.

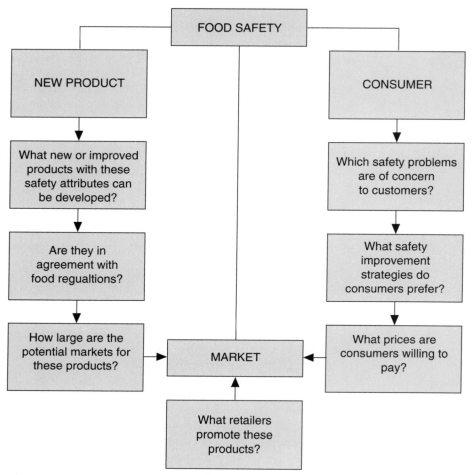

FIGURE 4-2   Introducing food safety into food marketing.

attribute would be a massive task in any food industry. The most important risks have to be identified and controls developed for them; gradually the process can be expanded into other risk areas.

HACCP is now being adopted by the regulatory authorities and is becoming a requirement mostly in processing facilities—for example, in meat and poultry plants in the United States.[9] The costs involved may force vertical coordination in agribusiness, because organizations further down the system have to rely on the earlier organizations and have to be responsible for their actions (Chapter 6). The sources of raw materials and their reliability need to be known. This could affect

[9]M. C. Easter, S. E. Mortimer, and W. H. Sperber, "The Role of HACCP in the Management of Food Safety and Food Quality," *Journal of Dairy Technology* 47.2 (May 1994): 42–43.

marketing structures where raw materials are sold through auctions or through international buyers and buying centers where little is known about the sources of the raw materials and how they have been produced.[10] The U.K. supermarket chain, Sainsbury's, runs a "Partnerships in Livestock" program, under which a Sainsbury representative visits each of their 1,200 producers at least once a year.

Food Quality Concerns

Processed food   All food is processed, unless it is eaten immediately upon harvest. It may be only washed and chilled, or simply pasteurized, like liquid milk, or blanched and frozen, like peas, or purified and formed into a manufactured product, like wheat in bread. There is a spectrum from minimal to complex processing. Consumers' concerns about processed foods may not be related to the position of the product along the scale of processing. They think of chilled products, even soups, as "fresh" foods, and bread, also, is not regarded as highly processed.

Consumers are more concerned about modern processing methods, such as canning and freezing; drying is more acceptable; raisins and currants, for instance, are very old, traditional products. They don't worry about whether the food is processed, but how it is processed. Processing may improve the nutritional value of a food by destroying natural toxins (both chemical and microbiological) and by making the raw material more easily available to digestion. On the other hand, there can be loss of vitamins and minerals and destruction of some of the nutritional value of the protein. These concerns lead consumers to divide foods into those that are good for your health and those that are low-quality or even junk foods.

Organic foods   "Natural" and "health" foods have no clear definition, but the consumer sees them as being free of additives and preservatives. People simply believe that foods described in this way are healthier—no matter what the nutrient content. An additive-free biscuit may be seen as "better for you," even though it contains large amounts of fat and sugar. A recent survey of New Zealand adults found that 60 percent of all adults believed that eating less preservatives would help to prevent heart disease.

Perhaps the most important marketing innovation to come out of consumer concerns about food safety and quality has been the development and marketing of organic foods. *Organic food* is fertilized with natural organic matter such as manure, rather than with chemical fertilizers, grown without application of pesticides, and processed without the use of food additives. Organic farming in the United States includes a range of farming systems, from using no man-made chemicals to low-input sustainable systems which are not necessarily chemical free. There are no general regulations for organic foods throughout the world, but various organizations have set standards, and their brand or name can be used only if the farmer is achieving their standards.

---

[10]J. E. Hobbs and W. A. Kerr, "Costs of Monitoring Food Safety and Vertical Coordination in Agribusiness: What Can Be Learned from the British Food Safety Act 1990," *Agribusiness* 8.6 (1992): 576–84.

Organic foods did not experience spectacular growth rates when they were introduced, because they were first sold in specialized stores, but they are now being marketed by a number of supermarket chains. There are problems: often, organic foods are not available in the quantities and at the times that the supermarkets need; also, some supermarkets suffer significant wastage because of deterioration in the product. Some buyers think that the food's quality is not as good as that of traditionally grown fruit and vegetables, that they have a worse appearance, and that they have low sales volume per area of shelf space because of low demand by consumers and lack of official labeling.[11]

Think Break

*What do the terms **natural, healthy,** and **organic** mean to you when they are used to describe foods? Look for food products in the supermarket marked with these names and note if they relate to your use of the words.*

In a British survey which included 29 percent organic food buyers, 64 percent nonbuyers, and 7 percent of respondents unaware of organic foods, the reasons given for purchasing and not purchasing are shown in Figure 4-3. These results are

[11]"Organically Grown Foods: Scientific Status Summary by Institute of Food Technology's Expert Panel on Food Safety and Nutrition," *Food Technology* 44.12 (1990): 123–30.

FIGURE 4-3 The demand for organically grown produce. *(Source: A. Tregear, J. B. Dent, and M. J. McGregor, "The Demand for Organically Grown Produce," British Food Journal 96.4 (1994): 21–25.)*

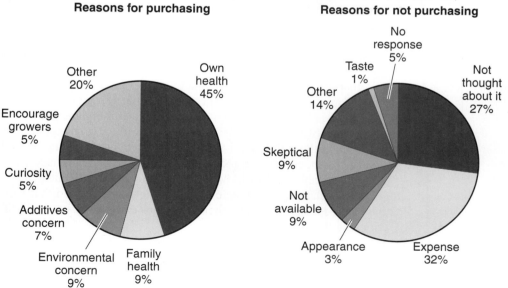

Reasons for purchasing

Other 20%
Own health 45%
Encourage growers 5%
Curiosity 5%
Additives concern 7%
Environmental concern 9%
Family health 9%

Reasons for not purchasing

No response 5%
Taste 1%
Other 14%
Not thought about it 27%
Skeptical 9%
Not available 9%
Appearance 3%
Expense 32%

generally similar to those of an American study in 1989, where consumers ranked their reasons for purchasing, from the greatest to least, as follows: safety, freshness, general health benefits, nutritional value, effect on the environment, flavor, and general appearance.[12]

Shelf Life of Foods

Consumers have always been concerned with the age of the perishable products they are buying and want to know if the food is still safe. Some microbiological deteriorative reactions, especially those they can see (mold and yeasts) or smell (putrefactive bacteria), can be detected when the product's appearance becomes unattractive or food odor becomes repulsive. Food poisoning may be caused by deterioration that is not always detectable. There are also chemical and physical deteriorations of which consumers are aware, such as rancidity in fats, bleaching of color, change of meat color from red to brown, souring of milk, and softening of apples, all of which can be easily identified by smell, appearance, and touch.

Date marking   The development of modern packaging made it difficult for consumers to determine the age of food by sensory testing (see Figure 4-4). Their concerns led to the introduction of regulations on *date marking* and the description of storage conditions on the package. Regulations control how this should be done, with "packed on," "best before," and "use by" among the suggested dates for food packs. Date marking started for short-life (10 days or less) products but has been extended in some countries to all products. The processor must guarantee the food's quality for its indicated life.

Packaging and carefully controlled conditions, as well as changes in the formulation and processing of the product, can extend the life of a food. Improved packaging and labeling may reduce concerns about *shelf life,* and new products, with different types of processing, are emerging. Also, sales of "fresh" foods (actually

---

[12]D. E. Jolly, H. G. Schutz, K. V. Diaz-Knauf, and J. Johal, "Organic Foods: Consumer Attitudes and Use," *Food Technology* 43.11 (1989): 60–66.

MISTER BOFFO   by Joe Martin

FIGURE 4-4   Life before date marking. *(MISTER BOFFO 1996 © Joe Martin/Distributed by UNIVERSAL PRESS SYNDICATE. Reprinted with permission. All rights reserved.)*

chilled food, very often under a controlled atmosphere) are growing rapidly, and it is predicted that in the future they will take a significant part of the frozen-food market.

SOCIAL AND ENVIRONMENTAL CONCERNS

There are increasing social and ethical concerns affecting food marketing, in particular concerns about the environment, methods of agricultural production, depletion of sea life, and reduction in the quality of soils.

Environmental Concerns

The environment looms as perhaps the single largest public concern of the nineties. Food packaging was criticized earlier, particularly aerosol cans and the tremendous amount of nonbiodegradable waste from food packaging. The "Green" bandwagon started to gather momentum in the '80s. With the agreement of countries at the 1993 international conference in Rio de Janeiro on such topics as protecting the ozone layer and stopping or slowing down the greenhouse effect of global warming, the environment has become an important subject worldwide.

Recently there have been increased consumer concerns about the effects of agricultural and fishing practices on the quality of the land and the sea. The effects of intensive fishing have perhaps been the most dramatic, with fishing grounds being depleted in European, Northern Pacific, and Eastern Canadian waters, and now in other areas, including the sea around Thailand. Perhaps the depletion of whales has attracted the most consumer concern.

At first the food industry was criticized for wasteful products and packaging, but the criticism has since expanded to methods of production and the general pollution caused by production and processing organizations along the food system. McDonald's were criticized not only for using polystyrene containers, but also for using beef from land cleared in South America from virgin forests. This instance is typical of the criticism that the food industry can expect.

Trends in Animal Production and Processing

The increase in animal production in the last 30 years has caused a reaction in the community—the small family farm with cows wandering in the fields and hens scrabbling in the yard had a cozy image, but large-scale beef lots and cage-produced chickens have not the same image, and there is resistance to this treatment of animals. Large-scale intensive production, both for export and for local markets, is widespread in the United States and Europe and is now increasing in the developing countries. For example, broiler production has spread into Southeast Asia and is now being introduced into China.

Concern for animals varies from country to country, by community and culture; it ranges from those who do not accept that animals should be used as a source of food and are vegetarians, to the other extreme of those preferring large-scale technological production of animals as an efficient method of supplying protein food. The positions of most consumers lie between these two extremes, but certainly they are now starting to criticize some production methods for cruelty to the animals and for possible effects on their own health. Animal protection groups have grown in recent years and have become more violent, especially in Europe. They will attack production units, processing plants, and products in the supermarket amidst a great deal of publicity. Although they are small in number, they have a strong effect on meat marketing, and likely they are the forerunners of stronger views developing in the general community.[13]

Biotechnology for New Plant and Animal Introduction

The use of recombinant DNA technology, variously described as molecular biology, biotechnology, or genetic engineering, to design new plants, animals, and microorganisms has developed rapidly in the last few years, although the number of new food products and food ingredients introduced is still small. Consumers have accepted plant and animal breeding for many years, but the ability to transfer genetic information from one species to another has caused concern. Consumers lack information, and these new methods, with media help, appear to them to be able to develop strange new life forms.

In a 1992 survey of United States consumers, 82 percent of the respondents had little or no knowledge of biotechnology. They were more accepting of its use for improving plants than for animals but felt that care must be taken to protect the environment in developing new plants. Most indicated that their primary sources of information were newspapers, magazines, and television, but they did not trust them. They trusted statements from health professionals and scientists, had moderate trust in government agencies and special interest groups, and had least trust in statements made by companies. They thought that the government should have some control over the products being introduced as foods but lacked confidence in government's ability to exercise such control. Their acceptance of products varied from 94 percent support for plants that were resistant to insects, therefore reducing the need for chemical insecticides, to 36 percent support for the use of genetic transfer to produce human medicines in the milk of dairy cows.[14]

Developing even faster is the use of biotechnology in the microbial and enzymatic production of food ingredients, such as conversion of starch to sweeteners, fruit-juice processing, cheese enzymes and a milk clotting agent for cheese manufacture, and genetically modified yeast for baking. No animal modified by DNA techniques is used in commercial agriculture, but the first plant product, a tomato, was launched in 1994 in the United States and then in Australia and Britain. Calgene Inc.'s Flavr Savr Tomato, the first genetically engineered consumer food cleared by federal regulations, was promoted for its summertime taste. Actually, the

[13]G. Harrington, "Consumer Demands: Major Problems Facing Industry in a Consumer-Driven Society," *Meat Science* 36 (1994): 5–18.

[14]L. Zimmerman, P. Kendall, M. Stone, and T. Hoban, "Consumer Knowledge and Concern about Biotechnology and Food Safety," *Food Technology* 48.11 (1994): 71–77.

change slowed the softening of fruit on the vine, so that the tomato could be ripened further before picking but was still firm enough to transport.[15]

Social and Environmental Concerns and Food Marketing

Retailers, particularly, have been active in environmental concerns; they have initiated recycling programs and have actively promoted environmentally friendly products. They are starting to ask suppliers to provide information on their environmental policy and performance and to rate them on ingredients, packaging, and use of pesticides. Only a minority of retailers are now doing this for food products, but the number is growing.

Eco-labeling has been very slow to develop and spread. The first environmental labeling plan was devised by the Germans in the mid-1970s, with the Blue Angel label recognizing environmentally friendly products. Environmental Choice labels were introduced by Canada and New Zealand in recent years. The German Blue Angel and a Japanese label can signify an improvement in one facet, or possibly several, but the Canadian and New Zealand labels require the whole production process and use of the product to be environmentally sound. However, the number of products under all these labels is small. A sampling of "Green" labels appears in Figure 4-5.

Essentially a purchasing choice which expresses a preference for less environmentally harmful goods and services, "Green" consumerism is introducing a different attitude into the marketplace. "Green" consumers are relating their food selection not only to the environment but to the whole social organization of the food system. "Development friendly" labeling may appear in addition to "eco-labeling." Some questions asked of food companies are: Do you have a policy to avoid driftnet caught fish? Do you have more than the required information on your labels? What policy do you have on additives? What happens to your wastes? What energy-saving programs have you initiated? How are you giving information to staff and customers on environmental issues? Have you changed your refrigeration system from chlorofluorocarbons?[16]

FOOD MARKETING ETHICS AND THE CONSUMER

There is no definitive list of consumer concerns about foods, because these concerns change with time and vary with the culture, social conditions, economic status, age, and education of consumers. Because of modern communication systems, these concerns about food products spread quickly throughout the world. "Consumer concerns" often are not just voiced by consumers, but are identified by experts, scientists, food-processing companies, advertisers, or retailers. One challenge for food marketers is to determine which consumer concerns should receive priority.

---

[15]Laurie McGinley, "U.S. Clears Calgene Tomato, The First Genetically Engineered Food to be Sold," *The Wall Street Journal* (19 May 1994): B8.

[16]R. Adams, "Green Consumerism and the Food Industry: Early Signs of Big Changes to Come," *British Food Journal* 92.9 (1992): 11–14.

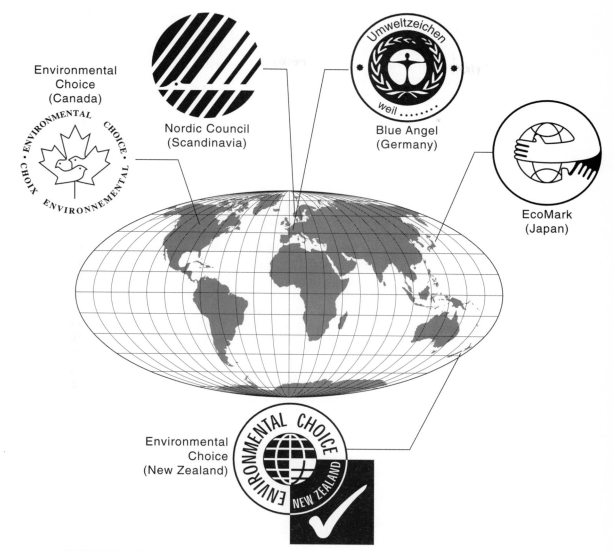

FIGURE 4-5   Green labels appear on products around the world.

Ranking of Consumer Concerns

The concerns that consumers identify themselves may be widely different from those of the experts. Experts usually base their concerns on the factual technical information available, and therefore they will list concerns that are identifiable as causing illness and death. Consumers base their identification and measurement of risk on three broad factors—dread, unfamiliarity, and the degree of exposure to the risk.[17]

The consumer balances the benefits with the risks involved. For any level of benefit, higher risk levels would be more easily tolerated for familiar, voluntary activities with well-known and immediate consequences than for unfamiliar, involuntary activities with unknown and delayed consequences. As the level of benefit increases, consumers will be more inclined to accept higher risks. For example, although fatty meat is known to be related to heart disease, consumers will not want it banned because they can make a voluntary choice to eat it or not. They want to have a choice of lean meat, but they do not want only lean meat. Nutritionists may rate high-fat/high-cholesterol foods as high-risk, but consumers may rate pesticides and food additives as higher risks because their knowledge and personal ability to control them is lower.

The dimensions of risk are not only psychological; individuals also consider the social, political, ethical, and economic issues attached to this concern. They may not trust industrial or governmental organizations to provide information about these risks. Their trust or lack of trust has a strong effect on consumers' appreciation of the risk, and thus concerns vary among groups in the community and between countries. Concern about food safety is very high in the United States and Japan, but even in Sweden and Norway, where consumer legislation puts high priority on safety issues, a significant proportion of consumers are concerned.[18]

Public and expert perception of risks from eating food do not coincide. Whereas experts judge hazard based on known deaths or cases of illness, the public has different criteria. There are several variations in comparisons of experts' views with those of consumers. The following ranking comes from a survey in the United States in 1990:[19]

RANK OF HAZARDS FROM EATING FOOD

Major food processors	Consumers
1. Microbiological	1. Spoilage
2. Pesticides	2. Pesticides
3. Mycotoxins	3. Improper canning
4. Package/product interaction	4. Spoilage/germs
5. Chemical additives	5. Chemicals
6. Carcinogens	6. Unsanitary handling by market workers
	7. Bacteria

This must not be considered an absolute listing, as other surveys have shown consumers ranking price, fat and cholesterol content, nutritional content, taste/

[17]B. A. Soby, A. C. D. Simpson, and D. P. Ives, "Managing Food Related Risks: Integrating Public and Scientific Judgments," *Food Control* 5.1 (1994): 9–91.

[18]Margareta Wandel, "Understanding Consumer Concern about Food-Related Health Risks," *British Food Journal* 96.7 (1994): 35–40.

[19]I. D. Wolf, "Critical Issues in Food Safety, 1991–2000," *Food Technology* 46.1 (1992): 64.

appearance, sodium content, and food safety as problem areas. A later survey in the United States found that consumers were concerned about fats and cholesterol, food poisoning, pesticide residues, preservatives and additives, salt content, hormones and antibiotics, and sugar content, in that order.

Once consumers move beyond the basic physiological need to satisfy hunger, they become increasingly concerned about the safety of foods, its immediate nutritional value, and finally its long-term effects, mostly in regard to illness and their health, and its social and environmental effects.

Think Break

Rank the following in order of how risky you think they are:

pesticides	*nuclear power*
food colors	*alcoholic beverages*
smoking	*food preservatives*
guns	*motor vehicles*
cholesterol	*junk foods*

Morals, Ethics, and Legislation

What ethics should govern the conduct of food marketing? *Ethics* basically refer to a systematic study of moral choices. They are related to, but distinguished from, morals and laws.

• Ethics are a system of principles of personal behavior which people use in their daily lives; ethics provide guidelines to relationships with other individuals.
• Morals are a set of principles used to distinguish right from wrong. Ethics and laws are based on moral principles.
• Laws are a set of rules passed by a government, including restraining and enabling legislation, as interpreted by courts and regulatory agencies.

A food marketer has the dilemma of having to match what is "right" according to general cultural standards with what is good business. Generally speaking, people have their own sets of standards of conduct, which they believe to be ethical, and abide by them. It is therefore doubtful if any marketers consciously engage in unethical practices, as they normally adhere to their own ethical standards. Why, then, is some of their behavior considered by society as unethical?

Ethical standards are set by the group (society), not by the individual, and therefore the group evaluates the individuals' judgments of what they think is ethical. The problem is, however, that society lacks commonly accepted standards of behavior. Standards vary from country to country, from industry to industry, from one situation to another, and even from one product to another. Figure 4-6 indicates the interplay of society's and marketers' ethical standards.

Marketers are also consumers and members of society; therefore, their moral standards are molded by society. In most cases they will have some consideration

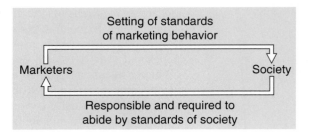

FIGURE 4-6 Ethics and the marketer.

for their fellow members of society, but there is still a need to set standards which relate to that society's standards. Marketers have the responsibility to continuously evaluate societies' ethics and abide by them as well as possible in the company and in the market. They need to look for places where higher standards should be set.

Codes of ethics are set by many marketing organizations, including advertisers and market researchers. Each code sets out guidelines for the members of the organization which governs their conduct. Suitable conduct in one organization may not be suitable in another; for example, accountants and bikers have different codes of ethics. The codes of ethics provide protection for the organizations, individual members of the organizations, and members of the general public. Basically, a code of ethics is based on the moral ideals of the society in which the organization operates. It is a written form of the most important "rules," according to the members of a particular organization.

SUMMARY

Consumer concerns are based on their past knowledge and the knowledge they receive currently. Therefore some concerns are very old and some are new, but the food marketer must be aware that they are constantly changing, because of new information and also because of the increasing affluence of consumers. Consumers may start with the basic concern of satisfying hunger but gradually become concerned about how the food is affecting them and then about how it is produced: Is it affecting the environment? Are people being exploited?

The international marketer needs to realize that markets and submarkets may be at different stages of development and their concerns different; therefore, a product may be sold in a market where cheap calories are important, in another market where decrease in calories or fear of food poisoning causing immediate death are the concerns, and in yet another market where long-term cancer effects may be important. The marketer needs to identify specific consumer concerns in the various markets.

Nutrition and food safety are very basic concerns of consumers—are they going to be healthy or sick after eating this food? Food marketers must understand consumers' basic nutritional needs and how these can be achieved through eating different types of foods. Then they can produce suitable products as well as advertising to educate consumers about the nutritional values of foods in the diet. Food science and nutrition data are constantly being updated by new research, so there is no final knowledge, and marketers must constantly update their information. Nutrition is an important part of marketing, both in product development and in promotion, and the needs of particular markets must be considered.

Food safety is vital to the ongoing health not only of the consumer but also of the company. It may be regarded as a hidden part of marketing, until a company has an emergency of food poisoning or of food contamination and markets itself by its handling of the situation.

Today consumers also have environmental and social concerns. In the future, these may cause major changes in agricultural and marine production and in methods of processing, but at present they are causing a great deal of criticism of the food industry.

New technologies are always suspect, and certainly the introduction of molecular biology to improve plants, animals, and microbiological materials used in the food industry will stir controversy in the near future. Although animal and plant breeding are familiar and accepted, the DNA manipulation of plants and animals to produce new types is causing some concern on the part of consumers.

Consumer concerns are the basis of much of food marketing, but the marketer must realize which of these are very superficial and which are lasting, genuine concerns. A great deal of food marketing time and effort can be wasted on gimmicks. Marketers should also adhere to ethical standards that reflect consumers' valid concerns.

IMPORTANT TERMS AND CONCEPTS

biotechnology   76
codes of ethics   100
date marking   93
essential nutrients   77
ethics   99
food-borne disease   83
food contamination   88

food safety   83
HACCP   89
malnutrition   77
nutrients   77
nutritionally modified foods   79
organic food   91
shelf life   93

CASE STUDY 4-1:   Butter and Margarine

Since heart disease became a major cause of death in Western countries and fats were identified as related to the causes of heart disease, there has been a controversy between butter and margarine which has been used as a basis for marketing by both industries. Margarines were first offered as a cheap substitute for butter in Europe and then in the United States, and at that time often had a high proportion of saturated fats. In their development during the forties and fifties, the main emphasis was on creating products with the flavor and texture of butter; later the emphasis was on offering a variety of products which were designed for specific uses, such as cake making, spreading on bread, or frying.

When the heart-disease controversy arose, margarine companies developed polyunsaturated margarines, because polyunsaturated fatty acids had been identified as beneficial, compared with the saturated fatty acids found to be related to blockages in the arteries. Finally, with growing awareness of obesity and the fact that fat spreads were high in calories, the margarine manufacturers developed margarines that had 30 to 40 percent fewer calories. Butter stayed essentially the same for many years, but now a range of products is starting to appear.

The butter industry is at a crucial point in its development, as it will continue to face very active competition from margarines and oils. What would you do if you were employed by a dairy company as product manager in charge of marketing dairy fat products?

a) Compare the butter and margarine products available in your supermarkets.

b) Discuss consumers' uses for fats and their present attitudes toward fats.

c) Write the consumers' ideal product concept of fats for different uses, and from this develop a list of product attributes.

d) Score the butter products against the margarines presently on the market on these attributes.

QUESTIONS

1 Discuss how increasing interest in nutrition and health has caused changes in types of foods sold and in the methods of marketing food in your community.

2 How is nutrition used to promote food products? Give three examples of products currently on the market which are based on nutritional promotion and discuss the validity of their claims.

3 Discuss the food safety and environmental concerns of the consumers in the following situations:

a) A teenage girl buying a bottle of Coca-Cola.

b) A young housewife with small children buying a cheeseburger from McDonald's.

4 A company has decided to launch a new celery which has been developed using biotechnology. What could be consumers' concerns about this new product? To alleviate consumer concerns, the company can ask a market researcher to identify the concerns and suggest how a suitable promotion could overcome them. Write a research brief, describing the information needed by the company.

5 A fishing company has been severely criticized by some consumer groups for depleting fish in the area by using high-technology methods. How could focus groups be organized to determine the attitudes of the consumers who continue to buy the company's products and those who have stopped buying them? How should the company act in the future to keep its sales growing?

6 Choose two dairy products which are sold as an industrial product, a food service product, and a consumer product, such as powdered whole milk, chilled cream, or liquid milk. Contrast the concerns of the food manufacturer, the restaurant chef, and the household buyer.

7 What are your principal concerns about the food industry in general and about specific food products? How do you find information about your concerns—what are your sources? How can the food marketer use advertising and promotions to increase consumers' knowledge and so reduce their concerns?

REFERENCES AND RESOURCES

Adams, R. "Green Consumerism and the Food Industry." *British Food Journal* 92.9 (1990): 11–14.

Buzby, J. C., and J. R. Skees. "Consumers Want Reduced Exposure to Pesticides on Food." *Food Review* 17.2 (1994): 19–22.

"Charting the Costs of Food Safety." *Food Review* 17.2 (1994): 1–35.

Coultate, T., and J. Davies. *Food: The Definitive Guide.* London: The Royal Society of Chemistry, 1994.

Farrer, K. H. F. *A Guide to Food Additives and Contaminants.* Carnforth, Lancs.: Parthenon Publishing, 1988.

Gibson, R. "Label Law Stirs Up Food Companies." *Wall Street Journal* (June 2, 1993): B1, B8.

Harrington, G. "1994 Consumer Demands: Major Problems Facing Industry in a Consumer-Driven Society." *Meat Science* 36 (1994): 5–18.

McKinney, L. C. "Setting Workable Regulatory Thresholds." *Food and Agricultural Markets: The Quiet Revolution.* Ed. L. P. Schertz and L. M. Daft. Washington, D.C.: Economic Research Service, U.S. Department of Agriculture, 1994.

Newsome, R. "Organically Grown Foods, A Scientific Status Summary." *Food Technology* 44.12 (1990): 123–30.

Sloan, S. A. "Top Ten Trends to Watch and Work On." *Food Technology* 48.9 (1994): 89–100.

Soby, B. A., A. C. D. Simpson, and D. P. Ives. "Managing Food-Related Risks: Integrating Public and Scientific Judgments." *Food Control* 5.1 (1994): 9–19.

Wandel, M. "Understanding Consumer Concern about Food-Related Health Risks." *British Food Journal* 96.7 (November 1994): 35–40.

Whitney, E. N., and S. R. Rolfes. *Understanding Nutrition.* Minneapolis/St Paul, MN: West Publishing Co., 1993.

Zimmerman, L., P. Kendall, M. Stone, and T. Hoban. "Consumer Knowledge and Concern about Biotechnology and Food Safety." *Food Technology* 48 (1994): 71–77.

Internet Source

U.S. Food and Drug Administration: http://www.fda.gov/fdahomepage.html

PART THREE

FOOD MARKETING
SYSTEM

The place and activities of the producers, processors, manufacturers, food services, and retailers in producing and marketing food products

Parts One and Two gave you a bird's-eye view of the Food System and an understanding of how consumers' food-product needs drive the system. Now you will look at the types of organizations in the Food System and how they change, or process, and move the food materials so that the consumer can buy the right product, at the right time, and in the right place.

Chapters 5 and 6 study the functions of the different organizations and their interrelationships and linkages in the Food System. Chapter 6 discusses the selection of the appropriate market channel for a food product.

The process by which food processors and food manufacturers change raw materials into consumer food products is studied in Chapter 7. This chapter also includes the industrial marketing of products between producers, processors, and manufacturers. The topic of Chapter 8 is the final marketing of food products by retailers and the food service industry.

The international Food System crosses the boundaries of countries. The economic and political factors affecting the movement of foods are discussed in Chapter 9.

5

STRUCTURE OF THE FOOD SYSTEM

CHAPTER OUTLINE

LEARNING OBJECTIVES

After reading this chapter and answering the questions in the Think Breaks and at the end of the chapter, you should be able to:

- Appreciate the scope of the food system and how it can cross country boundaries.
- Describe a channel of distribution for a food product of your choice.
- Develop an appreciation for the biological nature of food production and nature's impact on food-system operations.
- Understand efficiency and why participants in the food system are larger and fewer than just a few years ago.
- Explain how costs build in the food system from production to consumer.
- Explain what the marketing margin says and does not say about the food system.
- Relate the activities of marketing intermediaries (wholesalers and retailers) to the services they provide.
- Differentiate between brokers and merchant wholesalers.
- Develop an overall perspective of food retailing and of trends shaping the industry.

INTRODUCTION

In one sense, the food system begins with its raw materials (agricultural and fishery products) and ends with the consumer—domestic and worldwide. However, in today's world, food marketing is driven by consumer needs. Food-system participants focus on determining demographic and social trends that may signal a change in buying behavior. Therefore, in some ways it is more correct to think of the food system as beginning with the consumer.

In Chapter 1, discussion of the Marketing Concept stressed the importance of the company's having an outward view, rather than being production driven.

Demographic and lifestyle trends, as discussed in Chapter 3, are continually shaping the food industry. For example, the U.S. tomato-processing industry has increased production of diced/chunky product to meet the demand for salsa. The fastest-growing segment in the Asian food market is "nutraceuticals," products which lie somewhere between food and pharmaceuticals and are believed to ensure good health, such as ginseng (a plant) and complex milk proteins. Uncle Toby's, of Australia, has responded to consumers' concerns about chemicals in food by producing an organic breakfast cereal. Market-driven companies, whether in food manufacturing or in other sectors of the food system, will be today's survivors and tomorrow's success stories.

While all components of the food system, represented in Figure 5-1, ultimately work together to respond to consumer needs and wants, each type of company in the system has a particular role to play. This chapter begins a study of the various companies and organizations which make up the food system and an analysis of the functions they perform. Chapter 6 describes the different ways these organizations are linked to each other and how they interact. The functions of processors and industrial marketers, in particular, are the subjects of Chapter 7, and Chapter 8 focuses on wholesalers, retailers, and food service organizations.

FIGURE 5-1   The food system.

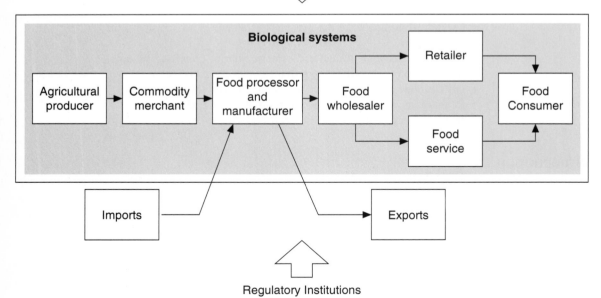

The food system includes suppliers of farm inputs, agricultural producers, suppliers of fish and game, producers of fermentation products (e.g., yeast), packaging suppliers, processors and manufacturers, commodity merchants, wholesalers, food retailers, restaurants, institutions (prisons, the military, airlines), and facilitating industries, such as transport, finance, and futures markets. Regulatory institutions affect all stages of the food system—from the chemicals used to spray a crop to permitting or forbidding two established retailers to merge their operations. Laws and regulations are particularly important in international food marketing, because they differ between countries and are often used to impose barriers to trade in food products. (See Chapter 9.)

The activities shown in Figure 5-1 often span international boundaries, as in the case of the Indonesian noodle industry, charted in Figure 5-2.

FIGURE 5-2   The Indonesian noodle industry: an illustration of how the food system crosses country boundaries.

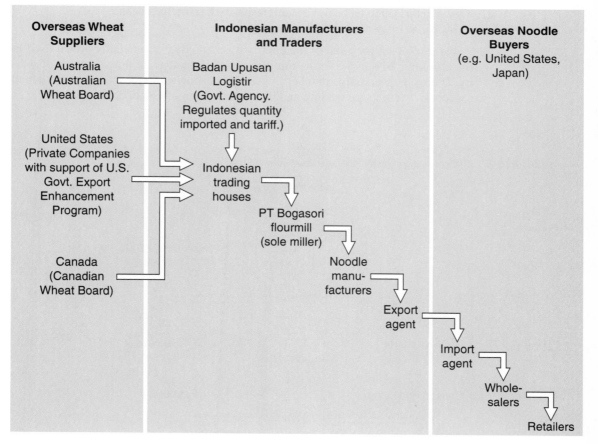

Think Break

Does the food system have a single identifiable beginning? Or many? Is any one participant in the food system more important than another? If your answer to this question was yes, justify your argument.

THE SYSTEM OF FOOD MARKETING INSTITUTIONS AND FUNCTIONS

Chapter 1 viewed activities in the food system in terms of the types of institutions involved (raw-material producers, processors/manufacturers, merchants, agents/ brokers, retailers, and facilitative middlemen) and the functions performed by each.

The sequence of institutions that delivers the final product to consumers is often referred to as the food value-adding channel. The activities in the channel comprise:

- Physical changes and movements: processing, transport, and storage.
- The flow of information. An efficient information channel is one that sends reliable information on buyers' requirements back down the channel.
- Change of ownership (title changes).

Figure 5-3 shows some of the alternative marketing channels for wheat used in bread baking. Figure 5-3 looks complex but is, in fact, a simplified version of reality. There are a very large number of possible channels for any agricultural product, especially when its processing and distribution span international boundaries.

FIGURE 5-3   The marketing channel for wheat used in bread baking.

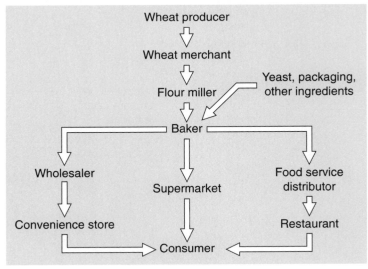

Note that there are two basic dimensions to the channel:

• A horizontal dimension: the structure of the industry at each level in the channel in terms of the number and size distribution of companies.
• A vertical dimension: the buyer/supplier linkages between levels in the channel.

Channels of Distribution

The food-system channel does not start with the farmer. In fact, it is difficult to define where it does begin. Manufacturers of farm inputs, such as fertilizer, agricultural chemicals, and tractors, buy raw materials from other manufacturers who, in turn, buy their raw materials from . . . and so on. Also, the final product may trace its origins to many places near the beginning of the system: a batter-fried fish may go back to a palm-oil plantation in Malaysia, a fishing company in New Zealand, a corn farmer in the United States, a salt company, and a chemical company.

Alternative routes coexist between most levels in the channel. For example, flour may be sold to the baker who sells bread to the supermarket, or the flour may be sold directly to a supermarket that makes bread on its premises. The flour miller/retailer link is shorter when the flour is supplied to a supermarket than when supplied to a restaurant.

Apart from the final consumer, every business in the system is both a buyer and a supplier. Most businesses have several types of customers. For example, agricultural chemical manufacturers need to consider the needs of their immediate customers, the farm input retailers and farmers. However, bread makers are also customers, (Will the chemical affect the bread-making qualities of the flour?) as are, of course, consumers.

The description of the food channel shown in Figure 5-3 focuses on wheat as one of the raw materials used to produce a loaf of bread. A yeast manufacturer would have a different view of the channel, as seen in Figure 5-4.

FIGURE 5-4   The bread marketing channel from the perspective of a yeast manufacturer.

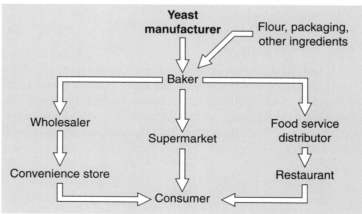

Similarly, the channel could be drawn from the perspective of a packaging supplier, or any other member of the value-adding channel. It is important to recognize that, while the dollar value-added contribution of each type of business may differ, they are all necessary to deliver utility to the final consumer.

As the wheat example indicates, channels may have many participants or few. For example, "farm-gate" sales of vegetables require a very short channel. Alternatively, the same producer may supply a supermarket directly, or use an even longer channel involving a broker, a central market, possibly a further wholesaler, and a restaurant. If the vegetables are exported to, say Singapore, the channel will be longer still. However, irrespective of the number of individual businesses in the channel, the same functions must be performed to deliver the specified mix of time, form, and place utility. (See Chapter 1 for a more detailed discussion of marketing functions.)

Think Break

Think about any food channel that you are familiar with. Identify the stages of the channel. What are the institutions, and what functions do they carry out?

If a company assumes ownership of the product (takes title), a price will be established. (Note that not all participants in the system take title, e.g., brokers, agents, facilitating middlemen.) If several sequential business activities are carried out by one company, obviously there will no change in ownership, and no price will be established.

A channel in which sequential activities are under the control of one organization is called an administered channel. The alternative form of channel organization, in which the activities are carried out by independent companies, is called a fragmented or open-market channel. There are three ways in which control is achieved in an administered channel:

- Common ownership (vertical integration)
- Contractual arrangements
- One channel member has enough *power* to influence and direct other channel members, without ownership or a formal contract.

A vertical market system does not necessarily change the competitive structure of the industry. For example, a vegetable producer who starts selling at the farm gate has, in fact, vertically integrated by ownership through to retail. However, the producer's market share is unchanged by this action, as is the competitive structure of the vegetable distribution sector. (These issues are discussed in more detail in the next chapter.)

Biological Influences

Most unprocessed food products, as well as the raw materials used in food manufacturing, come from farms, the sea or rivers, or occasionally from wild animals and plants. What all these food sources have in common is that they are biologically based. This means that food marketers face a number of unique challenges that marketers of other products do not have to contend with. In Figure 5-1, a representation of the typical channel of distribution from producer to consumer, the block "Biological Systems" envelops the entire food system.

Consider how biological systems affect the marketer. Apples are usually harvested over a four- to six-week period. With this seasonal production, if all apples had to be sold at harvest, there would be a tremendous glut and severely depressed prices. At the same time, consumer needs would not be met the other ten months of the year. But thanks to technology in the form of controlled-atmosphere (CA) storage, apples are available year round. This availability is not without its costs, however, for storage and the holding of inventory both cost money.

The beef industry experiences a different sort of time problem—the lag time between receipt of signals to increase production and delivery of the additional beef to the market. The beef producer does not have the luxury of hiring an extra shift, paying overtime, and immediately increasing production. Rather, if the producer is given a signal to increase production (presumably higher prices), it will be about 32 months before that increased production will reach the marketplace. Thirty-two months is the sum of the time required for a young heifer to reach breeding age, plus the gestation period for cattle, plus time for the new offspring to reach commercial slaughter weight (see Figure 5-5). Also, in the short term an increase in beef prices may actually result in less beef being available for slaughter, because breeding cows are retained, rather than being culled and sent to market.

FIGURE 5-5   Cattle feedlot in the Texas-Oklahoma panhandle. The biological cycle of beef production means that if producers decide to increase production, it will be about 32 months before greater supplies leave the feedlot. *(Source: U.S. Department of Agriculture.)*

Biology poses even more complex managerial problems for an industry such as fishing, because most fish are not farmed; they are caught in their wild state. The only influences that fishing industries can have on this situation are to regulate the quantity of fish caught and to try to slow down man-made water pollution.

Time is also a crucial factor in the marketing of perishable products. Perishable products cost a lot to transport and store—refrigerated handling requires energy and expensive equipment. Compounding the problem is product deterioration. It is estimated by the lettuce industry that 2 out of every 24 heads in a carton are not salable at retail. The end result is that the marketing bill for lettuce is very high, and the price to consumers is higher than what it could be with improved handling technology.

MEASURING EFFICIENCY IN THE FOOD SYSTEM

The functional and institutional approaches to studying marketing systems were introduced in Chapter 1. Combining these approaches provides an analytical framework by which to measure the efficiency both of individual companies and of the food system as a whole. For any activity, costs and margins must be evaluated in terms of the specific functions performed. For example, supermarket margins are less than those of a small grocer or convenience store, but the grocer may perform functions not performed by the supermarket—time utility (the grocer is open for longer hours), place utility for shoppers without cars (a type of transport function), and delivery (place utility and transport).

Each marketing function must be carried out. Bypassing an established intermediary does not bypass the function. Farmers who assume the storage function by building their own grain storage must be sure that this activity is properly costed and that their on-farm storage costs are fully competitive with alternative sources of storage.

Agricultural producers sometimes seek to "bypass the middle man" by engaging in processing/marketing activities through a cooperative or statutory marketing organization. Their success in this activity will depend on whether they carry out each processing/marketing function more effectively than competitive companies in this sector of the industry. Farmer ownership, in itself, does not guarantee success.

For the food system as a whole, it is more difficult to measure efficiency, or even to establish an appropriate definition of what is being measured. Efficiency measures the ratio of output to input. The most appropriate measure of the output of the food system is satisfied consumers, but how is consumer satisfaction measured? Questionnaires can yield potentially useful information, as can market-share data, but this type of information is more useful for individual companies or industries within the system (e.g., the beef industry) than for the system as whole. At this level of aggregation, all one can say is that the system should allow consumers a variety of alternatives and provide adequate information for them to make informed choices.

One measure of the denominator of the efficiency ratio is the cost of delivering the required product/service mix. There are two components to this cost: *technical (operational) efficiency* of all members of the industry (do operating costs meet world "best-practice" norms?) and *pricing efficiency* (is there sufficient competition at all levels in the system to ensure that technical efficiency is translated into value for consumers, rather than into monopoly profits?) In many countries, government agencies calculate costs and profits between the farm gate and the consumer as a measure of marketing efficiency. As will be seen later in this chapter, the dollar marketing margin tells very little about efficiency, but it still persists as one of the basic measures of performance in the food system.

Technical Efficiency

Driven to achieve technical efficiency—that is, to produce the product/service mix at the lowest possible cost—food-system participants, from producer to retailer, are becoming larger and fewer. The adoption of new technology has shifted input needs from labor- to capital-intensive resources. Capital-intensive inputs increase the optimal company size, since capital inputs tend to reduce unit costs of production only at higher levels of output. This gives companies the incentive to grow larger and to develop more concentrated market shares. For example, in the U.S. flour milling industry in 1990, the 4 largest companies processed approximately 58 percent and the 12 largest companies produced over 80 percent of all U.S. flour. Twenty years earlier, the 4 largest companies milled 34 percent and the 12 largest companies produced 68 percent of the flour output.[1] The same scenario has occurred in the soybean crushing (processing) industry. By 1992, the number of soybean crushing facilities had declined to 76, down from 115 in 1978, and the number of separate companies in the industry was reduced from 50 to 22. Worldwide, similar concentrations are occurring at the production, processing, manufacturing, and distribution levels.

The motivation for consolidation and larger plant size can differ from industry to industry, but the major force is that considerable economies of scale exist in food processing. Production costs are lowered primarily at high levels of output, with the result that optimal company size is increased and smaller companies are squeezed out. Work by Duewer and Nelson on economies in the beef-packing industry (Figure 5-6) shows the dramatic impact of *throughput* on costs of slaughter. Slaughter and fabrication (processing the carcass into the primal pieces) costs can differ by as much as 50 percent. Similar economies exist in other sectors of the food system, whether in distribution or in advertising. If a retail food chain in a geographic market area can double sales by a merger, it has effectively cut its advertising cost, as a percent of sales dollar, in half (assuming it keeps the same advertising budget).

Although production agriculture has undergone considerable consolidation over the past sixty years, consolidation is still continuing, and the U.S. pork industry

---

[1]*Milling Directory/Buyers Guide,* various issues as quoted in Michael L. Cook, "Structural Change in the U.S. Grain and Oilseed Sector," in *Food and Agricultural Markets* (Washington, D.C.: National Planning Assn., 1994): 119–20.

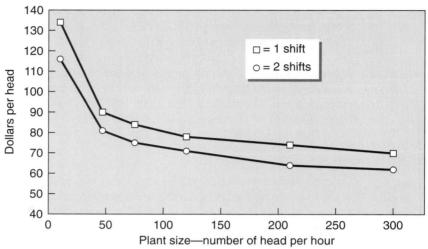

FIGURE 5-6 Costs of beef slaughter and processing per animal, six plant sizes, with 40-hour/week shifts. *(Source: Laurence Duewer and Kenneth Nelson,* "Beef Packing Costs Are Lower for Larger Plants," *Food Review (October–December 1991): 10.)*

illustrates this fact. The traditional system, where farmers mixed hog (pig) operations with other farm enterprises, especially soybeans and corn, is rapidly declining as the industry consolidates into fewer, larger, more specialized hog operations. During the 1970s and '80s, the number of hog farms dropped from nearly 900,000 to 250,000, and at the same time the total volume of pork production increased. Some industry observers believe that new technologies will place smaller farms at such a cost disadvantage that a swift decline in the number of farms will result, with only 100,000 remaining by the year 2000.[2]

The economies that reduce production costs are specialized technologies that push down all costs but particularly labor, which is nearly two-thirds less on large farms than on small farms. Production costs fall rapidly as the volume of production rises. As Figure 5-7 demonstrates, the average production costs on farms producing 3,000 hogs annually are over 30 percent lower than costs on small farms producing less than 500 hogs a year. These data suggest that larger production units will become more common. Moving to lower costs should improve the pork industry's competitiveness with other meats, especially with budget-priced poultry. Poultry's real price has fallen by more than a fourth during the past two decades, while beef and pork prices have remained nearly flat.[3]

[2]Chris Hurt, Kenneth A. Foster, John E. Kadlec, and George F. Patrick, "Industry Evolution," *Feedstuffs* 64:35 (1992): 1, 18–19.

[3]Barkema, Alan, "New Roles and Alliances in the U.S. Food System," in *Food and Agricultural Markets* (Washington, D.C.: National Planning Assn., 1994), pp. 102–106.

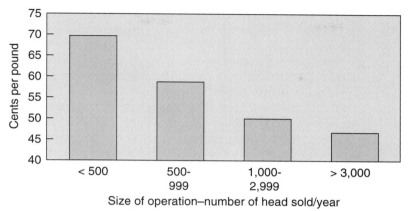

Size of operation–number of head sold/year

FIGURE 5-7   U.S. pork production costs, 1992. *(Source W.D. McBride,* "U.S. Hog Production Costs and Returns, 1992: An Economic Basebook," *Economic Research Service, USDA, AER 724, November 1995.)*

Think Break

You will often hear claims that one or another part of the food system in a particular country is highly efficient—for example, Australian production agriculture or the distribution system in the United States. How do you think efficiency is being measured when people make this sort of statement? What measure is being used as the numerator of the efficiency ratio?

Pricing Efficiency

Earlier in the chapter, the complex question of measuring the efficiency of the food marketing system was discussed. Efficiency is always measured as a ratio—for example, words typed per minute. It was suggested that the ratio of consumer satisfaction to total system costs might be an appropriate measure for the food system, but it is difficult to obtain reliable measures for both the numerator and denominator of the ratio.

The Marketing Margin   A marketing performance statistic that meets none of the desired characteristics of a measure of marketing efficiency is the *farm-retail spread* or *marketing margin*—the difference between farm price and consumer price. Despite its limitations, the marketing margin remains one of the most enduring, misunderstood, and misused statistics that comes out of food marketing. Marketing-margin data are produced in many countries, but their most persistent use (and abuse) is in the United States. For the market basket of food products sold from the supermarket checkout stand, American farmers in 1990 received 30 cents from each dollar. This decline in the farm share from 38–39 cents in the early 1960s gives rise to criticism that marketers are "ripping farmers off," or that the marketing sector is inefficient, resulting in higher marketing costs and lower prices to farmers.

The truth is that the farm-share figure cannot be used to arrive at the above conclusions. For example, the potato farmer receives a much smaller percentage of the retail price of frozen french fries than of the price for fresh potatoes, about 13 percent compared to 22 percent. Although the french fries cost a lot more at retail, the farm price remains about the same. There are other important considerations. For example, when selling processing potatoes, the grower often has a forward contract with the processor which limits his exposure to fluctuating prices. Such impacts on farm profitability are not even remotely considered in the farm-share number.

The potato example illustrates two important points. First, the farmer's share depends on how much value is added by subsequent processors and distributors. For an extreme example, what would be the farmer's share for potatoes sold as part of a meal in a high-class restaurant? The farmer's share has been declining in every food-producing country, simply because consumers are demanding more added value in terms of packaging, processing, and service. Second, price is only one component of farmers' agreements with the buyers of their products. As well as risk bearing, the farmer may carry out the grading, storage, transport, and processing functions to a greater or lesser degree.

Of what use, then, is the farmer's share? It does tell us something about marketing and its complexities, highlighting the fact that differing elements make up marketing costs. One of these elements is the amount of processing required. In Table 5-1, the contrast between eggs and a loaf of bread is dramatic. The contents of eggs come in nice neat containers, the shells. All that needs to be done is to protect them

TABLE 5-1 FARM-VALUE SHARE OF THE RETAIL FOOD DOLLAR—SELECTED ITEMS

Item	1980	1990	1994
Animal Products			
Grade A large eggs, 1 doz.	60%	64%	58%
Choice beef, 1 lb.	61	60	52
Fresh milk, 1/2 gal.	53	45	42
Crop Products			
Frozen orange juice, 12 fl. oz.	42	34	38
All-purpose wheat flour, 5 lb.	36	24	31
Northeast potatoes, 10 lb.	35	22	21
Lettuce, 1 lb.	10	16	18
Margarine, 1 lb.	28	23	29
Bread, 1 lb.	15	6	7
Average of all foods	37	30	24

Source: USDA Food Review, "From Farm to Retail," ERS, July–September 1991 and *Food Cost Review, 1995,* AER-729, USDA, pp. 8–9.

with a carton and sort them into standard weights. The loaf of bread has behind it considerable processing—wheat to flour, flour to bread.

One product characteristic that influences marketing costs is perishability. Highly perishable lettuce has a farm-gate value of only 18 cents of the retail dollar. Perishable products, frozen and fresh, require expensive equipment to store and transport them. The energy to run the cooling equipment is also costly. Even with special handling, fresh-produce marketers incur the cost of product deterioration. Obviously, retailers are going to build in a larger margin at retail for perishable products.

Another important consideration in the relationship between marketing costs and raw-product (farm-gate) value is how efficiently plant and equipment are used. Consider for a moment the tremendous investment in food-processing plant and equipment that is only utilized for a few months out of the year. The rest of the time it stands idle. A key factor in food-processing efficiency is throughput—in other words, the maximum volume that can be processed per hour and the portion of the available hours that the plant is operating.

Also contributing to marketing-cost differences are *transportation costs* and bulkiness in relation to product value. These two elements are often connected. Agricultural products are typically of low value and relatively bulky. Wheat, for example, may have a farm-gate value of $100 per ton, but, compared to a piece of machinery or some other manufactured item, it is bulky and very low in value. The simple mathematics of wheat marketing are that if wheat is transported considerable distances, its farm-gate value is relatively small compared to the delivered price. In today's world of specialization, agricultural products are often transported great distances: soybeans from Iowa to Japan, California lettuce to New York, Australian wheat to the Middle East.

The Need for Effective Competition   All of these elements, singularly or combined in some products, come together to explain why the marketing margin is, in many cases, rather large (and getting larger) compared to raw-product value, and why the difference between farm and consumer price varies so greatly from commodity to commodity. The key issues are consumers' requirements for more processing and services, the relative rates of improvement in technical efficiency—before and after the farm gate—and whether or not there is *effective competition* to ensure that efficiency gains are passed on to the consumer. Competition ensures that companies in the food system are motivated by profits to deliver services to the consumer at the lowest possible price. There is certainly no debate on whether or not effective competition exists in agricultural production. Farming is an industry that has low barriers to entry, and there is little opportunity for any one producer, or group of producers, to dominate. In fact, agriculture is often seen as approaching the economist's model of perfect competition (Chapter 2). The debate occurs over the processing and distribution sectors. This issue has been much studied in all parts of the world. Most of the studies show that, for the most part, effective competition ensures that food companies do not make excessive profits and that consumers are the beneficiaries of this competition.

In conclusion, the trend of increasing marketing margins is not a conspiracy, but the result of consumers demanding more processing, services, and year-round availability of quality food. Sometimes this is provided through imports, which involve higher transport costs, with a corresponding decrease in the share received by the farmer in the exporting country in comparison with the local producer.

Think Break

The preceding discussion has been somewhat negative about the value of the marketing margin as a measure of the efficiency of the food marketing system. Suppose you have been invited to join the affirmative side in debating whether "The Marketing Margin is the Best Thing Since Sliced Bread." What points would you make to support your case?

FOOD PROCESSORS AND MANUFACTURERS

The various participants in the food marketing system were introduced in Chapter 1. In this section and the next, the activities of two categories of participants will be discussed in more detail: *food manufacturers* and *marketing intermediaries*. The issues discussed here—food manufacturing and the major trends shaping it, coordination of raw-product procurement with manufacturing operations, and food service and food retailing industries—are explored in Chapters 6, 7, and 8. The section on marketing intermediaries that follows examines the different types and dimensions of the often-misunderstood distributors in food marketing and why they exist in their present forms.

Coordination between Processors and Producers

As discussed earlier, the food industry should be viewed as a system, in which there is considerable interdependence among all of the participants. For growers of fruits and vegetables, the processor must have the capacity to process their crops; otherwise, the produce will rot in the field, and the growers may face financial ruin. At the same time, the food processor has rather specific requirements as to raw-material quality. A freezer of green peas cannot make a product that meets consumer acceptance if the peas delivered were not harvested in a timely manner and are overripe and starchy, rather than sweet and tender. Today, food manufacturers' raw-product requirements are driven by consumer needs—whether they be for nutrition, safety, or taste.

Building a system requires coordination. The alternative systems of coordination discussed earlier are an open channel or an administered channel by ownership, by contract, or by power. In food marketing, coordination by administered channel has been increasing relative to coordination by an open-market system. In particular, contracting has been increasing relative to other coordination mechanisms. Administered channels may span country boundaries; for example, a palm-oil processor in

Europe may own plantations in Malaysia. Relationships between producers and buyers of agricultural produce continue to change.

Contracts may be either forward (production) contracts or marketing (sales) contracts. A forward contract is entered into prior to planting and therefore has an impact on future supplies. The advantage to the producer is that market risk is reduced with a known buyer and price for production. When a grower's capital investment in an orchard, per case of finished product, is about three times the canneries' capital investment per case, reducing uncertainty about price and market becomes an important component of a successful management plan.

At the same time, processors cannot operate efficiently with too much uncertainty about either quality or amount of raw-product deliveries. The importance of throughput in reducing fixed cost per unit was discussed earlier. In order to achieve greater throughput, the timing and availability of raw product must be assured. Forward contracting is a mechanism that regulates product flow to coordinate with expected demands and gives processors control over quality. For example, vegetable freezers control the planting dates and harvesting of peas. The director of operations for a major processor says, "Peas are probably more sophisticated than any other vegetable we do—we sometimes have three or four meetings a day on peas." The need for coordination becomes obvious when the biology of quality pea production is understood. Sweet tasty peas can become too mealy and starchy in just a few hours on a hot day. When peas are ready to pick, they are ready to pick; the giant combines are sent into the fields, and the processing plant must have the capacity to process them within four hours of picking, or the nutritional content and flavor will go downhill.

Vertical market coordination will be discussed in more detail in Chapter 6. At this point we need to understand what it is, why the food system has been moving toward more coordination over the past several decades, and that the trend is continuing. Major reasons for this trend are one or more of the following: risk management, quality assurance, raw-product availability, or efficient plant utilization. For example, breakfast-cereal manufacturers contract for high-protein oats to improve their oatmeal's protein content; growers expand their operations by using a portfolio of contracted crops, because the risk is less than on the fresh market, and their bankers will finance expansion; and a corn-chip manufacturer contracts for canola-seed production to be assured of a supply of this "healthy vegetable oil" for cooking the corn chips.

The Push toward Globalization

Food processors become international marketers in a variety of ways: exporting, establishing foreign subsidiaries, and entering joint ventures and licensing operations. Exporting goods has been the traditional way in which U.S. food companies (particularly commodity marketers) participate in a foreign market. In 1992, world trade in unprocessed products (commodities) was $120 billion, while processed foods exceeded $205 billion. Over half of processed food exports were from Western Europe and North America. The United States, France, and the Netherlands each accounted for about 9 percent of processed-food exports. Japan is the largest importer of processed-food products, accounting for 12 percent of the world total, followed by Germany and the United States.

Although processed-food exports are growing rapidly, the real internationalization of the food system is occurring from joint ventures, licensing, and subsidiaries. Sales by the foreign subsidiaries of large United States food companies are about nine times greater than their U.S export sales. The larger U.S. food-processing multinationals earned over 25 percent of their sales from their foreign direct investment (FDI) in 1991. For these same multinationals, exports from their U.S. processing operations accounted for only 4.1 percent of sales.[4]

Data for 64 of the largest U.S. food-processing companies provide insights into their international activities. Of these 64 companies, which account for nearly one-half of all U.S. food processing in 1988, 38 own food-processing plants in foreign countries. In total, these companies operate 2,518 processing plants, 27 percent of them overseas. Two companies, CPC International and Coca-Cola, make over 50 percent of their processed-food sales from foreign subsidiaries. There are 14 U.S. food processors that make over $1 billion each in annual sales from their foreign subsidiaries. The foregoing figures do not take into account earnings by U.S. companies from their international licensing and franchising. For example, many U.S. brewers license Canadian and British companies to produce their brands in the United Kingdom and Canada. Many food processors evidently find it more profitable to export capital, know-how, and trademarks than to export branded products from their U.S. facilities.[5]

While American companies have been active in expanding their global activities, the biggest multinational food companies are Swiss (Nestlé) and English/Dutch (Unilever). Both these companies have been around for over a century and have always had a substantial presence in both developed and developing countries.

MARKETING INTERMEDIARIES

Over the centuries distributors have not been well thought of and often have been cast in the role of villain—a necessary evil in bridging the gap between producer and consumer. Societies of yesterday were agrarian and saw the activities of traders (middlemen) as incidental to the activities of farmers and craftsmen. Plato held that trade was suitable for those weakest in body and unfit for any other work. Cicero stated, "All retail dealing may be described as dishonest and base, for the dealer will gain nothing except by profuse lying and nothing is more disgraceful than untruthful huckstering."[6]

---

[4]Charles R. Handy and Dennis Henderson, "Implications of a Single EC Market for the U.S. Food Manufacturing Sector," *Implications for World and Agricultural Trade,* Staff Report No. AGES 9133, USDA, ERS, 1991.

[5]Alden C. Manchester, *Rearranging the Economic Landscape: The Food Marketing Revolution, 1950–91,* Ag. Econ. Rpt. No. 660, USDA, ERS, September 1992: 48–55.

[6]Paul H. Nystrom, *Economics of Retailing* (New York: Ronald Press Company, 1930): 49.

While today there isn't the prejudice against distributors that existed in Plato's time, both producers and consumers still feel suspicion and ambivalence toward them. Consumers in today's supermarket take for granted the assortment of 15,000 items that greatly reduces their time devoted to shopping; farmers are often distrustful of any group that is involved in or responsible for forming or discovering farm prices.

What, then, do intermediaries accomplish? What is their rationale for existence? The fundamental role of wholesalers and retailers is to build assortments for their customers—the creation of possession utility. Also, intermediaries hold inventories where they are needed by buyers—the creation of time and place utility discussed earlier. If all the goods that are consumed in a village are produced in that same village, then intermediaries are not needed (situation A in Figure 5-8).

That is, if there is no specialization of production and there is no trade among different economic units, whether villages, districts, states, or countries, there is no need for wholesalers and retailers. Today the global community is not made up of thousands of isolated, disconnected subsistence units. The move toward industrialization and away from strictly agrarian economies around the world means that the distance (in terms of time, place, and product form) between producers and users widens. As this gap widens, the need for companies whose sole purpose is to organize the rate and timing of product flow between the two sectors increases (situations B, C, and D in Figure 5-8). These companies are the intermediaries of the food marketing sector.

FIGURE 5-8   Typical marketing channels.

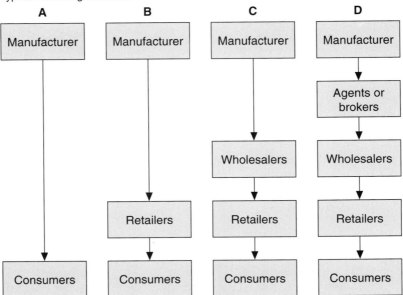

Functions of Marketing Intermediaries

Distributors are not involved in processing, changing product form, or adding value, and they do not produce and grow, so what do they do? A major function is to carry inventories. Food retailers have an inventory on the shelves so that their consumers' needs are satisfied immediately. Certainly the shopper doesn't expect to walk into the store and put in an order for a can of tomato sauce that will be received in two days. Backstopping the retailers is the merchant wholesaling operation. The wholesaler has purchased the tomato sauce from the manufacturer in large order sizes and received reduced transportation rates, since economical carload or truckload shipments are made to the wholesaler's warehouse. This wholesale supply can be on the shelves within 24 to 36 hours of the retailer's placement of an order.

Another major function of distributors is to reduce the number of contacts between seller and buyer. Figure 5-9 shows that in the absence of a marketing intermediary, sixteen different contacts are required to trade four manufacturers' products with four buyers.

The typical supermarket today has over 15,000 items on its shelves. Customers can walk into a well-stocked store and within an hour obtain everything they need for the next week or more. The basic assumption and rationale for intermediaries

FIGURE 5-9   Distributors reduce the number of necessary contacts between food manufacturers and retailers.

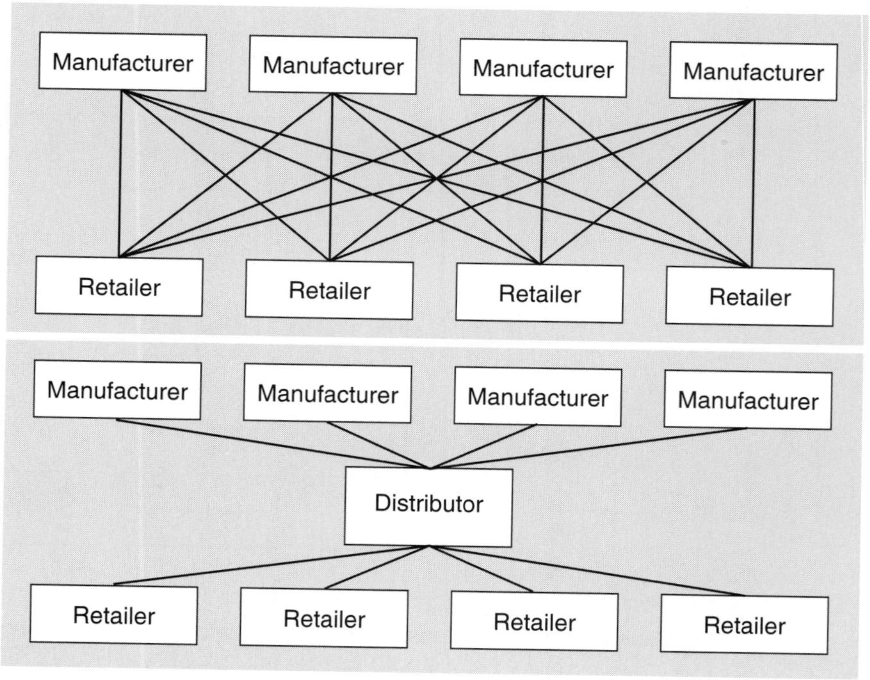

is that time is valuable to the consumer, and the efficiency of distribution systems reduces the effort and time required for the consumer to search out individual products. By building assortments, *wholesalers* and retailers reduce transactions and provide an inventory, making available the products that satisfy customer needs.

Other activities of wholesalers and retailers include assuming price and product risk (where ownership and title are taken) and providing a communication link between producer and consumer. Today, American farmers number fewer than 2 million and are separated geographically from the domestic market of nearly 260 million people and the global market of over 5.5 billion. Communicating with potential buyers is a major task. Taking advantage of the existing distribution network makes the task much easier.

BOX 5-1

JAPAN'S FOOD DISTRIBUTION SYSTEM

Distributors do not operate efficiently in all economies and situations. In Japan, over 625,000 stores retail food products to service a population of about 110 million while the United States, with a population of 260 million, has 128,000 grocery stores. In addition, Japan's distribution system is twice as long as the US system.

The traditional Japanese system has been criticized for its high cost and for restrictive trading practices that have been referred to as a nontariff barrier to foreign companies. Part of the high cost is due to the system's structure—it has several layers, so that a product passes through several intermediaries before reaching the retailer, and a large number of small retailers, with over half the stores operated by one or two people.

Source: "The Retail Food Market," Rabobank International, 1994: 32–34, and *Progressive Grocer: 63rd Annual Report,* April 1996: 13.

Think Break

Reflect on the comments from Box 5-1 on the Japanese food distribution system in terms of our earlier discussions on marketing efficiency. One reason why there are so many layers in the Japanese system is that, traditionally, Japanese housewives did not drive and liked to shop frequently, as much as three times a day. To facilitate such shopping behavior, many retailers were required. Having many small retailers requires a much more complex system of distribution than when retailing is carried out through large supermarkets with their own central warehouse.

Is the Japanese system of distribution inefficient or merely meeting consumer needs and fulfilling the marketing concept?

Wholesalers

Three types of wholesalers are found in the food system: *assemblers, brokers/ agents,* and *merchant wholesalers.* Table 5-2 shows which marketing functions are performed by assemblers, broker/agents, and merchant wholesalers, as well

TABLE 5-2 BUSINESS FUNCTIONS OF WHOLESALERS BY TYPE OF BUSINESS

Function	Business			
	Assembler	Broker/ agent	Merchant wholesaler	Retailer
Buy	Generally takes title	Brings buyers and sellers together	Takes title	Takes title
Sell	To merchants or processors	Agent of seller or buyer	Assortment builder for retailer	Assortment builder for consumer
Storage	Yes	No (may arrange)	Yes	Yes
Transport	Sometimes	No (may arrange)	Often	Sometimes
Processing	Rudimentary	No	Rarely	Yes
Grading/sorting	Yes, generally	No	Sometimes	Infrequently
Finance	Generally	No	Yes	Yes
Risk bearing	Generally	Limited	Yes (stock obsolescence)	Yes
Market information	Yes, particularly to farmers	Yes	Limited	Yes

as by retailers, which are usually the final link between food producer and consumer.

Assemblers are fairly easy to describe. They exist where products first leave the farm; they are the grain elevators, almond receiving and hulling stations, and fruit and vegetable packing houses. Assemblers do what their name indicates—assemble relatively small lots into larger lots and carry out commodity grading, that is, determine product characteristics and value. At times assemblers may do some very simple processing, such as cleaning and drying grains, hulling almonds, or packing fresh fruits and vegetables. For many commodities, assemblers do not exist in the marketing channel. Processing tomatoes go directly from field to cannery; there is an intermediate stop at a grading station, but it is only momentary, and the product stays on the truck.

The terms *broker* and *agent* are used in different industries for the same type of wholesaler. The essential element of a broker operation is that it does not take title or ownership of the product. This means that the broker does not have to worry about price risk or product deterioration. A produce broker can represent either the seller, a packing house for example, or the buyer, such as a chain store. If a load of lettuce goes bad on the way from California to New York, the broker does not have a financial obligation. Agents and brokers are paid on a fee or commission basis. In the packaged-food business a manufacturer may pay a commission, commonly 6 percent. In the produce industry the broker is paid a fee per unit sold (carton, crate, or sack). Marketers have a choice of having their own sales force out in the field contacting potential buyers or using a broker. Brokers/agents exist because they provide the same services as the sales force but are less expensive.

In contrast to brokers, merchant wholesalers take ownership of product. Merchant wholesalers, then, have warehouses and inventory a wide assortment of goods for retailers. In taking ownership or title, they have a risk position. For instance, in 1989 produce merchants importing grapes from Chile into the United States suffered losses of over $300 million when an incident of suspected cyanide poisoning of imported grapes was discovered by Food and Drug Administration inspectors.

Food wholesalers, particularly those known as general-line merchant wholesalers, are an important link between the food processor and the retailer. These wholesalers provide the broad range of products carried by today's food markets, everything from packaged dry goods and frozen foods to perishables. In addition to carrying manufacturers' branded products, like Kellogg's, Heinz, Coca-Cola, and Nestlé, these wholesalers have developed their own line of private-label products. In the produce business they often have their own buying office in the major producing areas, inspecting the product they buy and putting their stamp of approval on it before it is loaded on the trucks for shipment.

Wholesalers combined through mergers have set new records in the industry in recent years. For example, after several buy-outs and mergers, a major U.S. merchant wholesaler grosses over $20 billion. The merger push is motivated by the need to have substantial volume handled by a distribution center. The typical wholesaler warehouse services 150 to 200 stores. In wholesaling for the food service industry, the trend is much the same—mergers and a push to decrease costs on each unit handled.

Many of the large supermarket chains run their own general-line operation, which is referred to collectively as their buying office and distribution center. Their mode of operation is very similar to that described above, but now it is an integrated part of the chain-store operation, where buying, distribution, and retailing activities are all coordinated.

Food Retailers

The typical *supermarket* (defined in the United States as a store with at least $2 million in annual sales) carries from 15,000 to 17,000 items in a 30,000-square-foot store. A larger version, the superstore, has become increasingly popular in the past ten years, doubling its share of total supermarket sales. With larger size, 40,000 to 50,000 square feet, superstores offer an expanded assortment of goods, particularily non/food items. The superstore is also characterized by extensive service departments, such as delicatessen, bakery, and seafood departments. Many superstores incorporate kiosk operations in banking, laundry and dry cleaning, and video rentals.

While supermarkets account for over 50 percent of all retail food sales, a major development in food retailing has been the success of alternative formats, such as minimarts, operated as a part of petroleum retailing units, and wholesale clubs.

Wholesale clubs base their operation on the strategy of offering a more limited product assortment with a high inventory turnover, resulting in lower prices. Although expanding rapidly, wholesale clubs accounted for less than $20 billion of the $351 billion in grocery sales in the early 1990s.

Service and offering consumers choices are the key ingredients to supermarkets' success. On average about 50 percent of a shopper's grocery bill goes for perishables: meat, fruit and vegetables, frozen foods, and deli and take-out items. In these sections of the store supermarket operators see an opportunity to differentiate, to make their operation something special and different from the competition.

Chain supermarkets account for 55 percent of all U.S. grocery sales. A *chain* is defined as a retail organization with 11 or more units. Today the power in the food distribution channels lies with the retailer. In buying perishables the retailer has high expectations as to quality and delivery. Before putting an item on "special" and advertising it, the retailer requires certain assurance from the seller as to price and ability to deliver.

For the manufacturer of branded products, the battlefield is the supermarket's shelves. Shelf space is extremely difficult to capture. As mentioned, the typical supermarket has about 15,000 to 17,000 items on its shelves, up from 10,000 in 1985. Every year thousands of new products are introduced into the marketplace. With limited shelf space, the retailer is in charge, and slotting allowances or fees have become commonplace. Simply put, if a manufacturer wants to get shelf placement for a new untried product, it may cost as much as $50,000 to $100,000 in a chain or division of a chain supermarket, depending on the number of stores and their volume. Food marketing is a challenging business activity.

SUMMARY

Today's food system crosses country boundaries in a effort to provide at low cost the wide variety of products that consumers are demanding. There are several approaches to studying the food system: from the institutions involved (producers, processors, intermediaries), to the functions performed (exchange, physical, facilitating), to the type of supplier-customer relationship.

Food marketers face a number of challenges that general marketers do not have to contend with—these challenges are a result of the biology of production. Examples include perishable products that often cannot be stored for any length of time and a beef production cycle that can be 18 months or more, resulting in lagging adjustment to changing supply/demand situations.

The marketing margin measures the price spread between farm-gate value and the price at the retail-store check-out counter. While the marketing margin has experienced a long upward trend, this does not mean that the food system is becoming more inefficient. Rather, consumers are demanding more processing and services that contribute to the value-added share after the farm-gate.

Marketing intermediaries, such as wholesalers and retailers, provide a number of critical functions, including holding inventories and developing product assortments, thus reducing consumer search time. At the retail level, stores are becoming larger and providing more services, which range from delis to video rentals.

Within the system, there is considerable interdependence among all of the participants of the food industries. As a result, coordination is increasing between the different vertical levels of the system. For example, processors cannot operate efficiently with too much uncertainty regarding either the quality or quantity of raw-product deliveries, and so vertical control over raw-product production is exerted either through ownership, contracts, or relative power.

The many dimensions involved means that marketing cannot be carried out in a haphazard manner. Successful marketing requires skill and an understanding of the marketplace by both intermediaries and the consumer.

IMPORTANT TERMS AND CONCEPTS

assemblers   125
brokers/agents   126
chain   128
contracts   121
distributors   124
effective competition   119
farm-retail spread (marketing margin)   117
food manufacturers   120

marketing intermediaries   120
merchant wholesalers   125
pricing efficiency   115
supermarket   127
technical (operational) efficiency   115
throughput   115
transportation costs   119
wholesalers   125

QUESTIONS

1 What should be the major objective of participants in the food system?
2 Efficiency is defined as the ratio of output to input. What are the trends in food-processing size and efficiency?
3 What are some examples of technology "engineering" changes in the biological aspects of agricultural production?
4 Does the marketing margin measure the efficiency of the food system? If it does not, what does it tell us?
5 What influencing factors result in differing marketing margins for the various products listed in Table 5-1?
6 What forces result in more vertical coordination between the various sectors of the food system?
7 List the three types of wholesalers, describing each and how they differ from one another.

REFERENCES AND RESOURCES

"Agribusiness Spans National Borders." *Agricultural Outlook.* Washington, D.C.: U.S. Department of Agriculture, May 1993: 22–27.

Bucklin, Louis P. *Competition and Evolution in the Distributive Trades.* Engelwood Cliffs, NJ: Prentice-Hall, 1972.

"Food and Agriculture in the EC's Single Market." *Food Review* 15.1 (January–June 1992): 12–18.

"Food Wholesaling." *National Food Review* 12.2 (April–June 1989): 25–32.

"International Trade." *National Food Review* 12.2 (April–June, 1989): 40–48.

Lazer, William, Shoji Murata, and Hiroshi Kosaka. "Japanese Marketing Towards a Better Understanding." *Journal of Marketing* 49 (Spring 1985): 69–81.

6

ORGANIZATION OF THE FOOD SYSTEM

CHAPTER OUTLINE

LEARNING OBJECTIVES

After reading this chapter and answering the questions in the Think Breaks and at the end of the chapter, you should be able to:

- Explain alternative forms of channel coordination, ranging from administrative control to open-market coordination, in both the horizontal and vertical dimensions of the food system.
- Discuss the structural factors influencing power relationships in a particular industry.
- List and explain the principles of cooperative behavior.
- List and explain the sources of power for an individual company (or group of companies).
- Discuss the role of contracts in the governance of business-to-business relationships.
- Identify situations where vertical integration is the preferred form of vertical channel coordination.
- Understand the role of cooperatives in the food industry.
- State the principles of cooperative governance and discuss the issues involved in the application of these principles to a modern food-industry cooperative.
- Define and explain the term "industrialization" as it applies to intercompany relationships in the food system.
- Identify and discuss the variables affecting the design of the marketing (or supply) channel from the perspective of an individual supplier (or buyer).

INTRODUCTION

Chapter 1 and 5 introduced the idea of the food system comprising both marketing functions (the activities required to deliver the mix of time, form, and place utility required by consumers) and institutions (processors, distributors, brokers, and agents). This system can be viewed from a macro perspective (the efficiency of the system as a whole in delivering benefits to consumers in a cost-effective way) or a micro perspective (an individual company at any stage in the system seeking to maximize profits by managing raw-material procurement, production, pricing, promotion, and distribution effectively). Both perspectives recognize the role of the end consumer as the driving force of the whole system—"consumer sovereignty" in the macro model and the "marketing concept" in the micro, or managerial, model.

The concept of derived demand (for example, the demand for agricultural products) as being primary (consumer) demand less the marketing margin (the costs and profits of intermediary companies) was introduced in Chapter 2. Margin is influenced by the structure of processing and distribution sectors.

The *linkages* between agricultural producers, processors, distributors, and consumers require coordination. In Chapter 5, coordination is shown to be achieved by either a series of exchange transactions between individual companies—an *open market*—or by *administrative control,* where sequential activities are directed by one company.

The food system has both a horizontal and a vertical dimension. In either dimension, coordination can be at one of two extremes: one company controls all the activities through common ownership—administrative control; or, at the other extreme, control is by the "invisible hand" of the open market. Typically, the situation in the food system is somewhere between these two extremes. In the horizontal dimension, control by one company creates a monopoly, and market coordination by a large number of totally independent companies results in perfect competition. In the vertical dimension, one company controlling sequential stages in the channel by common ownership is called *vertical integration.*

In a perfectly competitive market system, an individual company has no direct communication with other companies—either the company's competitors in a horizontal direction, or its suppliers and customers in a vertical direction. The only links with the product and input supply markets are prices received for the company's output or prices paid for inputs. In the economist's model of how markets work, this is sufficient. Under perfect competition, all companies supply identical products. Prices provide complete information on how aggregate supply and demand are interacting in the market.

There are two significant changes when one moves from the perfect-competition model. First, every company does not supply an identical product—suppliers seek to differentiate their product from competitors' to some degree. Second, product differentiation means that companies do not act independently of each other. They are certainly aware of competitors and know that they need to communicate with suppliers and customers.

Alternative coordinative systems are illustrated in Figure 6-1. In this figure, the extremes on both the vertical and horizontal continua exist more in theory than in practice. It is rare to find a case of perfect competition or monopoly. It is equally rare to find a case where a whole industry is fully vertically integrated, or where

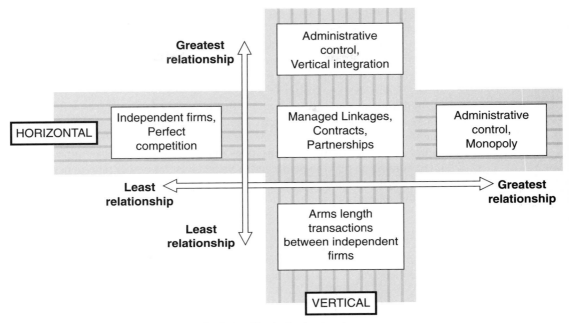

FIGURE 6-1   Vertical and horizontal relationships in the food system.

there are perfectly competitive markets at each stage in the marketing system. Most of the action, therefore, occurs in the center area. How companies interact, both with their competitors at the same stage in the channel of distribution and with their suppliers and customers, is the subject of the next three sections.

MEANS OF INFLUENCE

A company may seek in two ways to influence other companies in a business-to-business relationship. Company A may hold *power* over company B (because, for example, company B has no alternative buyer), or a company may seek to *cooperate* with another company to jointly achieve some mutually beneficial objective. For example, a food manufacturer may cooperate with an agricultural producer, or group of producers, to develop a new product that requires a new type of raw material. Of course, power relationships in business apply to individuals within companies as well as to relationships between companies. The principles are the same.

Power

Power can be simply defined as the ability to influence (or to resist being influenced by) the behavior of another individual or company. Power relationships can be analyzed at an industry level, between companies, and within organizations.

Impact of Industry Structure The economic model of industry structure and the behavior of companies within an industry, as discussed in Chapter 2, can be extended to provide a framework for analyzing power relationships in the food system. Figure 6-2 shows the application of the *Five Forces Model,* developed by Professor Michael Porter, from the perspective of a food manufacturer.

Conditions for Exercising Power In Figure 6-2, competition within the food manufacturing industry, barriers to entry, and potential substitute products are all variables that derive directly from the model of industry structure developed in Chapter 2. The remaining two variables, the bargaining power of suppliers and of buyers, remind us that the potential for the exercise of power (and hence profitability) is determined also by the relationship between the companies within an industry (in this case, food manufacturing) and their suppliers and customers. This relationship is, of course, very much influenced by the structure of the supplier (for example, agricultural production) and buyer (for example, retail) sectors of the industry.

Summarizing the impact of the five variables in Figure 6-2, the potential for the exercise of power is greatest when there is:

- little rivalry among existing companies

FIGURE 6-2 Structure and power relationships in the food industry. *(Adapted with the permission of The Free Press, a division of Simon & Schuster, from* Competitive Advantage: Creating and Sustaining Superior Performance *by Michael E. Porter: 5 Copyright © 1985 by Michael E. Porter.)*

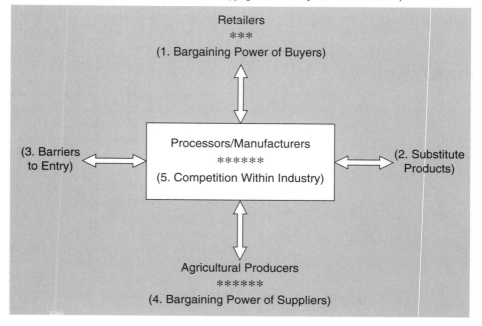

- no threat of new entrants (high barriers to entry)
- low bargaining power of suppliers
- low bargaining power of buyers
- no threat of substitute products.

As a general rule, the power held by companies at any level in the food system is positively related to industry concentration; that is, the fewer the companies, the more powerful they are relative to their suppliers and customers. In Figure 6-2, the number of asterisks is an indicator of industry concentration—the smaller the number, the more concentrated the industry. By this measure, retailing is the most concentrated (and therefore the most powerful) sector, followed by food processing. Agricultural producers are numerous and therefore lack power relative to both farm-inputs suppliers and food processors. These generalizations are broadly true, although power relationships differ from country to country. For example, food retailing is more concentrated in the United Kingdom and Australia than in the United States, and concerns about the power of retailers are more strongly voiced in these countries.

Potential power does not become real until it is excercised. Companies may choose not to exercise power for three reasons:

First, governments recognize that the exercise of power by food manufacturers and distributors may result in consumers paying more and farmers receiving less. Their response can be either to legislate to limit industry concentration, collusion, and other behavior that may be seen to be not in the public interest (antitrust in the United States, trade practices laws in other countries) or to support agricultural producers through legislation enabling collective behavior. For example, the Capper Volstead Act in the United States exempts agricultural cooperatives from antitrust legislation. *Statutory marketing boards* operate under specific legislation enabling agricultural producers to control their own marketing—for example, the New Zealand Dairy Board and the Australian Wheat Board are the only organizations permitted to export dairy products and wheat from New Zealand and Australia, respectively.

Second, the exercise of power may result in the other party in the relationship using *countervailing power.* For example, the union movement began as a response to the exercise of power by employers. If agricultural producers believe a food manufacturer is exploiting them by paying low prices, they will become more proactive in seeking alternative enterprises or, perhaps, will form a bargaining association to negotiate better prices and conditions of sale.[1]

The third reason is more subtle. The more powerful party in the relationship (for example, a food manufacturer) may wish to encourage cooperative behavior from the less powerful (for example, agricultural producers). Such behavior will not occur when the basis of the relationship is the use of coercive power by the manufacturer. The principles of cooperation will be discussed further in the next section.

---

[1]The formation and operation of collective bargaining groups are discussed in more detail in Chapter 11.

Individual Company Power   At the level of an individual company or collective bargaining group, power derives either from having power yourself or from facing a buyer or seller who lacks power. The key variables are:

• *Having alternatives.* An agricultural producer with land that can produce a variety of crops has more power in negotiating with a processor than one who can economically produce only one crop. A producer with a perishable crop has no alternative but to sell it when it is ready to market; a producer with a storable crop can choose when to market it. Product differentiation gives power if buyers can be convinced that other products are not a satisfactory alternative, thereby limiting their choices. A multinational food processor has the choice of supplying a particular product from a number of countries in which the company operates—thus increasing the company's power in relation to suppliers of raw materials or labor in any one country. Conversely, an agricultural producer group has power relative to a processor with no alternative sources of supply.

• *Switching costs.* The availability of alternatives is one thing; the cost of actually switching is another. For example, in the long run, a farmer can quit farming and become a merchant banker, but the *switching costs* may be very high, making this change an unrealistic alternative. A buyer who can easily switch to alternative suppliers has more power than one who cannot.

• *The financial importance of the deal.* If a particular input represents a small proportion of the total cost of a finished product (say, a particular spice in a canned soup), the spice supplier's bargaining power is increased, because the manufacturer will not be very concerned about the price.

• *Financial structure.* If a company is financed mostly by borrowed money (highly geared or leveraged), it will be more vulnerable in negotiations with either its suppliers or its competitors. Conversely, a company with little debt can "hold out" in a tough bargaining situation. Of course, as in other sources of power, financial vulnerability is relative. What is the financial position of the supplier or competitor?[2]

• *Potential for vertical integration.* If a food manufacturing company can offer a credible threat of backward integration into agricultural production, its negotiating power with agricultural producers will be increased. Credibility is enhanced if the company already sources some of its raw material from its own farm.

Cooperation[3]

The basic prerequisite for holding power in a relationship is having alternatives— the ability to walk away from the deal. Similarly, the power of one party in a relationship derives from the other party having no alternatives. The basic prerequisite for cooperation is the possibility of mutual gain. People (businesses) will cooperate with one another if they can see that there is something in it for them.

---

[2]Being very financially vulnerable may, at some stage, be a source of strength, because the buyer or supplier knows that there is no "fat" left to squeeze in the bargaining process.

[3]This section is a general discussion on the principles of cooperation in any sort of business relationship— to be distinguished from cooperation between agricultural producers in the formation of cooperatives, a specific legal and organizational entity to be discussed further in the section on horizontal linkages.

Of course, power and cooperation are not mutually exclusive—there are elements of both sources of influence in most business-to-business relationships. Some writers identify two sources of power: *opponent pain,* where power derives from the ability to hurt the other party (usually, in business, by reducing profitability) and *opponent gain,* where power derives from the ability to offer some type of benefit.[4] Of course, the possibility of opponent gain implies opponent pain if the favor is withdrawn.

In the food marketing system, the possibility of cooperation for mutual benefit occurs when cooperation either produces additional benefits for consumers (product differentiation) or reduces marketing costs. Because a commodity is undifferentiated by supplier, a commodity supplied by marketing channel A provides exactly the same buyer benefits as the same commodity supplied by marketing channel B. If all opportunities for reducing costs have been exploited—as will have occurred in an efficient marketing channel—a commodity marketing channel is, like poker, a *zero-sum game.* This means that increased profits for companies at one stage in the channel (for example, farmers) mean decreased profits for companies at other stages (e.g., processors). In this situation, there is no possibility of mutual benefits arising through cooperation.

The strongest incentive for cooperation occurs in situations of mutual dependency. Mutual dependency does not assure cooperation, however, unless the parties identify mutual benefits. The relationship between a dominant retailer and a dominant supplier of an established product, such as instant coffee, is certainly one of mutual dependence, but also it may be seen as a zero-sum game by both parties and therefore not one that yields opportunities for cooperative activity.

Mutual benefits are required for a cooperative relationship to get started. It also helps if people are comfortable at an individual level. In Asian cultures, socialization comes before business, an idea that American business people often find difficult to accept because they see it as being a time-wasting activity. They just want to get the contract signed and get on a plane back to the United States.

If mutual benefits and socialization are needed to begin a cooperative relationship, what makes it run smoothly once it is established? The main factors are:

- Both parties have about the same amount to lose if the relationship collapses.
- The relationship has the capacity to continually provide new benefits.
- Reciprocity. The ability to respond immediately to either positive or negative behavior by the other party in the relationship.
- Refraining from the use of coercive power, which reduces cooperation.
- Flexibility in making mutually determined adjustments to the relationship.
- The development of trust. Trust has been defined as "a bridge between past experiences and their anticipated future."[5] Trust develops when parties in a relationship are

[4] In the 1970s film *The Godfather,* the Mafia bosses were able to offer such attractive mixtures of opponent pain and gain that people always found their deals very difficult to refuse!

[5] D. Salmond, "Refining the Concept of Trust in Business-to-Business Relationships: Theory, Research, and Practice," in *Relationship Marketing: Theory, Methods, and Applications: 1994 Research Conference Proceedings,* Eds. J. N. Sheth and A. Parvatiyar (Atlanta, GA: Center for Relationship Marketing, 1994): 2.

confident, based on experience, that they can predict the behavior of the other party. Trust is also engendered by the supplier's or buyer's concerns for their reputation. You can trust McDonald's because of the massive amount of publicity that results from one bad hamburger.

The general principles of power and cooperation apply to both vertical and horizontal linkages in the food system. How these principles are applied in these two dimensions is discussed next.

VERTICAL AND HORIZONTAL LINKAGES

Vertical Integration

In Figure 6-1, vertical coordinative mechanisms range from vertical integration, where one company controls several sequential stages in the system through common ownership, to open-market coordination, where each stage is carried out by independent companies.

Reasons for Vertical Integration   The basic reason for companies to vertically integrate or contract with suppliers/buyers is control. Vertical integration gives the most control, as all decisions are made within one organization.

Vertical integration will tend to occur in the food system:

• When a company developing a new technology or market opportunity needs to control raw-material supply and/or distribution to maximize the benefits from its introduction. For example, broiler processors have been very successful in breeding for improved feed-conversion efficiency, growth rates, and meat quality (see Figure 6-3). To maximize the benefit from these genetic improvements, they need to control broiler production through contracts with broiler growers or vertical integration (most processors have some of both).

• When companies leading the development of an infant industry need to vertically integrate backward into input supply or forward into distribution because it is unprofitable for independent companies to carry out these functions. For example, a manufacturer exporting into a new market may buy a distributor or form a joint-venture company with a distributor. Conversely, as the industry grows, channel disintegration may occur as it becomes profitable for independent companies to assume functions formerly carried out by the integrated company.

• In a situation of *resource dependency*. A company that is dependent on a supplier with monopoly power may integrate backward into the supply sector. A manufacturer using a great deal of starch, for example, may buy an interest in a starch producer. Such integration does not need to be complete; a "window" into the sector (tapered integration) may provide sufficient countervailing power to enhance their bargaining stance.

• Where there is a risk that one party to a contract (Party A) will be able to exploit the other (Party B) because B has invested in plant and equipment specifically to meet the requirements of the contract and any alternative use of these assets is significantly less profitable than the established contract. Party A, on the other hand, has less contract-specific investment and is, therefore, more flexible in dealing with alternative

FIGURE 6-3   Broiler production. Over 99 percent of broilers are produced either on processor-owned farms or under contract with producers. *(Courtesy of Continental Grain Company.)*

suppliers—or buyers. (An example of this type of situation is given in the Think Break in the section on contracts, which follows). Party B may seek to avoid opportunistic behavior by Party A by vertically integrating backward or forward.

• Where the company has specialized and valuable knowledge and where the nature of the relationship with suppliers or distributors makes it difficult to keep this knowledge confidential.

Problems with Vertical Integration   Vertical integration, however, is not without costs and has several potential disadvantages. Vertical integration entails the risks of diversification because the company is engaging in business activities that are different from its established operation. Food retailing is a quite different type of business than food processing, and food processing and agricultural production are equally different. Also, there is a bureaucratic cost associated with trying to centrally control several stages of the food system.

If vertical integration occurs by the acquisition of an established business, there can be "flow-balancing" problems between the two stages in the system. For example, if a retailer acquires a manufacturing business, there can be problems if the output of the manufacturing business is greater than the retailer can handle. Sale of the excess production through other retailers may not be a viable alternative, because the supplier is now owned by a competitor.

In several respects, vertical integration reduces flexibility, which is especially important in times of rapid change. Vertical integration internalizes business functions and reduces access to outside technological and organizational information. For example, food processors who manufacture their own cans may find it more difficult to access information on both can-making technology and other packaging alternatives than manufacturers who deal with a range of packaging suppliers.

Contracts

A business-to-business relationship may be formalized in a legal *contract.* The use of contracts has been increasing in food marketing, especially between agricultural producers and their buyers, because both suppliers and buyers want more control than they would have under an open-market system.

Contracts can contain both coercive and cooperative provisions. In general, legal wording uses phrases that are more coercive than cooperative, and the more detailed the contract, the more coercive it is likely to be.

The basic problem with contracts is *bounded rationality.* In other words, it is impossible to incorporate all possible dimensions of a future relationship in a legal document. Attempts to do so limit the flexibility of the contract.

Other contractual issues are:

• *Adverse selection.* An example from the insurance industry is the couple who take out medical insurance that includes provisions for pregnancy and the birth of a child because they plan to start a family. In an actuarial sense, the dice are loaded against the insurance company, a fact that is reflected in the premiums charged for such insurance. A McDonald's franchise provides a lot of assistance to the franchisee, limiting his or her managerial discretion. There is a danger that this type of agreement might attract people who are not good managers because they believe that the support provided by the franchiser will compensate for their deficiencies. Of course, McDonald's process of selecting franchisees is designed to identify such people.

• *Moral hazard.* This is another quaint phrase from the insurance industry, embodying the idea that people who take out fire insurance on their house will not exercise enough care to prevent it from burning down. Moral hazard is a type of after-contract opportunism, as compared with opportunism before the contract, associated with adverse selection.

• *Balancing interests.* Contracts should be written to balance the parties' interests. Much thought is required in writing contracts to align the interests of the two parties, so that there are no circumstances where one party consistently benefits at the expense of the other. Broiler-production contracts usually stipulate that the processor will provide genetic material, feed, and veterinary care free of charge. The broiler producer receives a fixed price per pound (kilogram) of meat produced. The danger with this type of contract is that the producer will not take enough care to maximize feed-conversion efficiency because he does not have to pay for the feed—a type of moral hazard. Broiler processors have come up with an interesting way of handling this problem. The per-pound payment is based on an average standard feed conversion. Producers who do better than the average get a premium; those who do worse get a discount. One writer has called this type of payment system "tournament competition," because each producer competes against the average of all producers.[6] It is an effective way of balancing the interests of producers and processors for this major cost item in broiler production.

• *Equality of investment in relationship-specific assets.* Interests are aligned and opportunistic behavior discouraged if both parties have a similar investment in assets that have limited alternative uses if the contract is discontinued. Conversely, if Party A has a smaller investment than Party B, then A will be in a position to exploit this situation, especially at contract-renewal time.

Think Break

Consider a fortunate potato processor who has secured the contract to supply McDonald's with french fries for all their outlets in South East Asia. Both sophisticated specialized processing equipment and efficient local growers are needed to meet McDonald's requirements for price and quality. The processor therefore establishes contracts with both McDonald's and the growers. He is conscious that his company has invested a substantial amount of money in the venture and is concerned that both McDonald's and the growers (individually and collectively) have invested considerably less and can take advantage of this situation.

How likely is it that this will occur? Under what circumstances? (Think about these questions for both McDonald's and the growers.) How could the processor minimize the chances of its happening? What alternatives, other than contracts with local growers, does the processor have for a potato supply?

• *Importance of the relationship in the long term.* If a contract is for a single transaction, such as a forward delivery contract between a grain producer and a grain merchant, and both parties can easily find alternative markets/sources of supply in the future, neither will be very concerned about a longer-term relationship and will therefore be encouraged to engage in exploitative behavior within the legal boundaries of the contract. For example, a contract stipulating that the merchant will buy all grain harvested from a specified area at an established price subjects the merchant to moral hazard, because the grower has a strong incentive to underreport yield when the spot price at harvest is greater than the contract price. The merchant may know that this has occurred and can refuse to deal with the grower again, but the grower will not care much if he knows that there are many alternative buyers for future harvests. Of course, if the merchants have some mechanism by which such behavior is reported (like a credit agency), the number of such growers will fall. If the merchant and the grower both believe that there are benefits in a longer-term relationship, they will be less likely to engage in exploitative behavior. One writer has called this "enlarging the shadow of the future."[7]

---

[6]C. R. Knoeber, "The Real Game of Chicken: Contracts, Tournaments, and the Production of Broilers," *Journal of Law and Economic Organization* 5 (1989): 271–92.

[7]R. Axelrod, *The Evolution of Cooperation* (New York: Basic Books, 1984): 126.

In concluding this brief discussion about a complex topic, two points need emphasis: First, the complexities of all but the most simple business-to-business relationships cannot be captured in a legal document—the bounded-rationality problem. Second, attitudes towards contracts differ among cultures. Americans like to close the deal quickly with some type of legal document; Asians believe in a longer period of precontractual relationship building and consider the details of the contract unimportant. Box 6-1 summarizes a typical American contract, one written for a processing commodity.

Think Break

Think about the Tomato Growers Association contract (Box 6-1) in terms of the contractual issues outlined on pages 142–143. How could it be improved?

BOX 6-1

MASTER AGREEMENT BETWEEN THE CALIFORNIA TOMATO GROWERS ASSOCIATION AND (COMPANY NAME)

1 Canner acknowledges that the Association is the authorized agent to bargain for its members.

2 *Price Discrimination.* Canner will offer to purchase tomatoes from Association Members at equally favorable prices and economic terms as offered by Canner at that time to other tomato producers. The price shall include the reasonable value of any bonuses, premiums, hauling or loading allowances and deferred payments.

3 *Quantity Discrimination.* Canner agrees that it will offer to purchase from Association Members substantially the same percentage of Canner's total tomato purchases during the terms of this Agreement as the percentage of Canner's total tomato purchases which were made from Association Members in the immediately preceding crop season.

4 *Premium for Special Variety or Harvest.* Canner shall pay a premium as set forth in the Price Schedule for a variety that Canner and Association Member agree is experimental or unproven, or which Canner requires Association Member to harvest by hand or other special harvesting means.

5 *Minimum Tonnage Contract.* Any tonnage contract which requires an Association Member to produce or harvest the tomatoes to be purchased on a minimum acreage of land, shall also require Canner to purchase a minimum net tons of tomatoes computed on the average yield of the Association Member on such acreage or land during the preceding five years or less. In determining such average yield, a nonrepresentative high or low yield in any one year which is caused by unusual factors shall not be considered.

6 *Delivery Schedule.* A Weekly Delivery Schedule, specifying a minimum week delivery consistent with the normal practices in the area of production, shall be developed by mutual agreement between the Association Member and Canner. Canner agrees to adjust the Weekly Delivery Schedule to accommodate the delivery of tomatoes from the Association Member in excess of his Weekly Delivery Schedule provided that such adjustment would not restrict the delivery of tomatoes by other growers.

7 *Inspection of Tomatoes.* All tomatoes shall be weighed and inspected by the State of California Tomato Advisory Board. Time is of the essence in insuring the inspection occurs promptly.

8 *Reject Standards.* Tomatoes may be rejected by the Canner if mold is in excess of 5 percent of gross weight. This percentage may be reduced by prior written notice from Canner to process an acceptable finished product; provided, however, that if the Association believes that such reduced percentage is used by Canner to restrict the volume of deliveries, Association may, by written notice to Canner, require the percentage to remain at 5%. [There are other quality clauses relating to worm damage, material other than tomatoes, and color.]

Source: Abridged and simplified version of the 1995 contract. Produced with the consent of the California Tomato Growers Association, Stockton, California.

Horizontal Control

Basic Principles   The principles of power and cooperation are the same for both vertical and horizontal relationships in the food system. However, the opportunities for cooperation can be less obvious in the horizontal dimension, basically because companies operating at the same level in the system are primarily competitors. Furthermore, as discussed above, there can be legal barriers to cooperative activity between competing companies. The basic principle is to identify areas of mutual benefit and exclude areas of obvious competition. For example, small wine producers, who will be active and aggressive competitors on the local market, may collaborate in exporting, using the region where their grapes are produced as the promotional theme.

If an industry approaches the perfectly competitive model, overt competition between companies will be limited—each company is powerless to influence price and other conditions of sale. While this suggests opportunities for cooperation, realizing its benefits may be difficult because, under perfect competition, companies are small, numerous, and unaccustomed to collective behavior. In a dairy cooperative where there is excess capacity in the processing plant, there is both the motivation for, and the means of, cooperation among the producer members. The producers have an obvious motivation for sharing experiences on ways to produce more milk: it is in everyone's interest to increase the milk flow into the processing plant, because it reduces average processing cost.

Horizontal Alliances   Horizontal *alliances* are most likely to be established when mutual benefits can be clearly identified and boundaries of the alliance can be well defined, minimizing areas of possible competition. Horizontal alliances may occur in the food system when:

• An alliance is the only feasible way of entering a market. For example, many developing countries have high barriers to imports (discussed in Chapter 9). Therefore, the only way a foreign supplier can enter the market is to set up a manufacturing subsidiary in it. However, the developing country may also have laws that require a foreign investor to have a local partner.

• The costs of growth may be so great that even the largest companies need to combine with a partner. This is particularly true in international business. As one writer puts it: "Globalization mandates alliances, makes them absolutely essential to strategy."[8] An example of a global food-company alliance is General Partners Worldwide, established in 1989 between Nestlé and General Mills to sell ready-to-eat breakfast cereals outside the United States and Canada. The mutual benefit arises from combining Nestlé's strengths as global food manufacturer and distributor with General Mills' strength as breakfast-cereal supplier. The terms of the agreement limit the possibility of competition in General Mills' "home" markets.

[8]Ohmae, *The Borderless World* (London: William Collins, 1990): 10.

Many alliances and joint ventures fail. The successful ones are those that apply the rules for cooperation discussed above, working hard to ensure each other's prosperity in the alliance and to limit competition in other dimensions of the relationship. Mechanisms for reciprocity are built into the agreement.

Think Break

A trade association is a particular type of horizontal association (for example, milk processors or candy manufacturers). Identify a particular trade association and, if possible, talk to one of its executives. What are the association's main activities? What are the main benefits that it offers to its members? What are the legal constraints to the association's activities? What seem to be the factors contributing to the association's success (or lack of success)?

VERTICAL COORDINATION IN AGRICULTURAL PRODUCTION

Industrialization

The organization of the food marketing channel is changing from open-market, transaction-based relationships to contracts and alliances. This process has been called the *industrialization of the food system.*[9] Industrialization does not imply that plants and animals are produced using industrial-type production systems, although this may be true in some cases—for example, broilers. Industrialization is an organizational change, rather than a technological one, and is driven by the need for food manufacturers and distributors to have more control over the quantity and quality of products that they buy. Factors influencing the supply of and the demand for industrialization are shown in Figure 6-4.

Discriminating consumers are the basic force for change. For example, if consumers want "fresh," retailers must design procurement systems that deliver this attribute in a way that distinguishes them from their competitors. This is difficult to achieve if all retailers purchase produce at the same auction or market.

> When you buy a Big Mac or McChicken Sandwich, you'll find that it is garnished with lettuce. Iceberg lettuce. Fresh crisp iceberg lettuce every time. We know it's fresh, because we know when and where it was picked.[10]

Processors and retailers are increasingly concerned about their legal liability for the quality of the products that they buy. "Due diligence" provisions require them to be able to trace quality problems back to their source, which may be the farm or even the supplier of a farm input, such as animal feed or an agricultural chemical.

---

[9]M. Drabenstott, "Industrialization: Steady Current or Tidal Wave," *Choices,* 4th Quarter (1994): 5–8.
[10] Advertisement for McDonald's, quoted in *Breaking with Tradition: Building Partnerships and Alliances in the European Food Industry,* R. Hughes, Ed. (Kent: Ashford, 1994):48.

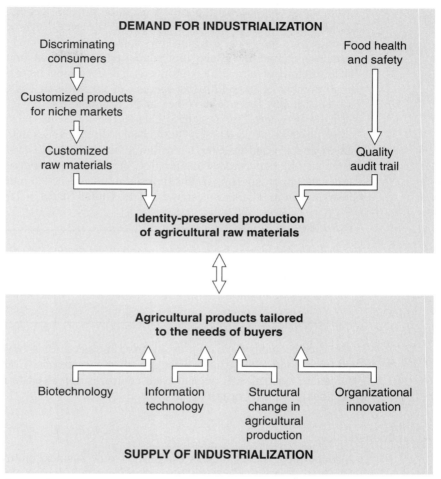

FIGURE 6-4 Supply of and demand for industrialization. *(Source: W. Schroder and F. Mavondo, "The Industrialization of Agriculture: Overseas Experience and Implications for Australia," Australasian Agribusiness Review 3.1 (1995): 23–35.)*

This means that we have to know where our animals come from and how they are managed. This cannot be done through the auction system. As soon as we can establish a network of three-cornered quality assurance partnerships with farm groups, abattoirs, and ourselves, we will refuse to handle any auction animals.[11]

---

[11]Chief Meat Buyer for Safeway in the U.K., quoted in J. E. Hobbs and W. A. Kerr, "Cost of Monitoring Safety and Vertical Coordination in Agribusiness," *Agribusiness: An International Journal* 8 (1992): 580.

On the supply side of the industrialization process, genetic engineering allows agricultural raw materials to be tailored to the needs of processors and retailers more quickly than can be achieved by conventional plant and animal breeding. Information technology allows more direct communication among all three groups. The structure of agricultural production is becoming increasing bipolar, with a small number of large farms at one end of the scale, an increasing proportion of specialist/hobby farms at the other, and a declining number of traditional "family" farms in between. This structural change facilitates the industrialization process. Large processors and retailers like to deal with businesses that are similar to themselves in scale and in approach to doing business. Large producers may also become the link between the smaller producers and processors or retailers—a type of organizational innovation. Industrialization has proceeded much faster in some industries than in others, as is shown for the United States in Table 6-1.

Think Break

In Table 6-1, why is the industrialization of the broiler system 100 percent while for feed grains it is only 2 percent? What changes have occurred in egg production and distribution that caused an increase in industrialization from 13 percent in 1960 to 94 percent in 1990?

Basically, industrialization arises from the need for a buyer (processor or retailer) to control the source of supply of raw materials. Conversely, commodity marketing systems will persist when control is perceived to be unnecessary, impossible to achieve, or too expensive.

Agricultural Cooperatives

A *cooperative* is a legal entity established to do business on behalf of its members. The first cooperative was established in Rochdale, England, in 1844. A group of

TABLE 6-1   INDUSTRIALIZATION IN U.S. AGRICULTURE

	Percentage of total production through contracts and vertical integration:			
	1960	1970	1980	1990
Feed grains	<1	<1	2	2
Hogs	<1	1	2	11
Market eggs	13	40	88	94
Broilers	95	96	98	100
Turkeys	35	42	79	93
Processed vegetables	75	94	98	97

Source: M. Drabenstott, "Industrialization: Steady Current or Tidal Wave." *Choices* (Fourth Quarter 1994): 6. Reprinted with permission, Federal Reserve Bank of Kansas City.

consumers, unhappy with the prices they were paying for food and other household items, established a cooperative in competition with established retailers. They laid down eight principles for cooperative organization: Open membership; Democratic control; Limited interest on shares; Dividends to members on the basis of patronage; Goods sold at current market rates for cash only; Neutrality in race, religion, and politics; Sale of fine and unadulterated goods; Continuous education of members.

Today cooperatives remain a major force in the food industry. Such well-known brands as Sunkist (United States) and Kerry Gold (Ireland) are produced by cooperative companies. In some countries, such as Denmark, cooperatives are the dominant form of organization in the food industry. The New Zealand dairy industry is 100 percent cooperative, and a statutory marketing organization, the New Zealand Dairy Board, which is controlled by the cooperative processing companies, is the second biggest international trader of dairy products. Both producer and supply cooperatives are important in the agricultural sectors of developing countries. As well as being a way for producers to integrate vertically, bargaining cooperatives can be used to achieve market power (horizontal control); they are discussed in Chapter 10. Cooperatives are also found in food wholesaling and retailing and are a major force in some Northern European countries. In the United States, cooperatives are powerful marketers of particular products; Blue Diamond Almond Growers (Figure 6-5) is just one example.

How well do modern cooperatives conform to the *Rochdale principles?* The principles are still hotly debated at cooperative conferences. Two remain as a basic feature of all forms of cooperative business organization: limited interest on shares and rebates to members on the basis of patronage. Payments to members on the basis of the extent to which they use the services of the cooperative is a fundamental of cooperative organization. The way that this works in practice for, say, a milk-processing cooperative, is that the payment for each month's milk supply is based on budgeted sales for the financial year less all expenses (apart from milk), with a final payment being made to each producer on the basis of milk supplied when the actual profit is known at the end of the year.

Cooperative Management Issues   Cooperatives face particular problems in raising equity capital. First, because remuneration is on the basis of patronage rather than investment, the signal to members is to maximize their use of the existing investment rather than to make new investments in buildings, plant, and working capital, and, in any case, members may feel that the money is better spent on their farming enterprise. Second, cooperative shares can usually be redeemed only at par value, so a member who quits farming and wants to sell his shares will not receive any benefit from capital appreciation.

In a conventional company, there is a clear distinction between the functions of the board of directors and those of management. Put simply, the board establishes policies and management executes them (hence the term "executive"). This model does not work well for cooperatives. The member directors often seek to play a more proactive role in the day-to-day management of the cooperative's activities.

FIGURE 6-5   Blue Diamond Growers, Sacramento, California. Owned by over 3,000 farmers, Blue Diamond Growers was started over 80 years ago and today processes nearly one-third of the world's almond crop each year. *(Courtesy of Blue Diamond Growers.)*

Cooperatives have both advantages and disadvantages with respect to quality assurance. It can be difficult to penalize members who do not meet quality standards and virtually impossible to expel them. Directors may use their authority to influence the grading of their own product. Pooling of product from different suppliers increases the difficulty of implementing quality programs (moral hazard). On the other hand, once agreement has been reached, there is the opportunity for rapid diffusion of quality initiatives among members. Cooperatives can be an effective governance structure for the production of high-quality products—Dutch vegetables and fruit, French wine.

A processing cooperative is a form of collective forward vertical integration by agricultural producers. Most of the problems faced by processing cooperatives arise from the fact that the board and management of a processing cooperative are required to address two sorts of organizational problems at the same time—

coordination of the producer network and diversification from the members' core business. A producer cooperative tends to be production, rather than marketing, oriented. There is pressure on management to focus on the member suppliers, rather than on the customers.

The fact that cooperatives survive and thrive suggests that these problems are not insurmountable. They remain, however, as major issues to be faced by cooperative boards and management. As the story in Box 6-2 relates, cooperatives can be effective competitors in the marketplace.

BOX 6-2

A PULP TALE: JUICE CO-OP SQUEEZES BIG RIVALS

When a little-known farmers' cooperative called Citrus World Inc. started to market its own brand of pasteurized orange juice, it looked like an improbable player in the $3 billion juice market. Citrus World, an 800-employee operation sitting on a lonely road near rural Lake Wales, Florida, was up against a couple of giants: Seagram Co., owner of Tropicana, and Coca-Cola Co., with its Minute Maid line.

But Citrus World knew exactly what to do: Squeeze that folksy image for all it was worth. To sell its Florida's Natural brand, it ordered commercials featuring sunburned farmers gulping down juice. In one current ad, growers holding boxes of oranges hold a "stockholders' meeting" in the back of a truck. Other workers cut "overhead" by chopping a branch from the orange tree.

Thanks to catchy ads and aggressive discounting, Citrus World has made a splash. A little over a year ago, it knocked Minute Maid off the No. 2 spot in the rapidly growing market for "premium" or pasteurized, not-from-concentrate orange juice. Citrus World spent just $12.5 million on its ads last year, while Coke spent $100 million to sell and promote new, fancier cartons for all of its juices. But Coke's Minute Maid is falling further behind. Last year, supermarket sales of Florida's Natural not-from-concentrate orange juice grew 27% to $135.4 million, according to A. C. Nielsen data supplied by Coca-Cola.

The co-op started in 1933 when a group of Florida orange growers decided to process their own crops rather than sell to big juice companies. It kept a low profile, offering frozen juice under inexpensive and private-label brands such as Donald Duck, Texsun, and Bluebird. But in 1987, the growers worried that frozen juice was losing popularity and decided to get into the small but fast-growing pasteurized market Tropicana had carved out for itself. With lower production costs than its competitors, who buy their oranges from outside suppliers, the co-op launched a copycat product, then called Fresh'n Natural—with a similar green logo on the carton.

After being sued by Tropicana for false claims in ads and being forbidden the use of the word "fresh" under a new nutrition-labeling law, the co-op's luck began to turn six years ago when it started running the ads with its farmers. In one, the narrator boasts that "recent mergers were fruitful," as the camera shows a bee buzzing around an orange blossom, and that "futures" look strong (a young orange twig). The consistent, long-running ads, along with frequent in-store promotions, helped boost sales, says Michael Cobb, a buyer at Roth IGA Inc., an 11-store chain based in Salem, Oregon. "They do a good job of showing they're out there in the fields."

"We have to be quick on our feet," says Walter Lincer, the co-op's sales and marketing chief. For the 1,100 growers who are the company's shareholders, "This is their only livelihood," he says. Tropicana executives argue that Citrus World is competing mainly on price, and vows Tropicana can stay ahead by promoting its strong brand name. Tropicana will boost its estimated $25 million annual ad budget "dramatically," says a spokesperson.

Citrus World's Mr. Lincer remains unfazed. "We understand the orange juice business," he declares, reciting the co-op's ad slogan: "We own the land, the trees, the company."

Source: The Wall Street Journal (January 30, 1996): B1, B9. Reprinted with permission of *Wall Street Journal,* ©1996 Dow Jones & Company, Inc. All Rights Reserved Worldwide.

CHANNEL DESIGN AND MANAGEMENT

The discussion so far has addressed the "macro" issues of the design and administration of the marketing channel—structure, power, cooperation, and control. An individual company addresses these issues from a "micro" perspective—how to design the company's marketing channel to best achieve its distribution (or supply) objectives. These objectives must, of course, be consistent with the company's overall marketing objectives, and the distribution strategy must be consistent with other elements of its marketing strategy—product, price, and promotion.

Rosenbloom defines the marketing channel as the "external contractual organization which management operates to achieve its distribution objectives."[12] The first aspect of this definition is that distribution involves managing activities external to the company, which inevitably means that management has less control over distribution than over other marketing activities. However, the definition assumes the company has some control—you can't manage something over which you have no control at all (as occurs in the case of a commodity supplier). The second aspect is that the definition is manufacturer focused (as are nearly all textbook discussions of channel management). In food distribution, the channel leader is often the retailer. The issues faced by the retailer are those of managing the supply channel, rather than distribution.

Channel Design

Figure 5-7 showed four types of marketing channel, ranging from direct selling by manufacturer to consumer, to a channel with three levels of marketing intermediaries. In any industry, or even for any one manufacturer, channels of varying degrees of complexity can exist in parallel. For example, a wine producer may sell wine at "cellar door," distribute directly to retailers or through a wholesaler, and, for export sales, use an agent in the importing country.

The second dimension of the distribution system is the number of companies at each level. For example, if it is decided to distribute through wholesalers, how many should be used? Extensive distribution is where there are many companies at each level; selective is where there are few; exclusive is where there is only one.

Factors Affecting Channel Design

The variables affecting *channel design* are the nature of the market, the product, company variables, the available distribution alternatives, and environmental variables. The impact of each of these variables is summarized in Table 6-2.

In Table 6-2, many of the linkages between the independent variables and channel structure are reasonably obvious. For example, many geographically dispersed customers located at a considerable distance from the manufacturer will require many levels of distribution and a large number of intermediaries at each stage. Perishable products, such as vegetables, require a short distribution channel, but there

---

[12]B. Rosenbloom, *Marketing Channels: A Management View* (Chicago: Dryden, 1986): 4.

TABLE 6-2   VARIABLES AFFECTING CHANNEL DESIGN

Variable	Dimension	Effect on number of	
		Levels	Companies
Market Variables			
Geography	Distance between manufacturer and customers	+	+
Size	Number of customers	+	+
Density	Number of buyers per defined area	−	−
Buyer behavior	Volume purchased at any one time	−	−
	Frequency of purchasing	−	−
	Involvement in purchase decision	+	−
Shopping behavior	Convenience goods	+	+
	Shopping goods	?	−
	Specialty goods	?	−
Product Variables			
Physical characteristics	Bulk	−?	?
	Perishability	−	+?
Unit value	High unit value	−	−
Degree of standardization	Product homogeneity	+	+?
Technical sophistication	Increased technical	−	−
Company Variables			
Size	Sales volume	−	?
Expertise	Distribution expertise in company	−	−
Distribution-System Variables			
Expertise	Distributor product and market knowledge	+	−?
Distributor power		−?	+?
Environmental Change	Rapidly changing environment	?	+?

+ indicates a postive relationship between variable and number of levels/companies
− indicates a negative relationship
? indicates relationship is uncertain

may be many companies at each level. Other linkages are less obvious and require further explanation.

Buyer Behavior   If consumers shop frequently, the quantity purchased at any one time will be less, and they are likely to be unwilling to travel long distances. Therefore shopping frequency will be positively related to the number of retail outlets. Many small independent retailers require a complex system of wholesalers to support them. This has been the case for food distribution in Japan (recall the discussion on the Japanese distribution system in Chapter 5), although this system is changing rapidly with the encroachment of supermarkets.

High-involvement purchases are those that buyers spend a lot of time thinking about, usually because they are "big-ticket" items in the household budget, or perhaps because the buyers are concerned about the impact of the product on their image, as in the case of fashion goods. High-involvement products require retailers with specialist knowledge to support consumers in their buying decisions. Clearly, food is usually a low-involvement product.

Products can be categorized into: convenience goods, where buyers are not brand aware; shopping goods, where they are brand aware but shop around to make their choice; speciality goods, where they know their favorite brand and look for a specialist supplier—of "up-market" brands of ice cream, for example.

Product Variables   Suppliers of products that are technically sophisticated and have a high unit value (for example, mainframe computers) tend to have a short distribution channel.[13] Products that are standardized and homogeneous (commodities) can, other things being equal, have quite long distribution channels with a variety of specialist intermediaries and facilitators.

Sales Volume   The volume and value of business also affects a company's choice of distribution method. For example, food manufacturers entering new export markets would, initially, be unlikely to have the volume of business to support the same type of specialist sales forces that they use in their home markets (new suppliers are also unlikely to have the expertise required to sell in an unfamiliar market). On the other hand, as markets grow, the volume may justify the manufacturers' setting up their own offices and sales forces.

A company may carry out its own distribution because management believes there are no distributors with sufficient expertise to handle their product. This situation is most likely to occur with technically sophisticated products. Also, a company may do its own distribution or, perhaps, appoint additional distributors, in response to the exercise of power by a distributor. Finally, multiple distributors provide more "windows" into the world in a rapidly changing environment.

Think Break

What channel design is appropriate from the perspective of a marketer of each of the following products? Breakfast cereal, specialized milk proteins used in food manufacturing, frozen boysenberries exported from New Zealand to Japan, regular ice cream, luxury ice cream, commodity wheat, specialized wheats, and a basic ingredient for a food manufacturer, such as salt.

Now think of the supply-channel design problem from the point of view of a) a family-owned delicatessen and b) a supermarket chain. For each of these two types of business, what channel design (in terms of both number of levels of suppliers and numbers of companies at each level) is appropriate for: specialty cheeses, regular cheeses, soft drinks, and soy sauce?

---

[13]IBM, the company which for many years dominated the computer industry, used to be vertically integrated through to retail. This system makes sense for mainframe computers, and they tried to retain it with the advent of the personal computer, setting up their own retailers to reach the wider market for this product. However, PCs were a low-value product seen as a shopping good by their buyers, who wanted to be able to compare a variety of brands in one location.

The examples given in the Think Break illustrate the point that there is no clear answer on channel design questions. The variables in Table 6-2 provide a guide, but it is an "other-things-being-equal" sort of guide. For example, if there are a large number of geographically dispersed customers for a new, technically sophisticated food ingredient, management will want to provide a high level of customer service using their own sales force, but this alternative is likely to be very expensive relative to using some type of distributor. Also, recall the point made at the beginning of the section, that your ability to "design" the marketing channel as a supplier or buyer depends on the amount of control you have. The supermarket chain in the Think Break has a lot more control over its suppliers than the deli.

Finally, remember that most food products are what marketing people call "fast-moving consumer nondurables." Buyers shop frequently and usually at the same retailers. Shopping behavior is routine. Brands, and the retailer's reputation, give buyers the security of being able to make a purchase without spending too much time worrying about it. Most buyers do not have a detailed shopping list. Cues to purchase decisions are given by the visual impact of the product display on the supermarket shelf. This type of buyer behavior means that the location of a product in the store and the height and length of its display have a significant impact on sales (see Chapter 8).

Channel Management

Having selected the "best" channel design (as far as it is possible to do so), the next task is the day-to-day management of distributors or suppliers. There are two main issues: distribution must be coordinated with other marketing activities, such as pricing and promotion; and distributors (suppliers) must be motivated to do the best possible job.

Distribution decisions must be compatible with decisions on product, pricing, and promotion. For example, the introduction of a new product requires close liason with distributors and coordination of promotion activities.

The price to the final consumer is, of course, the manufacturer's price plus the margins of one or more distributors. The basic principle is that each distributor's margin for a particular product line should equate with the next best alternative for the distributor. This basis for pricing distributor services can be illustrated by supermarket margins. The scarce resource in a supermarket is shelf area. Supermarket management wants to make sure that the total financial contribution per foot of shelf facing is about the same for each brand within a product category. The financial contribution comprises the number of units sold multiplied by the net margin (selling prices less buying price less direct costs) per unit, plus other contributions from the manufacturer, such as promotional assistance and direct payments for shelf space. Supermarket management recognizes that it will take time for a new product to become viable and will take this into account in their calculations. But, over time, the contribution from each product in a category must be about the same.

The promotional-strategy question for a food manufacturer is discussed more fully in Chapter 14. What share of promotional expenditure should go toward "pulling" the product through the distribution channel using mass advertising and promotion, relative to expenditure on "pushing" the product by supporting distributors directly? The problem for a manufacturer with a fixed promotional budget is that every dollar spent on trade promotion and direct payments to distributors means that less can be spent on advertising and other brand-supporting activities. The strength of the brand is the manufacturer's key weapon in negotiations with powerful retailers; therefore, the retailers' demands for more and more direct payments weaken the manufacturers' negotiating position because their brands are being continually eroded. Established manufacturers fight this trend as much as they can, but even the largest of them recognize they are on a downward spiral.

The principles of power and cooperation apply to the relationship between manufacturers and distributors in the same way as they apply to any other business-to-business relationship. The accompanying case study, "Power and Control in the Apple Basket," asks you to apply these principles to a specific case.

SUMMARY

The food marketing system has both a vertical and horizontal dimension. The vertical dimension is concerned with the coordination of business activities between food manufacturers and distributors, agricultural producers and manufacturers, and so on; in the horizontal dimension are relationships between businesses at the same level in the system. In either dimension, coordination can be by one company controlling all activities through common ownership, by the "invisible hand" of the market, or by contracts, partnerships, and alliances.

A company has two ways by which it may seek to directly influence other companies—by the exercise of power or by cooperating. The possibility of exercising power is altered by industry structure and organization. In general, the more concentrated an industry, the more powerful the companies in it are, relative to their suppliers and buyers. Recognizing that the exercise of power by manufacturers and distributors may result in consumers paying more and/or agricultural producers receiving less, governments may legislate to limit industry concentration or to support agricultural producers in their efforts to obtain countervailing power.

Basically, power derives from having a business relationship with someone who has few alternative buyers or suppliers, or conversely, being in the position of having alternative sources of supply or markets yourself.

The prerequisite for business-to-business cooperation is the possibility of mutual gain. In the food marketing system, this possibility is greatest when cooperation generates new benefits for consumers or reduces costs. Cooperative relationships run smoothly when both parties have about the same amount to lose if the relationship collapses, and when there are trust, flexibility, and reciprocity.

Vertical integration, where one company controls several stages in the food system by common ownership, achieves the highest degree of control but involves costs for the integrating company. Consequently, companies seeking to control supply or distribution are increasingly entering into some type of contractual relationship. Contracts should align the interests of the contracting parties and be balanced in terms of each party's investment in contract-specific assets. No contract can incorporate all possible dimensions of a future relationship in a legal document, and the contracts that work are those that recognize the principles of cooperation.

The principles underlying the establishment and operation of horizontal business-to-business relationships are the same as for the vertical. The opportunities for cooperation are, however, less obvious, and there can be legal barriers to cooperative activity between competing companies.

The trend to closer linkages in the food system has been called industrialization. Closer linkages are facilitated by biotechnology, information technology, and structural changes in agricultural production.

An agricultural cooperative is a legal entity established to conduct business on behalf of its producer members. Cooperatives are a major force in the food industry. Their distinguishing feature is limited interest on the members' investment, with the financial return to members being based on their use of the cooperative.

An individual company, such as a food manufacturer, seeks to design a supply and distribution channel that integrates supply/distribution with other marketing activities—product mix, pricing, and promotion. Channel design involves both the number of levels of suppliers and the number of companies at each level.

IMPORTANT TERMS AND CONCEPTS

administrative control   134
adverse selection   142
alliances   145
balancing interests   142
bounded rationality   142
channel design   152
contracts   142
cooperation   135
cooperative   149
countervailing power   137
equality of investment in
 relationship-specific assets   143
Five Forces Model   136

linkages   134
industrialization of the food system   146
moral hazard   142
open-market control   134
opponent gain   139
opponent pain   139
power   135
resource dependency   140
Rochdale principles   149
statutory marketing boards   137
switching costs   138
vertical integration   134
zero-sum game   139

CASE STUDY: Power and Control in the Apple Basket

Recall the definition of power as the ability to influence behavior. Power can be exercised in a coercive way (opponent pain) or in a cooperative way (opponent gain). We identified a number of sources of power and discussed the establishment and maintenance of successful supplier/buyer relationships. These can be summarized as follows:

The Porter Five Forces Model suggests that the first strategic decision is to be in the right industry—one with limited intraindustry competition, few substitute products, and high barriers to entry, and where both suppliers and buyers have limited bargaining power. (This might be easier said than done!)

A supplier has power in a business relationship where it has alternative buyers and/or enterprises and where the switching costs of changing to these alternatives are low. (Conversely, supplier power is increased where buyers have few alternatives and high switching costs.) Companies that are financially robust have more power than those that are highly leveraged.

A supplier of a raw material will have more power when the final demand for the manufactured product is inelastic and the cost of the raw material is a small proportion of the total manufacturer's cost. The possibility of a supplier negotiating a higher price is better when the buyer is making a profit than when he is not.

The principle of cooperation is that there must be benefits to both parties. Cooperative relationships are maintained when both parties have the same amount to lose if the relationship collapses and where there are trust, flexibility, and reciprocity.

You are a major apple producer in your area, accounting for about 25 percent of production. You have been selling your apples through the established marketing channel—the produce market in the state's major city. You are approached by a major supermarket chain (30 percent market share) to deal directly with them. Apply the principles of power and cooperation to establishing and managing your relationship with the supermarket.

QUESTIONS

1 Discuss the following statement: "Perfect competition is, in marketing management terms, no competition at all."

2 Define: power, countervailing power, switching costs, zero-sum game.

3 What are the main benefits of cooperation in a business-to-business relationship? How do you ensure that a relationship is based on cooperation, rather than conflict?

4 "Every business relationship should be formalized with a detailed contract." Discuss.

5 Think of examples of adverse selection and moral hazard in:
   a) fast-food franchise agreement
   b) membership agreement for an agricultural producer bargaining organization.

6 Give examples of opportunistic behavior in a contractual situation. How do you reduce the risk of such behavior?

7 What are the benefits and costs of vertical integration? Both contracts and vertical integration allow a company to achieve more control in its relationship with suppliers and/or buyers. Under what circumstances would vertical integration be preferred to a contract?

8 Why might food companies want to establish horizontal alliances? Discuss the reasons why horizontal linkages are usually more restricted than vertical.

9 What are the "Rochdale principles" of cooperation? How do these principles apply to a modern food-processing cooperative?

10 Global food companies are internationally unrestricted in terms of obtaining raw materials, locating processing plants, and finding customers. What problems might a cooperative food processor have in becoming a global company?

11 Define the term "industrialization" in food marketing. Do you think the term is appropriate? What are the main factors leading to increased industrialization in the food industry?

12 Think about the food-buyer behavior issues raised in Chapter 2 and in this chapter. How does buyer behavior affect the design of the food marketing channel?

REFERENCES AND RESOURCES

Axelrod, R. *The Evolution of Cooperation.* New York: Basic Books, 1984.

Drabenstott, M. "Industrialization: Steady Current or Tidal Wave." *Choices* (Fourth Quarter 1994): 5–8.

Hobbs, J. E., and W. A. Kerr. "Cost of Monitoring Safety and Vertical Coordination in Agribusiness: What Can be Learned from the British Food Safety Act, 1990." *Agribusiness: An International Journal* 8 (1992): 576–584.

Hughes, R., Ed. *Breaking With Tradition: Building Partnerships and Alliances in the European Food Industry.* Kent: Ashford, 1994.

Knoeber, C. R. "The Real Game of Chicken: Contracts, Tournaments, and the Production of Broilers." *Journal of Law and Economic Organization* 5 (1989): 271–92.

Kohls, R., and J. Uhl. *The Marketing of Agricultural Products.* New York: Macmillan, 1990.

Ohmae, K. *The Borderless World.* London: William Collins, 1990.

Porter, Michael. *Competitive Strategy.* New York: Free Press, 1980.

Rosenbloom, B. *Marketing Channels: A Management View.* Chicago: The Dryden Press, 1987.

Salmond, D. "Refining the Concept of Trust in Business-to-Business Relationships: Theory, Research, and Practice." In *Relationship Marketing: Theory, Methods, and Applications: 1994 Research Conference Proceedings.* Eds. J. N. Sheth and A. Parvatiyar. Atlanta: Center for Relationship Marketing, 1994: 12.

Schroder, W., and F. Mavondo. "The Industrialization of Agriculture: Overseas Experience and Implications for Australia." *Australasian Agribusiness Review* 3.1 (1995): 23–35.

7

FOOD PROCESSING AND INDUSTRIAL MARKETING

CHAPTER OUTLINE

LEARNING OBJECTIVES

After reading this chapter and answering the questions in the Think Breaks and at the end of the chapter, you should be able to:

- Understand the changes that occur in biological raw materials as they move through primary processing, secondary processing, and manufacturing.
- Differentiate between the different stages of food processing and manufacturing and understand their interrelationships.
- Understand systems for the preservation of "fresh" and "live" products.
- Explain how a formulated food product, such as bread, is built up from a number of food ingredients.
- Define the qualities needed in industrial food products.
- Know the different types of industrial food products and how they are used.
- Recognize the growth in number of food ingredients and in their volume of sales in global food marketing.
- Outline the buying process in industrial marketing.
- Understand the buyer/supplier relationship in industrial marketing.

INTRODUCTION

Often the study of food processing has been subdivided into the various industries, such as baking or meat processing. As food processing has developed from craft to technology, however, and the interaction of all food industries has grown more complex, it has become more useful to study the main processes. These can be divided into two major groups—food preservation and food-structure formation. Food preservation includes the processes used to extend the life of the food—chilling and freezing, drying, and canning. Some raw materials only need preservation, and the harvested product is the same in form as the consumer product. It is perishable and is often called a "fresh" product by the consumer, although it may have been stored many months. But many raw materials are refined and mixed with other raw materials to form new food structures; these are sometimes called formulated products by the food technologist, or processed foods by the consumer.

A number of ingredients—often as many as twenty—go into processed foods. These ingredients may come from many processors and even from a number of countries. For example, in making tomato-based sauces, such as ketchup, the food manufacturer could buy tomatoes from local farmers or tomato concentrate from Italy, California, or South America; gums from an ingredient supplier who imports them from the United States or Europe; vinegar from a local vinegar processor or acetic acid from a chemical company; salt from a national large salt processor or from a small sea-salt producer; and spices from the Middle East and Asia or essential oils from a Dutch processor. And ketchup is a simple product! It's obvious that the buying of ingredients in food processing is a very complex operation, possibly involving many people in many countries.

The marketing of these food ingredients is known as industrial marketing. It occurs at many stages in the food system—in fact, wherever there are suppliers and buyers, except at the final stage between retailer and consumer, which is known as consumer marketing. Supplier/buyer relationships are the core of industrial marketing.

THE BASICS OF FOOD PROCESSING

Food processing converts agricultural and marine raw materials into foods bought to satsify consumers' nutritional needs, reduce their food-safety fears, and agree with their other needs. Important influences on food processing in the last thirty years have been consumers' needs for convenience, variety, and sensory appeal.

The desire to cut down food-preparation time has prompted the advances from making flour by pounding grains, to crude mechanical mills, to modern mills producing different meals and flours, and the accompanying development from baking in the home to the large, modern bakery. The satisfaction of consumers' needs for convenience has been accomplished through technological advances.

The need for variety has meant an increase in food manufacturing and a consequent growth in the food-ingredient industry. Variety is often obtained by ingredient changes in formulation. For example, a line of six ice creams with different flavors may need not only different flavor ingredients, but also different stabilizers and emulsifiers. If these ingredients can be bought directly, then it is simple to change products and introduce new products.

The final stage, manufacturing the consumer food product, is becoming simpler—it is often a mixing operation combined with a heating operation to cook and/or preserve the product, and packaging and storage methods to give the necessary storage life. This may be a food service operation, such as McDonald's, which takes very standard food ingredients and changes them into the final food by simple cooking and presentation methods.

The food-processing industry is constantly evolving. At the beginning of this century small craft industries were, for the most part, replaced by very large primary processing plants and then by plants producing a variety of consumer food products. Today, the final stage of food manufacturing and the food service industry are generally located near the consumer in order to reduce transportation costs and give better service. Also, raw materials are now being refined and further processed in the areas near production. There has also been an increase in contract manufacturing, especially for supermarket brands, but also for some established food manufacturers and marketers. In much of the food processing industry, production and processing are linked by contracts between farmers and manufacturers.[1]

In studying food processing, it is useful to divide it into two areas—food preservation and food structure.

Food Preservation

Food is an active biological system and therefore is constantly changing. The rate of change depends on the conditions of storage—temperature, water activity (relative humidity), and the surrounding atmosphere. The type of change depends on the original condition of the food material—for example, chemical composition, biological condition, physical structure, and the presence of microorganisms. The change may cause deterioration in the food, such as food-poisoning organisms increasing or bread becoming stale, but it can also improve the food, causing the ripening of fruit or the growth of mold on cheese. *Food-preservation* techniques attempt to slow down or stop the deterioration of food, in particular by retarding the growth of bacteria, yeasts, and molds.

The most important preservation methods today are physical methods, including temperature control, heat processing, and drying. As the temperature is decreased, the rate of deterioration decreases. As the temperature is lowered below room temperature, some types of microorganisms will not grow, until finally, when the food is frozen to a low temperature, none will grow and indeed, some microorganisms may die. The storage life of a food could be increased from two or three days at ambient temperatures to possibly eight days by chilling it to 5°–8° C, to three weeks by reducing it to 1° C, and to three months or more by freezing to −20° C. In chilled storage, the temperature must be carefully controlled, as a slight rise in temperature will decrease the storage life markedly. The storage life of orange juice, the final form in which most oranges are consumed, is extended considerably through freezing (see Figure 7-1).

Heat processing can be mild and only pasteurize the product, or it can be such that it will sterilize the product. Pasteurized milk has a storage life of 2 to 3 days, but UHT (Ultra High Temperature) milk can last for many months. Canned products are also sterilized. Microorganisms can grow only at certain water levels,

---

[1]Two Rabobank International reports: *The International Food Industry,* 1995: 9, 25, 26; and *The Retail Food Market,* 1994: 17, 49.

FIGURE 7-1 Oranges on their way to becoming frozen juice concentrate. (*Source:* U.S. Department of Agriculture.)

called water activities; if a food is dried, or if sugar and salt are added to reduce the percentage of water, then its life is extended. Chemical preservation utilizes traditional food ingredients, such as acetic acid or vinegar, and preservatives, such as sorbic acid, sulfites, or benzoic acid.

Although the physical and chemical methods can reduce the effect of microorganisms, they may not stop chemical and physical deterioration. Chilling slows the growth of molds and yeasts on a fresh fruit salad, but browning of the fruit may still occur; similarly, the addition of propionic acid may stop molds on bread but will not stop the development of staleness. In some cases, these methods may introduce new deteriorations. Frozen storage may cause loss of moisture in foods, resulting in a loss of texture.

Control of oxygen in the surrounding atmosphere by the addition of gases, such as carbon dioxide and nitrogen, will also increase the storage life, especially if combined with chilling in controlled atmosphere storage. Such techniques can bring to Europe fresh apples from South Africa, tropical fruit from Southeast Asia, and bananas from Central America. New equipment and control methods will make this an important method of international distribution in the future, but dry products will still be important, because they can be transported cheaply at ambient temperatures.

Think Break

Choose one vegetable or fruit raw material, such as potatoes. Visit your local supermarket and identify some products containing this raw material which are preserved by chilling, freezing, canning, or drying. Compare the qualities of these products. Is the vegetable or fruit you chose preserved by any other method?

Food Structures

The other part of food processing is to take raw materials and convert them into attractive *food structures.* Some important structures are:

- emulsions of oil and water, such as mayonnaise, and margarine;
- carbohydrate and protein networks, such as bread or extruded snacks;
- sugar structures, such as hard candies and popsicles; and
- starch pastes, such as gravies or sauces.

Sometimes these can occur together: in ice cream there is an oil-and-water emulsion, but air is also incorporated to give an expanded structure, and sugar crystals are formed as the ice cream is frozen.

Food structures are basically made from oil/fat, proteins, carbohydrates, water, and air, in various combinations. In order to help these structures to form and to stabilize them, a wide variety of emulsifiers, stabilizers, and other texture-modifying substances are available, and this variety is constantly being expanded. Because the consumer wants low-fat products, fat is being replaced by new products, mainly based on carbohydrates, which give the same texture and "mouth feel" as the fat. In addition to appropriate textures and structure, processed foods need an attractive appearance, aroma, and flavor. These can come from the basic raw materials, such as the meat in sausages, and from added spices and flavors, or they can be developed during processing.

What does this mean to the marketer? It means that a vast variety of products can be developed by means of changes in formulations and processing. This is the basis of food-product development, which is an important part of food marketing today. The marketer can set up a product concept from discussions with consumers and, with the technical people, develop product design specifications, which are the basis for the design of the product. This will be discussed further in Chapter 13.

Think Break

Think of some products that are mixtures (emulsions) of oil and water, such as mayonnaise, aerosol cream, ice cream, or margarine, and study them in the supermarket. Which are thick liquids, thin liquids, creams, or solids? What ingredients are listed on the label of each type of product? On which label is oil higher on the list than water, meaning that there is more oil than water in the product?

TYPES OF FOOD PROCESSING

For food marketing, the types of processing can be divided into:

- perishable-food production—the whole product from land or sea is marketed.
- primary processing of the basic production materials
- secondary processing, where the materials are further changed
- consumer food manufacturing—producing final consumer products using materials from the other types of processing.

Perishable-Product Distribution

A *perishable* or fresh consumer *product* is sold as it grew in the soil or in the water, with minimal cleaning and preparation, and is preserved by chilling and controlled atmosphere. For many raw materials, such as fruit, vegetables, fish, and meat cuts, this is financially the most rewarding path for the farmer or fisher and the distributor. The product yield is high, and fresh food products command a higher price. But this often difficult-to-achieve result requires an effective harvesting system which reduces the temperature of the raw material as quickly as possible, a grading system which delivers a product of consistent good quality, controlled conditions to retain that quality in the distribution system and supermarket, and an attractive display.

Some fruits, such as kiwifruit, have a long storage life which allows time to organize marketing worldwide. The kiwifruit can be stored where grown, transported in temperature-controlled containers, and then stored in the market for distribution. Therefore it is reasonably simple to establish a marketing system. On the other hand, there are difficulties when exporting live fish: live lobster is a very delicate product which must be chilled and rested in water after catching and then airfreighted in insulated boxes.

An ever-increasing number and variety of sensitive and short-life products are being moved around the world as controlled storage becomes more technologically feasible and air freight more available. The markets for all these products are expected to continue to grow, and the internationalization of supply can only increase. Consumers are not happy with seasonal supply and will pay to have fresh products year round.[2]

Primary Processing

In *primary processing,* the plant, animal, or fish is slaughtered, cleaned, and/or separated. Beef animals produce primal cuts and offal products; fish are gutted and may be skinned and filleted; the grains of wheat are separated from nongrain material, such as straw, stones, and weed seeds, and cleaned of broken kernels and dust. The end products of primary processing are very often commodities, but recently more industrial products are being tailored to specifications for particular

---

[2]L. A. Gibson, "The Quest for Fresh," *Cereal Foods World* 40.3 (March 1995): R16–17.

companies. In the dairy industry, the product line of butter, cheese, and skim milk powder has gradually been expanded to include a wide variety of products for different food and nonfood industries.

The protein industries—animal and fish—are still the largest primary industries in many countries. In the past, beef-, sheep-, and hog-slaughtering plants needed sufficient capacity to cope with the peak demand of the farmers, and they had excess capacity at other times of the year. The hog- and beef-lot industries now have more predictable slaughter schedules, and with industry cooperation, plant capacity is being more effectively utilized (Figure 7-2).

The primary industries are being pressured by their customers (and indirectly by the consumers) to offer products of certain specifications. They are moving from supplying only simple commodity products to offering *specialized commodity products* for manufacturers and supermarkets, and, increasingly, industrial products prepared to manufacturers' specifications.

Secondary Processsing

Secondary processing takes a crude raw material and turns it into a specific industrial product; in some cases, primary and secondary processing can occur in one processing plant.

FIGURE 7-2   Hog slaughtering facility. By mechanizing and operating two shifts a day, meat-processing costs have been reduced. (*Source:* U.S. Department of Agriculture.)

In a dairy plant, the protein/lactose/minerals fraction can be separated from the butterfat to produce skim milk powder, and the skim milk separated into whey proteins, caseins, lactose, and minerals. Secondary processing is highly developed in the dairy industry—using process engineering techniques, they have developed a vast range of products with carefully controlled chemical, physical, and microbiological properties, such as a specific protein powder for Gerber, a baby-food manufacturer.

Secondary processing is often a separation and purification of proteins, fats, sugars, and complex carbohydrates, including starch and fiber. These are the basic ingredients of the food industry. There are also fruit and vegetable concentrates: tomato, orange, and tropical fruits; and dried and frozen vegetables, such as peas, corn, and beans. These products are usually prepared to specifications of the final manufacturer or group of manufacturers—for example, fruit-juice packers and makers of frozen and canned meals.

Consumer-Product Manufacturing

In *manufacturing* consumer products, very often a large number of raw materials are collected from various primary and secondary processing companies throughout the world and are mixed, processed, and packed as the final product. Consumer product manufacturing may be only a mixing and packaging operation; for example, dried ingredients are blended into a soup mix and packed in a film pouch; or frozen ingredients may be mixed with a stock made from dried ingredients, placed in a can, and sterilized, resulting in canned soup. Sometimes a basic fresh ingredient (milk or meat, for instance) may be mixed with micoorganisms for the development of a fermented product (yogurt or salami). Packaging complements the process at this stage; thus, packaging equipment and systems are crucial. Brand names and packaging are aspects of consumer-product marketing that are discussed further in Chapter 13. Discussing a food as simple as cookies, Box 7-1 gives an idea of the complex processes involved in manufacturing food products.

INDUSTRIAL FOOD PRODUCTS

Industrial food products are the raw materials for food manufacturing. This section describes industrial food products and discusses how they are marketed.

Types of Industrial Food Products

The variety of industrial food products has increased in recent years to include speciality starches, dairy proteins, fat fractions, special fats, and of course processed specialty products.[3] The latter are mainly supplied by the chemical industry, but

---

[3]C. O'Donnell, "European Ingredient Science Leads the Way," *Prepared Foods,* January 1995:35–37, 40. This article describes the ingredients at the 1994 Food Ingredients Europe Food Show.

BOX 7-1

MAN WALKED ON THE MOON BUT MAN CAN'T MAKE ENOUGH DEVIL'S FOOD COOKIE CAKES

If you think the space program has technical problems, consider Nabisco Biscuit Co.'s Snackwell's Devil's Food Cookie Cakes.

More than a year after the launch of the fat-free chocolate-and-marshmallow cookies, Nabisco is still unable to meet the consumer demand. Supermarkets nationwide say supplies of the cookie are tightly rationed and that the shortage has created a buying frenzy among some consumers, who view the fat-free cookies as the perfect food—healthy sweets.

So why can't Nabisco, which will bake some 600 million pounds of cookies this year, simply make more of this scarce cookie? The Snackwell's cookie center is covered on all sides with marshmallow, then it is com-

pletely drenched with chocolate icing, followed by a separate chocolate icing, followed by a separate chocolate glaze. The whole process takes four hours. This means that devil's food cookies require custom-made machinery, currently available in just one bakery. Adding capacity would be difficult and expensive, so its three production lines have to work overtime.

To keep chocolate lovers from growing too restive, the company is also rolling out new fat-free Snackwell's Double Fudge Cookie Cakes—two layers of cake with a dollop of fat-free fudge in the middle—an easier cookie to make. At the beginning it is only being sold in the northeastern states!

Source: K. Deveny, *Wall Street Journal* (September 28, 1993): B1, B3. Reprinted with permission of *Wall Street Journal,* ©1993 Dow Jones & Company, Inc. All Rights Reserved Worldwide.

THE COOKIE SCALE

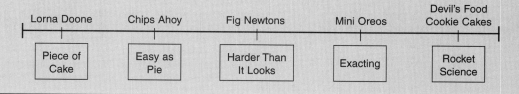

the biological industries have also developed gums, enzymes, and other specialty ingredients. Large chemical companies and their subsidiaries are involved in marketing these ingredients; for example Monsanto owns NutraSweet®, a noncalorie sweetener, whose sales increased from $59.6 million in 1982 to over $1 billion in 1992, fueled by the consumers' wish for low-calorie foods.[4]

A useful classification for food products, with examples of each type, is shown in Table 7-1. The difference between commodity products and specialized commodities is that commodity products are graded according to a recognized system agreed to by the farmers and the primary processors, and the specialized commodities are produced to the recognized specifications of manufacturers or supermarkets. (The grading and classifying of commodity products is discussed in Chapter 10.) Neither group of products has an identified customer at the time of production; they are produced for a general market. More and more commodities

---

[4]Detailed and updated information on synthetic and organic food additive markets and on flavors markets can be found in *A Competitive Survey of Flavor and Fragrance Markets, Synthetic and Organic Food Additive Markets,* by Leading Edge Reports, Cleveland Heights, Ohio.

TABLE 7-1   TYPES, DESCRIPTIONS, AND EXAMPLES OF INDUSTRIAL PRODUCTS

Industrial product type	Description	Products
Raw materials from farm or sea	When produced to specifications, these are industrial products	Peas for the vegetable-freezing industry Snapper for the live-fish trade Milk for dairy factories
Specialized commodities	Produced to specifications, but not designed for a specific process	Instant milk powder Specialized wheats
Bulk industrial products	Produced to specification and used in large quantities	Carbohydrates—cereals, flour, starches, dextrins, sugars Proteins—milk, soy, peanut proteins, meat powders Fats—vegetable, dairy, animal fats, fat fractions Fiber,—wheat, oat brans
Partially processed materials	Come from primary processing and need further processing before use in the final consumer product	Carcass beef, lamb, pork Boneless beef, lamb, and pork cuts Tomato concentrate Dried pumpkin powder Frozen blocks of fish fillets
Processed products	Further processed products, in a ready-to-use form for the final consumer product	Pastas—spaghetti, noodles Baked products—buns, biscuits, crackers Extruded products—puffed cereals, quick-cooking rice grains
Processed specialty ingredients	Sold in smaller quantities, having specific qualities to aid the processor and ensure the final product characteristics	Stabilizers—gums, starches, dairy proteins Emulsifiers—stearates, phosphates Colors and flavors—synthetic and natural Acids and salts—vinegar, salt, phosphates Nutrients—vitamins, minerals Fat replacers—malto dextrins, complex carbohydrates Preservatives—benzoic acid, sulfur dioxide, and sulfites.

are now produced as specialized commodities, and there is less demarcation between commodities and industrial products. In fact, the trend is for commodities to be developed into specialized commodities and then into industrial products designed for a particular process or customer (Chapter 6). Bulk, partially processed, and processed products are all industrial products at different stages of secondary processing.

Industrial Food-Product Characteristics

An industrial food product's most important characteristics are its uses in processing and its effect on the final product. The industrial product must be compatible with the process and at the same time provide the yields of finished product expected. It should allow uniform and stable processing, technical simplicity in processing, few equipment problems, and efficient use of staff. It must satisfy the composition, nutritional value, sensory qualities, and safety required in the final product and cause little variability in the product. Of course, cost is a factor: the basic raw-material cost, the cost of using it in the process, and the cost of the final product.

Convenience is also required in delivery and storage as well as in processing. Safety is another consideration—the processor must ensure that the ingredient does not contaminate the plant or result in an unsafe final product.

The industrial product can be divided, as shown in Figure 7-3, into the *tangible product,* the uses of the product, and the *services* that are marketed with the product, such as delivery times and technical information. The supplier must remember that it is the *total product* that is being marketed.

As shown in the diagram, there is a tangible product of specific composition, microbiological levels, physical properties, and sensory properties, but the wider product is also specified to cover the processing use, processing efficiency and processing costs, the storage life, and the quality of the derived product. These are all basic parts of the product. There are also characteristics that can show the uniqueness of the product–special features, quality and specifications, packaging and branding.

Services are also an important part of the product—for example product reliability, safety, availability and replaceability, technical information and help, delivery, and credit. It is not enough to sell the product—the company needs to sell the product and the services together. A product may be of high quality, but its delivery times are unreliable, so the buyer stays with a lower-quality product with exact delivery times. Products are not just a physical entity but an array of economic, technical, and personal relationships between buyer and seller. The company image and the salesperson's image are also part of the total product.

The industrial food product as described above is very different from the consumer product described in Chapter 13. The most important difference is that industrial products are sold on technical specifications, which may be specific to one manufacturer, to manufacturers using similar processes, or sometimes for different uses by a large number of manufacturers. Generally, today, industrial products are

FIGURE 7-3   The industrial food product.

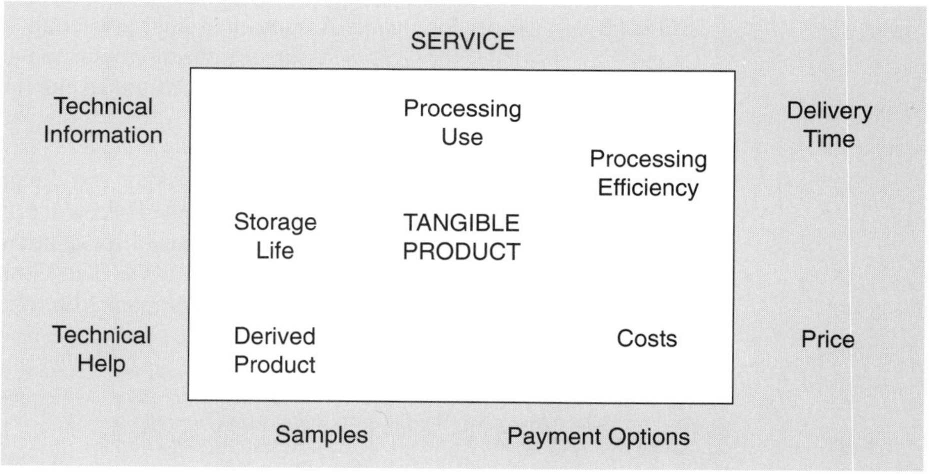

becoming more specifically designed for a particular process and type of final consumer product.

Think Break

Frozen blocks of boneless beef from Australia and New Zealand are used in the United States by large hamburger chains to make hamburger patties. Think about your nutritional needs and food safety concerns, what you enjoy when eating a hamburger, and the chains' experiences in making hamburger patties. Then list the product qualities, uses, and services that a hamburger chain might want from the importers.

Food-Product Specifications and Quality

Product specifications vary from product to product but generally include requirements such as:

- Chemical composition
- Nutritional composition
- Microbiological standard
- Physical properties
- Sensory properties.

They may also have specific requirements for use, packaging, storage, identification, and environmental and ethical standards.[5]

Very often now, the product, process, and production are required to meet ISO 9000 standards. *ISO 9000* are the International Quality Management and Quality Assurance Standards published by the International Organization for Standardization (ISO). There are three levels of Quality Assurance:

ISO 9003	Model for Quality Assurance in final inspection and test
ISO 9002	Model for Quality Assurance during production and installation
ISO 9001	Model for Quality Assurance in design/development, production, installation, and servicing.

Level 9003 ensures the product, 9002 processing and the product, and 9001 the product, processing, development, and servicing. There are private and government organizations which accredit companies for these ISO standards.[6]

As Golominski says in his paper on "ISO 9000–The Global Perspective," the choice of ISO standard is not difficult. A company that develops products and

[5]W. Gould, "Making Use of Specifications and Quality Standards," *Snack World,* March 1995: 65–70.
[6]W. A. Golominski, "ISO 9000–The Global Perspective," *Food Technology* 48.4 (December 1994): 57–59. A. J. M. Pallet, "ISO 9000–The Company's Viewpoint," *loc. cit.:* 60—62. J. G. Surak and K. E. Simpson, "Using ISO 9000 Standards as a Quality Framework," *loc. cit.:* 63–65.

manufactures them chooses ISO 9001; a contract manufacturer that does not do research and development chooses ISO 9002; a commodity supplier chooses ISO 9003. Other quality standards may apply—Malcolm Baldrige National Quality Award for Total Quality Management, and Hazard Analysis Critical Control Point (HACCP), as described in Chapter 4. HACCP and ISO standards are often combined in the food industry—total quality management is needed to ensure quality of the product (see Figure 7-4).[7]

Recently developed are the *ISO 1400* standards, which are guides on environmental management. The ISO 1400 covers environmental management systems, environmental auditing, environmental labeling, environmental performance assessment, life-cycle assessment, and environmental terms and definitions. It is interesting to see that life-cycle assessment is now included; the whole life of the product has to be environmentally acceptable, from the growing of the crop or catching of the fish to final consumption on the consumer's plate and disposal of all packaging and wastes.[8]

As well as these voluntary standards and certifications, there are statutory certificates from the country's food authorities, which may include licensing of the premises for food processing, product standards, labeling, food hygiene practices,

[7]Checklists for Handling and Distribution Functions and Customer Relations in Industrial Marketing are in J. P. Russell, "Quality Management Benchmark Assessment," *Quality Progress* (May 1995): 57–61.
[8]"Getting into the 1400 Series," *Food Technology in New Zealand* 30.8 (August 1995): 27.

FIGURE 7-4   Quality control technician. To meet ISO 9000 standards, HACCP systems may be used to ensure food quality and safety. *(Courtesy of Continental Grain Company.)*

food safety, and possibly HACCP. These standards must be complied with, and the buyer may require certificates confirming compliance. In exporting, both the exporting country and the importing country will have requirements which must be followed, or the products cannot leave one country or be admitted to the other. For example, in some countries, export products require Certificates of Origin and Health and Sanitary Certificates indicating that export plants and products are inspected; this inspection may also be overseen by officials of the importing country.

INDUSTRIAL FOOD MARKETS

The marketing activities that are undertaken to acquire and sell ingredients to be used in the further processing of industrial food products or in manufacturing consumer products are included in the term *industrial food marketing*. There are two broad types of industrial food markets:

User Market: companies that buy a product to use in the production of their own products, including food-manufacturing or food service companies, supermarkets—where the supermarket has a "manufacturing" operation such as bread or salad production—and small retailers, such as butchers and delis.

Repacker Market: companies who "sell on" the product to other companies. These ingredient suppliers may mix the ingredients or just repack.

Factors Affecting Industrial Food Marketing

Two important factors affect industrial marketing. Industrial food products have a derived demand (as discussed in Chapter 2)—the amount of an ingredient sold depends on the sales of the final consumer product. This can be hard for the farmer/fisher and the primary processor to realize, as they may be a long way from the final consumer, especially in export marketing. Also, the economic, political and social environment can affect industrial marketing—for both good and bad. For example, the forming of the European Community had a positive effect for countries inside the EC, but had a strong negative effect on countries who exported food raw materials and in many cases resulted in declining sales. Provisions in the GATT agreement may improve this situation (see Chapter 9).

Derived Demand In Industrial Food Marketing Demand for industrial food ingredients is derived from the demand for consumer food products. The sale of whole wheat flour is related to the demand for whole wheat bread. Box 7-2 sketches the uses of various flours, all of which influence wheat's derived demand. Industrial demand reflects the buyer's expectations of consumer demand, based on the buyer's optimism or pessimism about the future. Sales of hogs in August/September are related to the expectations for Thanksgiving and Christmas sales of hams. Industrial marketers can stimulate demand by stimulating the demand for consumer products; NutraSweet® is advertised on television to stimulate demand for low-calorie products containing NutraSweet®.

BOX 7-2

FLOUR IS NOT JUST FLOUR!

Flour is a general term used to describe a wide variety of industrial and consumer products; flours are designed in the wheat field and in the flour mill for these different purposes. An important characteristic is "strength"—strong flours are used in bread making and weak flours for biscuit and cake making—but there are also flours for making pasta, gravies/sauces, and other products. The strength of the flour depends on the quantity of protein in the wheat and the properties of the protein; these can be varied by plant breeding and agricultural practices. The amount of bran and therefore fiber in the flour can be varied during milling, by including various amounts of brans. Also, the coarseness of the flour can be varied.

Bread can be made by a slow fermentation process or by mechanical dough-development processes. Either process consists of mixing, fermentation, cutting, molding, and placing in the baking pans, proofing (holding at controlled temperature and humidity to allow the dough to recover), baking, cooling, cutting, and wrapping. Essentially the aim is to build up the dough structure and then set it, and also to develop the final color and flavor, during the baking. In slow fermentation, the dough structure is developed by expanding it with yeast-produced carbon dioxide; in mechanical dough methods, development depends on the mixing process.

Consumers buying standard flour may use it for making bread but will also use it for other baking, for sauces and gravies, and for thickening dishes.

Two demands must always be recognized in industrial marketing—the direct demand of the buying company and the demand for the consumer product made by that company. In selling an industrial product, it is necessary to know not only the characteristics desired by the buying company but also the qualities expected by the consumer in the final product. The size of the consumer market should also be determined, so that the supplying company has some indication of the overall size of the ingredient market and how it may grow in the future.

Think Break

Do you use a powdered coffee creamer (whitener) instead of milk in your coffee? What do you want the creamer to do in your coffee? In communicating with the dairy company that supplies the dairy powder (caseinate) for the creamer, what properties would you tell them you want their powder to have, to keep you buying the coffee creamer?

The Environment of Industrial Food Marketing   The quality and quantity of agricultural and marine raw materials available have a major effect on industrial food marketing. These can vary widely according to weather, the soil and water conditions, the technology available, and the agricultural organization of the country. No food processor can rely on the quantity, quality, and timing of raw material, and the whole industry has to be organized to deal with this: the factory must be able to run with low and high quantities, quality variations, and the daily, weekly, and monthly timing of raw material availability. These and several other factors affecting industrial food marketing are shown in Table 7-2.

TABLE 7-2   EXTERNAL FACTORS AFFECTING INDUSTRIAL FOOD MARKETING

Production of materials	Producers—farmers and fishers Climate Soils/waters
Movement and trading of raw materials	Brokers Auctions Futures markets Losses of raw materials Deterioration of raw materials
General environmental forces	Economic Ecological Technological Social
Political	Trade barriers Currency variations, controls Subsidies Internal laws and regulations International laws and regulations
Structure	Company Industry International structures

For an agricultural raw material that can be stored, the quantity supplied at any time is the amount traders release from storage. During transport and storage the product may deteriorate, so that it loses quantity and quality. Technological problems often arise in processing—availability of equipment and up-to-date technology, quality assurance accreditation, and food safety laws and regulations. Barriers to trade—tariffs and duties, food regulations, quota restrictions, internal subsidies on food raw materials, and "dumping" of subsidized raw materials in overseas markets—also strongly affect the marketing of industrial foods.

International Marketing of Food Ingredients

Ingredient supply is a global activity—the food processor may use ingredients from eight to ten countries in one product, more if the spices and flavors are included, and these ingredients may have gone through two or three processes in different countries. The basic raw materials can be harvested in one country, transported to another for refining and purification, and then to another country for treatment to give specific properties. Alternatively, ingredients for the final process can be grown, refined, and treated in one country and then exported.

Ingredients marketed globally vary widely: bulk carbohydrate materials—starches and sugars; bulk oils and fats—vegetable and animal; bulk proteins—skim milk powder, soy flour; specific fractions of oils, carbohydrates, and proteins; treated oils; fruit-juice concentrates, natural flavors and colors; and also other ingredients, such as synthetic emulsifiers, stabilizers, colors, and flavors. The estimated world markets in 1995 for some specialized food ingredients were, in $U.S. billions: food flavors—3.0, texturizing agents—1.0, gelatin—0.5, starch—1.0, cultures and enzymes—0.5, emulsifiers—2.5. Even for ingredients used in small amounts, the global markets are significant; texturizing agents sales were, in $U.S. millions: carrageenan—250, pectin—200, alginate—75, guar gum—30, locust bean gum—80, carboxymethyl cellulose—40, xanthan gum—165, and others—155.[9]

The United States and Europe are the main markets, but new markets are growing rapidly as consumer products become more varied in other areas, such as Asia and South America. Almost all food-related companies aiming to establish international business have targeted the Asian food markets, but as these are heterogeneous markets, it is usually preferable to export the ingredients rather than the consumer product. In order to understand consumer requirements, many ingredient companies have consumer and technical research centers to determine what the consumer needs in the products, relate this to the ingredients imported, and help the processing companies with processing and equipment problems. Thus they are building strong relationships with the buyers and indeed may form joint ventures with the local processing companies.[10]

If a company is to grow in the global ingredient market, it needs to develop global business acumen by taking the following steps:[11]

• Segment the different geographical markets and choose the market it wishes to enter.
• Improve products and services so that they are differentiated from other suppliers.
• Provide ingredients which meet consumer demands in a particular market.
• Organize reliable and timely transport and storage.
• Work closely with government to overcome political trade barriers, such as quotas, subsidies in competing countries, and nontariff barriers, such as food quality.
• Obtain Quality Assurance accreditation.
• Develop strategic alliances and insider presence in key markets.
• Continuously develop new technologies in production, processing, transport, and storage.
• Maintain environmental integrity in growing, processing, and packaging.

These marketing management principles are discussed further in Chapters 12 through 15.

INDUSTRIAL FOOD MARKETING

The Industrial Buying Process

The *industrial buying process* varies according to different buying situations, including a *straight rebuy, modified rebuy,* or *new buy.* Moving from straight rebuy

---

[9]S. Marshall, "Food Ingredients: The Role of Dairy Products," *Food Australia* 47.3 (March 1995): 105–7.
[10]"Meeting the Demands of Asian Tastes," *Asia Food Industry* (August 1995): 40–57.
[11]J. E. Lee, "Trends in World Agriculture and Trade in High Value Products," *Food Technology* 42.9 (September 1989): 119–27.

to new buy, the process becomes more complex. The straight rebuy may occur in response to a routine computer prompt when stocks reach a certain level, or may require a discussion among buyer, quality assurance, and production regarding past performance. Modified rebuy ranges from an examination of the alternative ingredients from a cost point of view to detailed testing by quality assurance. A new buy could entail detailed research by research and development (R&D), product development, production trials, and discussions by all involved.

The steps in the buying process are outlined in Figure 7-5.

Problems recognized by the buying company may have different causes. A major problem-solving operation may be triggered by cost of the product, variability in the product, processing breakdown, or new-product formulation. Company personnel may look to ingredients to solve these problems. For example, the buyer may persuade the production manager to use a cheaper ingredient to reduce costs, the quality assurance manager may suggest buying another ingredient so as to reduce the incidence of "out-of-spec" product, or the marketing manager may persuade the product developer to use another flavor to improve market acceptance.

Problem solving can develop into bargaining or even politicking. The buyer may bargain with the production manager to change the supplier if the production manager wishes to buy a new ingredient. The product developer may bargain with the quality assurance manager on the type of ingredient in a new product, and so on. At this point, the problem for the salesperson is to recognize when knowledge is needed and to know where to acquire the knowledge, how to transfer the knowledge, and when and how to involve other people from the supply company in the

FIGURE 7-5   The industrial buying process.

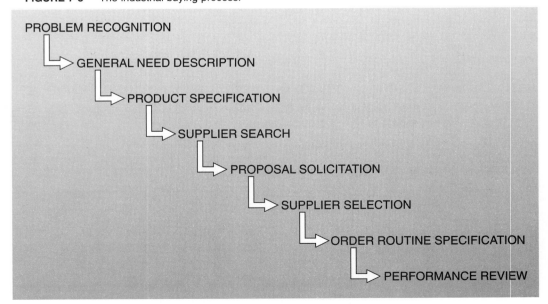

buying process. Besides the salesperson, the people in the supply company involved in the various stages are detailed in Table 7-3.

The small customer's buying process will not be as complex as this. The buyer, who may be the owner or manager, studies the needs of the company—its processing and storage capabilities, product specifications, and final consumer product needs, as well as the costs. Then a range of different competing products are identified and compared, and a product selected. A choice is often made on personal preference—a reassuring feeling about the brand, personal knowledge of the selling company, friendship with sales personnel. If the product is not satisfactory, the buyer looks for a new product, tests it, and buys or rejects.

The supply company needs a good information system to identify the changes that are occurring, so that the company and the salesperson can react quickly to these changes. Changes in the buyer organization will affect not only the buyer/supplier relationship and the buying process, but, more important, can affect the quantities and qualities of the products bought and services needed. Companies neglect this at their peril.

Think Break

The sales office has just received a new fat for breadmaking. Recently, there has been a large increase in the number of small bakeries, and the salespeople think they could find a good market for this product. A salesperson knows a small baker and takes a sample of the fat to him. The baker is busy that day but promises to try

TABLE 7-3 SUPPLY COMPANY ROLES IN THE INDUSTRIAL BUYING PROCESS

Steps in buying process	Supplier departments involved	Departments' role in buying process
PROBLEM RECOGNITION	R&D	Salesperson identifies problem, not just reacting to the buyer's recognition of it, and warns R&D early, as R&D takes time.
GENERAL NEED DESCRIPTION	R&D	R&D and salesperson help the buyer develop a general need description. Two-way information flow is needed.
PRODUCT SPECIFICATION	Production Quality Assurance R&D	General company effort to determine how product can be produced, and the predicted cost.
SUPPLIER SEARCH	Company	Company supplies information, and possibly also personnel, to give a good impression of itself.
PROPOSAL SOLICITATION	Marketing Finance	Marketing and/or Sales prepares the final proposed contract. If for a major buyer or order, senior company personnel presents and negotiates.
SUPPLIER SELECTION	Company	Everyone prays that the contract will be signed.
ORDER ROUTINE SPECIFICATION	Sales	An efficient, fast process with a good system of communication must be designed.
PERFORMANCE REVIEW	Quality Assurance R&D	Quality Assurance determines how the product is performing and alerts R&D to difficulties.

it the next morning. The next morning at 9 a.m. there is a telephone call, "Please remove this fat—I've had a disastrous morning. It's useless." What did the salesperson do wrong? How can the salesperson retrieve the situation?

Buyers and Suppliers in the Industrial Food Market

An industrial food buyer is any organization that buys food ingredients to be used finally in the preparation or manufacture of a consumer food product. *Buyers* range from the one-person bakery shop to the multinational food-processing company. Marketing methods do change for different buyers—from the product specifications and contracts offered to the large processor to the branded doughnut mix sold by the small bakery wholesaler—but all buyers are interested first in the ease of use of the ingredient in the process and second in the cost and quality of the final products. Much of the buying action is logically based on these needs, but there are still some psychological reasons for buying.

Suppliers must recognize that buyers operate at different stages of purchasing skills. In some companies, price and cost are the main bases for purchasing, but gradually technical properties are identified and related to cost; finally purchasing becomes part of the strategic management group. At the earlier stages, a group or person within the company (this may be the quality assurance manager, production manager, or product development manager) controls the product to be bought. Gradually, as the purchasing department becomes more skilled, other departments set the product specifications, but the purchasing department chooses the vendor and the product, and may even control the inventory-management, transport, and raw-material information systems. Even at this high level of competence in the purchasing department, industrial buying is often still a group decision within the company.

The buying department may be responsible for the final buying agreement, but they have been guided by other people in the company—R&D, production, quality assurance, finance, and general management. Very often, during development of a product, R&D personnel will determine the ingredients and usually the suppliers of the ingredients; production will identify the ingredients that most suit the process; quality assurance will set the specifications for the ingredients, and finance will set the costs and financing for the ingredients.

It is important in industrial marketing to understand the buying process in the company: who or what instigates the process, who influences it, who makes the final decision, and who does the actual buying. Box 7-3 lists contacts available to the marketer of one ingredient for one particular use. The buying could be done all by one person or by a committee of ten people, depending on the financial importance of the decision. The decision-making unit, the *buying center,* consist of those people within an organization who are significantly involved in the buying process. Individuals involved in the buying center have been found to assume certain social roles that have been identified. Industrial marketers will be more successful if they can identify these roles, understand their individual influences on the buying decision, and work to satisfy each one. The six roles that have been identified are:

• *Initiators* identify a problem or need that could be resolved by buying a product. Initiators work in various areas of the organization, from the purchasing department to quality assurance.

• *Influencers* have input into whether a purchase is made. Although usually found in supervisory or executive positions, influencers can come from any department or level within the firm or could be outside consultants.

• *Decision makers* make the actual yes-or-no decision about the purchase and choose or approve the product and supplier. It is important to understand that the initiators and decision makers are often not the same people.

• *Gatekeepers* control the flow of information in the buying center. A receptionist who screens salespeople acts as a gatekeeper, as does a purchasing agent who invites bids from suppliers.

• *Purchasers* order the good or service. Purchasers have little say in the actual choice but are expected to negotiate the best deal possible with chosen suppliers.

• *Users,* the ultimate customers of the product, are the production workers and other employees involved with it. Although users are often the initiators of a purchase, they may have little say in the purchase decision.[12]

Buyers' Needs, Motivations, and Actions   The basic needs of the industrial buyer are satisfactory sales and profits and a competitive advantage. Because the buyer needs some of the industrial-product characteristics described earlier but also

---

[12]Courtland L. Bovée, Michael J. Houston, and John. V. Thill, *Marketing* (New York: McGraw-Hill, 1992): 162.

BOX 7-3

WHICH DOOR TO KNOCK ON?

Casein is a dairy protein which can be used in processed-meat products, such as sausages or meatballs. A dairy company has decided to market casein products to meat processors. The industrial meat markets for casein products are large companies producing sausages, small specialized companies producing salamis, and retail butchers making their own sausages. Whom should the salesperson approach in the different companies?

   In large companies producing sausages:

• first, the product development, quality assurance, or senior technologist, with samples to test

• second, the buyer or buying department.

In small specialized companies producing salamis and other sausages:

• first, the sausage maker who has the specialized knowledge

• second, the owner or the person responsible for buying.

In retail butcher companies making their own sausages:

• a butcher supply company, who has a selling network to the butchers

• the ingredient buyer of the supply company.

wants the opportunity to make a choice between suppliers, the supplier must have some unique product characteristics or services to ensure the sale.

Different types of individuals in the company have specific needs:

Production	Reliability in delivery time and supply
	Constant required quality
Product Development	Ease of development
	Shortened time for development
	Final product quality
Quality Assurance	Raw-material specifications
	ISO standards
	Narrow range of quality variation
Purchasing	Reliability of supply
	Price
	Size of delivery
	Regular deliveries

The behavior of individuals in the company also needs to be recognized. These individuals may have technical knowledge but could also have a background in marketing or general management which they apply in the buying situation. Obviously, a highly educated production manager will view the selection of ingredients in a more technical way than a production manager who has little technical education. The production manager will have the goals to maximize yields and reduce costs, but the quality assurance assistant will have the goal to control quality. Therefore, their attitudes to ingredient selection and use can be quite different.

Supplier Characteristics   *Suppliers* have characteristics which are identified by the buyers: efficient/inefficient in fulfilling orders, good/poor technical knowledge, conservative/innovative, poor/excellent sales training for their staff, solid/shaky financial backing, excellent/poor physical distribution system, quality assurance accredited or not. Supplier features often identified by buyers as important are:

- Technical support services
- Supplier reliability and prompt delivery
- Service—quick response to customer needs
- Product quality ISO 9000
- Reputation
- Price
- Sales representatives' personality and technical knowledge
- Extension of credit
- Personal relationships with buyer
- Technical printed material.

In a recent survey of dairy processors, they ranked flavor suppliers' characteristics in the following order of importance: product quality, competitive prices, supplier reliability, technical sales personnel, dependable service.[13]

What are some of the suppliers' needs, motives, and attitudes? Ideally, the supplier would like a large buyer who stayed with a supplier for long time, bought regularly and in increasing amounts, and discussed future needs with the supplier so that new products could be developed together—in other words, a happy, rewarding present and a rosy future!

The supplier wants from the buyer:

- Clear product specifications which are not too tight
- Delivery schedule which is easy to achieve and maintain
- Forward contract with definite quantities and times
- Good communication
- Cooperative development
- Reliable and satisfactory price.

Today, to achieve these aims, buyers and suppliers are attempting to set up long-term relationships. This is particularly true of large companies procuring large-scale, important ingredients. Buyers and suppliers once considered themselves to be competitive, each trying to get the maximum share of the profit to be made at this point in the food system. Then, particularly with the introduction of Just-in-Time (JIT) distribution, they had to become partners. Now the relationship is considered to lie between these extremes.[14]

The Buyer/Supplier Relationship

The relationship is considered at two levels: company-to-company, and individual salesperson-to-buyer. The entire supply company, not just the product or the salesperson, has to take a principle role in the buyer-seller relationship. They have to decide if they are an innovative, reliable company, a stable, conservative company with good technical knowledge, or a reactive company supplying buyer-designed products quickly. It is crucial that salespeople act with the company behind them and not as sole agents. Everyone needs to build up the relationships with the buyers.

The conditions salespeople find when marketing to large food processors are:

- Relatively few customers
- Products and processes often complex
- Large-dollar-volume sales
- Service and technical assistance important.

---

[13]"Value Reigns," *Dairy Field* (November 1993): 40–44.

[14]For a detailed description of these relationships, see B. Leavy, "Two Strategic Perspectives of the Buyer-Supplier Relationship," *Production and Inventory Management Journal* (Second Quarter 1994): 47–51.

Therefore, personal selling is the major part of the promotional mix, and personal selling means different people in the supply company interacting with the buying company. The salesperson is often the go-between or the joining person between the two groups.

Selling Organization ⟷ **SALESPERSON** ⟷ Customer Organization

The central person in this relationship is the salesperson; salespeople must have a sense of identity both with customers and with their own company and be able to deal with the conflicts this can cause.

Salespeople need the knowledge of people in the following areas of their own company and must either transfer their knowledge to the buyers or bring the customer into direct contact with these people:

$$\left.\begin{array}{r} \text{R\&D} \\ \text{Production} \\ \text{Quality Assurance} \\ \text{Marketing} \end{array}\right\} \longleftrightarrow \textbf{SALESPERSON} \longleftrightarrow \text{Buyer}$$

The industrial salesperson is not just selling but doing market research, promoting the company and the product, and passing technical information between buyer and supplier.

At the individual level, salespeople deal with the personal reactions of the buyer or other company personnel. The salesperson meets many different types of buyers and has to adapt to each buyer's expectations of the salesperson and the company. This immediate relationship is affected by the individual's expectations and general reactions to the sales presentation, the reputation of the selling company, and the personalities of the people involved. This is the short-term, "meeting" interaction, but the company and the salesperson also have to build up the long-term interaction over months and years. Regular visits, joint seminars, and social activities at trade fairs and conferences are all methods of building up long-term relationships.

SUMMARY

A large proportion of food marketing occurs between raw-material producers and processors, and between processors and manufacturers. Products produced under a grading system and not specifically designed for a type of processing are marketed as commodities. Industrial products are designed either for a specific process in a company or for a process common to one or several industries.

Food processing can be divided into food preservation and food structuring. Preservation includes all the processes used to extend the life of foods: chilling, freezing, drying, pasteurization and sterilization, controlled atmosphere, and chemical methods with acids, salt, and other preservatives. Structuring is the building of food structures from basic raw materials—for example, breadmaking, sausage manufacture, or extruded-snack production.

Food ingredients for the final consumer product include agricultural and marine raw materials, some undergoing only primary processing; others receive secondary processing which purifies, separates, and treats the primary raw materials before final manufacture. Final manufacturing is becoming simpler, being very often a mixing and packing operation. This makes it easier for the consumer marketing company to design and manufacture the wide variety of products supermarkets and consumers demand.

Industrial marketing, although having the same basic marketing philosophies and functions as consumer marketing (discussed in Part Five), has differences in structure which dictate changes in the ways product, promotion, distribution, and pricing functions are used. In marketing to large food companies, there are very few customers and the relationship between the buyer and the supplier of food ingredients is crucial. This relationship, together with adherence to the technical specifications for the product and the services provided, forms the basis of industrial marketing.

Industrial buying is often a group activity involving different sections of the company, such as R&D, production, quality assurance, and finance, as well as the buying group. The supplier must involve all departments in the buyer/supplier relationship, not leave it only to the salesperson. Recently, buyers and suppliers are tending to develop partnerships, but the situation is still competitive, because both are trying to maximize their share of the added value at this point in the food system.

Global marketing of food ingredients is very old, dating from the early trading of spices among China, India, and Europe, but it has grown quickly in the last twenty years and is still growing. Final consumer food manufacturers in many countries are using imported ingredients in their products. The exporting company needs to be aware not only of what the food processor specifies for an ingredient, but also what the consumer wants in the final product. Therefore they need a presence in the overseas country if they are to be successful ingredient suppliers.

IMPORTANT TERMS AND CONCEPTS

buyers   180
buying center   180
food preservation   163
food structures   165
industrial buying process   174
ISO 1400   173
ISO 9000   172
manufacturing   168
modified rebuy   177
new buy   177
perishable product   166

primary processing   166
repacker market   174
secondary processing   167
services   171
specialized commodity products   167
straight rebuy   177
suppliers   182
tangible product   171
total product   171
user market   174

CASE STUDY: Comparing Dairy Proteins with Soya Proteins[15]

In the food industry, both dairy and soy proteins are used in a vast number of applications. As well as satisfying nutritional needs, both soy and dairy proteins can perform important food-processing functions, including water binding, emulsification, stabilization, gel firming, mouth feel enhancement, and viscosity improvement. The variety of protein products is increasing rapidly, and they are now being targeted at highly specific applications. One important application is in the manufacture of processed meats.

Dairy proteins include milk protein isolates, whey protein concentrates, sweet whey powders, whey protein isolates, lactalbumin, acid casein, rennet casein, sodium, calcium, potassium caseinates, modified whey proteins, protein hydrolysates. Those used in processed meat products are:

Dairy Proteins	Properties
Milk protein isolates	Excellent nutritional value, emulsifying capacity, whipability and foam stability, good dispersability, low viscosity, excellent water binding
Whey protein concentrates	Good nutritional value, emulsifying capacity, adhesives with excellent heat sealing ability, heat stable, highly soluble
Caseinates	Emulsifiers, fat binding, water holding, soluble, bland flavor, form gels

Soy proteins also come in many forms, including full fat and defatted soy flours, textured soy flour, soy protein concentrates, textured soy protein, soy isolates, soy protein hydrolysates. Four primary functions of soy proteins in food applications are emulsification, fat absorption, hydration, and texture enhancement. Soy proteins themselves have a limited emulsion ability, while soy isolates have good emulsification properties. The ability of soy proteins to hold and retain fat in a meat system is critical to retaining flavor and appearance, and achieving good cook yields. Although soy flours can absorb fat, they have limited ability to retain this property during cooking. Isolates are very effective fat absorbers, but their ability to absorb diminishes in the presence of salt. In meat processing, concentrates are used, as they absorb fat like a sponge and can hold it through multiple cooks, being unaffected by salt.

Major functionalities which cause competition between dairy and soy proteins include: solubility, emulsifying capacity, water and fat binding, protein content, salt tolerance, and allergy tolerances. Soy concentrates were the major proteins used in processed meats, because of their acceptable functionality and lower price, but they tended to have a slight flavor. The blander dairy protein products were more acceptable in chicken products, but in recent years the soy concentrates have become blander. Whey proteins are more acceptable in the manufacture of fish surimi, because they form gels similar to fish protein. The combination of emulsifying and gelling properties has advantages in patés and hams.

[15]This summary, from "Pinpointing Protein Performance," in *Food Ingredients and Analysis International* (January 1995): 28 to 32, also includes information from commercial promotional material.

Consider these questions:

1 Identify some industrial markets for dairy proteins and for soy proteins in the meat and fish industries.

2 Contrast the characteristics of dairy proteins and the soy proteins.

3 How would you suggest the dairy proteins be positioned against soy proteins in the market segments of the meat industry—poultry, pork, and beef?

4 Do you think that there might be more uses for dairy products now that consumers prefer lower fat in meat products? Explain why or why not.

QUESTIONS

1 Compare and contrast commodity marketing and industrial marketing of food ingredients.

2 Discuss these different types of industrial marketing:

  a) a farmer growing peas to specifications of quality and pesticide levels for a frozen vegetable processor

  b) a processor who manufactures a range of corn starches, selling to a dessert manufacturer

  c) a distributor who markets a wide range of ingredients to bakeries.

3 Discuss why derived demand is important in industrial marketing, giving two food-industry examples to illustrate your answer.

4 Describe how, in the buying of food ingredients, group buying is important. List the people in the company who may be involved in the buying and what they want from the product and the service.

5 Contrast the industrial marketing of food ingredients to large bakeries and to small bakers, discussing the needs of the different customers, their possible buying methods, the types of products, the services needed, and the selling methods the company uses.

6 Show how the buyers and suppliers in industrial food marketing are interdependent and what effects this has on the marketing methods used and the relationships between the companies.

REFERENCES AND RESOURCES

Deveny, K. "Man Walked on the Moon, But Man Can't Make Enough Devil's Food Cookie Cakes," *Wall Street Journal* (September 28, 1993): B1, B3.

Giese, J. "Proteins as Ingredients: Types, Functions, Applications." *Food Technology* 48.10 (1994): 50–60.

Haas, R. W. *Business Marketing: A Managerial Approach.* 6th ed. Cincinnati, OH: South-Western Publishing Co., 1995. Chapters, 2, 5, 6, and 7.

The International Food Industry. Nederland: Rabobank, Department of Food and Agribusiness Research, 1995.

Jelen, P. *Introduction to Food Processing.* Reston, VA: Reston Publishing Co., 1985.

Kawazoe, K. "Market Trends of Functional Foods and Food Ingredients in Japan." *International Food Ingredients* 5 (1994): 43–45.

Leavy, B. "Two Strategic Perspectives of the Buyer-Supplier Relationship." *Production and Inventory Management Journal* (Second Quarter 1994): 47–51.

Manchester, A. C. "Food Manufacturing and Product Changes." *Rearranging the Economic Landscape: The Food Marketing Revolution, 1950–91.* Ag. Econ. Report No. 660. Washington, DC: USDA, Economic Research Service, 1992. 42–87.

Paine, F. A. *Modern Processing, Packaging, and Distribution Systems for Food.* Glasgow: Blackie, 1987.

The Retail Food Market. Nederland: Rabobank, Agribusiness Research, 1994.

Russell, J. P. "Quality Management Benchmark Assessment." *Quality Progress* (May 1995): 57–61.

Unger, L. "Food and Beverage Additives, Part I." *The World of Ingredients* (September/October 1995): 28–33.

8

FOOD RETAILING AND
FOOD SERVICE

CHAPTER OUTLINE

LEARNING OBJECTIVES

After reading this chapter and answering the questions in the Think Breaks, you should be able to:

- Understand supermarkets and chain stores and how the food retailing industry classifies the various food-system retail participants.
- Describe the various sectors of the food service industry.
- Compare and contrast the food service distribution/wholesaling industry with the food retailing distribution/wholesaling industry.
- Appreciate the global expansion of the food service industry, particularly the fast-food sector, and realize how important understanding the culture and economics of foreign countries is, if global expansion is to be successful.
- Recognize consumer motivations for eating out and their implication for the food service industry of the future.
- Understand how the Universal Product Code (UPC) and related information technology are transforming marketing and logistics by providing store-generated data.
- Relate the Wheel of Retailing concept to the retail food industry today and to its continuing evolution.

INTRODUCTION

The last stages of the food system, the parts the consumer usually deals with, are the food retailing and food service industries. The root of the word, retailing, is *tailor*—that is, to cut. In the days before self-service supermarkets, this important function of retailing was more obvious than it is today, when most of the cutting and snipping is done behind the scenes or even back at the food manufacturer's operation. Today, food retailers bring together a wide assortment of products at locations that are convenient to the consumer. Food service has become a key player at this stage in the food system, as consumer lifestyles have increased the need for value-added food products that are characterized by ease of preparation and are often served outside the home.

Although wholesale club stores have grown in popularity the past decade, they represent a relatively small market share in the retail market. Stores that are categorized as supermarkets still account for over 75 percent of all U.S. grocery sales, and over two-thirds of these stores are chain operations. Today the major force shaping the retail industry is information technology. The Universal Product Code (UPC) provides customer information that the retailer can use to focus in on particular segments of the customer population, often as many as 200 different segments. *Point-of-sale (POS)* information that is generated at the retail level and other information technologies are used by retailers in inventory management and in micromarketing.

The food service industry includes all the businesses and institutions that sell or provide meals. Insofar as food service companies transform raw materials into meals, they are a type of food manufacturer, and the principles of industrial marketing discussed in Chapter 7 apply in supplying food service buyers. The food service industry is expanding in the United States, as well as around the world. Much of the U.S. growth in the next decade will come from changing demographics, particularly from the increasing ethnic diversity and the graying of America explored in Chapter 3. The fast-food industry has been vigorously pursuing international markets because growth in domestic fast-food sales has slowed and has fallen behind growth in international sales. Fueling this international growth is the attraction American fast foods hold for most consumers around the world. It seems that along with Levi's, the golden arches of McDonald's are synonymous with American culture and the "good life" associated with it.

FOOD RETAILING AND FOOD SERVICE

An Overview of the Food Retailing Industry

In the United States, modern food retailing traces its roots back to 1859, when Charles Gilman and Huntington Hartford started the Great Atlantic and Pacific Tea Company (A&P). A few years later a line of groceries was added to the tea. From this single store, A&P expanded to 200 stores by 1900; however, A&P grew most rapidly in the 1915 to 1930 period, with over 16,000 stores and over $1 billion in annual sales by 1930. Other chain organizations developed during this time: Grand Union was organized in 1872, Kroger in 1882, and Safeway in 1915.

By 1928 there were 315 chains (then defined by the industry as a company operating four or more stores; today, a *chain store* is defined as a company that operates 11 or more stores), and their share of retail grocery sales rose from 8 percent in 1900 to 32 percent in 1929. In 1994, chains accounted for about 55 percent of all grocery sales, a figure that has been relatively stable over the past two decades. A similar expansion of chain stores has occurred in the United Kingdom, where today chains claim over 60 percent of grocery sales. Since the 1950s, supermarkets have expanded in Northern Europe and more slowly in Southern Europe and are now growing in the urban areas of Southeast Asia and South America.

Why did chain stores explode in numbers during the early part of this century? There is no single reason; a number of advantages over independents came together during this time. One advantage that has been well documented is the bargaining power that chains had over suppliers. Another factor is that large chains integrated back into wholesaling and set up their own distribution systems, as opposed to using several smaller distributors, thus reducing the cost of purchasing. Chains also experienced certain economies of scale by being able to spread advertising costs over several stores, and they were aggressive in their real estate operations, making sure they had prime locations that would support stores.

Supermarkets had their beginning with Clarence Saunders, who introduced food retailing self-service in 1912 in his Piggly-Wiggly grocery stores. In a radical departure from conventional grocery retailing practices of the time, customers in Saunders' stores selected their merchandise and carried it to a check-out counter, where they paid cash. In its early days, the self-service idea was not immediately successful, and many of the national chains ignored it and instead concentrated on acquiring and building small, clerk-operated stores.

Michael Cullen, a Kroger branch manager, is credited with bringing the self-service innovation to fruition. In 1930, he proposed building a 6,400-square foot store with ample parking space and set a goal of weekly volume of $12,500. Compared with today's supermarket of 35 to 50 thousand square feet, Cullen's proposal seems rather modest, but the average chain store at the time had weekly sales of $500 to $600 and an area of 500 to 600 square feet. After Kroger turned down the idea, Cullen opened his own store on Long Island, New York. Advertising as "King Kullen the Price Wrecker," he lowered gross margins to 12 to 13 percent, compared with the chain's 18 to 19 percent, and in the process was able to earn higher net profits.[1]

Others imitated Cullen, and eventually the national food chains were forced to move to the supermarket format. Today, the retail food industry defines a supermarket as a store with annual sales of at least $2 million and offering the full assortment of food (and, in most cases, many nonfood items); now, 75 percent of all groceries are sold through supermarkets. As grocery retailing evolved, various types of store formats were developed.

In 1995, the average supermarket had grown from a 1930s King Kullen of 6,500 square feet to 28,000 square feet, and the number of identifiable items *(SKUs— stock keeping units)* in a supermarket topped 20,000. As a point of contrast, Japanese supermarkets are only one-third the size of those in the United States, but they carry an assortment of 30,000 SKUs. While a supermarket is defined as a retail store with sales of at least $2 million a year, the average chain supermarket has sales around $12 million annually. Table 8-1 shows that while supermarket numbers declined over a ten-year period, their share of the total retail food market remained around 75 percent.

Table 8-1 also reveals that *wholesale club stores* such as Costco, Sam's, and Pace, which have limited assortments of 3,500 to 4,000 items but up to five times

---

[1]Joel B. Dirlam, "The Food Distribution Industry," in *The Structure of American Industry,* ed. Walter Adams, 5th ed. (New York: Macmillan, 1977): 41–42.

TABLE 8-1   U.S. GROCERY STORE SALES, BY NUMBERS, VOLUME, OWNERSHIP, AND FORMAT, 1985 AND 1995

	NUMBER OF STORES				ANNUAL SALES			
	1985		1995		1985		1995	
	No. of stores	% of total	No. of stores	% of total	$ Sales (billions)	% of total	$ Sales (billions)	% of total
Supermarkets:								
Chains	17,220	11%	18,500	14%	143.7	49%	240.3	58%
Independents	13,285	9%	11,300	9%	66.1	23%	71.4	17%
Total supermarkets	30,505	20%	29,800	23%	209.8	72%	311.7	76%
Convenience stores	45,400	29%	56,000	44%	20.4	7%	27.3	7%
Wholesale club stores		0%	710	1%		0%	19.6	5%
Other stores	78,095	51%	41,490	32%	61.9	21%	53.9	13%
All grocery stores	154,000	100%	128,000	100%	292.2	100%	412.5	100%

Source: Progressive Grocer: 53rd Annual Report, April 1986, and *63rd Annual Report,* April 1996: 13. Reprinted with permission from *Progressive Grocer.*

the square footage of a conventional supermarket, account for about 5 percent of all grocery sales. While they experienced tremendous growth in the late 1980s and early 1990s, it appears that their growth has slowed. *Convenience stores,* such as 7-11, combined with Other stores, the category on Table 8-1 including everything from small, family groceries (mainly in cities) to specialty stores, whether selling ethnic foods, confections, or health and organic foods, make up over 77 percent of all food stores in the United States but account for only about 20 percent of all food sales. Gasoline service stations are increasingly becoming combination convenience stores/fast-food outlets.

The implication of Table 8-1 for most food manufacturers is that if they focus on the nearly 30,000 supermarkets in America, they have tapped into 75 percent of the retail food market. Of course this can differ by manufacturer—Frito-Lay, as a snack-food manufacturer, will need to have their product in all 128,000 grocery stores, as well as in other outlets, including vending machines.

Internationally, distribution structures differ by region and country. In Northern Europe, most food is sold through supermarkets and hypermarkets operated by large-scale retail chains. The two largest food retailers in the world are Metro/Asko and Rewe AG, two German companies; in France, with over 120,000 food outlets, 7,000 supermarkets and hypermarkets account for a combined market share of over 40 percent of all food sales. However, in Southern Europe, the role of small grocery stores is still significant. In Greece, Italy, Spain, and Portugal the number of food outlets per 1,000 inhabitants is four to five times higher than in the United Kingdom and France. Even in these countries, the trend is toward declining numbers of food outlets and growth in large-scale retailing, often being brought in by foreign companies.

In Asia the food retailing sector is, as one might expect, even more fragmented. The Japanese food retail market is characterized by its large number of small outlets. Only 12 percent of outlets are supermarkets and 7 percent are convenience stores, with the bulk of Japanese food stores being small grocery stores, specialty stores, and produce shops. In Indonesia, food retailing is by far the largest sector of the national economy, with 850,000 food and nonfood retail outlets, of which 500,000 are open market stalls. The market stalls, or wet markets, as they are called in Hong Kong, account for 90 percent or more of fresh food sales in most Asian countries. The situation is similar in the Philippines (see Figure 8-1). A manufacturer or retailer developing a marketing strategy and plan for exporting to or operating in a new area must recognize country differences in food distribution structures.[2]

An Overview of the Food Service Industry

The food service industry as we know it today has developed in just the past three decades. In that time, food service has moved to center stage as a major player in

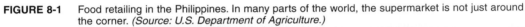

[2]*The Retail Food Market* (Nederland: Rabobank, Agribusiness Research, 1994): 27–40.

FIGURE 8-1   Food retailing in the Philippines. In many parts of the world, the supermarket is not just around the corner. *(Source: U.S. Department of Agriculture.)*

delivering a final product to consumers. Today nearly 50 percent of all food dollars spent in the United States go for *food service,* with total 1995 sales of over $285 billion dollars. Around-the-world market growth has kept up with and, in many instances, surpassed that of the United States. Currently, Japan has one restaurant for every 117 persons, while in the United States the ratio is one for every 400 persons. In the past fifteen years, the Japanese food service industry has grown nearly 50 percent, and its annual growth rate of 5.7 percent is about 1 percent ahead of Japan's gross national product. Thoughts of French fine food and exquisite cuisine bring to mind such delicacies as *escargots* and *pate de foie gras.* However, over the past 20 years, more than 290 McDonald's have opened in France. Today, the Big Mac can be purchased in over 70 countries around the world.

Growth in the food service market is attributed mainly to rising consumer income and changing lifestyles/demographics: more women working outside the home, smaller households, and an increase in the number of single households. Another contributing factor is the desire by peoples around the world to participate, for better or worse, in the American "good life." The French schoolboy wearing Lee jeans and Nike sneakers wants *Le Big Mac.* In Japan, where guests have long been entertained in restaurants, rather than in the home, and men frequently eat daily meals in restaurants, the change is a strong shift toward Western-style eating.

When one hears the words "food service industry," the ubiquitous fast-food sector most often comes to mind and is sometimes mistakenly thought of as synonymous with food service. While *fast food* accounts for about 30 percent of U.S. food service sales, the industry is made up of a diverse array of participants, ranging from prisons and hospitals to child care/nursing home/elder care facilities. An industry trade magazine, *Restaurants and Institutions,* annually examines the performance and trends of the following sectors:[3]

- *Fast food*—any restaurant that emphasizes quick service and take-out. Chains and franchising dominate this segment. Fast food has led the industry in annual sales growth over the past 20 years.
- *Full service*—sit-down restaurants, which are further segmented into Casual, Medium, and Fine-Dining establishments. While these account for about 30 percent of all food service sales, this annual sales growth lags behind that of the fast-food industry.
- *Schools/colleges*—offering more choice to their constituents, these will be a growth area for fast-food chains. Market share is about 10 percent, with total sales of over $25 billion.
- *Health care*—including hospitals, nursing homes, and elder/life care. With pressures on hospitals to cut costs and shorten the length of patient stays, hospitals will, at best, be a stable market in the near future. Nursing homes, however, are providing more acute-care services, which call for specialized diets and feeding methods.
- *Retail sales*—food service in supermarkets, convenience stores, and other nonfood stores, such as K-Mart, Wal-Mart, and department stores. Supermarkets are improving the quality of prepared foods in their establishments, along with providing

---

[3]"The Big Picture—R&I's 1994 Foodservice Industry Forecast," *Restaurants and Institutions* (January 1, 1994): 50–88.

greater variety in their delicatessen operations. In larger supermarkets, national-brand kiosks and food courts are being added.

• *Other government*—the military market is shrinking in the United States as force size and locations are decreased. At the same time prison numbers are increasing.

• *Lodging*—the market share for hotels/motels is 3.5 percent, with very little growth. Many hotels are moving their food operations to more casual approaches and, in some instances, national-chain restaurants such as Pizza Hut are replacing in-house operations.

• *Recreation/transportation*—a wide assortment of outlets, from cruise ships to baseball parks and race tracks. As with other segments, variety seems to be the major development in this market. Orient Lines has commissioned famed Los Angeles area chef Wolfgang Puck to develop a menu for its 800-passenger flagship, *Marco Polo*.

• *Social caterers*—although they hold a small market share, growth is expected to be over 5 percent, owing largely to the change in tax laws. The reduced deductibility of business meals is causing corporations to do more in-house, catered entertaining.

DISTRIBUTION ALTERNATIVES

Food Service Distribution

Although the food service distribution industry has undergone considerable consolidation in recent years and has some major players, it is still a very fragmented industry. The top five U.S. companies, as large as they are, account for less than 20 percent of total sales. The top company, SYSCO, with sales of $8.9 billion in 1992, has an 8 percent share of the market. The other companies in the top five are Kraft Foodservice, $3.5 billion; Martin-Brower Company, $3.4 billion; PFS, $2.8 billion; and Rykoff-Sexton, $1.6 billion. The total industry has over 5,000 companies, and the 50 largest of these account for 30 percent of sales. *Distributors* are classified among four typical types: broad-line distributor, systems distributor, self-distributor, and specialty distributor.[4]

Broad-line distributors sell a full line of food service products and nonfood items, such as kitchenware, paper products, chemicals, and equipment. While broad-line distributors offer many thousands of items, as many as 185,000 systemwide, the companies' individual distribution centers routinely stock only 5,000 to 10,000 items and average about 8,000 (see Table 8-2). Broad-line distributors have their own manufacturing facilities, and between 20 and 30 percent of their sales are from their own brands. Some broad-line vendors encourage multiunit food service operators to develop primary-vendor relationships, whereby the buyer can achieve savings in price and delivery charges in exchange for agreeing to purchase most of their products from that vendor.

Systems distributors service only large chain accounts and maintain minimal inventory relative to the typical distribution facility. Essentially delivery specialists, they contract to accept deliveries from various vendors and manufacturers with

[4]Gregory X. Norkus and Elliot Merberg, "Food Distribution in the 1990's," *Cornell Hotel and Restaurant Administration Quarterly* (June 1994): 50–62.

TABLE 8-2   COMPARISON OF THREE TYPES OF FOOD SERVICE DISTRIBUTORS, 1992

	SYSCO (broad-line)	Martin-Brower (systems)	PFS (self)
Sales	$8.89 billion	$3.37 billion	$2.75 billion
Distribution facilities	160	28	25[1]
Units serviced	245,000	11,500[2]	14,000[3]
Average sales per unit	$36,297	$293,043	$194,643
Line items per distribution facility	8,000	450–3,600[4]	—

[1]Including one each in Canada and Mexico.
[2]Involving 16 accounts.
[3]Involving 3 accounts.
[4]The centers that service only McDonald's restaurants stock about 450 line items. The other centers service about eight chain accounts each and inventory about 3,600 items.
Source: "Food Distribution in the 1990s," *Cornell Hotel and Restaurant Administration Quarterly* 35.3 (June 1994): 54. Used by permission. All rights reserved. ©Cornell University.

whom chain restaurants have negotiated price agreements. Their main tasks are to maintain the appropriate level of inventory to keep the chain supplied, and to deliver items according to contract requirements. Their clients agree to pay a purchase fee for these services. The largest systems distributor in North America is the Martin-Brower Company, which supplies McDonald's in some geographic areas, as well as other chains.

Self-distributors are restaurant companies who accept deliveries from vendors and manufacturers at their own warehouses. In certain cases, self-distributors act somewhat like broad-line distributors by reselling their products to franchisees. An example of a self-distributor is PFS. PFS sells to franchisees—Pizza Hut, KFC, and Taco Bell—and is also the largest self-distributor. Hardee's is an example of another fast-food chain that has its own captive distribution network.

Specialty distributors include smaller local distributors that either specialize in a product line (examples: produce, beverages, meats) or serve the full range of product needs of a particular type of restaurant. Specialty distributors are particularly strong in serving ethnic restaurants, concession stands, and vending outlets. The fundamental business of food service distribution involves purchase, stocking, sale, and delivery of food and other food service products.

Food Retailing Distribution and Procurement

The wholesaling sector, referred to today as the distribution sector of the food business, is generally unknown and taken for granted not only by consumers but also by students of food marketing. Noisy, busy warehouses, with pallets and trucks backing up to loading docks, are just not as glamorous as the production of a new commercial for Kellogg's. However, making distribution more efficient can save billions of dollars, as is discussed in the section on information technology. General-line distributors all perform pretty much the same functions in the marketing channel—bringing together the assortment of products needed by a retailer and delivering them in a cost-efficient manner. The differences lie more in who owns and controls the distribution function and in the type of alliance (if any) between the retailer and the distributor. Today, there are essentially four types of wholesalers or distribution arrangements that supply the assortment of food products found in a supermarket.

- *Chain-store integrated* or chain-store owned—the large chains, such as Kroger (U.S.), Sainsbury (U.K.), and Woolworth's (Australia), operate their own distribution centers and buy direct from grocery manufacturers.
- *Voluntary*—the distributor has developed alliances with independently owned retail stores. The retail store carries the logo (brand) of the voluntary, such as I.G.A. or Supervalu.
- *Cooperative*—the distributor is owned by its patrons (retailers), and at the end of their financial year any profits (called patronage refunds in a cooperative) are returned to the retailers, based on their patronage in dollars. In Europe, most of the major retailers are members of a buying/wholesaling cooperative of some type, because they provide bargaining power with suppliers and economies of scale in distribution.
- *Independent*—if a distributor is not organized in one of the above manners, it operates as an independent.

Figure 8-2 shows that most chain stores (72 percent) are supplied from their own *distribution centers*. As chains have grown, they have tended to develop their own warehouses, store delivery fleets, and procurement systems. However, as the technologies and the economies of scale required for low-cost distribution-center operations have increased, many medium to fairly large chains have turned to outside wholesalers to supply some of their needs. For example, frequently retail chains

FIGURE 8-2 Suppliers of supermarkets in the United States—1994. *(Source: Progressive Grocer: 61st Annual Report (April 1994): 33. Reprinted with permission from Progressive Grocer.)*

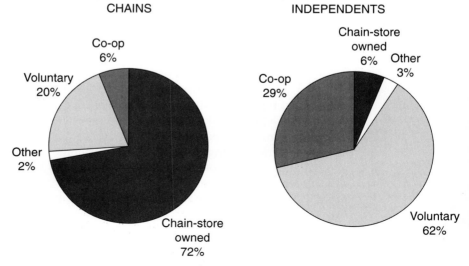

CHAINS

INDEPENDENTS

Co-op 6%

Voluntary 20%

Other 2%

Chain-store owned 72%

Chain-store owned 6%

Other 3%

Co-op 29%

Voluntary 62%

expand into new geographical regions where they do not have the store density and volume to warrant establishing their own distribution center.

In the United States, the wholesale/distribution sector has undergone tremendous change in the past ten years. While there were almost 400 general-line grocery distributors in 1984, by 1994 the number was less than 200. The two leading non-chain-owned distributors are Fleming and Supervalu. Fleming's 50 distribution centers in 45 states serve more than 8,000 stores, about one-third of them chains. In the mid-1990s both companies made several acquisitions, with Supervalu becoming the nation's largest food wholesaler, with sales of over $22 billion. The driving economic forces behind the wholesale mergers and acquisitions are increased use of technology (discussed in the next section) and the cost savings that result when warehousing operations are merged and some smaller, less efficient, facilities are closed.[5]

In Europe, retail buying alliances, where several retailers join together in a co-operative purchasing effort, have become the norm, the exceptions being a few of the largest food retailers, such as Sainsbury and Tesco (U.K.) and Aldi and Tenglemen (Germany), who have remained independent. There are over 18 such groups involving more than 130 companies. Many of these alliances have sales of $60–70 billion and are able to achieve considerable economies of scale and bargaining power. Among the activities of alliances are coordination of distribution activities, monitoring of product quality control, and sourcing of own-label (private-label) suppliers. As in the United States, the aim of these European alliances is to achieve the scale of operations necessary to underwrite investments in distribution infrastructure and information technology.[6]

GLOBAL EXPANSION

Globalization of Food Service

With the U.S. market reaching saturation, expansion overseas has become a key element in the strategic plan of many food service companies, particularly the fast-food industry. Of the top twelve U.S. fast-food chains operating outside the United States, Kentucky Fried Chicken takes the lead with 45 percent of its over 9,400 units abroad (Table 8-3). In 1995, McDonald's had only a 7 percent growth in domestic sales, compared to 27 percent growth internationally. Found in over 90 countries, McDonald's earns 47 percent of its income from outside the United States.[7] Most of the fast-food chains that operate internationally report a higher growth rate in these markets than in their domestic operations.

Since chain-market penetration is low and incomes are relatively high in many foreign countries—European countries, for example—many chains see expansion opportunities in these countries. In 1995, U.S. chains were estimated to command a 20 percent market share of Europe's food service establishments. KFC hopes to triple its number of European units over the next five years, with plans for Spain,

[5]Ryan Mathews, "Street Smart," *Progressive Grocer* (August 1994): 56–57.
[6]*The Retail Food Market* (Nederland: Rabobank, Agribusiness Research, 1994): 56–58.
[7]*McDonald's Corporation Annual Report* 1995: 20.

TABLE 8-3   U.S. FAST-FOOD CHAINS PENETRATE FOREIGN MARKETS, 1994

Restaurant franchises	Total sales (millions $)	Total units	Foreign units	Percent foreign (%)
Kentucky Fried Chicken	7,100	9,407	4,258	45
McDonald's	25,986	13,993	5,461	39
Baskin Robbins	1,008	3,765	1,300	35
Dunkin' Donuts	1,413	3,453	831	24
Churchs	590	1,171	233	20
Burger King	7,500	7,684	1,357	18
Domino's Pizza	2,500	5,079	840	17
Dairy Queen	3,170	5,542	628	11
Arby's Restaurants	1,770	1,548	168	11
Subway Sandwiches	2,500	9,893	944	10
Wendy's	4,277	4,411	413	9
Taco Bell	4,290	5,615	162	3

Source: "Tops in Sales" and "Tops in Size," *Restaurant Business* (1 November 1995): 36–41. Reprinted with permission of *Restaurant Business.*

France, and Germany. Arby's has plans to open 90 units in the United Kingdom and the Netherlands over the next five to seven years.

Think Break

You are on the management team of a large fast-food chain that currently has only domestic operations. What kind of information would you collect, and from what sources, in developing a plan to establish foreign operations?

The rush to globalization is not without its perils. Often chains jump into areas without stable joint-venture partners or solid franchisees. A few years ago, McDonald's had to go through a protracted court battle with its French partner before they could replace him. In all countries a thorough understanding of the local culture, customs, and economy is essential. Domino's home-delivery pizza business in Poland is limited by the lack of telephone service—and to suit local tastes, cabbage is available as a topping, along with salami and spicy pork. Dunkin' Donuts has found that over 80 percent of their international business is eat-in (versus the U.S. scenario where 80 percent is take-out). Upper-income Asian teenagers turn the doughnut shops into dating bars after sunset. And, when ordering a Dunkin' Donut in Jakarta, Indonesia, one may choose a filling of durian fruit, which has been described as tasting somewhat like a well-matured blue cheese.

It is obviously not enough just to bring "America" abroad. Respect for the host culture, no matter how foreign or strange it seems to the introduced culture, is required. In Muslim countries, such as Saudi Arabia, restrictions on the mixing of the sexes mandate special seating arrangements, as Long John Silver's discovered. In their Saudi stores they have a separate dining room, separate order area, and separate entrance for lone men versus families. Any time a woman and children come in, they use the "family" side. A husband who comes in without his family must go to the "men's" side, but if he comes in accompanying his family, he goes to the family side. In the family side, small screens are issued so that women are not seen when they remove their veils to eat.[8]

In South Korea, McDonald's was criticized by the government for introducing a "Happy Meal" special for children, like the one it sells in the United States. Government officials asked McDonald's executives why the chain was trying to push children to spend more money. In India the "Golden Arches" will have to come up with a beefless Big Mac, since four out of five Indians are Hindu and eat no beef. The beef substitute may be lamb, but according to McDonald's, it will look at consumer preferences, supply systems, and market research before making a decision. Box 8-1 describes the McDonald's scene in Rio de Janeiro.

[8]Joan Oleck, "When Worlds Collide," *Restaurant Business* (July 1, 1993): 48–56.

BOX 8-1

MCDONALD'S HAPPY MEALS IN RIO: CHAMPAGNE, WAITERS, AND MUSIC

RIO DE JANEIRO—It was Friday evening, the end of a long workweek; Niraldo Aburque and his friends in downtown Rio were in the mood for a happening Happy Hour. So they cleared their desks, locked the office and headed for the one place they knew where for two hours the beer would be flowing, a live band would be playing, and there was plenty of food to be had. They went to McDonald's.

Welcome to the Golden Arches, Brazilian-style, where a Big Mac can be washed down with a cold beer, partrons can gobble their Quarter Pounder and fries to the sounds of live samba and, on certain nights, meals are served under candlelight by waiters bearing champagne. "It's Brazil," explains Peter Rodenbeck, a top executive in McDonald's eighth-largest market. A burger and beer is not unique to Brazilian McDonald's, but across this country, Brazilians are putting their own special stamp on the McDonald's image, most noticeably with the creation of their Happy Hours, complete with suds and salsa bands, or disc jockeys and jukeboxes.

Restaurants wanted to serve beer and have music. Rodenbeck said, "We investigated and gave them permission to do it. It's a cultural thing." Salim B. Maroun, the Lebanese owner of a McDonald's downtown, started his Happy Hours four months ago after watching his lunch patrons walk past his outlet on Friday nights en route to beer-serving restaurants. "*Cariocas* (Rio de Janeiro natives) like to have their beer on Friday," said Maroun. "They were asking for it, so I said, 'Why not give them beer for two hours?' I don't want anybody not to come to McDonald's because they can't find what they want."

The first beer is on the house. Others cost 70 cents. "It has been very good for business," Maroun said. "We've probably increased it by 60%." Alex Apolinario, 23, and a fellow salesperson, Andrea Oliveira, 24, are enjoying the change. "It's nice because of the beer and the atmosphere," said Apolinario, who also frequents the restaurant for lunch, "and the music is good, too." "Yeah," Oliveira said, "People go to the other bars to listen to *pagode* (a more raucous Brazilian music). This is better. The atmosphere here is more classy." "Being in this place is more sophisticated," said Roberta do Carino, 23, a cashier at a local store. "People don't abuse the place. They don't drink too much. They don't get too loud."

Classy and *sophisticated* are not words usually associated with McDonald's restaurants, but in Brazil, where a Big Mac is equivalent to half a day's pay for many, the restaurants hold a different position in the dining hierarchy. The owner of the McDonald's in upscale Ipanema has been trying to capitalize on that perception. Every Tuesday night, from 8 to 10, the restaurant becomes the equivalent of Chez McDonald's. The house lights are dimmed, soft jazz is piped through the restaurant, and tables are set aside for candlelight dining.

Source: Los Angeles Times, World Report Section, "McDonald's Happy Meals in Rio: Champagne, Waiters and Music" (September 13, 1994): 1.

One challenge that faces global fast-food operators is the cost of real estate. To combat this expense, kiosks and carts are the new locations in many countries. In the Moscow subway system, Taco Bell has taken such an approach and is moving toward its goal of having 220,000 points of access around the world by the year 2000. With extremely high real estate costs in Japan, Baskin-Robbins fits 20 of its 31 ice-cream flavors into a 131-square-foot unit, compared with their 800–1,000 square-foot U.S. stores. KFC configures many of their units in two- or three-story designs, with seating on the upper floors, to cut down on costly ground-level space. KFC is also opening "twinning" or food-court operations in Japan, where KFC, Pizza Hut, and Taco Bell are all under one roof.[9]

To assure sufficient and quality raw material, food service operations, domestic and foreign, develop systems for *sourcing*. However, in foreign situations they often become involved in agricultural production, actually farming or supervising the farming operations that supply raw material. In Hong Kong, the McDonald's staging post for entering the Chinese market, they have been working with Chinese farmers for the past seven years. They have improved the quality of the food so that this source can be used for all of the Hong Kong operations, as well as those in China.

In establishing their Moscow store, McDonald's brought potato growing and handling technology from Western Europe and grew the quality of potato that would in turn make french fries they can be proud of. Setting up operations in Israel, McDonald's found that they were going to have to import potatoes temporarily because the farming group that they wanted to use did not have sufficient volume. Underscoring the need for quality and reliable raw-materials sources, a McDonald's spokesperson said, "We could never open a McDonald's without the proper french-fry sources. We will use the local potato farming group as soon as they are ready."

Globalization of Food Retailing

The food retailing industry does not have the international flavor that characterizes food manufacturing or food service, as there are no Nestlés or McDonald's organizations in food retailing. However, there is an international dimension to food retailing. The largest U.S. supermarket groups are shown in Table 8-4, along with country or state of ownership. Of these top ten retailers, three are foreign owned. The granddaddy of all chains, Atlantic & Pacific Tea Co. (A&P), has belonged to Germany's Tenglemann Group since the 1970s. The North Carolina-based Food Lion, one of the most Southern of all supermarket chains, belongs to Delhaize "Le Lion" SA, of Belgium. Today Delhaize and the Dutch company, Royal Ahold do more business in the United States than in their home countries. J. Sainsbury PLC, a British supermarket chain, has invested $325 million in Giant Food of Washington, the sixteenth largest U.S. food chain.[10]

---

[9]Jeff Weinstein, "Big News Over There!" *Restaurants and Institutions* (July 1, 1994): 135–39.
[10]Ahold's Supermarkets 'Go Native' to Succeed in US," *Wall Street Journal* (October 4, 1994): B3.

TABLE 8-4   LARGEST U.S. SUPERMARKET GROUPS

Company	Control	Number of stores	Annual sales (billions) 1995
Kroger	U.S. (Ohio)	2,160	$23.9
American Stores	U.S. (Utah)	797	17.5
Safeway	U.S. (California)	1,064	16.4
Albertson's	U.S. (12% German-owned)	764	12.5
Winn-Dixie Stores	U.S. (Florida)	1,173	11.8
Atlantic & Pacific Tea Co.	Germany	1,034	10.1
Publix Super Markets	U.S. (Florida)	518	9.2
Ahold USA*	Netherlands	677	8.8
Food Lion	Belgium	1,073	8.2
Wal-Mart Supercenters/ Hypermarket	U.S. (Arkansas)	334	6.4 (est.)

*Ahold operates supermarkets in the United States under the following names: Bi-Lo, Giant (PA), Finest, Edwards, and Tops.
   Source: *Progressive Grocer's Marketing Guidebook,* September 1996: 85–87. Reprinted with permission from *Progressive Grocer.*

The motivations bringing European chains to America vary, but for the most part they come for growth. Ahold's small home market in the Netherlands is saturated with stores, and its growth there is limited. Not all foreign entries into the U.S. market have been successful, however. In the 1980s the French failed in bringing to the United States their 200,000-square-foot hypermarkets that sell everything from automobiles to lettuce. Their prices were not competitive and Americans found the stores unwieldy, with over 60,000 SKUs under one roof. However, in the 1990s Carrefour, a French retailer, has taken its hypermarkets to Brazil, Argentina, and Taiwan. By one report, over half of Europe's 30 biggest retailers have foreign operations, though many are rather modest. America's Wal-Mart has a joint venture for bringing warehouse clubs into Mexico, and Costco is expanding internationally, looking to Britain and other foreign locations.

COMPETITION AND TRENDS IN FOOD SERVICE

Consumer Motivations for Eating Out

Success in food service depends on a number of factors internal to the company: having the right product or "concept," as the industry refers to it; location and real estate costs; effective and motivated employees; and quality/dependable product sources. As important as all the above are, the first step to success is understanding the consumers, their social and economic situations, the extent to which they are used to eating away from home, and their potential for attitude and lifestyle changes. To develop a restaurant concept, one must understand consumer preferences as to food, price, atmosphere, and the reason for eating out on a particular occasion. The NRA (National Restaurant Association) and CREST (Consumer Reports on Eating Share Trends), a market research company, have conducted various studies on consumer behavior and market segmentation in the eating-away-from-home market.

Why does a consumer eat at a certain restaurant on a given occasion? The NRA did a study in 1989 to explore the influences and circumstances surrounding the dining decision. Five basic reasons for dining out were identified:[11]

• *Having a fun time.* The consumer wants to go out for a treat, a reward, or a celebration. Plans are made in advance, and table-service restaurants with average bills above $10 are favored. Concepts might include upbeat decor and theme, attentive service, food with eye appeal, a table-side presentation, experimental dishes, and perhaps live music.

• *Having a nice meal out.* The motive is the pleasure of eating out. The decision is made impulsively, with expectations of good food, quality service, hearty portions, and exceptional value. Typical choices are table-service restaurants with average checks below $10 and self-service cafeterias. The focus is on the completeness of the meal, rather than on the event. Efficient, constant service is important.

• *Satisfying a craving.* This is the most impulsive decision. It can be triggered by the aroma or sight of a food. It is a key to the home-delivery and carry-out segment. Important aspects are the price and the freshness and quality of the food. Foods that might be craved are pizza, barbecued or ethnic food, and bakery products. A restaurant operator can stimulate the craving by using signs, advertising, cooking aromas, and food displays.

• *Making sure everyone is satisfied.* The family group with fragmented schedules and preferences makes this decision on the basis of convenience and the ability of the restaurant to meet various needs. The consumer is not concerned with a complete meal but just wants to make sure everyone gets something. Such consumers want familiar fare and are not willing to experiment. The service needs to be fast; these consumers go to fast-food restaurants, get carry-out, or have the food delivered.

• *Doing the easy thing.* People who are tired and pressed for time want a hassle-free experience while obtaining food. Convenience and speed of service are critical. To attract this group, a simple process for obtaining the food must be offered. Fast-food restaurants dominate, and restaurant carry-out, supermarkets, and delis are also popular.

Market segmentation, including age-group analysis, and product positioning are discussed in detail in Chapter 12; therefore, a study of market segmentation and some of the segmentation schemes that have been developed by market research companies, such as SRI, Simmons Research, Claritas, and CREST, is reserved for that chapter.

To Eat Healthy or Not to Eat Healthy—That Is the Question

The importance of nutrition and public awareness of it continues to grow. According to a 1993 report by the American Dietetic Association, 82 percent of Americans

---

[11]Keith Goldman, "Concept Selection for Independent Restaurants," *Cornell Hotel and Administrative Quarterly* (December 1993): 59–72.

rate nutrition as moderately to very important, compared with 79 percent in 1989. Surveying 1,000 consumers, *Restaurants and Institutions* magazine and the ICR Survey Research Group examined the nutritional expectations of adults (Figure 8-3).[12] In general, the results showed concern that menus should offer more salads, fruits, and vegetables, and that products contain less fat and cholesterol. Fewer than 10 percent of the respondents said that restaurant food is nutritionally satisfactory the way it is.

While surveys such as the above and other anecdotal evidence say that consumers are concerned about nutrition, their purchasing actions often do not match their talk. The American Dietetic Association report cited above found that the number of Americans who said they are doing all they can to achieve a healthy diet dropped to 39 percent in 1993 from 44 percent in 1991. And while more people said that they are monitoring fat and cholesterol consumption, only 6 percent could

[12]"The Healthy Menu: Part III," *Restaurants and Institutions* (June 15, 1994): 37.

FIGURE 8-3   What customers say they want. *(Source: "The Healthy Menu: Part III,"* Restaurants & Institutions Magazine, *(June 15, 1994): 37. Reprinted with permission of Cahners Publishing Company.)*

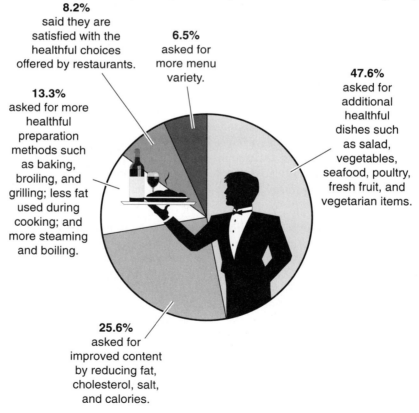

8.2% said they are satisfied with the healthful choices offered by restaurants.

6.5% asked for more menu variety.

47.6% asked for additional healthful dishes such as salad, vegetables, seafood, poultry, fresh fruit, and vegetarian items.

13.3% asked for more healthful preparation methods such as baking, broiling, and grilling; less fat used during cooking; and more steaming and boiling.

25.6% asked for improved content by reducing fat, cholesterol, salt, and calories.

correctly state the guideline for daily fat intake and virtually no one could identify the cholesterol intake guideline.

What are the causes for this apparently schizophrenic nutritional behavior? Some would argue that at some point taste becomes more important than nutrition. While recipes and preparation methods have made great improvements in nutritional flavor enhancements (flavored vinegars, fruit juices, natural carmelization, herbs), the fact remains that salt- and fat-free foods are still less palatable to most people. Examples of "nutritionally correct" product failures are McDonald's McLean burger and Long John Silver's broiled fish.

While restaurant operators may often become frustrated with consumer indecision regarding proper nutritional practices, a few common-sense truths come out of the research conducted. Foremost, consumers want variety and choice. They may not want to eat healthy all the time, but they want the option to do so.

COMPETITION AND TRENDS IN FOOD RETAILING

Information Technology

The U.S. food retailing industry's entry into the information age began with the adoption of the Universal Product Code (UPC) bar-code scanning system in the mid-1970s. In its early years the technology was adopted slowly; it was expensive, and consumer advocacy groups and retail store labor unions put roadblocks in the way. Consumer groups were distrustful of the accuracy of the scanning and demanded that the cans and boxes on the shelf be price-marked so that the consumer could check the accuracy of the check-out register receipt. Labor unions saw the technology as potentially eliminating retail-clerk jobs and also protested the adoption of scanners. While only a handful of scanners were in place in 1975, by 1985 more than 10,000 were installed, and by 1995 over 25,000 supermarkets, 83 percent, were using electronic scanners (see Figure 8-4).

Obviously some real benefits result from the adoption of the scanner technology. The front-end operations (check-out) of supermarkets require less labor. Productivity is improved in the shelf-stocking area as well, now that not price-marking individual items is accepted. But the technology is also being put to several other uses, including inventory management and development of a customer data base for *micromarketing* to specific customer groups. A look at micromarketing shows how the technology is utilized.

Micromarketing with Store-Generated Data   The system used by Von's, the largest supermarket chain in the Southern California market, works likes this: customers are given a VonsClub card; when customers swipe the magnetic card at Point-of-Sale (POS), they receive automatic deductions on selected items. At the same time, detailed purchase data is transmitted to a central computer. At Von's headquarters, customers are sorted into one or more of 200 groups based on products bought, ranging from antacid to wine, and also into lifestyle groups (which will be discussed more fully in Chapter 12) such as young parents: consumers of

FIGURE 8-4   Bar-code scanning system at the check-out stand. *(Source: U.S. Department of Agriculture.)*

children's products. Von's then provides these lifestyle and purchasing categories to manufacturers, who can develop promotions, even pinpointing purchasers of competing brands. A mailing of individually laser-printed discount coupons is sent to each VonsClub member. The key to success is the precision that micromarketing provides. McCormick & Co. promotes its Cake Mate icings and decorations only to those who have previously bought cake mixes. A coffee roaster with an upscale brand offers a $1-off coupon, but only to coffee buyers who regularly purchase premium brands of other goods.

The next step in the Von's micromarketing program will be to issue new VonsClub cards with memory chips that store data such as the cardholders' birthdays and how much they spent the last month. With this technology, discounts can be determined according to demographic and past purchase data while the basket is being scanned at checkout. Once the shopper is identified, the system will look at past purchases to determine whether a buy-two-get-one-free coupon is warranted today. Micromarketing or data base marketing, as it is often called, is just one of the offshoots of the information age.[13] Another recent computer application— grocery shopping on-line with home delivery—is the topic of Box 8-2.

[13]Coupon Clippers, Save Your Scissor," *Business Week* (June 20, 1994): 164–66.

BOX 8-2

PEAPOD'S ON-LINE GROCERY SERVICE CHECKS OUT SUCCESS—CUSTOMERS SHOP ELECTRONIC AISLES

While several national on-line computer shopping services have failed in the grocery business, tiny Peapod is growing by focusing on a few markets and having superior software. The company serves about 7,000 customers in the Chicago and San Francisco markets and plans to expand to Boston later this year.

Operating through contracts with established stores, such as Jewel Food Stores in Illinois and Safeway in California, Peapod sends their grocery pickers into the stores to make up orders that have been placed by customers using Peapod's software. Customers browse electronic "aisles" such as "Cereal and Breakfast" or "Ethnic Foods" just to get ideas, or to select a grocery category or brand name. They can compare prices, scan for specials, use coupons, and rank items by price. Special features of the software allow lists to be kept for weekly shopping, party planning, or guests on special diets. Other instructions allow substitutions for out-of-stock items and buying "half the bananas green."

The order comes to Peapod via computer, telephone, or fax for delivery between 9;30 a.m. and 9 p.m. weekdays and until 2 p.m. on weekends. The customer picks

a 90-minute delivery window, paying by check or credit card, or through a computer account. The pricing structure varies: Chicagoans pay $4.95 a month, $5 per delivery, and 5% of the final bill, or about $35 monthly for somebody with an average $100 grocery bill who shops three times a month. San Franciscans pay a flat $29.95 monthly fee, and in both locations there's a $29.95 setup fee.

As with all computer systems, Peapod is only as good as the information inputted. About three-fourths of all customer orders include an item that is listed but is out of stock. On the supermarket floor Peapod's pickers or shoppers use what the company calls the "lasagna theory" for deciding what is crucial: For instance, if the customer has ordered lasagna noodles, tomato sauce, mozzarella, and ricotta cheese, the picker should guess that lasagna is being made for supper and find the closest substitution for any out-of-stock ingredients. And when critical items, such as baby food or diapers, aren't available, Peapod shoppers call customers. The electronic superhighway can bring much of the supermarket into the home, but not its virtual reality.

Source: Wall Street Journal, "Peapod's On-Line Grocery Service Checks Out Success," June 30, 1994, p. B2. Reprinted by permission of *Wall Street Journal,* ©1994 Dow Jones & Company, Inc. All Rights Reserved Worldwide.

Inventory Management   The food industry is undergoing a major revolution in distribution—that is, warehousing, amount of inventory required, and transportation. Linking manufacturers to retail point-of-sale (POS) information by *Electronic Data Interchanges (EDI)* has vastly improved inventory management. One example is Spartan Stores, Inc., in Michigan, where warehouse inventories were cut from $55 million to $33 million under what the grocery industry calls *ECR (Efficient Consumer Response).* Continuous-replenishment systems also go by other acronyms: JIT (Just in Time), or QR (Quick Response).

All continuous-replenishment systems start with the POS data that each store generates (Figure 8-5). This on-line immediate sales information is then fed into a software program that examines what is being sold at each store, what remains in inventory, and what is in the pipeline (in transit). Some of these software systems utilize artificial-intelligence/expert-system technology to forecast more accurately future demand for goods. The focus is on eliminating inventory; the old logistics systems duplicated inventory at the supplier, in the supplier's field distribution system, at the retailer's distribution center, in the retailer's store, and in transit between all of these points. In the above example of Spartan Stores, the $22 million reduction in inventory would result in a cost saving of $1,760,000, if borrowing to finance that inventory was at an interest rate of 8 percent.

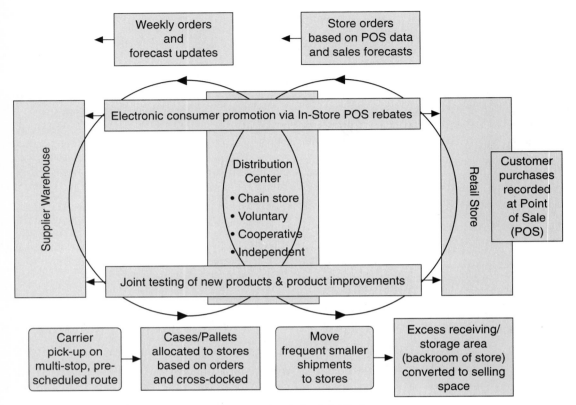

FIGURE 8-5 Efficient consumer-response system in food distribution.

One way in which the electronic data interchange (EDI) between retailer and supplier reduces inventory is by facilitating cross-docking. Cross-docking describes a system in which the product is not consigned to storage, but rather flows across the warehouse floor from inbound supplier trucks directly to the retailer outbound transportation. How can this be accomplished? Through EDI the manufacturer knows sales, inventory, and need for products by individual store. The manufacturer then assembles, by pallet, store shipments that can move right across the distribution-center dock to the truck going to that store. In some cross-docking systems, the merchandise is held at the dock less than half a day before heading to the store. As the time window on cross-docking is tightened, greater inventory savings result, but the coordination between buyer, seller, and any third parties, such as transportation providers, becomes more precise.

Other uses of EDI allow the food manufacturer to develop individualized programs for supermarkets and for various consumer segments, based on their lifestyles and demographics. By analyzing one of their major customer's dairy categories using POS-generated information, Kraft Foods was able to increase sales 22 percent and reduce out-of-stock situations. Kraft benefited by obtaining better shelf position for their high-demand products, plus increased profits from selling more product.[14]

Large, fast-growing retailers, such as Wal-Mart, receive a lot of attention from manufacturers in their effort to effectively implement continuous replenishment. Proctor & Gamble, marketer of such brands as Crisco, Folgers, and Duncan Hines, has a 40-person team at Bentonville, Arkansas, the head office of Wal-Mart. At the same time, retailers apply pressure on suppliers to perform. One retailer levies a $20,000 fine if a supplier's product is incorrectly bar coded. Another, Home Depot, in home and building supplies, has a "three strikes and you're out" policy on bar-code readability.

Coping with the challenges of "information-age" technology is a problem for smaller suppliers and retailers. For instance, will smaller food manufacturers join in some type of cooperative or alliance to provide the same level of service that Proctor & Gamble, Nestlé, and Quaker Foods provide to their customers? Or perhaps they will follow the European model, where many retailers, recognizing the technology, expertise, and scale of operations required for efficient low-cost distribution operations, opt to utilize a third party for all or part of their logistics operations.

Competing for the Consumer's Food Dollar

This section concentrates on the food retailer's strategic marketing mix choices. Part Five of the book explores the marketing mix in greater depth, and although it is particularly oriented toward the food manufacturer, the principles developed there also apply to food retailers' marketing strategy.

Grocery retailers market branded differentiated products, using the same marketing-mix tools as manufacturers do: place, product, price, and promotion. Of course there are differences: In product strategy, retailers have a wide assortment by category (dry grocery, meats, health and beauty aids, etc.) and by brand (manufacturer, private label, generic). And in pricing, retailers are concerned about the price mix for their assortment of SKUs and the consumer's perception of their overall pricing approach. When consumers are asked what is important to them in supermarket selection, "low prices" always ranks high; however, it is interesting that in a 1995 survey reported in *Progressive Grocer,* factors such as "all prices clearly labeled" and "accurate price scanning" were also ranked high by consumers (Table 8-5). Evidently consumers remain somewhat skeptical of information-age technology—they worry whether retailers are using it to take advantage of consumers.

Pricing   There are two major pricing strategies that retailers adopt. The everyday-low-prices (ELP) strategy emphasizes that for a representative market basket of grocery products, the consumer will pay less than at a competitor's, where deep-cut price specials are offered on a limited assortment of products and perhaps other promotional approaches, such as double coupons, are used. These price-specialing

---

[14]"The Keys to High Performance Retailing—Partnering with Vendors," *Chain Store Age Executive* (January 1994): 6MH–10MH.

TABLE 8-5   SUPERMARKET ATTRIBUTES IMPORTANT TO
CONSUMERS, 1995

Rank	Characteristics
1	Cleanliness
2	Low prices
3	All prices clearly labeled
4	Accurate price scanning
5	Accurate, pleasant check-out clerks
6	Freshness date marked on products
7	Good produce
8	Convenient store location
9	Good meat
10	Good layout for fast, easy shopping

Source: Progressive Grocer, 63rd Annual Report,
April 1996. Reprinted with permission from *Progressive
Grocer.*

retailers are using "high-low" or variable price merchandising (VPM). Further discussion of ELP and VPM pricing, along with other aspects of food retail pricing, is found in Chapter 15.

Location   Store location is a crucial aspect of retailing success. A marketing professor was asked, "What are the three most important factors that determine the success or failure of a retailing venture?" He replied (so the story goes): "Location, location, location." (Also see Figure 8-6.) While these examples somewhat overstate the importance of location, it is true that no amount of marketing effort can overcome poor location strategy. For example, most shopping malls are anchored by major department stores or mass retailers, with the idea that the anchors will both attract customers to the mall and create flow between anchors, providing customers to the specialty shops that often depend on impulse buying.

The following cautionary tale is true: A California town built a small shopping mall anchored at one end by a department store but at the other end by a hotel! The

FIGURE 8-6   The importance of location! *(©1993, Washington Post Writers Group. Reprinted with permission.)*

city fathers (and mothers) in their wisdom had not allowed a major department store to move from its downtown location to the mall, so as to preserve the downtown shopping. The end result was that the mall had a 50 percent vacancy rate, and in the end the downtown department store left town because the store was too small to be viable in the 1990s.

Consumers rank location as important in store selection (Table 8-5). Evidently, unlike those who, advertisers once said, would "walk a mile" to buy a particular brand of cigarettes, shoppers won't walk a mile to get to the supermarket. And in order to grow, chains must be aware of the demographic trends. Where is population growth occurring in the state, region, and city, and what is the make-up of this growth in terms of age, ethnicity, and income? Utilizing market research, either from their own staff or from outside companies, the large chains track these demographic trends; then their aggressive real estate departments acquire or lease desirable sites.

Product   The product offered by a supermarket includes not only the 20,000 items on the shelf, but also the atmosphere and a bundle of other services it provides. For example, few supermarkets accepted credit cards five years ago; today over 80 percent accept credit cards. From Table 8-5, it is clear that store attributes such as "cleanliness" and "layout for fast, easy shopping" are important to consumers.

As to product assortment, supermarkets have extended heavily into service departments, such as delicatessens, and offer ready-to-eat items in fast-food or bakery departments that compete with the best stand-alone stores. Supermarkets have been extending themselves into the nonfood territory for many years—first into health and beauty aids, then more extensively into household goods, and even into automotive supplies.

Private-label branding and branding strategies are discussed in more depth in Chapter 13. Private-label products can be low-priced "generics" or, as in the case of retailer brands in Europe, quality brands priced similarly to manufacturer brands. Private labels also provide the retailer leverage in dealing with branded-product manufacturers, such as Nestlé or Heinz. Other product lines, such as generics and club-packs, have not had the same sustained success as private labels. Generics became popular in the late 1970s, as supermarkets responded to consumer dismay over food-price inflation of 10 percent or more per year. Generic products, rock bottom in price and quality, were added to the supermarket assortment. Club-packs, in large containers or multiunit packs similar to those sold by such warehouse clubs as Sam's and Costco, were introduced in the early 1990s in the supermarkets' fight against the encroachment of clubs into their sales base. In recent years generics have been declining as a product category, and a decreased emphasis is being put on club-packs.

Promotion   Supermarket promotion in the 1990s is centered on advertising, with over one-half of it going to newspapers and 30 percent to free-standing inserts that may be delivered to households in newspapers or by other means. Radio and television advertising are used sparingly, as the detail to be communicated to consumers in the grocery business does not lend itself to these media.

An economic factor that makes chains more competitive than independents is the ability to spread fixed costs, such as advertising, over a greater sales base. For example, advertising costs average about 0.5 cents of the supermarket sales dollar, but are about 4 percent of the retailer's gross margin. If a chain with sales of $200 million in a market area spends $1 million on advertising, this would equate to 0.5 cents on the sales dollar. If by a merger the chain can increase sales in the same market area to $300 million, while keeping the same advertising budget, advertising costs will go down to 0.33 cents on the sales dollar, and store profit margins will improve (assuming all else remains constant). Such economies that result from multiple-store operations have been an important force in retail grocery mergers and acquisitions over the past 30 years. In most market areas, which are defined by the Census Bureau as metropolitan census areas (MSAs), the four largest retailers have a combined market share of 65 percent. This figure has risen persistently over the past 30 years, from about 50 percent in the mid-1960s.

Besides advertising, supermarkets have used a variety of promotional approaches to get consumers to come through their doors. In the '50s and '60s it was trading stamps, where for every dollar spent at a store the consumer would receive stamps that could then be redeemed for merchandise. Later, premiums such as dinnerware and encyclopedias were given away or sold at reduced prices with purchases. In the 1980s, double couponing became popular—supermarkets would allow double the face value of manufacturers' coupons against purchases.

Obviously all of these approaches have a life cycle of their own, fading as: 1) consumers have acquired all the dinnerware or encyclopedias they need, and/or 2) competitors have all jumped on the same promotional wagon, so that the effectiveness of the promotional approach wanes. Also, as supermarkets have emphasized price as a major competitive weapon, these nonprice promotional efforts have declined in use. Chain executives are using a variety of tactics, such as improving and stressing their private-label products, emphasizing quality and assortment of perishables, and expanding in-store product demonstrations and sampling, to differentiate their store from the one down the street.[15]

THE WHEEL OF RETAILING

The *wheel of retailing* is a concept that explains the changes in retail strategies and formats over time. Described by M. P. McNair, a pioneer in bringing modern management thought to the retailing sector, this theory says that change in retailing is often sparked by a low-cost, low-price store that enters the market (King Kullen in 1919; Wal-Mart in the 1980s). Their low prices are made possible by a reduction in services, and/or the adoption of new technology that results in lower costs. Successful in attracting customers and taking business away from other retailers, the

---

[15]"Databank—How Does Your Store Stack Up?" *Progressive Grocer—61st Annual Report of the Grocery Industry* (April 1994 Supplement): 56–58.

"new" company at some point broadens its appeal in order to improve margins or gain customers, moving from the low-price image to one with more services. Offering higher-quality products or greater assortment means higher costs and higher prices. Eventually, consumers begin to perceive the "low-cost" store as not low cost, and this gives a new low-cost, low-price type of retailer an opportunity to enter the market. So the wheel of retailing continues to turn.

In the grocery business the wheel began with chains challenging independents; then supermarkets revolutionized chains and nonchains alike; low-cost warehouse stores and other economy formats forced supermarkets to use Everyday Low Pricing; and club stores, such as Costco and Sam's, while also pressuring ELP supermarkets, provided them with opportunities to expand services, meeting the demands of busy consumers who want everything at one stop. Perhaps tomorrow's low-cost innovator will be a version of Peapod, where people shop from their computers and the orders are filled from a warehouse using computers and robotics. While it is always dangerous to project the future from the past, it probably can be said with some certainty that new participants in food retailing will be diverse in formats and services provided. Success will go to those who are quick and agile in adopting new technology that assists in responding to consumer wants in a cost-efficient manner.

SUMMARY

Supermarkets, defined by the industry as retail food stores with a broad assortment and sales of at least $2 million per year, dominate the U.S. retail food industry. Over 75 percent of all grocery sales are through supermarkets and over 50 percent of the supermarkets are owned by chains. While warehouse club stores have grown in numbers over the past decade, from virtually none to over 600, they account for less than 5 percent of all grocery sales in the United States. When thinking of the food service industry, a person most likely calls to mind the fast-food industry and its stores that are found across the geographical and retail landscape of America. However, the full spectrum of food service is much broader, including other sectors such as full-service sit-down restaurants, schools/colleges, health care, retail sales, government (military and others), lodging, recreation/transportation, and social caterers.

The food wholesaling/distribution industries are the unknown and unsung heroes of the food system; they supply the logistical expertise in offering a ready product assortment and low-cost transportation to the retail store, whether it be grocery or food service. Food distribution companies are incorporating the latest in electronic data technology and becoming larger through mergers to provide efficient, low-cost services. Today most chain stores, 72 percent, are supplied by distribution centers owned by the retailer. Also, many of the food service providers, such as PFS (Pizza Hut, Taco Bell, KFC) and Hardee's, operate their own distribution network.

In recent years the food service industry has looked to international markets for growth opportunities, and today many companies are operating overseas. The reason for their aggressive move into foreign markets is simple—growth. For example, McDonald's domestic growth has recently been about 3 percent per year, compared to 14 percent internationally. At the same time U.S. food retailers have been reluctant participants in foreign expansion efforts. However, many foreign retailers, for example, Sainsbury (UK) and Royal Ahold (Netherlands), are buying into U.S. food retailing. Their motivation for entering the U.S. market is also growth.

Companies serving the consumer will find success if they understand consumer motivations and focus on those market segments with growth opportunities. Consumer research also shows that while consumers may be somewhat schizophrenic about eating healthy foods, they do want variety and choice. Food retailers are utilizing scanner data to target consumer groups in a very specific way. An example of this micromarketing, or data-base marketing, as it is also called, is one California chain that sorts customers into one or more of 200 groups based on products bought.

Food retailers utilize a number of competitive tools—price, promotion, product assortment, and location—to attract consumers. The product that retailers offer is not only the assortment of items on the shelf, but also other services that it provides. Retailers' promotional efforts vary, from newspaper advertising to in-store premiums and games, in an effort to make their store unique and different. Pricing policies also differ, from the Everyday Low Price (ELP) approach to one where price specials receive greater emphasis (VPM). The wheel-of-retailing idea explains the evolution of retail strategies that occurs when new low-cost, low-price stores enter a market. They take advantage of market opportunities created by other retailers who have moved to a higher level of service, and hence to higher prices, but gradually change their strategy to differentiate themselves from other retailers who have followed suit.

IMPORTANT TERMS AND CONCEPTS

chain store   192
convenience store   194
distribution center   199
distributors   197
efficient consumer response (ECR)   209
electronic data interchanges (EDI)   209
fast food   196
food service   196
food service distributors   197
  broad-line   197
  self   198
  specialty   198
  systems   197

micromarketing   207
point-of-sale (POS)   192
retail distributors   199
  chain-store-integrated   199
  cooperative   199
  independent   199
  voluntary   199
sourcing   203
stock keeping unit (SKU)   193
supermarket   193
wheel of retailing   214
wholesale club store   193

QUESTIONS

1 Provide the industry definition of a supermarket; what is their share of the retail food markets and has it been growing, stable, or declining over the past ten years?
2 How are the distribution/wholesaling operations of the food service industry similar to, and different from those of the food retailing industry?
3 Describe some of the difficulties and challenges food service operators have faced in entering foreign markets.
4 Your friend wants to get into the restaurant business as a small, independent, non-fast-food operator. After reading the section "The Competition and Trends in Food Service," what recommendations do you have as to market segment and menu selection that she should pursue?
5 What are some of the uses of the UPC code and the information that it generates other than improving labor productivity in a retail food store?

REFERENCES AND RESOURCES

"The Big Picture—R&I's 1994 Foodservice Industry Forecast." *Restaurants and Institutions* (January 1, 1994): 50–88.

Progressive Grocer: 63rd Annual Report of the Grocery Industry. Supplement. April 1996.

Fisher, William P. *Creative Marketing for the Foodservice Industry.* New York: John Wiley & Sons, 1982.

Grunert, K. G. *Market Orientation in Food and Agriculture.* Norwell, MA: Kluwer Academic Publishers, 1996.

"The Keys To High Performance Retailing—Partnering with Vendors." *Chain Store Age Executive* (January 1994): 6MH–10MH.

Melaniphy, John C. *Restaurant and Fast Food Site Selection.* New York: John Wiley & Sons, 1992.

Messersmith, Ann M., and Judy L. Miller. *Forecasting in Foodservice.* New York: John Wiley & Sons, 1991.

Paul, Ronald N. "Status and Outlook of the Chain-Restaurant Industry." *Cornell Hotel and Restaurant Administration Quarterly* (June 1994): 23–26.

The Retail Food Market. Nederland: Rabobank, Agribusiness Research, 1994.

Sullivan, Catherine F., ed. *Management of Medical Foodservice.* 2d ed. New York: Van Nostrand Reinhold, 1990.

INTERNATIONAL FOOD TRADE

CHAPTER OUTLINE

LEARNING OBJECTIVES

After reading this chapter and answering the questions in the Think Breaks and at the end of the chapter, you should be able to:

- Show how international trade increases economic welfare.
- Use economic tools to analyze the impact of trade.
- Show the impact of exchange-rate movements on importers and exporters.
- Outline the role of food in world production and trade, the major products and commodities traded, and the principal suppliers.
- Show how food consumption changes with changes in population and income.
- Identify and classify barriers to food trade.
- Analyze the impact of trade barriers on importers and exporters.
- Define and illustrate the producer subsidy equivalent.
- List alternative mechanisms and institutions for reducing trade barriers.
- Compare free trade areas with multilateral trading arrangements.
- Show how food processing companies are affected by agricultural policy.

INTRODUCTION

In Chapter 1, marketing was defined as a process of exchange between buyers and sellers. This process is unique to the human species and results in two main benefits: it broadens the assortment of goods available for consumption, and it encourages more efficient production by allowing specialization. The first humans had access to only the limited range of foods that they could catch or harvest locally. Then the development of primitive tools allowed the production of food crops. The beginning of food marketing occurred when, after a generation or two of attempting to take each other's food by force, these primitive food producers decided that it would be more efficient to develop a system of barter, through which they could exchange food and other items with each other.

If specialization benefits consumers within a country, specialization and exchange between countries should provide even more benefits. Underpinning international specialization is the concept of factor abundance. The idea of *factor abundance* is that countries specialize in producing products for which local inputs are abundant and cheap. For example, countries like the United States and Australia have abundant land, and they are relatively efficient producers of crops such as wheat. The factor-abundance model was developed in the nineteenth century; it still provides some useful insights into the conduct of international business, but its relevance is decreasing in the modern trading world.

There are two basic differences between an exchange when the buyer and seller are located in the same country and one when they are located in different countries. The first is that there are usually few barriers to trade within a country—in fact, such barriers are prohibited in the constitutions of many countries. The second is that each country has its own currency, but transactions between countries require a conversion from the seller's currency to the buyer's currency. The rate at which this conversion takes place is called the exchange rate.

Despite the apparent benefits from unrestricted trade between nations, countries erect barriers to trade by making imported goods more expensive in one way or another than those locally produced. This is especially true for food and agricultural products. Trade barriers for manufactured products have fallen since 1950, and there has been a 12-fold increase in the volume of world merchandise trade, significantly more than the growth of overall economic activity. Agriculture has moved in the opposite direction. Barriers to agricultural trade have increased, and agriculture's share of total merchandise trade has fallen. Apparently, governments see food and agriculture differently than they do other products.

At the same time as governments erect barriers to trade, they also participate in bilateral (two countries) and multilateral (many countries) negotiations to dismantle them. The best-known forum for such negotiations is the General Agreement on Tariffs and Trade (GATT), succeeded by the World Trade Organization in 1995.

INTERNATIONAL COMPETITIVENESS AND TRADE

International trade in food raw materials and finished goods occurs because: a) companies located in a particular country can produce a product that is either cheaper or better than that supplied by competing producers in other countries, and b) no country can be internationally competitive in everything. Introductory economics textbooks often use the example of guns and butter. Two countries can each produce both products but choose to specialize and trade to their mutual advantage. It helps if the two countries have political or other ties. For example, for nearly a century countries like Australia and New Zealand were among the most affluent in the world, using their close ties with Britain to be, along with other former colonies, her favored food suppliers. Britain produced the guns (and other manufactured products) while New Zealand and Australia produced the butter.

More Choice and Better Products Result from Trade

Climate is one of the more obvious ways in which countries differ, and food production, as compared with most manufacturing activity, is particularly climate dependent. It is possible to overcome climatic disadvantages, but at a cost. For example, bananas could be produced at the South Pole, but they would be quite a bit more expensive than those produced in Costa Rica or Fiji! Even if a country can produce a food efficiently, it may not be able to do so all the year round. Nevertheless, today's affluent consumers demand quality produce every day of the year, which means that imports are required in the local off-season. These seasonal windows may be for quite short periods—Kenyan cabbages find their place on the shelves of the English food retailer, Marks and Spencer, for less than three weeks of the year, but they ensure continuity of supply of quality produce. For all these reasons, international specialization in food production occurs and consumers benefit from being able to buy a wider assortment of better-quality products.

Think Break

At your local supermarket, which products are manufactured locally? Which are imported? Can you identify local and imported easily by their labels? Classify imported products in terms of the three reasons for trade discussed above: cheaper than the local alternative, providing more choice for buyers (for example, Swiss chocolates), or because the local product is seasonally unavailable.

Trade Improves Competitiveness of the Food System

In addition to a cheaper, better, and a wider assortment of food, an additional benefit of free international trade is that it extends competition between companies across country boundaries, as exemplified by U.S. exports of wheat (Figure 9-1). Countries foster competition at home through antitrust laws and trade practice regulations. If domestic competition is seen to be desirable, extending the competitive arena globally should be even more beneficial. (Individual companies, of course, seek to avoid competition and will seek comfortable havens in countries that restrict competition by imposing barriers to imports.) However, for agricultural products in particular, the benefits of international competition are apparently not self-evident to the governments of most industrialized countries. These countries impose a variety of barriers to food imports, reducing the volume of international trade in food products and increasing their price.

Trade barriers encourage a more internationally dispersed pattern of investment than would occur under unrestricted trade, and the giant food multinationals, such as Nestlé and Unilever, operate in most countries of the world for this reason. As trade barriers are reduced, plants in high-cost locations may be closed and these countries supplied from their more efficient neighbors. Of course, the threat of international competition may be enough to encourage inefficient producers to

FIGURE 9-1   Grain barges on the Mississippi River. Most years, 50 percent or more of the U.S. wheat crop is exported. *(Source: U.S. Department of Agriculture.)*

become more efficient. For example, the American multinational, H. J. Heinz, used the Closer Economic Relations (CER) agreement between Australia and New Zealand to achieve increased operating efficiencies in their Australian operation by threatening to shut the Australian plant down and to supply Australia from their more efficient plant in New Zealand.

What makes an industry in a particular country internationally competitive? Cheap *factors of production,* such as land, sunshine, and labor, are still important, but their importance is declining relative to other variables. It is not only factor abundance, but also the efficiency by which factors are converted into products, that determines international competitive advantage. Conventional economic theory argues that in the long run, conversion efficiencies will tend to equate across national boundaries because technology (such as plant varieties, cultivation equipment, and agricultural chemicals) will eventually become available in all countries. A good example of a food industry which seems to operate at a similar level of efficiency in most parts of the world is broiler production. This is basically because the technology of breeding, housing, feeding, and processing is easily transferred between countries.

Factor Abundance and Efficiency of Production

Professor Michael Porter, in *The Competitive Advantage of Nations,* asks why some countries seem to be able to nurture industries that remain internationally competitive for long periods.[1] Porter distinguishes between *basic and advanced factors*—basic being natural resources such as climate and minerals, advanced factors being such things as the educational level of the people. Basic factors are inherited; advanced factors are created. The possibility of factor creation means that the factor pool is not fixed. An obvious example is Japan, a country that lacks basic factors but has worked hard in creating advanced factors—in particular, a highly educated workforce. If factors of production can be created, no country can expect to have sustained international competitiveness based only on inherited factors of production. An industry that is based on cheap inherited factors is always vulnerable to an even lower-cost competitor. For example, America is a low-cost producer of oranges and soybeans and, for many years, dominated world production and trade for these crops. In the 1960s Brazil emerged as a major competitor, with production based on abundant land previously in forest or used for cattle production. Furthermore, created factors, in particular educated people, are increasingly internationally mobile—another reason why the factor pool in any country is not fixed.

Porter goes as far as suggesting that basic factor abundance may actually be a disadvantage to a country, because it encourages the inefficient use of resources and discourages innovation. On the other hand, if a factor of production is scarce, clever countries will find innovative ways of using it more efficiently—for example, energy use in Japan after the oil price increases of the 1970s and '80s. Porter gives the example of the Dutch flower industry. Holland exports over $1 billion of cut flowers per year, despite its cold, gray climate. The Dutch have been innovative in greenhouse techniques, energy conservation, plant breeding, and distribution, and, in any case, the new varieties and consistent quality of Dutch flowers allows them to overcome any price disadvantage caused by the inhospitable environment in which they are produced. In Australia, a small dairy company, King Island Dairies, operates on an island south of the Australian mainland. This location allows them to produce cheap milk, but transport costs mean that they can't compete with mainland suppliers of conventional dairy products. Their response was to produce King Island Brie, a high-value cheese that can bear the cost of transport to the mainland and which uses the isolated location as a marketing advantage.

What do Porter's ideas mean for food production and marketing? For agricultural producers, the suppliers of raw materials in the food system, it means that any competitive advantage based on cheap land or fishing rights, sunshine, and labor is always vulnerable to lower-cost competition. Also, most of the technology of agricultural production transfers readily across national boundaries, further eroding the competitive advantage of any one country.

Think Break
───

How well do Professor Porter's ideas about the use of basic and advanced factors apply to food processing? To food retailing?

───

[1]Michael Porter, *The Competitive Advantage of Nations* (New York: The Free Press, 1990): 75.

Ultimately, international success is determined by productivity, the efficiency with which labor and capital are used either to achieve the lowest cost of production or to develop differentiated products that can command a premium price. What determines productivity? Specialization, which in turn is encouraged by competition, both within a country and from imports. Efficient industries use the most up-to-date technology and management, which may require foreign investment. If there are barriers to increased productivity (such as the efficiency of the labor force), manufacturers may overcome these by moving their operations to other countries.

If productivity is encouraged by allowing the free movement not only of goods and services but also of labor, technology, management, and capital, the nation state becomes increasingly irrelevant in international commerce. Globally oriented companies operate in many countries. Their "home base" country may represent a very small proportion of their total sales, investment, and staff. The biggest food company in the world, Nestlé, is Swiss, but this fact is not particularly relevant to the way it operates. Home-country sales are less than 5 percent of total, and more than 50 percent of the company's executives are non-Swiss. Other major food companies such as Cargill, H. J. Heinz, and Unilever follow a similar model.

One writer who argues strongly that the role of nation states in international business is declining is Kenichi Ohmae. He believes that "for the growing proportion of firms that serve global markets or face global competition, nationality will disappear."[2]

Think Break

The two writers mentioned above have quite different views on the importance of the "nationality" of a business or industry. Porter thinks that the country where a business has its home base is still important. Ohmae does not. Who is right? (This would also be a good topic for a class debate.)

SUPPLY-AND-DEMAND ANALYSIS OF INTERNATIONAL TRADE

The role of supply-and-demand analysis in analyzing commodity price formation was studied in Chapter 2. In particular, the importance of the responsiveness of quantity supplied and demanded to price changes (price elasticities) was outlined. Supply-and-demand analysis can also be used to provide insights into the impact of international trade on prices and quantities traded and to study the impact of trade barriers.

Figure 9-2 illustrates the situation for an exporting and an importing country before and after international trade.

Before trade, the equilibrium price in the (potentially) exporting country is P_1 and the equilibrium quantity is Q_2 (Figure 9-2A). Similarly, in the (potentially)

[2]Kenichi Ohmae, *The Borderless World* (London: William Collins and Co., 1990): 46.

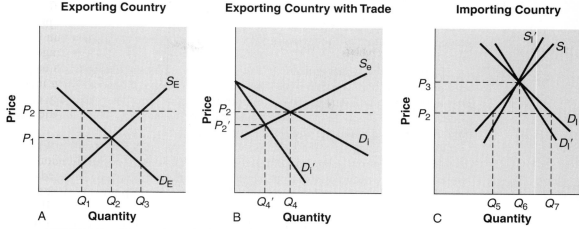

FIGURE 9-2 Price and quantity impact of international trade.

importing country (Figure 9-2C), the equilibrium price is P_3 and the equilibrium quantity is Q_6.

Because P_1 is less than P_3, there is an opportunity for the exporting country to compete with the local suppliers in the importing country. What quantity will be supplied and at what price? The demand for imports equals demand less supply at prices less than P_3 in the importing country, while the supply of exports is the excess supply at prices greater than P_1 in the exporting country. The demand for imports is D_i in Figure 9-2B, while the supply of exports is S_e.

S_e and D_i intersect at an equilibrium price of P_2, and the quantity traded is Q_4. Note that Q_4 equals Q_3-Q_1 (in Figure 9-2A) and Q_7-Q_5 (in Figure 9-2C.)

The impacts of trade on the exporting country are:

- Price increases from P_1 to P_2.
- Quantity supplied increases from Q_2 to Q_3.
- Quantity consumed falls from Q_2 to Q_1.
- Quantity exported is Q_3-Q_1.

Similarly, in the importing country:

- Price falls from P_3 to P_2.
- Quantity consumed increases from Q_6 to Q_7.
- Quantity produced falls from Q_6 to Q_5.
- Quantity imported is Q_7-Q_5.

The Effect of Trade on Producers and Consumers

Trade is usually beneficial to producers in the exporting country and to consumers in the importing country. Consumers in the exporting country face a price rise, while suppliers in the importing country face a price fall. The obvious losers are the importing country producers, and this group is usually most active in opposing trade and encouraging their government to erect trade barriers against competing imported goods.

The price and quantity impacts of trade are affected by the elasticities of supply and demand in both the exporting and importing country. Suppose, for example, that both supply and demand in the importing country were less elastic—as illustrated by $S_I{'}$ and $D_I{'}$ in 9.2C. The demand for imports is now $D_i{'}$. The volume traded falls from Q_4 to $Q_4{'}$ and the equilibrium price falls from P_2 to $P_2{'}$.

Of particular interest is the situation where imports are a very small proportion of total consumption in the importing country. In this case, one would not expect price in the importing country to be significantly affected by changes in the quantity of imported product. That is, the demand for imports is highly elastic. The extreme case is where the price in the importing country is not affected at all by changes in the quantity of imports. That is, the export supplier is a "price taker" (as is any supplier with a small share of a homogeneous commodity market). Economists call such a supplier a "small country." Similarly, an importing country with a very small share of the exporter's total production cannot significantly affect the price paid and is a small-country price-taking buyer.

Of course, as previously discussed, no supplier needs to be a 100 percent price taker, because it is always possible to differentiate even commodity products to some degree. The objective of product differentiation and branding is to achieve some monopoly power for the supplier (this may be both partial and short-lived). In this situation, it is irrelevant that the supplier is located in a small country or, for that matter, whether the supplier produces small volumes relative to competing products. The supplier in fact has a 100 percent share of the market for his brand. If this brand is clearly differentiated from competing brands, the supplier has some market power in all the markets in which he operates. Economic models designed for the analysis of commodity markets have limited applicability in this situation.

IMPACT OF EXCHANGE RATES ON TRADE

The currency of any country is like any other commodity; its price is established where the supply of and demand for the currency intersect. This price is the *exchange rate*. For example, the exchange rate of the U.S. dollar for the Japanese yen (say Y100 per $U.S.) tells us that the "price" of U.S. dollars is 100 yen per dollar.

What factors influence the supply of and demand for a currency? Buyers of a currency (say the U.S. dollar) include:

• Importers of U.S. goods or services who buy U.S. dollars to pay for their purchases.
   • Overseas tourists visiting the United States.
   • Overseas investors who buy U.S. dollars to invest in the United States, in the form of either equity investment or loans to American borrowers.

Similarly, sellers of U.S. dollars (buyers of other currencies) include:

- American importers buying goods from foreign suppliers.
- American tourists traveling out of country.
- Americans investing offshore.

Figure 9-3 illustrates the impact of these variables on the U.S. dollar/yen exchange rate. The initial exchange rate is Y100/$U.S. Buyers of U.S. dollars (for investment, tourism, or to buy U.S.-produced goods) move the demand for the currency to the right, increasing its value to 107 yen per $U.S. Sellers of U.S. dollars (importers of overseas-produced goods, Americans investing offshore, and outbound tourists) move the supply curve to the right, devaluing the currency to Y94/$U.S.

For the United States and many other countries, imports consistently exceed exports, placing the U.S. dollar under continuous downward pressure relative to the currencies of more competitive economies such as Japan and Germany. Changes in the U.S. dollar/Japanese yen exchange rate from 1968 to 1995 are shown in Figure 9-4.

Impact of Exchange-Rate Changes on Exporters and Importers

Changes in exchange rates obviously affect the profitability of international transactions in food products. Their impact depends on whether the supplier is a "price taker" or a "price maker" in the importing country. (Recall the discussion on this question earlier in this chapter.) When the exchange rate, Japanese yen for U.S. dollar, increases, either the price of the American product to the Japanese buyer increases, or the American seller receives less, or both—as detailed in Table 9-1.

FIGURE 9-3   Effects of supply and demand on the exchange rate, Japanese yen/U.S. dollar.

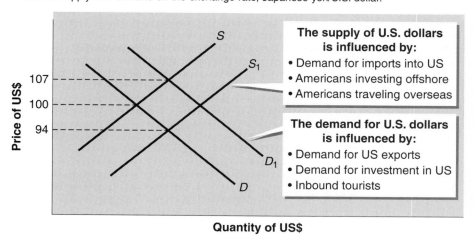

Quantity of US$

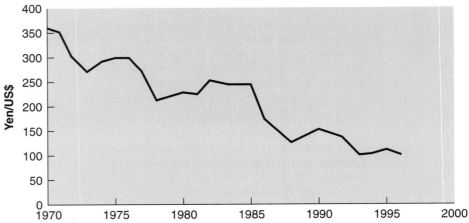

Which of these cases is most likely to occur? It depends on the elasticity of demand for the American product in the Japanese market. This, in turn, depends on how much competition the American seller faces in the Japanese market. If the product faces little competition (perhaps because it has identifiable unique features and strong brand recognition), the buyer has no choice but to pay the price increase arising from the exchange-rate increase; that is, the supplier has some ability to be a price maker. If, on the other hand, the product has many substitutes, the Japanese buyer can easily switch to a local or an alternative foreign supplier. An extreme case is when the product is a commodity—a product that is totally undifferentiated by supplier. In this case, the American supplier is a price taker. There will be no change in the Japanese yen price, and the American supplier will bear the full burden of the exchange-rate increase.

TABLE 9-1   ALTERNATIVE IMPACTS OF EXCHANGE-RATE CHANGES

U.S. seller	Price received in $U.S.	Exchange rate yen/$U.S.	Price paid by buyer in yen
Before exchange-rate increase	1.00	100	100
Exchange rate $U.S./yen increases from $0.01 to $0.011:		110	
Case 1: No change in yen price to Japanese buyer	0.91	110	100
Case 2: No change in $U.S. price to U.S. seller	1.00	110	110
Case 3: Buyer and seller share burden of exchange-rate increase	0.96	110	105.6

As discussed in Chapter 13, competition in any market increases as a product moves through its life cycle. Thus, the impact of exchange-rate movements is greater in the maturity phase of the life cycle, when there are many competing products, than in the introductory phase, when there are few. For example, in the 1980s, cheesecake was a relatively new product in the Japanese market, finding its place in the rapidly expanding family-restaurant sector. The main supplier was the American company, Sara Lee. By the 1990s there were many suppliers. Sara Lee, facing more competition, became more vulnerable to changes in the $U.S./yen exchange rate.[3]

In all cases, it appears that an increasing exchange rate reduces the competitiveness of American suppliers in the Japanese market. Another view is that high exchange rates have the same beneficial effect as factor scarcity; they encourage internationally competitive industries, because they force companies to differentiate export products to overcome the price disadvantage. Certainly, Japanese and German exporters have grown and prospered over more than a decade of rising exchange rates.

INTERNATIONAL TRADE IN FOOD AND AGRICULTURAL PRODUCTS

Although the volume of food trade is increasing, food's share of both world economic output and trade is falling. In rich countries such as the United States, agricultural production's share of the total output of the economy is less than 5 percent (about 30 percent in developing countries). Of course, when food processing and distribution is taken into account, the food sector's share of the economy is higher, but still small relative to manufacturing and services. Food's share of world merchandise trade has declined from over 50 percent in the 1950s to less than 15 percent in the 1990s. It is to be expected that food's share of a growing world economy will fall. As people get richer, they spend a smaller proportion of their income on food and a greater proportion on manufactured goods and services.

Importance of Trade to U.S. Agriculture

However, when looked at from other perspectives, agricultural trade is important—for the U.S. economy and for agricultural producers. As Figure 9-5 shows, agricultural exports have always exceeded imports, thus achieving a positive trade balance of $30.5 billion in 1996. Agriculture is one of four U.S. industries that show a positive merchandise trade balance. This helps reduce the overall trade deficit, in which imports of petroleum and automobiles figure most prominently.

Agricultural exports also provide markets for producers. For example, the $60.0 billion of 1996 U.S. agricultural exports resulted in a home for over one-fourth of U.S. harvested acreage. The export share for major crops in 1996 is 58 percent for

[3]In fact, the value of the U.S. dollar generally fell in relation to the yen over the period, making it easier for U.S. suppliers to withstand competition in the Japanese market. In any case, multinational food companies such as Sara Lee would be able to supply from other countries if the $U.S./yen exchange rate were seriously affecting the profitability of the Japanese market.

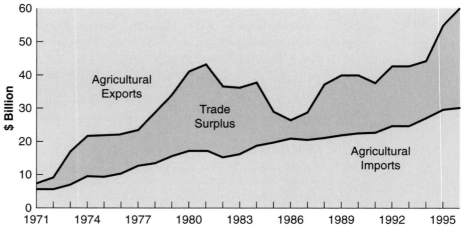

FIGURE 9-5 U.S. agricultural trade exports and imports, 1971–1996*. *1996 figures are forecast. (*Source: Desk Reference Guide to Agricultural Trade, USDA FAS, Agricultural Handbook No. 683, April 1994, and* 1996 Agricultural Outlook, *USDA ERS, April 1996.*)

wheat, 30 percent for feed grains, 48 percent for rice, 38 for soybeans, and 41 percent for cotton. Exports are also important for red meats, almonds, citrus fruits, and wines.

Food Self-Sufficiency

Most countries produce most of their own food requirements. A measure of a country's ability to feed itself is the *self-sufficiency ratio,* production/consumption expressed as percentage. Self-sufficiency ratios for seven major food categories are given in Table 9-2.

TABLE 9-2 SELF-SUFFICIENCY RATIOS BY COMMODITY (PERCENT)

Commodity	Industrial Market		Centrally Planned		Developing Economies	
	1961–64	1983–86	1961–64	1983–86	1961–64	1983–86
Wheat	139	182	98	88	81	82
Coarse grain	98	122	103	92	105	93
Rice	100	115	37	84	102	102
Ruminant meat	97	106	100	97	105	96
Nonruminant meat	99	102	101	102	100	99
Dairy products	103	108	100	99	96	91
Sugar	69	87	85	72	103	98
TOTAL	99	113	99	94	103	98

Source: R. Tyers and K. Anderson, *Disarray in World Markets: A Quantitative Assessment* (Cambridge: Cambridge University Press, 1992): 23–24.

The data in Table 9.2 show that:

- The industrial market economies are, on average, 113 percent self-sufficient for the seven food categories listed. Putting this figure in another way, these countries generate surpluses for export of about 11.5 percent of their total production. On the other hand, the (formerly) centrally planned European economies and the developing countries are not quite self-sufficient, their requirements for imports being 6 and 2 percent of total consumption, respectively.
- The emergence of *export surpluses* in developed countries is a relatively recent phenomenon. The turnaround has been dramatic. In the early 1960s, Western Europe accounted for about 40 percent of world food imports; it now accounts for over 15 percent of exports. These surpluses have been generated by substantial subsidies paid to both agricultural producers and exporters.
- While the industrial market economies have, with the assistance of various types of subsidies, moved toward being net exporters of most foods, the developing and centrally planned economies have become less self-sufficient. In the developing countries both production and consumption have expanded rapidly, but consumption has grown slightly faster than production, owing to both population and income increases, thus increasing the requirement for imports.

High self-sufficiency ratios mean that a relatively small proportion of world food production and consumption is traded internationally. For example, about 7 percent of beef production and 5 percent of dairy is traded. One implication of this fact is that relatively small increases in production in the major producing regions (such as the European Union) translate into export surpluses that represent a substantial increase in volume of international trade.

Food Trade by Product Category and Supplying Country

As might be expected from the self-sufficiency data in Table 9-2, the developed industrial economies dominate the export of basic food raw materials—90 percent of wheat, 76 percent of beef and sheepmeats, and 95 percent of dairy products. An increasing proportion of food trade is in highly processed consumer products, as shown in Table 9-3.

The European Union is the leading exporter of consumer food products, while the United States is the major supplier of bulk commodities in the world market (Table 9-3). However, among U.S. agricultural exports, consumer-oriented products have nearly doubled in the past six years. Today fresh and processed fruits and vegetables account for $3.2 billion of U.S. consumer exports, while red meats also account for over $3 billion. Other major consumer-ready products include tree nuts, snack foods, and wines and beer.

BARRIERS TO FOOD TRADE

Barriers to trade can be overt, such as a tariff or an import restriction, or can be of a "nontariff" type, such as unjustified restrictions to imports on the grounds of

TABLE 9-3   MAJOR SUPPLIERS BY PROCESSING STAGE (PERCENT SHARE OF EXPORTS)

	Average 1970–74	Average 1980–84	Average 1990–92
Total			
United States	20%	23%	19%
European Union	11	14	18
Australia	6	4	5
Canada	4	4	4
China	2	3	4
Bulk*			
United States	28	32	30
Canada	6	7	7
European Union	2	4	6
Australia	3	4	5
Brazil	7	5	5
Intermediate†			
European Union	11	19	18
United States	19	18	17
Australia	11	7	8
Malaysia	2	5	6
Argentina	3	4	5
Consumer-oriented‡			
European Union	19	25	27
United States	8	10	14
Australia	6	4	4
Thailand	2	3	4
New Zealand	5	4	4

***Bulk** commodities include wheat, rice, feed grains, soybeans, peanuts, cottonseed, flaxseed, safflowerseed, other bulk oilseeds, unmanufactured tobacco, pulses, and raw sugar. Tropical products, such as green coffee, cocoa, and natural rubber, are also included in this category.

†**Intermediate** products are principally semiprocessed products in the intermediate stage of the food system, such as wheat flour, feeds and fodders, hops, live animals, planting seeds, oilseed meals, vegetable oils, hides and skins, wool, and refined sugar.

‡**Consumer-oriented** or consumer-ready products are fundamentally end-use products that require little or no additional processing for consumption. Included in this group are such items as fresh and processed horticultural products, fresh and processed meats, snack foods, pet foods, beer and wine, and other processed food products.

Source: Desk Reference Guide to Agricultural Trade, USDA FAS, Agric. Handbook No. 683, April 1994: 47.

plant, animal, or human health. Subsidies to local producers are also a type of trade barrier.

The most common trade barrier is a *tariff* or duty. A tariff is simply a tax on imports. The tax may be levied either on the value of the imported product (ad valorem) or on a per-unit basis. A *variable levy* is a tax that changes as the price of the foreign good changes, the objective being to keep the landed price of the good constant. Variable levies are one of the devices used by the European Union to limit agricultural imports.

Impact of Tariffs and Duties

Table 9-4 compares three forms of tariff established on two exporters' prices, $100 and $90. The exporter's price is basically the price landed on the importing country's wharf. The per-unit tariff is $10. The ad valorem duty is 10 percent of the landed price. The landed price equals the exporter's price plus the duty. At an exporter's price of $90, the ad valorem duty falls to $9, while the per-unit duty is unchanged. The variable levy increases from $10 to $20 to keep the landed price unchanged at $110.

Tariffs may be established in other ways—for example, on the basis of raw-material content or on the value of the product at an earlier stage in the export channel (ex-warehouse or FOB).[4]

Think Break

A jar of English jam being exported to the United States is priced at £0.50 FOB (the exchange rate is U.S. $2 per British pound). Freight and insurance are £0.20 per jar. The U.S. tariff is 20 percent on the U.S. dollar FOB value, and U.S. wharf charges are 10 cents per jar. What is the ex-dock price of the jam?

An import *quota* is a quantitative restriction on the volume of the import (in total or from specified countries) that is allowed into the country. For example, the United States imposes a quota on beef imports when domestic beef production reaches a predetermined level.

The Economic Effect of Tariffs and Quotas   Both tariffs and quotas generally:

- Raise the price to consumers in the importing country
- Reduce the price received by the exporter (the terms of trade effect)
- Increase production in the importing country
- Reduce consumption in the importing country.

[4]"FOB" (Free On Board), one of the standard terms in international commerce—"Incoterms," is the price of a product at the seller's factory or at a named port of exportation or a named vessel at a port of exportation. Other terms are "FAS" (Free Alongside Ship), where the product is priced at dockside in the exporter's country, and "CIF" (Cost, Insurance, Freight), a price quote for delivering the product to the port of the importing buyer. In Table 9-4 the exporter's price is a CIF price.

TABLE 9-4   IMPACT OF TARIFFS AND DUTIES

	Ad valorem tariff (10%)		Per-unit tariff ($10 per unit)		Variable levy (per unit, variable)	
Exporter's price	100	90	100	90	100	90
Tariff/duty	10	9	10	10	10	20
Landed price	110	99	110	100	110	110

Figure 9-6 shows the impact of a tariff on imports and prices of an importing country. The demand for imports is D_i and the supply of imports is S_i. The equilibrium quantity of imports is Q_3 and the equilibrium price is P_3. A tariff, t, is established by the importing country. This has the impact of moving the supply of imports after payment of duty in the importing country to S_i'. (The supply of imports before payment of duty remains unchanged at S_i.) The impact of the duty is to decrease the quantity imported from Q_3 to Q_2. The price paid by the importer increases from P_3 to P_4, while the price received by the overseas supplier falls from P_3 to P_2. In this example, it appears that the price effects of the tariff are borne about equally by the importer and the exporter.

However, suppose the demand for imports is infinitely elastic—as shown by D_i'. Infinitely elastic demand for imports from a particular country is approached when the quantity supplied by that country represents a very small share of total consumption. In this case, the quantity imported falls from Q_3 to Q_1, and the price

FIGURE 9-6   Impact of a tariff on an importing country.

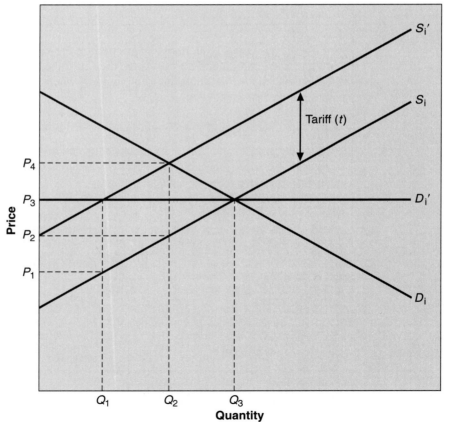

received by the exporter falls from P_3 to P_1. The price paid by the importer is unchanged at P_3. That is, the full effect of the tariff is borne by the exporter. This accords with common sense. New Zealand supplies less than 3 percent of American beef consumption. New Zealand suppliers know that if the United States imposes a tariff on New Zealand beef, this will have no effect on the U.S. beef price but simply reduce the price received by New Zealand suppliers. If the supply of exports is inelastic (which it will be in the short term for most commodity products), the impact of the tariff on quantity supplied will be small—the end result being that the exporting country supplies about the same amount, but at a reduced price.

The impact of a tariff can be compared with the impact of exchange-rate changes discussed above. A price-taking supplier is not able to pass on an exchange-rate appreciation in the form of an increased price to the overseas buyer. Of course, if the exporter's currency depreciates, the full benefit of the depreciation will be received in the form of a higher local-currency price.

One potential impact of a tariff imposed by an importing country is that supplier countries may impose retaliatory trade restrictions of their own. The issue, then, is the impact of a possible trade war on the total commercial relationship between the two countries. The United States justifies the Export Enhancement Program (EEP), where sales of grain and other products to certain countries are subsidized, on the grounds that it is designed specifically as a retaliatory measure against subsidized exports of agricultural products by the European Union. It is not clear that the program has actually had any effect on the behavior of European Union exporters.

The Producer Subsidy Equivalent

One feature of trade in food and agricultual products is that the most important barriers to trade are not tariffs and quotas, but the subsidies and other forms of assistance given to agricultural producers.

Subsidies may be used to increase prices received by agricultural producers or to decrease the price of inputs, or in other ways. Increasing the price received by agricultural producers naturally encourages them to produce more, which generates surpluses that can only be exported with a further subsidy. Efficient agricultural producers such as New Zealand, Australia, and Thailand are thus doubly penalized. They not only face having reduced or no exports to the subsidizing country; they also have to compete with subsidized exports in other markets.

Recognizing that all forms of assistance to producers in any country are a barrier to imports from other countries, economists have devised various measures that attempt to incorporate all types of assistance in one figure. The most common of these is the *producer subsidy equivalent (PSE)*. For example, if the PSE in a particular country is 10 percent, this means that if all the different types of assistance (tariffs, subsidies, etc.) were added together, they would be equivalent to a single subsidy of 10 percent of the unassisted price.

The figures in Table 9-5 show that PSEs have been increasing in all of the selected countries/regions except New Zealand. For the 1989–93 period, subsidies

TABLE 9-5   PRODUCER SUBSIDY EQUIVALENTS IN SELECTED COUNTRIES

Country	Producer Subsidy Equivalent	
	1979–81	1989–93
Australia	9	10
Canada	24	37
European Union	37	46
Japan	57	67
New Zealand	18	4
United States	16	21

Source: R. Tyers, and K. Anderson, *Disarray in World Food Markets: A Quantitative Assessment* (Cambridge: Cambridge UP, 1992): 56, and *Desk Reference Guide to Agricultural Trade,* USDA FAS, Agric. Handbook No. 683, April 1994: 17.

represented 67 percent of income received by Japanese farmers (compared with 21 percent in the United States, close to 50 percent in the European Union, and only 4 percent in New Zealand). In 1993, the European Union budgeted U.S. $44 billion on farm support programs.[5]

AGRICULTURAL POLICIES

As well as limiting trade, the agricultural policies of industrialized nations raise prices to consumers and cost governments billions of dollars. Why, then, do countries establish complex mixtures of import restrictions, subsidies, and other forms of assistance?

Agricultural policy objectives include:

• A "fair" standard of living for agricultural producers relative to the rest of the community. (In Japan, this relativity is enshrined in "The Agricultural Basic Law.")
• Price stability to producers and/or consumers.
• Regularity and security of food supplies.
• Adequate nutrition.
• Reasonable prices for consumers.
• Productivity and technical efficiency in agricultural production.
• Improving the country's balance of payments.
• Environmental objectives, such as reducing pollution from fertilizers and pesticides or retaining woodland in agricultural areas.

These objectives are given different emphases in different countries. In rich countries, the emphasis is usually on food security, a fair standard of living for rural people, and, increasingly, environmental issues. Developing countries, on the other

[5]"Spudsidies," *The Economist* (10 April 1993): 17.

hand, tend to emphasize balance of payments, reasonable prices for consumers, and adequate nutrition.

Agricultural policy objectives can be achieved in a number of ways, including measures to improve productivity of production, processing, and distribution and measures to improve technical efficiency or reduce farm costs, such as farm-input subsidies. Prices received by farmers may be increased by subsidizing local or export prices, by restricting imports, or by restricting domestic supply through quotas or "set-aside" programs.

Some measures are not directly concerned with farm profitability. The provision of public services such as schools, mail, and telephone is more expensive in rural areas, and the additional cost of providing a service equivalent to that provided in urban areas is a form of subsidy. Cash grants and welfare payments, while not limited to agricultural populations, often further agricultural policy objectives.

Governments may choose to facilitate the provision of off-farm income by de-centralizing their own activities and encouraging industrial development in rural areas. Also, structural policies may be aimed at getting farmers off farms (for example, the Rural Assistance Scheme in Australia).

A cost-effective policy measure is one that: a) clearly identifies the policy ob-jective(s) that the measure seeks to achieve and b) achieves the objective at the low-est possible cost to taxpayers and consumers. For example, if the objective of agri-cultural policy is to provide income support for poor farmers, price subsidies are unlikely to be cost effective, because they provide more support for rich farmers than for poor.

Consider the case of a hypothetical small European country called Mecklenberg Holstein (MH). There are 40,000 dairy farmers in MH. The objective of govern-ment policy is to ensure that they all get a net income (from dairying) of $20,000 per year. The government is considering two possible forms of assistance: a milk price subsidy or direct income support for any farmer whose net income does not meet the income target.

The two alternatives are compared with the situation before any assistance in Table 9-6. A price subsidy sufficient to increase the net income of the 10,000 small farmers to the target level of $20,000 per year costs the taxpayers of Mecklenberg Holstein $1,620 million, 92 percent of which goes to the large and medium farmers—who meet the minimum net income target without assistance. Income supplementation, targeted at the small farmers costs only $120 million, 7 percent of the price-subsidization alternative.

This is a hypothetical example, but a realistic one. Research shows that less than 1 in 10 dollars from farm support programs actually reaches needy farmers—and the rich farmers certainly do get a whole lot richer. In 1986 a Californian cotton producer, Jim Boswell, collected $12 million in government payments. Every American sugar producer receives subsidies equal to twice the nation's average family income.[6]

---

[6]"Agriculture Survey: The New Corn Laws," *The Economist* (December 12, 1992): AS7.

TABLE 9-6   A COMPARISON OF ALTERNATIVE FORMS OF ASSISTANCE

	Size of farm			
	Large	Medium	Small	Total
No assistance				
Number of farms	5,000	25,000	10,000	40,000
Cows per farm	150	20	10	
Milk gross revenue*	450,000	60,000	30,000	
Expenses	360,000	40,000	22,000	
Net income	90,000	20,000	8,000	
Subsidize milk price by 20 cents per liter				
(Volume & expenses unchanged)				
Gross revenue	630,000	84,000	42,000	
Net revenue	270,000	44,000	20,000	
Cost to taxpayer ($ million)	900	600	120	1,620
Direct income support for small farmers				
Net farm income	90,000	20,000	8,000	
Direct payment	0	0	12,000	
Cost to taxpayer ($ million)	0	0	120	120

*6,000 liters per cow at 50 cents per liter.

Think Break

Once you have determined the agricultural policy objectives of your country you can identify the mechanisms used for achieving these objectives. Do you believe these mechanisms are cost effective?

If price subsidies are not a cost-effective way of helping needy farmers, why are they used? The reasons are the political power of large farmers, often in coalition with farm-input suppliers, and the fact that no one likes to be seen as a recipient of charity. The idea of "uncoupling" prices and farm-family incomes has been around for a long time. University of Chicago economist Theodore W. Schultz proposed direct welfare payments instead of subsidized prices as a means of supporting needy farm families in 1943.

In countries like Japan and Sweden, food self-sufficiency is an important policy objective. If the underlying objective is to have sufficient food so as not to be dependent on imports in the case of major shortages, perhaps holding substantial stocks of basic foodstuffs, imported when prices are low, is more cost effective than local production. In any case, agricultural production is increasingly dependent on purchased raw materials, which, in many cases have to be imported.

As Box 9-1 indicates, agricultural policy has more to do with politics than rational economics. Any policy measure will have both winners and losers, and the most effective way of influencing the political process is to establish a coalition of potential winners. These may be a diverse and influential group. For example, in the

BOX 9-1

SPUDSIDIES

While the costs mount and a trade war looms, Europe is extending the common agricultural policy to a new crop

Nowhere is the Eurocrat more powerful than in the continent's verdant fields and tidy farmyards. His charge, the common agricultural policy (CAP), was for decades the European Community's one genuinely big idea. With its incomprehensible language of "stabilizers" and "co-responsibility levies," its "monetary-compensatory amounts" and "export restitutions," and a budget this year of 36 billion ecus ($44 billion), the CAP survives as a luxuriant creation of bureaucratic ingenuity. Repeated efforts to prune and pare this extraordinary growth have failed. Even so, one great crop has been cruelly excluded from the financial fertilizer. Until now, that is. This month the CAP is preparing to embrace the potato.

If the EU's northern countries have their way, farm ministers will establish common potato standards and producer groups, and monitor imports. Southern countries want more intervention to gobble up surplus spuds when prices fall too low. With this small difference ironed out, Europe can within the month exult in a common potato policy.

The potato farmers' triumph is just one example of the CAP's almost supernatural resilience. Far from cutting the milk-output quotas, as was agreed last year, the commission has frozen them at current levels and has even talked of raising them in some countries. Chaos surrounds the reform for cereals as farmers are asked to complete the paperwork needed to receive subsidies: a 17-page form in Portugal, a 79-page explanatory booklet in Britain, nothing at all so far in Greece.

Another half-baked idea

In truth, the already over-managed CAP is growing not towards free farm-trade, but towards more bureaucracy and ever more intricate subsidies and controls. Whatever their intent, reforms are always partially implemented and subverted by entrenched interests. Hence, tomorrow's CAP will be more wasteful and just as remote from world markets as yesterday's. Those in Europe who want genuinely freer food markets have only one choice: the discipline of a GATT deal on farm trade.

Source: Excerpts from an editorial, "Spudsidies," *The Economist* (April 10, 1993): 17. ©1993. The Economist Newspaper Group, Inc. Reprinted with permission, further reproduction prohibited.

European Union, the main policy mechanism is direct price subsidies. All farmers benefit from this policy, large farmers considerably more than small.

There are a number of other winners:

- Farm-input suppliers
- Exporters (who handle the subsidized exports resulting from the surpluses generated by the subsidies)
- Environmentalists who believe that the rural environment would be damaged by the reduction in the number of farmers that would occur without the subsidy
- Rural politicians
- Bureaucrats who are employed administering the policies and can think up creative ways of pleasing their political bosses by inventing new vote-catching policy mechanisms
- Consumers, because they have a secure supply of locally produced food.

Against this formidable list of winners is a smaller, less influential list of losers:

- Farmers from other countries
- Environmentalists (because subsidies encourage excessive use of fertilizers and agricultural chemicals that pollute air and water)
- Consumers, because they pay higher prices
- Taxpayers.

Of course, assisting farmers costs consumers and taxpayers—an average of $1,400 per nonfarm household in 1990 (Tyers and Anderson, 1992). However, despite the costs imposed by farm support programs, the price of food continues to fall in real terms, as does food's share of the household budget. Individual consumers have much less to gain from removing farm programs than individual farmers or fertilizer manufacturers have from keeping them.

Note that two groups in the European Union, consumers and environmentalists, are both winners and losers. This is often the case with any policy measure; there are tradeoffs, both between and within groups. Whether consumers care more about the cost of food than about food security is debatable. Surveys of Japanese consumers consistently show, for example, that they are aware that the cost of locally produced rice is three to five times the cost of imported rice, but they are willing to accept this situation for the sake of having a secure local supply of rice.

Recall that food is of declining importance in the household budget and that the farm price is a declining portion of the retail price. Perhaps consumers see a small increase in weekly household expenditure as a reasonable price to pay for what they believe is a secure food supply.

Think Break

Who are the winners and losers for the agricultural policies that you identified previously?

REDUCING AGRICULTURAL PROTECTIONISM AND TRADE BARRIERS

Barriers to trade in food and agricultural products have been increasing (while barriers for manufactured goods and services have decreased). Historically, agricultural lobby groups have been able to persuade governments to leave agriculture out of trade negotiations and to leave domestic support arrangements intact. There is evidence that this situation may be changing. New Zealand's traditionally efficient farmers briefly enjoyed levels of support approaching their counterparts in Europe in the early 1980s. They now receive virtually none. Sweden, one of the most heavily subsidizing countries, is abolishing some of the worst trade-distorting practices. Japan has liberalized imports of beef, oranges, and, because of local shortages in 1993 and 1995, even rice (see Figure 9-7).

For the first time since its establishment in 1947, the General Agreement on Tariffs and Trade included serious discussions on agriculture in the "Uruguay Round" of negotiations (started in 1986 and completed in 1993).

Free Trade Areas, Customs Unions, Economic and Political Unions

Negotiations on reducing barriers to international commerce may occur between two countries (bilateral) or between several (multilateral). Trade liberalization may include all goods and services or a few. A *Free Trade Area* is a bilateral or

FIGURE 9-7   U.S. beef exports to Japan increased in the mid-'90s. *(Courtesy of U.S. Meat Export Federation.)*

multilateral agreement under which there are (theoretically) no restrictions on trade between the participating countries. Examples of Free Trade Areas are NAFTA (North American Free Trade Agreement), EFTA (European Free Trade Agreement), and the CER (Closer Economic Relations) agreement between Australia and New Zealand. One of the problems with a free trade agreement is that the individual member countries may have different tariffs on nonmembers' goods. Suppose countries A and B have an agreement under which there is no tariff on (say) cheesecakes that are traded between the two countries. Country A, however, has a 50 percent tariff on cheesecakes imported from a third country (C), while Country B's tariff on Country C's imports is only 20 percent. There will be an incentive for an enterprising businessperson in Country B to import cheesecakes from Country C and reexport them, possibly with a new label, to Country A.

This leads us to the next level of economic integration—a *customs union.* In a customs union, members agree to have a common external tariff. So far, only trade in goods and services has been mentioned. International commerce also involves movement of investment capital and people. An *economic union* seeks to harmonize commercial laws and establish a common currency, allowing free movement of labor and capital as well as goods and services.

The final level of integration is a *political union,* under which the power of individual governments is reduced relative to that of the collective government. Over the course of its history the European Union has changed its name from a "Common

Market" to an "Economic Community" to its present title, "European Union," as it has evolved from a free trade area, to an economic union, to a political union.

Think Break

The country in which you live is very likely to belong to one or more economic alliances of the type described above. Describe any one of these.

The World Trade Organization

The established vehicle for multilateral trade negotiation is the *World Trade Organization (WTO)*. The WTO replaced its predecessor, the *General Agreement on Tariffs and Trade (GATT)*, in 1995. The GATT provided agreements binding on its member countries. There have been eight negotiating "rounds" since the GATT was established in 1947. There is no doubt that the GATT has been a major contributor to world prosperity, having liberalized trade over the past 45 years. For food and agriculture, however, the GATT has been much less successful. A former GATT director general is quoted as saying (in 1985): "Agriculture has been virtually excluded and insulated from the processes of trade liberalization. Unlike industrial products, the attempts to liberalize agricultural trade have remained ineffective."

Until the Uruguay Round, there were two clauses in the agreement that impacted specifically on agricultural products: Article XI, which allowed quantitative restrictions on agricultural imports, and Article XVI, which allowed subsidized agricultural exports as long as the exporting country stayed within its equitable share of trade. The first of these was, in fact, somewhat restrictive on importing countries, restrictive enough that the United States, in 1955, obtained a "temporary" waiver, which was still in place nearly 40 years later! This example illustrates agriculture's general situation in the GATT. There were so many official and unofficial violations of the rules that the GATT administration seemed to have given up. Furthermore, countries that might challenge violations because they are obviously injured by them tend to be smaller countries, such as New Zealand, that have a lot to lose if the offending country (such as the United States) chooses to retaliate.

The latest negotiating round of the GATT was completed in December 1993, seven years after it was launched in Punta del Este, Uruguay. The negotiations took so long mainly because agriculture was seriously on the agenda for the first time. Prior to the beginning of the round, fourteen food-exporting countries established the Cairns Group to represent their interest. In 1987 the United States tabled a plan to scrap all farm subsidies, but it backed down in 1989. A ministerial meeting in December 1990 that was supposed to conclude the round foundered over agriculture. In general, the strongest opponents to reducing agricultural subsidies were the European Union (in particular, France) while the strongest proponents were the Cairns Group (generally smaller countries, such as Australia and Thailand). In the end, there were significant benefits for agricultural trade—a reduction in the subsidization of exports, substitution of tariffs for nontariff barriers, and a planned reduction in tariffs over six years.

These changes are expected to lead to increases in prices for agricultural products of 10 to 20 percent. The new body, the World Trade Organization (WTO), oversees the implementation of the Uruguay Round agreements and provides a forum for future negotiations and the settlement of disputes. If the reforms are implemented as planned, the big winners will be the Cairns Group; the biggest losers in the short term will be developing countries paying more for food imports (in the longer term, the increase in world prices will encourage food production in developing countries). A cynical observer of GATT history might say to wait and see if the anticipated benefits come about.

Free Trade Areas

The GATT includes nearly all the major trading countries. Smaller trade agreements such as the North American Free Trade Area (NAFTA) include fewer countries, usually in a defined geographical region. Which is the best? The answer to this question is not obvious. Some of the arguments for both viewpoints are:[7]

For Free Trade Areas (FTAs):

- FTAs can move faster than the GATT, because they have fewer members.
- FTAs can force economies to become more efficient.
- Until the Uruguay Round, the GATT had achieved very little for agriculture. There have, however, been some recognizable achievements within FTAs.

For Multilateral Trading Arrangements (MTAs):

- The GATT still provides the best way to work toward global free trade.
- FTAs can be highjacked by political considerations (for example, the Common Agricultural Policy of the European Union).
- FTAs lead to complex administrative systems—for example, in terms of determining a product's country of origin when it may include components from several FTA members, as well as imports from outside the regional trading arrangement.
- FTAs are especially unsuitable for agricultural trade.

(As for the GATT, agriculture has usually been excluded from regional trading blocs, the European Union being a notable exception.)

In general, small countries benefit most from MTAs, because they lack power in bilateral negotiations with larger trading partners (and negotiations with countries of a similar size do not provide access to important markets). On the other hand, a large powerful country such as the United States can use its negotiating strength to force change in a bilateral relationship (for example, with Japan).

Implications for Food Marketing

The discussion in this chapter has focused mainly on agricultural producers, the suppliers of raw materials at the beginning of the food system. This is partly

---

[7]C. Goodloe and T. Rainey, "Trading Blocs: Pro or Con for Agriculture," *Choices* (Second Quarter 1992): 26.

because agricultural policies are oriented toward farmers, not toward food manufacturers, retailers, or consumers, and partly because the economists who have researched this area address the issue in terms of aggregate product categories such
as "dairy products," which may include anything from commodity milk powders to
aerosol cream in retail packs. Discussion at this level of aggregation is not very useful for understanding the behavior of food processors and retailers.

Forecasts of the impact of trade liberalization can go awry because of this aggregation problem. For example, analysts of the Japanese beef market overesti-
mated the impact of the more liberal import policy implemented in 1991, because
they did not take into account the quality differences (as perceived by Japanese buyers) between imported and locally produced beef. Furthermore, most imported beef
is consumed at some type of restaurant where the cost of meat is only 15 to 20 percent of the cost of the meal. So, even if the full cost of a beef price reduction of
(say) 20 percent was handed on to consumers, this would mean a meal price reduction of only 3 to 4 percent, hardly enough to change consumption very much.[8]
Even if there are no discernible differences between an imported and a locally produced product, consumers may still have a strong preference for the local, as is the
case with rice in Japan—their consumers not only want Japanese rice, they want it
to come from the area of the country that they, their relatives, or their ancestors
came from.

Food processors seek: a) access to cheap raw materials, and b) as little competition as possible in their product market. In trade-policy terms, this is achieved in a
particular country when there is no tariff on raw materials and a high tariff on the
final product. The other variables determining the economics of food manufacturing in any country are: raw-material cost as a proportion of total manufacturing
costs, costs other than raw materials (such as labor), and the existence of substitute
products. If raw materials represent a small proportion of the cost of the finished
good and there are no close substitutes for it, the processor is able to raise prices in
response to raw-material price increases without affecting sales or profitability very
much. If all manufacturers buy their raw materials in the same market, they should
be able to collectively hand these price increases on to consumers with only small
impact on sales volume.

Impact of Trade Barriers Depends on Stage of Processing   The application of
these principles can, in practice, be quite complicated. For example, the Indonesian
government wishes to encourage the development of local milk production, both
for nutritional reasons and to provide a source of income for smallholder farmers.
Milk-processing plants are also required. Local processors are also helped by high
tariffs and import quotas on any fully processed milk products. However, local raw
milk production is insufficient for the needs of Indonesia's expanding and increasingly affluent population. Therefore, imported dairy raw materials are needed to
produce reconstituted milk. This source of raw materials is much cheaper than locally produced milk, giving the milk-processing companies high profits on this part

---

[8]D. Chadee and H. Mori, "The Japanese Beef Market in Transition," *Choices* (Fourth Quarter 1993): 32.

of their operation. The Indonesian government takes some of this profit by imposing a tariff on raw materials and, at the same time, encouraging the processors to buy local milk by limiting their raw-material imports to a specific ratio of their local milk purchases. Multinational dairy companies, such as Nestlé, can make a profit whatever the Indonesian government may do—as processors of local milk and as importers of both raw materials and processed-milk products.

In general, tariff rates are higher for finished goods than for raw materials, encouraging local manufacturing. If a government wants to protect local raw-material suppliers, it must also provide protection in the finished-goods market. The worst situation for a food manufacturer is where there is intense competition in either the local or export market, combined with high raw-material costs resulting from distortions in the input market. Canadian food manufacturers faced increased competition from U.S. suppliers with the establishment of the U.S./Canada Free Trade Agreement, but also had higher input costs due to Canadian agricultural policy.[9]

Response by Food Companies to Trade Barriers   Globally oriented food companies can operate profitably in a variety of environments, either manufacturing locally or supplying from other countries as cost and tariff structures dictate. The sugar market is the most controlled of all the major food commodity markets, but multinational sugar manufacturers such as the English company, Tate and Lyle, are able to operate profitably in most parts of the world, using either beet or cane as a raw material. Nestlé is to be found in most countries where there is a dairy industry, adjusting their raw-material sourcing, manufacturing, and sales strategy in line with local government policy. Perhaps it is the flexibility of such companies that makes them relatively relaxed about protectionist agricultural policies.[10]

Think Break

Barriers to trade in food and food products have certainly increased over the past 30 years. There is, however, some evidence that this situation is changing. Do you think the world has reached a turning point; is it now on a new trend of declining agricultural protectionism?

SUMMARY

Although food's share of world production and trade is relatively small and most countries are largely self-sufficient in basic food products, international trade in food and agricultural products is of great importance to agricultural producers and food manufacturers. Trade provides benefits in terms of increasing

---

[9]C. Goodloe and T. Rainey, "Trading Blocs: Pro or Con for Agriculture," *Choices* (Second Quarter 1992): 26.

[10]William Schroder, Tim Wallace, and Felix Mavondo, "Cooperatives, Statutory Marketing Organizations and Global Business Strategy," *Agribusiness: An International Journal* 9.2 (1993): 175.

world production by international specialization, encouraging more efficient industries through international competition and giving consumers more choice.

Introducing trade between two countries usually has the impact of lowering
prices and increasing consumption in the importing country and increasing prices
and production in the exporting country.

A basic difference between trade within a country and trade between countries
is that each country has its own currency. The exchange rate is the value of a currency expressed in terms of units of another currency (for example yen per U.S.
dollar). Exchange rates are determined by the demand for a country's exports, its
imports, the demand for services such as tourism, and capital movements in and
out of a country. Generally, an appreciating exchange rate discourages exports,
because currency appreciation increases the price to the overseas buyer and/or decreases the price received by the exporter. A currency depreciation has the opposite effect. However, the exports of countries such as Japan and Germany have
continued to grow despite substantial increases in the value of these two countries' currencies.

The main food-consuming countries of the world are also the main producers.
That is, most countries are self-sufficient in basic food products. A relatively small
share of food production is traded internationally. Food trade in agricultural raw
materials is dominated by the United States, while the European Union leads in
processed foods.

Changes in food consumption can be explained by changes in population and income. This model shows that the newly industrializing countries of Asia will be the
main markets for imported food in the future.

Overt barriers to food trade are tariffs and quotas. Less obvious, but probably
more important, are health and phytosanitary restrictions and subsidies and other
forms of assistance given to agricultural producers in the "rich" countries of the
world, such as the European Union, United States, and Japan. Tariffs, quotas, and
other assistance measures can be combined to give an aggregate measure of assistance, the producer subsidy equivalent.

Agricultural policy objectives include: price stability, regularity and security of
food supply, nutrition, reasonable prices to consumers, productivity and technical
efficiency in agricultural production, balance of payments, and environmental objectives. The weighting given to these objectives differs between countries, but, for
a given set of objectives, it is important that the agricultural policy measures used
are a cost-effective way of achieving them. The most-used forms of assistance are
price-support measures. It is easy to demonstrate that price support is not a cost-
effective way of providing income assistance to poor farmers, because most such
assistance, in fact, goes to rich farmers. Farm-input suppliers and food processors
and distributors can also benefit from protectionist measures and will form political coalitions with agricultural producers.

Barriers to trade between countries can be reduced by free trade agreements and
customs unions and through multilateral agencies such as the GATT/WTO. The
most recent GATT negotiating round has yielded significant benefits for agricultural trading countries.

Global food processors such as Nestlé can manage trade protectionism to their advantage through flexibility in sourcing raw materials, in the location of their manufacturing activities, and in distribution of finished products.

IMPORTANT TERMS AND CONCEPTS

basic and advanced factors   223
customs union   241
economic union   241
exchange rate   226
export surplus   231
factor abundance   220
factors of production   220
free trade area   240
General Agreement on Tariffs and Trade (GATT)   242

political union   241
producer subsidy equivalents   235
quota   233
self-sufficiency ratio   230
tariff   232
variable levy   232
World Trade Organization (WTO)   242

QUESTIONS

1 How can a country overcome being "poor" in basic factors such as climate and natural resources?

2 Describe the effect of trade to producers of an exporting country and consumers of an importing country. Should consumers of an exporting country be concerned about trade?

3 What major factors influence exchange rates?

4 Why have industrial market economies become self-sufficient food producers and net exporters of most foods?

5 In recent years, an increasing share of world agricultural exports is consumer-oriented (value-added) products. Is the United States participating in this trend?

6 Describe the difference between a quota and a tariff.

7 What was the overall effect on agriculture of the GATT Uruguay Round of negotiations?

8 Discuss various types of trade agreements that are not as comprehensive as GATT. What are their relative advantages and disadvantages, compared to GATT?

9 Does a more liberal or open trade policy always result in more trade? Why or why not?

10 How do multinational food companies deal with the environment of "less than completely" free trade around the world?

REFERENCES AND RESOURCES

"Agriculture: The New Corn Laws." *The Economist* December 12, 1992: AS7.

Carter, C. A., A. F. McCalla, and J. A. Sharples, eds. *Imperfect Competition and Political Economy: The New Trade Theory in Agricultural Trade Research.* Boulder, CO: Westview Press, 1990.

Chadee, D., and Mori, H. "The Japanese Beef Market in Transition." *Choices* (Fourth Quarter 1993): 32.

Dolinsky, Diane. *Desk Reference Guide to Agricultural Trade.* Agricultural Handbook No. 683. Washington, D.C.: U.S. Department of Agriculture, revised April 1994.

Goodloe, C., and T. Raney. "Trading Blocs: Pro or Con for Agriculture." *Choices* (Second Quarter 1992): 26.

Halcrow, H. G. *Agricultural Policy Analysis.* New York: McGraw-Hill, 1984.

Legg, Wilfrid. "Direct Payments for Farmers." *The OECD Observer* 185 (December 1993/January 1994): 26–28.

Medium-term Prospects for Agricultural Commodities: Agricultural Projections to 2000. FAO, 1993.

McCalla, A. F., and T. E. Josling. *Agricultural Policies and World Markets.* New York: Macmillan, 1985.

Mellor, J. W., and R. H. Adams. "The New Political Economy of Food and Agricultural Development." *Food Policy,* November 1986: 289–297.

Ohmae, K., *The Borderless World.* London: William Collins and Co., 1990.

Porter, M. *The Competitive Advantage of Nations.* New York: The Free Press, 1990.

Schroder, W., T. Wallace, and F. Mavondo. "Cooperatives, Statutory Marketing Organizations, and Global Business Strategy." *Agribusiness: An International Journal* 9.2 (1993): 175–187.

Tweeten, L. T. *Agricultural Trade: Principles and Policies.* Boulder, CO: Westview Press, 1992.

Tyers, R., and K. Anderson. *Disarray in World Food Markets: A Quantitative Assessment.* Cambridge: Cambridge UP, 1992.

Internet Sources

University of Texas's Latin America general information menu for USAID, economic and social data on Caribbean and Latin American countries, regional maps, and other information: http://lanic.utexas.edu/la/region.html

International travel information, including planning aids, tip sheets, and links to other pertinent Web sites: http:nearnet.gnn.com/gnn/meta/travel/index.html

PART FOUR

COMMODITY MARKETING
MANAGEMENT

The management of the marketing of raw materials and unbranded food products

Three types of food marketing were identified in the previous chapters—consumer, industrial, and commodity. Industrial marketing management is in Chapter 7, and the marketing of branded food products will be considered in Part Five. Basic to the Food System is commodity marketing, which provides raw materials and undifferentiated food products.

Controlling product quality by grading is studied in Chapter 10, along with a discussion and evaluation of such pricing mechanisms as auction markets, individual negotiation, and bargaining cooperatives. Chapter 11 describes the operation of futures markets, their role in determining the price of commodities, and the use of the market to manage the risk of changes in prices in the future.

10

COMMODITY GRADING SYSTEMS AND PRICING MECHANISMS

CHAPTER OUTLINE

LEARNING OBJECTIVES

After reading this chapter and answering the questions in the Think Breaks and at the end of the chapter, you should be able to:

- Understand the purposes of commodity grading systems.
- Evaluate commodity grading systems on their objectivity, cost effectiveness, and measurement of factors important to end users.
- Differentiate between intrinsic factors and other physical factors that are used in determining a commodity grade.
- Appreciate the importance of adjusting grading systems to allow for changing consumer preferences and agricultural production technology.
- Understand how seller and buyer arrive at price under the six different pricing mechanisms.
- Identify and discuss the main issues in the establishment and success of agricultural producer price bargaining groups.
- Discuss the criteria by which pricing system performance can be evaluated.
- Compare and contrast the performance of the six pricing methods, using the criteria discussed.

INTRODUCTION

In Chapter 1, commodities are defined as raw materials that are not branded or differentiated by supplier. Since commodity suppliers are "price takers," the elasticity of demand facing an individual supplier of a commodity product is infinite: that is, the supplier can sell any quantity at the established (market) price, but can sell nothing at all at any price above this (see Chapter 2). Commodity suppliers are, however, increasingly seeking to tailor their products to the needs of buyers, thus moving them out of the commodity category into the category of industrial products (discussed in Chapter 7).

Because raw materials needed by the food system come in various qualities, owing to differences in variety, cultural practices, and the impacts of weather and disease, grading systems are used to determine the quality and value of commodities. Grading systems should be judged on how well they meet the needs of the buyer and, ultimately, of the consumer. Commodities should be objectively measured, and the grading system cost effective. Problems encountered in established grading systems, particularly when changing consumer tastes render them ineffective, are explored.

Placing a particular lot of a commodity in its appropriate slot in a standardized grading system is only one part of the process of marketing that commodity; the other component is determination of the price the producer will get for a wheat crop, lettuce, or beef cattle. The second half of this chapter will explore the various pricing mechanisms that are found at the farm level, review the recent trends in methods of price discovery—the process by which buyers and sellers arrive at a specific price—and evaluate the different pricing mechanisms on several performance criteria.

COMMODITY GRADING AND STANDARDIZATION

The following definition of *grading* will be used: "the sorting of a product into quality classifications according to standards that are agreed upon by the industry."[1] *Quality* also has a particular meaning in commodity grading: it refers to the attributes of a commodity that influence its acceptability to a group of buyers, and, therefore, the price they are willing to pay for it. It is important to understand that quality in this definition does not mean whether something is good, better, and best, but rather is synonymous with "characteristic," which is actually Webster's Dictionary's first definition of quality. For example, a potato-chip processor has different quality requirements than a packer of fresh-market potatoes. The chip processor is concerned with the specific gravity of the potato, because that attribute determines the crispness of the chip. The fresh-market packer is not concerned about specific gravity but is concerned about the outside appearances of the potato and whether it is appealing in the supermarket produce section.

The Purpose of Grading Systems

The purpose of grading is to have identifiable standards of quality so that prices can be established for each grade. Without grading, the price received by a supplier will: a) be some sort of average across quality attributes, limiting the ability of the marketing system to signal price/quality relationships to producers, and b) be discounted by the buyer because the quality is unpredictable. As will be discussed in Chapter 11, the grade is one of the defining characteristics of a futures contract. Stating the minimum quality that can be delivered by sellers who enter into a futures contract standardizes one of the major variables influencing price.

[1]V. James Rhodes, *The Agricultural Marketing System,* 4th ed. (Scottsdale, AZ: Gorsuch Scarisbrick, Pub., 1993): 222.

Another advantage of grades is that with them commodities can be *sold on description.* In procurement activities, buyers can compare grades and prices at several different locations and do not have to personally inspect each lot to determine its worth or value.[2] In this respect, grading systems improve pricing efficiency, because with the product descriptors, communication and competition is improved. A buyer of wheat, for example, can compare price offers from Canada, Australia, and the United States, knowing how much end product—flour—will result from milling a tonne (1,000 kg) of wheat and what that flour can be used for: baking bread, which requires high-protein and higher-quality flour; or manufacturing noodles and crackers, which use a flour of lower protein (gluten) content.

Although grades facilitate the trading of commodities by description, it must be noted that in many commodities personal inspection and approval of lots *(buying on actuals)* still plays a large role in food marketing. For example, in perishable marketing, grades and/or shipper labels are used to differentiate various qualities. However, buyers often employ "bird-dogs," who go out in the field as the produce is being harvested and packed in cartons, to inspect the quality of the pack and whether it meets their buying specifications. In coffee, important quality distinctions can only be uncovered by personally inspecting a lot and by taking a sample that is roasted and brewed into a cup of coffee. It is then tasted for off-flavors, bitterness, and to determine whether that particular lot has the qualities wanted by a specialty gourmet roaster or should be relegated to the manufacture of generic brands of instant coffee.

Setting Up and Evaluating Grading Systems

Grades for commodities can be set by government departments or agencies, agricultural producer boards, trade organizations, processor groups, or a consortium of several of these groups. Which group sets a product's grades depends on the strengths of these various organizations, the homogeneity or variety of its end-users, and the political concerns of the governments involved.

New Zealand's Meat Producers' Board sets its standards for beef and lamb, while in the United States, the grading of meat is under the auspices of a USDA Agricultural Marketing Service division, the Federal Marketing and Inspection Service (FMIS). Within one country, different organizations may set the grades for different products; for example, in addition to meats, FMIS sets grades for fruits, poultry, dairy products, and nonfood commodities, such as cotton, tobacco, and naval stores (turpentine), while the USDA's Federal Grain and Inspection Service (FGIS) administers grading programs for grain, rice, beans, and lentils. Figure 10-1 shows USDA graders at work.

Internationally there are often several grading systems for one type of product, especially when government agencies are involved. The standards for meat cuts may also vary a great deal, because they are based on traditional methods of

---

[2]George L. Mehren, "The Function of Grades in an Affluent, Standardized-Quality Economy," *Journal of Farm Economics* (December 1961): 1377–83.

FIGURE 10-1   Grading poultry at Perdue plant in Accomack, Virginia. Over 75 percent of the poultry produced in the United States is graded by the USDA. Along with the grades, most poultry producers, such as Perdue, market a differentiated product in extensive branded-product programs. *(Source: U.S. Department of Agriculture.)*

cutting a carcass. However, when an international consortium of processors or producers has set the grades, these grades are usually internationally recognized as the standard for the product.

Certain criteria are used both in establishing grades and in evaluating a grading system; these are discussed in the next sections.

Accepting the Marketing Concept in Grading   Grades based on production types may not reflect the material's *intrinsic value* to the buyer, but realities of agricultural production must also be recognized—there is no point in having grades which farmers cannot produce. When a wide variety of buyers use a raw material, only the most significant uses may be reflected. Also, grade standards can be, and often are, revised to reflect shifts in consumer preference, product evolution, or new measurement techniques. Of course, if grade standards are changed too frequently, price/quality signals to producers and traders may become confused. With any change, extensive education on the reasons for it is required.

In determining grade standards and administering a grading system, the basic principle should be the Marketing Concept. It makes no difference what agricultural producers believe a "quality" product is or is not. The question is what the buyer of the product expects and wants from it. Disregard of this concept occurs on a regular basis. At a conference on peanut production and marketing, one speaker made the following observation, "If one were to criticize any part of your impressive program, it would be to note a major omission. Only one of your 120 presentations mentions the final judge of our product. I would like to make amends for this and tell you something about that person who makes all our occupations and investments possible—the consumer."[3] Ross goes on to explain that manufacturers and importers are concerned about excessive foreign material, size inconsistency, and the need to provide a reliable, consistent product. Of particular concern is aflatoxin, a mold that is dangerous to animal and human health. Higher levels are allowed in the United States than in many countries of the world, and in some, no measurable aflatoxin is allowed.

Grading Must Be Cost Effective   Because of the time and costs involved, only a few properties can be tested. Grading systems must be cost effective. Because the sampling of lots and grading procedures are repeated over many lots at various locations, grading procedures must be fast and must utilize cost-effective technology. (The cost of setting up the system and conducting the grading, which occurs in the plant or on the production line, must be added to the price of the product.)

Grading is repeated thousands of times in an industry. In the meat industry each carcass is inspected and graded, and an Instrument Grading System (IGS) must be able to perform on-line in a commercial packing facility. For example, the time required per carcass for on-line scanning allows for a speed of about 100 carcasses per hour. Also, it only requires a few hours of training for an on-line scanning technician to perform accurate and consistent evaluations. Any IGS system adopted by the industry must perform similarly. Many times grading is done in environments that are hot, dusty, or may in some other way adversely affect the accuracy or longevity of testing equipment. This, and the fact that grading is often done at thousands of locations, means that testing equipment must be relatively inexpensive and reliable under a variety of conditions. The early moisture meters for use in grain had difficulties in consistency and reliability under normal use at grain elevators.

Identifying the Physical, Chemical, or Sensory Characteristics Important to the User   Too often, commodity grading standards are not adjusted to reflect the end-use value of the commodity. For example, the grade standards in soybeans include bushel weight, foreign material, and other physical properties. While oil and protein content of soybeans were identified as important characteristics for indicating value as early as 1925, and by 1954 the USDA had developed a quick method of determining the oil and protein content of soybeans, this measure of intrinsic value

---

[3]Douglas T. Ross, "Peanut Quality: The Needs of International Users," in *Peanut Quality: Its Assurance and Maintenance from the Farm to End-Product,* Agricultural Experiment Station Bulletin 874 (technical) (Gainesville: University of Florida, July 1986): 55–60.

was never incorporated in the U.S. grain standards.[4] In wheat, a similar problem has been partially corrected. In 1978, the USDA established an official test of protein as part of its inspection responsibilities. This information is not a part of the grade; however, it can be entered on the inspection certificate upon request.

Hill, in his book *Grain Grades and Standards,* is quite critical of U.S. grain standards, where few grade factors measure the physical and chemical properties that are most important in terms of the products for which the grain is to be used: flour from wheat; feed, starch, or oil from corn; oil and meal from soybeans. Quoting Hill, "Many of the factors in the current standards describe physical and biological characteristics of the grain, but fail to provide information about the yield of intermediate or final products made from it after processing. For example, the relevance of test weight (weight per bushel, which varies since the bushel is a measure of volume), is a grade-determining factor that has been questioned repeatedly since it was first introduced into the corn standards in 1916."[5]

Objectivity in Measuring Characteristics   In the past, experts depended on their eyes, nose, and hands, but today chemical, physical, or microbiological testing is used where possible. If only sensory testing is available, trained sensory-testing panels are used instead of single experts.

Objectivity is desired in grading, just as it is in the refereeing of a football or basketball contest—inconsistency in calling fouls interferes with determining which team really is superior. Grades help determine the value of a commodity, and consistency is important because end users, whether industrial or consumer, don't like rude surprises—like a tough steak when they thought they had purchased a piece of meat that should be tender. The importance of following a set procedure in an effort to achieve consistency in grading is demonstrated in Box 10-1, "Peanut Grading Is Not Peanuts."

Another problem in grading is that often the method of ascertaining quality is applied subjectively. For example, under the current U.S. beef grading system, the measured traits to determine whether a carcass grades USDA Choice or Select (or some other grade) are: the distribution and amount of intramuscular fat (or marbling), the subcutaneous fat thickness, and the rib-eye muscle size. The amount of marbling is determined visually by certified inspectors who compare the amount of marbling to USDA standards. Errors can be made in the judgment call as to whether the marbling percentage is sufficient for a carcass to grade Choice (the most popular grade of beef) or Select, the grade level below Choice. Also, there have been instances of bribery and fraud in beef grading; presumably, instrument grading would help eliminate these problems.

Subjectivity and errors that are made in assessing carcass value have resulted in the beef industry calling for the development of an instrument to replace the visual assessment. A prototype *Instrument Grading System (IGS)* has been developed by researchers at Iowa State University, using ultrasound technology to evaluate the intramuscular fat percentage. The IGS results were correlated against actual fat

[4]Lowell D. Hill, *Grain Grades and Standards* (Urbana: University of Illinois Press, 1990): 287.
[5]*Ibid.:* 289–90.

BOX 10-1

PEANUT GRADING IS NOT PEANUTS

The US Department of Agriculture's Agricultural Marketing Service (AMS) administers the peanut grading program for US peanuts. In order to achieve uniform peanut grading among all the states, the AMS standardizes the grading procedures used by state inspection services. The AMS also provides training, licensing and federal supervision for the inspectors. Domestic peanuts are graded at least twice by the inspection service—first, when the peanuts have been delivered to the sheller (handler), where they are referred to as "farmers' stock" peanuts, meaning they have not been shelled. They are again inspected as "milled" peanuts after going through the milling process of sizing, cleaning, and removing shells for lots shipped as shelled peanuts.

The procedure for grading farmers stock peanuts is specific by the AMS. The following is a brief summary of the procedure used by the state inspection services.

Sampling Procedure: Take a sample from the lot. If in bags, use the prescribed hand sampling procedure. If the peanuts are in bulk, use the pneumatic sampler or the spout sampler. Subdivide the sample to about 1800 grams with a sample divider.

Whole Nut Inspection: Separate foreign material (FM) and shelled kernels (LSK) from the sample. Determine the % FM and % LSK based on the total weight of the sample. Pass a 500 gram subsample of the pods through the presizer. Shell the subsample in the sampler

sheller and determine the % hulls based on the weight of the subsample.

Kernel Inspection: Measure the % moisture in the shelled kernels with an approved moisture meter. Use the mechanical screen shaker to screen the sample of kernels over a grading screen with $16/_{64} \times 3/_4$-inch openings. Divide the material that fell through the grading screen into splits (kernel cotyledons and broken pieces of kernel that are between $3/_4$ and $1/_4$ of a kernel) and other kernels (small whole kernels and small pieces of kernels). Pick out the splits that rode the screen and combine them with the appropriate group of splits that passed through the screen. Calculate the % sound splits; % other kernels (OK); % damage splits, % concealed RMD, % freeze damage, % total damage, % sound, mature kernels (% SMK), and total % kernels. Enter these data on inspection certificate.

Mold Inspection: Examine all kernels from the kernel inspection for visible *A. flavus* mold growth and use a microscope to confirm the identification of mold that appears to be *A. flavus*. If *A. flavus* growth is found at this point or in earlier inspections, indicate it on the inspection certificate.

Source: James W. Dickens, and Ligon W. Johnson, "Peanut Grading and Quality Evaluation," in *Peanut Quality: Its Assurance and Maintenance from Farm to End-Product*, by Esam M. Ahmed and Harold E. Pattee, eds., Bulletin 874 (technical), Agricultural Experiment Station, University of Florida, Gainesville, July 1987.

---

content, as determined by laboratory chemical tests, and found to have a high degree of correlation. Further expansion of the IGS system to determine the quality factors other than marbling, so that a completely *objective measure* of retail value may be obtained as the carcass moves through the slaughtering facility, is planned.[6] Research similar to the Iowa State work is also being conducted at the University of Illinois and at other research institutions around the world.

Meaningful Divisions—Not Too Many, Not Too Few Grades   The number of grades should correspond to the number of quality categories buyers feel are important. The proliferation of grade categories has been a concern in many industries. A few years ago the olive industry examined their size designations and found

---

[6]Viren Amin, et al., "Computerized Ultrasound System for On-line Evaluation of Intramuscular Percentage Fat in *Longissimus dorsi* Muscle at a Commercial Packing Facility," in *1995 Beef Research Report*, AS-630 (Ames: Iowa State University, January 1995): 19–23.

that the nomenclature for various size designations was not consistent. For example, Jumbo and Extra Large were being used for the same olive size category. Also, an excessive number of size categories were being packed. (How many different sizes of olive does the consumer need?)

In the early days of grain grading, the number of different grades was so great that it made them virtually meaningless. A 1906 study of the grain trade showed 133 names or grade titles for wheat, 63 for corn, 77 for oats, and 53 for barley. In addition, there were dozens of terms, such as "moderate, reasonably, fit, strictly, sufficiently, enough, limited," that required subjective value judgments by inspectors?[7] When considering the number of grade categories, the major concerns should be: does the buyer want and need the various grade categories? Is there a different end use and/or value for each product category?

Think Break

Select one of the following commodity groups with which you are familiar and, using the performance criteria, evaluate how well the grading system for that commodity performs. The commodity groups are: grains, livestock and meats, fresh fruits and vegetables, and tropical crops, such as coffee, sugar, and cocoa.

Verifying Grading Systems

If a commodity is not graded by a governmental agency but by the producing company, its grading system must be subject to outside review, or the system's validity and value in the market may be questioned. There are several ways in which a grading system can be verified: by government inspectors or graders, such as the USDA; by official body inspectors—for example, the Meat Producers' Board; by an official or industry-recognized testing organization; or by the company's quality assurance staff, either under government or official supervision or in a recognized Total Quality Management system.

The trend in many countries today is toward company, rather than government, inspection. Company inspection systems which are integrated into Total Quality Management systems may be verified by the appropriate government agency or by quality auditors either for the internationally accepted ISO standards or for specific industry standards. ISO standards are widely accepted in certain areas of the world, such as the European Community, and internationally for some raw materials (see Chapter 7 for more detail).

Independent laboratories used for testing should also be officially recognized, either by government agencies or by a laboratory certification authority. Countries exporting materials must ascertain whether results from laboratories in their own country will be recognized as valid in the destination countries.

---

[7]C. Louise Phillips, *History of Grain Inspection in the United States, 1838–1936* (Washington, DC: USDA, 1936) and C. W. Kitchen, "Standardization and Inspection of Farm Products," *Yearbook of Agriculture, 1940* (Washington, DC: USDA, 1940), as quoted in Hill: 44.

There are two aspects to verification of a grading system—technical and commercial. Technically, the system should:

- Sample the product correctly
- Measure the product characteristics within the parameters of the grades
- Be consistent over time
- Have control mechanisms for checking the system and for dealing with variations.

Commercially, grading system costs should not be more than the product can stand, and the grades and their measurement should be acceptable to the buyer.

PROBLEMS WITH GRADING SYSTEMS

Failed Grading Systems

The Australian beef industry has undertaken a major revamping of its grading system. The system previously in place was described as follows by an industry official: "The beef industry has failed to describe its product to our customers so that eating quality is easily identified . . . for many years the Australian beef industry has fudged the issue of identifying eating quality to our customers."[8] The new grading system employs technology similar to that of the IGS program previously described, in an effort to achieve objective measurement that consistently meets customer and consumer needs. The examples discussed underscore the all-encompassing principle that all grading systems must reflect consumer demands, or the industry will sooner or later find demand for their product dwindling.

In one test of applesauce, Cornell University put USDA grades to a consumer test. Taste-testing eight different applesauces that USDA inspectors had graded, 652 people tasted all eight and registered their preferences. The results of the study were that most people preferred the two applesauces graded USDA Grade C.[9] Evidently, in determining applesauce grade standards, someone forgot to ask consumers what they want in applesauce.

In California, for decades peaches had been graded under the auspices of a state marketing order, where policies were set by a board of directors made up of both producers and processors. From the perspective of Tri Valley Growers (TVG), a fruit and vegetable canning cooperative, the problems with the old grading system were many. They included variability in applying grade standards from grade station to grade station; a compromise on maturity standards which resulted in delivery of too-green peaches, and not meeting consumer needs. The canning-peach grading system was failing the industry on at least two criteria: objectivity and determining intrinsic value. Besides being inconsistent, it did not provide producers incentives to deliver what consumers wanted.

[8]Kevin Roberts, "Producing to meet the Market," *Outlook 96 Conference* (Canberra, Aus.: Australian Bureau of Agricultural Research and Economics, February 1996): 225–31.
[9]*Perspectives on Federal Retail Food Grading,* Office of Technology Assessment (Washington, D.C.: U.S. Congress, June 1977): 37.

Because of all these problems, TVG opted out of the state's grading system and in its place developed grade standards and a grading system that would be managed by an independent third party under contract. According to the president of TVG, "These changes will give growers the incentive to produce higher-quality products and provide TVG with greater control over the consistency of the product we supply customers."[10]

The Political Economy of Grading

Grading systems vary from country to country and change over time. The fact that grading does not occur in a vacuum but responds to the current cultural and political environment is illustrated by the following discussion of the beef grading system in the United States.

The U.S. beef grading system and changes to it have been at the center of a controversy for the past several decades. Established in the 1920s, beef grading was voluntary and originally was instituted to differentiate between lower-quality grass-fed beef and higher-quality—that is, more highly marbled—grain-fed animals. However, by 1940, less than 8 percent of all beef was graded, which indicates that only a small proportion of beef was high quality. In the twenty years following World War II, the demand for beef increased dramatically as incomes rose and large-scale cattle feeding operations were developed. The U.S. Choice grade became the one preferred by retailers; the grade was identified by consumers as one in which they could have confidence that the product would be tender and juicy.[11]

Over the years, beef grading standards have been changed so that the carcass requires less fat to grade Choice. The most recent change was in 1975, when the amount of marbling required for an "A"-maturity (less than 30-month-old) carcass to grade Choice was lowered. This change was made after considerable consumer research by the beef industry, which clearly demonstrated that tenderness, juiciness, and flavor of meat from this age category of animal did not depend on the extra marbling and fat that the existing standards required. The change was controversial; consumer groups brought suit in Federal Court, claiming that as a result, consumers buying the new Choice grade would receive a product that was inferior to the old. After the legal challenges to the USDA's move were defeated in court, the change finally went into effect in 1976.

Another effort was made in the early 1980s to further reduce marbling requirements because consumers said that they wanted less fat, but that change was defeated by consumer and other groups down the marketing channel from the producer. Beef grading became more a political battle than a scientifically based procedure. Studies by Texas A&M University researchers concluded that further reducing the marbling requirements would result in less excess fat being produced,

---

[10]"TVG Raises Grading Standards," *California Farmer* (February 1996): 41.
[11]V. James Rhodes: 232–34.

but because changing beef grades is a political minefield, the industry (producers) is not going to propose or argue for the change.[12]

A major challenge in the beef industry is to produce a high-quality carcass (flavorful and tender, with low amounts of fat) that is at the same time high-yielding (producing a large percentage of salable product to total carcass weight). Yield grades (YG) measure the leanness of the carcass, because the yield of retail cuts is largely a function of the amount of fat. Yield grades are numbered 1 to 5, with 5 being the poorest. An industry study estimates that 97.4 pounds of fat are trimmed from each carcass to produce boxed-beef (the primal cuts that are vacuum packed at the processing facility and shipped to wholesalers, food service, and retailers) with $\frac{1}{4}$-inch fat-trim specifications. If all YG 5 and YG 4 carcasses are eliminated from this calculation, the amount falls to 91.8 pounds, and if YG 3's could be eliminated, the average amount of fat trimmed would fall to 81.9 pounds. Retailers point out that excess fat costs them about $70 per head, and the salvage value of fat for rendering is just a few cents per pound.

While excess fat is an important problem in beef marketing, another problem is insufficient muscling in many carcasses. The *National Beef Quality Audit* observes that while Yield Grading does take into account some muscling differences, the current US marketing system isn't structured to identify categorical differences in muscle-to-bone ratio. Nevertheless, muscling has a substantial indirect influence on value via its effect on live-animal and carcass weight, dressing percentage, muscle-to-bone ratio, marbling score, and rib-eye/loin-eye size."[13]

The conclusions of the *National Beef Quality Audit* support the use of USDA grade standards to determine beef value and to provide incentives for producers to grow a product that meets consumers' needs. However, many of the quality concerns in Table 10-1, expressed by industry experts, are not being addressed by the current grading system. Specifically, the *Audit* recommends changes to the current grading system that: 1) identify rib-eyes that are too large or too small and carcass weights that are too heavy or too light; 2) change pricing logic from the present

---

[12]Jeff W. Savell, "Value-based Marketing of Beef," Paper presented at the Farmland Industries, Inc., University Advisory Board Meeting, Kansas City, MO, July 22, 1993.
[13]*National Beef Quality Audit—Executive Summary* (Englewood, CO: National Cattlemen's Association, 1992): 14–17.

TABLE 10-1   "QUALITY" CONCERNS VOICED AT U.S. BEEF QUALITY AUDIT WORKSHOP, 1995

1. Low overall uniformity and consistency	6. Excessive weights of cuts and boxes of cuts
2. Low overall palatability	7. Too high incidence of injection-site lesions
3. Insufficient marbling	8. Price too high for quality received
4. Inadequate tenderness	9. Excessive live and carcass weights
5. Excessive external, seam, and beef-trim fat	10. Too frequent hide problems

Source: National Beef Quality Audit—1995 (Englewood, CO: National Cattlemen's Beef Association, 1995): 8. Reprinted with permission.

"dressing percentage" (untrimmed carcass weight divided by live weight times 100) to a new "red meat yield" (weight of carcass trimmed to quarter-inch fat-trim divided by live weight times 100). How fast the industry moves to adopt these and other recommendations is a function not only of the political economy external to the industry (consumer groups and government) but also of the industry's internal political economy among competing interests thoughout the marketing channel— producer, packer, purveyor (wholesaler), food service, and retailer. Grades are only one part, but a significant part, of the puzzle as to how competitive beef will be in the race against poultry and pork for the consumer's meat budget.

COMMODITY PRICING MECHANISMS

The manner in which a commodity price is set is as important as grading in determining the returns that a producer receives. The various methods of price discovery can be categorized as follows:[14]

• *Negotiation between individuals or firms.* Sometimes referred to as decentralized individual negotiation (DIN), this method is commonly used in direct marketing, where buyer and seller consummate the transaction without using an intermediary.

• *Auction markets or organized exchanges.* Most auctions are cash or physical-delivery markets, with buyers, sellers, and products present. Futures markets, on the other hand, are price-discovery but not physical-delivery markets (Chapter 11).

• *Electronic markets,* where products are not brought into a single location, such as a livestock auction yard, but are described and portrayed visually through videotapes and other long-distance communication devices, such as telephones and computer terminals.

• *Formula pricing,* by which a mathematical formula relates the transaction price to one or more indicators of value.

• *Collective bargaining* between producers and processors, where often a bargaining cooperative is established as the means for producers to achieve group action.

• *Administered pricing,* which is typified by government price support programs.

Price-discovery methods differ by commodity and within a commodity by country. Most fruits and vegetables in the United States are priced by individual negotiation. That is, a packer/shipper has a sales desk where lettuce is sold by telephone to retail chains, terminal market buyers, and anyone else who wants to buy lettuce. Each sale can involve negotiation as to price and other terms of the sale. Outside the United States, perishable fruits and vegetables are often priced by auction at a regional market or large urban center terminal market, such as in New Zealand and Scandinavia.

In many commodities, the pricing system may be thought of as a mixed system. A farmer who sells grain to a local elevator may contact two or three potential buyers and may bargain and negotiate to some extent. But the prices that the various

---

[14]William G. Tomek and Kenneth L. Robinson, *Agricultural Product Prices,* 3d ed. (Ithaca, NY: Cornell University Press, 1990): 200.

elevators offer are based on futures-markets prices, which are auction prices. In fact, grain pricing in this instance includes a bit of formula pricing, as the cash price at the local elevator is the futures auction price adjusted by the basis (discussed in Chapter 11).

In some sectors, different pricing systems are used for the various products in an industry. In beef marketing, auction markets are the major method used by cow-calf operators when selling their 450-pound weaners that are going to another owner for further weight gain. However, for animals going to the packing plant, 1,100-pound Choice steers, auction marketing is rarely used; the price at the feedlot is the futures price, adjusted by basis, and the animals are marketed direct, much the same as in grain pricing.

Think Break

> *For the following commodity products in your country, state, or region, define the price-discovery mechanism that is in place.*
>
> - *Milk*
> - *Fresh vegetables*
> - *Grains*
> - *Livestock—beef and pork*
> - *Eggs*
> - *Fruits for freezing, canning, and drying*
>
> *If possible, also tell whether the mechanism has been in place for some time and whether it is currently undergoing change and modification.*

Individual Negotiation

Around the world, millions of prices are established by private negotiation between the buyer and seller. Mid-East bazaars, the new "free markets" of the Former Soviet Union countries that are more like flea markets, and the open markets in many cities of the world, such as Victoria Market in Melbourne, Australia, are all examples of private treaty markets. Negotiating for price has an appeal to some people who have skill in bargaining and trading. For others, the whole process is distasteful and gives rise to pricing alternatives, such as the "no-haggle" automobile pricing which is becoming increasingly popular in the United States.

The advantages of *individual negotiation* are that there is no "up-front" cost to the method—that is, there is no auction house or other intermediary to be paid—and that it can be done anywhere. The two parties can be thousands of miles apart, as in perishables marketing, and conduct business. While there may not be an up-front cost for the farmer, there is the cost of time involved. To a farmer in many developing countries this cost may be little if there are few alternative uses of labor and the half-day spent in a market or bazaar also has a social aspect—an offset that cannot be quantified by the economist.

One disadvantage of individual negotiation is that the farmer often has incomplete knowledge of marketing alternatives. This key point needs emphasis—in order for individual negotiation to be efficient, obtaining a "fair" price for the producer, market information as to alternatives and prices is necessary. Also, producers may lack negotiation skills if they have not studied the available body of knowledge about effective negotiation.

Auction Markets and Exchanges

The essence of both auctions and exchanges is that competitive bidding is used to establish the price. In an auction, only buyers bid, sellers are passive; in an exchange, both buyers and sellers participate in the bidding process. Bidding may be carried out by assembling the buyers and sellers in one location, or they may bid by telephone or computer.

Because of their openness and the bidding process, auctions and exchanges are described as the most "efficient" by economists. Efficiency in this context means that the price arrived at is the correct price for that quality and quantity of a product at that moment in time.

Auction markets can adopt various procedures: in a Dutch auction, the price is started above the expected sales price and it is then lowered until a buyer accepts. This process is used extensively in Canada and Europe. Compared to the English auction, the Dutch auction is faster but often results in a less efficient and lower price. The English auction is most common in the United States, where bidding is started at a lower level and then incrementally increased (the Latin root of auction, *auctus,* comes from the verb *augere,* "to increase"). Other auction systems exist around the world; for example, the Japanese fish markets require all bidders to submit single bids for the lot being sold at the same time, on the auctioneer's signal. Sales are concluded almost instantly upon going up for bid. Sealed-bid auctions are sometimes used for large transactions where considerable effort goes into determining the bid or offer.[15]

Auction markets bring all the supply and demand together at one location and, through an open and competitive process, arrive at the price. Another advantage of auctions is that price can be determined for a wide range of qualities, since each lot is priced separately and often is physically inspected by buyers. (Inspection takes place before and during Australian cattle auctions, as seen in Figure 10-2). For this reason, auction markets are popular for sales of wine, feeder cattle, and especially breeding stock, where, because of bloodlines and performance, one animal that looks just like the one next to it can be worth thousands of dollars more or less. The major disadvantage of most auction systems is that the product has to be physically taken to the auction location, whereas transportation costs would most probably be much less if the animal or product went directly from the seller's location to the buyer's. If buyers and sellers have enough confidence in the grading/appraisal

---

[15]Bruce W. Marion, *The Organization and Performance of the US Food System* (Lexington, MA: Lexington Books, 1986): 69–70.

FIGURE 10-2   Livestock auction, Eastern Victoria, Australia. Auction pricing and marketing is still popular in some sectors of the livestock industry. A competitive price is arrived at through the auction process, but one disadvantage is its relatively high cost, compared to other pricing methods. *(Courtesy of William Weitkamp.)*

system, auctions can be conducted without the physical presence of the product being sold; bidding is based on a description of each lot in the auction catalog.

In an exchange, both buyers and sellers bid. Futures (discussed in the next chapter) and stocks and shares are traded in exchanges. Like an auction, an exchange can be operated either by assembling the buyers and sellers in one location or electronically (or both, as in the case of the Sydney Futures Exchange, which operates on a face-to-face basis during the day and uses a computer network (Sycom) the rest of the time).

Electronic Markets

The first commercially successful *electronic trading* system in North America was launched by the Ontario Pork Producers Marketing Board in 1962. While the Ontario system has flourished, similar systems were tried and eventually abandoned in several other Canadian provinces. Other efforts in eggs and lamb have met with partial success. In Australia, Computer Assisted Livestock Marketing (CALM) was established in the 1970s.

The major premise behind electronic marketing is that the pricing efficiency that results from using large-volume central terminal markets can be combined with the technical efficiency of direct marketing (individual negotiation), where the product moves directly from the seller's location to the buyer's. Generally, pricing in electronic markets is through some type of auction or exchange.[16] (The electronic video market process for cattle is described in Box 10-2.)

Studies of electronic markets, both experimental and commercial, have found that in comparison with individual negotiation, direct markets, and some physical auction markets, electronic marketing results in: 1) enhanced competition among rival buyers, 2) greater availability and accuracy of market information, and 3) improved market access for geographically remote and smaller traders. As a result, electronic marketing achieves more efficient prices and reduces monopolistic price distortion. A key requirement of electronic marketing is that buyers are confident that the information available to them in the auction catalog, possibly supported by a video, is sufficient, without their having to actually see, feel, or smell the product.

The cost per unit marketed under electronic trading has generally been high; electronic marketing needs greater volume in order to be competitive with direct marketing. As communication technology evolves and becomes more flexible, and at the same time less expensive, electronic markets may find new cost-effective applications in commodity marketing.

Formula Pricing

In a *formula-pricing* system, the price for any given transaction is established on the basis of a mathematical formula that relates the transaction price to one or more other indicators of value. Milk is an excellent example of a commodity for which farm-level prices are determined by a formula. In California, the formula consists of the price of manufactured milk as established by the federal milk price support program, adjusted for the cost of feed and other production inputs in California, and finally, the Consumer Price Index. In essence, the California milk price is a function of the price in competitive producing states, the costs to produce the product, and how much inflation food prices have been experiencing. Another example is egg prices, which are generally formulated relative to the Urner Barry quote, a figure that is published daily and recognized as the reference price in most of the United States. Also, carcass beef prices quoted in the *National Provisioner* (often called the Yellow Sheet) are frequently referred to in formulas.

A major issue in formula pricing is whether the published price, which is used as a base, is really representative of the market. If the published price is based on one or two auction markets that account for only a small proportion of total sales (a "thin market"), the prices arrived at do not really represent the equilibrium price that would be determined under the true supply/demand situation. Also, thin-market prices are more susceptible to manipulation, and sometimes these markets are markets of last resort for sellers as well as for buyers. Sellers may use them as a dumping ground for temporary surpluses, or chain-store buyers may use them

---

[16]Marion: 80–82.

ELECTRONIC MARKETING IN BEEF—SATELLITE VIDEO MARKETING

In recent years, video cattle auctions have grown in popularity. The photos below portray part of this process. For the video auction presentation, the animals are filmed in their natural surroundings and are also described in a sales catalog as to breed type, weight, number of head, frame size and condition, feeding program, weighing conditions, and health program.

The video is edited for the auction; on the day of the auction, buyers bid either from the auction site or by telephone from any location where a satellite transmission can be received. All buyers must register in advance of the sales and undergo a credit check to participate.

Cattle are sold F.O.B. (free on board) the seller's ranch or F.O.B. a nearby scale. This makes transportation the responsibility of the buyer, who can adjust bidding accordingly. A video auction representative oversees the sorting and delivery of the cattle onto the buyer's truck. At delivery, the seller is issued a check that has been drawn on the auction company's bonded custodial account.

Advantages of the video auction are that overall trucking costs are reduced and that generally more buyers participate in this type of auction than in traditional regional physical delivery auctions, such as those in Oklahoma City, Oklahoma, Greeley, Colorado, and Dodge City, Kansas. Bypassing the auction lots, the animals reach buyers less stressed and with reduced exposure to disease or infection. Also, buyers are offered larger lot sizes and are given more information about the animals, such as their vaccination history.

Source: Dee Von Bailey, "Video Auctions are Viable Marketing Alternatives for Cattle," *Cattle Producer's Library,* CL815, Utah State University Cooperative Extension System, 2d ed. reprint, July 1995; and Superior Livestock Auction, Fort Worth, TX.

Photos Courtesy of: Superior Livestock Auction, Fort Worth, TX.

only to source supplies when produce from other sources, bought directly through individual negotiation, is insufficient for their needs.[17]

When a large firm buys or sells a large percentage of its volume on a formula-priced basis, a thin cash market may provide an environment in which relatively small shifts in that firm's cash buying or selling activity can influence prices in its favor. Thin markets also hamper such firms if they have relatively large positions in a market and then find that the lack of market liquidity makes it difficult to adjust to a new supply/demand situation—their exit from a cash or futures position has a disastrous effect on the market price. These types of illiquid market situations magnify price volatility and render market participants vulnerable to exploitation.

Collective Bargaining

Bargaining cooperatives provide agricultural producers greater power by enabling them to take collective rather than individual action. They are different from marketing cooperatives, described in Chapter 6, in that although they usually take title to their members' produce in order to represent them in negotiations, bargaining cooperatives do not process, warehouse, or otherwise handle the physical product. The unique characteristics of agricultural production that give rise to problems (and sometimes, opportunities) in designing and managing agricultural producer organizations are:

- Agricultural producers are usually small, numerous, and geographically dispersed.
- Because they are small, agricultural producers have limited expertise beyond managing their farming operation.
- Agricultural production can be unpredictable and seasonal.
- Agricultural products are often perishable.

The first characteristic increases the cost of collective behavior. The second means that farmers face problems when they try to extend their expertise into processing and marketing. The last two make the management of any collective processing and marketing activity more difficult, although perishability can be a positive motivation for establishing a processing and bargaining cooperative, so as to better coordinate production with market needs.

In a bargaining association, producers combine to negotiate with processors and/or distributors regarding prices and other terms of sale. In the United States, bargaining cooperatives can be formed by producers under the auspices of the Capper-Volstead Act, which allows agricultural producers to join together for collective action without violating federal antitrust statutes. Consider a producer bargaining group supplying a raw material—for example, peas—to a processing company. A variety of factors are associated with the success of such a group:

- **The proportion of pea production controlled by the grower group.** Bargaining associations must control a substantial proportion of production. While there is no

---

[17]Tomek and Robinson: 204–5.

magic amount that must be controlled in order for a bargaining association to be effective, in general it can be said that controlling at least 50 percent of total production—ideally, 75 percent or more—will give it power in negotiations. Support of enabling legislation establishing the group as the recognized negotiating body is a major benefit in promoting the effectiveness of bargaining efforts. Such legislation may control "free riding" by requiring all growers to become members. However, in the United States, with few exceptions (such as the 1973 Michigan Marketing and Bargaining Act, which applies to perishable fruits and vegetables), there is no legal sanction for exclusive agency bargaining. In other words, bargaining is a voluntary activity, and with its voluntary nature comes the problem of "free riders," those producers who do not join and contribute to the association but reap the benefits.

• **The ability of the group to control the quantity of peas produced by group members.** This control depends mainly on the availability and profitability of alternative crops for the growers and on the cost of switching from peas to one of these alternatives, but also on several other factors: group cohesiveness; the geographic dispersion of producers; similarity of producers in terms of size, enterprise, and mix; and the social bonds between producers. Bargaining is generally more successful in commodities that are produced in a relatively small geographical area; peaches for canning in California and red tart cherries in Michigan are examples.

The most famous effort in farmer bargaining was led by Aaron Sapiro in the years following World War I. Sapiro's efforts in convincing farmers to withhold grain and livestock from the market in order to raise prices soon collapsed. Despite so-called "iron-clad" contracts requiring members to market through the association, they left when nonmembers benefited more from the cooperative's action than they did. Nonmembers continued to sell and received higher prices because the cooperative was withholding product from the market, while members received little or nothing, since their product was not being sold.[18]

• **Price elasticity of demand for the processed product.** If the retail demand for frozen peas is inelastic (increasing the retail price does not decrease sales very much), then the processor can add a raw-material price increase onto the price of processed peas without significantly affecting sales. Also important is whether the processor has alternative sources of peas—perhaps in another growing region where producers have fewer crop alternatives and different costs of production. It is also helpful if the bargaining organization offers real benefits to the processor, such as quality control, scheduling, or reducing the costs and uncertainty involved in procuring raw product.

Think Break

Think of an agricultural production situation with which you are familiar. The producers are thinking of establishing a bargaining group to negotiate with processors. Considering the above discussion of factors that influence the success of bargaining efforts, do you think the group will succeed?

---

[18]Tomek and Robinson: 207–10.

Administered Prices

With this pricing method the seller establishes a nonnegotiable price in advance of the sale. Since individual farmers fit the model of pure competition, they rarely, if ever, have the opportunity to control or administer prices. In general, in order for a firm to administer prices, it needs to have a differentiated product; that is (from the Chapter 2 discussion), the individual firm must face a demand curve that is not perfectly elastic. Of course, even firms that market a differentiated product have limited power over the range within which they can price. If suppliers attempt price "gouging," buyers will go to competitors, substitute products will be developed, or new firms will enter the industry.

There have been instances of governmentally *administered prices* in the food system. During times of war, price ceilings were placed on basic food foodstuffs, and during the 1970s, price ceilings were imposed in the United States in an attempt (unsuccessful, by the way) to control inflation. Agricultural subsidy programs that try to control production, establishing floor prices for commodities as part of the program, may be thought of as a system of administered prices. Of course, the Soviet Union's economic system of dictating what should be produced, when, and with what inputs, was an example of administered prices for a total economy. The collapse of that system was largely due to the ineffectiveness of administered prices in organizing the economy and providing for consumer needs and wants.

EVALUATING PRICING MECHANISMS

The criteria or dimensions by which the various pricing systems can be evaluated are transaction costs, access to market information, equity or fairness, and price stability. For example, the desire to minimize *transaction costs* has been a major force for change in the marketing of agricultural commodities. Transaction costs include the cost of searching for alternatives, the costs added because of the uncertainty of exchange, and the costs associated with the physical exchange. For example, with increases in transportation costs, direct marketing utilizing individual negotiation became more popular than auction markets.

For individual negotiation to work, the producer must have *access* to market information and to the various selling alternatives. This makes market information a vital public good and leads governments to take a major role in reporting price and other market intelligence for agricultural products. However, some information has costs associated with it that a small producer may not be able to afford, or which may not be accessible to the individual.

In one study of southeastern U.S. hog packing plants, it was found that the price the producer received was established by formulas which varied by packing plant. Various factors are used in the formulas, such as premiums for back fat less than 25 mm, yield of the carcass compared to live weight, and weight within the desired range of 172 and 194 pounds. Only about half of the plants publish the details of their pricing system, and even with the information, it would be difficult for most producers to make the comparison without a computer. Many packing plants, which use direct negotiation, prefer to discuss their pricing program privately with each producer, thus denying producers easy access to the market information necessary to make a reasoned choice among available marketing alternatives.[19]

Also of concern is whether the pricing system is *equitable.* This equity can be viewed in the sense of equal treatment of all system participants to the extent that they can deliver equal performance. Differences in quality, location, and timing must be recognized by the pricing system. Also, equity requires that rewards and penalties be assigned to those who have control over the product attributes involved. For example, contracts that place production practices or harvesting under the control of the buyer and then penalize the grower for problems caused by the buyer are considered inequitable.[20] In these situations, a bargaining association may be helpful to producers who, individually, are fragmented and powerless to affect price and terms of sale in negotiating with processors, who are few and have greater market power and information.

In some contract situations, producers are paid a fee per unit produced which is not related to the price of the raw product. In Australia, broiler producers are paid a per-bird growing fee, which is derived from the target figure for a producer's salary plus return on investment in the land, buildings, and equipment to grow the birds. In the state of Victoria, the contractual agreement between processors and growers is under the authority of the Victorian Broiler Industry Committee (VBINC). The VBINC often employs an outside expert to analyze the costs and returns to growers and recommend a particular growing fee. As might be expected, the issue of equity is at the core of these discussions. What is a fair salary for growers? What percent return on investment should be used in the calculations? What is the investment required to produce a given number of chickens per year? The list of questions goes on and on.[21]

Regarding pricing systems, *price stability,* particularly the question whether the auction market of the futures markets adds to price volatility unnecessarily, is an issue. It must be recognized that the nature of commodity prices is one of instability—weather, political action (such as the Gulf War), and other factors make for markets that are continuously searching for an equilibrium price that will succeed in allocating or rationing supplies efficiently among competing uses. Various studies, including the often-cited examples of onion futures, have examined the futures markets' ability to "unduly contribute to price volatility." Onion futures were traded for many years, and then Congress banned their trading. The various studies of onion price behavior with and without futures-contract trading demonstrated that, if anything, onion price volatility increased after they ceased being traded. Other studies in soybeans failed to demonstrate any connection between futures and increased price volatility.

Table 10-2 summarizes the six price discovery systems as evaluated by the performance criteria.

---

[19]David Kenyon, John McKissick, and Kelly Zering, "A Comparison of Carcass Value Pricing Systems of Southeast Hog Plants," *NCR-134 Conference Applied Commodity Price Analysis, Forecasting, and Market Risk Management,* Chicago, IL, April 24–25, 1995; 215–32.

[20]Marion: 65–66.

[21]"Chicken Meat Group Eatmore Branch," conference proceedings, VBINC Decision 1994, Branch Meeting, September 9, 1994.

TABLE 10-2   PRICING METHODS RANKED BY PERFORMANCE CRITERIA

Method	Equity	Transaction costs	Access	Price
Auction— Physical Product at Location	High	High	Medium (geographically isolated producers)	Low
Electronic Marketing	High	Medium to High	High (may be limited for small producers)	Low
Decentralized Individual Negotiation	Variable (need market information)	Low	High (may be limited for small producers)	Low
Formula Pricing	Variable (depends on age of formula)	Low	High	Variable
Bargaining	Medium to High (depends on effectiveness)	Low	Medium to High	Medium (viewed as more stable than under individual negotiation)
Administered Governmental Pricing	Variable	High (plus poor resource allocation)	Variable	High

Agricultural producers base production decisions on priceexpectations, which, in turn, tend to be based mainly on current prices. Thus, if current prices are high, producers usually expect them to remain so and increase plantings accordingly. The result is an oversupply in the next season with correspondingly low prices (signaling producers to reduce production). This results in both price and production instability.[22] One goal of government and private sources in providing market information is to allow producers to make the production adjustments necessary to prevent either excessive production, and the waste that accompanies it, or shortages, which result in less than optimum consumer satisfaction.

If price stability is a prime goal of the pricing system, then government involvement is often invoked. For example, it has been determined that it is in society's best interest to have plentiful supplies of and stable prices for milk. The advantages accrue to both the supply side—dairymen, who have large fixed investments in milking barns and facilities with no alternative use, and to the demand side—consumers who enjoy reasonably priced, readily available milk. Shortages and high prices can be tolerated in discretionary diet items—artichokes, plums, and Alaska king crab, as examples—but not for staple products (thus society, through its

---

[22]This phenomenon has been called the "Cobweb theorem" by agricultural economists because the supply/demand graph traces a cobweb over time.

elected representatives, has said). However, along with this price stability have come periods of overproduction and surpluses, a major disadvantage of governmentally administered price systems.

Clearly no single pricing system ranks high on all criteria. Auction markets competitively arrive at a market clearing price but generate high transaction costs. Individually negotiated pricing, popular because of its efficiency, often is not equitable. Bargaining can redress the inequities due to an imbalance of power; however, owing to the voluntary nature of bargaining and other limitations, only a small proportion of agricultural production is priced through bargaining. Price volatility is inherent in agricultural commodities; greater price stability can be achieved through governmentally regulated prices, but at the expense of inefficient resource allocation.

SUMMARY

This chapter addresses two major areas of study in commodity marketing: 1) grading and standardization and 2) price-discovery mechanisms. Commodity grading is necessary, since the raw products that are produced on farms and fisheries come in various qualities, owing to differences in variety, growing practices followed, and the impacts of weather and disease. These variations in quality dictate the optimum end use, and hence the value, of commodities.

The two important concepts are *grading*—the sorting of a product into quality classifications according to standards that are agreed upon by the industry, and *quality*—the attributes of a commodity that influence its acceptability to a group of buyers, and, therefore, the price they are willing to pay for it. Two important functions of grades are: 1) to establish the price for a commodity, and 2) to facilitate the sale of commodities on description, so that the buyer does not have to physically inspect samples from each lot purchased.

Too often, grading systems have not measured the real value of the commodity to the end user, whether that end user is a consumer or an industrial buyer, such as a food processor, manufacturer, wholesaler, retailer, or food service institution. For this reason, many industrial buyers have established their own quality standards and in effect set up their own grading systems, bypassing those established by government or producers. Objectivity helps ensure that the graded product is of consistent quality and that the grading process is conducted fairly. It is through grades that value is determined, producers are paid equitably, and end users obtain a product from which they can expect a certain level of performance.

Another important criterion in grading systems is that the system must reflect the Marketing Concept in determining quality. Quality is the package of attributes important to the consumer, not necessarily what producers believe quality is about. Other criteria include the need for grading systems to be cost effective, and also to have not too many grade categories, so that the system does not become unnecessarily complicated and confusing. It is important that a grading system meets these various criteria, or the end result may be that competitive products or competing countries take market share away from an industry.

Commodity pricing at the farm and first handler levels can be accomplished in a number of ways: physical auction markets, electronic markets that may utilize auction or other means of price discovery, direct negotiation between seller and buyer, formula pricing, collective bargaining, and government-administered pricing.

Pricing mechanisms differ by commodity and vary around the world. Direct negotiation has become the primary method of price discovery for perishable fruits and vegetables in the United States, while in many other countries auction markets are used. Within a commodity, such as beef, different market sectors may employ different pricing methods: auctions, physical and electronic, for calves coming off ranches; direct negotiation for animals purchased by packing houses from feedlots.

Individual negotiation has become the major commodity pricing system in the United States because it is less expensive. It does not involve the transaction cost, or commission, charged by physical assembly markets such as auction markets. Also, transportation costs are often lower with direct negotiation, as the commodity goes directly from the seller's location to the buyer's, bypassing the intermediate auction location. However, for direct negotiation to result in an efficient and "fair" price to the producer, market information is a necessity. Electronic markets, which can combine the best aspects of auction and direct marketing, have become popular for marketing cattle and hogs in the United States.

Other types of pricing are used exclusively in some industries. For example, formula pricing, which is sometimes also tied to government-administered schemes, is used for milk products. Formula pricing is more common in industries that have become or are becoming industrialized (Chapter 6), such as poultry and pork. An issue in formula pricing is whether the published price, which is used as a base, is really representative of the market.

In some commodities—processing tomatoes, cherries, and other processing crops—bargaining associations have been established. These associations provide producers greater market power in negotating price and terms of sales with processors in oligopsonic industries (having few buyers) and in sectors of the food system where the general trend is toward fewer and larger firms.

Pricing mechanisms can be evaluated on at least four criteria: transaction costs, producer access, equity or fairness, and price stability. Although none of the systems scores high on all of these criteria, it is clear that the advantages of individual negotiation have made it the most common pricing mechanism in the United States.

IMPORTANT TERMS AND CONCEPTS

CASE STUDY: An Example of U.S. Grade Standards—Wheat[23]

PROBLEM: Wheat is not a homogeneous product. The U.S. produces five major classes of wheat and a large number of genetic varieties within each class. Each class and variety has different end-use characteristics. These wheat varieties are grown across the U.S. under a large number of growing conditions, introducing additional variations in their end-use properties. Wheat quality can be described as having three dimensions: (1) physical condition, including purity and soundness, (2) intrinsic characteristics, and (3) uniformity shown in the figure below. Each of these characteristics affects wheat's performance in terms of its processing and end-use properties.

[23]Bendt T. Hyberg et al., *Economic Implications of Cleaning Wheat in the United States,* Agricultural Economic Report No. 669 (Washington, D.C.: USDA, December 1993): 4–6.

Wheat quality dimensions. *Source:* Hyberg et al., as adapted from the National Wheat Improvement Committee.

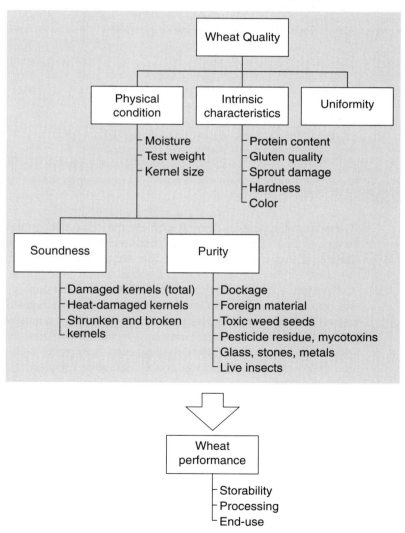

Test weight and moisture content are also indicative of soundness because test weight suggests likely milling yields and the moisture content affects wheat's storability. Damaged kernels are correlated with lower test weight and lower milling yields.

OFFICIAL U.S. DEPARTMENT OF AGRICULTURE GRADES AND STANDARDS FOR WHEAT

			Maximum limits of:						
			Defects					Wheat of other classes[1]	
Grades[2]	Hard red spring wheat or white club wheat[3]	All other classes	Heat-damaged kernels	Damaged kernels (total)[4]	Foreign material	Shrunken & broken kernels	Defects (total)[5]	Contracting classes	Wheat of other classes (total)[6]
	Pounds		Percent						
1	58.0	60.0	0.2	2.0	0.4	3.0	3.0	1.0	3.0
2	57.0	58.0	0.2	4.0	0.7	5.0	5.0	2.0	3.0
3	55.0	56.0	0.5	7.0	1.3	8.0	8.0	3.0	10.0
4	53.0	54.0	1.0	10.0	3.0	12.0	12.0	10.0	10.0
5	50.0	51.0	3.0	15.0	5.0	20.0	20.0	10.0	10.0

[1]Unclassed wheat of any grade may contain not more than 10 percent of wheat of other classes.
[2]There is a limit of 31 insect-damaged kernels per 100 grams.
[3]These requirements also apply when hard red spring wheat or white club predominates in a sample of mixed wheat.
[4]Includes heat-damaged kernels.
[5]Defects included damaged kernels (total), foreign material, and shrunken and broken kernels. The sum of these three factors may not exceed the limit for defects for each numerical grade.
[6]Includes contrasting class.

Intrinsic characteristics are the biochemical and structural properties inherent in the product. Important intrinsic characteristics for wheat include protein content, gluten quality, hardness, color, fat acidity, crude fiber, and ash. Measuring these intrinsic characteristics of wheat can be difficult and time consuming.

Uniformity refers to the degree of variation in wheat quality, either physical or intrinsic, within a shipment and between shipments. Fine materials in bulk grain naturally segregate during shipment by gravitating to the bottom middle of the grain vessel. When discharged, the entire cargo is rarely reblended into separate sublots for each buyer. Lack of uniformity frequently is a source of disputes, because wheat in a shipment can be shared by several different buyers. Variation in wheat quality between shipments can cause disruption to buyers' milling operations.

Complicating matters even further is the fact that wheat's end uses are diverse: bread, crackers, pasta, and animal feed. Each of these uses requires wheat with a specific set of end-use characteristics. The ultimate test of wheat quality for each use lies in its performance in manufacturing the final product. Flour used to make bread, for example, requires hard wheat with a high protein content, whereas wheat flour used to make crackers or cakes must have less protein, which is available from soft wheat. Baking properties of flour could be affected by gluten qualities even when the protein content is the same.

Questions

Evaluate the U.S. wheat grading system on the following points:

1 Is the system objective? That is, can the various measures be repeated with consistent results?
2 Does the grading system measure the quality attributes important to various end users?
3 Does the system appear to be cost effective?

QUESTIONS

1 Define *quality* as the word is used in commodity grading, and relate it to the definition of the Marketing Concept.
2 Put yourself in the position of a consultant who has been asked to evaluate the grading system for a fresh fruit, say kiwifruit or grapefruit. How would you proceed in conducting the analysis and in making your evaluation?
3 Beef grading has undergone a number of revisions over the years. What forces have prompted these revisions? What are the various difficulties encountered by an industry when changes to a grading system are proposed?
4 In what different ways can the objectivity criteria be applied to a grading system? If you were a meat buyer for a large supermarket chain, why would you be concerned about objectivity in the meat grading system?
5 List and briefly describe the various pricing mechanisms that are used in determining farm-level prices.
6 The transaction costs for producers using direct marketing through individual negotiation are lower than at physical auction markets. However, to obtain a "fair" price under this system, producers must possess two key ingredients or factors. What are they?
7 What are the relative advantages of electronic markets compared to physical auction markets?
8 Define a "thin market." What problems are associated with thin markets, particularly with regard to formula pricing?
9 What are the performance criteria by which pricing mechanisms can be evaluated?
10 What pricing system ranks best when evaluated by the criteria in the previous question? What system generally performs worst?

REFERENCES AND RESOURCES

Ahmed, Esam M., and Harold E. Pattee, eds. *Peanut Quality—Its Assurance and Maintenance from the Farm to End-Product.* Bulletin 874 (Technical). Gainesville: University of Florida Agricultural Experiment Station, July 1987.

Amin, Viren, et al. "Computerized Ultrasound System for On-line Evaluation of Intramuscular Percentage Fat in *Longissimus dorsi* Muscle at a Commercial Packing Facility." *1995 Beef Research Report—Iowa State University.* No. AS-630. Ames: Iowa State University, January 1995: 19–23.

Executive Summary—National Beef Quality Audit. Englewood, CO: National Cattlemen's Association, 1992.

Hill, Lowell D. *Grain Grades and Standards.* Urbana, IL: University of Illinois Press, 1990.

Hyberg, Bengt T., et al. *Economic Implications of Cleaning Wheat in the United States.* Agricultural Economic Report No. 669. Washington, D.C.: U.S. Department of Agriculture, December 1993.

Kenney, M. C. "Commodity Grades Help Consumers." *National Food Review* 27. Washington, DC: U.S. Department of Agriculture, Commodity Economics Division, Economic Research Service, 1984: 1–3.

Kenyon, David, John McKissick, and Kelly Zering. "A Comparison of Carcass Value Pricing Systems of Southeast Hog Plants." *NCR-134 Conference Applied Commodity Price Analysis, Forecasting, and Market Risk Management.* Stillwater, OK: Department of Agricultural Economics, Oklahoma State University (1995): 215–32.

Marion, Bruce W. *The Organization and Performance of the US Food System.* Lexington, MA: Lexington Books, 1986.

Mehren, George L. "The Function of Grades in an Affluent Standardized-Quality Economy." *Journal of Farm Economics* 5 (December 1961): 1377–87.

Perspectives on Federal Retail Food Grading. Washington, D.C.: Congress of the United States, Office of Technology Assessment, June 1977.

Tomek, William G., and Kenneth L. Robinson. *Agricultural Product Prices.* 3d ed. Ithaca, NY: Cornell University Press, 1990.

Roberts, Kevin. "Producing to Meet the Market." *Outlook 96 Conference.* Canberra, Aus.: Australian Bureau Agricultural and Resource Economics (February 1996): 225–31.

Savell, Jeff W. "Value-based Marketing of Beef." Paper presented at Farmland Industries, Inc., University Advisory Board Meeting. Kansas City, MO, July 1993.

11

COMMODITY PRICE RISK AND THE FUTURES MARKETS

CHAPTER OUTLINE

LEARNING OBJECTIVES

After reading this chapter and answering the questions in the Think Breaks and at the end of the chapter, you should be able to:

- Understand the types of risk in the production and marketing of commodities and the various methods of managing these risks.
- Appreciate the role of futures markets in commodity price discovery and price risk management.
- Understand the motives of speculators and hedgers in trading futures contracts.
- Take a position in the market and calculate profits and losses upon roundturning.
- Explain the difference between volume and open interest and how open interest is created.
- Explain the factors that determine the basis of a storable commodity, such as wheat, and how the basis of cattle is different from that of a storable commodity.
- Understand when a market is inverted and what the supply-demand conditions are that result in an inverted market.
- Differentiate between owner and needer hedgers and what each is attempting to achieve by hedging.
- Execute a short hedge utilizing the concept of localization, as used by an agricultural producer.
- Understand the mechanics of a buying or long hedge as used by a grain exporter or by a processor who is buying product for future requirements.

INTRODUCTION

Agriculture is a risky business. If you don't believe it, just ask any farmer or anyone else involved in the agricultural production end of commodity marketing.

Will the weather cooperate this year? What will the government do to help or hurt marketing opportunities? What kind of demand will there be for the crop, and how much will be produced around the world to compete for that demand? What kind of transportation will be available when the crop needs to move to market, and what will it cost?

The main types of risks facing a commodity supplier or buyer are:

- physical risks associated with unpredicted variations in yield and quality
- financial risks: credit risk, exchange-rate risks (discussed in Chapter 9), and interest-rate risk.
- price risks

The common feature associated with all three types of risk is our inability to predict the future 100 percent accurately. Risk occurs because managers make decisions today and the results of these decisions happen in the future. This chapter introduces risk-management principles and discusses in detail the management of price risk using the futures markets and a technique known as hedging.[1]

RISK-MANAGEMENT PRINCIPLES

Investors, boards of directors, company management, and family businesses have one thing in common—they want maximum financial return for minimum risk—but there is always a tradeoff between these two objectives. The basic idea underlying *risk management* is this risk/return tradeoff. Some managers are more risk averse than others, and risk management must take into account the decision maker's attitude toward risk. For example, farmers can take out cash forward contracts on their grain crops and "lock in" a known price, or they can wait and sell in the cash market, because they believe they can get a better price this way. Forward contracts (Chapter 6) are less risky than selling in the cash market; therefore, the farmer might be willing to accept a contract price that is lower than the forecast cash price as a tradeoff for the reduced risk. The ways of managing the three main types of risk are introduced below.

Physical Risks

Risks associated with unpredictable variations in quantity and quality are important for agricultural producers. In a country with wide variation in rainfall, such as Australia, or in the western part of the U.S. grain belt, wheat yields can vary from season to season by over 100 percent. Processors also face physical risks: variations in quality and deterioration of raw materials or finished product in storage. There are few external mechanisms for managing such risks. Insurance is available for major losses, but the main ways of reducing physical risks are internal to the firm—

---

[1]Options, traded on underlying futures contracts, will be described only briefly in this chapter, owing to space limitations. They are a different but important tool that can be used in risk management. One succinct reference explaining options is *Commodity Marketing* by Keith Schap, listed in this chapter's references.

diversifying the mix of enterprises, better management practices, and better quality control.

Financial Risks

Credit risks occur because the seller relinquishes control of the product before payment is received. For some overseas transactions, it may be three months between shipment of the product and receipt of payment. Banks will take over credit risks in international transactions, guaranteeing payment on arrival of shipments through letters of credit at a cost to the exporter—reducing risk is never free. Managers can also carry out credit checks on buyers. Of course, the best way of reducing credit risk is not to give credit, but credit terms may be essential to make the sale.

Interest costs occur in any business, because costs are incurred before revenue is received. The risk is that interest rates will rise over the "cash-to-cash" cycle. Exchange-rate risks arise in international transactions, for the reasons outlined in Chapter 9; an increase in the exchange rate disadvantages exporters, commodities being more disadvantaged than branded products. Again, banks provide ways of reducing these types of financial risk—for example, forward contracts that fix the interest or exchange rate for a specified period. Futures and options on interest and exchange rates are also available.

Price Risks

Buyers and sellers of commodities are particularly vulnerable to price risks because, as discussed in Chapter 2, they are price takers. Also, commodity prices can change sharply, even on a day-to-day basis.

Participants in commodity markets can be owners or needers: *owners* hold inventory of the product (for example, a grain elevator at the end of harvest), or they expect to hold inventory (a farmer prior to harvest). Owners run the risk that prices will fall. Alternatively, processors need commodities in the future; or traders may not hold stocks at the time they make commitments to supply product under fixed-price forward contracts but expect to purchase sufficient product to meet the contracts (such arrangements are common in commodity trading). These participants, *needers,* face the risk that the price will rise in the cash market.

A common way of managing position risk is to forward contract. Owners sell forward—a contract for future delivery at a known price; needers buy forward—a contract to take delivery at a specified date and price. For a merchant trader, such as Cargill or Continental Grain, risk is minimized when buying and selling contracts are "back to back"; that is, timing, grade, and price are aligned. Hedging, using futures, is a special type of forward contract that is discussed in detail later in this chapter.

Risk management is important for all participants in the food marketing system. Broadly, it involves identifying all types of risk, recognizing the impact of the worst possible situation for each risk category individually and in combination, and developing specific policies for managing them. Remember that reducing risk is not without cost, and managers must make decisions on the proportion of each category of risk that is covered. The rest of this chapter will discuss an important institution in managing both price and financial risks—the futures market.

Think Break

In each of the following situations, does the trader face the risk that prices will rise or fall? Identify each trader as an owner or needer.

> *1 A farmer harvests corn in September and chooses to store the product for future sale.*
> *2 Grain merchants contract with a miller for forward delivery. They anticipate buying the wheat to meet the contract.*
> *3 A soybean crusher holds inventories of soybeans, soybean meal, and oil.*
> *4 A tomato processor has forward orders for ketchup but has not yet signed contracts with growers.*

FUTURES MARKETS AND CONTRACTS

More than 150 years ago, farmers—who sold their grain at central markets—and buyers of grain, such as flour millers and bakers, wanted to establish the price before the grain was available on the market. Those who produced, owned, or processed grain entered into forward contracts to protect themselves against adverse price changes due to product destruction from natural hazards, such as drought or flood, or due to an unforeseen change in export demand as markets around the world became interrelated by trade.

The first futures exchange in the United States, the Chicago Board of Trade, came into existence in 1848; traders dealt in cash commodities and "forward" or "to arrive" contracts, which were essentially deferred-delivery contracts. The seller was required to deliver a specific amount of grain at a future period and for a predetermined price. These contracts provided economic incentives to store wheat and thus resulted in a more rational flow of the product to market over time. Postharvest prices rose because some grain was placed in storage rather than sold. Preharvest prices were reduced because grain was removed from storage and sold.

However, a major problem remained. Because of the forward contracts' heterogeneity and lack of assurance that all parties would perform according to the contract specifications, traders were reluctant to trade them. With the Chicago Board of Trade's introduction of futures contracts for grain in the 1860s, these problems were eliminated. Futures contracts were similar to the forward contracts, except that standards for quality, quantity, and delivery at a specific location and time were guaranteed for the commodity that would be delivered in the future. At the same time, contract integrity was assured—and a major difference from the forward contract was that contract obligations could be met by making the offsetting transaction. This process of the roundturn will be further discussed later.

While Chicago remains the trading center for global futures and options on futures, other markets—in particular, those in London, Paris, and Tokyo—are becoming increasingly important. Table 11-1 lists the major exchanges worldwide, in order of their 1995 trade volume.

Today, futures contracts are traded on agricultural commodities, raw industrial products, foreign currencies, and financial instruments, such as treasury bonds. Commodities on which contracts are traded tend to be available in abundant quantities and not subject to price manipulation by any individual or group of individuals. Additionally, energy products—crude oil, gasoline, and heating oil—are now priced on futures markets, since OPEC has lost much of its power as a cartel. The growth in these nonagricultural futures contracts has been amazing; however, agricultural contracts are still important, with nine making the list of the top 25 contracts traded in 1995.

Two basic concepts apply to futures markets: they are markets where prices are discovered, and their major purpose is for owners and needers of the physical product to establish a price for future delivery. Price is discovered by the buying and

TABLE 11-1 EXCHANGES AROUND THE WORLD TRADING FUTURES CONTRACTS, 1995

Exchange*	Contracts traded, 1995 (millions)
Chicago Board of Trade	165.6
Chicago Mercantile Exchange	146.7
Bolsa Mercantil & de Futuros, Brazil	130.8
London International Financial Futures Exchange	107.4
New York Mercantile Exchange	63.6
MATIF, France	56.7
London Metal Exchange	43.4
Tokyo International Futures Exchange	36.4
Tokyo Commodity Exchange Industry	35.1
Sydney Futures Exchange	23.2
Simex, Singapore	22.2
Tokyo Stock Exchange	16.7
Tokyo Grain Exchange	14.3
International Petroleum Exchange, U.K.	14.3
Coffee, Sugar, Cocoa Exchange, U.S.	8.9
New York Cotton Exchange	4.7
Kobe Rubber Exchange, Japan	4.0
Osaka Textile Exchange, Japan	2.9
Kansas City Board of Trade	1.7
Winnipeg Commodity Exchange	1.6
Yokohama Raw Silk Exchange, Japan	1.3
Minneapolis Grain Exchange	.94
Toyahasi and Maebashi Dried Silk Cocoon Exchanges, Japan**	.93

*This table dos not list all exchanges and emphasizes some smaller exchanges that trade agricultural commodities.

**Combined only for this report, because both are dried silk cocoon exchanges.

Source: Futures Industry Association, Inc., *International Report,* 1995. Reprinted with permission of Futures Industry Association.

selling of contracts on an exchange. All available market information, as well as expectations as to future developments, is brought into the pit, the trading arena for the futures contract. (Figure 11-1 shows the fast-paced action on an exchange floor as contracts are bought and sold.)

Futures contract prices fluctuate in response to supply and demand. If a new piece of market information comes into the pit that says world wheat production is going to be 10 percent below previous expectations, traders will want to buy wheat contracts. The buying pressure will be greater than the selling pressure, resulting in wheat futures contracts increasing in price. Of course, just the opposite scenario can occur, with wheat prices declining in response to news of increased production.

Futures Markets Participants

Futures markets provide the opportunity for *hedgers* of commodities, currencies, and financial instruments to fix, or lock in, a price that is quoted in the market today for future delivery, on a date which could be as close as 2 to 3 weeks in the future or as far as 2 to 3 years. Thus, a futures hedge provides a form of risk management, similar to that of a forward contract. Hedgers are both those who will be selling a commodity and those who need inventory and will be buying physical product in the future. Hedgers don't want to be exposed to the vagaries of the marketplace and seek to shift the risk of adverse price changes to others.

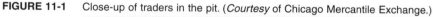

FIGURE 11-1   Close-up of traders in the pit. (*Courtesy* of Chicago Mercantile Exchange.)

Speculators are willing to place their money at risk with the idea that they will be able to correctly forecast the direction of future prices—up or down (more on the mechanics of how this works later). The root of the word speculator is the Latin *speculari,* which means "to observe, or spy out." Speculators use various tools to observe and discern what they see as future price direction and then are willing to expose themselves to financial risk in an attempt to profit from ever-changing prices.

A specialized type of speculator is the scalper. Scalpers trade on very small price fluctuations and rarely have an open position longer than 10 minutes. They do not leave the floor with an open position. Scalpers play an important and vital role because they give markets volume and liquidity, two essential ingredients for the smoothly functioning market required by hedgers.

In summary, the speculator assumes the risks which the hedger—the owner, producer, or user of a commodity—seeks to avoid. Futures markets function because speculators seek risk and opportunities to profit and hedgers seek to avoid risk. Sometimes speculators are unjustifiably maligned as to their role in the futures market. In truth, futures markets could not exist without speculators.

Futures Contracts

A futures contract is a legally binding commitment to deliver (to sell or *go short*) or take delivery of (to buy or *go long*) a commodity at some time in the future. The delivery month may be as close as next month, or it could be several months or years in the future—hence the term *futures contract.* The contract stipulates and standardizes the quantity, quality, price, and place of delivery. Soybean futures, for example, are traded on the Chicago Board of Trade. They must be at least USDA Grade #2 Yellow, are sold in 5,000-bushel units, and are delivered to authorized warehouses. The contract months traded are: January, March, May, July, August, September, and November. Each month will be priced differently because of the seasonality of production and cost of storage—soybeans are harvested in October/November and placed in storage; end users, processors, and exporters buy out of these storage stocks, which will not be replenished until the next harvest.

How are futures contracts created? Unlike shares in the stock market, which are authorized and issued by a company, a futures contract is created by a willing seller and a willing buyer agreeing on a commodity's future price. The buyer and seller execute their trades on a futures exchange. All that is needed is someone who is willing to make a trade opposite your trade or desired *position.* If your expectation is that prices will rise in the future, you would buy a contract today and would be said to have an obligation in the market or a position. *Bulls* are speculators who anticipate price increases, so they "go long" (buy). Simultaneously, others—*bears*—will "go short" (sell) because they anticipate price declines in the future.[2] Futures markets work because there are differences of opinion as to what the price will be in the future.

---

[2]Understanding futures markets requires mastering the language or vocabulary of the business. The glossary defines terms that may be used in context in this chapter and require further elaboration.

A. A speculator SHORT the market is forecasting declining prices.

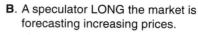

B. A speculator LONG the market is forecasting increasing prices.

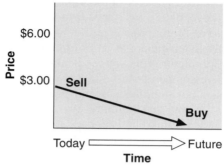

FIGURE 11-2   A speculator either sells or buys a futures contract to take a position in the market.

As is seen in Figure 11-2, profits can be made from either falling or rising prices. A bull makes money by buying today and then selling when and if the price rises in the future. A bear does the opposite, selling today and buying back the contract at a profit when and if the price falls. For every futures contract traded, there must be a buyer and seller.

A question frequently asked is, "Will I ever have to take delivery of (or deliver) the commodity?" It is possible but highly unlikely. While there is some delivery on futures contracts, for the most part producers, who want to sell, and end users, such as processors and exporters who need to buy, use various cash (spot) markets around the world to trade the physical product, whether it is wheat or orange juice. Speculators are rarely, if ever, interested in making or taking delivery.

Rather than making or taking delivery, traders make offsetting transactions in the futures market before the delivery date of the contract. If one buys a contract of wheat for delivery six months in the future and then sells a contract prior to the delivery date of the contract, the combination of buying and selling voids one's original obligation. Likewise, one's obligation is also nullified if a short original position in the market (sell) is subsequently followed by a buy order prior to the delivery date of the contract. This process of offset, or liquidating one's position in the market, is also known as roundturning. With the *roundturn,* traders no longer have a position in the market, and their profit or loss is calculated and delivered to them by the brokerage firm with whom they are trading.

Making a profit, of course, is one reason contracts are offset prior to the delivery date. The speculator who correctly anticipated the sudden rise in soybean prices during the summer of 1993 (due to the massive flooding in the midwestern United States, could have gone long one contract in early June, when the price was $5.90/bushel, and offset this position by selling a contract in late July after the market price had risen to $7.00. This trade would have resulted in a gross profit of $5,500.

$7.00   Sell
 5.90   Original long position
$1.10   Profit ($1.10 × 5,000 bushels = $5,500)

Deliveries of the physical commodity against futures contracts occur in less than 3 percent of the total contracts traded. It is common, however, to have more futures contracts traded than there is actual production of that commodity during a given year. For example, 53 billion bushels of soybeans (10.6 million contracts × 5,000 bushels per contract) were traded on the Chicago Board of Trade in 1995—a year in which 2.15 billion bushels of soybeans were produced on American farms.

The commodity futures markets, therefore, are not merchandising markets where the actual product changes hands. Futures markets are pricing markets where producers and users of commodities establish price in advance of delivery and shift the risk to someone who is willing to assume that risk.

Think Break

A speculator, forecasting a bear market in canola prices, goes short at $420 Canadian per metric tonne and later roundturns this short position at $375. What is the speculator's profit or loss per contract on this transaction? Canola (an oilseed) is traded in 20-metric-tonne contracts on the Winnipeg Futures Exchange.

When buying or selling a contract, the trader must make a *margin* deposit. These deposits serve as earnest money—an assurance of performance on the contract. (It is important not to confuse margin with down payment). The individual commodity exchanges establish the minimum margin requirements for the contracts traded on their floor. The amount of margin a commodity broker requires of a client is determined on the basis of market risk. Just as the broker requires a margin deposit from the buyer and seller, the clearing house requires a security deposit on each contract from the brokerage firm. The margins are usually between 5 and 15 percent of the value of the contract. Such low margin requirements make the leverage, also referred to as gearing, factor very attractive to the speculator. That is, the profit (or loss) potential on the risk capital committed to a futures position is very high compared to many investment alternatives.

Volume and Open Interest

Two measures of market activity followed by traders are volume and open interest. *Volume* is the more straightforward of the two; it is the number of contracts traded over a given time period and is measured on a daily basis. Remember that for every seller of a futures contract there must be a buyer, so volume is the total number of either purchases or sales, but not the sum of the two. As a measure of total market activity, volume figures include those trades that are day trades and scalp trades—

those that are roundturned during the day's trading. Open interest is a different type of measure and does not include those trades.

Open interest is the number of unliquidated contracts at any point in time and is a cumulative figure that shows the total number of contracts in the market with an obligation. This obligation can be met in two ways: roundturning and taking profits or losses through the roundturn, and making or taking delivery, depending on whether you are short or long the contract. As with volume, open interest is measured by the number of either the open long positions or the open short positions, but not the sum of the two.

Table 11-2 illustrates how open interest and volume are calculated. Suppose that on day 2 a new contract begins trading and individual A buys two contracts from B. At the end of the day the clearing-house records would indicate that individual A has two open long positions and individual B has two open short positions. Both the daily volume and open interest at the end of the day would be two contracts. On day 3, suppose there is a sale of one contract by individual D (a "new" seller) to individual C (a "new" buyer). At the end of day 3 the cumulative open interest will be increased from 2 to 3 and the daily volume will be recorded as one contract. More trades are made in Table 11.2 for days 4 through 7, and you are encouraged to work through the impact of these trades on volume and open interest. As is demonstrated, if there is a purchase by an "old" seller from an "old" buyer, open interest declines. On the other hand, if there is a purchase by a "new" buyer from an "old" buyer, open interest is unchanged.[3]

An Options Contract

Options on futures are contractual obligations that are traded on organized futures exchanges through an auction system of trading with open outcries of bids and

[3]Steven C. Blank, Colin A. Carter, and Brian H. Schmiesing, *Futures and Options Markets* (Englewood Cliffs, NJ: Prentice-Hall, 1991): 20–22. This section, as well as several other figures in this chapter, comes from Blank, Carter, and Schmiesing, courtesy of the authors.

TABLE 11-2   ILLUSTRATION OF OPEN INTEREST AND VOLUME CALCULATIONS FOR FUTURES CONTRACTS

Day no.	Buyer	Seller	Open "longs"	Open "shorts"	Daily volume	Open interest
1					0	0
2	A(2)	B(2)	A(2)	B(2)	2	2
3	C(1)	D(1)	A(2), C(1)	B(2), D(1)	1	3
4	B(1)	E(1)	A(2), C(1)	B(1), D(1), E(1)	1	3
5	D(1)	C(1)	A(2)	B(1), E(1)	1	2
6	E(1)	A(1)	A(1)	B(1)	1	1
7	B(1)	A(1)			1	0

Note: Numbers of contracts either bought or sold are in parentheses. Letter A . . . E denote individual traders.
Source: Steven C. Blank, Colin A. Carter, and Brian H. Schmiesing, *Futures and Options Markets: Trading in Financials and Commodities.*

offers. These characteristics they share in common with futures contracts, but there are some important differences between the two. An option, as the name implies, gives its buyers the right, but not the obligation, to exercise the option and take possession of a futures contract at a predetermined price. Options sold on futures contracts specify delivery of either a long or short futures contract. A call option specifies that the seller must deliver a long futures position to the option buyer, and a put option specifies delivery of a short futures position. Therefore, the buyer of an option has the right to either purchase (in the case of a call option) or sell (in the case of a put option) a futures contract at a preestablished price within a given period of time. The predetermined price is referred to as either the *strike price* or the exercise price.

For example, in April, a person who expects soybean prices to increase may decide to purchase a call option, specifying delivery of a July soybean contract at a strike price of $7.00 per bushel. If the current July futures price in trading is in the $6.50 range, then the *premium* paid for this call option may be approximately 10 cents per bushel. If the July soybean futures price rises above $7.00 before the option expires in July, then the holder of the option will most likely exercise the option and take possession of a long July futures position at the $7.00 price.

The financial obligations involved in options trading are different from those in futures trading. Futures traders have obligations to deliver (in the case of a seller) or accept delivery of (in the case of a buyer) a specified product at a specified price and time in the future. (Of course, physical delivery hardly ever takes place, because traders offset positions by roundturning.) With options, in contrast, option buyers have no financial obligations after the payment of the premium and can walk away from a put or call, but option sellers are obligated to comply.

When a call option is exercised, the holder of the option will acquire a long futures position at the option strike price. If a call option is exercised, the exchange (through the clearing house) assigns a short futures position to the person who previously sold the call option. Alternatively, when a put option is exercised, the option holder acquires a short futures position at the option strike price, and the long futures position is assigned to the person who sold the put that is exercised. An option can be exercised by its holder at any time before it expires.

The prices of options are reported publicly in the same manner as are futures prices. For each product, call and put options with different strike prices and expiration dates are listed. The settle prices reported are for the option, not the product, and are quoted in dollars per bushel, pound, or ton—however the commodity is priced and marketed.

THE EXCHANGE

The commodity exchange functions very much like a stock exchange. The exchange provides the facility (the trading floor and the trading pits—see Figure 11-3) for futures trading, a governing board which establishes and enforces trading regulations, and the *clearing house,* which operates the mechanism of "clearing" all transactions on a daily basis and accounts for the flow of funds on each trade.

FIGURE 11-3   Overview of trading floor. (*Source:* Chicago Board of Trade.)

Orders to buy and sell arrive by telephone or telex at members' stations near the pits. Messengers carry instructions from these areas to floor traders. In Box 11-1 the newsworthiness of a minor event on an exchange floor indicates the extent to which all levels of activity are regulated. The actual trading of contracts takes place in octagonal or polygonal "pits," which are center ring areas surrounded by ascending steps. Traders stand in groups around the individual pits and offer to buy

---

BOX 11-1

CHAOTIC ACTIVITY FOLLOWS THE RULES, USUALLY

"At the Chicago Board of Trade, people hardly notice when a futures trader eats a $1 million loss. But on May 26, the feast consisted of a 2-inch cockroach, and that halted all other activity in the treasury note pit. The bug was perched on the tongue of Brian Waller, a trader's clerk who consumed *la cucaracha* in response to a $200 dare. 'He bit it and turned around so everybody could see it, including the visitors' gallery,' said Geoffrey Getz, a trader who witnessed the incident.

Waller's feat amazed traders and runners from adjacent pits, who flocked to the spectacle and chanted: 'Eat it, eat it.'"*

Even on normal days, the CBOT may appear to the observer to consist of chaos and confusion, but the activity is actually well regulated. Waller's little snack "bugged floor officials," who collared Waller and began disciplinary proceedings leading to a $1,000 fine for disrupting trading. Waller, who couldn't be reached for comment, was later fired. There's another entry in the CBOT rule book that might better fit his offense, though: No eating on the floor."*

*"It Doesn't Pay to Eat a 2-Inch Roach,"*Business Week*, June 12, 1989, p. 32.

or sell contracts for a specific commodity, calling for delivery within a specific month. The offers are communicated by open outcry and a system of hand signals. In some countries, trading is carried out by linked computers, but in the United States the traditional system still predominates, with traders physically present on the floor.

Market reporters surrounding the pits record the price changes as they occur and pass the information along for display on chalkboards or electronic display boards surrounding the trading floor. The boards also display prices from other exchanges. The price information is passed along to other exchanges and public reporting services, as well.

Clearing-House Operations

The clearing house is a corporation separate from the commodity exchange and is responsible for the daily settlement of thousands of transactions executed on the floor of the exchange. As is shown in Figure 11-4, every trade consists of a buy and

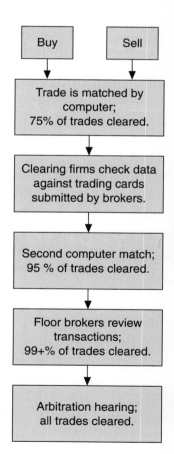

FIGURE 11-4   How commodity trades are cleared. (*Source:* Steven C. Blank, Colin A. Carter, and Brian H. Schmiesing, *Futures and Options Markets* [Englewood Cliffs, NJ: Prentice-Hall, 1991] p. 12.)

a sell order, and one of the functions of the clearing house is to make sure all these trades are matched and that there are no discrepancies in price, number of contracts traded, or the futures months traded.

Buyers and sellers do not create financial obligations with one another but rather create obligations to the clearing house through member firms of the clearing-house corporation. Clearing-house members include most major brokerage firms, major banks, and commercial firms, such as Cargill and General Mills in wheat and Nestlé and Hershey in cocoa. All trades must be made through a clearing-house member, although members of the exchange need not be members of the clearing-house corporation.

The clearing-house becomes, in effect, the buyer for every seller and the seller for every buyer. Initially, when the trade is executed, a clearing-house member takes the opposite side of each contract. At the close of trading each day, after each contract has been cleared (the process of matching all purchases with a corresponding sale), the opposite clearing member is replaced by the exchange clearing house, which has become responsible for verifying and guaranteeing each contract. This is an important difference between a futures and a forward contract. With a forward contract, there is always the risk of either party defaulting. This risk becomes negligible with a futures contract. All transactions must be cleared prior to the opening of the market on the next day. Each clearing member must pay the clearing house its previous day's debt, or collect its previous day's gain. This no-debt system is the primary reason why the exchanges have a record of financial integrity.

In most countries, regulation of commodity exchanges and futures exchanges by a governmental agency also contributes to the integrity of futures markets. In the United States, this agency is the Commodity Futures Trading Commission (CFTC), an independent agency of the federal government. The CFTC is authorized to prevent price manipulation and excessive speculation and to protect all parties involved in futures trading from unethical and illegal activities. In addition, the exchanges have various committees and mechanisms in place to help assure that ethical and fair trading practices are followed.

Under the Commodity Futures Trading Commission Act, the CFTC is authorized to establish *position limits* on all commodities. Position limits are the maximum number of open long or short positions any person or group of persons acting together may hold in a particular commodity. Position limits reduce the chances of anyone's unfairly manipulating prices or forcing delivery of commodities.

THE BASIS

Hedgers want to reduce risk. In order to understand how and why hedging works, it is essential first to understand the relationship between cash and futures prices. The *basis,* the difference between the two prices, is calculated by subtracting the futures price from the cash price. Normally, the basis is negative; that is, the cash price that the farmer receives is below the futures price because of transportation and storage costs. However, owing to differences in cash-market locations and quality factors, at times cash can be above futures. For example, traders talk about the basis of a grain at New Orleans being "30 cents over" (meaning 30 cents above a quoted futures contract price), because the cash price includes the cost of barge or rail transportation to get the grain from the upper Midwest to the Gulf for export shipment. On the same day, the same type of grain at a cash-market location in western Nebraska may be quoted at "40 cents under," or 40 cents a bushel below the futures quote because of the cost of shipping from that market to a terminal market.

As is shown in Figure 11-5, there is an interaction between cash and futures markets, because prices in each market are influenced by the same global forces. For example, in the world wheat market, Australia is a major player; the 1994 drought in Australia influenced both cash and futures markets in the United States. Remember that a futures contract is simply a type of forward contract, standardized in terms of quality, quantity, and delivery location and time. Therefore, the cash price

FIGURE 11-5   The relationship between futures-market and cash-market prices.

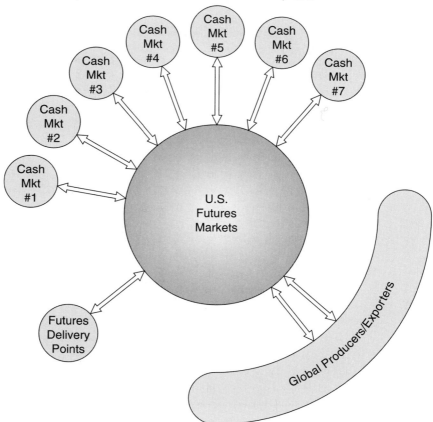

in Australia would be expected to be related to the futures price in Chicago, allowing for quality differences between Australian and U.S. wheat, transport and storage costs, and local factors in each market.

Producers and users of commodities recognize the tendency for cash and futures prices to move in the same direction, reacting to the same economic influences. Generally cash prices are below futures, reflecting transportation costs from a cash or local farm market location to the terminal market. The infrequent situation where cash may be at a premium to futures is referred to as an inverted market and is discussed later in this section. Factors which can influence the basis include:

- Cost of transportation between the cash market and the futures market.
- Supply and demand conditions at the cash market as opposed to those at the futures market.
- Differences between the quality of the cash-market product and the grade specifications of the futures market.
- Availability of storage space at the cash and futures markets.

For a storable product, such as wheat, soybeans, coffee, or frozen concentrated orange juice, the typical basis pattern between cash prices and a futures contract is demonstrated by Figure 11-6.

Three aspects of the cash-futures price relationship become evident as this figure is studied. They are:

- Futures prices are above cash.
- Over time, cash and futures prices tend to converge as the basis becomes less.
- Futures and cash prices fluctuate together, or are said to "dance together."

FIGURE 11-6   Theoretical cash-futures price relationships for a storable commodity, over time, ending in the delivery month.

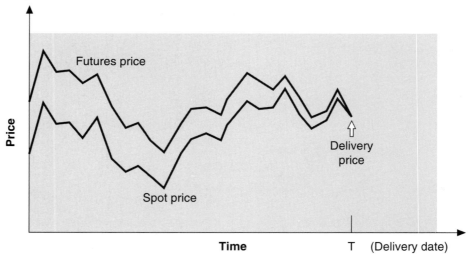

First, why are futures prices above cash? The reason is storage or *carrying charges*. For a storable product, the cost at a future point in time has to be today's cash price plus the cost of storage (interest on product value, because funds are tied up in the stored stocks; insurance on such losses as fire, theft, and others that can be insured; and the costs of the warehousing facility). Thus, carrying charges also explain the observation that over time the basis becomes less: the remaining months and weeks until contract maturity are fewer, and so the cost of carry becomes less. If it helps, put December on the far left of the horizontal axis and May as the delivery date.

The tendency of futures and cash prices to "dance together"—that is, when futures prices move up, cash moves up and vice versa—is a result of *arbitrage* between these two markets. Arbitrage is buying on one market and selling on the other to profit from a discrepancy in prices. For example, if futures prices went up but cash prices did not follow, what would the arbitrage opportunity be? The astute speculator would buy cash and deliver on the futures contract, pocketing the difference between the two prices; all proceeds above the full cost of carry would be profit. Obviously, in an efficient market, where market information is available to a number of competing participants, such a scenario is not going to happen. And so futures and cash prices fluctuate together. This is not to say that arbitrage opportunities never exist—they do, but generally for very short time periods and for relatively small amounts. Arbitrageurs will take advantage of all opportunities that result in a gain above the transaction costs, but also will assume any risks that exist in making the trade.

Basis relationships also exist in the cattle markets. While cattle cannot be stored and therefore basis has no carrying-cost component, basis in cattle does depend on location. In Figure 11-7, the April Live Cattle (slaughter cattle coming out of the feedlot) contract price is subtracted from the cash price in the Texas-Oklahoma Panhandle. Over the 12 months prior to April, cash prices are sometimes at a

FIGURE 11-7   Basis relationship: Texas-Oklahoma Panhandle cash price minus April live cattle contract price, 5- and 15-year average, 1981–95.) (*Courtesy of* Moore Research, Eugene, Oregon.)

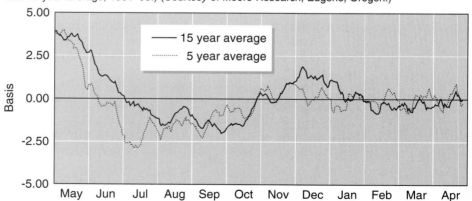

discount and sometimes at a premium to futures. The important point is that at contract expiration in April, cash and futures prices are at par; that is, the basis is close to zero. This is the expected situation, since Panhandle feedlots are delivery points for the live-cattle contract.

However, a similar analysis of California cash prices compared to futures would show that cash cattle are generally one to two cents below futures during most of the life of the contract and at delivery. As will be seen in the next section, cattle hedgers must understand what cash-futures price relationships are typical in order to effectively use the market for forward pricing. As Schap concludes "livestock hedgers, no less than grain hedgers, must track the basis, study it, and be alive to the opportunities *[and potential problems]* it can create."[4]

Think Break

Work out what you would do as an arbitrageur if, on the last day of trading for the May cocoa contract, it was trading for $1,260 per metric tonne, but you could buy cash/spot cocoa that met the contract quality standards and was in a warehouse approved by the exchange for delivery, for $1,220 per metric tonne. What would the end result be to you as a speculator, and what would happen to the difference between cash and futures cocoa prices?

The Inverted Market

Normally, as Figure 11-6 shows, futures prices are higher than cash commodities prices because of the carrying costs (storage, insurance, and interest). However, exceptions occur—cash and nearby futures prices can be higher than deferred futures contract prices. The nearby contract can be priced at a premium to the more distant month. This is known as an *inverted market*.

An inverted market generally occurs when there is a current tight supply-demand situation in which high prices ration available supplies. If this happens toward the end of the marketing year, say March to June in grains, futures prices for the "old crop" or nearby contracts in February and March will be at a premium to the deferred contracts, reflecting added supply coming from the "new crop." With an inverted market, there is an economic incentive to deliver the commodity immediately, as the market is not paying for storage. In fact, there is a "negative" price for storage.

Figure 11-8 demonstrates how the market priced wheat in early February 1992 for future delivery. It shows an inverted market, with the contracts for May and July delivery discounted relative to the nearby March contract. "Crossing over the crop year," along with the low wheat supplies in 1991–92, are the main reasons for this inverted market. Also, notice from Figure 11-8 that with the September

---

[4]Keith Schap, *Commodity Marketing: A Lenders & Producers Guide to Better Risk Management* (Chicago: American Bankers Association and Chicago Board of Trade, 1993), p. 60.

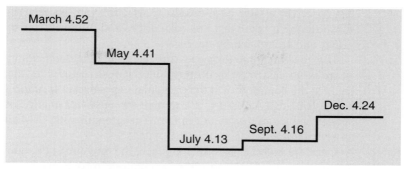

FIGURE 11-8   Wheat futures prices, early February 1992.

contract, when virtually all of the Northern Hemisphere crop will be harvested and in storage, the normal carrying-charge market relationship resumes. The September 1992 settle price is above July by 3 cents, and December (4.24) is above September (4.16) by 8 cents, reflecting carrying charges.

HEDGERS AND HEDGING

As noted previously, in futures markets the physical commodity need not change hands between buyer and seller. A distinguishing feature of futures contracts is that delivery is not mandatory if an offsetting trade is made. For instance, a long position in the market can be settled by performing the roundturn transaction, which would be a sell transaction; only in a small percentage of cases will the long-position holder take delivery of the commodity in fulfillment of the contractual agreement. The fact that two separate but connected markets (cash and futures) exist allows for hedging.

Hedging can be defined as:

Holding equal and opposite positions in the cash and futures markets.

Or:

The substitution of a futures contract for a later cash-market merchandising transaction.

A close look at the above definitions explains much of what hedging is all about. Take an Iowa farmer, who in May is planting soybeans for late October harvest and sale. The agricultural producer and his banker would like to know now what price he will receive for his soybeans in October. Given the price in May of the November soybean futures contract price and the expected October cash-futures price relationship, the soybean producer can fix or lock in a price for October sale.

The mechanics of the hedge will be seen in a later example, but what the farmer does is to call his broker and tell him to "sell November soybeans 'at the market'." In our definition of hedging, this is the substitution of a futures contract (short, in this case) for a later cash-market transaction (an October sell). What allows this substitution? It is the fact that cash prices and futures prices move up and down together and are related by the basis.

The pivotal point to successful hedging is understanding basis relationships. There is no easy way to do this, since it first requires developing historical basis data for the commodity at the particular cash-market location where it will be marketed. It is also necessary to examine the basis for change over time. Sometimes economic factors may result in the basis strengthening or weakening, or becoming more volatile.

Once the hedge program is in place, the basis must be monitored constantly. As the next section on hedging shows, changes in basis can cause a hedge to result in a profit or loss, or to break even. Understanding why cash price levels may deteriorate relative to futures (weakening basis) or why cash prices may gain relative to futures (strengthening basis) is important for successful monitoring.

Hedgers are more concerned with the change in the basis than with the change in the price of the commodity. In fact, commodity prices are frequently quoted by their basis. A grain exporter may quote a cash price of "25 cents under," meaning that today's cash price is 25 cents lower than the futures price for the next active trading month, or the nearby contract.

Hedging works because futures prices and cash prices follow a generally predictable pattern. More importantly, the risks of change in the difference between the cash price and the futures price (the basis) are much less than the risks inherent in actual price movement.

Hedgers can be classified as either owners or needers. Hedgers enter the futures market opposite their position in the cash market with the hope that the net result of the hedge will be to prevent a loss due to adverse price movement. Specifically, the risk of potentially adverse price movement is shifted to someone else, who may be either a speculator or another hedger.

Producers or owners of a commodity are concerned that the value of their inventory will decline. The wheat grower in Kansas, in Manitoba, Canada, or in Queensland, Australia, has no way of knowing what wheat prices will be three to six months in the future. The producer faces a risk and is, in a sense, speculating on what the cash price will be at harvest, or later if the crop is placed in storage.

Users or needers of a commodity are concerned that the supply will tighten when they need a product, and rising costs will squeeze profit margins and/or result in their having to increase the prices of their manufactured product. Manufacturers such as Keebler (Box 11-2) face price risk—fluctuating and potentially higher raw-material costs.

Hedging can be utilized by both owners and users to "lock in" a price before the physical product is sold or bought. Hedging, therefore, is utilized primarily as a means of minimizing risks due to price fluctuations.

The Short Hedge as Used by Agricultural Producers

The purpose of the *short hedge* is to protect the price at which the product will be sold in the future. It is used by owners (crop and livestock producers) and can be

BOX 11-2

HOW KEEBLER TRADERS SMOOTH OUT MARKET PEAKS AND VALLEYS

Thomas Finn is senior vice president of purchasing for Keebler, the second largest cookie and cracker company in the country. Keebler is the largest soft wheat buyer in the United States and has direct access to brokers on the Chicago Board of Trade floor. As head of Keebler's hedging operation Finn has two other persons assisting him in trading multiple futures markets: wheat, corn, the soybean complex, cocoa, and sugar. They also consult with Keeblers' treasury department on how to manage foreign currency risk on major overseas equipment purchases.

As Finn describes their major strategy, "Our goal is to try and make market prices smooth and less disruptive than, let's say, what has happened because of the drought (1987). And I think we have done that. In other words, we are trying to level out these impacts so you can run this fairly low margin business. You can't have those types of disruptions without having an immediate impact on margins." As a hedger, Keebler is a buyer against requirements and a seller against inventories. However, this does not mean that they don't bring a little bit of speculative philosophy into their operations. For

example, they look for abnormalities in price volatility, such as the price run-up that took place during the Chernobyl nuclear meltdown. If their analysis indicates that the market is overbought and there will be a retracement, Keebler will probably lighten up a little on their long hedge positions and get long again when the prices come back down.

Along with outside consultants, the Keebler hedging group is constantly on the phone with analysts and suppliers. Finn believes in working closely with suppliers, as they should know more about the particular product than the buyer. He says, "We're not ashamed to be humbled: we want to learn as much as we can from our supply base. A good working relationship can benefit both of us." The Keebler group is developing a computerized expert-type purchasing system, which borders on artificial intelligence and says how much they should be covered (hedged) in a particular commodity. Some of their computer expertise is provided by Steven Brunner, who gained his computer knowledge earning a master's degree from Purdue University in agricultural economics, and recently joined the firm.

Source: Ginger Szala, and Jim Wiesemeyer, "How Keebler Traders Smooth Out Market Peaks and Valleys," *Futures Magazine* (October 1988), pp. 45–47. Reprinted with permission of *Futures Magazine,* 219 Parkade, Cedar Falls, IA 50613.

executed before the crop is planted, during the production period, or at harvest to earn a storage return.

Example of an Owner-Selling Hedge   Kansas dry land wheat is planted in the fall and harvested the next June to July. A Kansas farmer expects to harvest 50,000 bushels of wheat. The farmer projects that $3.40 per bushel is needed to cover costs. In March, the farmer looks at the futures price for wheat to be delivered on the Kansas City market in July, which is the time the crop should be ready for market. The expected or forecast July basis, from historical records, is normally −30 cents. On March 15, July wheat is trading at $4.40, so the farmer fixes (establishes) a price of $4.10 for the wheat by going short 10 July wheat contracts.[5]

In late June the farmer is ready to sell the wheat, but—as feared—the market price has fallen drastically since the hedge was initiated. (Assume that there had been no change in the basis; that is, in the forecast basis of −$0.30.) On June 21, the farmer sells the wheat for $3.75, 35 cents below the price objective, and

---

[5]Sometimes in hedging literature this fixed price is referred to as the price objective. As this example unfolds, it will become apparent that the $4.10 fixed price is dependent on whether the July basis of − $.30 forecast in March actually comes true.

simultaneously offsets the future position by going long 10 July wheat contracts. The futures price had also dropped 35 cents on June 21 to $4.05 per bushel. The 35-cent loss in the cash market is offset by a 35-cent gain in the futures market, thus preserving the farmer's locked-in price of $4.10.

Date	Cash market		Basis	Futures market	
March 15	Fixes July Delivery of 50,000 bushels @	$4.10	−$0.30	Sells 10 July wheat contracts @	$4.40
June 21	Sells 50,000 bushels of wheat @	$3.75	−$0.30	Buys 10 July wheat contracts @	$4.05
	Cash loss (The sale price is 35 cents below the locked-in or fixed price.)	−$0.35		Gain on hedge	+$0.35

Hedge analysis:

Cash-market sale	3.75
Futures gain or loss	+0.35
Realized price*	4.10

*Realized price is the term given to the final hedge results—that is, the combination of the cash-market sale and the hedge gain or loss.

The above example is what is referred to as a perfect hedge, where the gain in one market exactly offsets the loss in the other. The likelihood of a perfect hedge's occurring, especially over the long run, is remote. A narrowing or, in some instances, a widening of the basis would be more likely to occur. The short hedger benefits from the narrowing of the basis (a strengthening basis). For example, if the cash price had dropped to $3.95 and the futures price dropped even further to $4.05 (a −10-cent basis), the result would have been a 20-cent increase over the original price objective.

Cash market		Basis	Futures market	
Fix price @	$4.10	−$0.30	Sell @	$ 4.40
Sell @	3.95	−0.10	Buy @	4.05
Cash loss	$−0.15	+$0.20	Gain on hedge	+$0.35
(Sell @ $3.95 + Gain on hedge 0.35 = 4.30 − Fix price 4.10 = 0.20 strengthening of basis)				

On the other hand, if the cash price had been $3.95 at the time of sale and the futures price dropped to only $4.30 (a −35-cent basis), the original price objective would have been missed by 5 cents. This is an example of a weakening basis. In this example cash prices deteriorated relative to the decline in futures prices.

Cash market		Basis	Futures market	
Fix price @	$4.10	−$0.30	Sell @	$4.40
Sell @	3.95	−0.35	Buy @	4.30
Cash loss	$−0.15	−$0.05	Gain on hedge	+$0.10
(Sell @ $3.95 + Gain on hedge 0.10 = 4.05 − Fix price 4.10 = 0.05 weakening of basis)				

The above examples demonstrate the importance of correct basis calculations as a prerequisite to successful hedging.

The Process of Localization   The futures price is converted to a fixed price by subtracting the basis from the futures price for the month of expected cash delivery (futures ± basis = fixed price). This is sometimes referred to as *localization,* because the futures price is being localized to the cash price that the producer can expect at his local market.

To fully convert futures to expected cash, two other adjustments need to be made:

1 Hedging costs must be considered. For every contract hedged, commission must be paid on the roundturn, and margin money must be on deposit with the commission house. In some situations, treasury bills may be accepted as margin collateral money, but if this is not the case, interest costs on the margin for the length of time the hedge is put on must be calculated. These two costs of hedging commission and interest on margin must be subtracted from the realized price.

2 Quality adjustment must be made to fit the producer's own situation. Futures contracts price a specific quality. Using cattle as an example, the cattle futures contract specifies Choice, 1050#–1250# steers, yield grade 1 & 2. A commercial feedlot would rarely expect a lot of finished animals to uniformly grade Choice, 1050#–1250#, yield grade 1 & 2. In this situation, the producer must adjust downward the fixed or locked-in price that he can expect to receive. In some situations the quality allowance may be a premium, instead of a discount.

Think Break _____

Using Figure 11-7 basis information, help a Guymon, Oklahoma, (Texas-Oklahoma Panhandle) feedlot operator calculate the fixed price for 1050–1250 pound Choice steers that will be ready for market in April. Other needed information: the cost of hedging (commission plus interest) is 0.25 cents/pound and the quality adjustment is 1.50 cents/pound; that is, the quality of this lot of steers is 1.50 cents below futures quality, and the packer will offer a price reflecting this discount when buying them from the feedlot.

_____

The Long Hedge as Used by Processors and Exporters

The buying hedge is used by needers or users of a product—those who do not have or need the product today but will need it in the future. Prime users include grain exporters, coffee roasters, and food manufacturers—Frito-Lay needs corn and soybean oil; General Mills needs to buy wheat. The buying hedge, also known as the *long hedge,* is especially valuable to those who have made forward sales contracts on the cash market but do not have the product purchased to deliver on these sales contracts. The long hedge involves initially buying futures contracts to protect against possible price increases of the physical commodity prior to its purchase.

Example of the Buying Hedge   On September 10, a grain exporter, such as the one in Figure 11-9, receives an order for 100,000 bushels of corn to be shipped to Thailand in late March of the following year. Not having the storage facility to buy the corn now and store it until March, the exporter must be protected against the risk of price increases between now and the time the corn is bought. The price could go down, which would be to the exporter's benefit; however, the price could go up, too.

The exporter buys 20 March corn contracts (100,000 bushels, 5,000 bushels per contract) on the futures market on September 10, at $3.00. The exporter locks in the cash purchase price at $2.80 ($3.00 less basis of 0.20) and contracts to sell the corn at $2.90 to the Thai feedmill operator (the difference between the locked-in cost of $2.80 and the selling price of $2.90 goes toward the exporter's costs and presumably a profit margin on this sale).

FIGURE 11-9   Traders at a multinational grain exporting firm. (*Courtesy of* Continental Grain Co.)

Toward the end of February, both cash and futures prices for corn have risen 25 cents per bushel. On February 27, the exporter buys 100,000 bushels of corn for $3.05 and simultaneously closes the futures position by selling 20 March corn contracts at $3.25. The 25-cent loss in the cash market is offset by a 25-cent gain in the futures market, thereby locking in the price objective.

Date	Cash market		Basis*	Futures market	
Sept. 10	Locks in cost of corn @	$2.80	−$0.20	Buys 20 March corn contracts @	$3.00
Feb. 27	Buys 100,000 bushels of corn @	$3.05	−$0.20	Sells 20 March corn contracts @	$3.25
	Additional cash cost (The purchase price is 25 cents above the locked-in or fixed price.)	−$0.25		Profit on hedge	+$0.25

Hedge analysis:	
Cost of cash corn	3.05
Futures profit or loss	−0.25
Net cost of corn	2.80

*The −$0.20 basis that is used here is the expected or forecast late February cash versus March corn futures contract price relationship.

Had the exporter not taken a position in the futures market, the losses would have been 25 cents per bushel because of the higher cost of corn. The buying hedge protected the exporter against rising corn prices, and the parallel movement of cash and futures prices insured the price objective.

Think Break

A soybean processor located in Rotterdam buys a cargo (shipload) of soybeans every month. It is early summer, and concerns about the Northern Hemisphere crop prospects have begun to push soybean prices up. The processor wants to hedge his December requirements. The November contract is currently trading at $7.25/bushel.

What would be the processor's hedged price per metric tonne, dockside Rotterdam? Needed information:

1 Cost to ship soybeans from U.S. gulf ports: $75 per metric tonne.
2 Barge freight from upper Midwest to Gulf ports is 30¢ per bushel.
3 Metric tonne = 2,200 pounds, and soybeans weight 60 pounds/bushel.

Show what happens if soybean prices go up to $8.50 by December.

Hedging Recap

The examples of selling and buying hedges were simplified here in order to illustrate that:

- Cash and futures prices do tend to move up or down in a parallel fashion and fluctuate due to the same economic factors.
- Hedging is a valuable tool in minimizing risk due to potential adverse price movement.
- Hedgers understand basis patterns and fluctuations and strive to profit from favorable basis movements.

As is evident from this discussion, futures markets and hedging are complex subjects, and it takes a fair amount of education and effort to understand the principles and apply them in the context of changing market conditions. For this reason, some participants in the food system utilize the futures market only indirectly. For example, while grain farmers may not hedge for themselves, grain-handling companies often offer cash forward contracts (Chapter 6) to farmers and in turn use a futures hedge to manage their price-risk exposure. The complexities of the market and the numerous alternative risk-management products also provide opportunities for specialized consulting services to the various participants in the food system.

SUMMARY

There are three types of risk in commodity markets: physical, price, and financial. Price risk can be managed by forward contracts or by hedging on the futures market. Commodity futures markets exist for two major reasons: to provide a forum for price discovery and to provide a mechanism (hedging) whereby owners and needers of the physical product can establish a price for future delivery. Participants in futures contract trading can be categorized as either hedgers or speculators. By definition, hedgers buy or sell the actual physical commodity, either for current delivery or at some date in the future, and use the futures market for managing price risk. Speculators, on the other hand, are not interested in becoming involved in the physical commodity, but put their money at risk with the idea of profiting from correctly forecasting the direction of future prices.

Futures contracts are legally binding commitments to deliver or to take delivery of a commodity at some future date. The contracts are standardized so that all parties understand the commmon quality, quantity, and delivery location of the commodity being traded. This standardization also facilitates the process of offset—the ability of a trader to roundturn out of a position in the market. Market integrity is assured by individual exchange regulations. Also, the Commodity Futures Trading Commission, an independent governmental regulatory organization, establishes various ground rules for exchange operation, as well as auditing brokerage firms and investigating claims of wrongdoing and fraud in the markets.

Before a hedging program can be implemented, it is crucial to understand the basis relationships for the commodity that you are trading. Basis is defined as the difference between a futures contract price and a cash market price. For commodities where the price discovered impacts worldwide prices, a basis relationship can be established for cash markets around the world. For example, the price that an Argentine, Australian, or Canadian wheat farmer receives is directly influenced by wheat futures contracts traded on the Chicago Board of Trade. Some of the factors that influence basis are: storage costs, transportation costs, quality differences, regional supply-demand balances, and the overall "macro" supply-demand situation for the commodity.

Understanding the basis relationship for a cash-market location also involves ascertaining whether there are seasonal patterns to basis and whether the basis is changing over time due to some longer-term trending influences. The bottom line is that for a successful hedge, cash and futures prices must move up and down in unison, and while the two prices are not perfectly matched in their moves, the statistician would say that there is a high correlation between the two price series.

Hedgers enter the futures market with one objective: to establish a price for future delivery of a commodity. Producers and other owners of a commodity are concerned that price levels are going to decline in the future, relative to the prices currently quoted in the market. They sell futures contracts as a temporary substitute for their later cash-market sale. The mirror image of owner hedgers are needers—those processors, exporters, and other end users who are going to need a commodity in the future but do not now have it physically in their inventory. Needers buy or go long futures contracts to hedge their later cash-market purchases. The substitution of futures contracts for later cash-market transactions is made possible by basis relationships, where cash and futures prices move up and down together as they are influenced by the same economic factors. Although the underlying motives and hedge mechanics differ by type of agribusiness firm—farmer, processor, merchant, exporter—all have the same objectives, to establish a price for forward delivery and not be exposed to the tremendous risks of commodity price fluctuations.

IMPORTANT TERMS AND CONCEPTS

QUESTIONS

1 Since futures markets are not for the marketing of the physical commodity, what are the two major purposes of these markets?

2 Define speculators and hedgers. How can one differentiate between these two types of futures-market participants?

3 Explain the activities of the clearing house and the role of clearing houses in assuring the financial integrity of futures markets.

4 What is the function of margin requirements in futures trading, and what does it mean if your broker says that you have just received a margin call on a futures position?

5 Two measures of market activity or market liquidity are volume and open interest. Explain each of these measures, how they differ from one another, how open interest is created, and what happens to the open interest after the bell rings on the last trading day of any contract.

6 What are the various factors that can make up the basis between a futures contract and a cash-market price?

7 Trace the theoretical cash-futures price relationship for a futures contract over time. Why do the two price series behave as they do?

8 What are the various conditions that can cause an inverted market? What is an inverted market saying to holders of inventory?

9 Identify the hedging situation of an owner (short hedge) or needer (long hedge).

10 Describe the process of localization that agricultural producers use to convert a futures price to a fixed price at their cash market.

11 Explain the impact when the basis or localization widens (becomes larger) from the time the hedge is put on to the later roundturn, when the cash-market transaction is made. Develop an example for both the owner and needer hedge.

REFERENCES AND RESOURCES

Blank, Steven C., Colin A. Carter, and Brian H. Schmiesing. *Futures and Options Markets: Trading in Financials and Commodities.* Englewood Cliffs, NJ: Prentice-Hall, 1991.

Schap, Keith. *Commodity Marketing: A Lenders & Producers Guide to Better Risk Management.* Chicago: American Bankers Association and the Chicago Board of Trade, 1993.

Schwager, Jack. *Schwager on Futures: Fundamental Analysis.* New York: John Wiley & Sons, Inc., 1995.

Hieronymus, Thomas. *Economics of Futures Trading.* 2d ed. New York: Commodity Research Bureau, 1977.

Murphy, John J. *Technical Analysis of the Futures Markets.* New York: New York Institute of Finance, 1986.

Internet Sources

Chicago Board of Trade: http://www.cbot.com
Chicago Mercantile Exchange: http://www.cme.com
Commodity Futures Trading Commission: http://www.clark.net/pub.cftc/
Futures Magazine: http://www.futuresmag.com

BRANDED-PRODUCT
MARKETING MANAGEMENT

*Identifying the target market segment, positioning the food product, and selecting
the marketing mix that will attract customers and convince them to buy*

You have been introduced to the management of both industrial (Chapter 7) and
commodity marketing (Chapters 10 and 11). The marketing of branded food
products to consumers, the subject of this section, is carried out by food manufacturers and, increasingly, by food retailers.

To market branded food products, first identify the market—the target
customers—then design food products that suit their needs, and position these
products in the market against competing products (Chapters 12 and 13). Next,
develop the marketing mix of place, price, and promotion, so that the product
reaches the consumers and they are encouraged to buy. The place—the market
channel—was discussed in Chapter 6; pricing and promotion are the topics of
Chapters 14 and 15.

This study ends with a chapter on marketing strategy and planning, an important aspect of all food marketing—if the marketing strategy is not developed as
part of the company's business strategy, there is no direction for marketing. The
plan, which provides the blueprint for marketing decisions, draws on your understanding of the entire Food System.

12

SELECTING AND RESEARCHING
TARGET MARKETS

CHAPTER OUTLINE

LEARNING OBJECTIVES

After reading this chapter and answering the questions in the Think Breaks and at the end of the chapter, you should be able to:

- Understand how a market can be divided into market segments to aid marketing.
- Know the methods of market segmentation and how to select the most appropriate way to segment the target market.
- Identify the information needed about market segments so that a marketing-segmentation strategy can be developed.
- Select market-research methods to find the information needed.
- Understand the uses of the two types of market research: primary and secondary.
- Use market-segment information to develop a market-segmentation strategy and the marketing mix for each market segment.

INTRODUCTION

When a company enters a new market, the question is, where to start? The company must identify groups of consumers, industrial customers, or distributors into coherent groups which have similar behavior and attitudes toward the product, so that the same marketing method can be used for all the members of the group. Such a group is called a market segment and the process is called *market segmentation.*

This chapter discusses some of the ways a market can be segmented, how information can be found to choose the best type of market segmentation, and how to develop a market strategy for each segment. Segmentation varies with the product and the market.

Once market segments have been identified, the next task is to find information on which to base the marketing strategy and organization. The information needed varies with the type of market, the product, the company, and its competitors. In consumer marketing, information on the consumers' attitudes and behavior toward the product is needed; in industrial marketing, the customers' uses of the products and their requirements for product quality and services are important.

The information can be found using various types of market research—secondary research, utilizing the available information already gathered by other sources, and primary research, collecting new information by market and consumer surveys. Market research needs to be well planned and organized so that the most reliable information is found at the lowest cost.

The chapter ends with a discussion on choosing the market segment, planning product positioning for the segment, and developing a marketing strategy for that segment. Segments chosen must have a sufficiently high sales potential for the product; thus, a number of market segments might have to be combined to give the company an adequate return. Segmentation depends on the size of the total market—New Zealand, with 3 million people, cannnot have many segments, as this would result in each segment being uneconomic; Australia, with its much larger population, can be divided into more market segments of sufficient size, and the United States into even more. As you are reading this chapter and visiting the supermarket, recognize the market segments a company's products are serving.

MARKET SEGMENTS THROUGH THE FOOD SYSTEM

Segmentation may be applied to all the buyers in the food system: consumers, industrial users, food service, and retailers. The number of segments into which the pizza market has been divided (Figure 12-1) is not atypical.

FIGURE 12-1   Which piece of the pie provides the greatest rewards? The pizza market has been segmented into bake-it-yourself, home delivery, casual pizza parlor, and higher-priced signature pizza makers, each after a particular group of customers. *(Courtesy of R. Lamberts, New Zealand Institute of Crop and Food Research.)*

Consumer-Market Segments

A consumer market may be segmented in many different ways; five common ways are shown in Figure 12-2. Depending on the country you are in and the type of product, the importance of these segmentation variables will differ.

Examples of market segmentation are:

- *Age*—children, teenagers, young adults, middle aged, elderly
- *Usage*—do not use, light, medium, heavy; or nonuser, intermittent, constant
- *Brand loyalty*—brand loyal, brand fickle, brand indifferent.

Some segmentation categories, discussed below, are more commonly used in food marketing than others.

Sociocultural   As an example, almost all cultural groups have subgroups, referred to as social classes. Great Britain and the United States have clearly defined social classes, which have different food-buying and eating behavior, while in other countries the differences are not so marked. Some of the social classes identified in the United States are:[1]

FIGURE 12-2   Consumer market-segmentation categories.

Sociocultural	Geographic
Religion	Country
Ethnic group	Region
Nationality	City size
Social class	Urban/rural
Household life cycle	Climate

Demographic	Psychographic
Age	Life style
Sex	Behavior
Income	Personality
Education	Attitudes

User Behavior

Usage rates
Brand loyalty status
Purchase occasion
Benefits sought:
- Sensory appeal
- Nutrition
- Convenience
- Status

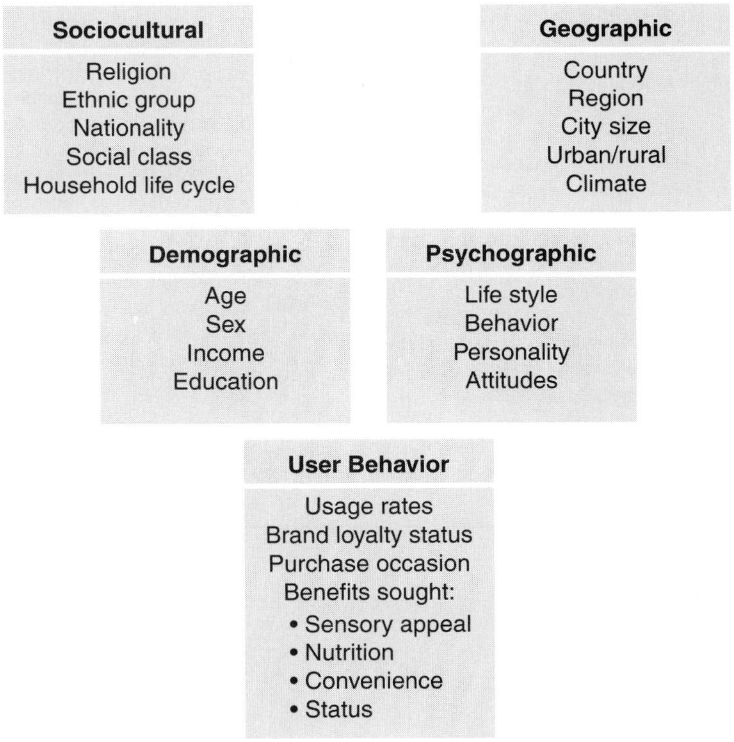

[1]See Philip Kotler and Gary Armstrong, *Principles of Marketing,* 5th ed., chap. 5, for details.

Upper-upper   —old families, aristocracy
Lower-upper   —"new rich," top executives, successful lawyers, doctors
Upper-middle—moderately successful businessmen, lawyers, doctors
Middle   —white-collar workers, office workers, salespersons, technicians,
              skilled blue-collar workers
Working   —blue-collar, semiskilled
Upper-lower   —employed but poorly paid
Lower-lower   —chronically unemployed.

Consumers are often segmented according to their type of household and at what stage they are in the life cycle of households:

Singles   —one person, young or middle aged, living alone
Couples   —two people living together, young or middle aged
Room/house mates—a group of people of either same or mixed sex, who have
                 no family ties

BOX 12-1

DO DISTINCT CLASS PREFERENCES FOR FOODS EXIST?

The classes in Britain were identified as:

Bourgeoisie:	Employers (large and small establishments), self-employed professionals, farmers (employers and managers)
Petite bourgeoisie:	Own-account workers and farmers
Authority:	Manager, professional workers, and supervisors
Workers:	Ancillary workers and artists, skilled/unskilled, manual and non-manual, agricultural workers, personal service workers.

A survey of 7,265 households indicated class preferences for certain food items. The workers and the bourgeoisie had stronger class preferences than the middle groups. The authority group appeared to be more heterogeneous in its consumption habits.

Some class patterns were apparent. The strongest patterns appeared to be the desire among workers for staples such as bread, potatoes, flour, and canned vegetables, along with a propensity to consume alcohol away from the household—as opposed to the bourgeois preferences for beef, restaurant food, take-aways, cheese, fresh vegetables, and fruit juice. The workers (and to a lesser extent the petite bourgeoisie) maintained an element of "convivial indulgence," while the upper social class was more fond of restaurants, fresh vegetables, and fruit ("sophisticated and healthy").

The spectrum of food from the bourgeoisie to the workers is shown in the diagram.

Source: Summarized from M. Tomlinson, "Do Distinct Class Preferences for Foods Exist: An Analysis of Class-Based Tastes," *British Food Journal* 96.7 (1994): 11–18.

Bourgeoisie tastes ⟵——————————————————⟶ Worker tastes

| Restaurants | Cheese
Take-aways
Fruit juice
Fresh
  vegetables
Spirits at home
Beef/veal | Cooked
  cereal
Ham | Fish
Processed
  fruit
Biscuits | Food at work
Fats
Alcohol away
  from home
Coffee
Flour | Canned
  vegetables
Potatoes
Bread | Cooked
  meats |

Young families   —two adults or a single parent with small children
Maturing family   —one or two adults with teenage/adult children
Adult family   —a number of related adults living together
Empty nest   —a couple whose children have left home
Survivor   —the partner, usually elderly, living alone after the other
                    partner has died.

These households often have different food needs, so this method of segmentation is meaningful to food marketers.

In Australia, with the mixture of ethnic groups, it is useful to segment into Italian, Greek, Chinese, Thai, and Polynesian, because of the needs of these groups for particular foods. In New Zealand, the ethnic groups for segmentation are Pakeha (White) New Zealander, Maori, European, Pacific Islander, and Chinese, but, as each is such a small market, they were seldom differentiated until recently. In the United States, Asians, African-Americans, and Hispanics are large ethnic groups, all of which have their favorite foods.

Psychographic   In recent years, segmentation into lifestyle groups, one aspect of psychographics, has become popular. For example, men have been grouped into socially active young men, mature family men, success-oriented men, and elderly, traditional men; and women are identified as young social women, devoted young mothers, active professional, active retired, or elderly women. Some "couple" categories are: DINKs (Double Income, No Kids), traditional married (only husband working), house husband (husband at home); and households are typified as sophisticated social, relaxed casual, home lover/renovator, traditional, and so on. These labels change with time as lifestyles change and also in relation to the products being marketed.

A comparison of five global psychographic types, based on a wide variety of attitudes and consumer values, as well as on media use, viewing habits, product use, and buying patterns, is shown in Table 12-1. Strivers are young people living hectic, time-pressured lives; achievers are slightly older and have experienced

TABLE 12-1   GLOBAL SCAN SEGMENTS IN THREE COUNTRIES

	Japan %	United States %	United Kingdom %
Strivers	22	26	29
Achievers	17	22	18
Pressured	19	14	12
Adapters	22	14	17
Traditionals	18	12	16
Unassigned	2	12	8

Source: Rebecca Piirto, *Beyond Mind Games: The Marketing Power of Psychographics* (Ithaca, NY: American Demographic Books, 1991): 149. Reprinted with permission.

some success; the pressured group spans all ages and is largely composed of women who face financial and familial pressure; adapters are older people who are content with themselves and their lives and also manage to live comfortably in a changing world; traditionals hold fast to the oldest values of their countries and cultures.

User Behavior   One aspect of user-behavior segmentation is the benefits sought from a purchase. For instance, food market segments may be based on the nutritional benefits the consumer desires:

Food faddist	—frequents health food stores, takes vitamins and minerals, eats yogurt to promote longevity
Calorie-conscious buyer	—looks for ways to lower calorie intake
Dieter	—goes on frequent diets to lose weight
Fearful consumer	—aware of the effects of salt and saturated fats on health, particularly in relation to heart disease and cancer
"Don't-care" buyer	—not interested in health or in the nutritional aspects of foods.

Think Break

The consumer-market segments attracting beef marketers in the US have varied. When beef was criticized by nutritionists, marketers targeted nutrition-conscious segments, such as dieters and calorie-conscious weight watchers, teenage girls wanting to stay slim, and fearful consumers concerned about protein and iron. The market strategies emphasized low-calorie beef, diet-sized servings, 300-calorie recipes, and nutri-fact programs.

A recent consumer survey divided beef consumers into three segments: "beef dominant"—very loyal beef users, buying all cuts of beef and also premium cuts of poultry and pork; "beef rotator"—heavy meat users who purchase beef, poultry, and pork about equally and choose promoted cuts; and "budget driven"—purchasers of inexpensive cuts of meat with the emphasis on poultry.

Compare these two methods of segmenting the beef market, and show how the marketing strategies would change if the usage segmentation were adopted.

Demographic   In market research, sex, age, salary/wage, and occuption segments are still used. This information is easily obtained from national and international statistics and can be used to determine the sizes of different market segments. This segmentation is particularly helpful for studying a new market in an overseas country and developing potential market data. The following are some examples of demographic categories:

Sex	Age	Salary/wages	Occupation
Male Female	6–10 years 11–14 years 15–20 years 21–30 years 31–40 years 41–55 years 56–70 years >70 years	<$10,000 $10,000–20,000 $21,000–30,000 $31,000–40,000 >$40,000	Manager Professional Office worker Manual worker Technician Homemaker Unemployed Retired

Demographics are fundamentally significant to food marketers—in particular, the increasing proportion of people over 60, the decreasing size of the average household (25 percent of households in the United Kingdom now comprise only one person), and a sharp increase in the proportion of married women in full-time employment. Married people aged 50 to 60, the years immediately prior to retirement, are in the "empty-nest" phase of their life cycle and have high levels of discretionary income. They are major users of restaurants. Elderly people can have problems with reaching products on supermaket shelves and opening modern packaging. Working women seek quality convenience products; for example, in Australia, the beef industry has promoted the "Short Cuts" line of products—quick-cooking, high-quality beef cuts.

Industrial-User Market Segments

For industrial-market segmentation, two stages are often used: macrosegmentation, in which companies are grouped according to some easily identified factor such as location, size, or type of processing; and microsegmentation, by internal company factors such as buying processes, technical expertise, or product and service needs. For example, a supplier marketing pastry margarine could group the large companies as pie manufacturers, frozen pastry manufacturers, croissant manufacturers, and biscuit manufacturers. These could also be microsegmented as nationally owned or multinational companies; large or small; low-, medium-, or high-volume purchasers; and strict, moderate, or not demanding regarding particular technical specifications.

Buyers can also be segmented by their buying characteristics: average order size; frequency of purchase; customer history—past, present, or never a customer; loyalty—one source or users of several suppliers; or even their financial situation and reliability. Product and service characteristics and benefits are often used to group customers; for example, users of emulsifiers could be segmented on emulsifying needs—oil in water, water in oil, thin liquid, thick liquid, cream. Service segments could include delivery speed required or degree of technical support needed.

Subgroups of innovators, influentials, followers, and diehards exist in industry, as well as among consumers. Often the innovators will be small companies that want to capture a market without having to compete with large companies; their ideas will then be adopted by larger, influential companies, followed finally by the conservative companies.[2]

Food Service Market Segments

Food service divides into two broad spectrums: commercial and institutional. Commercial customers can be further segmented by the type of organization: fast food, fine food restaurants, family restaurants, coffee bars, or food services. Or they can be divided by company organization: chain, groups, or caterers; by size: small, medium, large; by the cuisine offered: French, Italian, Thai, Chinese, Indian; steak and salads, limited menu, buffet, a la carte, vegetarian, seafood; or even by the times of service or meals served: daytime, evening, night, 24 hours; breakfast, lunch, or dinner. Institutional markets are generally subdivided by type of institution, by size, and finally by type of service.

Retailer Market Segments

Retailers may be segmented by size/type—chain supermarkets, individually owned supermarkets, small supermarkets or superettes, corner or convenience stores, or specialty shops; or according to ownership—Kroger, Winn-Dixie, Safeway. For example, in France, food markets could be segmented by:

Type of retailer:	Hypermarket, supermarket, independent specialist, butcher, dairy
Geographic:	Urban—Paris, Lyon, Rouen
	Region—Normandy, Limousin, Lorraine, Aquitaine
Supermarket chain or group:	LeClerc, Intermarché, Carrefour, Promodès

Segmentation varies from country to country because of the use of different outlets, and care must be taken not to ignore an important segment, such as department stores in Japan. Although the number of department stores selling food is less than 500—a small portion of the over 600,000 food outlets in Japan—they are located in high-traffic areas such as the Ginza, in Tokyo, and have high food sales, often accounting for more than 20 percent of total store sales.[3]

Think Break _____

Fast-food companies segment markets in different ways—for example, according to age, usage (once a week, once a month, less than once a month, never), or

---

[2]R. W. Haas, *Business Marketing,* 6th ed. (Cincinnati, OH: South-Western College Pub., 1995), chap. 9, "Segmentation in Business Markets."

[3]A. M. A. Heijbroek, W. M. H. van Noort, and A. J. Van Potten, *The Retail Food Market: Structures, Trends, and Strategies* (Netherlands: Rabobank International, Agribusiness, 1994): 33–34.

needs (economy, speed, enjoyment).[4] Select the market segment you think you are in and consider what you want when going to two different types of fast-food restaurants—for instance, McDonald's and a steak house.

Requirements for Effective Segmentation

As the previous discussion demonstrates, the variables that can be used to segment a market are endless: age, lifestyle, geographical location, and a long list beyond. The crucial question is which segmentation scheme is useful to the marketer. For example, is religion a valid variable for segmenting the salt market? As a matter of fact it is, as salt marketers have developed a coarse kosher salt for the Jewish market. But would psychographics prove to be useful in segmentation—do "achievers" have different requirements for salt than "traditionals"? Probably not. To be of value, market segments must have the following characteristics:[5]

- *Measurability*—the degree to which the size and purchasing power of the segment can be measured.
- *Accessibility*—the degree to which the segments can be reached and served.
- *Substantiality*—the degree to which segments are large or profitable enough for a company's purposes.
- *Actionability*—the degree to which effective programs can be designed for attracting and serving the segments.

Smaller companies cannot operate in all segments at once. The need to limit the number of segments served leads into the following discussion of company strategies toward segments.

MARKET-SEGMENTATION STRATEGIES

The company's marketing objectives should be determined first, and then the market-segmentation strategy developed to meet these objectives. The objectives reflect the company's business plan, company image, and general philosophy. These indicate the general market area, product type, sales volume required, and the project aim—whether to launch an innovative product or to expand a product mix.

The market-segmentation method chosen must be appropriate to the overall marketing strategy. The company can decide not to differentiate the product and to market one product across all market segments *(undifferentiated strategy),* to aim at all market segments with different products *(differentiated strategy),* or to aim the

---

[4]Keith Goldman, "Concept Selection for Independent Restaurants," *Cornell Hotel and Administrative Quarterly* (December 1993): 59–72, and A. W. H. Grant and L. A. Schlesinger, "Realize Your Customers' Full Profit Potential," *Harvard Business Review* (September–October 1995): 65–66.

[5]Phillip Kotler and Gary Armstrong, *Principles of Marketing,* 6th ed. (Englewood Cliffs, NJ: Prentice-Hall, 1994): 230.

product at only one or two segments *(concentrated strategy)*. Obviously, a large company can choose among all strategies, but smaller companies may be limited to the concentrated strategy. Figure 12-3 compares these strategy choices.

How the product can be differentiated also affects the choice of strategy. It is difficult to differentiate a commodity product such as manufacturing beef, so an undifferentiated strategy is appropriate; a branded processed product can easily be developed into a series of products differentiated for various market segments.

FIGURE 12-3   Strategies toward market segments.

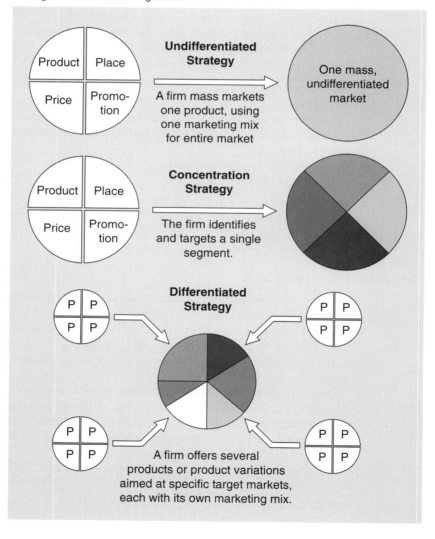

Variations in consumers' needs and wants, some of which consumers may not identify until the products are presented to them, also help to determine the best strategy. For example, when there were only two or three products in the bread market, consumers might not have been able to visualize the wide variety of breads available today, all designed for particular market segments.

MARKET RESEARCH FOR MARKET SEGMENTATION

Market research is needed to determine the needs of consumers or customers, to identify the different market segments and select those most suitable, and finally to select the products, prices, marketing channels, and promotion for the final marketing strategy. For a new product, this research is usually conducted during the product development process (see Chapter 13); developing a new market for a present product requires extensive research in the new market; for an improved product, a great deal of the information is already available and it is a case of pinpointing the inadequate knowledge.

Stages of Market Segmentation

Research occurs at each of the three stages in the selection of market segment(s):

• *Preliminary Selection of Market Segments*—Secondary research study to identify the different possible segments and to predict their possible sizes
• *Selection of Market Segment(s) and Product Positioning*—Both a study of products competing for the market segments and a consumer/customer study to give information on the segments' needs, attitudes, and behavior toward the products
• *Final Decision on Market Segment(s) and Product Positioning*—A consumer or customer study to determine market and sales potentials for the selected market segments.

Market research for consumer marketing usually starts with secondary market research. Some information may already be available in international or national statistics and in company records. This data will help to define different market segments and to assess their fit with the marketing objectives. The relative market shares of the different competing products can be determined from retail audits and buyers' diaries. Consumers' needs and attitudes and their positioning of the products on the market can be determined by in-depth interviewing or, more likely, through focus groups or consumer discussion panels. These would be conducted with different groups of consumers to determine the possible market segments. Finally, a consumer survey can be conducted to finalize the market segmentation and also to obtain quantitative buying data to predict sales and market potentials.

For industrial marketing, the overall structure is the same, but the researcher may obtain information on competing products from discussions with buyers or by testing in the supppplier's own pilot plant. The market shares and the total market size may be available from industry statistics, but a better source would be to survey customers. The customers' needs for the products and services and potential

TABLE 12-2   PROBLEMS IN OVERSEAS MARKET RESEARCH

Secondary research	Primary research
Limited availability of published data	Difficulty in locating respondents
Long delays between collecting and publishing	Difficulty in identifying the correct respondents
Inaccuracies in published data	Translation of questions into the language
Changes in basis of data	Meanings/politeness in other language
Difficulties in locating information	Local names of foods, products, ingredients
	Differences in cooking methods, processing
	Compatibility of interviewers with respondents
	Different seasonal variations

volume of usage could also be obtained from discussions with the buyers, as well as from observation in their plants.

International Markets

Because countries differ in many ways—language, foods and their characteristics, processing methods—market research must be conducted in the country where the product is to be sold. Information systems in multinational companies are global as well as national, with each country subsidiary developing a data base available to the other countries, as well as the head-office marketing team. Research projects may also involve cooperation between countries. Table 12-2, above, outlines typical problems encountered in searching for information in other countries. It is usually more efficient to use local market-research companies to overcome these problems.

In international research, interviews with government officials, chambers of commerce, consultants, importers, manufacturers, and retailers help build an understanding of an industry, its marketing structure, and limitations on it.

SECONDARY MARKET RESEARCH

Secondary market research uses data from appropriate government reports and trade statistics. Researchers analyze that information to estimate quantities consumed and identify trends in the consumption of particular products. There are many sources of information, and one of the problems is to identify and find the suitable source. To give some idea of the detailed information available, Box 12-2 contains a sampling of secondary sources on Japan's canned-beverage market.

International, National, and Industry Statistics

Governmental organizations, business institutes, and educational institutions, as well as information services found within larger companies, are valuable sources for secondary research. They can be broadly categorized as follows:

International Statistics and Reports   The United Nations Food and Agricultural Organization (FAO) develops food consumption, production, and trade data by combining statistics from individual countries. The United Nations Industrial Development Organization (UNIDO), reviews industries by country.

Country Statistics   Most countries produce food balance sheets or food statistics on the average per capita consumption of groups of foods. Usually rather crude, these statistics are calculated by starting with production data, adding imports and subtracting exports, and allowing for losses, storage, and animal feeding. Time and privacy problems make it difficult to collect accurate data from the various processing plants in many countries. As long as the base has not been changed, food balance sheets are useful for following trends in food consumption.

Country Surveys   In order to monitor the nutritional changes occurring in a country as a basis for health policies, many countries conduct diet surveys. These can be a 24-hour recall interview, a 2-to-7 days recording of what is consumed, or a careful weighing and itemization of the meals eaten. These surveys give a much more detailed analysis of the foods eaten and have the reliability of the usual sample survey, which depends on the size of the sample and the variability of the population.

Commercial Statistics   Various banks, newspapers/journals, trade associations, and commercial research organizations issue regular and special reports on the food industry in various countries. Unlike government statistics, these usually have to be purchased. These may give details of specific product areas, such as a breakdown of dairy products into liquid milk, fermented products, and ice cream.

BOX 12-2

JAPAN'S CANNED-BEVERAGE MARKET: RECENT TRENDS, CURRENT DATA

- Japan's canned-beverage market is experiencing growth due to low-sugar and sugar-free drinks. *Tradescope,** January 1996, 2–4.
- Sports and health drinks in Japan. Figures including annual sales, container types, sales by market leaders, and trends over several years. *Japanscan,*** September 1995, 25–26.
- Japan's mineral-water market. Reviews demand trends, domestic production, import trends, distribution, and import-related regulations and tariffs. *Tradescope,* October 1995, 9–16.
- Fruit juice consumption in Asia. Potential markets for investors considering this growing market are highlighted. *Asia Pacific Food Industry,* July 1995, 46–48, 50, 52.
- Japanese soft-drink market. Annual production of soft drinks, types of packaging, and sales by market leaders. *Japanscan,* January 1995, 20.

*Published by Jetro International Communication Department, Tokyo, Japan.
**Published by Anville, Upper Quinto, Stratford-on-Avon, England.

Research Studies by Universities and Institutes   Groups of researchers study food consumption patterns, sometimes in general nutritional areas and sometimes in particular food groups.

Before starting secondary research, it is useful to refer to international and country-specific catalogues of statistics and to do a computer search in food science and food technology abstracts and in nutrition abstracts. The USDA has published production and consumption statistics for many years, and excellent data on long-term trends in U.S. food consumption are available.

The Company's Internal Sales Information

The company has two main internal sources of sales information—salespeople and their records, and shipping records. The company may also track total industry sales, obtained from trade associations or from government statistics. Sales analysis, which in smaller companies may be the only type of research done, helps define the problem and guide the more expensive external research. Sales volumes may be measured over some historical period on the following bases:

- Total sales volume
- Product sales
- Territorial or geographic sales
- Customer or customer-type sales
- Size and timing of orders.

Salespeople may also provide information about the competition and their activities, new products, general trends in product sales, industry changes, and company changes. It is useful if sales data from several sources are used in analysis; if they agree, then forecasters can use the data with more confidence. If they do not agree, it is a signal to continue researching.

Purchased Market-Research Data

Retail Audits   Commercial companies regularly audit food products in retail outlets in many countries and sell this information. A representative sample of supermarkets and other outlets is selected and audited at regular intervals. The quantity of food products received into the store, on the shelves, and in storerooms is counted to determine sales. Data on the whole range of products and brands are collected so that the company product can be compared with competing products both at a particular time and over time. This method of tracking product sales is especially useful for monitoring the progress of a newly launched food product.

Supermarket Electronic Data (Check-out Scanners)   Today, because all sales are recorded electronically at the check-out stand, supermarket chains have a record of sales of each individual product, down to its different sizes. Each product is marked with a computer-readable bar code, and its sales recorded over time. Food manufacturing companies can buy this data, which provides a fast and accurate record of sales in that supermarket chain. The computer has completely revolutionized the collection and use of retail data; there are now continuous records of sales in different outlets and under different conditions. Consumer data collected at the supermarket can be related to the sales data. Sales can be related to shelf space, products, branding, promotion, and pricing.[6]

The data shown in Table 12-3 is from scanner data, gathered by Information Resources, Inc., from 2,700 supermarkets, 500 drugstores, and 250 mass-merchandise outlets selected to represent the national American market place. One can see how Van Den Bergh Foods launched a new product line, Ragu's Today's Recipe, and cannibalized its own present product line, Ragu Fino Italian, but the market leader, Classico, with 19 percent sales growth, grew 2 percent faster than the total market.

Buyers' Diaries   Retail audits measure only total sales and do not indicate the pattern of buying, nor do they identify the actual people buying. Some market-research companies hire panels of consumers who continually record what they buy. These panels of from 200 to 1,500 consumers detail not only how much they buy of which product, but also how often they repeat-buy or switch types and/or brands of products. Again, the change in sales and market share over time can be followed, and this information helps in forecasting future sales.

Trade Publications, Directories, Trade Shows

As a secondary source in industrial marketing, trade publications and directories provide company names, addresses, sizes, and production volume, as well as types of products, companies marketing the products, and brand names. Trade shows, where companies and products are on display, offer information on competing

---

[6]K. Grikitis, "EPOS—Threat or Benefit," *Food Processing* (April 1993): 17–19, and M. Penford, "Continuous Research—Art Nielsen to AD 2000," *Journal of Market Research Society* 36.1 (1994): 19–28.

TABLE 12-3   ITALIAN SAUCES IN THE US IN 1992

Brands	Sales, $ millions	% Change vs. year earlier	Current market share, %
Classico	15.8	19	32
Ragu Today's Recipe	12.1	—*	25
Ragu Fino Italian	7.4	−41	15
Progresso	5.8	7	11
Francesco	1.9	40	4
Others	6.2	n/a	13
Total Market	**49.2**	**17**	**100**

*New product
Source: K. Devenny, "Marketscan," *The Wall Street Journal* (October 6, 1992), p. B-1. Reprinted by permission of *Wall Street Journal,* ©1992 Dow Jones & Company, Inc. All Rights Reserved Worldwide.

products and their qualities, on new products and product uses, product comparisons, technical data, new customers, and customer needs.

PRIMARY MARKET RESEARCH

Primary research can determine the present usage patterns for particular types and brands of products—buying, preparing, eating—and also consumers' attitudes toward different products. Primary research methods include *interviewing* and *observation, focus groups,* and in-depth interviews. In interviewing, consumers are asked about their past and predicted future actions; in observation, their present behavior is watched by a trained observer.

Consumer Surveys

The most common consumer survey method is the formalized (or structured) personal interview, either face-to-face or by telephone or mail. The personal interview consists of asking questions of consumers (usually called respondents) in a face-to-face situation. The questionnaire may be structured, with simple behavior questions, or an in-depth interview seeking attitudes and motives. Sometimes respondents are asked to complete the questionnaire themselves (self-administered). In a telephone interview, used to obtain limited information which is wanted quickly and inexpensively, respondents are asked a short series of questions from a structured questionnaire. In mail interviews, questionnaires are mailed to respondents, who are asked to complete and return them by mail. Only short, simple questions can be asked, and return percentages are low—often less than 30 percent.

The consumer survey is organized in ten stages:

1 Research brief—determine the information required and the target consumers.
2 Research proposal—design the overall survey plan, including timing and cost.
3 Research design—detail the survey plan, selecting research methods and the consumer sampling plan.
4 Preparation—design and print the questionnaires and train interviewers.
5 Pretest—check questionnaire and methods with a small batch of respondents.
6 Survey—conduct the complete survey.
7 Data collection—edit, tabulate quantitative data, and transcribe qualitative data.
8 Data analysis—perform statistical analysis of quantitative data; summarize qualitative.
9 Report—write and present report to decision makers.
10 Action—decide on the action indicated by findings.

Note the final stage—taking action. Consumer research is expensive and needs to lead to decision making. The survey should be designed with this end result in mind.

Important Aspects of the Consumer Survey

Research Design   The two parts of research design—selection of research methods and selecting the consumer sample—are interrelated. Several factors affect these choices: type of information desired, accuracy needed, time available, cost considerations, and the ability of the researchers. For quantitative data, such as the number of people eating X brand of frozen peas, to an accuracy of ± 2 percent, a personal interview with a random sample of consumers is suitable, but for information on consumers' attitudes toward peas, an in-depth interview with a representative sample of consumers could be more useful.

Only *random-sampling* designs allow statistical inferences about a population to be made from a sample. Because the sample closely resembles the population, proportions, ratios, averages, and other similar measures computed from the sample are predicted to be true of the population within a certain accuracy range. This accuracy depends on the size of the sample and the amount of variation within the population. Pure random sampling is often difficult in consumer research, and adaptations of it are used:

Systematic sampling—Names are chosen from a population list by randomly selecting a starting number and using every nth name to gather the required sample size.

Stratified sampling —The population is divided into groups or strata, and a random sample is chosen from each stratum.

Area sampling   —The entire area or country is divided into districts, and a sample is taken from each district.

Cluster sampling   —Points on the map of an area are selected randomly, and a cluster of respondents is selected around each point.

In nonrandom sampling, the most common method is *quota sampling.* Interviewers are assigned the numbers of people of various kinds that they must interview. Provided that the specifications are fulfilled, they are free to interview whomever they wish.

Questionnaire Design   This skill must be learned by experience. The questionnaire is a communication mechanism on which the rest of the survey and the reliability of the resulting data depend. Before starting to formulate actual questions, it is advisable to list in detail all the information needed. This gives a broad indication of types of questions to ask and the length of the questionnaire. Questions can be completely structured with a list of possible answers, which are usually coded for ease of data entry, or open questions, allowing any answer. The interview need not follow a straight question-and-answer format; the interviewer can hand the person statements to read, pictures and samples to examine, or lists to be studied. The questionnaire must be designed to keep the respondent interested and communicating, while at the same time providing data that will be useful for analysis.

Interviewer Selection and Training   The interviewer's role is to contact respondents, ask the desired questions, and record the answers obtained. Interviewers are selected carefully to be capable of intelligent and friendly interviewing and able to write, speak, and record information clearly and accurately. Training, a necessity, must be carried out for every new survey interviewers are asked to conduct, regardless of how experienced they may be. They should be trained in the office by the researcher who designed the questionnaire, as well as in the field where they can be supervised while undertaking several interviews. Field supervision provides support when difficulties are encountered, verifies that the interviews are genuine and that the correct respondents have been interviewed, and keeps the work of different interviewers accurate and uniform.

Editing   The completed questionnaires need to be edited to ensure that there is consistency in the results and that they are in a suitable form for collating. In structured interviews, the possible responses on the questionnaires are precoded, ready for entry into the computer. Answer categories are mutually exclusive—there is a clear and unambiguous boundary between categories, with sufficient categories for all possible responses. Coding requires careful interpretation to ensure that the meaning of the response and the meaning of the category are consistently and uniformly matched. In unstructured interviews, the responses to open questions are recorded by interviewers, then transcribed and summarized.

Summarizing the Data   The data is usually tabulated into frequency distributions and then used to determine percentages, means, and some measure of the distribution, such as range or standard deviation/error. Scatter diagrams are also useful to give an indication of the relationships between the variables, before using correlation and regression techniques to calculate their statistical relationship.[7]

Industrial-Market Surveys

In industrial marketing, surveys are used to study customers' processes, ingredients used, qualities needed in ingredients, methods of using ingredients, quantities of ingredients used now and anticipated future needs, the types and qualities of final consumer products, sales of consumer products, and the customers' experiences with the company's and competitors' products in their plants.

Industrial-market surveys vary from consumer surveys in that the numbers of respondents are small and the questions are usually technical. The smallness of the numbers also makes it difficult to take random samples; therefore, either a complete census or a sample representative of the various types of companies is surveyed. Face-to-face, mail, and telephone interviews are used, but the use of fax and e-mail, faster methods of communication, is increasing. Fax and e-mail surveys cannot be long and detailed; for more information, face-to-face or telephone interviews are used.

Usually a formal questionnaire with structured questions is completed by the interviewer in face-to-face or telephone interviews, but self-administered questionnaires are used in mail, fax, and e-mail surveys. The interviewers must be technically competent in the customers' area and therefore are often either

---

[7]This is only an outline on consumer surveys; more information can be found in a good basic text, such as *Research for Marketing Decisions* by P. E. Green, D. S. Tull, and G. Albaum, Prentice-Hall International Editions, 5th edition, 1988.

salespersons or technical people within the company. Market-research companies do undertake industrial market research, but usually more in the general management and marketing areas, rather than in the product and processing technical surveys.

Table 12-4 outlines a survey on the use of milk powders by bakers.

Focus Groups

Focus groups are commonly used to study product characteristics, benefits, and positions. The focus group is six to eight people who have a discussion on a specific area, a process which can be repeated several times so that the total group of people taking part better represents the market. The main advantage of focus groups over individual, in-depth interviews is that respondents interact and stimulate each other, leading to more creative thinking. Focus groups are also flexible—the areas discussed can be varied in response to information being provided. They also cost less than other attitudinal research; a three- or four-hour interview study can be conducted, analyzed, and reported in less than a week.

Focus groups need an experienced moderator or group organizer and a relaxed atmosphere. Photographs, sketches, or products can be used to stimulate

TABLE 12-4   AN INDUSTRIAL MARKET SURVEY

PROBLEM	Determine the types of bakers buying skim milk powders and baking mixes which include skim milk powder. Are baking mixes replacing skim milk powder? What are the comparative sales?

AIM	Detailed study of industrial milk powder users, providing—
	  Quantitative information: tonnage, suppliers, products, prices.
	  Qualitative information: service and new-product opportunities.

METHOD	**Possible sources:** industries and companies listed in available secondary data, such as Business Who's Who and telephone books.
	Primary data collection: full census of industrial users:
	  Large companies—semistructured personal interviews.
	  Small and geographically dispersed companies—telephone interviews.
	Secondary data collection: background research using company data, company interviews and government statistics

ANALYSIS	**Quantitative:** market share, customer analysis of usage, historical sales. **Qualitative:** current product mixes for different companies and different market segments, their present and predicted future needs, image of company and the company's products, service levels of different companies. **Development of information for decision making:** company brainstorming, customer forecasting, researching expert opinions on future outcomes.
USE/DECISION MAKING	**Product-mix management:** deletions, additions, or improvement to the product mix, leading to product development and subsequent changes in the marketing mix.
FINAL OBJECTIVE	**A strategic five-year marketing plan,** including a timed product and customer mix for milk powder products.

discussion. Sessions, best when limited to about twenty to thirty minutes but sometimes lasting one to two hours, are recorded and transcribed later. Theoretically, the results cannot be generalized, because samples are invariably small and not selected randomly, questions are not asked the same way each time, responses are not independent, and results are difficult to quantify. However, focus-group findings are often confirmed by later consumer surveys using random sampling.

PRODUCT POSITIONING IN THE MARKET SEGMENTS

Once marketers have identified the market segments appropriate to their company, the next step is to position their product in the marketplace. The term, *product positioning* was popularized in the 1981 book, *Positioning: The Battle for Your Mind.* Its authors, Ries and Trout, state that the consumer is bombarded with thousands of messages each day; many competitors want the attention of the consumer; and there are a limited number of positions for products in the consumer's mind. The marketer's task is to find these positions and, through the marketing mix, to place their product in the most ideal position.[8]

Selecting the Product Position and the Market Segment

A product position is the place that consumers perceive a product holds in the marketplace as compared with competing products. Product positioning follows four important steps:

- Consumers identify the key product characteristics.
- Consumers place competitive products with regard to these key characteristics.
- The company positions its product relative to competitive products by product design and promotion.
- Consumers confirm the product's position.

Consumers may compare products on price, convenience, appearance, nutritional value, healthiness, or any other important product characteristic. For example, cheese could be positioned on price:

Low price	Processed cheese	Mild cheddar	Tasty cheddar	Blue	Camembert	Brie	High price

Calorie-reduced foods might be positioned on their similarity to "real" foods:

Looking like real food	Trimmed pork	Low-calorie yogurt	Low-fat cookies	A liquid meal substitute	Not looking like real food

[8]Al Ries and Jack Trout, *Positioning: The Battle for Your Mind* (New York: McGraw-Hill, 1981): 5–35.

The consumer may compare products on one dimension or several, on product characteristics or on product benefits (see Chapter 13). Identical competing products will occupy the same position; differentiated products, unique positions.

The product position and the market segment are interrelated, and their selections are considered together.[9] Below are comparisons of the product positions of margarines and butter and the related market segments:

CALORIES

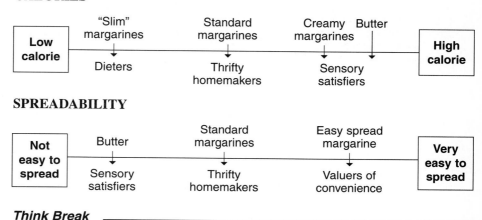

SPREADABILITY

Think Break

In a supermarket, look at the cheeses in the deli case. Select two important characteristics of cheeses, draw a scale for each, and position the products on the scales. Other products you could position are yogurts or cereals.

Different market segments may give different positions to the product. For example, in positioning cheese on price, an upper social class may regard blue cheese as cheap, with special European cheeses on the expensive end.

Not only the product itself, but also the brand and packaging must relate to a particular segment and position. When aiming for market integration—marketing to more than one segment—brand names must not contain words which have bad connotations for any segment. Foods aiming at a range of segments are usually more bland, but may be highly flavored for specific niche markets. Also the packaging, aesthetically acceptable to all the segments, may be differentiated for specific niche markets.

Market Segment and the Marketing Mix

When the market segment and the products are identified, the remainder of the marketing mix can be chosen to support and enhance them.

[9]C. L. Bovée, M. J. Houston, and J. V. Thill, *Marketing,* 2d ed. (New York: McGraw-Hill, 1992): 224–27.

BOX 12-3

**PRODUCT-POSITION MAPPING WITH
MULTIDIMENSIONAL SCALING (MDS)**

Perceptual mapping using a research technique called
Multidimensional Scaling shows how customers perceive products in the market, according to their most important attributes. Hopefully, gaps can be found where
there are no products. For example, in this perceptual
map of the U.K. yogurt market, there are gaps at the top
around *healthy* and a big gap at the bottom between
creamy and *Greek*.

The one important thing MDS doesn't tell is whether
there is a market in these gaps, but other quantitative
techniques are combined with MDS to predict sales potentials for products in the gaps. In brand-strategy mod-
eling, where gaps are found, various "what-if" models
measure brand-share potential, helping to avoid canni-
balization of a company's own products and existing
brands, and measuring the extent to which a new product/
brand might take market share from competitors.

Source: C. H. Wilson, "Brand Development and Marketing in
Europe in the 1990s," *Journal of the Society of Dairy Technology*
44:2 (1991): 37–40.

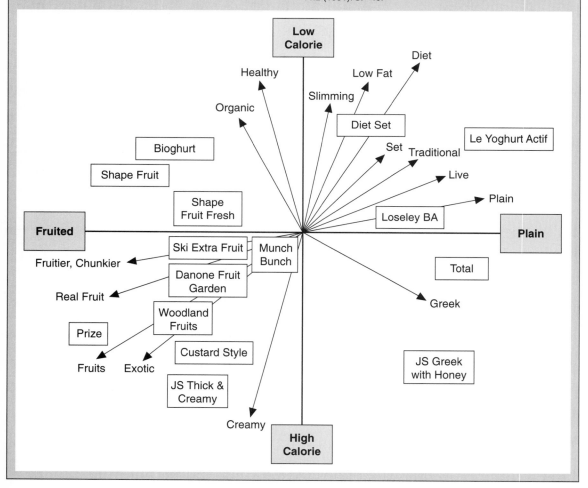

The market channel (place) delivers the product to the chosen market segment with the appropriate quality and quantity, and, of course, the right image. In consumer marketing, the type of retail outlet is related to the market segment. The upper-upper-class British consumer buys food at Fortnum and Mason; the middle- and lower-class British consumer buys at the corner shop or supermarket. In the United States, supermarkets are also related to social class—the specialized supermarket for the upper-class Californian, the basic no-frills supermarket in the working-class area, and in some inner-city areas few supermarkets and numerous small groceries. In some Southeast Asian countries, the middle class, likely educated overseas, goes to the supermarket; everyone else goes to the open market. Exporters must identify the retail outlets used by the various market segments in the overseas market, as well as the importers and distributors providing imported foods to these retailers.

The direct relationship between different consumer groups and restaurants is even more marked. For example, in the United States, children up to the age of 17 prefer fast-food restaurants. Although 18–24-year-olds eat out in restaurants more than any other age group, they eat mainly fast food. Ethnic cuisines, particularly Mexican or Italian, are popular with 25–34-year-olds, but still 50 percent of their visits are to fast-food places. People aged 35–44 are expected to move from fast-food to full-service concepts, while those 45–54 support midscale restaurants, with a third of their visits to family-style steakhouses and cafeterias. The 55–64-year-olds also patronize midscale restaurants, but ethnic restaurants are less popular. Americans over 65, many on fixed retirement incomes, are historically light restaurant users. Although their patronage has increased in recent years, they buy mainly fast food.[10]

The value (price) of a product varies with the social group. For example, a cheese regarded as everyday in Scotland can be sold at double the price in a London shop; a New Zealand lobster paté may double or triple in price when sold in Paris, where patés are expected to be expensive. Consumers have an expected price range for a product, but different consumer groups have different expected price ranges. An "organic" carrot in a health food store is expected to cost more than a carrot in a supermarket. A special wine priced low would be regarded as suspect by the wine buff.

The preferred forms of promotion vary for different market segments. The type of promotion—advertising, in-store promotion, public relations—is selected for the market segment, and then the specific message and media. In integrated marketing, where one product is marketed to several segments, the message has to be generally acceptable and delivered by widely received media, such as television. In specific segment marketing, the media used by the target segment is identified. For example, the elderly family woman most likely reads daily newspapers and weekly magazines, particularly women's magazines; she disdains sexy advertisements and

---

[10]Keith Goldman, "Concept Selection for Independent Restaurants," *Cornell Hotel and Administrative Quarterly* (December 1993): 59–72.

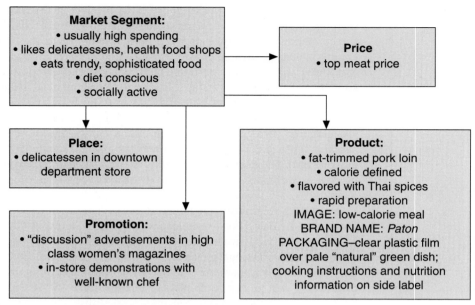

FIGURE 12-4   Meat product for the urban professional woman.

messages aimed at children and is interested in food education, reading the recipe pages and food articles. The young mother is more likely to pick up books on food and cooking, while the professional woman reads sophisticated women's magazines, bestsellers on food and diets, and news magazines. Figure 12-4 traces the development of a new meat product aimed at a specific market segment, the urban professional woman.

Think Break

Is the menu in your favorite restaurant becoming boring? What new dish would you like to add? Describe this dish and how it would be positioned on the menu. What should its price be? How would you promote it if you owned the restaurant?

SUMMARY

Market segmentation, product description, and product positioning are central to marketing and are necessary for the development of a marketing strategy. Once these are decided, then the rest of the marketing mix falls into place.

The identification and selection of the market segment(s) is not simple because there are so many methods of segmentation. The selection depends on the type of market, the company, and the product. A commodity product reaches the total market, but an industrial product may be directed at a market segment of large companies with high technology. A large food manufacturing company may wish to combine several consumer segments so that it can have a market of viable size and so must design a product which is acceptable to all these segments. The small company may identify one market segment and design a product with the unique qualities this market segment wants or needs.

Segmentation and development of a product for that segment require information which is obtained through market research. What research the company chooses to do depends on the money and time available and the risk attached to the decision it is going to make. Secondary research draws on information available in government and industry statistics, in the company's sales records, in specialized reports, or from companies who sell retail information continuously recorded from retail audits, electronic scanning, or buyers' diaries.

Detailed consumer or industrial customer information comes from primary research, particularly consumer or industrial surveys to determine product needs, product uses, and market shares. Focus groups provide details about products and consumer/customer needs; they are especially valuable in developing new-product ideas and product concepts and for positioning the product.

Through the use of this information the market segment, the product, the positioning of the product in the market, and finally the marketing mix can be developed.

IMPORTANT TERMS AND CONCEPTS

concentrated strategy   319
differentiated strategy   319
focus group   329
interviewing   326
market segmentation   311
market segments—
   demographic   316
   geographic   313
   psychographic   315

sociocultural   313
  user behavior   316
observation   326
primary research   326
product positioning   330
quota sampling   327
random sampling   327
secondary research   332
undifferentiated strategy   319

CASE STUDY: Market Research—The Importance of Defining the Problem and Research Objectives

Market research is often conducted by market-research companies for food companies. If the two companies communicate well, the research provides the information a food company needs for decision making. A request for research takes the form of a market-research brief.

In this case study, a large bread company is marketing bread in two large urban areas. They are worried about decreasing sales caused by the increasing amount of bread being baked in supermarkets. To help decide what new products would most improve their market share, they want to know what market segments are in this market. With that information, they plan to select a specific segment(s) and develop a product(s) targeting that segment. They wrote the following brief for their market-research company.

MARKET-RESEARCH BRIEF

Company:	Best Bake Bread.
Product:	All types of bread.
	Own and competitive brands.
	Supermarket bread.
Aim:	To identify the buyers of different types of bread at different outlets.
Use of Information:	To identify market segments as future targets for new products.
Geographic Areas:	City A—pop. 3 million; City B—pop. 1 million; and surrounding districts.
Segmentation:	Demography, lifestyle, consumption rate.
Accuracy:	Plus or minus 10 percent.
Research Budget:	$120,000.
Timing of Research:	Information needed before development of next year's plans.
Company Data:	Best Bake Bread owns three bakeries, two in City A and one in City B. It has 30 percent of the market in City A and 35 percent in City B. The product line includes white bread (8 types, sliced and unsliced), whole-wheat breads (4 types, sliced and unsliced), a fruit loaf, and 8 varieties of rolls and buns. All bread is sold under the brand "Fresh Maid"; no products are individually branded.

Questions

1 If the company presented you with this brief, what other questions would you ask them?
2 What other information would you need before you could start to write a research proposal? How could you find this information?
3 How could this market-research brief be improved?

The market-research company developed a research program and presented the following research proposal to Best Bake Bread.

MARKET-RESEARCH PROPOSAL

Aim:	Identify the buyers of the different types of bread at different outlets.
Place:	City A and City B urban areas only.
Retail Outlets:	Supermarkets.
Respondents:	Shoppers from different age groups.
Research Method:	Interview, using a structured questionnaire.
Sample:	25 supermarkets—15 in City A, 10 in City B—chosen randomly from different city areas.
Questionnaire:	Types of bread bought.
	Brands of bread bought.
	Reasons for buying, not buying.
	Quantity of bread bought.
	Demographic details—age, occupation.
Timing:	Over 2 weeks, 3 weeks after agreement.
	Report 4 weeks after interviewing.
Cost:	$100,000.

Questions

1 If you were the marketing manager of the bread company, what would be your reaction to this proposal?

2 Would the proposal give you the necessary information for segment selection and product positioning?

3 How could it be improved without making the research more costly?

4 What secondary information could be found or bought to combine with this primary research and help the company make its decisions.

5 Do you think the research program would give the company sufficient information to develop its product development strategy?

6 What information would the company need in order to develop a market strategy to sell new products to this market segment?

QUESTIONS

1 What effect is the changing population age structure likely to have on the future age market segmentation for beef and dairy products?

2 Discuss nutritional market segmentation in the breakfast-cereal market, outlining the consumers in each segment. Briefly summarize the product characteristics you perceive as important in targeting each segment.

3 The "type of household" is often used to identify market segments in food marketing. For three different types of households, describe their methods of buying foods: how, when, where, and what.

4 List some of the sources of secondary market-research information. What types of information can be obtained through these sources?

5 Where would you look for information on the trends in total bread sales over the last fifty years in a particular country? In a city or metropolitan area?

6 Looking at the shelf-space usage in your supermarket, what would you estimate are the market shares for the larger companies in the frozen-vegetables market? Where would you look for information to confirm your guess?

7 An American company is interested in building a starch manufacturing plant in New Zealand using wheat, maize, and potatoes as raw materials. As a New Zealand-based market-research company, you have been asked to find information on both the raw-material supply and the industrial market for starches in New Zealand. Your information will be used to decide whether or not to build the plant. Discuss the development of your research proposal.

8 A customer interview survey was chosen to investigate restaurants' use of portion-controlled meat. Outline the various stages you would include in such a survey. Who will be the respondents, and what information will be sought in the questionnaire?

REFERENCES AND RESOURCES

Askegaard, S., and T. K. Madson. *European Food Cultures: An Exploratory Analysis of Food Related Preferences and Behavior in European Regions.* MAPP (Market Process and Product Innovation in the Food Sector) Working Paper No. 26. Aarhus, Denmark: Aarhus School of Business, September 1995.

Churchill, Gilbert A., Jr. *Marketing Research: Methodological Foundations.* 6th ed. New York: The Dryden Press, Harcourt Brace College Publishers, 1995.

Green, P. E., D. S. Tull., and G. Albaum. *Research for Marketing Decisions.* Englewood Cliffs, NJ: Prentice-Hall International Editions, 1988.

Grunert, K. G., et al. *Marketing Orientation in Food Agriculture.* Boston, MA: Kluwer Academic Publishers, 1996.

Haas, R. W. *Business to Business Marketing and Management.* 6th ed. Cincinnati, OH: South-Western College Pub., 1995.

Hobert, N. B., and M. W. Speece. *Practical Marketing Research: An Integrated Global Perspective.* Englewood Cliffs, NJ: Prentice Hall, 1993.

Penford, M. "Continuous Research: Art Nielsen to AD 2000." *Journal of Market Research Society* 36.1 (1994): 19–28.

Piirto, R. *Beyond Mind Games: The Marketing Power of Psychographics.* Ithaca, NY: American Demographic Books, 1991.

Stanton, W. J., M. J. Etzel, and B. J. Walker. *Fundamentals of Marketing.* New York: McGraw-Hill, Inc., 1994.

Usunier, J. C. *International Marketing: A Cultural Approach.* New York: Prentice-Hall, 1993.

13

FOOD-PRODUCT MANAGEMENT AND DEVELOPMENT

CHAPTER OUTLINE

LEARNING OBJECTIVES

After reading this chapter and answering the questions in the Think Breaks and at the end of the chapter, you should be able to:

- Identify the important characteristics of a food product.
- Name the different types of branding strategies that a manufacturer can adopt.
- Understand under what conditions brand extension is a desirable strategy.
- Show how the product life cycle can be used to manage the product mix.
- Explain product mix and the difference between product-mix width and product-mix depth.
- Understand the product management approach to organizing the marketing function in a company.
- Know when products could be improved or eliminated, or new products introduced.
- Understand the product development process and how it can be planned and controlled.

INTRODUCTION

The previous chapters have introduced the various types of food products—commodity, industrial and consumer—and in Chapter 7 industrial products were discussed in some detail. This chapter opens by studying consumer food products, in particular the characteristics that identify the product and the benefits that the consumer sees in the product. A product profile can be drawn to identify product characteristics; this profile can be compared with competing products and with an ideal product profile identified by the consumer. This analysis shows how the competing products differ from the company's present product and how that product can be improved to compete more effectively. Identification of product characteristics and building of product profiles and product concepts is a fundamental part of product improvement and development of new products.

Companies usually have not just one product but a series of product lines combined in a product mix. There are different types of product mixes from which a company selects the one that fits with their marketing strategy and business plan. The product mix needs to be analyzed and controlled to yield the sales revenues and profits required by the company. Regular product-mix audits indicate poorly performing products that can be removed (product elimination) or improved (product development). Adding new or improved products to the mix requires product development.

The product development process has been refined over the last thirty years and is still evolving. It consists of seven clearly defined stages—from the setting of project objectives to analysis after the product launch on the market. Although the stages occur in all product development processes, the activities at each stage vary with the type of product—consumer or industrial—and with the company's size and risk-taking philosophy.

WHAT IS A FOOD PRODUCT?

Food   —a material eventually consumed by humans to satisfy physiological and psychological needs.

Food product—a food designed for sale to the public.

The term *product* can be defined from the company's or the buyer's viewpoint. For example, a definition showing that the product is a function of processing and marketing is:

Product   —those characteristics of a food arising from materials or ingredients, processing, formulation, design, storage life, sensory qualities, packaging, and service.

A definition from the buyer's viewpoint is:

Product   —a complex of tangible and intangible attributes, including packaging, color, price, manufacturer's prestige, retailer's prestige, and manufacturer's and retailer's services, which the buyer may accept as offering satisfaction of wants or needs.

Figure 13-1 shows how a total consumer product is built up by the company, but also how consumers see it in the market and home environments. From this viewpoint, consumers develop their own product concept.

The tangible product is the physical entity; the extended or total product is the tangible product plus its aesthetic appearance and/or packaging, plus advertising and services. The product concept, also called the product image, is the product as the consumer sees it and includes the consumer's psychological reactions to the

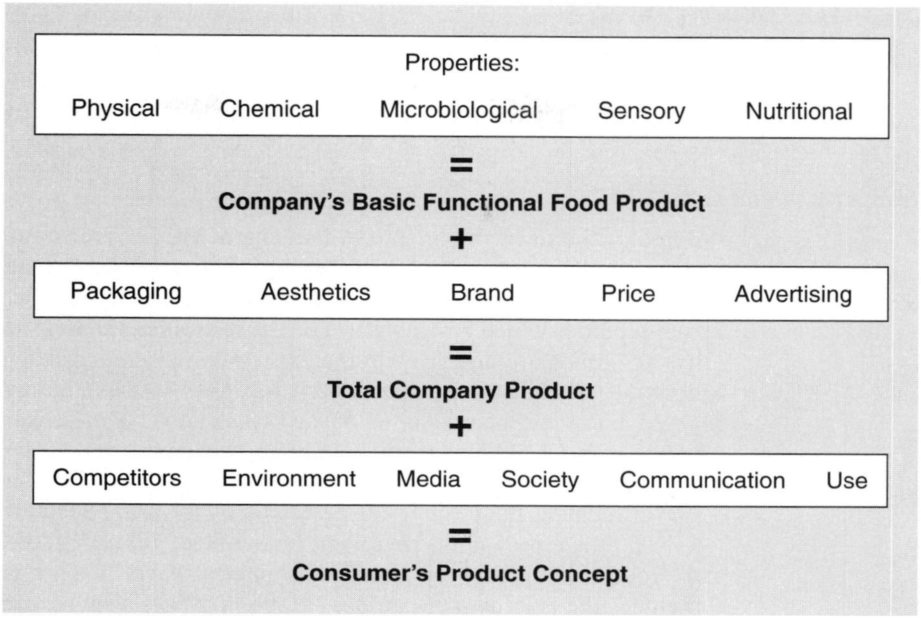

Properties:				
Physical	Chemical	Microbiological	Sensory	Nutritional

=

Company's Basic Functional Food Product

+

Packaging	Aesthetics	Brand	Price	Advertising

=

Total Company Product

+

Competitors	Environment	Media	Society	Communication	Use

=

Consumer's Product Concept

FIGURE 13-1   Food product as viewed by company and by consumer.

product. The response to simple products such as bread can be rather basic, but products like a bottle of wine may also have social connotations, or a box of chocolates may produce emotional responses.

Think Break

Compare this outline of a consumer food product with the industrial product in Figure 7-1.

A product usually has an identifiable and readily recognizable form and can be placed in a *product category,* each product category carrying a commonly understood descriptive name, such as apples, frozen peas, or corned beef. The separate products in the product category can be identified by their brand name, for example, Safeway frozen peas and Birdseye frozen peas. The brand name suggests a product difference to the consumer. In fact any change in the product, however minor, creates in effect a "new" product. If consumers recognize a difference, then it is a new product to them. Some separate products are identified as product types, such as Red Delicious apples, Granny Smith apples, or Gala apples.

THE TOTAL FOOD PRODUCT

The *characteristics* of a food product, summarized in Table 13-1, can be divided into product, package, and service. Many of these characteristics have been described in Chapters 3 and 4 for consumer products and in Chapter 7 for industrial products.

Product Characteristics

Some of the most important product characteristics are sensory; not only do consumers judge food quality by the sensory characteristics, but attractive sensory properties add to eating enjoyment. Sensory characteristics are the physical and chemical properties which have an effect on the consumer's senses: nose, ears, eyes, touch, mouth. Foods are bought with the expectation of certain definable sensory properties: the aroma of wine, fizz of champagne, softness of a peach, crunch of an apple, bitterness of coffee, or flavor of ketchup. Other sensory properties include temperature—cold ice cream, hot coffee; and pain—hot curries, whisky "straight."

Sensory characteristics are classified as appearance, aroma, flavor, and texture. Flavor includes the basic tastes perceived by the tongue (sour, salty, sweet, and bitter) and the aroma notes perceived by the nose. Flavor is detected in the mouth as the food is being chewed and also as an after-flavor when it is swallowed. Texture includes the crispness or hardness at the first bite, chewiness as the teeth grind the food, and the feeling of the food in the mouth, such as fattiness or slipperiness. Sensory characteristics present the greatest problem to food manufacturers, because, although it is relatively easy to recognize the need for a good "nose" on a wine, or a flavorful orange juice, or an elastic-textured salami, it is extremely difficult to define what a good bouquet is, or what flavor a "flavorful" orange juice has, or exactly what the right texture for salami should be.

Think Break

Have a glass of fruit juice and describe the flavor in detail, from the first sip to the final swallow. Then eat an apple and another fruit and compare their textures, from first bite to last.

TABLE 13-1   CHARACTERISTICS OF A FOOD PRODUCT

Product	Package	Service
Physical	Aesthetic	Consistency of quality
Chemical composition	Brand	Consistency of safety
Nutritional	Price	Product availability
Sensory	Value for money	Product replacement
Use and convenience	Ease of use	Cooking information
Safety	Protection of product	Storage information
Storage life	Ease of storage	
Psychological	Information	

Packaging Characteristics

The *package* is an integral part of the consumer product and may also be important in food service products. The package protects, promotes, and educates, as well as complying with any government regulations. A package protects the product from water, oxygen, foreign odors and flavors, and foreign objects. It should also provide ease of storage and use. The package's aesthetic design (color, shape, graphics) describes the product qualities and attracts the consumer's eye. Information can be given about ingredients, nutritional value, cooking and serving, and alternative recipes. Regulations may specify information to be included: ingredients, weight/volume, manufacturer's name and address, and, in some cases, nutritional information. Regulations may also specify the size of printing and type of information allowed, such as nutritional claims.

In international marketing, care needs to be taken with colors of packaging and symbols. For example, death is sometimes associated with white, black, or purple; in Hong Kong white is for funerals, yellow is imperial, and red is warm and friendly. Also, the size of packaging may vary in different countries—salad dressings sell in small bottles in Britain and in large 1-liter jars in New Zealand.

Think Break

Look at a food package from the supermarket and decide what image that package projects. Then decide what package characteristics create that image.

The brand can add value and is therefore an intrinsic part of the food product. A simple product such as frozen peas can appear different to a consumer if it has no brand, a retailer brand, or a food-company brand. The brand identifies the product and also gives it uniqueness, adding a great deal to the consumer's perception of it. For example, two competing soups could be tasted unidentified and consumers would say they preferred Brand A to Brand B; identify Brand B as Smith's, a popular brand, however, and they may then say they prefer Brand B to Brand A.

Brand —name, term, symbol or special design that is intended to differentiate the products of one seller from those of another seller. It can be:

Brand name—words, letters, or names that can be vocalized.

Brand mark —nonverbal design or symbol that can be identified with a product by sight.

Trade marks—a brand or part of a brand given legal protection of the seller's exclusive rights to use that brand name and/or brand mark.

Foods may be branded with manufacturers' *national brands*—"Birdseye," for instance, or with *private brands*—retailers' or wholesalers' brands, also referred to as distributors' labels, house brands, or own-label products, such as "Woolworth's" or "Safeway." Foods may be packaged with *generic brands* or as *plain packs,* on which only the generic name of the food is used—for example, Instant Coffee. Generic brands are usually established by wholesalers or retailers.

Generics usually have simple packaging, lower quality, and the lowest pricing. Private brands vary according to the quality image desired by the retailer—budget brands, low-quality and cheap, or value-oriented brands, with strict quality specifications and promotion as top-quality foods. A *family brand,* such as Heinz, (pictured in Figure 13-2) may cover all, or at least a significant number of, the company's products. Product-line brands identify groups: Dolmio sauces, Schilling herbs and spices, Pal dog foods. Single-product brands label individual products—Mars Bar (of the Mars Group), Folger's Coffee, and Crisco (both marketed by Procter & Gamble).

International brand names must avoid sounding like words with bad connotations in any language and must be easily pronounced by speakers of all languages. It is preferable to retain the home brand abroad, unless it has different, undesired meanings in other countries. Well-known international brands usually have status when entering a new country. However, the in-country industry also recognizes this, and the brand may be in use in that country before the international producer enters the market.

FIGURE 13-2   The Heinz product line. Heinz uses the family brand of Heinz on many of its products, but also uses single-product and local brands, as well as product-line brands, such as Weight Watchers. *(Courtesy of H. J. Heinz.)*

Think Break

Compare two family brands, for example, Heinz and Campbell's, and describe the image you have of these companies and their products. Is this image formed by the company's promotion or by your eating experiences?

What single-product brands do you know? Why do you think they have been given their own brand name?

Service Characteristics

Surprisingly, *product availability,* including the place and time, is an important food-product characteristic. For example, a Scottish cheese specialist making a traditional Scottish cream cheese coated with oatmeal could decide to market it through an upscale grocer in London; the product would then be a specialized cheese; if marketed though a discount supermarket chain, it would become an everyday product. Pizza sold between meals might be regarded as a snack, but when sold in the evening, as a meal.

Consistency in quality and safety are usually desired in a food. Consumers would find unacceptable canned peas with varying amounts of peas in the cans or canned sliced peaches with thick and thin slices. The modern food industry is based on ensuring a uniform and dependable quality, but sometimes "natural" or "organic" foods are produced with variable qualities to emphasize the naturalness of the products.

Think Break

Look at different sauces which can be added to food for flavoring. Identify the characteristics which are common to all the sauces and the unique characteristics of individual products.

BRAND STRATEGIES

Brands can be valuable company assets, and the term *brand equity* is used to describe this value. This is evident when food companies change owners, as they frequently do. The value of the "intangible assets," or "goodwill," is usually three to five times that of inventory and fixed assets (buildings and plant). Brand equity is based on brand loyalty, name awareness, perceived quality, brand associations, and other proprietary brand assets, such as patents, trademarks, and channel relationships.[1]

The food manufacturer first decides either to have its own brand or to market under a retailer's private brand. In 1994, in the United Kingdom and the United States, private-label products were respectively 28 percent and 14 percent of total

---

[1]For more on brand equity, see David A. Aaker, *Managing Brand Equity: Capitalizing on the Value of a Brand Name* (New York: Free Press, 1991).

grocery sales; other European retailers' use of private labels fell between these extremes but is increasing rapidly.[2]

A manufacturer without sufficient money for promotion may enter a particular market by agreeing with retailers to manufacture for their label. Large companies often provide basic foods, such as canned beans or frozen peas, under retailer labels, but will also maintain their company brand. A few retailers, such as Marks and Spencer in Britain, whose philosophy is to provide products of consistently high quality and who have very strict specifications for the food manufacturer, do market high-priced products under their own label.

The next brand choice is whether to employ *brand extension* or to create a new brand. Brand extension means using an existing brand for a new product targeting a new market segment. Trading on existing consumer recognition, brand extension requires less promotion and advertising. A brand is usually extended within the company, but it can be extended to another company. For example, Sunkist is the well-known brand used for oranges by a California citrus marketing cooperative. They extended the brand to Sunkist juice drinks and Sunkist fruit snacks by licensing the brand to Lipton's for these products. Extending brands requires care: there is no point in using a brand with a poor reputation, nor a brand that does not relate to the product, nor adding a product which will damage the present products. As David Aaker states, "There is little point in extending mediocrity."[3]

There are other pitfalls in brand extension. Does the extension brand create undesirable attribute associations? General Mills, the maker of Cheerios, was reluctant to interfere with Cheerios' brand association of being a low-sugar cereal. They tested Honey Nut Cheerios for a long time to assure that such an extension would not damage Cheerios' image and core market. Neither Honey Nut Cheerios nor Apple Cinnamon Cheerios had an effect on Cherrios' core market. It is argued that potential negative associations from the extension to the original are less likely to occur if: 1) the original brand associations are very strong, and 2) there is a distinct difference between the original and the extensions, but the difference between the original and extension is not so extreme as to make the extension appear incongruous. Thus, the Cheerios brand extension worked because all the products were associated with oats and the doughnut shape, and the new Cheerios products were distinctly different from the original but not incongruous to the original product and brand. Probably, a line extension to a Cheerios candy bar would not work as well.

Another strong argument for developing a new brand, rather than relying on continual extension, is that the new brand may provide new opportunities for growth. Campbell's introduced the Prego brand for a line of spaghetti sauces after research had found that consumers had an unfavorable association of the Campbell's name with spaghetti sauce. Evidently Campbell's was not red enough, rich enough, or thick enough. With the Prego brand association established in the sauce area,

[2]David Hughes, ed., *Breaking With Tradition: Building Partnerships and Alliances in the European Food Industry* (Wye, Ashford, Kent: Wye College Press, 1994): 24.

[3]David A. Aaker, *Managing Brand Equity: Capitalizing on the Value of a Brand Name* (New York: Free Press), 1991: 213.

Campbell's could extend that brand to a line of Italian soups. These soups would be positioned to attack the Progresso brand line of Italian-style soups which had been taking market share from Campbell's.[4]

The promotion required by a new brand makes it expensive. However, if the product is really innovative and unique to the market, a new brand is appropriate, especially if the product can be developed into a product line or even into a group of related products. Also, the present company brands may not be related to the new product; in fact, they may give the product the wrong image. For example, if the company's brand is associated with low-price products and the company has decided to launch a line of gourmet meals, a new brand should be developed.

Another decision is how many brands to show on the package. A family brand may appear with an individual brand if the product gains from the company's reputation, but showing more than two brands risks confusing the consumer. The family brand lends an image to the product which may encourage the consumer to trust the new product sufficiently to buy it, but the failure of a new product might adversely affect the family brand. The discussion in Box 13-1 highlights the

[4]*Ibid.,* 206–37.

BOX 13-1

NESTLÉ'S BRAND-BUILDING MACHINE

Nestlé represents a thumping rejection of the one-world, one-brand school of marketing. The company prefers brands to be local and people regional; only technology goes global. Nestlé has poured nearly $18 billion into acquisitions over the past decade and now owns nearly 8,000 different brands worldwide. Of those 8,000 worldwide brands, only 750 are registered in more than one country, and only 80 are registered in ten. In new markets Nestlé alights with a mere handful of labels, selected from a basket of 11 strategic brand groups. The idea is to simplify life, limit risk, and concentrate the attack; brand survival becomes managers' top priority. Nestlé can then pour advertising and marketing into just two or three brands per country and gain huge market shares. Not believing in life cycles for brands, they expect a well-managed brand to survive a long time.

Nestlé had a problem in Thailand in 1987. Coffee sales were growing, but the company had to decide whether to launch other Nestlé brands into the market or invest in building more coffee sales. The general manager of Nestlé Thailand had worked there for Nestlé for 30 years and is one of about 100 managers worldwide who spend their entire careers in just one region of the globe. Says he: "In ten years we had established coffee for breakfast in the cities. Sales were growing by about 7 percent to 10 percent a year. The economy was growing so fast, it was overheating." The group gambled that this mounting wealth held more for coffee than for any other product it could push or acquire. Soft drinks lacked the satisfaction or romance of coffee.

The locals junked the traditional taste, aroma, and stimulation strategy for advertising coffee on TV. Instead, ads played on urban stress, showing a man kicking a taxi door in frustration. Coffee was promoted as a way to relax from the pressures of traffic, the office, and even romance. Within Nestlé, the switch caused a ruckus. The zone manager for Asia stalked out of a screening of the first TV ad for the campaign. But the local group still had authority for Thailand and held firm. They also adapted a summer coffee promotion from Nestlé Greece, for Nescafé Shake, a cold coffee concoction.

Coffee sales in Thailand grew from $25 million in 1987 to $200 million in 1994. Nestlé sales are forecast to climb at three times the economic growth rate of Thailand, or about 25% a year. Nescafé now owns 80% of the market.

Source: Carla Rapoport, "Nestlé's Brand Building Machine," *Fortune* (September 19, 1994): 147–156. ©1994 Time, Inc. All rights reserved.

complexity added to the decision-making process when a company markets internationally.

PRODUCT LIFE CYCLE

Products are born, that is, they are launched onto the market, and they may also die, when they are dropped from the market. However, there are great variations in a *product's life cycle* between its birth and death. The classic product life cycle is shown in Figure 13-3. The Introduction is a period of slow initial sales growth; then sales grow rapidly during the Growth period, until the product finally reaches a maximum at Maturity, with sales decreasing during the Decline.

In the Introduction, there is usually a loss because of the costs of development, new production, and marketing; with efficiencies in production and the rapid increase in sales reducing marketing costs, profits peak during the Growth period. As the product matures, profits decrease owing to costs of product improvement and increased promotion. If costs are not carefully controlled during Decline, profits may rapidly devolve into losses.

Two product life cycles are involved: that of the overall product category and that of the individual product. The overall life cycle is easier to predict, as the factors affecting it are reasonably long term, but the individual product life cycle, which depends on competitor's actions, is more difficult to predict. Some companies may be strong initially but unable to maintain their market shares during the growth period, owing to the entry of competing products. The level of sales reached by the overall product category during maturity depends on the total industry marketing effort, which includes the quality of the marketing effort, as well as marketing expenditure. Similarly, company sales depend on the company's marketing effort.

FIGURE 13-3   The theoretical product life cycle.

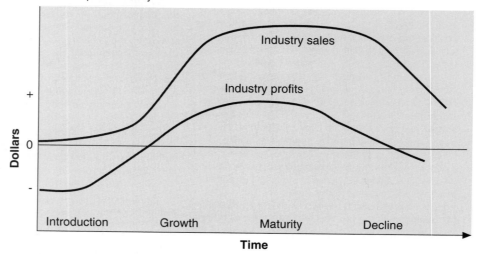

A product life cycle varies in length from three months for a special summer ice cream to over 100 years for Kellogg's Corn Flakes or Coca-Cola, but the average lives of food products have shortened in the last twenty years. Product life depends on how the product diffuses into the market—it may be fast because of the consumers' recognized need, the efficient distribution of the product, and educational, attractive promotion; or it may be slow because of consumers' resistance to the product or a poor marketing effort. The length of maturity and decline depends on continuing need for the product and lack of competition from improved products.

The product life cycle varies with the type of product, the effectiveness of the marketing activity, the effect of the competitors in the market, economic conditions at the time, technological developments, and company policy. Many of these factors are hard to predict, and therefore the product life cycle is hard to predict; hence the criticism of the product life cycle as a marketing tool.

Although the product life cycle is not a good predictor of future sales, it can be used to determine when to launch, improve, relaunch, or eliminate a product. Usually, products are improved during the growth period and relaunched when maturity appears to be approaching. Early product improvement is often in the area of product quality, but as the growth period continues, a redesigned package or variations of the product can be introduced. For example, a passion-fruit cheesecake may be extended to four new flavors, such as berry fruit, chocolate, lemon, and tropical. If a new product is the first of its kind launched, product improvement should start quite early in the growth stage, so that the market share is maintained when competitive products enter the market.

When the decline begins, product costs and price should be reduced to keep control of the dying market. At this time or earlier, during the maturity phase, a new product should be launched. Product maturity and decline can cause problems. In the early 1990s, the U.S. microwave food market experienced fierce price wars and quality reductions—sales of entrees, pizza, vegetables, soups, and sandwiches decreased. Large companies started to move out of the market, but when some smaller companies moved in, the large companies considered relaunching with higher-quality products and improved packaging.[5]

The amount spent on promotion is greatest in the introductory and early growth stages; it decreases at maturity, until it becomes cheap reminder advertising at decline. Promotion varies in content: the message during the introduction is "Try the product," in growth, "Choose our brand," and in maturity, "Be brand loyal." Supermarkets may influence the product life cycle through high shelf charges or even product refusal during the introduction, by promotion charges during growth, by requesting private-label product during maturity, and by removal from shelves during decline.[6]

Industrial products also follow a product life cycle, but the cycle is highly affected by technological changes in either the supplying or the buying industry.

---

[5]Patricia M. Dillon, "Reinventing the Microwave Market," *Food Engineering* (August 1993): 83–89.
[6]Philip Kotler, *Marketing Management,* 8th ed. (Englewood Cliffs, NJ: Prentice-Hall, 1989): 372–74.

Introduction may be slow, because innovations are usually adopted by one or two companies who have product-testing capabilities and are able to decide quickly to try new products. If the product/process is successful, then other companies will try it. Buyers may be very conservative if they have invested a great deal in their present plant and processes, because they lack technical knowledge, or because they have a bureaucratic buying system and change slowly. The risk associated with adopting an innovative product influences its sales increase in the growth period, especially if changes in processing are required and the company is not sure how the new ingredient might affect their end product. If risk of failure is high, then adoption may be very slow, unless the rewards are even higher.

Think Break

Monitor microwave meals in your supermarket freezer over a few weeks. Note the space they are allotted, types of products, brand names, and differences in packaging. Over the weeks note any changes that occur, particularly the products that disappear and new products that appear.

What do you think are the trends occurring with this group of products?

PRODUCT MANAGEMENT

The Product Line and Product Mix

Food products are seldom marketed as individual products, but rather as product lines. Most food companies market several product lines and a large number of products. Their total product mix may consist of hundreds or even thousands of products.

The *product line* is a group of products that are closely related, either used for similar purposes or possessing similar characteristics. Examples are the Heinz line of canned soups, Birdseye line of frozen mixed vegetables, and Nabisco line of cookies.

The *product mix* is a list of all products offered for sale by a company. It can be described by its width—number of product lines, and its depth—number of types, flavors, or sizes within each product line. For example, Figure 13-4 outlines Campbell Soup Company's product mix. In large companies like Campbell's, each product area could be identified as an individual product mix.

Organizing for Product Management

Many consumer food marketing companies with large product mixes subdivide them for management purposes. The marketing manager is responsible for the whole product mix, and *product managers* are responsible for product groups. Product managers serve as focal points for the planning and coordination of all the activities required for the growth and profitability of products they oversee. They

Product Mix Width

Canned/Bottled Products	Canned Soups	Dried Soups	Frozen Foods	Bakery/ Confectionery

Sauces
  Prego spaghetti
    sauces
  Pepperidge Farms
    gravies
 	
Juices
  V-8 tomato based
  Spring Valley
    (Australia)
 	
Canned Meats
  Fray Bentos (U.K.)
  Swift Armour
    (Argentina)
 	
Pickles/Relishes
  Vlasic
 	
Canned Pasta
  Franco-American
  SpaghettiOs
	Regular
	  Campbell's
	
	Health
	  Healthy Request
	
	Full-Bodied
	  Chunky
	
	Home Style
	  Home Cookin'
		Original
		  Campbell's
		  Ramen Noodle
		  Sanswa
		  Soup Co.
			Meals
			  Swanson
			  • "Hungry Man"
			    meals
			  • pot pies
			  • dinners
			
			Seafood
			  Mrs. Paul's
			
			Breakfast/
			Sandwich
			
			  Great Start
				Crackers/Cookies
				  Arnotts' (Australia)
				  Pepperidge Farms
				  Delacre (Belgium)
				
				Confections
				  Lami-Lutti (France/
				    Belgium)
				  Godiva Premium
				  Chocolates

Product Mix Depth (vertical axis label)

FIGURE 13-4   Campbell Soup Company: product-mix width and depth around the world.

also develop marketing plans which are used as marketing documents for a budget year. To develop strategies, as well as to control the marketing of the product mix and to measure its success or failure, managers conduct product audits.

An organizational chart for a company that follows the product-management concept is shown in Figure 13-5.

Product-Mix Management

Product-mix decisions refer to the company's strategy and overall plan. Responding too quickly to customers' requests, as industrial marketers, and sometimes even consumer marketers, tend to do, results in an uncontrolled product mix. A firm's business strategy and its marketing strategy form the basis of the product-mix plan. Part of the strategy is to have products at various stages in the product life cycle. Charting the life cycles of individual products provides some of the information necessary to conduct a rational overall product development and product retirement plan.

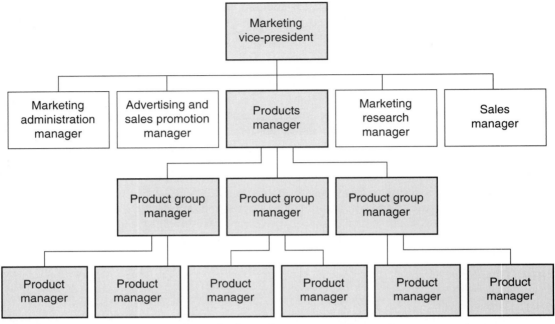

FIGURE 13-5   Company organization under the product-management concept.

The long-term aim of product-mix management is not only to have an evolving product mix which is currently profitable, but also to plan for profitable future mixes.[7]

In product-mix management, the first step is to organize records of the product mix with sufficient information so as to make short-term and long-term changes. The product mix should be reviewed or audited at least once a year, so that additions and eliminations of products are conducted systematically. *Product audits* vary from company to company, but information may be collected in these areas:

- Industry and product background—product type, product-line description, principal markets, industry structure and practices, competitors and their products and marketing strategies, present total market potential, and reasons for market shares.
- Business, political, and social environment—business cycles, political changes, government regulations, social changes, and social concerns.
- Product—importance of product in product mix, compatibility of product with other product lines, comparison with competing products, the product life cycle, sales and profits forecasts, present sales and profitability as compared with other products in the mix, present and future costs of production and marketing, production capabilities

[7]Robert D. Hisrich and Michael P. Peters, "Strategic Management of Product Mix," *Decisions for New and Mature Products,* 2d ed. (New York: Maxwell, Macmillan International Editions, 1991): 43–62.

and constraints, inventory needs, cost problems, and vulnerability to technological obsolescence, substitution, or loss of appeal.

• Markets—segmentation, geographic areas, buying habits and their trends, market channels and possible changes, company coverage of segments and geographic areas, seasonality of markets, and market growth, contraction, or leveling.

• Company marketing—present prices and price trends, production costs and trends, factors affecting production costs, suitability of market channels, promotion spending, effectiveness of promotion, agreements with agents on percentages, and agreements with customers on discounts, rebates, or payment.[8]

Product-Mix Adjustments

The product audit may indicate that marketing improvement, product improvement, product development, or product eliminations are needed. Product-mix adjustments should not be made in an ad hoc manner—such rash decisions may not be in the company's long-term interests. There can be constraints on the mix, such as production capacity, the promotional or marketing budget, and the total market potential for each product. A frequent problem in such analyses is that products are often interdependent—one product in the mix may affect the sales of other products.

Market performance does not identify reasons for product change—are downward trends long-lasting consumer changes, or are they caused by poor product performance or poor marketing? For example, the decline in sales of frozen vegetables over the last few years is predicted to continue as consumers turn to fresh vegetables, which, with improved long-distance refrigerated transport and long-term storage techniques, are now available year round. Private brands have grown in the U.S. frozen-vegetable market to a 42 percent market share, making manufacturer-brand frozen vegetables a low-margin commodity product. The two large companies dominating the market had to decide how to exit the business—sell out or reduce in size.[9]

In another case, cooking sauces were launched on the market in the early 1990s, but they rapidly lost sales and in 1994 were listed among the fastest-declining categories. Not as convenient in cooking as desired, the sauces had flavors that were not attractive to the whole family, particularly children. Is this a product with a short life, or did it fail because of poor quality at a fairly high price? Some companies believed the latter and launched what they thought were improved products, with shorter cooking times and milder flavors. There is a time to stay and a time to get out, and those times are often not easy to identify.[10]

[8]Adapted from the Product Audit in John M. Brion's *Corporate Market Planning* (New York: Wiley, 1967): 214–18.

[9]Richard Gibson, "Declining Vegetable Prices Wilt Processors' Earnings," *Wall Street Journal* (February 20, 1996): B4, and "Fresh Produce Melts the Vegetable Ice Age," *Wall Street Journal* (September 30, 1993): B1.

[10]Laura Bird, "Makers of Chicken Tonight Find Many Cooks Say, 'Not Tonight'," *Wall Street Journal* (May 17, 1994): B1.

Much is written on product development but little on *product elimination.* A summary from Philip Kotler says that the weak product:

- tends to consume a disproportionate amount of management's time
- often requires frequent price and inventory adjustments
- generally involves short production runs in spite of expensive set-up times
- requires both advertising and sales-force attention that might better be diverted to making the "healthy" products more profitable
- by its very unfitness can cause customer misgivings and cast a shadow on the company's image.[11]

Some products may be dropped easily, but others present difficulties because they are a significant part of production, or they support other products. Also requiring consideration are raw materials and products in inventory, the compensation to be made to people in the market channel, particularly the customers, and the effect of eliminations on staff and plant.

NEW-PRODUCT DEVELOPMENT

Systematic Approach to Product Development

During the past 20 years, rapid technological changes and a steady increase in the standard of living have resulted in greater opportunities for product development in the food industry. This, coupled with increasing competition in the marketplace, has forced many companies to rethink their approach to product development.[12]

In the past, one of the greatest stumbling blocks to product development in industry was the gulf between the scientists and the marketers—the scientists keeping their intellect bent toward technical issues of product development and the marketers only looking at the world outside. The result was product failures in many companies. Through the product development process, the different research techniques— marketing, processing, and engineering—are coordinated into one type of research, which has become a method of industrial research in its own right.

The aim of product development research is to invent and develop a product which consumers or industrial customers will buy. The two parts of product development— customer knowledge and technological know-how—are both equally important; there should be no domination by either component, but rather a marrying together of all research. Figure 13-6 shows the interdisciplinary nature of the product development process. Nabisco attributes its success in product development to a rigorous planning process, a separate new-product organization, senior-manager support up front, strong cross-functional teamwork, and a proactive product development group—a combination of communication skills and teamwork throughout.[13]

---

[11]Philip Kotler, *Marketing Management,* 8th ed. (Englewood Cliffs, NJ: Prentice-Hall, 1989): 369–72.

[12]A. L. Page, "Assessing New Product Development Practices and Performance: Establishing Crucial Norms," *Journal of Product Innovation Management* 10: 4 (1993): 273–90.

[13]Diance L. Hnat, "A Cross-Functional Strategy for Product Development," *Food Technology* (August 1994): 62–65.

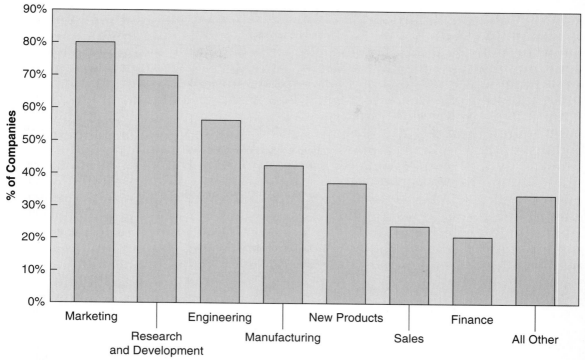

FIGURE 13-6 Functional areas involved in new-product development. (*Source:* Reprinted by permission of the publisher from Albert L. Page, "Assessing New Product Development Practices and Performance: Establishing Crucial Norms," *Journal of Product Innovation Management,* Vol. 10, page 278. Copyright 1993 by Elsevier Science Inc.)

The stages of the product development process are exactly the same in industrial marketing as in consumer marketing, but the marketer's guiding influence is the industrial/food service customer, who in turn responds to the derived demand of the food product's ultimate consumer. If the food manufacturing company buying the food ingredient has full knowledge of its final consumers' behavior, needs, and attitudes and has developed its own product concept and product design specifications, then the supply company's path in product development is very clearly defined. However, if the buying company has poor knowledge of its final consumers, the supply company must also do some consumer research, in order to reduce the buying company's risk of product failure.

The Product Development Process

The system of research for product development varies in detail from project to project but overall retains the same structure. As shown in Table 13-2, the seven stages, each of which has a specific outcome, combine market, consumer, product,

TABLE 13-2   THE PRODUCT DEVELOPMENT PROCESS

Stage	Interim analysis	Results
1. PROJECT SET-UP		AIMS, OBJECTIVES, CONSTRAINTS
	Business Strategy Go/No-Go Decision	
2. PRODUCT IDEA GENERATION AND SCREENING		PRODUCT CONCEPT AND DESIGN SPECIFICATIONS
	Critical Analysis of Product and Target Market	
3. PRODUCT DESIGN		PRODUCT PROTOTYPES
	Evaluation of Technical Success and Costs	
4. PRODUCT TESTING		FINAL PRODUCT, TARGET MARKET
	Evaluation of Market Success Quantitative Analysis of Market, Prices, Costs, Investment	
5. PRODUCTION AND MARKETING DEVELOPMENT		PRODUCTION SYSTEM, MARKETING STRATEGY
	Quantitative Prediction of Outcomes of Launching	
6. PRODUCT LAUNCH		CONSUMER/CUSTOMER ACCEPTANCE
	Analysis of Sales, Buying Behavior, Marketing Methods	
7. POSTLAUNCH REVIEW		PRODUCT and/or MARKET IMPROVEMENT
	Analysis of Product Quality, Efficiency	

ACCEPTANCE OF NEW PRODUCT INTO THE PRODUCT MIX

Source: Adapted from Marvin J. Rudolph, "The Food Product Development Process," *British Food Journal*

and processing research. These different types of research are combined and not done in sequence—there is little point in developing an advanced-technology product if the consumer does not need it or the market rejects it; also, there is little point doing a great deal of consumer research on a product the company does not have the technical ability to develop and make.

The project and the products are evaluated between each stage—first qualitatively: does the product fit with the company? is there a consumer need? can the product be developed?—and then quantitatively: costs, time frame, prelaunch investment, predicted sales, expected launch date. After each project evaluation the decision is made either to stop the project or to set the scene for the next stage. To continue, the information obtained is compiled as the basis for the next stage's activities. For example, by the end of Stage 3, Product Design, the following are available: the final product prototype, including its technical qualities and consumer benefits, an outline of the process and processing conditions, target market segments, and predicted costs.

Stage 1.   Set Up the Project

Stage	Interim analysis	Results
PROJECT SET-UP		AIMS, OBJECTIVES, CONSTRAINTS
	Business Strategy Go/No-Go Decision	

The *project aim* is developed within the framework of the company's overall business strategy:

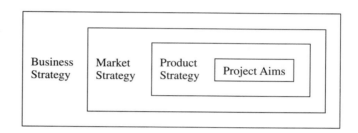

Product development must be based on the business and marketing strategies, and in particular on the product strategy for overall development of the product mix. These guide the selection of the project and the project aim. Thus, at the beginning of the project, everyone knows exactly what the company is trying to achieve overall and also the objectives for each stage of the project. (The marketing planning process is discussed in detail in Chapter 16.)

Every *project* operates within *constraints*. Various factors may impose limits on a project: the product itself—its specific nutritional quality, for instance; processing—specific equipment; marketing—existing distribution channels; financial—maximum investment; company—expertise available within the company; or environmental—government restrictions. For foreign markets, the food and entry regulations can be significant constraints and need to be identified early in the project.[14]

The situation of a U.S. food manufacturer with a large plant in Britain, Beans Unlimited, will be followed through all the stages of new-product development. Beans Unlimited wants to reverse the decrease in sales of their canned beans in

[14]Andrea H. Allen, "Designing for the World? Get the Facts First," *Food Product Design* (May 1995): 28–50.

tomato sauce by introduction of new canned-bean products. After discussion of their vague initial project aim, "to increase sales of canned beans," the staff sets a more specific aim, "to develop new types of canned bean products for the British market which will increase usage by the present customers or/and encourage new market segments to eat canned beans." Beans Unlimited's project must work within several constraints: use present equipment, market within Britain, price competitively, and keep total development and launching costs below $2 million.

After setting the aims, recognizing constraints, and making the go/no-go decision, the company reaches the creative part of the process.

Stage 2. Creating and Screening Ideas

Stage	Interim analysis	Results
PRODUCT IDEA GENERATION AND SCREENING		PRODUCT CONCEPT AND DESIGN SPECIFICATIONS
	Critical Analysis of Product and Target Market	

A creative company environment is important for idea generation. Ideas come from advances in technology and from market/consumer needs. Often, advancing technology supplies innovations, and the market recognizes product improvement. For example, new technologies of fat hardening and treatment brought new margarine products; then consumers' desires for easy-to-spread margarine inspired the technology of fat blending to produce softer margarine, and the need to reduce calorie intake led to low-fat spreads. The first products had 40 percent fat, which was reduced to 25 percent fat, and then to 3 percent fat.[15]

Normally, between twenty and fifty ideas are required for every successful product. The creative thinking is aided by studying local and foreign markets, reviewing technical literature, consumer research, and such techniques as brainstorming, synectics, and *product morphology.*[16]

Beans Unlimited decides to use product morphology to develop ideas, as shown in Box 13-2.

From this product morphology, Beans Unlimited comes up with a number of product ideas, including red beans in hot tomato sauce with bacon pieces, lima beans in a white cheese and onion sauce, mushy beans in tomato sauce with meatballs, and a rich meaty sauce with beans for pouring on steak.

Think Break

Note the product characteristics identified on the product map in Box 12-3 (Chapter 12) for yogurts on the British market. Using different blends of these

---

[15]M. Byrne, "The Creative Advantage," *Food Engineering International* (February 1994): 44–47.

[16]Christian Wagner and Albert Hayashi, "A New Way to Create Winning Ideas," *Journal of Product Innovation Management* 11 (1994): 146–155.

BOX 13-2

PRODUCT MORPHOLOGY

Product morphology is the breakdown of a product into the specific characteristics that identify it to consumers, by analysis of the product family and the individual product. An individual canned-bean product might exhibit a combination of the following ingredient and sensory characteristics:

Raw materials:	navy beans, lima beans, red kidney beans
Liquid:	tomato sauce, cheese and onion sauce, beef sauce, white sauce

Ratio of beans to liquid:	high, medium, low
Other ingredients:	bacon, beef
Flavor:	spicy, bland, hot
Texture:	firm, chewy, mushy
Color:	red, creamy, brown
Aroma:	bland, spicy, meaty

The beans could also be differentiated on size of can, nutritional value, psychological features, and value for money.

Morphology identifies the characteristics important to the consumer so that the marketer can concentrate on these when developing new products. This analysis of product morphology is also useful in determining a product's position against competing products.

---

characteristics, develop ten ideas for new yogurt products. Rank these products from "definitely would buy" to "definitely would not buy." Identify the factors that you used in ranking the products.

Product-idea screening views produce ideas from two angles: Can the product be made? Can the product be marketed? The product needs to satisfy the project's original aim and constraints. At this stage, using secondary sources and previously collected data is preferable to costly market or customer research. Technical information is obtained from textbooks, review articles, and abstracts.

> Beans Unlimited rejects some of their product ideas; for example, mushy beans cannot be made using present equipment, so all products containing mushy beans are eliminated. Because supermarket sales data reveal that competitors' meatballs with beans products have very low sales, meatball-containing products are also rejected.

For the products remaining after screening, discussion groups and surveys determine what the customer/consumer wants, how many customers/consumers there are, and how much they will buy. Discussions with company staff, consumers, retailers, or industrial customers help identifying needs, attitudes, and behavior, but surveys are used to make quantitative predictions. Technical information searches may include preparation of "mock-ups" of proposed products.

> Beans Unlimited makes ten different bean products in its experimental kitchen and conducts focus groups in Southern England, Northern England, and Scotland, with consumers tasting all ten products. The white products, such as beans in cheese and onion sauce, are not popular; the southern English prefer sweetish flavors and the other areas prefer hot, spicy flavors. The consumers show interest in the products' nutritional value, in particular their fiber content. Processing tests find

that white beans darken during heat sterilization, so these products are dropped. Because a consumer survey of 300 people on the five remaining products predicts low sales on two products, the project is narrowed to three products: lima beans and beef in sweet and sour tomato sauce, mixed beans in curry sauce, and red kidney beans with bacon in a hot tomato sauce.

The *product concept* includes the product characteristics, benefits, and position, all as identified by the consumer. To build up and test a product concept, competitive products or preliminary product prototypes are presented to consumer focus groups; then the results are discussed in-company. During development, product benefits—the product characteristics important to consumers—are emphasized.

Beans Unlimited organizes focus groups segmented by age, who develop product concepts for the three products. Their product concept for red kidney beans with bacon in a hot tomato sauce is, "brown kidney beans with small bacon pieces in a bright red sauce, with a sweet tomato flavor, not too hot but spicy, firm but not too chewy, high in fiber and protein, to be eaten alone or with sausages or hamburgers." Teenagers and young adults are identified as the target market segment. Product benefits are listed by teenagers as easy-to-eat, with a bright appearance, and by buyers and cooks as low-priced and filling.

Think Break

For the yogurt product idea you ranked first in the last Think Break, develop a product concept. Identify yourself as a target market segment and list the product benefits you expect from your yogurt product.

Product-design specifications are developed from the product concept, with reference to technical aspects of the product, processing, and distribution. Consumer testers develop an ideal product profile, which measures the "strength" they desire for each product characteristic. Combining the profile with the technical qualities of the product, food designers write technical specifications for the functional product. These steps enhance the design process and ensure that the design is developing in the right direction, both for production and for the consumer.

For Beans Unlimited's kidney-bean product, a panel of teenagers develops an ideal product profile using experimental products, including:

Excitement	Everyday _____|_____	Star Wars excitement
Sauce color	Pale red _____|_____	Dark red
Bacon size	Tiny _____|_____	Large bits
Chewiness	Soft _____|_____	Very chewy

Food designers correlate these consumer scores with physical measurements to determine technical standards in the product-design specifications. Marketers use the ideal product profile to develop the product image and packaging aesthetics.

Think Break

From your yogurt product concept, develop an ideal product profile. Identify the important characteristics, draw a scale for each characteristic, and position your ideal yogurt product on each scale.

Stage 3. Product Design

Stage	Interim analysis	Results
PRODUCT DESIGN		PRODUCT PROTOTYPES
	Evaluation of Technical Success and Costs	

The food technologist designs and tests the product against previously defined standards. Different raw materials and processing conditions are also investigated. For instance, the marketer of seafood products pictured in Figure 13-7 may

FIGURE 13-7   Seafood specialty processor designs new products. Food processors, whether large multinationals, such as Nestlé, or small specialty firms, depend on new products for growth and competitiveness in the marketplace. *(Courtesy of R. Lamberts, New Zealand Institute of Crop and Food Research.)*

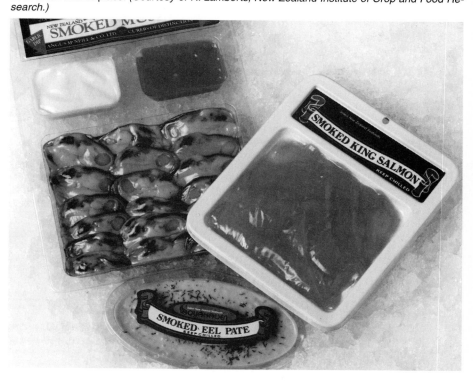

consider new fish varieties, new flavorings, or new preservation and processing methods. During their *product-design* stage, test procedures must be related to the qualities identified by the user. As early as possible in development, consumers or industrial customers test *prototypes* of the product. Changes made to a formulation are comparatively inexpensive at this stage, but very expensive later.[17]

> Beans Unlimited has developed three bean products: red kidney beans with bacon in hot tomato sauce, lima beans and beef in sweet and sour tomato sauce, and mixed beans in curry sauce. A panel of twenty consumers tests the prototypes during development, placing important product characteristics on scales, as in the ideal product profile.

Think Break

Buy a plain yogurt and any ingredients available to make your yogurt product. Try mixing these in different amounts to create product prototypes and test them against your ideal product profile.

Stage 4.   Product Testing

Stage	Interim analysis	Results
PRODUCT TESTING		FINAL PRODUCT, TARGET MARKET
	Evaluation of Market Success/Quantitative Analysis of Market, Prices, Costs, Investment	

The final prototype product is tested by consumers using in-home tests and central-location tests or, in industrial marketing, in-plant tests. After these tests, it is possible to evaluate much more accurately both the product and its acceptance by the target market.

> Beans Unlimited organizes central-location tests of its three products in urban shopping malls in Southern England, Northern England, and Scotland. Consumers passing through the malls are asked to taste the products, rate the products' acceptability, and indicate their degree of willingness to buy the products.

Think Break

Ask some friends to rate the acceptability of your yogurt products and to identify their good and bad qualities.

From outline process plans, including raw-material specifications and quantities, a product cost is determined. Product tests indicate the consumer/customer

---

[17]Marvin J. Rudolph, "The Food Product Development Process" *British Food Journal* 97:3 (1995): 3–11.

price range for the products. The process plan, costing analysis, and consumer/ customers' evaluation tests together give excellent information for a final feasibility study before the very expensive steps of factory and market development. At this stage, any necessary legal or government approval for the product is sought.

Stage 5.   Development of the Marketing and Production Plans

Stage	Interim analysis	Results
PRODUCTION AND MARKETING DEVELOPMENT		PRODUCTION SYSTEM, MARKETING STRATEGY
	Quantitative Prediction of Outcomes of Launching	

Technical experiments with processing conditions, either in a pilot plant or on small runs in the standard plant, find out if the product can easily, consistently, and economically be made to the quality standards. A new industrial product is used in the buyer's plant. Preliminary designs are drawn for new-process equipment or for adaptation of present equipment.

Packaging design is crucial in marketing. Based on consumer needs and uses of the food product, it must also have aesthetic appeal. Computer design software has streamlined packaging design techniques, but designer creativity is still the key element. The package is tested for product protection during storage and transport in order to determine the product storage life under expected conditions of distribution, sale, and use. Then consumers test the final, packaged product.[18]

> Beans Unlimited adopts a can with a rip-off top and an attractive white inside lacquer, which provides both convenience and protection of product color during storage. Although united by Beans Unlimited's family brand, the three labels are each given a distinctive design to emphasize their different flavors and uses.

Think Break

Design a package for your yogurt product. Look at different types of dairy-product packaging in the supermarket to get ideas.

Marketing managers use the information gained from all the previous research to develop the marketing strategy and launch plan. This plan covers market trials, promotion and advertising, pricing, and distribution. Financial analysis includes costs of launching and production, prediction of revenue, costs, and profits, and a final prediction of product success. Then comes the final decision whether to stop or to allow the product to be launched.

[18]Ken Goddard, "Focus on Packaging Design," *Food Manufacture* (June 1995): 37–40.

From the market research, Beans Unlimited finds that appearance, eating sensations, and high protein and fiber content are its new products' most salable features and therefore decides not to advertise on TV. Instead, tasting promotions with young sports stars and media releases by a well-known nutritionist will be directed at teenagers and young adults. The products will be distributed to supermarkets through Beans Unlimited's usual channels.

Think Break

Outline a marketing strategy for your yogurt product.

Stage 6.   Product Launching

Stage	Interim analysis	Results
PRODUCT LAUNCH		CONSUMER/CUSTOMER ACCEPTANCE
	Analysis of Sales, Buying Behavior, Marketing Methods	

Once the decision is made to invest in a *launch,* the plans for both production and marketing are finalized. Production may require the design, construction, and commissioning of a new plant, and staff training. Product inventory is built up before distribution to retailers begins. With industrial products, salespeople are briefed and begin marketing the product to customers.

Now the problem is to secure supermarket acceptance of the product. New products are presented at supermarket chain headquarters by the company's salespeople or by a food broker and are reviewed by a buying executive and/or a buying committee. They accept or reject based on the product's qualities and uniqueness, on growth in the product category, and on profit contribution (discussed in Chapter 15). Buyers are also influenced by strong advertising and promotion budgets, both nationally and for the supermarket chain. Supermarket chains charge for putting new products on the shelves and may set a time limit for reaching a certain sales level.

All is then ready for the launch—the advertising is placed in the media, and the product is faced up on store or supermarket shelves. The only step remaining is for the consumer to buy the product and to keep on buying it. In the United States, 44 percent of new products are accepted by supermarket chains, and one-half of these are removed from the shelves within a year.[19] Despite careful adherence to the product development process, new-product launching is still a chancy business.

[19]Edward W. McLaughlin and Peter J. Fredericks, "New Product Procurement Behavior of US Supermarket Chains: Implications for Food and Agribusiness Suppliers," *Agribusiness* 10.6 (1994): 483.

Beans Unlimited's efforts have paid off: their three new products are accepted by three major supermarket chains in Britain for national distribution, and publicity for their healthy, appealing products is well received.

Stage 7. Postlaunch Review

Stage	Interim analysis	Results
POSTLAUNCH REVIEW		PRODUCT and/or MARKET IMPROVEMENT
	Analysis of Product Quality, Efficiency of Production, and Distribution	
	ACCEPTANCE OF NEW PRODUCT INTO THE PRODUCT MIX	

The retailers' attitudes toward the product, their placement and promotion of it in the supermarket, and, of course, the consumers' attitudes and behavior toward the product are postlaunch concerns. Are they rebuying? How much are they buying? What do they like/dislike in the product? On the production side, the yield and quality of the product are monitored. This monitoring usually leads to product adjustments, production and quality assurance refinement, and changes in distribution and marketing methods. The results are constant improvement of the product, reduction in production costs, and increased effectiveness of marketing methods.

In industrial marketing, the postlaunch stage includes a study of the customers' processes and their products. In recent years, the manufacturer's and the supplier's product development processes have become intertwined. Technical support at all stages has always been provided, but there is an increasing trend for the supplier to also conduct consumer and market research. For example, the supplier of a new fat replacer not only helps with formulation of the reduced-fat product, but may even consumer-test the final product to prove that it is acceptable to the consumer. This involvement is occasioned by the increasing complexity of food ingredients and reductions in food manufacturing companies' R&D staff.[20]

Managing the Product Development Process

Responsibility within the company for product development can be assigned in various ways. Project teams, reporting to top management, may be organized in response to business-strategy decisions or set up to combine the research of various departments. Top management can also give middle management a budget for product development and the job of organizing it; then product developers report to the marketing manager or to the research and development manager. If product development is conducted completely in the product area, usually it comprises part of the

[20]Larry L. Hood, Raymond J. Lundy, and Donald C. Johnson, "New Product Development: North American Ingredient Supplier's Role," *British Food Journal* 97:3 (1995): 12–17.

product manager's responsibility. The importance of product development to the company determines which method is used. There are two considerations in managing product development: integration of the multidisciplines involved, and control of the costs and timing of the process. Failures usually result from poor integration and poor timing.[21]

In a typical company, with not one but several product development projects running side-by-side, very good coordination and control are required. Proper timing assures that staff and facilities are working at an even pace, with the quiet and busy periods of various projects offset.

Although the product development process should include all the stages, the type and quantity of research in each stage varies by product and project. The amount of innovation in the product, the resources available, the knowledge and expertise in technology and marketing, and company size all influence the amount of research conducted. The company's risk-taking attitude enters the equation—low risk takers do more research, high risk takers do less—but timeliness is also important: the new-product development process may need to be accelerated in response to competition. Top management usually dictates the attitude toward research by the amount of resources it allocates to product development.

SUMMARY

The product is the central element of food marketing. The product characteristics include the physical, nutritional, chemical, sensory, and safety qualities that can be identified in the tangible product, as well as the services it offers—reliability, information, uniformity, and the social and psychological properties, such as healthiness or fun. Package and brand characteristics are also identified, with reference to the entire product life, from the consumer's first view to disposal. Product benefits are Package characteristics that the consumer identifies as filling some need. Once the product characteristics and benefits are identified, the product concept, the consumer's perception of the product, including its benefits, can be defined. The product concept provides the basis for selecting the other marketing functions: price, promotion, and place.

Products are born and die, but the time between, called the product life cycle, varies a great deal. All product life cycles include the following stages: introduction, growth, maturity, and decline—but the cycle length and the rates of growth and decline depend on the type of product, the company's and the total industry's resources, the effectiveness of marketing, the need of the consumer for the product, and the technological knowledge and expertise of the company and the industry.

The product mix in a consumer food marketing company is often large and in need of constant management. Although the industrial marketing company's

---

[21]D. L. Hnat, "A Cross-Functional Strategy for Product Development," *Food Technology* (August 1994): 62–65, and N. Karagozoglu and W. B. Brown, "Time-based Management of the New Product Development Process," *Journal of Product Innovation Management* 10 (1993): 204–15.

product mix may be narrower, it still needs careful control to prevent company re-action to every customer request at the expense of its business strategy. Products should regularly be introduced, be improved, have costs decreased, and finally be eliminated. A regular product audit will identify the products that are performing poorly and why. Then product managers decide what to do with these products—improve the marketing, improve the products, or gradually drop them.

The product development process is a systematic method for the development and launching of new products. The process has seven stages from the initial setting up of the project to the postlaunch evaluation. When a company launches a large number of products annually, as happens in the food industry, the product development process requires careful management of timing and resource allocation.

IMPORTANT TERMS AND CONCEPTS

brand   345
brand equity   347
brand extension   348
brand mark   345
brand name   345
family brand   346
generic brand   345
national brand   345
package   345
plain pack   345
private brand   345
product availability   347
product audits   354
product category   343
product idea screening   361

product characteristics   344
product concept   362
product design   364
product design specifications   362
product elimination   356
product launch   366
product life cycle   350
product line   352
product manager   352
product mix   352
product morphology   360
project aim   359
project constraints   359
prototypes   364
trade mark   345

QUESTIONS

1   Identify and compare the product benefits that you see in the following pairs of products:

Birdseye frozen peas—Green Giant frozen peas (or any two brands with which you are familiar)
Mixed-grain loaf   —White bread
Fruit juice   —Beer
Ketchup   —Salsa sauce

2   Choose a large food company with which you are familiar. Look up the company's annual report in the library. What are the main brands that the company owns? What types of brands are they: family, product line, international, local, or single product?

3   Develop a list of potential brand extensions that have logical links to a favorite food brand that you find in your supermarket. Analyze the brand extensions that you come up with in terms of their suitability for the company, the market, and the consumer.

4 What roles do product characteristics and consumers' perceptions of product characteristics play in positioning a product in the market? How can a characteristic held by several competing products be used in a successful positioning strategy?

5 A company wishes to launch a line of prepared entrées—curried chicken, chili con carne, beef stew, vegetarian goulash—into the hotel market. Sketch a product development process for this project.

6 Discuss how you would develop a brand name for the following products: a specialty industrial product such as dried berry fruit concentrate to be used in cold cereals; a food service product such as fish fillets in batter; and a consumer product such as a luxury ice-cream dessert.

7 State the four basic tastes in foods and give examples of food products where each of the basic tastes is important.

8 Frozen peas are in the decline stage of the product life cycle, and the market is dominated by two major brands. One company wants to leave the market; the other company wants to stay. What actions could each take to achieve their aims?

REFERENCES AND RESOURCES

Assael, H. *Consumer Behavior and Marketing Action.* 4th ed. Boston: PSW-Kent, 1992.

Allen, D. *Developing Successful New Products: A Guide to Product Planning.* London: Pitman Publishing, 1993.

Andreasen, M. M., and L. Hein. *Integrated Product Development.* Springer-Verlag, Berlin: IFS (Publications), Ltd., 1987.

Earle, M. D. "Changes in the Product Development Process." *Trends in Food Science and Technology* 8.1 (1997): 19–24.

Earle, M. D., and A. Anderson. *Product and Process Development in the Food Industry.* New York: Harwood Academic, 1985.

Fuller, G. W. *New Food Product Development from Concept to Market Place.* Ann Arbor, MI: CRC Press, 1994.

Graf, E. and I. S. Saguy, eds. *Food Product Development from Concept to Market Place.* New York: Van Nostrand and Reinhold, 1991.

Hisrich, R. D., and M. P. Peters. *Marketing Decisions for New and Mature Products.* 2d ed. New York: Maxwell, Macmillan International Editions, 1991.

Lehmann, D. R., and R. S. Winer. *Product Management.* Burr Ridge, IL: Irwin, 1994.

Moskowitz, H. R. *Food Concepts and Products: Just-in-Time Development.* Trumbull, CT: Food and Nutrition Press, 1994.

Rudolph, Marvin J. "The Food Product Development Process." *British Food Journal* 97.3 (1995): 3–11.

14

PROMOTION OF FOOD PRODUCTS

CHAPTER OUTLINE

LEARNING OBJECTIVES

After reading this chapter and answering the questions in the Think Breaks and at the end of the chapter, you should be able to:

- Identify the four major promotional methods available to the marketer.
- Appreciate why grocery manufacturers are tending to allocate more of their promotional budget to trade and consumer promotion rather than media advertising.
- Understand the choice manufacturers make in using a push versus a pull strategy to stimulate demand in a market.
- Recognize the various consumer promotional methods and the relative advantages and disadvantages of each.
- Understand the methods used to allocate budgets to advertising and why the objective-and-task method is the most logical.
- Develop the basics of a media plan.
- Describe the concepts of reach and frequency and their interrelationships in media planning.
- Recognize the market and product variables that indicate personal selling should receive greater emphasis than advertising in the promotional mix.
- Understand commodity advertising and the concept of predatory versus cooperative goods.
- Explain the potential benefits of commodity advertising and commodity promotion programs.

INTRODUCTION

Communicating effectively to potential buyers is not a recent development in the food system. A hundred years ago Kellogg's had to convince Americans brought up on cooked, hot oatmeal breakfasts to switch to cold, packaged cereals. The fresh, crispy taste of corn flakes and its convenience for the housewife turned oat-meal lovers into cold-cereal enthusiasts. Today, Kellogg's spends over $800 million a year in advertising around the world, convincing potential buyers that their Rice Bubbles (Australia), Banana Bubbles (United Kingdom), or Miel Pops (France) should be taken off the shelf and purchased. While advertising is the most pervasive method of communicating, the marketer has four major tools available in the promotion mix:

• *Advertising* is any paid message by a sponsor that is delivered, usually by media such as newspapers, magazines, radio, or television. This delivery is nonpersonal and can also be accomplished by using billboards, posters on buses or taxis, and other means.

• *Sales Promotion* covers a wide range of activities, from direct payment to supermarkets for shelf space to free samples that are delivered to the consumer via the Post Office. Coupons are also considered sales promotion, even though often they are delivered by media.

• *Public Relations* includes building good relations with the company's various publics by obtaining favorable publicity, building up a good "corporate image," and handling or heading off unfavorable rumors, stories, and events.

• *Personal Selling* is oral presentation in a conversation with one or more prospective purchasers for the purpose of making sales, a much more important tool for the food processor and manufacturer than for the retailer.

The promotional mix depends on many factors, including the nature of the market, the nature of the product, the target market segment, the message to be transmitted, and the amount of money and the promotional methods available. As Figure 14-1 shows, in business-to-business marketing—for example, selling ingredients to a food manufacturer—the promotional mix is heavily weighted toward personal selling.

FIGURE 14-1 Relative importance of advertising to personal selling.

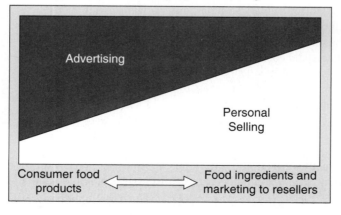

Personal selling predominates in industrial markets, because the market is often geographically concentrated, with few customers and few firms. Also, the products often are technical, complicated to use, and, if not expensive in themselves, expensive if their use in the manufacturing process does not go right.

The general promotional mixes for consumer marketing and business-to-business marketing (including industrial marketing and marketing to wholesalers and retailers) are shown below.

	Consumer market	Business-to-business market
Promotional mix	1. Advertising 2. Sales promotion 3. Personal selling 4. Public relations	1. Personal selling 2. Sales promotion 3. Advertising 4. Public relations
Advertising media	Television, radio, newspapers magazines, outdoor signs	Trade journals, direct mail, directories
Sales promotion media	Displays, contests, recipes, demonstrations, samples	Trade exhibitions, formulas, processing assistance, samples

This chapter first considers promotional techniques used by food-product manufacturers to obtain reseller and consumer support. The management of advertising—budgeting, message considerations, and media strategy—is discussed next. Finally, commodity advertising is examined, as carried out by such industry groups as the pork, beef, and citrus industries.

PROMOTION IN GROCERY DISTRIBUTION

The heading *promotion* covers a variety of techniques used by grocery manufacturers to obtain the support of distributors and retailers for their products. In recent years, new-product introductions have grown tremendously to over 15 thousand new food products annually in the U.S. grocery market, up from around 5 to 6 thousand new product introductions a decade ago. During this same period, grocery-store size, measured in square feet, grew by only 40 percent. Obviously, space constraints are a primary limitation on the acceptance of new products by grocery-store buyers. In addition, retailers are carefully screening new products for potential profitability.

Manufacturers can choose from two opposing strategies for stimulating market demand—push and pull. In a *push strategy,* the manufacturer uses the various promotional elements, mainly sales force and sales promotional methods, to "push" the product through the distribution channel (Figure 14-2). This approach may also involve the use of price incentives to get wholesalers and retailers to carry the product. The alternative is a *pull strategy* where the manufacturer communicates directly with the consumer and depends on the consumer to request that the retail outlet carry the product, thus pulling the product through the channel. In practice, most food manufacturers use a combination of both push and pull—their "pull" advertising to consumers complements their "push" strategy of sales promotion

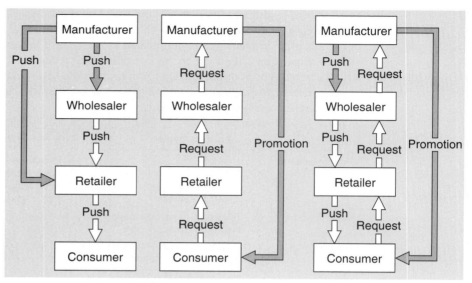

FIGURE 14-2 Strategies for promotion in grocery distribution.

techniques. Cooperative advertising allowances and sales-force incentives encourage their sales force to convince wholesalers and retailers to carry a product and make room for it on the shelf. Figure 14-2 shows wholesalers and retailers as the potential audiences for the push strategy. The sales force may also be the target for promotional techniques, such as motivational meetings, training programs, selling aids, and monetary and nonmonetary incentive plans, all aimed at improving sales-force performance. However, these topics, which are included in sales-management books, will not be discussed here.

Promotions by manufacturers to distributors and retailers are known as *trade promotions.* This "push" marketing is employed by most major manufacturers, and today, with manufacturers competing for increasingly scarce shelf space, more promotional dollars are being spent by packaged-good manufacturers on "trade deals" than on consumer promotion (Figure 14-3). These trade deals are directed to members of the channel of distribution (such as supermarket chains) and can take the form of off-invoice-price *trade discounts,* cumulative volume rebates, inventory financing, free goods, point-of-purchase (POP) displays and materials, cooperative advertising, contests, and direct payments for shelf space. Retailers play manufacturers off against one another to secure the best trade deals, and some retailers will hardly consider a new item without requiring some form of trade allowance.[1] Trade promotion is crucial to the success of a brand, for without retailer support the prod-

[1]Peter J. Fredericks and Edward W. McLaughlin, *New Product Procurement: A Summary of Buying Practices and Acceptance Criteria at U.S. Supermarket Chains,* A. E. Research 92–12 (Ithaca, NY: Cornell University Department of Agricultural Economics, December 1992): 4–5.

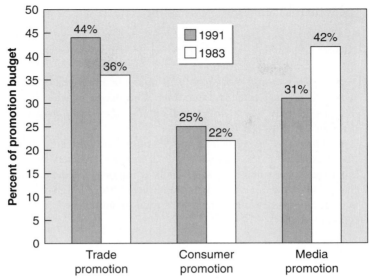

FIGURE 14-3 Promotional dollars spent by packaged-goods manufacturers. (*Source: Peter J. Fredericks and Edward W. McLaughlin,* New Product Procurement: A Summary of Buying Practices and Acceptance Criteria at U.S. Supermarket Chains *(Ithaca, NY: Cornell University Department of Agricultural Economics, December 1992): 5. Reprinted with permission of the Food Industry Management Program, Cornell University.)*

uct does not receive distribution, and the consumer cannot buy it.

Promotions that manufacturers address directly to consumers, bypassing the retailer (although at times the retailer may be involved in delivering the promotion), are known as *consumer promotions*—the basis of the "pull" strategy. The purpose of these incentives is to encourage trial or usage of the product by the final consumer.

Consumer Promotion

Various types of promotional offers are used by manufacturers to obtain trial of a brand and to increase usage. Some methods—sampling, coupons, price-off techniques, and trade coupons—are more appropriate for generating consumer trial, the first step in new product introduction. Other promotional efforts, such as bonus packs, premiums, contests, and sweepstakes, are more helpful in increasing usage. This discussion will review these techniques, their use, and some limitations.

In generating consumer trial of new food products, demonstration and taste *sampling* is one of the most effective methods. Compared to advertising, however, it is also very expensive. To be cost effective, the consumer trial must be converted into repeat usage—the ultimate goal of any new-product introduction. Most sampling programs are aimed at the subsets of a target market that the marketing manager feels are most favorably inclined to try using the sampled product. However, there are various situations where sampling is the best trial-generating promotion:

• *New-product-category introduction.* When a new product category is being introduced to the market, speed of trial is important, because consumers will often settle on the first "good" brand tried.

• *Superior-brand introduction.* If a new or improved brand is introduced in an established product category, sampling is an excellent way to obtain trial. Sampling is perhaps the only way to obtain trial among *other-brand loyals* who are one of the most difficult target audiences to convert.

• *When advertising is inadequate to demonstrate the brand's benefit or benefits.* In the consumer market, sampling works well for products such as food and beverages, where sensory evaluation (taste, smell) is important to the consumer purchase decision. Sampling can also be useful at another level, to sell high-involvement, high-risk products, such as a new ingredient for a food manufacturer's formulation in the industrial market.

There are several methods for delivering samples: door-to-door, mail, central location (in-store), or newspaper and magazine. Each method has its pros and cons; for example, door-to-door is fast, but it is also the most expensive and is obviously not feasible for perishable products such as ice cream. The method chosen is a function of product characteristics (perishability and product size) as well as of time and money available and segment being targeted.

Coupons are defined as certificates that entitle the buyer to a price reduction on the couponed item and sometimes may require the consumer to purchase multiple units of the product, a related item in the manufacturer's product line, or a different manufacturer's complementary product. For example, a coupon for a large discount on tuna fish might require the purchase of crisp rye crackers. The shopper in Figure 14-4 is weighing the merits of a new product at a reduced price against the regularly priced, known brand.

As with samples, coupons can be delivered to the consumer in many ways: consumer-direct by mail or door-to-door, as free-standing card inserts in newspapers, in Sunday newspapers, in magazines, in/on the pack or product, or in retailer coupon books. Various studies have shown that about 80 percent of U.S. households use coupons at least occasionally; on any given day about 25 percent of consumers carry coupons into the store; about 19 percent are able to use them.[2] The average time that it takes consumers to redeem a coupon is 2 to 6 months; therefore, coupons work best in an established product category where the effort is toward extending the brand to new users and time is not a consideration.

It should be noted that if the marketing objective is to increase trial, coupons can fail. A few years ago, General Foods decided to cut back on the use of coupons in promoting their Maxwell House brand. At first glance the Maxwell house 40-cent coupon that went out to consumers every five weeks was a success, achieving an 8 percent redemption rate compared to the coffee industry average of 5 percent. How-

---

[2]As cited in John R. Rossiter and Larry Percy, *Advertising & Promotion Management* (New York: McGraw-Hill, 1987): 346.

FIGURE 14-4   Coupons are an example of sales promotion used by food manufacturers. *(Source: U.S. Department of Agriculture.)*

ever, further consumer research for Maxwell House showed that the coupons were mainly being redeemed by current Maxwell House users. In essence Maxwell House was "buying their own customers."[3] The marketer in Figure 14-5 is avoiding a similar situation.

The *price-off* and bonus-pack techniques are used particularly to stimulate usage. Because of manufacturer abuse of price-off promotions in the United States, the Federal Trade Commission has set out the rule that no more than three price-off promotions may be offered in a year on a given size of the brand, and no more than 50 percent of the brand's annual total distributed volume can be sold at price-off by the manufacturer. (Retailers are free to use price-offs as often as they like.) Price-offs are fast to implement and are a valuable tool to maintain usage rates (market share) against competitive inroads. The problem is that rather than being used as a short-term tactical tool, too often price-offs are overused; consumers become less brand loyal and more price sensitive, switching from brand to brand. Bonus packs are often used when a new competing brand is about to enter the category. This encourages consumers to load up, preventing them from trying the new brand—at least until the consumers' inventories run out.

Premiums are items that are offered free or at a price less than their retail value as

---

[3]*Ibid.,* 350.

FIGURE 14-5   Jackie, Andy Capp's pub owner, understands when promotion works and when it doesn't! *(Reprinted with special permission of North America Syndicate.)*

an incentive to buy one or more units of the brand. Premiums are not widely accepted by consumers; one often-quoted figure is that less than 10 percent of all households have ever sent in for a premium, whether it is free or "self-liquidating"—where the consumer mails in the proof-of-purchase and money which covers the cost of the premium and handling charges. Premiums can be effective, however, in holding present users through a multiple-purchase requirement, or they can be used to appeal to a particular subgroup of users. For example, a "classy" self-liquidator, such as a Perrier umbrella, may be used to increase "upmarket" usage and effectively enhance Perrier's brand franchise.

Trade Promotion

Trade promotions are frequently used by manufacturers to encourage retailers to stock the product and, in many cases, to provide a special display space or favorable shelf space. The manufacturer's primary motive is to obtain distribution of new products and increase usage of existing products. (This perspective sometimes conflicts with the retailer's objective of getting people into the store to buy anything.) Both the reputation of the manufacturer and the supermarket decision maker's attitude toward a potential supplier are very important in the new-product acceptance process.

Factors important to the retail buyer can be categorized as product attributes and supplier attributes. Product attributes—Is the new item in a strong, growing product category? Is the item just another "me too" line-extension product or a fundamentally new product?—influence the decisions of the "gatekeepers" of new product introductions, the retail buyers.

The three most highly ranked supplier attributes can be collectively classified as vendor financial support. Very important to 76 percent of the buyers queried are promotion (in-store sampling, coupons, or POP materials), and vendor advertising (TV and other media). Providing adequate channel development funds (for cooperative advertising and slotting allowances—payments to retailers for shelf placement) is very important to 70 percent of buyers.[4] Grocery buyers note that since it is not easy to predict the sales potential of a new item, the amount of advertising

---

[4]Fredericks and McLaughlin, 49–53.

and promotion support that a manufacturer offers with a new item often becomes a deciding factor in new-item acceptance. These promotion efforts by the manufacturer to ensure the product's short-term profitability, as well as long-term viability, are all forms of vendor financial support.

Point-of-purchase (POP) displays, trade promotions frequently offered by manufacturers to increase consumer interest in their products, are often cited as resulting in sales increases of 200 to over 1,000 percent. However, these results must be compared with the costs of producing displays and setting them up. Too often, displays are not very profitable either to the manufacturer or to the retailer. Also, POP displays are retailer-controlled, and only a small percentage offered to retailers are actually used. Despite these problems, POP remains an important tool in the marketer's promotional bag, and it is widely used in some industries, such as beer and wine—witness all the neon signs and other materials for Guinness and Fosters in pubs, taverns, and bars around the world.[5]

Cooperative advertising is a cash contribution from the manufacturer to the retailer's advertising budget. Depending on how much the manufacturer "cooperates," that is, the percentage contribution to the retailer's advertising budget, manufacturers can buy lesser or greater control over how their brands are portrayed. Cooperative advertising allowances can range from 5 percent (low control) to 100 percent (high control) and depend on how important it is for the manufacturer to oversee the communication and presentation of the brand in the retailer's advertising presentation.

The power of retailers in the food system has been increasing, particularly in Europe and Australia. The food manufacturers' main weapons in this battle are their brands. The problem is that every cent of the promotional dollar spent on trade promotion leaves less for media and other types of brand-supporting promotion. Also, retailers actively promote private or own-label brands, further eroding the standing of manufacturers' brands. Unless actively supported, food manufacturers' brands suffer a downward spiral. Aware of this, major global food companies, such as Kellogg's and Nestlé, support their brands with continuous massive media expenditure.

THE MANAGEMENT OF ADVERTISING

Problem to Be Solved

Depending on the product and its stage in the product life cycle, the immediate objective of promotion may be to generate awareness, stimulate first trial/rebuy, increase sales, establish or change attitudes (brand image), or build consumer loyalty. The first step in moving consumers toward purchase is brand awareness—are they able to recognize or recall the particular brand with sufficient detail to make a purchase? For a new brand, this process takes time—one of the reasons that line ex-

---

[5]For a very practical discussion of POP and how to implement it, see Menin and Benning's *The Power of Point-of-Purchase Advertising.*

tensions, new products that use an existing brand, are popular with marketers.

Once the consumer is aware of the product, the next step in the consumer buying process (Chapter 3) is "buying action" or product trial. A combination of promotional tools, such as coupons, in-store sampling, and other point-of-purchase efforts, may be involved in leading the consumer to action in the marketplace.

Brand image or differentiating the product is another important function of promotion. If the brand is not unique in the mind of the consumer and correctly positioned, as discussed in Chapter 12, the product will not survive the pressures of competing with new and exsiting products in today's supermarkets. Brand image development has both logical and emotional components, which will be considered under the creative approach to media strategy. The entire process of advertising management is diagrammed in Figure 14-6.

Through creative and judicious application of the promotional mix, the marketer works to build the brand's consumer franchise—a relatively permanent preference for that brand, referred to as brand equity. Putting it in the economist's framework, the goal is to increase demand—the product's sales volume at any given price—and also to affect the product's demand elasticity. The marketing manager wants to make the demand inelastic when its price increases—so that sales decline very little and total revenue increases; and elastic when its price decreases—to increase sales considerably, which will also increase total revenue.[6] The picture just painted, which may be described as "Marketer's Heaven," is one that is difficult to achieve.

Budgeting Decisions

Various models are presented for determining the amount of money that a company spends on promotion. Some are more appropriate than others; in some instances, a combination of methods may be utilized. According to the ideal model, the company sets out what it wants to accomplish (objective) and then determines what is necessary to accomplish that objective (task). In practice, the difficulty is in isolating the impacts of advertising on revenues, and also, on the task side, in arriving at a formula that accurately predicts the results of a given level of advertising intensity. The models that are used generally fall into one of the following categories.

Percentage of Sales   Companies usually make up future promotional budgets in terms of percentage of sales, using the preceding year as a base. If competitive pressures are severe, they may have to increase the budget to maintain the brand's share of market (assuming that one of the objectives of the firm is to maintain or increase market share, which would be typical). The pitfall of this method is that there is no evaluation of the profitability of a given level of advertising expenditures, and in fact, monies could be expended with little chance of increased profit.

---

[6]William J. Stanton, Michael J. Etzel, and Bruce J. Walker, *Fundamentals of Marketing,* 10th ed. (New York: McGraw-Hill, Inc., 1994): 459. Also, see the discussion of demand elasticity in Chapter 2.

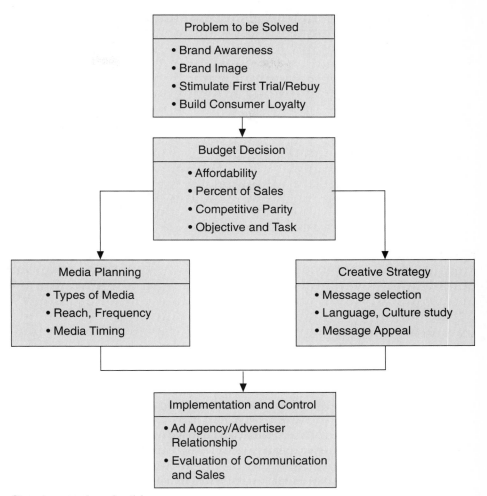

FIGURE 14-6 Steps in managing advertising.

Competitive Budgeting Few if any advertisers operate in a vacuum, without action by competitors. Industries exhibit norms or averages regarding how much is being spent on promotion. For example, processed foods differ from candy and gum in advertising expenditures, and the fast-food industry has another advertising environment (Table 14-1).

Within an industry there can be a wide variation in expenditures, in total and by percentage of sales. Table 14.1 shows that the average spending as a percent of sales of the fast-food industry is 6.0 percent. However, in a firm-by-firm look at this industry, McDonald's stands out, with the highest expenditure on advertising. In 1994, the "Golden Arches" spent over $880 million in advertising, making it the

TABLE 14-1   EXAMPLES OF TOP U.S. FOOD SYSTEM ADVERTISERS, 1995

Primary business	Company	U.S. advertising expenditure (millions $)	U.S. sales (millions $)	Advertising as percent of sales (%)
PACKAGED FOODS	Campbell Soup Co.	253.4	4,561.1	5.6
	CPC International	164.4	2,885.0	5.7
	H. J. Heinz	246.9	5,235.8	4.7
	Average—Packaged Foods:			5.2
CEREAL	General Mills*	489.9	5,204.5	9.4
	Kellogg Co.	739.7	4,080.3	18.1
	Average—Cereal:			13.2
CANDY & GUM	Hershey Foods	429.9	3,218.9	13.4
	Wm. Wrigley Jr. Co.	160.1	922.2	17.4
	Average—Candy & Gum:			14.2
BEVERAGES	Cadbury-Schweppes	179.6	1,972.8	9.1
	Coca-Cola	433.2	5,261.0	8.2
	Average—Soft Drinks:			8.5
FAST-FOOD RESTAURANTS	McDonald's Corp.	880.0	15,905.0	5.5
	Taco Bell	172.0	3,503.0	4.9
	Wendy's Int.	206.8	1,403.0	14.7
	Average—Fast-Food Restaurants:			6.0
GROCERY RETAILERS	American Stores	114.0	18,309.0	0.6
	Kroger	67.9	23,398.0	0.3
	Average—Grocery Retailers:			0.4

*Includes noncereal business, such as Yoplait, Betty Crocker foods, and Bisquick.
Source: "100 Leaders by Most Advertised Segment," *Advertising Age* (September 30, 1996): S51.

most advertised single brand in the world. There are companies who spend more on advertising, but it is spread over several brands. Just-for-fun calculations show that $880 million a year equates to over $2.4 million spent on advertising daily, or $100,000 an hour, or $1,650 a minute! The concern of McDonald's competitors is how they can effectively cut through this massive barrage of messages being sent to consumers and obtain a favorable response to their message to "come eat my taco" or "try my rotisserie chicken."

Affordability   Many companies, especially smaller ones, use the affordability method; that is, they budget what they think the company can afford. This method obviously ignores the effect of promotion on sales volume and can result in over-spending, but more often results in underspending. Although it lacks a rationale, studies have shown that between 20 and 30 percent of companies utilize this method.

Objective-and-Task   The most logical budget-setting method is to "determine what we want to do and what has to be done in order to do it." As mentioned earlier, the objective-and-task method forces management to: 1) define advertising objectives in terms of market share, sales growth, or other goals, 2) determine the tasks that need to be performed in order to accomplish these objectives, and 3) decide what it will cost to perform these tasks. The tasks will differ, depending on several factors:[7]

- *Stage in the life cycle.* Early in product introduction, large advertising budgets build awareness and gain consumer trial.
- *Market share.* High-market-share brands usually need more advertising spending as a percent of sales than low-share brands.
- *Competition and clutter.* In a market with many competitors and high spending, a brand must advertise more heavily to be heard above the clutter and noise in the market.
- *Product differentiation.* A brand that is similar to other brands in its product class (cigarettes, beer, soft drinks) requires heavy advertising to differentiate itself.

Media Planning

Given that the objective-and-task method is the most appropriate approach in developing a promotional strategy, the first step in media planning is to establish objectives. Objectives may be stated in terms of consumer awareness (in the case of a new product), sales volume, market share, or some combination. The media plan translates these objectives into advertising action. It also forces the marketer to develop the most cost-efficient plan possible. With a prime-time 30-second television spot costing $100,000 or more, it is imperative that the media plan reaches the largest number of prospects at the lowest cost and with the greatest effectiveness (meaning that the particular media environment—program content or print vehicle—supports the brand image). The media plan has a number of components, and, while there is no standard format, the following elements are found in most plans:[8]

- The target audience
- Communication requirements and creative elements
- Geography—Where is the product distributed?
- The efficiency/effectiveness balance—Shall reach, frequency, or continuity be stressed?
- The pressure of competition
- The budget.

Since market segmentation, target markets, and product positioning have been treated in Chapter 12, those topics will not be discussed here. Also, for a complete understanding of such a complex and ever-changing aspect of marketing as advertising, a specialized reference book is a must.

[7]Donald E. Schultz, Dennis Martin, and William P. Brown, *Strategic Advertising Campaigns* (Chicago: Crain Books, 1984): 192–97.

[8]J. Thomas Russell, Glenn Verrill, and W. Ronald Lane, *Kleppner's Advertising Procedure,* 10th ed. (Englewood Cliffs, NJ: Prentice-Hall, 1988): 141.

After identifying the target market, the media planner must choose the appropriate media for the advertising message. Messages with a lot of technical data may best be delivered via print or direct mailings. As a contrast, the beer industry has found television and sporting events to be a natural fit, not only in terms of reaching their target audience (virtually a perfect fit), but also in terms of the environment—competition, excitement, and male bonding—that supports the message content of most beer advertising.

Too often in advertising planning, the media and creative functions are not closely enough coordinated. The result, according to critics, is that advertising often does not fully utilize the communicative strengths of the various media vehicles.

The media planner must also deal with budget allocation by geographic area. Are prospects concentrated in a geographic area, as perhaps consumers of ethnic foods are? In that case, special newspaper sections or narrowly defined radio and TV programs may be used to reach prospects concentrated in one area. If the target audience is not concentrated geographically, budget allocations are made by comparing sales and population of a market. For example, different markets with equal population may have differing sales potentials. If an area has sales potential only 67 percent as great as another area of equal population, the media planner would reduce that area's budget allocation proportionately.

From country to country, advertising expenditures and the characteristics of various media differ considerably. As might be expected, the U.S. populace is at or near the top on a per capita basis, with over $450 per person spent on advertising. Most other industrialized countries, such as Sweden, Australia, Great Britain, and Canada, are around $200, and in many developing countries the figure is often little more than $1 per capita. In countries where some media are nonexistent or their availability is limited, the promotional program will be restricted by a lack of options.

Differences in media behavior are also exhibited. For example, Mexico has about 800 radio stations, with over 60 in Mexico City. On most of these stations there are 24 minutes of commercials and 11 breaks per hour, with 2 minutes of news during each break. With this type of programming, listeners cannot tolerate listening to one station continually and are constantly changing stations. Advertisers buy a quantity of media space for the same time block across several stations, as opposed to the U.S. practice of purchasing advertising on a limited number of stations that reach their target market over several time frames and are not particularly coordinated among the stations used.[9]

The Impact of Reach and Frequency   The heart of a media plan is balancing reach and frequency in a specific advertising campaign. *Reach* refers to the total number of people to whom a message is delivered. It is also sometimes stated in terms of the percentage of people in a target market who are exposed to the

---

[9]Jean-Claude Usunier, *International Marketing: A Cultural Approach* (Hemel Hempstead, Hertfordshire, UK: Prentice-Hall International (UK) Ltd., 1993): 340–84.

advertising campaign during a period of time. Note that exposure to a message does not mean that the subject actually sees or hears the message. Delivery of the message means just that—the newspaper is delivered to a residence or a television is turned on. The subject may or may not read the newspaper or watch the television. *Frequency* is the number of times the advertisement is delivered within a given period (usually figured on a weekly basis for schedule planning). *Continuity* refers to the length of time a particular advertising schedule runs. In practice, reach and frequency are the primary considerations in developing a media schedule.

All advertising campaigns are limited by funds available. In this example, the budget will purchase 2,000,000 exposures. These exposures can be bought in different ways but cannot exceed the 2,000,000. As exposures per prospect are increased (frequency), the number of prospects that can be reached is reduced:

Frequency		Reach		Exposures
2 exposures	×	1,000,000 prospects	=	2,000,000
5 exposures	×	400,000 prospects	=	2,000,000
10 exposures	×	200,000 prospects	=	2,000,000

For a given advertising budget, there is a tradeoff between the total number of people in the target audience reached and the number of times each person is exposed to the message. It might seem a good idea to reach every member of the target audience at least once, but on the other side of the coin is the concept of effective frequency. Research has shown that to break through the clutter and to be effective—to be above a threshold frequency level—requires a minimum amount of repetitions. It is only after the third exposure that the consumer is likely to take action. This three-exposure effectiveness level is just a guide (based on packaged-goods testing) and can be adjusted up or down on a client-by-client, campaign-by-campaign basis.[10]

To achieve maximum reach and frequency efficiencies, it is likely that a combination of media will be the best solution, mainly because potential customers in most target markets differ in their media preferences. For instance, in the United States, about 33 percent of adults are heavy magazine/light TV users, while 39 percent are heavy TV/light magazine users, and 13 percent are light TV/light magazine users.

An important measure of advertising intensity and advertising purchasing is *Gross Rating Points (GRP);* 1 gross rating point is 1 percent of the universe of the market being measured; for example, in television, 1 GRP equals 1 percent of the households having TV sets in a geographic area. If a particular program has a rating of 12, it means that 12 percent of all sets are tuned to that program. The advertiser builds up the advertising schedule in differing geographical markets using GRPs; 1 GRP in Tokyo has the same relative weight as 1 GRP in Osaka. However,

[10]Steve Lonning, "Effective Frequency: A Planner's Perspective," *Journal of Media Planning* (Fall 1986): 47.

the cost of media is going to be much higher in Tokyo, with its population of over 11.9 million compared to Osaka's 2.5 million.

Scheduling Advertising   Once the appropriate reach and frequency balance is reached, the next question is how to schedule the advertising. Some product sales are seasonal in nature: candy at Christmas and Easter, barbecue sauce during the summer. For these products, advertising is scheduled to reflect the seasonal peaks, appearing ahead of the consumer buying season, when people begin to think of buying such products.

When the sale of a product is uniform throughout the year (bread, for example), advertising can be scheduled in one of three typical *timing patterns,* portrayed in Figure 14-7: continuous, flighting, or pulsing. A *continuous* schedule provides a constant level of advertising over time, but maintaining threshold frequency levels continuously would be an extremely expensive solution. Rather than reduce costs by spreading advertising at a lower level over 12 months, marketers prefer to concentrate advertising over shorter time periods. Also, in the United States during the summer, reading and TV watching decrease and radio listening increases; therefore, some advertisers decrease their TV expenditures in favor of radio or take leave of TV for the summer months. Two alternatives to a continuous advertising schedule are flighting or pulsing: *flighting* schedules advertisements in bursts with gaps between, during which no ads are run; *pulsing* varies the frequency of ads but maintains a threshold level.

Creative Strategy

The message content and how that message will be portrayed are crucial components to an advertising program. The two major types of appeal that are used in

FIGURE 14-7   Three patterns of media continuity.

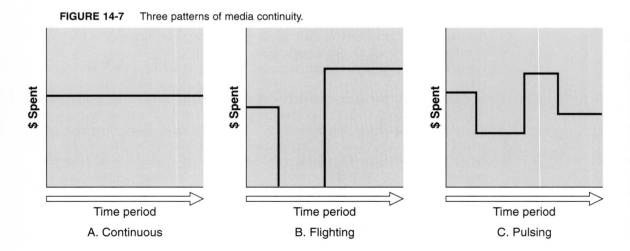

A. Continuous   B. Flighting   C. Pulsing

food marketing are rational appeals, such as nutrition, and emotional appeals, which motivate purchase through desire, fear, guilt, or shame. The use of appeals varies by culture: French and Italian ads often appear as very dream oriented—viewers and readers are supposedly desirous of escape from the real world. Germans, however, are known to prefer advertising that is rational and informative.

Other challenges in international advertising include the use of language and the roles represented in advertising. Advertising uses colloquial language which is very precise as far as meaning is concerned. This language is generally not found in "official" dictionaries, and translating colloquial speech is difficult, since there is little literal equivalence. For example, the California Milk Processor Board wanted to extend their national hit advertisement, "Got Milk?" to Hispanics. However, in a Mexican-American focus group the "Got Milk?" punch line translated roughly to "Are you lactating?" The focus-group research also found that not having milk or rice in Hispanic households is not funny; having run out of milk means that you have failed your family. Armed with this information, the Board's Hispanic ad agency, Anita Santiago Advertising, in Los Angeles, created "Generations," an advertising campaign designed for the Mexican-American culture.[11]

In depicting people, especially women, in character roles, advertisers have to be very careful. Whether it is the character's age, dress, or situation which is represented, nothing should be left to chance in advertising messages. What is conventional wisdom is often not borne out upon closer examination. For example, in a study of the advertising industry's attitude toward sex roles in Australia, Mexico, and the United States, it was expected that a more traditional image of women would be the norm in Mexico, with a more modern image in the United States and Australia somewhere in between. It was found, though, that in the United States and Mexico (as opposed to Australia) women were more often shown in roles of consumers and men were more often shown in roles of authority or expertise with respect to the product.[12]

As marketers move into new international markets, they should study a representative sample of local advertising messages. With a systematic analysis of the content of newspaper, magazine, and television advertising, a good idea of acceptable portrayal of the sex roles, age roles, typical everyday situations, and social relations in a particular country can be achieved.

For a multinational food company, communication with a market segment that is specific to a certain country needs to be delegated to the local level. While there are aspects of promotion that are global, such as the core values conveyed by a company's corporate image—innovativeness, social responsibility, and healthfulness—even in internationally standardized ads, the messages need to be reviewed by someone of that culture as to their various linguistic/cultural contexts.

[11]Leon E. Wynter, "Group Finds Right Recipe for Milk Ads in Spanish," *Wall Street Journal* (March 6, 1996), B1.

[12]Usunier, 347–48.

Evaluation of Communication/Sales

Measuring the effectiveness of advertising is not easy. If a company looks just at the dollar sales figure over a time period, the sales increase or decrease can be a result of many factors outside the control of the advertiser. Actions by competitors, whether promotional efforts or pricing tactics, can mask the real impact of an advertising campaign. Also, changes in the economy, unemployment, and whether the economy is growing or in recession, all have a potential impact on a product's sales.

The communication effect of a specific advertisement is somewhat easier to measure than the sales effect. The two major approaches to testing advertising copy in printed, television, or radio advertisements are *pretesting* and *posttesting.* In pretesting, a consumer panel looks at alternative ads and rates them in terms of attention getting and their affect on the panel members.

In posttesting, two common techniques are used: aided recall, where respondents are shown an ad and asked whether they remember it, and unaided recall, where respondents are questioned without prompts. Recall scores measure an ad's ability to be noticed and remembered, which is the key to the communication process. Recall scores can also be useful to compare an advertisement's effectiveness in different market segments and with competitors' ads. Along with recall, the audience's behavior, attitude, beliefs, or whatever variables the advertiser is targeting to influence with the ad may also be tested.[13] If a chicken-meat marketer wants to convince the target audience that an advertised product is fresher and safer than competitors', then the beliefs of the audience should be measured with both a pretest and a posttest.

To conduct the research described above and to execute advertising programs or campaigns, most food marketers, particularly manufacturers, use an advertising agency. The agency's advantage is its specialized expertise in buying media, creative services, and research. Today, many agencies provide a full array of marketing services, including public relations and new-product development assistance. With the internationalization of advertisers, agencies have also increased their operations in foreign countries. Often conflicts arise between client and agency as to the creative strategy to be followed, and operating across country borders adds to the challenges inherent in the relationships between advertiser and advertising agency. In the end, results such as brand awareness, brand image, and sales increase tell the story of a particular advertising campaign's effectiveness.

PERSONAL SELLING

Different types of marketing apply to different stages in the food system: commodity marketing for agricultural raw materials, industrial marketing to food processors and manufacturers, reseller marketing to retailers, and branded-product marketing to consumers. While advertising is the main promotional method for marketing to

---

[13]C. L. Bovée, M. J. Houston, and J. V. Thill, *Marketing,* 2d ed. (New York: McGraw-Hill, 1992): 564–65.

consumers, and sales promotion is used mainly in reseller marketing, personal selling, the third element of the promotional mix, is the main promotional activity used to market industrial products.

The basic difference between personal selling and other types of promotional activity is that it is interactive: the supplier and the customer meet on a face-to-face basis. The two main functions of the salesperson are to help the customer buy and to provide feedback from the customer to the company.

Personal selling is the most expensive form of promotion on a per-customer basis. Therefore, it should be used only if it offers clear benefits in comparison with advertising or sales promotion. Table 14-2 shows when personal selling is likely to be cost effective relative to advertising.

Table 14-2 shows why personal selling is used to a lesser extent in retailing food products: they are usually nontechnical, have a low unit price, and so on. On the other hand, marketing a complex piece of food-processing machinery requires a substantial personal selling input: the product is high-priced, technical, purchased infrequently, and requires demonstration.

Personal selling is a part of the total buyer-seller relationship. In industrial marketing, the relationship is often multidimensional, especially for major-cost items. Customer companies may have established buying centers, which could include manufacturing, R&D, and financial staff, as well as the designated buyer (see Chapter 7). The supplier must recognize this in determining the composition of the selling team.

TABLE 14-2   PERSONAL SELLING COMPARED WITH ADVERTISING

Product variables	
Use ADVERTISING when the PRODUCT is:	Use PERSONAL SELLING when the PRODUCT is:
Standardized	Nonstandardized
Low unit value	High unit value
Nontechnical	Technical
Purchased frequently	Purchased infrequently
Simple to use	Needs demonstration
Low psychological involvement	High psychological involvement
Low unit price	High unit price
Market variables	
Use ADVERTISING when the MARKET is:	Use PERSONAL SELLING when the MARKET is:
Geographically dispersed	Geographically concentrated
Many customers	Few customers
Price is nonnegotiable	Price is negotiable

The Sales-Management Process

Managing the sales force involves eight main activities:

1 Define the role of personal selling in the promotional mix and establish sales-force objectives.

2 Determine the size and structure of the sales force.

3 Select salespeople.

4 Train salespeople.

5 Decide the basis of sales-force remuneration.

6 Determine sales-force organization.

7 Set performance standards.

8 Evaluate performance.

It is beyond the scope of this text to discuss all these activities in detail, but the first and sixth activities, defining the role of the sales force and determining how it should be organized, require further comment.[14]

How does one define the role of the sales force? At first glance, the answer to this question appears simple. Surely the role of a salesperson is to make sales. However, in industrial and reseller marketing, getting the order is usually a relatively small part of the salesperson's job. The salesperson is a link between the company and the customer. A major function is to serve as a conduit for information, both from company to customer and from customer to company. Salespeople also have a role in servicing industrial customers and motivating resellers.

The sales force can be structured on a territory basis, a product basis, or a customer basis (one salesperson is responsible for a specified set of customers). The advantages of a territory basis of organization are reduced travel costs, good identification of the salesperson with the company, and ability to establish a clear link between responsibilities and performance. The big disadvantage is that the salesperson has to be a generalist, which becomes increasingly difficult as the product range becomes more complex.

Think Break

Given the variables discussed above, what are some situations in which the product-based or customer-based forms of sales-force organization are preferable?

Determining the size of the sales force is like the objective-and-task method of determining the advertising budget. You must begin the process with a clear statement of what the sales force is expected to achieve. Salespeople can have one or more of the following three roles: order getters (generating new business), order takers (serving established business), or sale supporters (providing technical advice). The sales-force objective is defined in terms of the level of service received

---

[14]See a text such as Johnson, Kurtz, and Schueing, *Sales Management: Concepts, Practices, and Cases* (McGraw-Hill).

by each customer from each category of salesperson. The sales task can then be specified in terms of the number of calls per year required to service each customer properly and, allowing for travel and call time, to calculate how many salespeople are required to do the job.

COMMODITY PROMOTION

Industry groups expend considerable effort on increasing the demand for their product category by carrying out commodity promotion and advertising programs. Forker and Ward define generic or *commodity advertising*[15] as "the cooperative effort among producers of a nearly homogeneous product to disseminate information about the underlying attributes of the product to existing and potential consumers for the purpose of strengthening demand for the product."[16]

A key point of commodity advertising is that these programs are funded through a coordinated effort. In the United States, participation of producers is required by special legislation or under the auspices of federal or state marketing orders. In most cases the producer is required to participate, given the rationale that everyone benefits from commodity promotional programs so everyone should pay—there should not be free riders. Other ideas contained in the definition are: 1) the homogeneous nature of the product limits what can be said in the promotional/advertising efforts, and 2) the end purpose of any commodity advertising program is to strengthen demand by attracting new consumers and by increasing existing consumers' usage of the commodity.

Commodity Organizations

A commodity organization is most often managed by a staff hired and directed by its producer board of directors, who have been appointed by the state or federal agriculture department with program oversight responsibilities. Some organizations may have a board that represents both producer and processor interests, and often a consumer or public member is required by the legislation.

As with brand advertising, commodity advertisers may contract with other firms to implement the advertising or promotional program. Market-research firms are used to conduct surveys, and advertising agencies are hired to create advertisements and place the ads with the media. Programs with larger budgets tend to have large media advertising campaigns to communicate the beneficial attributes of the commodity to consumers. Smaller-budget programs often emphasize other promotional

---

[15]The terms *commodity* and *commodity promotion organization* are used in this context to refer to the industry as a whole, and in contrast to individual brand advertising. As an example, the dairy industry promotes consumption of cheese as a food product, while Kraft and Land o' Lakes promote and advertise their specific brands. The term *generic* is sometimes used as a synonym for *commodity;* however, to avoid confusion with the use of *generic* earlier in the text, the term is not used here. It should also be noted that the definitive book on the subject, Forker and Ward, while somewhat ambivalent in the title of their book, *Commodity Advertising: The Economics and Measurement of Generic Programs,* use the term *commodity* throughout.

[16]Olan D. Forker and Ronald W. Ward, *Commodity Advertising: The Economics and Measurement of Generic Programs* (New York: Lexington Books, 1993): 6.

tools, such as publicity and various in-store merchandising techniques. Some invest heavily in research, whether it is technical research to improve product quality and usage or marketing research that assists all brand marketers to improve their performance.

There are over 100 commodity-promotion organizations in the United States, with total expenditure of over $750 million. The dairy industry, with various state and national programs, makes the largest single industry effort, spending over $200 million in promotional programs. Commodities that have programs range from catfish and ginseng to one of the most visible and active programs over the years, the Florida Citrus Commission. The Florida program, established by a special act of the legislature in 1935, with recent annual budgets of over $60 million, is the largest of any state-legislated promotion program.

The Florida Citrus Commission carries out a substantial media advertising program which accounts for 53 percent of its budget. The Commission also conducts economic analysis and outlook, scientific research, and other marketing efforts, including merchandising at the retail level, food service programs, and international market development. The focus of the Florida program is on processed products, as its strategy is to persuade consumers to choose Florida orange juice over other juices, claiming great taste and nutritive values that other juices and juice drinks do not have.

Several studies have shown that the Florida program is effective in increasing sales and that, while brand advertising has a more immediate effect than commodity, the carryover effect of commodity advertising is greater than that of brand advertising and is greater in later periods. However, brand advertising was found to be slightly more effective in increasing sales than commodity advertising.

The major problem the Commission faces is the "free-rider" issue. In the past decade, juice imports, mainly from Brazil, have increased tremendously. The Florida industry is able to collect assessments only on juice that is imported through Florida ports. Also, perhaps more importantly, the long-run success of the Florida program hinges on how well it is able to differentiate 100 percent Florida juice from orange juice in general. If it is unable to make this differentiation, the Florida industry will become disenchanted with the idea of building markets for the Brazilians and other competitors.

Commodity and Brand Advertising

While the Florida Citrus Commission experience raises an important issue relating to commodity promotional program effectiveness—that of the free rider, another problem area is synergy or lack of synergy between brand and commodity advertising. First, it is useful in understanding commodity-group advertising to view products on a continuum as to their cooperative or predatory nature.[17] Products that cannot be differentiated are considered *cooperative goods*. Advertising these goods may increase total demand, but it cannot change market shares among sellers. In

---

[17]James Friedman, *Oligopoly and Advertising* (Cambridge, MA: Cambridge UP, 1983): 143.

this case commodity and brand advertising would have identical results on consumer behavior, and there would be little incentive for individual brand advertisers to promote their goods, since all other sellers would benefit without paying their share of the advertising cost. For example, why would Kansas producers of USDA #1 hard winter wheat advertise their product when millers around the world know that USDA #1 hard winter wheat from Oklahoma is the same product? The Kansas wheat producers are not going to invest in developing markets for their fellow hard red winter wheat producers in neighboring states. An answer in this case would be a coordinated effort by all hard winter wheat producers to promote their product to end users around the world.

Products are called *predatory goods* when expansion in total consumption is difficult to achieve, but the products can be differentiated by brand. Advertising by brands in this case shifts market share but does not increase total consumption. While predatory goods are usually thought of in the situation of brand substitution, one can also view this concept as being operational in a broader cateogry, such as foods in general. The issue is whether the advertising of one food group leads to switching from other categories or to growth in total food consumption. Often, in public policy discussions as to the desirability of commodity advertising, the full-stomach argument is used to support the idea that commodity advertising is contrary to the public interest. That is, if there is a limit to total food consumption, and for the most part in developed countries we have reached or overextended that limit, then one food group may be predatory on another.

Think Break

> *Do you accept the full-stomach argument? That is, in developed countries we have reached the limit to total food consumption, so that commodity-group advertising efforts are predatory on other group efforts, for example, pork on beef. If this is the case, then the end result of such advertising is simply a tax on the product and raises the price to consumers. Should not commodity advertising efforts be banned by governments?*

Probably most agricultural commodities lie somewhere between the purely co-operative and the predatory situations. We can look again at Forker and Ward's example, Florida Citrus, where both brand and commodity advertising have been beneficial to the industry. The characteristics of orange juice are such that the basic commodity remains nearly identical across suppliers (although surely they would disagree even on this point), but differentiation occurs through different product forms and packaging.

To be supported by the industry, commodity advertising should be brand neutral. It calls consumers' attention to the product group and product attributes that are common to the category; there should be no information in the message that leads consumers to believe that one brand is different from another. Commodity advertising may benefit a "brand" in an industry that has a strong private-label presence.

The argument here is that commodity advertising favors the private label by providing an advertising base for the entire industry and perhaps in the process negates some of the differentiation claims made by brands.

Figure 14-8 provides three views of the interplay between commodity and brand advertising. In case I, the inner circle represents total sales of the three brands (shown as A, B, and C). If commodity advertising is effective, then demand growth should occur, and if the commodity is a completely cooperative good, market shares do not change—all market participants share equally in the growth. In case II, brand advertising is occurring within a group of predatory brands. In this example the total market is not growing, but brand A is increasing sales by taking market share from B and C.

In case III, the total market grows while brand shifting also occurs. In this case the total market growth could be due to commodity advertising or brand advertising, or a combination of both. In the orange-juice market, Tropicana Pure Premium orange juice has been heavily advertised and its market share has grown. According to market research, the brand's advertising has substantially contributed to growth in the demand for all orange juice, but research by the Florida Citrus Commission shows that their advertising has also been effective in increasing the overall consumption of orange juice.

The Benefits of Commodity Advertising

The objective of all commodity advertising organizations is to increase the total demand for the commodity. This larger demand results in a larger volume being sold for higher-value uses or higher prices for a given supply, and higher total revenues

FIGURE 14-8   Commodity and brand advertising effects on markets. *(Source: Forker and Ward, p. 41. Reprinted with permission from Olan D. Forker and Ronald W. Ward,* Commodity Advertising: The Economics and Measurement of Generic Programs. *Copyright ©1993 Jossey-Bass Inc., Publishers. First published by Lexington Books. All rights reserved.)*

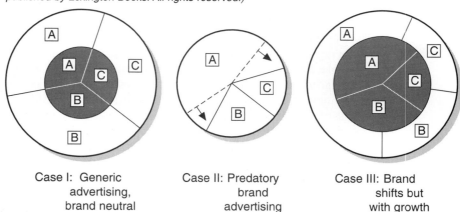

Case I: Generic advertising, brand neutral

Case II: Predatory brand advertising

Case III: Brand shifts but with growth

for all producers. Research in various commodities—apples, orange juice, dairy—has shown commodity advertising to be effective, with some exceptions. Advertising of cheese did not influence households that normally buy natural cheese (as opposed to processed) to increase their consumption. It was found that commodity advertising of fresh potatoes was not effective, but at the same time, both brand and commodity advertising of frozen potatoes, primarily french fried, did have a positive impact on consumption. In addition to advertising, commodity organizations carry out merchandising efforts at retail, as shown in Figure 14-9.

Below are several of the conclusions Forker and Ward drew as to the overall performance of commodity advertising:

• Commodity advertising and promotion programs can have positive impacts on sales. Several empirical studies show that these increases have been large enough to benefit producers.

• In the evaluation of market impacts, it is important, even essential, to account for the carryover effects of an advertising or promotion program.

• Brand advertising, as well as commodity advertising, can increase aggregate demand for a commodity. Commodity and brand advertising can complement one another.

• Commodity-promotion organizations, in addition to increasing demand directly, have been able to influence the rate of technical change in production and marketing.

FIGURE 14-9   Promotion by the California Strawberry Commission. The California Strawberry Commission uses advertising, POP materials, and other merchandising efforts to maintain strawberry display space in the produce department, where the number of items has increased from 200 to 350 in recent years. *(Courtesy of California Strawberry Commission.)*

This kind of collective action has enabled the beef and pork industries to develop more rapidly products with the qualities and attributes that are strongly in demand by consumers.

SUMMARY

Food marketers can take a variety of avenues in promoting their product, whether that product is an industrial product, such as a flavoring or other ingredient, or a consumer product, such as a can of soup or bag of potato chips. The promotional mix consists of advertising, sales promotion, public relations, and personal selling. In marketing consumer packaged goods, the promotional mix is generally weighted more toward advertising.

The food manufacturer has two potential targets for promotional efforts: wholesalers/retailers and consumers. Efforts directed toward distributors and retailers are known as trade promotions and can take the form of off-invoice price discounts, inventory financing, free goods, point-of-purchase (POP) displays, and cooperative advertising. In recent years, manufacturers have moved their promotional dollars more toward trade promotion and away from consumer media advertising.

In advertising management, budgeting is a major issue, and several models can be used to determine how much money a company should spend on advertising. According to the ideal model, the company sets out what it wants to accomplish (objective) and then determines what action (task) is necessary to accomplish that objective; in practice, often the percentage-of-sales, competitive budgeting, or affordability method is chosen.

An advertising campaign begins with a media plan. While the media plan has a number of components, it should always state the objectives—what the advertising is expected to accomplish. Other aspects of the media plan include definition of the target audience, the media to be employed, the schedule (reach and frequency), the creative elements of the advertisements, and the budget.

Commodity-promotion organizations exist to strengthen demand for a commodity by attracting new customers and to increase usage by existing consumers. In the United States more than 100 commodity-promotion organizations, which are set up under special legislation or under the auspices of federal or state marketing orders, spend over three-quarters of a billion dollars on commodity promotion and advertising efforts.

The concept of cooperative goods and predatory goods is important in understanding the effect of commodity advertising. Products that cannot be differentiated, for which advertising may increase total demand but not change market share among sellers, are referred to as cooperative goods. Products are called predatory goods when expansion in total demand is difficult to achieve, but the products can be differentiated by brand. Most food products are somewhere between purely cooperative and purely predatory—for Florida Citrus, for example, both brand and commodity advertising have been beneficial.

Commodity advertising can have a positive impact on sales sufficient to benefit producers, and commodity and brand advertising can complement one another.

In addition to directly increasing demand, commodity-promotion organizations have been able to influence the rate of technical change in production and marketing. Thus, it is argued that commodity-promotion organizations in industries such as beef and pork have fostered improvements in product quality and in other product attributes more quickly than would have occurred in their absence. The competitiveness of industries such as beef and soybeans in global markets is said to be due, at least in part, to the activities of their commodity-promotion organizations.

IMPORTANT TERMS AND CONCEPTS

advertising 374	Point-of-Purchase (POP) 381
advertising timing patterns: 388	posttest 390
continuous 388	predatory goods 395
flighting 388	premiums 380
pulsing 388	pretest 390
commodity advertising 393	price-off 379
consumer promotion 377	public relations 374
continuity 387	pull strategy 375
cooperative advertising 381	push strategy 375
cooperative goods 394	reach 386
coupons 378	sales promotion 374
frequency 387	sampling 377
Gross Rating Points (GRP) 387	trade discounts 376
personal selling 390	trade promotion 376

CASE STUDY: Do Advertising and Packaging Make the Sale?

In 1994, fruit flavored teas, bubbly waters, and concoctions with mystical names like Fruit Integration and Strawberry Passion Awareness were all the rage in the U.S. beverage industry. Brands like Fruitopia Real Fruit Beverage, Fruit Box Fruit Drink, and Nestea (all Coca-Cola brands) had also spread to New Zealand by 1995, and had captured shelf-loads of refrigerator space in the shops. These New Age beverages appeared to be the marketing triumph of the decade.

In the United States, Coca-Cola had launched one line of trendy drinks, Fruitopia, in early 1994 and poured $30 million into the launch, giving it a psychedelic image complete with kaleidoscope television ads and such cosmic slogans as, "Fruitopia: For the mind, body, and planet." However, sales were only $60 million for the first year, instead of the $400 million predicted. In October, 1995, the *Wall Street Journal* reported that sales were falling and the big winners for the summer of 1995 were Mountain Dew and Coca-Cola Classic.

Some of the reasons given for the "flat" market in the United States were:

• The health kick that launched the New Age drinks had faded.

• People got tired of the tastes of distinctive juices and unusual teas—colas are more neutral and less memorable.

- The too trendy marketing attracted attention, but quickly faded.
- Prices were too high.

But could it be that the products do not deliver anything really new? *New Zealand Consumer Magazine* describes them as only sugar and water; high fructose corn syrup is the sweetener in several drinks, but this is no healthier than ordinary sugar. Several New Age beverages claim to "contain real juice," but none contain very much: Oasis Raspberry Iced Tea—5 percent, Fruitopia—13 percent. Some use more sugar than Coke and Lemon-lime sodas. So is flavoring the only difference besides the lack of bubbles and a wide-mouthed bottle that is easy to swig from and recap?

An analysis of various beverages provided the following cost and nutrition comparisons:

Brand	Price per 250-ml glass	Sugar (teaspoons)	Energy (Kj)	Caffeine (mg)
Fruitopia Real Fruit Beverage	$1.06	6.3	550	—
Twinings Iced Tea	1.59	4.2	360	45
Nestea Iced Tea	1.00	4.1	350	98
Fizzy soft drinks: Cola	.70	5.6	480	23
Lemonade	.70	5.6	480	—
Orange juice (unsweetened)	1.20	4.0	345	—

Questions

1 What are the advantages of the New Age beverages?
2 Are the advertising images portrayed related to these advantages?
3 If you do not think the advertising portrays the advantages, you have two choices. Would you redesign the product to fit the New Age image or find a new image to portray the product?
4 Discuss Coca-Cola's decision to introduce Fruitopia internationally after its slow sales in the United States.

Sources: "Would You Swallow This?" *Consumer (N.Z.)* (December, 1995): 36, reprinted with permission of *Consumer Magazine;* and Robert Frank, "Fruity Teas and Mystical Sodas are Boring Consumers," *The Wall Street Journal,* 9 (October 9, 1995): B1, Reprinted with permission of *Wall Street Journal* ©1993 Dow Jones & Company, Inc. all Rights Reserved Worldwide.

QUESTIONS

1 How does an advertiser utilize the objective-and-task method of determining advertising budget? What factors determine the amount of advertising expenditure required for success in the marketplace?

2 At the heart of a media plan are the concepts of reach and frequency. Define each and describe the underlying theory behind the number of repetitions required for advertising to be effective.

3 What is "one Gross Rating Point," and how would a marketing manager use gross rating points in building a media plan?

4 What are some examples of trade promotions? What is the concept behind the trade-promotion techniques as opposed to consumer-promotion techniques?

5 Point-of-purchase displays and cooperative advertising are popular trade-promotion techniques in the grocery industry but suffer serious problems in their application. What are these problems?

6 What has research revealed about consumer use of coupons and the effectiveness of coupons in attracting new users to a product?

7 Describe what is meant by a cooperative good and a predatory good as applied to commodity advertising. How does a commodity or food product's cooperative or predatory nature influence whether the industry should financially support a commodity-advertising program?

8 Discuss the performance of commodity advertising and in what situations it is effective.

REFERENCES AND RESOURCES

Forker, Olan D., and Ronald W. Ward. *Commodity Advertising: The Economics and Measurement of Generic Programs.* New York: Lexington Books, 1993.

Fredericks, Peter J., and Edward W. McLaughlin. *New Product Procurement: A Summary of Buying Practices and Acceptance Criteria at U.S. Supermarket Chains.* A. E. Research 92-12. Ithaca, NY: Cornell University Department of Agricultural Economics, December 1992.

Margolin, Victor, Ira Brichta, and Vivian Brichta. *The Promise and The Product—200 Years of American Advertising Posters.* New York: Macmillan, 1979.

Menin, Ben, and Arthur Benning, Sr. *The Power of Point-of-Purchase Advertising.* New York: American Management Association, 1992.

Montgomery, D. B. "New Product Distribution: An Analysis of Supermarket Buyer Decisions." *Journal of Marketing Research* 12.3 (1975): 255–64.

Rossiter, John R., and Larry Percy. *Advertising & Promotion Management.* New York: McGraw-Hill, 1987.

Russell, J. Thomas, Glenn Verrill, and W. Ronald Lane. *Kleppner's Advertising Procedure.* Englewood Cliffs, NJ: Prentice-Hall, 1988.

Quelch, John A. "It's Time to Make Trade Promotion More Productive." *Harvard Business Review* (May–June 1983): 130–36.

Stone, Randy, and Mike Duffy. "Measuring the Impact of Advertising." *Journal of Marketing Research* (November/December, 1993): RC 8–12.

"What Happened to Advertising?" *Business Week* (September 21, 1991): 66–72.

15

PRICING FOOD PRODUCTS

CHAPTER OUTLINE

LEARNING OBJECTIVES

After reading this chapter and answering the questions in the Think Breaks and at the end of the chapter, you should be able to:

- Show how pricing relates to company objectives.
- Relate pricing to the other elements of the marketing mix.
- Understand how the various business functions are coordinated in price setting.
- Apply cost accounting to price establishment through break-even analysis.
- Show how industry structure influences pricing.
- Appreciate how buyers' valuation of product/service attributes can be used in setting prices.
- Identify variables influencing buyers' sensitivity to price.
- Apply market-segmentation concepts to price setting.
- Explain how competitors influence the pricing decision.
- Be aware of the legal issues involved in setting prices.
- Understand alternative strategies for pricing in relation to the product life cycle.
- Understand different geographical pricing approaches, including export pricing.
- Apply pricing principles to the four different types of marketing found in the food system: commodity, consumer, industrial, and reseller marketing.

INTRODUCTION

Price is one of the four elements of the marketing mix. That is, price, along with product characteristics, promotion, and distribution, influences the purchasing decision. Price is also a key determinant of profitability, as shown in Figure 15-1.

Figure 15-1 shows that a 1 percent increase in price results in a much higher profit increase than that obtained by increasing volume or decreasing costs by 1 percent.

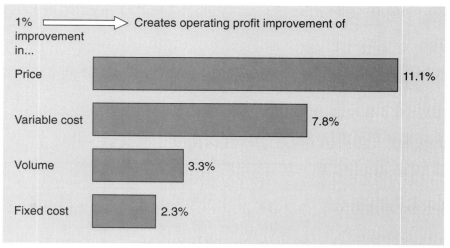

FIGURE 15-1   Comparison of profit determinants. *(Reprinted by permission of* Harvard Business Review *from "Managing Price, Gaining Profit," by Michael V. Marn and Robert L. Rosiello (September–October 1992): 85. Copyright ©1992 by the President and Fellows of Harvard College; all rights reserved.)*

While pricing principles are the same for commodity, industrial, reseller, and consumer marketing, their application is different. Suppliers of commodity products are price takers; they do not actively price their products. A supplier of a complex specialized food ingredient will attempt to price it in terms of the value of the technical benefits it offers the food processor relative to competitive suppliers' products. Manufacturers of branded food products must take into account the profitability of their chosen distributors (resellers), as well as the price reactions of the consumer and the availability of competitive products.

Chapter 2 discussed the concept of derived demand—the idea that the price at each stage of the value-added chain derives from the subsequent stage and that ultimately, all prices derive from the price paid by the final consumer. But price is also related to the cost of the basic raw materials; the pressure on prices is two-way, from each end of the food system. Also, price is established in the food system only when there is change of title. If subsequent activities in the food system are carried out by one firm (vertical integration, as discussed in Chapter 6), there will be no market price, although there may be an internal transfer price within the firm.

Price establishment by a company is influenced by internal (marketing strategy, costs) and external (customers, competitors) factors. In commodity markets, external factors dominate—there is little market strategy, and the cost of production for an individual firm does not affect price. In contrast to the commodity marketer, the manufacturer of a branded food product does establish a selling price as a part of the marketing mix. Ultimately, however, price is determined in the marketplace, and the price received by any supplier cannot guarantee a profit.

This chapter first looks at the role of internal and external factors in pricing decisions and shows how these are applied in practice at the various stages of the product life cycle. It then explores various concepts from accounting and economics that must be understood by the marketer in making pricing decisions. Finally, pricing practices are examined by stage in the food system.

PRICING AND THE FACTORS AFFECTING IT

Prices can be set by calculating all the costs in the system and allowing a margin for profit. As detailed in Figure 15-2, the "price" evolves as the product moves through the food system from food manufacturer to consumer—manufacturer's price, distributor's price, retailer's price.

FIGURE 15-2   The elements of food prices.

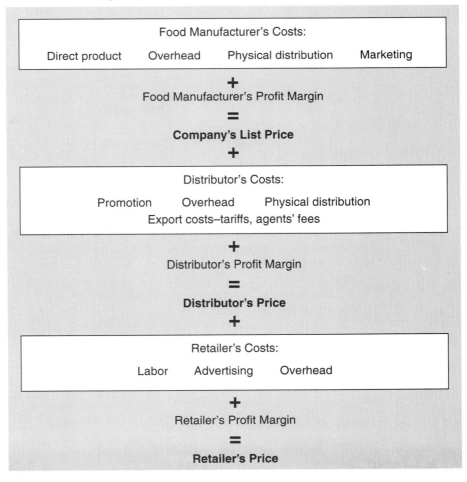

The final price in the market place is affected by many other factors. Changes in material and labor costs, the actions of competitors, and of course consumers' attitudes and behaviors toward prices also influence the determination of a product's price. Figure 15-3 groups these and other influences as internal or external factors.

Factors Internal to the Company

Company and Marketing Objectives   The basic objective of most firms is profitability. Simply expressed,

$$\textbf{Profit} =$$

Sales (units sold $\times$ price per unit)

minus

Marketing Expenditure (product development, promotion, distribution)

minus

Manufacturing Costs[1]

minus

Overhead Costs

Both marketing and manufacturing costs can be *variable* (costs that vary directly with the number of units produced/sold) or *fixed* (also called "allocated" or overhead costs; costs that don't change with the number of units sold). At first glance, it seems that the role of price in achieving the profit objective is straightforward—simply set the price so as to achieve the target profit level. On closer investigation, however, the situation becomes more complicated for a number of reasons.

First, price and quantity sold are not independent of each other; if the price is increased, the quantity sold decreases, this relationship being determined by the elasticity of demand—the more elastic the demand, the greater the impact of a given price change.[2] In the extreme case of a commodity product, the demand facing individual suppliers is infinitely elastic, which means that they have no price-setting discretion; any price increase results in zero sales, but, on the other hand, suppliers can each sell as much as they want at the prevailing market price.

Second, marketing activity influences both the position and slope of the demand curve (Figure 2-5) and enters into the cost side of the profitability equation as well. For example, promotional activity would be expected to move the demand curve to the right and make it more inelastic, but it is also an expense. Promotion and pricing are related in the sense that if promotional activity does, in fact, make demand more inelastic, it will allow the firm to increase prices. The question facing the

---

[1]In the case of resellers, such as wholesalers and retailers, substitute Cost of Goods Sold for Manufacturing Costs.

[2]Elasticity of demand is defined in Chapter 2.

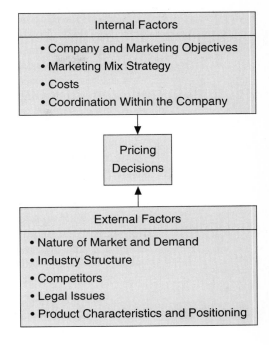

FIGURE 15-3   Internal and external factors influencing pricing decisions.

marketing manager is, "Will the increased sales resulting from a promotional activity more than cover its cost?"

Third, if we accept that profitability is the objective, we need to specify the *profit time horizon* over which it is to be maximized. In the short term, a high-price strategy may appear attractive, especially for a new and novel product. After considering the longer-term implications, however, management may decide to introduce the product at a low price and sacrifice short-term profits. This strategy may help to keep a high market share by discouraging new competitors and to build volume, leading to economies of scale and improvements in production and marketing efficiency (known as the "experience effect").

Market share is, in fact, often stated as a strategic objective, and many studies have shown links between market share and profitability. Why this is so is not immediately obvious. Probably, the reasons relate to the volume/cost-of-production effects discussed above and to the ability of a firm with high market share to exercise some power over its competitors.

Think Break

A number of strategic objectives for a firm have been identified: cost efficiency, growth in market share, short-term profitability, and long-term profitability. What other strategic objectives might a firm have? How might these affect pricing policy?

Marketing-Mix Strategy Along with the other elements of the marketing mix, price signals the product's position in the market to the buyer. "No frills" food retailers signal their position in the marketplace through price, as well as the other elements of the retail merchandising mix—a smaller number of lines, basic store design, no carry-out service, and so on. At the other end of the food retailing scale, a five-star restaurant signals quality by its high prices, combined with the quality of its food and service.

For products such as wine, there are "price bands" that signal quality/price relationships. Wine buyers know that if they pay over $25 for a bottle of wine, it will be of reasonable quality. On the other hand, an $8 bottle, while being good "value for money" for the many buyers in this segment of the market, would never be expected to have the subtle and complex combinations of bouquet and flavor found in the $25 bottle. These price/quality relationships are partly based on cost—the more expensive wine should have been produced from selectively harvested grapes and may have been matured longer in French oak barrels—but, equally importantly, they are based on perceptions in the minds of consumers of what quality they expect for each price band.

Other marketing-mix influences on price can be summarized as follows:

Market considerations:
- Distribution channels used
- Amount of promotion required by distributors
- Extent of service required
- Distributors' costs and mark-ups
- Margins required to maintain distributor loyalty

Product considerations:
- Positioning of product in the market
- Stage in product life cycle
- Agreement with overall product-line/product-mix pricing strategy

Think Break

Think how pricing is coordinated with other elements of the marketing mix for:

- *A "full range" food service supplier of family restaurants. ("Full range" in this context means everything the restaurant might require—from napkins to all types of food products.)*
- *A "no frills" supermarket.*
- *The manufacturer of a novel, "light" dairy dessert.*

Costs If one accepts that profitability is the basic reason for being in business, then pricing without reference to the costs of production and distribution would appear to be a recipe for disaster. Certainly, in the long term, a firm that did not achieve prices that covered all costs (including fixed or overhead) would not survive. However, a pricing strategy that does not cover all costs for all product lines may be entirely appropriate in the short term. Sometimes a company's new products are priced to cover only their own variable or direct costs, and overhead costs are absorbed by the existing product line. Similarly, in developing a new export market, domestic sales may often cover the company's overhead, and the exports may be charged only direct manufacturing costs plus distribution costs.

Coordination Within the Company Within any organization, there can be many participants in the pricing process. The marketing department sets the price as a part of the marketing mix. Salespeople, on the other hand, like to discount prices to make the sale, especially if they are being paid on commission. The accounting department wants prices that will provide an acceptable contribution to overhead costs. The company's lawyers may be involved if the pricing policy appears to break the law—for example, if there is government price regulation or if the price could be seen as a predatory attack on a competitor. Firms need a mechanism for coordinating these functionally related pricing activities. Pricing is important enough that the final decision needs to be made by someone senior in the organization, perhaps a vice-president. However, to make decisions on hundreds of products quickly, many large food companies depend on computer-based pricing systems.

External Factors Influencing Pricing Decisions

Nature of Market and Demand Understanding customers—here the term covers all stages in the food system, including manufacturers, distributors and, of course, the end consumer—is as important for pricing as it is for the other elements of the marketing mix.

The idea is to find out how buyers value the product along with its bundle of services offered. For example, whey protein, a product of the dairy industry, is used as a substitute for egg white in the manufacture of foods such as mayonnaise and prepared desserts. Buyers of whey protein are concerned about its functional properties: whipping, gelling, or emulsifying. As discussed in Chapter 7, they are also concerned about the product's research and development support, the company's technical service competency, frequency and reliability of delivery, credit terms, and so on. All these attributes of the "total product" contribute to the *buyer's valuation* of it.

Identifying the components of value for a food consumer is not as obvious as it is for the buyer of an industrial product. For example, one attribute that food consumers all want is security—regularity of supply, reliable quality, and, most of all, an assurance that the product will not endanger their health. Security is provided by an established brand and/or the reputation of the supplier. However, security having been recognized as important, placing a value on it for price-establishing purposes is not easy.

Of course, not all customers value the various attributes of a product in the same way. These different viewpoints provide a basis for segmenting the market. Pricing products differently for each segment, called price discrimination, is discussed in the section on price setting.

Think Break

Look at the different products and their prices in your favorite fast-food restaurant. Which market segments are they priced to attract?

Industry Structure   The most important external variables influencing the price-establishment process are the *industry structures* of both the supplying and buying industries. Four main types of (seller) market structures and the pricing behavior identified with these structure are shown in Table 15-1.

In the food industry, oligopolistic market structures can be found among food manufacturers—for example, the makers of breakfast cereals or colas. The structure of the supermarket sector of food retailing is becoming increasingly oligopolistic in

---

BOX 15-1

CHICKEN MARKETERS SCRATCH FOR PROFITS

In New Zealand, the poultry market has changed radically in the last decade—consumption has increased and sales of fresh and value-added products are gaining momentum. Already New Zealanders eat more chicken than lamb. By the end of the decade, if the trend continues, they will eat more chicken than beef. The fact that poultry prices have decreased by about 12 percent, compared to red meats, has clearly contributed to its increased popularity.

Tegel Foods currently holds 65 percent of the market; Australia-based Inghams is Tegel's biggest competitor. Chubby Chicken, a smaller but significant player, supplies only the basic chicken product and no value-added products, and is quick to deal with supermarkets. Vertical integration of the poultry industry keeps costs down. Companies control the breeding regime by contracting out to growers, and many own their own feed suppliers, factories, transport, marketing, and distribution systems.

The group marketing manager of Tegel Foods comments, "It's always been a price competitive commodity market. Although we have excellent brand awareness, if the price goes up by too much, we soon lose the competitive edge. Supermarkets heat up the competition by offering chicken specials at very low prices simply to generate store traffic." A supermarket buyer adds, "When frozen chicken is discounted, it gets rid of stock. But at the same time, it creates a low price point which affects the fresh chicken, as the consumer does not expect to pay any more for it. There is a need for producers and retailers to coordinate supply and demand."

Tegel keeps its market share with a widespread distribution system able to deliver fresh product daily, television and magazine advertising, and a large sales force. Advertising and promotion maintain the strong image of Tegel's own brand, which appears only on their own product, not on the unbranded product Tegel sells to supermarkets for their own preparation and packaging. The Tegel sticker is its guarantee of quality, and Tegel wants supermarkets to buy the prepackaged, labeled product.

Tegel, Ingham, and the supermarkets are trying to move away from the low price for chicken by promoting fresh and value-added products, such as crumbed fillets. In the United States, over 80 percent of chicken is sold fresh, compared to about 50 percent in New Zealand. Supermarkets will prepare value-added products to give consumers more choices, but it appears that New Zealand consumers prefer to prepare chicken themselves, rather than pay a premium price for the ready-to-cook product.

Regardless of new products offered and new approaches to marketing, a marketing manager states that the product must be priced within the "consumer's price barrier to be successful. We notice products fail quite dramatically if the prices aren't what the consumer is prepared to pay for it. People from all income groups are conscious of value for money."

Source: S. S. Lindsay, *Marketing Magazine* (New Zealand) 13.8 (September 1994): 26–28.

TABLE 15-1   PRICING UNDER DIFFERENT MARKET STRUCTURES

Industry Structure	Likely pricing behavior
Monopoly	One supplier. Considerable discretion in price setting. May be subject to government surveillance.
Oligopoly	Few suppliers. High barriers to entry. Each firm knows that any price change is likely to provoke a response from its competitors.
Monopolistic competition	Usually many suppliers. Few barriers to entry. Some product differentiation between suppliers. Suppliers are aware of the prices of competing products, but price is only one element of their marketing mix.
Perfect competition	Many suppliers. Low barriers to entry. No product differentiation. Individual firms cannot influence the market price and are price takers.

parts of Europe and Australia, but other food distribution systems, such as restaurants and their suppliers (the food service industry), tend to have monopolistically competitive market structures. As stated before, the structure of the agricultural production sector often approaches perfect competition.

Think Break

Think of counterexamples to these generalizations. Are there agricultural producers who are not *in a perfectly competitive market? Does some food retailing approach the perfectly competitive model? (As a student of international marketing, look for examples beyond the borders of your country.)*

The structure of the industry supplying the food product is only one side of the equation. The other side, of course, is the structure of the buying industry. Concentration in the food retailing sector increases the power of retailers relative to their suppliers, thus limiting the ability of the suppliers to set prices.

Competitors   The number and behavior of competitors influence price setting. There are three alternatives:

- Meet competitors' prices.
- Price below competitors.
- Price above competitors.

Obviously, a supplier of a commodity product has to accept the market price. In fact, pricing for a commodity supplier is not an active decision; the supplier knows that he will get the market price at the time of sale. Any supplier of a product that is not distinctively different from competitors' would be foolish to try to price above the prevailing price. Stable price relationships between suppliers can also occur under oligopoly, because the few suppliers are very conscious of each other's prices and will always match a price drop. If this occurs, they will all end up with the same market share and lower revenues. On the other hand, if one supplier raises his price, the others will not follow, and the lone supplier who increased his price suffers a sharp reduction in sales. This situation gives rise to a *kinked demand curve,* as shown in Figure 15-4.

In Figure 15-4, the prevailing price is establishd at P_1 on the demand curve D. Under the conditions outlined above, a price increase by one supplier results in a sharp decrease in sales, while a price drop (which is matched by competitors) has a small impact. A kinked demand curve will therefore tend to result in stable prices. Supermarkets in a particular location often engage in oligopolistic price competition, scanning their competitors' prices and matching any price reductions.

Pricing below competitors on a sustained basis makes sense when it is a part of a considered strategy to be a low-cost producer or distributor, achieving efficiencies through volume while still offering value to buyers. Discount stores of all types operate in this way. Customers recognize that everyday low prices (ELP) are accompanied by reduced services, but are happy with the tradeoff.

Legal Issues   In most developed countries, various laws govern price setting. Some of these are:

- Manufacturers are not permitted to collude in setting prices.
- Manufacturers are not permitted to dictate the retail price, often referred to as *retail price maintenance.*
- A manufacturer must supply all buyers at the same price, unless price differences can be justified on the basis of cost (the Robinson-Patman Act in the United States). Price differentials may be acceptable if it can be shown that they do not substantially injure competition.
- A manufacturer or distributor may not engage in *predatory pricing* activities—for example, selling below cost for a prolonged period with the objective of driving a competitor out of business.

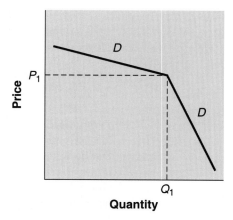

FIGURE 15-4   Kinked demand curve.

• Basic food items, particularly in developing countries, are often under direct price control.

This is a very brief summary of a complex group of laws. In marketing food or any other product, managers must remember that they are not free to price however they wish; they need to be aware of the legal issues.

Think Break

You supply cartoned milk to retailers. Your price for supermarkets is lower per gallon than for small convenience stores. A competitor argues that this is illegal in the United States under the Robinson-Patman Act. What evidence would you assemble for your defense?

PRICE SETTING

In arriving at a price, companies must recognize and take into account the external and internal factors just discussed. For example, a company must understand the impact of industry structure to accurately analyze competitors' reactions to price changes. Internally, each company has its own "hurdle rates" for return to capital and stockholders' investment that must be met by existing products, as well as by any potential new-product introductions. Break-even analysis and price discrimination, concepts from managerial accounting and economics, respectively, also apply to price setting. Other aspects of pricing are price setting in relation to the stage of the product life cycle and the process used to price products in international trade.

Break-even Analysis—Using Cost and Volume Relationships in Pricing

This example of a potato-chip manufacturer illustrates cost/volume relationships. The variable cost of producing a standard bag of potato chips (raw materials, allocated labor, and packaging) is 60 cents. The overhead cost of running the potato-chip line (depreciation, interest on capital, and management overheads) is $500,000 per year. A useful first step in establishing the per-unit price is to calculate the profit (or loss) in relation to the volume of production.

The cost/volume relationships are as follows ($\times 1,000$):

Volume (bags)	Fixed Cost ($)	Variable cost ($)	Total cost ($)
0	500	0	500
500	500	300	800
1,000	500	600	1,100
1,500	500	900	1,400
2,000	500	1,200	1,700

The plant capacity at this cost structure is 3,000,000 bags. The manufacturer hopes that the chips will retail for $1.20, and an acceptable retail mark-up is 20 percent, leaving $1.00 per bag.

We can now add revenue and profit columns to the cost data (×1000):

Volume (bags)	Fixed cost ($)	Variable cost ($)	Total cost ($)	Total revenue ($)	Profit (loss) ($)
				($1.00 per bag)	
0	500	0	500	0	(500)
500	500	300	800	500	(300)
1,000	500	600	1,100	1,000	(100)
1,500	500	900	1,400	1,500	100
2,000	500	1,200	1,700	2,000	300

It appears that the *break-even* volume of production, at a manufacturer's price of $1.00 per bag, is between 1 and 1.5 million units. We can calculate this volume with some simple algebra:

$$Y = Q \times P - (FC + Q \times VC)$$

Where: Y = net profit
Q = volume of production
P = manufacturer's selling price
FC = fixed cost
VC = variable cost per unit.

The break-even profit is where $Y = 0$. Therefore,

$$Q = FC/(P - VC) = 500,000/0.4 = 1,250,000$$

These relationships are shown graphically in Figure 15-5.

The discussion so far has assumed that the manufacturer can sell every bag produced at a per-unit price of $1.00. That is, the demand curve facing the manufacturer is infinitely elastic (refer to Chapter 2). If the demand curve sloped downward, each extra unit would have to be sold at a lower price. In practice, manufacturers would not be able to calculate price/quantity relationships with the precision shown in Figure 2-2, but they might be able to estimate, for instance, that they could sell up to 1,000,000 units through regular supermarket chains at $1.00, but additional sales would have to be through discount stores at $.80. The demand curve for this sales/price pattern is shown in Figure 15-6.

Production cost is unchanged. The total cost, revenues, and profits are now (×1,000):

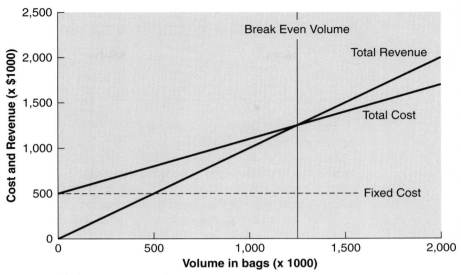

FIGURE 15-5   Volume/cost/price impacts on profit.

FIGURE 15-6   Price/quantity relationships.

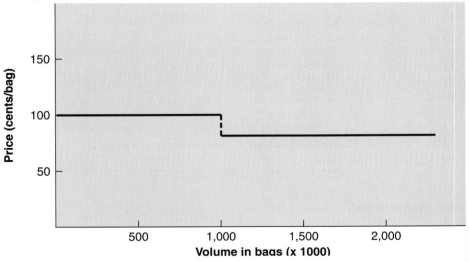

Volume (bags)	Total cost ($)	Total revenue ($)	Profit loss ($)
0	500	0	(500)
500	800	500	(300)
1,000	1,100	1,000	(100)
1,500	1,400	1,400	0
2,000	1,700	1,800	100

The impact of the downward-stepped demand curve is to increase the break-even volume from 1,250 to 1,500 bags.

As mentioned in the earlier discussion of organizational objectives, cost-based approaches to pricing need to be used cautiously. While prices for the firm's product range must cover all costs in the long term, the price for a particular product does not need to cover the cost of producing it. As discussed above, prices may be set below cost in the short term to gain market share and increased volume of production which, in turn, leads to improvements in production and marketing efficiency. Some products in a product line may never cover their costs, even in the long term, but are retained because they are seen as being necessary to complete the line.

Finally, a financially stressed firm may price below cost in the short term to reduce stocks and to generate cash—*survival pricing.*

Think Break

A lettuce producer finds that when the crop is ready for market, there is a glut of lettuce and the price per head is only 25 cents. The producer has costed the production of lettuce and has come up with the following figures:

Item	Cost per head (cents)
Land preparation	7
Seed and planting costs	9
Irrigation	9
Harvesting	6
Transport to market	2
TOTAL	37

Apparently, the market price is below the cost of production and delivery to market. What should the lettuce producer do?

Price Discrimination

When different market segments have different elasticities of demand, the marketer can use this information in setting prices. The practice of *price discrimination* is simply selling the same basic product in different markets at different prices, with price differences that are greater than the differences in the cost of servicing the market. For price discrimination to work, the markets must be separable, so that a purchaser cannot act as trader, buying in the cheaper market and selling in the higher-priced market.

An example of price discrimination is the marketing of eggs. There are three main markets for eggs: the fresh retail market, the food service market for fresh eggs, and the processing market for egg pulp and powder. The elasticity of demand in each of the three markets is shown in Figure 15-7.

In Figure 15-7, the fresh retail market has the most inelastic demand, while the demand facing the egg supplier in the processing market is infinitely elastic. The decision facing the egg supplier is how to allocate the total quantity of eggs produced to each of the three markets in such a way as to maximize revenue. Quantities Q_1 plus Q_2 plus Q_3 equal Q, the total quantity of eggs produced.[3]

Think Break

An apple producers' cooperative identifies three potential markets for apples: fresh, juice, and apple concentrate. Which of these markets would you expect to have the least elastic demand; which would you expect to have the most? Which market would you expect to yield the highest return to growers—net of any processing costs?

---

[3]The details are beyond the scope of this text, but, in economic terms, the revenue-maximizing allocation of eggs is given where the **marginal revenues** (net of the costs of servicing each market) in the three markets are equal. If one of the three markets is a commodity-type market with an infinite elasticity of demand (processed eggs in Figure 15-7), the allocation to the fresh market(s) will be as shown in Figure 15-7 and, irrespective of the total volume of production, Q, any surplus will be processed. It is possible that the net profit in the processing market may be negative, in which case the egg producer would want to restrict the total supply to Q_1 plus Q_2.

FIGURE 15-7   Price discrimination in egg marketing.

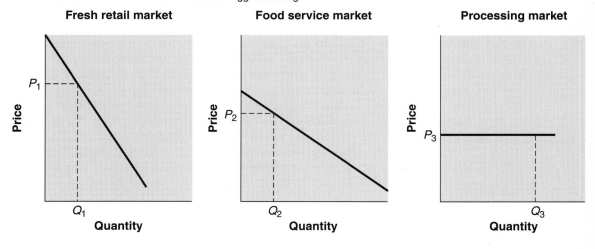

TABLE 15-2   VARIABLES AFFECTING PRICE SENSITIVITY

Variable	Impact on pricing
The product's share of the household (or manufacturer's) budget	If the product is a major item in the budget, buyers will be more sensitive to price changes.
The ability of the firm to "hand on" price increases	If the buyer of a raw material sells finished product in a market that is not price sensitive (inelastic demand), the buyer will be able to "hand on" a raw-material price increase. Therefore, the demand for the raw material will be inelastic.
The cost of "shopping around"	Is the buyer able to "shop around" and compare alternatives in a cost-effective way?
Switching costs	A food manufacturer may face a high cost of switching raw-material suppliers if the plant has been designed to use a particular type of raw materials, implying a more inelastic demand for it.

Other variables affecting customers' sensitivity to price are described in Table 15-2, above.

Think Break

How do the factors influencing price sensitivity (Table 15-2) apply to:

- *Your choice of supermarket for your routine shopping?*
- *McDonald's choice of french-fry supplier?*
- *A food manufacturer's choice of salt supplier?*

Pricing by Stage of the Product Life Cycle

The concept of the product life cycle was discussed in Chapter 13. In the very early stages of the cycle, there may be only one supplier. If the product is truly unique, the supplier may be able to price significantly above cost of production and still achieve sufficient sales volume to make a handsome profit *(skimming-the-cream pricing)*. However, this may not be the best long-term strategy, because the high price limits sales volume and may encourage competitors. The supplier may choose *penetration pricing* to discourage competition and to obtain a higher sales volume and market share. Experience-curve effects and economies of scale will allow the firm to retain its competitive position in the growth phase of the product life cycle.

Various factors, including those discussed above, affect the choice between a high (skimming) or low (penetration) pricing policy at the introduction phase of the product life cycle.

- The initial price sensitivity (elasticity of demand)
- The slope of the cost/volume and cost/experience curves

- Potential competitors
- Legal protection from competitors through patents and the like
- The desired image of the product.

As the product life cycle progresses into the growth and maturity stages, price becomes increasingly important. Competition in mature markets approaches that found in commodity markets, where price is the only important variable in the marketing mix.

Think Break

Development of new products in the food industry generally tends to involve rather small variations on existing products (Chapter 13). For such products, which new-product pricing strategy is appropriate—skimming the cream, penetration, or neither?

Geographic Pricing Considerations, Including Export

Obviously, it costs more to supply cheese manufactured in France to a buyer in the United States than it does to supply the same cheese to a local French buyer. The question, then, is: should the manufacturer or the buyer pay the additional transport costs? There are two extreme points of view on this question. The first point of view is that the buyer should bear all transport costs, with the manufacturer establishing the price on an *FOB* basis. (FOB stands for "free on board" the freight carrier at the manufacturer's plant, sometimes referred to as "ex-plant." However, in international marketing, FOB specifically refers to on board a ship or aircraft—which would include the manufacturer's cost of shipping from the plant to the seaport or airport.)

The second view is that the manufacturer should bear all transport costs. The manufacturer's location is, after all, of little concern to the buyer. There are all sorts of alternatives in between these two extremes: *uniform pricing*—every buyer pays the same price, which means, in effect, the nearby buyers subsidize the more distant ones; zone pricing—every buyer in a specified zone pays the same price; and *freight-absorption pricing*—a manufacturer located further away from the buyer charges only the same freight as a nearer one.

As in other aspects of pricing, there is no easy answer. Ultimately, price must be determined by the elasticity of demand facing a particular supplier. If this demand is inelastic, the supplier has more chance of pricing on an FOB basis, with the buyer bearing the freight cost. If the demand facing the supplier is more elastic, the manufacturer will have to absorb freight costs or lose sales. An individual supplier of a commodity, facing an infinitely elastic demand, knows that the price received ex-farm will be the price in the distant market less all grading, handling, and freight charges. For example, the pricing center of the world wheat market is probably the U.S. Gulf ports. Australian farmers can calculate their farmgate price by starting with the New Orleans price and deducting all storage and handling costs (allowing for exchange rates and quality differentials).[4]

In export marketing, buyers may request a product to be priced on an FOB basis—its priced delivered to the port, either sea or air—or on a *CIF* basis. The term CIF stands for cost, insurance, and freight, and if a product is priced CIF, it includes all the relevant costs of export to the buyer's port. These costs can include, but are not limited to the following: freight costs (ocean or air), marine insurance, documentation fees, the exporting port fees, and other types of fees (for example, quality assurance).

An example of the calculations an exporter would make in determining whether to pursue an export market is given in Table 15-3. In this case, a New Zealander visited the United States and saw a retail consumer food product that could be manufactured in New Zealand. The New Zealand product would be a "me-too" product, selling at the same price as the U.S. version. The retail price was $2.00 U.S., and the calculation determined that a New Zealand company could compete at a profit.

---

[4]In futures markets, the difference between the futures price, which is just the price for a specified grade of a commodity delivered at a specified time and place, and the current cash price is called the **basis.** (See Chapter 10.)

TABLE 15-3 PRICING BACK FROM THE EXPORT MARKET

	Charges (cents)	Balance (cents)
Retail price (assessed market price)		U.S. 200.00
Less standard retail margin (20% of retail)	40.00	
Wholesale price		U.S. 160.00
Less wholesale margin (5% of wholesale)	8.00	
Importer's price		U.S. 152.00
Less: Importer's margin (15% of import price)	22.80	
Local advertising reserve (5%)	7.60	
Spoilage allowance (1%)	1.50	
Importer's cost of customs clearance	2.10	
Customs duties (10% of CIF value)	10.70	
Total U.S. marketing costs	44.70	
CIF Price at U.S. port in U.S. cents		U.S. 107.30
CIF Price at U.S. port in N.Z. cents (60 US/100 N.Z.)		N.Z. 178.80
Less: Ocean freight and insurance	16.30	
Exporter's FOB vessel price		N.Z. 162.50
Less: Export documentation costs	2.50	
Plant-to-port distribution costs	5.00	
Maximum price exporter can charge ex-plant		N.Z. 155.00
Less production costs	120.00	
GROSS PROFIT CONTRIBUTION		**N.Z. 35.00**

With an industrial product, the gross profit contribution would be calculated by starting from the selling price of the material or ingredient and deducting a distributor's and/or agent's margin, instead of retailer and wholesaler margins.

Think Break

You are an ice-cream manufacturer in Australia, planning to export to Malaysia. Suppose, for simplicity, that there are only two alternatives for pricing: FOB plant, Australia, or into cold storage in Malaysia. What are the advantages/disadvantages of each of these two alternatives from the buyers' point of view and from your point of view as an exporter?

Overview: Benefit-Based Pricing

From a marketing perspective, the logical approach is to ask these three questions and base your price on the answers:

1 What benefits does my product offer to buyers that are not offered by competitive suppliers? Conversely, what limitations does my product have relative to competitors'? In this question, "product" refers to the whole mix of product and service attributes—product reliability, delivery time, delivery reliability, after-sales service, and so on.

2 How can I use these relative benefits/limitations in setting my price?

3 Is the price established on the basis of 1) and 2) one that will allow me to make a satisfactory long-term return, remembering that, for a number of reasons, I may price below cost temporarily?

For suppliers of industrial products, answering the first two questions requires knowledge of the buyer's business as well as their own. In particular, they need to know whether their product has properties that provide measurable benefits relative to competitors in terms of: a) reducing the buyers' manufacturing costs, or b) enhancing the buyers' end product in a way that will allow the manufacturers to increase their selling price. The manufacturer of a consumer product will require a lot of expensive research to know how that product is positioned relative to competitors' in the mind of the consumer. And, of course, all buyers are not the same. Segmentation requires in-depth research for each major segment. Finally, the question of whether the average selling price provides a satisfactory profit, which might, at first glance, appear to be a straightforward cost-accounting exercise, turns out to be complicated by the stage of the product life cycle, economies of scale, experience-curve effects, and other factors.

PRICING BY STAGE OF THE FOOD SYSTEM

Pricing principles may also be viewed in relation to the three main types of marketing: commodity, manufacturer, and reseller—wholesaler and retailer—marketing.

Producers' Pricing of Commodities

A commodity product is undifferentiated by supplier. The demand facing the individual supplier of a commodity is infinitely elastic. For an individual commodity supplier, the internal factors in Figure 15-3, such as organization objectives and cost of production, have no influence on the price received. External supply and demand variables are the only determinants. In the commodity market, the individual firm is a price taker, and pricing is a passive activity. The processes of commodity price formation are discussed in Chapters 2 and 10.

Manufacturers' Pricing of Consumer and Industrial Products

Consumer Goods   There are two key words in consumer marketing—segmentation and positioning (Chapter 12). The economic result of segmentation is a set of demand curves, one for each market segment. For example, segmenting the fresh-produce market on the basis of consumers' concerns about chemicals in food might identify an "extremely concerned" segment representing 5 percent of vegetable buyers. The demand for organically produced vegetables by this segment would be expected to be quite inelastic, allowing high margins for organic suppliers. Another (larger) segment might be described as "moderately concerned" and have a more elastic demand. The "not at all concerned" segment would not see organic produce as offering any benefits relative to conventional production and would be unwilling to pay any premium for it.

Positioning is how consumers see your product relative to competitors' products. Applying the principles of segmentation and positioning to pricing consumer products allows us to apply the ideas outlined above—identifying benefits relative to competitors for each market segment and using this information to set prices. However, the basic problem that food manufacturers face is that, while they may have plenty of market research to support a particular retail price, the actual price is under the control of, and set by, the retailer.

Industrial Products   Industrial buyers' sensitivity to input-price changes depends on the input's share of the total cost of production, the manufacturer's ability to hand on price increases, and the cost of switching to another supplier. (For more detail, review the section on customers earlier in this chapter.)

In comparing the pricing of industrial products with the pricing of consumer goods, industrial pricing is:

• Based more on "objective" factors—manufacturing costs, consistent technical performance, end-product quality—than is consumer-goods pricing
  • Often negotiated and, as a result, different for different buyers
  • Less transparent (not public information)
  • Often based on competitive tendering or bidding.

Industrial buyers and suppliers often have a high degree of awareness of each other's businesses. This leads to a mutual understanding of what is a "fair" price. Manufacturers are concerned with the technical characteristics of an industrial input, as well as with its cost. How well does the input perform in reducing processing costs and/or improving the quality of the finished products?

Retailer Pricing of Food Products

Food retailers usually adopt one of two pricing strategies: variable-price merchandising (VPM) or everyday low pricing (ELP). Large retailers have popularized the ELP approach—Wal-Mart Stores, Inc., has used it while becoming the number-one retailer in America. The main argument for ELP is that under VPM consumers become very price conscious, or "cherry pickers," waiting until an item comes on special to purchase. The other stated advantage of ELP is that merchandising and inventory control are easier. Prices are not being changed every week on a large number of items, and the retailer does not experience the extreme peaks and valleys in demand that can result in stock-outs, meaning "rain checks" and unhappy customers. Also avoided is excess inventory that must be disposed of in some manner, either through in-store very deep-cut specials or through sales to outside liquidators, who take such inventory at a small fraction of its value.

Retail management must decide which strategy is most profitable. A study conducted in 88 stores of a Chicago-area chain found that ELP resulted in sales being a little higher but showing less profit. Some stores had converted to ELP, reducing prices and keeping them low in 19 product categories, and other stores had pursued the VPM strategy. Overall, profits in the categories that used ELP were about 17 percent below those of stores where VPM was used. According to the researchers, the superior performance of VPM was due to higher profit margins on items that were not on sale.

These results are not really all that new—for years, retailers have been told at conventions and in trade publications to review their pricing practices and that pushing up prices on nonfeatured items just a little (2 or 3 percent) can improve profits substantially. The effect is so great because of the dynamics of grocery retailing pricing. Often the profit on a dollar of sales is only 1 cent; therefore, a 1 percent increase in gross sales doubles the profits. This translates into considerable improvement in the firm's total profitability, return on investment, and return to the shareholders.[5]

The same pricing research found that price specials add excitement to what can otherwise be a rather boring and tiring chore. As Stephan J. Hoch, a marketing professor overseeing the research, says, "Everyday low pricing goes against what shopping's all about." It was found that some items are much more responsive to discounting than others. Frozen entrees and soft drinks moved more quickly when specialed than did dishwashing detergents. People are not going to wash dishes more often if soap is cheaper, but they will drink more soda pop if it is sold at a discount.

[5]"Broad Grocery Price Cuts May Not Pay," *Wall Street Journal* (May 7, 1993): B1.

In retailer marketing, profit is determined by:

- Volume
- Margin—selling price minus cost
- Payments from manufacturers for sales promotion and shelf fees
- Variable and overhead expenses, including interest costs.

Supermarket managers, with 15,000 or more product lines, do not have time to think much about pricing any one of them. They tend to follow simple rules based on an established mark-up for a product category, combined with a close watch on what their nearest competitors are doing. A manufacturer who wants to convince the retailer to change these simple rules will need to show that the change results in more profit for the retailer—either through the retailer's margin or through the various "below the line" payments that manufacturers make to support their product on the retail shelf.

When grocery retailers talk about mark-up, they are talking about the amount that is added to the product's cost to arrive at the selling price. In the grocery business, mark-up is calculated as a percentage of the product's selling price. That is, if a product is marked up 15 percent and sells for $1.00, the cost of goods sold is 85 cents. The retailer then has 15 cents available to pay for labor, utilities, fixed investment in building and equipment, advertising, taxes, and profit.

Some examples of mark-ups and direct product profitability on grocery lines for a supermarket chain in the United States are given in Table 15-4. This chain can be described as following the VPM strategy.

How does the retailer determine these margins, and hence the retail price? The most important variable is "price sensitivity" (in economic terms, elasticity of demand). Basic foods, such as eggs, soup, and flour, are more price sensitive than infrequently purchased items, such as seasonings and spices, and retailers accept low margins on them. The other factor that can play a role is the extent of product differentiation; as Table 15-4 shows, items such as dips/sour cream, candy, and ice cream carry a higher gross margin than other items in each of their individual categories.

Cost factors play a part, as well. Margins are higher for produce than for non-perishable items such as soup because of wastage and the cost of cool display areas. Gross margins do not take into account the cost of coolers, freezers, and behind-the-scenes costs of warehousing, shipping, and handling, nor other in-store costs directly attributable to a product. For this reason, the retail industry has come up with direct product profitability (DPP) as a truer measure of product and product-category profitability. (See Table 15-4.)

Manufacturers directly influence retailer profitability through advertising (increasing volume), direct payments for sales promotion and shelf space, and credit terms. But inventory-related costs—storage, interest, ordering costs, out-of-stock costs, order cycle time, and delivery reliability—are also costs to resellers and are major considerations in their choice of manufacturer with whom to do business. Wholesalers and retailers follow the basic principle that, over time, any product should about equal the competing line's return on shelf space (DPP). As we have

TABLE 15-4   GROSS MARGINS AND DIRECT PRODUCT PROFITABILITY (DPP) BY FOOD CATEGORY, WITH SELECTED PRODUCT EXAMPLES

Category	% Gross margin	% DPP*
Grocery	20.6	12.2
Soup	18.6	7.0
Flour/meal	4.9	−11.1
Candy	32.7	8.6
Pickles/relishes/olives	35.1	27.9
Canned fruit	22.7	13.2
Salt/seasonings/spices	38.2	32.9
Dairy	27.6	15.6
Cottage cheese	27.6	13.0
Dips/sour cream	39.8	24.7
Eggs	16.9	4.6
Frozen foods	33.5	24.1
Pot pies	29.4	16.9
Ice cream	39.2	25.9
Juices/drinks	27.6	22.0
Service deli	37.9	10.9
Meat/seafood	25.0	16.8
Produce	38.7	18.5
Floral	42.4	37.8

*DPP (Direct Product Profitability) measures the profitability of a product after accounting for warehousing, direct labor, spoilage, shelf space utilized, and other costs that can be directly attributed to the product.
    Source: "Profitability: Where It's Really At," in "The Marsh Super Study," *Progressive Grocer* (December 1992): 26–31. Reprinted with permission from *Progressive Grocer.*

seen, this return is influenced by many variables other than the manufacturer's price.

SUMMARY

Price establishment by a firm is influenced by internal and external factors. External factors dominate in commodity markets where suppliers are price takers. Suppliers of branded food products, on the other hand, establish a selling price as part of the marketing mix.

The basic objective of most firms is profitability, and profit equals sales minus marketing, manufacturing, and overhead expenses. Dollar sales equal the quantity sold multiplied by the price per unit, but these two variables are not independent; they are linked through the demand curve (Chapter 2). The time horizon needs to be considered when discussing profitability; a manager may net better profits in the long term by reducing the price to gain market share and/or by reducing manufacturing costs.

Within a company which has many participants in the pricing process, including accountants who want a price that covers all costs and sales staff who want to be able to discount prices in order to make sales, someone senior in the organization needs to coordinate pricing decisions.

Marketing costs have a fixed and a variable component. The break-even sales volume is where total cost equals total revenue. Marketing activity such as advertising enters the cost side of the profitability equation but will also, if it is successful, move the demand curve to the right and make it more inelastic.

A major external factor is the structure of both the supplying and buying industries. For example, under monopoly one seller has considerable discretion in setting prices; under perfect competition, with many suppliers, an individual supplier cannot influence the market price.

Companies choose from three pricing alternatives in relation to competitors: pricing above, pricing below, or meeting competitors' prices. A supplier of a commodity product, along with the other suppliers, meets the market price. Stable price relationships can also occur in oligopolistic situations (small number of suppliers) because no individual supplier wants to rock the boat.

Most developed countries have various laws influencing price setting; for example, manufacturers are not permitted to dictate reseller prices or to collude in price setting.

The key to pricing is to understand how buyers value the product. This is easier for an industrial food ingredient than it is for a consumer product, but the principles are the same. Of course, within a particular market, not all customers value the various attributes of a product in the same way. In economic terms, this allows us to segment the market on the basis of elasticity of demand (price discrimination). The most important variables influencing elasticity of demand are the availability of substitutes, the product's share of the household (or manufacturer's) budget, the ability of the buyer to "hand on" price increases, and the costs of shopping around and switching.

The stage in a product's life cycle affects pricing strategy: at first it may dominate the market, allowing the supplier to price well above the cost of production and make substantial short-term profits, skimming the cream. On the other hand, setting a low price will discourage competitors, making it possible for the supplier to increase sales volume and reduce production costs.

In setting the price of a product delivered to the buyer, the question arises, who should pay the freight cost—the supplier or the buyer? The answer depends on how competitive the market is. Suppliers facing little competition may be able to price on an FOB basis, requiring buyers to bear the freight costs. If the market is highly competitive, suppliers will have to meet competitors' prices irrespective of freight or any other costs.

The marketing principles of segmentation and positioning can be used to identify product benefits for each market segment. Prices for consumer products are set using this basic information. However, food manufacturers usually do not sell directly to consumers; they supply resellers, such as wholesalers and retailers. The basic principle of pricing to resellers is that the price should allow a net return similar to that of competing lines, recognizing that food manufacturers also make a number of "below-the-line" payments to retailers, such as promotional incentives or shelf-space allowances. Pricing of industrial raw materials, including farm products used in food manufacturing, is based on the technical properties of the raw material. The price also takes into account credit, servicing, and inventory-related costs.

IMPORTANT TERMS AND CONCEPTS

break-even pricing 414	penetration pricing 418
buyer valuation of products 409	predatory pricing 412
CIF (Cost, Insurance, Freight) 420	price discrimination 416
fixed and variable costs 406	profit time horizon 407
FOB (Free on Board) 419	retail price maintenance 412
freight absorption pricing 419	skimming-the-cream pricing 418
industry structures 410	survival pricing 416
kinked demand curve 412	uniform pricing 419

QUESTIONS

1 Explain how price signals the market position of each of the following products/services:
   a) A "Big Mac" hamburger
   b) Generic brand foods
   c) Truffles.

2 The variable cost of producing a can of baked beans is 20 cents. The fixed cost of the baked-bean processing line is $100,000. Graph revenues and costs. Calculate the break-even volume of production if the manufacturer's ex-factory price per can is:
   a) 60 cents
   b) 70 cents.

3 Supermarkets essentially price on a cost basis. Discuss the limitations of cost-based approaches to price setting.

4 How would you expect competitive structure to influence pricing behavior in the case of:
   a) Retail outlets for beer
   b) Suppliers of malt to the brewing industry
   c) Suppliers of malting barley to malt manufacturers
   d) Suppliers of glass packaging to the brewing industry.

5 Flour is, of course, a raw material for the baking industry. What functional properties are required for particular products, such as bread or pastry? How might these properties be valued in setting the price of flour to a bread or pastry manufacturer? (This question might require some research. If you know a food science major, ask your friend. If you like, choose another raw material—for example, malting barley for the production of beer.)

6 What factors influence the elasticity of demand for a raw material purchased by a food manufacturer? How would these apply to the beef purchased by a major hamburger chain?

7 You are a manufacturer of specialized food and beverage enzymes. Your R&D department has come up with an enzyme that allows accelerated maturation of red wine without aging in oak barrels. There is some cynicism in the industry about this product,

but blind tastings show that experts cannot tell the difference. How would you price this new product to the different segments of the wine-production market?

8 You have developed a new type of orange juice, not only based on a new, sweeter variety of orange, but also using a type of packaging that allows the juice to stay fresh-tasting at room temperature. How would you price this product to food retailers? (You have relatively limited volumes for the first three years.)

REFERENCES AND RESOURCES

Branch, Alan F. *Export Marketing and Management.* 3d ed. London, U.K.: Chapman and Hall, 1995.

Dolan, Robert J. "How Do You Know the Price is Right?" *Harvard Business Review* (September–October, 1995): 174–183.

Haas, Robert W. *Business Marketing.* 6th ed. Cincinnati, OH: Southwestern College Publications, 1995.

Hisrich, Robert D., and Michael P. Peters. *Marketing Decisions for New and Mature Products.* 2d ed. New York: Macmillan Publishing Co., 1991.

Marn, Michael V., and Robert L. Rosiello. "Managing Price, Gaining Profit." *Harvard Business Review* (September–October, 1992): 84–94.

Pappas, James L., and Mark Hirschey. *Managerial Economics.* Chicago: Dryden Press, 1987.

Stanton, William J., Michael J. Etzel, and Bruce J. Walker. *Fundamentals of Marketing.* 10th ed. New York: McGraw-Hill, 1995.

16

PLANNING AND IMPLEMENTATION OF FOOD MARKETING

CHAPTER OUTLINE

LEARNING OBJECTIVES

After reading this chapter and answering the questions in the Think Breaks and at the end of the chapter, you should be able to:

- Outline the stages of the corporate planning process and relate the stages to each other.
- Develop a mission statement for a company or organization.
- Know the criteria for writing corporate and marketing objectives and be able to prepare objectives for a company or organization.
- Use the product/market matrix as a basis for identifying and analyzing strategies.
- Understand the concept of gap analysis.
- Be able to link objectives in a hierarchy of objectives.
- Understand the key role of segmentation and positioning in developing marketing strategies.
- Develop an action plan based on the marketing strategy plan.
- Design a control system for the implementation stage of planning.
- Be aware of the reasons why planning is not always as successful as it should be.

INTRODUCTION

In the previous three chapters, we discussed food marketing management in terms of the three categories of decisions that marketing managers need to make: product, price, and promotion. The fourth category, distribution, was discussed in Chapter 6. These marketing-mix decisions are, in turn, driven by higher-order decisions about customers—segmentation, target marketing—and where the firm's products are positioned relative to competitors (Chapter 12).

These activities require coordination. This is the function of marketing planning; making the basic decisions regarding the firm's product range and its customers, establishing objectives and strategies for achieving them, implementing the plan, and monitoring performance.

The planning process occurs at a number of levels. In a large company, comprising a number of divisions producing quite different products, the highest level is the corporate strategic plan. Planning at this level addresses a very basic question—what portfolio of business activities best positions the company for sustained long-term profitability?

The divisions of a large company are called *Strategic Business Units (SBUs)*. A smaller company may comprise only one SBU. At the SBU level, there are three further levels of planning. The first level is the strategic plan for the SBU (or company), where management defines the mission, analyzes the external and internal environments of the company, sets objectives and then selects appropriate strategies to achieve them. The second level is the development of separate strategic plans for each functional area—marketing, production, finance, research and development, and human resource management. The third level is the action plan, which turns strategies into specific actions. Whereas a strategic plan has a long-term focus (say five years), the action plan is focused on the short term—one year or less.

Plans are not worth very much unless they are implemented—the last stage of the planning process. Implementation involves monitoring (checking actual performance against planned) and control (taking action when actual performance differs significantly from planned). Figure 16-1 illustrates the planning process.

The activities shown in Figure 16-1 are complex, time consuming, and expensive. This leads to a question: Why plan? Some reasons for planning are that, if properly carried out, planning results in:

- Clear thinking about the objectives of the organization
- A better understanding of anticipated environmental changes
- A unified vision of the direction of the organization
- Better coordination within the organization
- Establishment of performance standards that are well understood and achievable
- Effective mechanisms for coping with contingencies.

Many companies, especially smaller ones, don't really plan, or if they do, their planning is not effective. Some of the reasons managers give for not planning are:

"It's too time-consuming."
"Changes happen too fast for planning to be of any use."
"We've done OK in the past."

The planning process activities shown in Figure 16-1 are detailed in this chapter.

CORPORATE STRATEGIC PLANNING

For a large company, the highest level in the planning process is selecting the SBU portfolio. For a smaller company with only one SBU, the principles are the same, but the portfolio comprises product/market combinations. The discussion in this section incorporates both levels.

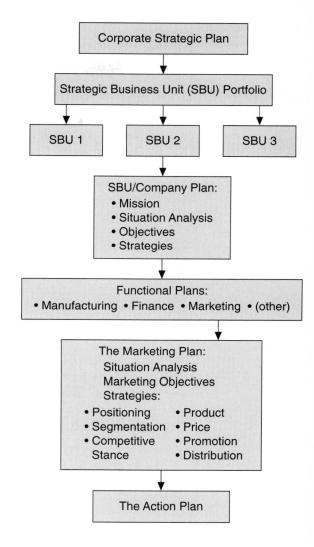

FIGURE 16-1   The planning process.

The stages of *corporate strategic planning* are listed below.

CORPORATE STRATEGIC PLANNING

- Write the Mission Statement
- Establish Corporate Objectives
- Analyze the External Environment
- Analyze the Company's Strengths and Weaknesses
- Develop Strategies

Mission Statement

For both corporate and *SBU* plans, the driving vision for the planning process is the *mission statement,* which, if properly designed, will give people, both within and outside the organization, a ready understanding of its strategic direction.

The mission statement seeks to encapsulate the strategic plan in two or three easily understood sentences. It comprises a broad statement of objectives, strategies, and the firm's sources of competitive advantage. Take, for example, a small cooperative dairy manufacturing company called "The Really Efficient Butter Company" (REBC).

REBC specializes in the production of butter, which is sold in bulk packs to manufacturer/distributors for repackaging as a branded product. The mission statement for REBC might be:

Broad statement of objectives	"REBC will consistently pay its suppliers more per liter of milk than other processors in the Southeast region of Holsteinland"
Strategies	"by specializing in the production of nonbranded butter tailored to the requirements of individual industrial buyers"
Source of competitive advantage	"at a lower cost than our competitors."

The REBC mission statement includes the key elements required to articulate the company's vision—a broad objective, a strategy specified in terms of products and customers, and an identified source of competitive advantage.

Think Break

Professor Michael Porter argues that there are basically two ways that a company can gain competitive advantage: by producing at a low cost or through product differentiation. Clearly, the REBC has chosen the low-cost route. Design a mission statement for REBC if its focus is to produce branded dairy products.

A real-world example is the Kerry Group, a diversified food company that has grown into a global business from its beginnings as an Irish Dairy Cooperative. This is Kerry's corporate mission statement:[1]

The Kerry Group will be:
—a significant consumer foods company in Europe, and
—a major international food ingredients corporation.
Kerry will be a leader in selected markets through
—technological creativity

[1]From Kerry Company documents. Used with permission.

—superior product quality
—superior service to customers, and
—the unique wholehearted commitment of each employee.
The Kerry Group will continue to grow
—at an annual rate of 15 percent over each five-year period.

Kerry's Mission Statement reflects its global orientation—"a significant consumer foods company in Europe" and "a major international foods supplier." Kerry's growth has been in terms of both product range (from dairy products to a wide range of consumer foods and food ingredients) and geography (from its home base in Ireland to the whole world).

Kerry's Mission Statement also illustrates the idea that large organizations have a number of *stakeholders*. A stakeholder is anyone who has an interest in the company. In Kerry's case, this includes customers, employees, farmer suppliers (the Kerry farmer cooperative is the largest individual shareholder in the Kerry Group), other suppliers, and the financial community (banks, stockbrokers, investment advisers etc.).

Think Break

Think of any business or organization you know about. This may be a family business, a professional organization, a sports club, or any other type of organization. Design a mission statement for this organization.

Corporate Objectives

The mission statement represents the organizational vision. It is brief and not quantified. Objectives, on the other hand, should be detailed, quantified, and achievable. *Corporate objectives* may be:

• Financial (profits, indebtedness, return on shareholders' funds)
• Growth (sales, share value)
• Market oriented (market share, rate of new-product development, customer satisfaction)
• Employee related (staff turnover, employee commitment)
• Social (environmental practices, employment practices).

Other types of objectives are possible. Achieving a satisfactory financial performance must always be on the list of objectives, because if this does not happen, the company will not survive.

Returning to the Really Efficient Butter Company, suppose management developed the following objectives:

1 Increase the price paid to cooperative members for milk.
2 Reduce manufacturing costs.
3 Price REBC butter 50 percent lower than nearest competitor.
4 Add value to niche products.

Think Break ────────────────────────────────────

Critically evaluate Really Efficient Butter Company's objectives.

────────────────────────────────────

Following are the above objectives together with some critical comments. Compare these comments with your evaluation in the Think Break.

Objective	Comment
1. Increase the price paid to cooperative members for milk.	By how much? By when?
2. Reduce manufacturing costs.	By how much? By when?
3. Price REBC butter 50 percent lower than nearest competitor.	Unlikely to be achievable.
4. Add value to niche products.	Jargon. "Motherhood" statement. Not quantified. Probably not compatible with objective 2.

Think Break ────────────────────────────────────

Design objectives covering a one-year planning period to correspond with your company or organization's mission statement.

────────────────────────────────────

Situation Analysis

Situation analysis involves a detailed look at both the opportunities and threats posed by changes in the company's external environment as well as an internal analysis to identify the company's strengths and weaknesses. These activities can be summarized by a useful acronym, *SWOT.*

Internal Analysis —Strengths
                        Weaknesses
External Analysis—Opportunities
                        Threats

Analysis of the *external environment,* carried out at two levels—the *macroenvironment* and the *industry environment*—involves five stages:

- Identify important factors.
- Research each factor, getting relevant facts from primary and secondary data.
- Analyze these facts.
- Forecast the direction and extent of change for each factor.
- Analyze the impact on the company.

The Macroenvironment   Changes in the macroenvironment include:

- Changes in the economic environment
- Demographic changes

- Social and lifestyle changes
- Technological changes
- Legal and political changes
- Changes in the natural environment.

The economic environment includes the well-known macroeconomic indicators, such as employment, inflation, the exchange rate, balance of payments, household income, income distribution, GDP (Gross Domestic Product) growth, and so on. The general trend has been that, on average, people in developed countries are better off (measured by GDP and household income growth), but there is increasing inequality of incomes; that is, the rich are getting richer, and the poor are getting poorer. The impact of economic changes, or any other external variable, on food consumption depends on which food product is being talked about (Chapter 2). For example, consumption of a basic food such as bread or rice is not much affected by changes in employment, income, and economic growth. On the other hand, consumption of food sold through an expensive restaurant is quite sensitive to the state of the economy.

Demographic changes in Western countries include a decline in both birth and death rates, with the result that the proportion of the population over 60 and the average age are increasing. The number of single-person households is also increasing. Migration rates have generally increased, with the result that the population in most countries is becoming more ethnically diverse.

Examples of lifestyle changes that impact on food consumption are an increasing proportion of working women, generally longer working hours (for those fortunate enough to be employed), increased international travel, and a growing interest in recreational cooking.

Technological change has always been a major driving force in the food industry—from the advent of freezing as a means of preserving food in the nineteenth century to genetically engineered plants and animals today. Overall, the impact of technology at all stages of the food chain has been to reduce the cost and increase the quality and variety of food available to consumers.

Political and regulatory changes are also important to food producers. Consumers are increasingly concerned about food safety and demand protective legislation. In some countries, governments regulate the quantity of food that farmers are allowed to produce. Nowhere is the impact of politics and regulation more apparent than in the European Union (EU). Farm output is regulated by quota but, on occasion, still exceeds domestic consumption. Then the surplus has to be sold with the support of subsidies that require more regulation (Chapter 9).

Concern about the impact of agriculture on the natural environment is on the rise. For example, in countries such as the Netherlands, the rate of artificial fertilizer application and quantity of animal manure required to be recycled by spreading it on pasture land are strictly regulated.

The Industry Environment   For a manufacturer, the industry in which the manufacturer's firm operates comprises competitors, buyers, and suppliers.[2]

---

[2]For an overview of the impact of competitive structures on an industry, see Chapter 6.

One of the most difficult challenges for a planning analyst is to define an industry in operational terms. The boundaries of an industry as defined in official statistics may be quite inappropriate from the perspective of a manager considering the competitive environment of his/her firm. For example, a five-star restaurant is likely to be grouped with many other types of restaurants under the "restaurant" category in the official statistics. McDonald's is not a close competitor for an exclusive restaurant, but a night at the theater probably is. Manufacturers of dairy desserts know that their competitors are other manufacturers of ready-to-eat desserts, but for statistical purposes, such manufacturers may be categorized under "miscellaneous dairy products," which could include dairy-based food ingredients and specialty yogurts as well as dairy-based desserts. Similar problems apply to the analysis of industries supplying raw materials to food manufacturers and to the food distribution sector.

What is the nature of competition within the industry? According to Porter, the most intense rivalry occurs when there are:[3]

- low *barriers to entry* (for example, food service)
- numerous, equally balanced competitors (the standard "perfect competition" model)
- slow industry growth
- diverse competitors[4]
- high fixed costs
- low buyer switching costs
- excess capacity
- high *exit barriers.*

Beef processing, for example, meets many of the requirements for intense competition—declining industry growth, excess capacity, high exit barriers (due to specialized plant and, possibly, agreements with unions preventing lay-offs).

Information about competitors is not easy to obtain. Ideally, managers should know as much about competitors as they do about their own business. A competitor profile should include:

- *Financial position,* taking particular account of how the company is leveraged, because a high level of debt limits its competitive flexibility and makes it vulnerable to attack.
- *Marketing performance.* Sales and market share by market segment.
- *Technical strengths/weaknesses.* Cost of production technological knowledge.
- *R&D and new-product capability.*
- *Competitive strategy.* Are the competitors aggressively seeking market share or satisfied to stay where they are? Is the basis of their strategy low cost or product differentiation?

---

[3]Michael Porter, *Competitive Advantage: Creating and Sustaining Superior Performance* (New York: The Free Press, 1985): 4–11.

[4]Diverse competition could occur, for example, in vegetable production, where there are large-scale "corporate" producers, middle-sized commercial family farmers, and immigrant workers farming a small leased area while also working as laborers for commercial producers. The small producers do not demand a market return on their labor and capital, which makes the commercial producers very vulnerable to competition from this source.

The other elements of the "industry" for a food manufacturer are suppliers and the distribution sector. For a complete industry analysis, research similar to that described for competitors should be carried out for suppliers and buyers. Table 16-1 looks at changes in the distribution and supply sectors and their potential affect on the food industry.

In most European countries and Australia, retail concentration is already very high. (It is not uncommon for the top five supermarket chains to be responsible for over 80 percent of food sales at retail.) In these countries, the rate of increase in retail concentration will inevitably slow. On the other hand, retail concentration is likely to increase in other parts of the world, especially the newly industrializing countries of Asia. Relationship marketing is concerned with extending marketing beyond the traditional marketing mix to build closer relationships with customers (consumers, resellers, or industrial customers). For example, "smart cards" may include information on consumer preferences that could be used to develop a customized shopping list as the shopper enters the store.

The Internal Environment   The next stage in the situation analysis is to study the *internal environment* of the firm—the company's strengths and weaknesses in each of the functional business areas: finance, manufacturing, marketing, research and development, organization and administration, and human resource

TABLE 16-1   SHOPPING BEHAVIOR AND DISTRIBUTION TRENDS

Item	Recent Trend to 1996	Trend to 2010
Away-from-home eating	++	++
Electronic shopping	+	++
Recreational shopping	+	++
Late/early shopping	+	++
Retail concentration	++	+?
Retailer power	++	+?
Retailer brands:		
Europe	+++	+
Australia, United States	+	++
JIT, ECR, and EDI*	+	++
Relationship marketing		
Retailers/suppliers	++	++
Retailers/consumers	+	+++
Globalization	0	++
International retail alliances	+	++
Independent full-range wholesalers	−	−−
Specialist wholesalers	+	++

Code: +/− = Small increase/decline   ++/−− = Moderate increase/decline
+++/−−− = Large increase/decline   0 = Static
*These three-letter acronyms are all concerned with offering the best service to customers at minimum cost (see Chapter 8). JIT = "Just in Time," ECR = "Efficient Consumer Response," and EDI = "Electronic Data Interchange."

management. What follows is not a detailed checklist, which can be found in books on business strategy,[5] but simply a highlighting of some of the major points.

The most important financial variable is the company's debt-equity structure. As discussed in relation to competitor analysis above, debt limits flexibility to move in strategic terms—either defensively or offensively. Other financial variables involve the management of cash flow: inventories, accounts receivable, and accounts payable. For example, an important source of profitability for food retailers is the fact that they are paid in cash, but have credit terms on purchases.

Manufacturing strengths and weaknesses relate to labor and plant productivity: downtime, production flexibility, human resource management, and quality control.

The marketing SWOT analysis will be discussed in detail later in the chapter. Some of the important variables are: positioning, segmentation, brand recognition and acceptance, product quality and reputation, distribution facilities and costs, and customer service.

Research and development can be oriented either to product (development of new products and improving the quality of existing products, as depicted in Figure 16-2) or to process (reducing manufacturing costs). What are the company's strengths and weaknesses for both of these types of R&D?

[5]For example, David W. Craven, *Strategic Marketing,* 2d ed. (Homewood, IL: Irwin, 1987).

FIGURE 16-2 Marketing planning as a continuous process. At Hubbards Foods Ltd., a small cereal manufacturer, the new-product development philosophy is not to have endless meetings about new products, but to have a discussion about every three weeks to review ongoing progress and brainstorm new ideas. *(Courtesy of Hubbards Foods Ltd., Auckland, New Zealand.*

Organization, administration, and human resource management are increasingly recognized as sources of *competitive advantage*. Does the company have a lean, flat management structure and an "empowered" workforce? How effective are the management information and internal communication systems? How does the company's industrial relations record compare with that of competitors?

Each company should design its own checklist. For example, a food manufacturer today would have a substantial list of variables under the heading "quality management," including management of the procurement of raw materials and a "quality audit trail" going back to the farm or even to the farm-input supplier. For each variable in the checklist, management should evaluate their organization in relation to competitors—ranking it from "Clearly better than the top company in the industry" to "A disaster—bottom performer."

Think Break

Develop a strengths-and-weaknesses checklist for the business, club, or organization you have been thinking about in previous sections of this chapter. Devise a five-point scale to compare this organization with its competitors.

Strategy Development   Two basic questions are involved in strategy development.

What business(es) are we in?
What business(es) do we want to be in?

Corporate objectives express the goals of the board and management, SWOT analysis defines the environment in which they will be achieved, and *strategies* show the path to be followed.

Strategic planners have a number of useful tools for identifying and analyzing alternative strategies. One of these, developed by Ansoff, structures the product/market alternatives available to the firm as shown in Figure 16-3. (The Ansoff matrix was developed originally to apply to one country only. However, Market development, Sector III, can include exporting and investment activities in other countries, and Ansoff has developed a more complicated matrix that recognizes these alternatives.)

Sector I of the matrix promotes "business as usual, but more of it." It is a low-risk strategy but may be difficult to achieve if the company already has a high market share or is constrained in other ways from growing its established business (for example, limited raw-material supplies). Growth in this sector may be either *organic* (growth within the present organizational structure) or by *acquisition* (buying similar companies).

Product development, Sector II, is an alternative often used in the food industry (discussed in Chapter 13). New markets for existing products (Sector III) may be geographical (for example, exporting) or in new market segments. A company that has specialized in consumer food products might consider entering the food service industry.

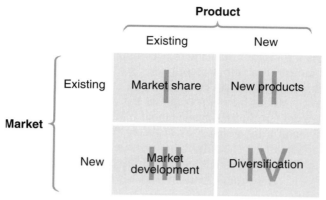

FIGURE 16-3 The product/market matrix. *(Adapted from H. Igor Ansoff,* Corporate Strategy *New York: McGraw-Hill, 1965: 109.)*

The last alternative, diversification (sector IV), is the most extreme change from the established business and is therefore the highest-risk strategy. The largest food company in the world, Kraft-Phillip Morris, is the result of Phillip Morris's move to diversify away from their declining, but still profitable, cigarette business into processed food. This initiative also illustrates another strategy—using established "cash cows" to fund acquisitions in growth businesses.[6]

Another direction for growth in the food industry is to look at input suppliers and customers as potential acquisition opportunities—integrative growth. Forward vertical integration is, in fact, a type of diversification, because to a company manufacturing industrial food ingredients, like the Really Efficient Butter Company discussed earlier, manufacturing consumer food products really is a new product/market.

Gap Analysis In the strategic-planning sequence, strategies followed the establishment of objectives. A reasonable question could be, "How do you know these objectives are achievable until you have chosen strategies and calculated their financial implications?" The answer is that you don't. Strategic planning is a cyclical process which allows revision of both objectives and strategies until a feasible match is achieved. Operationally, this means that, after the first objectives/strategy review, you look at the "gap" between the objective and what can actually be achieved using the proposed strategies—as shown in Figure 16-4.

Closing the gap involves revising either the strategies or the objectives, or both. As a first review, managers should investigate strategies in sector I of the matrix in Figure 16-3 to see if these will achieve the objective(s), because this quadrant offers the lowest-risk alternatives. If, after this revision, the strategy does not achieve the targeted financial, marketing, or other objectives, then sectors II and III can be

[6]This is a key element of the Boston Consulting Group portfolio analysis matrix, another tool for strategic planners [David W. Craven, *Strategic Marketing,* 2d ed. (Homewood, IL: Irwin, 1987].

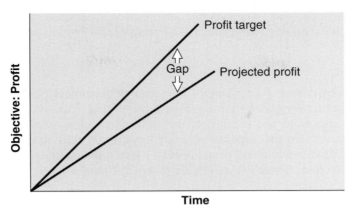

FIGURE 16-4   Gap analysis.

considered. Because it is the highest-risk alternative, sector IV should be considered last.

Going sector by sector is a rather cautious approach to strategy. A manager with leadership and vision might leapfrog sectors I, II, and III, going straight for the high-risk/high-yield strategy in sector IV.

A company expanding internationally may begin by exporting commodity products through an agent. As sales volume increases, it eventually becomes sufficient to support the company's own sales office in the importing country. The company begins to differentiate its range of commodity products into industrial raw materials. Eventually, the company may acquire one of its customers and become a food manufacturer—forward vertical integration/diversification, sector IV. Once in the manufacturing business, the company may recognize opportunities for expanding to other products required by its customers—sector II. Globally oriented companies see the whole world as providing opportunities, not only for product and market development, but also for raw-material sourcing and the location of processing and manufacturing activity.

Kerry, the company whose mission statement was discussed earlier in this chapter, is an example of sustained growth—using all four sectors of the product/market matrix. Kerry was established as a dairy cooperative in 1974. Early growth came through acquisitions of other dairies in Ireland—the existing-product/existing-market sector. However, Kerry management recognized that there was an upper limit to this type of growth, imposed mainly by the likely imposition of milk production quotas in the (then) European Economic Community. Further acquisitions in the 1980s were in meat processing—basically an existing-market/new-product initiative. (It was also easy to deal with a familiar type of supplier, farmers.) However, since the late 1980s, most of Kerry's growth has been in sector IV of the matrix—diversification. They have acquired food-ingredient companies in the United States, Mexico, and Canada, as well as in the rest of Europe. Kerry's earnings growth has averaged over 16 percent per year—a remarkable achievement, considering the very high rate of failure for acquisition-based diversified growth in the food industry.

MARKETING PLANNING

The marketing plan is one of the series of functional plans (along with finance, manufacturing, etc.) shown in Figure 16-1. The corporate mission, situation analysis, objectives, and strategy are the basis of marketing-plan objectives. The tools of analysis used for corporate planning can also be used for marketing planning. We will discuss marketing planning at two levels: the *strategic marketing plan* and the *action plan*. These two stages are shown in Figure 16.5.

Strategic Marketing Plan

In the strategic marketing plan we begin with the situation analysis, then define marketing objectives, and finally develop marketing strategies. The principles are the same as for corporate planning, but the focus is on marketing variables.

Situation Analysis: External   The first step in the external analysis is to define and quantify the market for each product/market segment in which the firm competes. As discussed earlier, this may be quite difficult. Competition should be seen from the perspective of the consumer, not the producer—the marketing concept is the underlying principle. Once the market has been described, the next step is to identify the key driving forces, how these drivers have changed in the past (and can be expected to change in the future), and the expected impact of these forces on both the industry and the company.

The environmental factors fall into two main areas—the macroenvironment and the microenvironment(s) for the firm's set of product/markets. The main driving forces in the macroenvironment are:

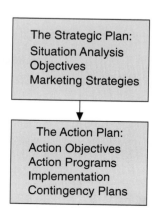

FIGURE 16-5   The marketing planning process.

- *Economic:* Income, income distribution, employment
- *Demographic:* Birth/death rates, age structure, migration
- *Lifestyle:* Work/recreation, travel
- *Attitudes:* Environmental issues, food health concerns

A possible tabular format for analyzing the external environment and its impact on the company is shown below.

			Impact on:	
Factor	Past trend	Future trend	Industry	Company
Macro Environment:				
Economic:				
Income distribution	+3	+1	−1	+2

0 = No obvious historical (or future) trend; no expected impact on industry (or company).
+5 = Strong historical (or future) trend; major expected positive impact on industry (or company).
−5 = Strong historical (or future) trend; major expected negative impact on industry (or company).

Microenvironmental variables are detailed in Table 16-2. This list is illustrative only. Other variables may be included, depending on the particular product/market.

TABLE 16-2   MICROENVIRONMENTAL VARIABLES WHICH MAY IMPACT THE MARKETING PLAN

Consumers/customers	Changes in demographic profile of the product's buying population Buying behavior Changing food preferences (such as health concerns) Changing segmentation (emergence of new segments) For industrial products: industry structure, technology, etc.
The product/market	Stability of demand (cycles, seasonality) Product adoption rates (innovators, early adopters) Stage of product life cycle Manufacturing: costs, experience curve, technology Legal and government
Competitors	Positioning Segments served Historical and current performance (sales, market share) Marketing mix (products, pricing, promotion, distribution) Strengths and weaknesses (marketing, manufacturing) Competitive stance (aggressive retaliator, follower)
Distributors	Structure of distribution sector Characteristics of customers served by each distributor Relationships with other suppliers Strengths and weaknesses (financial, for example) Purchasing terms and conditions Cooperative/competitive stance
Suppliers	Structure of supply sector Relationships with other buyers Strengths and weaknesses with respect to technology, service Purchasing terms and conditions Cooperative/competitive stance

The interpretation of the sample tabular analysis is that changes in income distribution have been significant in the past, but will be less significant in the future. For the industry as a whole, the impact of future changes is expected to be slightly negative, but for the particular firm, the impact will be slightly positive (perhaps because the firm specializes in producing "no frills" generic brands).

Situation Analysis: Internal   The internal analysis proceeds in a similar fashion: first identify the key variables, and then weigh their importance from a company perspective. The list should include at least those variables shown in Table 16-3.[7]

A more detailed list would be developed for a complete marketing audit (see Chapter 13, product audit). As for the external analysis, organizations should develop a checklist most appropriate to their needs and devise some measure of the organization's strengths and weaknesses relative to competitors.

Marketing Objectives   *Marketing objectives* derive from corporate objectives, and, within the marketing function, objectives for specific marketing activities such as advertising and distribution derive from the marketing objectives. There is thus a *hierarchy of objectives* in the company and marketing plans. Strategies at one level define objectives at the next lower level, as shown in Figure 16-6. As well as

---

[7]Loosely based on Phillip Kotler, W. Gregor, and W. Rogers, "The Marketing Audit Comes of Age," *Sloan Management Review* (Winter 1989): 49–62.

TABLE 16-3   INTERNAL (COMPANY) VARIABLES WHICH MAY IMPACT THE MARKETING PLAN

Strategy	Objectives clearly defined and operational?
	Long-term growth targets achievable, given the company's position in the market and resources committed to growth?
	Company's position in each market segment it serves is well defined, defensible?
Effectiveness of strategy	Market share (present position, trends)
	Profitability by product and market segment
	Cost-effectiveness
Organization	Real organizational commitment to the marketing function
	The organization's structure and lines of authority reflect this commitment
	Communication within the marketing function and between marketing and the rest of the organization
Systems	Marketing information
	Planning and control
	New-product development
Marketing functions	Products (product-line objectives, products that should be added or deleted)
	Pricing (pricing in relation to marketing objectives, costs)
	Promotion, Advertising and publicity (Advertising objectives properly linked to marketing objectives? Adequate budget? Adequate evaluation?)
	Sales force (Objectives appropriate? Adequate number of salespeople? Organization? Strengths/weaknesses?)
	Distribution (Objectives, adequacy, cost-effectiveness)

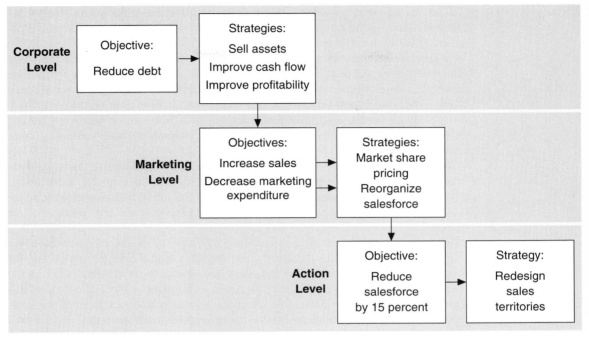

FIGURE 16-6   A hierarchy of planning objectives.

being internally consistent within the plan, objectives should be quantifiable, measurable, actionable, and motivational.

Marketing Strategies   As for nearly all marketing activity, the two key words are segmentation and positioning. What market segments does the company seek to serve? How will the company's product(s) be positioned in these segments relative to competing products?

Market segmentation was discussed in Chapter 12. For planning purposes, the different ways to segment a market may be summarized as follows:[8]

Who the customers are:	Demographics, psychographics
What and where they buy:	Product features, purchase locations
Why they buy:	Perceptions, attitudes, preferences
Customer type:	Volume purchased (particularly important for industrial marketing)
	Function performed by purchaser (e.g. processor or reseller)
	Heavy/light users
Benefit segmentation:	Benefits offered to buyers by the product

[8]Peter Reed, *Marketing Planning and Strategy* (Sydney, Australia: Harcourt Brace Jovanovich, 1992):100.

The last of these provides a particularly powerful basis for segmentation, because it addresses the fundamental marketing question, "What needs does the product meet for each category of customer?"

Marketing strategy is also influenced by the stage of the product life cycle (Chapter 13) the product has reached. For example, at the introductory stage, the basic marketing objective is to create awareness and encourage trial. Distribution is likely to be limited and selective at this stage. With intense competition at the maturity stage of the life cycle, strategies are likely to be based on defending market share and on production efficiency (to remain profitable under increasing price competition).

Another important element of strategy is the firm's competitive stance. A firm may be a market leader proactively defending its dominant share, a challenger aggressively seeking to wrest market share from the leader, a follower with a "me too" type of product, or a niche marketer specializing in a small segment of the market.

The key strategy issues at the marketing-mix level have already been discussed in previous chapters. Once the basic questions regarding the target market and the product's position in it have been answered, the development of strategy relating to the four elements of the marketing mix becomes relatively easy. For example, it is a straightforward task to determine advertising strategy and tactics when the categories of customer a company wishes to reach and the positioning statement it wishes to make to them are known. There should be clearly identifiable links a) between marketing-mix strategies and marketing objectives and b) between the marketing strategies themselves. (Do product, price, advertising, and distribution all convey the same positioning message to buyers?)

IMPLEMENTATION AND CONTROL

Implementation and control issues occur both at the strategic planning level and on a month-to-month or even day-by-day basis.

Strategic Implementation Issues

As shown in Figure 16-1, strategic planning involves establishing a portfolio of strategic business units (SBUs) and developing a strategic plan for each one. SBU plans, in turn, include detailed plans for each functional business area, such as manufacturing, research and development, finance, or marketing.

Three basic questions need to be answered in implementing the strategic plan:

• How should business activities be configured geographically? For an international company, this involves decisions on the number and location of manufacturing plants, raw-material suppliers, sales offices, advertising agencies, and so on.

• What business activities should be carried out by the company itself and what should be handled by suppliers, distributors, or some type of subcontractor? In manufacturing, this becomes the "make-or-buy decision"; in marketing the decision may be whether to use some type of agent or distributor or to establish a sales office.

Another way of looking at this question is the degree to which the company is vertically integrated—a high degree of vertical integration means that the company has chosen to keep most manufacturing and marketing activity "in house" (Chapter 6).

• How should the activities of the company be coordinated? Should local managers be given a high degree of autonomy, or should everything be tightly controlled from the head office?

These three questions apply to each business function. For example, should marketing be centralized, with the same brand, advertising theme, and campaign for each country, or decentralized, using many brands and giving the marketing managers in each country a high degree of autonomy in choosing advertising themes and agencies?

The three dimensions of international business organization are shown in Figure 16-7.

FIGURE 16-7   Organization of international business activities. *(Source: W. Schroder, T. Wallace, and F. Mavondo, "Cooperative Statutory Marketing Organizations, and Global Business Strategy," Agribusiness: An International Journal 9.2 (1993): 177.)*

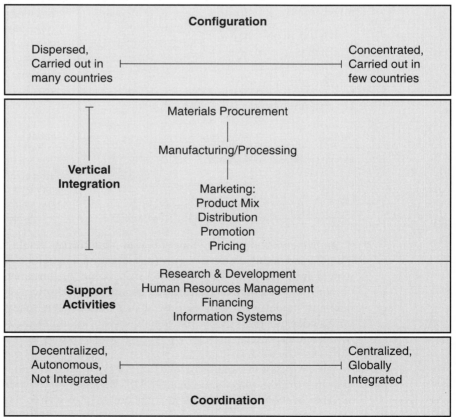

Nestlé, the second largest food manufacturing company, operates over 400 plants located in 60 countries. The only business functions that are tightly managed from the head office in Switzerland are finance (for major investments) and research and development. Marketing is decentralized, and most Nestlé products are not sold under the Nestlé brand. The international activities of Kerry, the Irish company discussed previously in this chapter, are even more decentralized. Kerry's strength lies in the ability to select and price good candidates for acquisition and to give its competent managers a high degree of autonomy.

Short-Term Planning, Implementation, and Control

Strategic planning focuses on the medium to long term, usually one to five years, whereas short-term planning is based on a planning cycle of one year or less. Annual plans relate marketing planning to financial planning. While there is no particular logic in choosing a one-year planning cycle for a marketing plan, financial planning is inevitably on an annual basis, and it is necessary to integrate the marketing plan, along with the other functional plans, into the financial reports.

Action planning turns strategies into actions. It addresses four important questions:

What is to be done?
When is it to be done by?
Who does it?
How is it to be done?

For example:

Strategy		Actions
Increase personal selling effort	*What:*	Advertise three new sales positions
	When:	Advertisements: November 1 Interviews: December 15
	Who:	Sales Manager, Personnel Manager

Implementation of the plan involves *monitoring* actual performance versus planned and taking action to *control* the situation if actual performance deviates too widely from planned. This deviation may occur for three reasons: the forecast of one or more external variables (such as raw-material prices) may be incorrect; the planning model itself may be flawed (for example, the relationship between proposed sales of a product and the general level of economic activity); or the planning model and the forecast values for external variables may be acceptable, but the plan is poorly executed.

The process for monitoring and control is shown in Figure 16-8. When is a deviation from the plan "significant"? This depends on how strongly the particular variable in the plan influences key performance measures. For example, variation from planned sales of a product that accounts for 5 percent of total sales will have

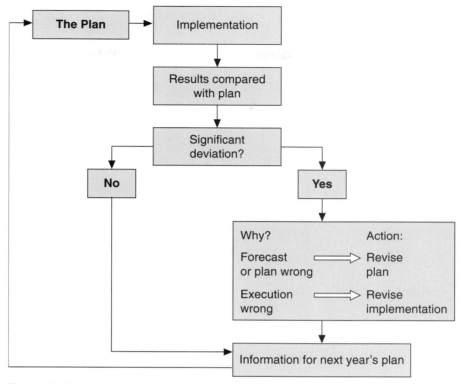

FIGURE 16-8   The monitoring and control process.

a much smaller influence on profits than a similar variation for a product that accounts for 50 percent of sales.

A significant deviation from the plan signals management to take some action—the control part of the implementation process. In Figure 16-9, the variable being monitored is advertising expenses as a percentage of sales. The planned level for this variable is 6 percent. Deviations of 1 percent either way are acceptable to management, but outside these limits some action is required. The trend at month 5 should be ringing warning bells to management. At month 7, it is time for corrective action.

The use of control charts facilitates *management by exception.* In this particular example, the person responsible for advertising (perhaps the advertising manager) is free to implement the advertising plan in whatever way he or she feels appropriate, as long as expenses and sales lie within the specified limits. The exception to this operating guideline occurs when the expenses/sales ratio strays outside the limits. When this happens, the advertising manager's boss (probably the marketing manager) notices, and action is taken.

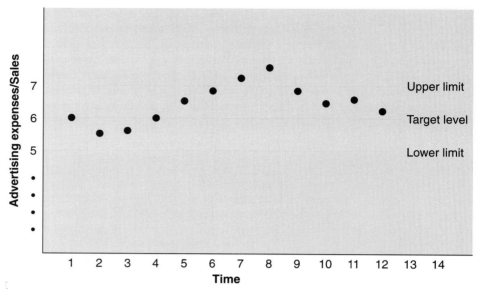

FIGURE 16-9   Planning control chart.

What control measures are appropriate? Basically, anything that may significantly influence high-level objectives, such as net profit or return on capital, should be tracked. This involves separating the objective into its component variables. For example, suppose a company has experienced increased dollar sales. How might this have come about? Dollar sales may be expressed as an equation:

$$\text{dollar sales} = \text{units sold} \times \text{price per unit}$$

We can further break down the independent variables:

$$\text{units sold} = \text{total market volume} \times \text{market share}$$

$$\text{price per unit} = \text{base price} \times \text{inflation factor}$$

Therefore:

$$\text{dollar sales} = (\text{total market volume} \times \text{market share}) \times (\text{base price} \times \text{inflation factor})$$

The final form of the equation shows what variables should be monitored in the planning process. It also breaks up the performance measure "dollar sales" into those variables that can be influenced by management (market share, base price) and those that probably cannot (total market volume, inflation).

In the longer term, the *marketing audit* is a basic control activity. At the completion of the planning cycle—say one year—management reviews actual performance against planned and thinks deeply about where they went right or wrong. What strengths and weaknesses has the implementation of the plan revealed? This information, along with targets and forecasts for the new planning period, feeds into the planning process for the next planning cycle.

While most larger companies use some sort of planning, few would claim that it is 100 percent successful. Perhaps this is because formal plans impose a degree of rigidity on an organization which limits their flexibility to act in a fast-moving world.

> The crucial problems in strategy were most often those of execution and continuous adaptation: getting it done and staying flexible. And that, to a very large extent, means going far beyond strategy to issues of organizing.
>
> —Peters and Waterman, *In Search of Excellence*[9]

Other reasons that have been advanced for the failure of planning to achieve its potential are:

• Planning is carried out in isolation within the organization by planning specialists with insufficient involvement from other staff. "Planning is too important to be left to planners."

• Closely related to the first reason is the NIH (Not Invented Here) syndrome. People will resist change when they have not been actively involved in designing it.

• Plans are often too general, not detailing the specifics of implementation.

• Especially in smaller organizations, managers are too busy managing from day to day to take the time to plan. This might be referred to as the AIC (Armpits in Crocodiles) syndrome: "When you're up to your armpits in crocodiles, you don't have time to plan draining the swamp."

SUMMARY

Marketing planning provides the framework for coordinating the marketing activities of a company. The marketing plan is one of a series of functional plans (manufacturing, human resource management, research and development, and financial) which, in turn, are a part of the overall planning process (refer to Figure 16-1).

Strategic planning at the corporate level involves five steps:

The Mission Statement
Objectives
Analysis of the external environment of the company (opportunities and threats)
Analysis of the internal environment (strengths and weaknesses)
Strategies

The mission statement encapsulates a broad statement of objectives, strategies, and sources of competitive advantage in two or three sentences. It provides a public statement of the firm's strategic direction.

---

[9]Thomas J. Peters and Robert H. Waterman, *In Search of Excellence: Lessons from America's Best Run Companies* (New York: Harper & Row, 1982): 4.

The marketing plan has a similar structure but usually includes only the last four of these steps. Planning objectives should be measurable, quantifiable, achievable, and have a specified time dimension. Examination of both the external and internal environments of the firm comprises the situation analysis. The external environment includes both the macroenvironment and the industry environment.

Analysis of the internal environment includes a statement of the company's strengths and weaknesses with respect to the following areas: strategy development, key performance indicators (past and forecast trends), organization, systems, financial (indebtedness), manufacturing (cost of production), research and development (product development and cost reduction) and marketing (positioning, segmentation strategy, product range, pricing, promotion, and distribution).

Strategy development involves exploring four broad alternatives. Sales may be increased (I) for an existing product range in existing markets, (II) for an existing product range in new markets, (III) with new products in existing markets, or (IV) with new products in new markets. Manufacturers may also consider expanding vertically, into the domain of their suppliers or of their customers.

The key elements of marketing strategy are the identification of target markets (segmentation) and the positioning of products relative to competitors in each target market. Product, price, promotion, and distribution strategies flow from these two key elements.

Action plans translate strategies into action by addressing the questions:

What is to be done?
When is it to be done by?
Who does it?
How is it to be done?

Implementation involves monitoring actual performance versus planned and taking action to control the situation if actual performance deviates from planned.

IMPORTANT TERMS AND CONCEPTS

QUESTIONS

1 Search your library for information of one of the top food companies—for example, Nestlé, Unilever, or Kraft-General Foods. Identify the company's strategic business units.

2 Locate a small business (less than 100 employees). Find out about the planning process in this organization.

3 Comment on the following Mission Statement:
Company X will achieve excellence in the production and distribution of widgets by operating at a lower cost than our competitors and providing the highest level of service to our customers.

4 Comment on the following objectives for a company producing food flavors:
a) Increase sales by 10 percent.
b) Increase market share by 5 percent.
c) Reduce sales force by 60 percent.

5 Using any food manufacturing company as an example, identify the six most important changes in the company's macroenvironment. How have these changes trended over the past ten years? How do you expect them to trend in the next ten?

6 Using the same literature base as in question 1, prepare a brief SWOT analysis for one of the companies listed.

7 Referring to the product/market matrix in Figure 16-3, suggest alternatives in each quadrant for the Really Efficient Butter Company.

8 Choose any food product. Locate this food product in the official statistics of your country. Does this industrial classification make sense in terms of defining the competitive arena for the chosen product? Comment on other limitations of the statistics.

9 Express the components of net profit as an equation. Derive the components of this equation. What variables might management be expected to be able to control and what variables are uncontrollable?

10 *The Big One!* You have already completed several sections of a plan for your favorite company or organization. You are now ready to combine them with some additional detail to prepare a complete marketing plan. This should include:

- Mission Statement
- Situation Analysis
- Corporate Objectives
- Marketing Objectives
- Strategies
- Action Plan
- Financial Implications.

Note: This exercise offers a practical review not only of the concepts in this chapter, but also of those learned in the rest of the book, particularly in the previous three chapters.

REFERENCES AND RESOURCES

Ansoff, H. Igor. *Corporate Strategy.* New York: McGraw-Hill, 1965.

Cravens, David. *Strategic Marketing,* 2d ed. Homewood, IL: Irwin, 1987.

Kotler, Phillip, W. Gregor, and W. Rogers. "The Marketing Audit Comes of Age." *Sloan Management Review* (Winter 1989): 49–62.

Peters, Thomas J., and Robert H. Waterman. *In Search of Excellence: Lessons from America's Best Run Companies.* New York: Harper & Row, 1982.

Porter, Michael. *Competitive Advantage: Creating and Sustaining Superior Performance.* New York: The Free Press, 1985.

Reed, Peter. *Marketing Planning and Strategy.* Sydney: Harcourt Brace Jovanovich, 1992.

Schroder, W., T. Wallace, and F. Mavondo. "Cooperatives, Statutory Marketing Organizations, and Global Business Strategy." *Agribusiness: An International Journal* 9.2 (1993): 175–87.

GLOSSARY

access   The ability to obtain information about the market and about various selling alternatives necessary for a producer to use individual negotiation successfully.

action plan   Stage of planning process which turns strategies into actions. It addresses four important questions: What is there to be done? When is it to be done by? Who does it? How is it to be done?

additives   Materials added intentionally to foods during processing and manufacturing to aid processing and to give specific properties to the food product.

administered prices   Pricing method by which the seller establishes a nonnegotiable price in advance of the sale. Agricultural producers, who are in the model of pure competition, have no opportunity to control or administer prices. Generally refers to government intervention in price determination, for example, farm price support programs in the U.S. and the European Union and the pricing practices of centrally planned economies such as the now defunct Soviet Union.

administrative control   One company controls all the activities in a marketing channel through common ownership.

adverse selection   A contractual arrangement that attracts participants who are able to take advantage of the contract terms to the detriment of the other party.

advertising   A process of relatively indirect persuasion delivered by media such as newspapers, magazines, television, radio, and outdoor billboards. The message delivered by advertising is designed to create favorable mental impressions that "turn the mind toward" purchase. Includes all the activities involved in presenting this non personal, sponsor-identified message regarding a product, idea, or organization.

advertising timing patterns   How advertising is scheduled to allow for seasonality or other variations.

alliances   Partnerships or networks established when mutual benefits can be clearly identified and boundaries of the alliance can be well-defined, minimizing areas of possible competition.

arbitrage   Simultaneous purchase of cash commodities or futures in one market and the sale of cash commodities or futures in the same or a different market to profit from a discrepancy in prices.

assemblers   Wholesalers who gather relatively small lots into larger lots, carry out simple processing, such as cleaning grain or hulling almonds, and are often located where commodity grading is accomplished.

attitudes   A person's consistent, favorable or unfavorable evaluations, emotional feelings, and opinions in regard to a product and/or toward any tangible or intangible aspect of marketing.

auction   Competitive bidding by persons wanting to buy or sell, whether in a futures market or country livestock auction. Because of their openness and the bidding process, auction markets are described as the most "efficient" markets; that is, the price arrived at represents supply and demand at a given time.

balancing interests   Ensuring that no party can consistently benefit at the expense of another in a contractual situation.

bargaining cooperatives   Cooperatives that take title to their members' produce in order to represent them in negotiations with buyers, generally food processors, but do not process, warehouse, or otherwise handle the physical product.

barriers to entry   Difficulties for new entrants to an industry. An industry with low barriers to entry experiences greater competition than one with high barriers.

barriers to exit   Difficulties for companies wishing to cease operations in an industry— for example, a redundancy (guaranteed employment) agreement with a labor union.

basic food groups   The grouping of foods by nutritionists according to their type and nutritional value: cereals, fruit, vegetables, meat and other protein foods (including fish, eggs, and beans), dairy products, fats and oils, and sweeteners.

basic food tastes   The sensory characteristics with which food flavors are discerned: sweetness, saltiness, sourness, and bitterness.

basis   The difference between the spot price and the price of futures. Computations of basis include location, as well as time differentials.

bear   One who believes prices will fall.

benefit-based pricing   Setting prices on the basis of identified benefits to buyers.

biotechnology   The development of new plants, animals, and microorganisms based on recombinant DNA technology.

bounded rationality   The inability to fully define any future situation—for example, in establishing a contract.

brand   A name, term, symbol or special design that differentiates the products of one seller from those of other sellers.

brand equity   The value of a brand to a company, based on brand loyalty, name awareness, perceived quality, brand associations, and other proprietary brand assets, such as patents, trademarks, and channel relationships.

brand extension   A new or modified product launched under an already successful brand name, very often aimed at a new market segment.

brand loyalty   Consumers' level of commitment to a brand, indicated by their continuing purchase of that brand.

brand mark   A nonverbal design, symbol or color in a brand that can be identified with a product by sight.

brand name   Words or letters in a brand that can be vocalized.

branded consumer products   Also called differentiated products, where many products and product variations are developed which are aimed at specific segments, using a marketing mix (product, price, promotion, and distribution) adapted for each segment.

break-even pricing   A per-unit price that covers both fixed and variable costs of production at a particular volume.

break-even volume   The volume of production at which profit equals zero for any particular price.

brokers/agents   Broker and agent are terms that are used in different industries for the same type of wholesaler. The essential element of broker operations is that they do not take title to or ownership of the product, but represent the seller in carrying out the personal selling function of marketing.

bulk industrial products   Raw materials and ingredients marketed in large quantities to a food processor or manufacturer.

bull   One who expects prices to rise.

buy on actuals   Buying process which includes personal inspection and approval of lots. Buying on actuals still plays a large role in food marketing.

buyer valuation of products   The valuation of a product by industrial buyers and consumers, which can be used as a basis for pricing.

buyers   Representatives of a food processing, manufacturing or retailing company who interact with suppliers, arrange the terms of sale, and process the actual purchase order.

buyers' diaries   Daily recordings of purchases by consumers, which are summarized and the data sold by market research companies.

buying center   The individuals and groups who participate in the buying decision process within a food processing, manufacturing or retailing company. The center may include initiators, influencers, decision makers, gatekeepers, purchasers (buyers), and users.

buying motivations   The reasons why a person or an organization buys a specific product or makes a purchase from a specific company, including technical reasons, such as product quality; distribution reasons—size and timing of deliveries; finance reasons—discounts; and personal reasons—cooperation with individuals in the supplying company.

calories   The energy available in foods, approximately 4 calories per gram of carbohydrate or protein and 9 calories per gram of fat.

carrying charges   Cost of storing a physical commodity over a period of time, including insurance and interest on the invested funds, as well as other incidental costs.

cash commodity   The actual physical commodity, as distinguished from a futures commodity. The term "spot" mean the same as cash.

cash cow   A business activity at the mature stage of the product life cycle that generates cash which is often used to invest in new businesses.

central location test   The consumer testing of a new or improved product held in a central place, such as a shopping mall.

chain store   A company that operates 11 or more stores.

channel design   Organization of the marketing channel from the perspective of one of its participants.

CIF (Cost, Insurance, Freight)   Selling price includes all costs to deliver the product to the buyer's port, including all the relevant costs of export: freight costs—ocean or air, marine insurance, documentation fees, exporting port fees, and other types of fees.

clearing house   A separate corporation associated with a futures exchange that is responsible for matching the transactions executed on the floor of the exchange. It also collects and maintains margin moneys, regulates delivery, and reports trading data. Clearing houses guarantee all futures and options contracts, acting as a buyer to every clearing member seller and a seller to every clearing member buyer.

codes of ethics   Guidelines for the members of an organization which govern their conduct and provide protection for the organization, individual members of the organization, and members of the general public.

commodity   An agricultural product that has had little or no processing and is often a raw material for further processing, such as raw sugar, wheat, or oilseeds. Because the product is undifferentiated by supplier, suppliers of commodities face an infinitely elastic demand.

commodity advertising   The cooperative effort among producers of a nearly homogenous product to disseminate information about the underlying attributes of the product by existing and potential consumers for the purpose of strengthening demand for the product.

competitive advantage   Strengths relative to competitors. Sources of competitive advantage are specified in a company's mission statement.

competitor profile   Information concerning competitors including: financial position, marketing performance, technical strengths and weaknesses, R&D capability, and competitive strategy.

complement products   Products that "go together" in the minds of buyers. Complements have a negative cross price elasticity of demand.

concentrated strategy   A strategy where a single market segment is targeted for a single product or limited line of products.

consumer survey   The collection of primary data by interviewing consumers face-to-face, by telephone, or by mail.

continuity   The length of time a particular advertising schedule runs.

continuous advertising timing pattern   Schedule providing a constant level of advertising over time.

contract   A legally binding association or arrangement.

contracts   May be either forward (production) contracts, or marketing (sales) contracts. Forward contracting is a mechanism that regulates product flow in line with expected demands and gives processors more control over quality.

control   Action taken by management when actual performance deviates from planned.

convenience store   A retailer that develops a limited product assortment of convenience-oriented groceries and nonfoods, has higher prices than found at supermarkets, and offers few customer services; for example, 7-11 or Circle K.

converging food preferences   The increasing similarity of consumer food preferences as consumers grow more affluent.

cooperation   Organizations/individuals working together for mutual benefit.

cooperative   A legal structure that allows individual businesses to invest collectively in purchasing inputs or processing outputs. The distinctive feature of a cooperative is that the return to members is based on their patronage of the cooperative, rather than their investment in it.

cooperative advertising   (1) Joint promotion of a national advertiser (manufacturer) and local retail outlet on behalf of the manufacturer's product on sale in the retail store. (2) Joint promotion through a trade association for firms in a single industry. (3) Advertising venture jointly conducted by two or more advertisers.

cooperative goods   Products that cannot be differentiated and for which advertising may increase total demand, but will not change market shares among sellers.

corporate objectives   The highest level objectives of the organization; these objectives can be financial, market-oriented, employee-related, or social.

corporate strategic planning   Establishing objectives, carrying out an internal or external analysis, and developing strategies for the long-term future of the organization.

countervailing power   The attempt by one party in a relationship to develop sources of power in response to the exercise of power by another party.

coupons   Vouchers or certificates that entitle the buyer to a price reduction on the couponed item. Trade coupons are offered by both manufacturers and retailers and are usually are paid for by the manufacturer and retailer jointly.

cross-price elasticity of demand   The percentage change in the quantity of product A demanded in response to a one percent change in the price of product B.

culture   The set of basic values, perceptions and wants created by society as determinants and regulators of human behavior and learned by the individual from family and other groups in the society.

date marking   The methods of stating the dates on foods to allow the consumer to identify the predicted life of the food. Regulations control date terminology, with "packed on," "best before," and "use by" among the suggested dates for food packages.

debt/equity ratio   Also called leverage or gearing, this ratio is important in strategic terms because a high level of debt limits decision-making flexibility.

demand   A measure of the desire that potential customers have for a product and their ability and willingness to pay for it.

demand curve   A curve which graphs the schedule of quantities sold at various prices.

derived demand   Demand at food manufacturer door or farm gate deriving from primary customer demand at retail.

dietary guidelines   The recommendations from government, health and nutrition departments, and committees regarding the quantities of foods from the different food groups to be eaten daily to provide optimum nutrition.

differentiated strategy   A strategy offering many products in two or more market segments of a market, each segment having different products, prices, promotion, and distribution.

distribution center   The warehouse used to accumulate food products from processors and distribute them to retailers. The distribution center includes store delivery fleets and procurement systems.

distributors   Their major function is to carry inventories and the assortment of items that their customers—retailers and food service firms—need. It is common for distributors to operate their own truck fleet and deliver products to their customers. Also referred to as merchant wholesalers.

E numbers   Numbers used in Europe to identify food additives on food labels, keyed to a reference book.

eco-labeling   The labeling of foods to show that they have been produced under environmentally sound conditions and in some cases also may be consumed so as to cause no pollution.

effective competition   The level of competition which ensures that companies in the food system are motivated by profits to deliver services to the consumer at the lowest possible price and that efficiency gains are passed on to the consumer.

ECR (Efficient Consumer Response)   The system that manufacturers and distributors use (relying on EDI—Electronic Data Interchange) to efficiently supply retailers with a minimum of inventories being held at various levels and at the same time avoiding occurrences of insufficient stock. ECR also goes by other acronyms: JIT (Just In Time), or QR (Quick Response).

elastic demand   The percentage change in quantity consumed in response to a one percent change in price or income is greater than one percent.

elastic supply   The percentage change in the quantity supplied in response to a one percent increase in price is greater than one percent.

elasticity of supply   Percentage of change in quantity supplied in response to a one percent change in price.

EDI (Electronic Data Interchange) The information exchange between retail point-of-sale (POS) and manufacturers. EDI allows efficient inventory management and feedback of marketing information.

electronic trading Using electronic methods to link sellers and buyers in some type of auction market. The pricing efficiency of the auction market combines with the technical efficiency of direct marketing, where the product moves directly from the seller's location to the buyer's.

ELP (Everyday Low Pricing) Using the same retail prices for long periods, offering no "specials" or other deals.

Engel Curve The relationship between the quantity of a product consumed and household income.

equality of investment in relationship-specific assets Both parties to a contract have similar investment in assets that have limited alternative uses if the contract is discontinued.

equilibrium price The price established at the intersection of the supply and demand curves.

equitable In a pricing system, giving equal treatment to all system participants to the extent that they can deliver equal performance. Differences in quality, location, and timing must be recognized.

essential nutrients The nutrients which need to be consumed to support the necessary physiological functioning of the body, in particular to provide energy and to build or repair tissue and bone.

ethics The rules and standards of moral behavior that are generally accepted by society at one point of time.

ethnic diversity In food eating habits and preferences, the variations among individuals belonging to different races, as Celtic, Hispanic, Anglo-Saxon, Thai, Chinese, or Indian.

exchange The voluntary act of providing a person or organization something of value in order to acquire something else of value in return.

exchange functions Those functions which provide the utility added to a product by transferring title from seller to buyer. Along with the actual buying and selling of a product are other exchange activities, such as price determination and risk bearing.

exclusive distribution A supplier uses only one distributor.

experimental research The collection of primary data by organizing planned situations in which variables are set at different levels and measuring the outcomes, for example, setting different prices in supermarkets and measuring the sales.

extensive distribution A supplier uses many distributors.

external environment The macroenvironment of an organization (social, economic, and physical) together with the industry (competitors, suppliers, and buyers) in which the organization operates.

external factors influencing price Price is influenced externally by market characteristics, industry structure, competitors, legal issues, and product characteristics and positioning.

facilitating functions Those functions which make possible the smooth performance of the exchange and physical functions. Facilitating functions include standardization, grading, financing, market intelligence, communication, advertising, promotion, and public relations. Although not directly involved in the exchange of title or physical handling of food products, they are crucial to the operation of the food marketing system.

family brand A brand which covers all, or at least a significant number, of a company's products. Very often a form of the company name.

farm-gate demand   The schedule of quantities of farm output sold at various prices. This demand is derived from consumer demand less the margin for processing and distribution.

farm-retail spread (marketing margin)   The difference between farm price and consumer price. Despite its limitations, the marketing margin remains an enduring, though misunderstood and misused statistic.

fast-food   Any restaurant that emphasizes quick service and take-out. Chains and franchises dominate this segment. Fast-food has led the industry in annual sales growth over the past 20 years.

Five Forces Model   The attractiveness of an industry as an investment depends on: the bargaining power of buyers; the bargaining power of suppliers; barriers to entry of new firms; substitute products supplied by other industries; and competition within the industry.

fixed and variable costs   variable—costs that vary directly with the number of units produced/sold; fixed—costs that don't change the number of units sold. Also called "allocated" costs.

flighting advertising timing pattern   A variation in the pulsing advertising schedule, in which ads are massed in bursts with complete gaps between the bursts, during which no advertisements are run.

FOB (Free on Board)   Selling price includes any freight and handling to place product on board the freight carrier. The buyer pays freight charges plus all costs, including insurance.

focus groups   A primary research method in which small groups of people, led by trained moderators, discuss a defined aspect of a product being researched.

food availability   The degree of ease with which consumers can obtain food from their surroundings. Available food may be food grown locally, but in developed countries includes the foods available through retailers and can be from many regions.

food borne diseases   The diseases transmitted through foods to humans. These diseases can be from animals, or by microbiological contamination from soil, water, food handlers, equipment, other foods.

food buying decision process   The series of actions that a consumer goes through in buying and using a food product: preaction, search action, buying action, preparation action, eating action, and postaction.

food consumption   The food consumed daily by an individual or by a group, measured either in the quantities of the different food groups eaten or on a nutrient basis.

food contamination   Any foreign material that is absorbed by the food during production, processing, distribution, and food handling in the home. It includes chemical substances, such as pesticides and cleaning preparations, metals, stones, bandages, and biological materials including viruses and microorganisms causing food borne diseases.

food diversity   The variety of food products made available through the absorption of different ethnic foods into the mainstream food market.

food manufacturers   Companies that combine ingredients produced by food processors in value-added products for sale to consumers and for the food service industry.

food poisoning   Illness and possibly death caused by toxins in foods, usually from biological sources, but sometimes from chemicals.

food preservation   Processes used to extend the life of foods: temperature control (chilling and freezing), drying, heat processing (sterilization and pasteurization), chemical, and mechanical (packaging).

food quality   A food characteristic or attribute recognized by consumers as important, and the strengths of this characteristic in the food. Food qualities include sensory, safety, nutritional, physiological, physical, compositional, and shelf-life characteristics.

food regulations   The standards set by government for foods, including hygienic requirements of plant, equipment, and people, processing methods, compositions of foods, additives allowed, naming of foods, labeling of foods.

food safety   Methods used to control the different types of materials which can adversely affect people consuming the food. These materials can be broadly divided into biological and chemical, or natural and added.

food service   The provision to consumers of complete meals or ready-to-eat snacks and beverages, combining a product and an intangible service, the importance of each varying with the type of food service outlet; for example, service is very high with upscale restaurants, and low with fast food outlets. The industry is made up of a wide array of participants, including prisons, hospitals, child care/nursing home/elder care facilities, and airline caterers, as well as eating places.

food service distributors   Wholesaling operations that serve the food service industries, classified as one of four types: broad-line distributor, systems distributor, self-distributor, and specialty distributor.

food service distributors—broad-line   Distributors who sell a full line of food service products and nonfood items, such as kitchenware, paper products, chemicals, and equipment.

food service distributors—self   Distribution systems owned by the restaurant company and/or franchise they service. An example is PFS, who service their Pizza Hut and KFC (Kentucky Fried Chicken) units.

food service distributors—specialty   Smaller local distributors that either specialize in product line (examples: produce, beverages, meats) or serve the full range of product needs for particular types of customers, such as ethnic restaurants or concession stands at sports events.

food service distributors—systems   Distributors who service only large chain accounts and maintain minimal inventory relative to typical distribution facilities. Essentially delivery specialists, they contract to accept deliveries from various vendors and manufacturers with whom the chain restaurant has negotiated price agreements, such as the Martin Brower Company, which supplies McDonald's in some geographic areas.

food structures   The various combinations of oil/fat, proteins, carbohydrates, water, and air to provide the basic physical forms of foods, as oil and water emulsions, carbohydrate and protein networks, sugar crystal and glass structures, starch pastes, and gels.

food system   Beginning with raw materials (agricultural and marine products) and ending with the consumer—domestic and worldwide, this system includes all the participants directly involved: producers, manufacturers, resellers, retailers, food service operators, and consumers, as well as the input and facilitating industries and regulatory institutions.

food value-adding channel   The sequence of activities from the supply of raw materials, through processing and distribution, to purchase by the final consumer.

form utility   The functions by which agricultural products are changed from the form in which they originally grow, including grading and processing, into forms ready for consumption or further processing.

formula pricing   Basing the price for any given transaction on a mathematical formula that relates the transaction price to one or more other indicators of value.

freight absorption pricing   A manufacturer located further away from a buyer charges only the same freight as a buyer that is nearer.

frequency   The number of times an advertisement is delivered within a given period, usually figured on a weekly basis for schedule planning.

functional approach   Study of the food system in terms of the activities carried out: processing, transport, finance, etc.

futures contract   A legal agreement made on the trading floor of a futures exchange to make or take delivery of a commodity. Futures contracts are standardized by commodity as to the quality, quantity, delivery date, and location, leaving price as the only variable.

gap analysis   Identifying the "gap" between the initial objectives in a plan and the outcome of the initial strategies, for the purpose of revising the objectives and/or the strategies.

generic brand   Not bearing a brand name or mark. Labeled with product type, such as coffee, sugar, flour, or spaghetti. Packaging is plain to give a "no frills," low cost image. Generic brands are really retailers' brands.

go long   Buy a futures contract to establish a market position. A buyer is "long" until the market position is closed out through an offsetting sale. A long position obligates the holder to take delivery. Opposite of going short. It is, of course, also possible to be long in the cash commodity.

go short   Sell a futures contract to establish a market position. A seller is "short" until the market position is closed out through an offsetting purchase. A short position obligates the holder to make delivery. The opposite of going long.

government market   Purchasers of foods for government employees, such as the armed forces, or for government institutions such as schools, hospitals, and prisons.

grading   Sorting of a product into quality classifications according to standards that are agreed upon by the industry.

GRP (Gross Rating Points)   A measure of advertising intensity and advertising purchasing; one gross rating point is one percent of the universe of the market being measured: in TV, one percent of the households having TV sets in an area; for an outdoor sign, one percent of the number of people passing that sign in one day. Gross rating points represent the total of the schedule in that medium in that market per day, week, or month.

growth by acquisition   Expansion by purchasing an established business.

HACCP (Hazard Analysis Critical Control Points)   A preventive system to eliminate or minimize potential biological, chemical and physical hazards to the safety and quality of foods.

hedger   One who hedges. One who, in the normal course of business, either handles, processes, stores, or produces the physical commodity in which a futures market position is taken to limit risk due to adverse price changes.

hedging   The purchase or sale of a futures contract as a temporary substitute for a merchandising transaction to be made at a later date. Usually the process involves taking opposite positions in the cash market and the futures market at the same time.

hierarchy of objectives   In company and marketing plans, strategies at one level define objectives at the next.

horizontal alliance   An alliance, partnership, or network between businesses at the same stage of the food system.

horizontal channel relationships   Relationships between businesses at the same stage of the food system—for example, food processors or farmers.

identity preserved production   Food production where the output of an individual farm is uniquely identified through the food system.

implementation   The action phase of the planning process, involving carrying out the plan, monitoring the implementation process, and taking action to control the situation if the actual performance deviates too widely from the planned.

impulse food   A food bought when seen for sale, with no previous intention to buy it.

income elasticity   The percentage change in quantity demanded in response to a one percent increase in household income.

individual negotiation   Setting price and other terms of sale by discussion between two parties—a seller and a buyer. Generally there is no "up front" cost to the method—that is, there is no auction house or other intermediary to be paid—and it can be conducted by phone or other electronic means.

industrial buying process   The steps taken by food processing, food manufacturing, and food service companies when buying industrial food products, which vary according to the buying situation: straight rebuy, modified rebuy, new buy.

industrial food products   Partly processed raw materials that are used by food manufacturers and/or the food service industries in producing value-added products for consumers.

industrialization of the food system   Organizational changes to achieve closer linkages between agricultural producers, food manufacturers/processors, and distributors.

industry environment   For a manufacturer, the industry's suppliers, customers, and competitors.

industry structure   How an industry is organized in terms of: number and size distribution of suppliers; barriers to entry of new suppliers; product homogeneity/differentiation; collusion/cooperation in setting price and other terms of sale; and availability of competing products from related industries. Industry structure is the most important external variable influencing the price establishment process.

inelastic demand   The percentage change in quantity purchased in response to a one percent change in price or income is less than one percent.

inelastic supply   The percentage change in quantity supplied in response to a one percent change in price is less than one percent.

institutional approach   Study of the food system from the perspective of the different categories of businesses involved—brokers, agents, merchants, processors, retailers, etc.

instrument grading system   The use of a mechanical instrument to replace visual assessment, for example, ultrasound technology to evaluate the intramuscular fat percentage in beef carcasses. Instruments were introduced to reduce subjectivity and errors.

internal environment   The company's strengths and weaknesses in each of the functional business areas: finance, manufacturing, marketing, research and development, organization and administration, and human resource management.

internal factors influencing price   Price is influenced internally by costs, company objectives and marketing objectives, the marketing mix strategy, and coordination within the company.

international business organization   The strategic decisions on the configuration of business activities in different countries, how these activities are coordinated, and the extent to which they are vertically integrated across country boundaries.

interviewing   A primary research method in which consumers or industrial customers are asked questions about their knowledge, past behavior, attitudes, motives, preferences, and their predictions for their future behavior.

intrinsic value   End-use value of a product. A grading system can be judged on its measurement of intrinsic value—the real value of the commodity to the end user, whether consumer or industrial buyer, such as a food processor.

inverted market   A futures market in which the nearer months are selling at premiums to the more distant months.

ISO 1400   The international standard on environmental management set by the International Standards Organization, which includes environmental management systems, environmental auditing, environmental labeling, environmental performance assessment, life cycle assessment, and environmental terms and definitions.

ISO 9000   The international standards for quality management and quality assurance set by the International Standards Organization, including three standards: 9001 for design/development, production, installation and servicing, 9002 for production, installation and final product inspection, 9003 for final product inspection and testing.

kinked demand curve   The curve which occurs for an individual supplier in an oligopolistic market structure, because an increase in price above the prevailing industry price will cause an immediate reduction in sales.

knowledge   The range of information a person has gained by experience and education to give a theoretical and practical understanding of the subject.

law of demand   The economic principle stating that other things being equal, the quantity demanded falls as the price increases.

linkages   Connections between agricultural producers, processors, manufacturers, and distributors which require coordination and are achieved by a series of exchange transactions between individual companies or by sequential activities directed by one company.

localization   Adjusting a futures price to a local fixed or locked-in price. Components of the localization adjustment are: (1) forecast basis, (2) cost of hedging—interest on margin and futures commission, and (3) quality adjustment from futures contract deliverable quality to the quality that is expected to be marketed on the cash market.

long hedge   The purchase of a futures contract to offset the forward sale of an equivalent quantity of a commodity not yet owned. Used by processors or exporters as protection against an increase in the cash price.

luxury food   A food that is sold mainly on its prestige and identification with upper class consumption.

macroenvironment   The physical, demographic, economic, legal, social, and cultural environment in which a company operates.

malnutrition   An imbalance in the diet causing ill health because of not eating enough of all essential nutrients or eating too much of some nutrients, particularly high energy producing materials such as fats.

management by exception   A control system where management takes action when some measure of performance falls outside an established guideline.

manufacturing   The production of consumer foods, usually a mixing operation, sometimes combined with a heating operation to cook and/or preserve the product, and packaging and storage operations to give the necessary protection and storage life to the food product.

margin   The cash amount which must be deposited with a commodities broker for each futures contract held as a guarantee of fulfillment of the contract. It is not considered as part payment on purchase.

market   A group of consumers that has needs to satisfy, money to spend, and the authority and willingness to spend it.

market segment   A group of consumers or industrial customers with similar behavior and attitudes towards a product so that the same marketing mix can successfully be used for all the members of the group.

market segmentation   The process of dividing the total market into several, smaller, coherent groups; the members of each group have similar characteristics regarding a product(s), but each group has different needs, attitudes and behavior, from the other groups.

market segments: demographic   Groups within the total market based on sex, age, education, income, occupation, or other variables.

market segments: geographic   Groups within the total market based on geographic divisions, as country, region, city size, urban/rural, or climate.

market segments: psychographic   Groups within the total market based on life-style, behavior, personality, attitudes, or benefits sought.

market segments: sociocultural   Groups within the total market based on religion, ethnic group, nationality, social class, or household life cycle.

market segments: user behavior   Groups within the total market based on usage rates, brand loyalty status, purchase occasion, or reaction to new products.

marketing   The process of planning and executing the conception, pricing, promotion, and distribution of goods and services to create exchanges that satisfy individual and organizational objectives.

marketing audit   A review of the company's external environment and the company's marketing strengths and weaknesses.

marketing concept   The ideal of meeting customer needs and wants while maximizing the long-term profitability of the firm.

marketing ethics   The rules and standards of moral behavior as specified by professional marketing organizations, and which are generally accepted in society.

marketing intermediaries   People or organizations, generally classifed as wholesalers, retailers, or food service companies, that assist in the flow of products in a marketing channel.

marketing management approach   Study of the food system from the perspective of the system of business activities designed to plan, price, promote and distribute products to target markets in order to achieve the objectives of the firm or organization.

marketing margin   The difference between prices at various stages of the food system—for example, between retail and farm gate.

marketing mix   The combination of the four primary elements that comprise a company's marketing program—product, promotion, pricing, and distribution.

marketing objectives   Objectives for the marketing plan which derive from the corporate objectives and may include financial objectives, market share objectives by market segment or product, and distribution and promotion objectives.

marketing planning   Making the basic decisions regarding a company's product range and its customers, establishing objectives and creating a plan for achieving them, implementing the plan, and monitoring performance.

marketing research   The systematic gathering, recording and analysis of information for company use in developing marketing strategy and for monitoring marketing performance.

merchant wholesalers   See distributors.

micromarketing   The sorting of customers into one of perhaps as many as 200 groups based on products bought and lifestyle; chains provide this information to manufacturers, who can develop promotions, even pinpointing purchasers of competing brands.

mission statement   Two or three easily-understood sentences which seek to encapsulate a company's strategic plan. It comprises a broad statement of objectives, strategies, and the firm's sources of competitive advantage.

modified rebuy   An industrial buying situation in which the customer wants to modify product specifications, prices, terms, services or suppliers. It ranges from an examination of the alternative ingredients from a cost point of view to detailed testing of competing ingredients.

monitoring   Tracking actual performance versus planned.

monopolistic competition   An industry structure where there are a relatively large number of suppliers and some degree of product differentiation between suppliers.

monopoly   An industry structure where there is only one supplier and there are barriers to entry for new suppliers and products.

moral hazard   Condition which occurs when one party in a contract is able to take advantage of another.

motives   The internal factors that activate and direct an individual's behavior to achieve satisfaction or a goal.

national brand   The brand of a food manufacturer who distributes food products nationally through retailers.

needers   Individuals or firms that will need a commodity in the future but do not now have it in inventory; classified as long hedgers. Needers are concerned that commodity prices may increase before the date of planned purchase on the cash market. Examples of needers are coffee roasters, flour millers, poultry companies needing soybean meal and corn, and exporters.

needs   Differences between consumers' actual conditions and their desired condition.

new buy   An industrial buying situation in which the customer purchases a product or service for the first time. The new-buy process varies from a study of suppliers' reported qualities of alternative ingredients, laboratory analysis and testing of the ingredients, to full scale test production in the buyer's plant.

nutritional intake per capita   The quantity of calories, protein, fat, carbohydrates, vitamins, and minerals absorbed by an individual on a daily basis. Usually estimated as a mean nutritional intake per capita, by calculating for the total population the total intake of foods, converting to the nutrients and dividing these values by the number of people in the population.

nutritional value   The composition of a food, including the main nutrients—energy (calories), protein, fat, and carbohydrates, and also the minor constituents—vitamins and minerals.

nutritionally modified foods   Food products that have been changed from the standard product by removing or adding nutrients or by replacing the nutrients with non-nutrient substances, e.g., fat reduced milk, vitamin fortified cereals, sugar replaced by aspartame in soft drinks.

objective measures   Measures which do not depend on the grader's skill or on consistency from one grader to another for fair and even application of a grading process.

observation   Recording of consumer behavior by a trained observer or by video camera, or, in industrial marketing, the study of a customer's process.

oligopoly   An industry structure with a small number of suppliers who interact with and are responsive to the behavior of other suppliers.

open interest   Total number of futures contracts in a given commodity that have not yet been offset by an opposite futures transaction nor fulfilled by delivery of the commodity. For open interest, only one side of the open contract is counted, even though each transaction has a buyer and a seller.

open market control   Marketplace where the suppliers and buyers relate to each other on an "arms-length" basis (the opposite of administrative control).

opponent gain   The ability to benefit the other party in a negotiating situation.

opponent pain   The ability to hurt the other party in a negotiating situation.

organic food   Food that has been grown using natural organic matter such as manure, without chemical fertilizers or herbicides, and processed without the use of food additives.

organic growth   Growth in an established business (compared with growth by acquisition of established companies).

owners   Individuals or firms who will be marketing a commodity in the future and either have the commodity in storage or are in the process of producing it. Owners are concerned that commodity prices may decrease before the future date when they plan to sell the product on the cash market and protect themselves by using the short hedge. Examples of owners are farmers producing grains, feedlot operations with an inventory of cattle in the feedlot, or a country grain elevator with an inventory of grain.

package   Integral part of the consumer product, which protects, promotes and educates about the product, as well as complying with any government regulations.

penetration pricing   Pricing low at the introduction stage of the product life cycle to deter competition, build market share, and take advantage of the experience curve effect.

perfect competition   An industry structure where there are many suppliers acting independently of each other and no barriers to the entry of new suppliers.

personal selling   The direct, one-to-one communication of information to persuade a prospective customer to buy a good, service, idea, or other product.

physical functions   Those activities that involve handling, movement, and physical change of a food product. Examples are: manufacturing, processing, packaging, transportation, and storage.

place utility   The utility created when a product is made readily accessible to potential customers through transportation. Consumption does not usually occur at the point of production; agricultural products must be transported.

plain pack   See generic brand.

POP (Point-Of-Purchase)   Displays and materials for in-store use, offered to retailers as a form of trade promotion.

POS (Point-Of-Sale)   The electronic scanning technology used at the checkout stand to generate marketing information at the retail level utilized by retailers, distributors, and manufacturers for inventory management and in micromarketing.

position   An interest in the market, either long or short, in the form of open contracts.

position limits   The maximum position, net long or short, in one commodity future or in combined futures of one commodity which may be held open or controlled by one person or firm in its own name, as prescribed by the Commodity Futures Trading Commission. Does not apply to bona fide hedgers.

possession utility   The utility created when a product is priced and ownership transferred as part of the marketing transaction. Exchange is a fundamental component of any marketing transaction. It involves establishing the price and transferring ownership from seller to buyer.

posttest   Evaluation of the effectiveness of an advertising campaign through tracking studies that are compared to pre-campaign or benchmark surveys. Items measured include advertisement recognition and recall and market share.

power   The ability to influence (or to resist being influenced by) another individual or company.

predatory goods   Goods for which brand advertising shifts market share but does not increase total consumption.

predatory pricing   Selling at or below cost for a prolonged period with the objective of driving a competitor from the market.

premium   (1) An item, other than the product itself, given to purchasers of a product as an inducement to buy. Can be free with a purchase (on the package, in the package, or the container itself) or available upon proof of purchase and a payment (self-liquidating premium).

(2) The amount by which one futures contract price exceeds another. Also, the difference between one spot commodity price and that of another grade of the same commodity or that of another spot commodity.

pretest Testing of advertisements before they are placed in the media to improve the chances that finished ads will work as planned. Both rough executions of the ad and finished ads are tested.

price One of the four elements of the marketing mix, ideally established at the intersection of the supply and demand curves.

price discrimination Selling the same basic product in different markets at different prices, with price differences that are greater than the cost of servicing the market.

price elasticity The proportional change in quantity sold for a specified proportional change in price.

$$PED = \frac{\Delta Q/Q}{\Delta P/P} \text{ (usually expressed as a percentage)}$$

price flexibility The percentage change in the price received in response to a one percent increase in the quantity supplied.

price off Manufacturer initiated promotion where the container is marked "_____ cents off" the regular price.

price sensitivity Equivalent to price elasticity of demand, it is influenced by: the availability of substitutes, the product's share of the household's or firm's budget, the ability to "hand on" price increases, switching costs, and the costs of "shopping around."

price stability A possible goal of a pricing system. If price stability is a prime goal, then government involvement is often invoked.

pricing efficiency Sufficient competition at all levels in the food system to ensure that technical efficiency is translated into value for consumers, rather than into monopoly profits.

primary demand Consumer demand for food products at retail.

primary processing The initial processing of raw materials from land or sea. The plant, animal, or fish is killed, cleaned, and sometimes separated. The materials from primary processing are usually graded.

primary research The gathering of new data for a project, for example by interviewing consumers about their attitudes in a consumer survey, recording consumers' behavior in observation research, or organizing tests of brand recall from different commercials in experimental research.

private brand A brand owned by a reseller, usually a retailer or wholesaler, but can be an industrial products distributor. Also referred to as distributor's label, dealer brand, house brand, or own-label brand.

product audit A detailed study of the products in a product mix to analyze their performance in quantitative and qualitative terms.

product benefits The product characteristics identified by consumers as important to them in buying and using the product.

product category A group of products carrying a commonly understood descriptive name, such as apples, frozen vegetables, fruit juices.

product characteristics Also known as product attributes. The specific qualities of a product, which can be divided into product, package and service.

product concept Detailed description of a product, with consumers identifying product characteristics and product benefits and marketers defining the target market segments and product position.

product design The arrangement of the tangible and intangible elements in a product to give the desired product. The stage in the product development process at which the technologist designs and makes the product, then tests it against the standards defined in the previous stages of product development.

product design specifications A set of technical specifications for a functional product with reference to the aspects of product design, processing, distribution, and consumer needs. It is developed from the product concept and the technical product qualities.

product elimination The decisions involved in the process of dropping a poorly performing product from the product mix.

product launch Full-scale marketing of a new product after the successful development of the product, production, and marketing strategy.

product life cycle The course of a product's sales and profits during its lifetime, through Introduction, Growth, Maturity, and Decline. This can be for the generic product category or for the single branded product.

product line A group of products that are closely related, either used for similar purposes or possessing similar characteristics.

product manager The person responsible for planning new products and managing established products for a specific group of products, such as canned soups and vegetables, or for a specific brand. Sometimes called a brand manager.

product mix The set of all products that a company offers for sale. It can be described by its width—number of product lines, and depth—number of types, flavors, or sizes within each product line.

product morphology The breakdown of a product into the specific product characteristics that identify a product to consumers.

product positioning Through the marketing mix, placing or positioning a product in the most ideal location relative to competing products, and in one of the limited number of positions or locations in the consumer's mind.

product reliability The ability of an industrial ingredient to behave consistently over time in the buyer's process and to produce a consistent quality in the food product.

product/market matrix A matrix defining four alternatives for growth: same product mix/same market, same product mix/new market, new product mix/same market, or new product mix/new market.

profit time horizon Time period over which profit is to be maximized, which influences pricing because of market share and experience curve effects.

project aim The goal for a product development or marketing development project, which sets the project's direction. A clear definition of the aim lessens confusion and difficulties during the project.

project constraints Factors which limit the area of the project, arising from various elements: product, processing, marketing, financial, company, or environmental.

prototypes Sample products created during the design/development stage.

public relations Building good relations with the company's various publics by obtaining favorable publicity, building up a good "corporate image," and handling or heading off unfavorable rumors, stories, and events.

pull strategy A manufacturer's promotional effort directed primarily at end users so they will ask middlemen (wholesalers and retailers) for the product.

pulsing advertising timing pattern   Advertising schedule which allows threshold frequency levels to be reached by overlaying bursts of advertising in a few markets at a time, while maintaining a reduced schedule of advertising in the market at all times.

push strategy   A manufacturer's promotional effort directed primarily at middlemen who are the next link forward in the distribution channel.

quality   An attribute of a commodity that influences its acceptability to a group of buyers, and, therefore, the price they are willing to pay for it; does not mean whether something is good, better, or best, but rather is synonymous with "characteristic."

quality assurance   The management procedures and techniques used to ensure the quality of the final product.

quota sampling   A method of selecting a sample of individuals or companies for research, in which the selection is free as long as the numbers (quota) required in each specified category are fulfilled.

random sampling   A method of selecting individuals or companies for research, in which every member of the population has an equal chance of being included. This sample selection method allows statistically sound inferences about a population to be made from the sample.

reach   The total number of people to whom an advertising message is delivered.

reciprocity   Responding to either positive or negative behavior by another party in a relationship.

Recommended Dietary Allowance (RDA)   Recommended nutritional intake of the basic nutritional components of foods: calories, protein, fats, carbohydrates, and the minor components—vitamins and minerals.

relationship-specific assets   Assets directly employed in a contractual situation that have limited alternative uses.

repacker market   Companies or individuals in industrial marketing who "sell on" the product to other companies; that is, they acquire food products for the purpose of selling them with minimum change; they may mix or repack the ingredients.

resource dependency   Condition of dependence on a supplier with monopoly power for raw materials.

retail audits   Regular, systematic recording of sales in retail outlets.

retail distributors   The warehouses and systems used to distribute the assortment of products provided by manufacturers to retailers.

retail distributors: chain-store integrated   Large chains, such as Kroger (US), Sainsbury (UK), and Woolworth's (Australia), which operate their own distribution centers and buy direct from grocery manufacturers. See Distributors.

retail distributors: cooperative   Distribution companies owned by their patrons (retailers); at the end of their financial year any profits (called patronage refunds in a cooperative) are returned to the retailers, based on their patronage in dollars. In Europe, most of the major retailers belong to wholesaling cooperatives.

retail distributors-independent   If a distributor is not organized as a chain-store integrated, cooperative, or voluntary distributor, it operates as an independent.

retail distributors-voluntary   A distributor who has developed alliances with independently owned retail stores. The retail store carries the logo (brand) of the voluntary distributor, such as I.G.A. or Supervalu.

retail price maintenance   The practice by which manufacturers dictate, or attempt to dictate, the retail selling price, illegal in most countries.

risk management   Understanding the various risks that a firm is exposed to, such as physical, financial, and price risks. Also, developing strategies such as hedging, cash forward contracts, insurance, and diversification to appropriately manage the particular risk exposure.

Rochdale Principles   Eight principles for the organization of a cooperative.

roundturn   Procedure by which a commodity trader's long or short position is offset by an opposite transaction or by accepting or making delivery of the actual commodity.

sales promotion   Technique used to stimulate product demand, including a wide range of activities, such as free samples, coupons, celebrity appearances, and contests.

sampling   The method of introducing and promoting merchandise by distributing a miniature or full-size trial package of the product free or at a reduced price.

SBU (Strategic Business Unit)   A grouping of closely related business activities (such as a division) within a company. A smaller company may comprise only one SBU.

secondary processing   The processing of a crude raw material into a specific industrial product, to be marketed to another food processor or more likely to a food manufacturer. Primary and secondary processing may occur in the same plant; for example, starch is separated and its purified form is treated to give it specific properties.

secondary research   The searching of data and information that already exists, having been collected for another purpose. For example, data on a country or district's quantitative consumption by food groups may be gathered from appropriate government reports and trade statistics.

self-administered questionnaires   Respondents record their own replies to questions on an interview form.

sell on description   To market commodities based on their grades and prices. Buyers can compare grades and prices at several different locations and do not have to personally inspect each lot to determine its worth or value.

sensory properties   The physical and chemical properties which have an effect on consumers' senses: taste, smell, sight, feel, and hearing. Classified as appearance, aroma, flavor, and texture.

services   Activities that a company offers to another company or a consumer that are intangible and do not result in ownership. They can be marketed with a product, such as delivery times and technical information, or offered separately, such as market research.

shelf life   The time that a food will remain at an acceptable quality to the consumer under specified conditions.

shipping records   The company's data on the types and quantities of a company's products that leaves its warehouses. They show what leaves the company but not necessarily what consumers buy.

short hedge   The sale of futures contracts approximately equal to the amount of a commodity currently owned to reduce the risk of loss due to possible decline in its value.

situation analysis   A detailed study of the company's internal environment (strengths and weaknesses) and external environment (opportunities and threats).

skimming-the-cream pricing   Selling at a high price because of lack of competition at the introduction stage of the product life cycle.

social classes   Ranking sub-divisions in a society based on family birth status, economic status, occupation, or education.

sourcing   Obtaining raw material and ingredients of sufficient volume and quality for food service operations by contracting with growers and, in some cases, operating self-owned processing plants.

specialized commodity products   Industrial ingredients with certain specifications that could fit the needs of food processors and manufacturers, but are not designed for specific buyers, as a whole milk powder produced to the supplier's specifications which are thought to be some buyers' specifications. Fresh products produced to supplier's specifications may also be marketed as specialized commodity products to supermarkets.

specialty ingredients   Ingredients with specific qualities to aid the processor and ensure the final product characteristics, used in small quantities, as colors, flavors, or emulsifiers.

speculators   Commodities traders who attempt to anticipate price changes and through market activities to make profits; they are not using the futures market in connection with the production, processing, marketing or handling of a product.

stakeholders   Everyone who has an interest in the company, including shareholders, staff, customers, and suppliers.

staple food   A basic food, mainly providing energy, which is eaten regularly, usually daily, as bread or rice.

statutory marketing boards   Organizations that are given statutory authority through industry-specific legislation. Examples are the Australian Wheat Board and federal and state marketing orders in the United States.

SKU (Stock Keeping Unit)   An identifiable inventory item (with a Universal Product Code number). Today supermarkets carry 20,000 or more SKUs in their product assortment of food and nonfood items.

straight rebuy   The buying action of a food processor, food manufacturer or retailer, in which the buyer routinely reorders without seeking any further information or alternative suppliers.

strategic marketing plan   A plan which includes a situation analysis, marketing objectives (developed to be in line with corporate objectives), and marketing strategies.

strategies   Broad approaches to achieving corporate objectives.

supermarket   As defined by the industry, a store with at least $2 million in annual sales.

suppliers   Individuals or companies supplying food ingredients and services that food processor and food manufacturers need to produce their food products. They have the following characteristics identified by the buyers: efficiency in fulfilling orders, technical knowledge, conservative/innovative, sales staff training, financial backing, physical distribution system, quality assurance accreditation.

supply curve   Schedule of the quantity supplied at different prices.

supply curve shifters   Factors affecting the supply curve, including input prices, prices of alternative products that may be produced, technological change, weather, disease, etc.

survival pricing   Pricing below cost to reduce stocks and generate immediate cash.

switching costs   The cost of changing from a current activity.

SWOT (Strengths, Weaknesses, Opportunities, Threats)   Internal analysis (strengths and weaknesses) and external analysis (opportunities and threats) of a company's situation.

tangible product   A food product of specific composition, microbiological levels, physical properties, and sensory properties.

target market   A group of potential customers (people or organizations) the marketer thinks are most likely to want a company's product and at whom the seller directs the marketing program.

tastes and preferences   All factors other than price and income that influence the demand for a product.

technical (operational) efficiency   The ratio of output to input; for example, retailing dollar sales per square foot, or, in manufacturing, quantity produced per man hour. Measures of technical efficiency can determine whether operating costs meet world "best practice" norms.

technological change   Improvements in methods that allow the production of more output from the same input mix, that is, greater efficiency.

technology   The total system used to produce and market goods and services. It includes technological knowledge, techniques and implementation methods and can be divided into different types according to products, as baking technology or fresh vegetable production, or according to the stage in the food system, as production technology, processing technology.

throughput   The tons, pounds, or kilograms of a material processed in a given time period by a company's plant and equipment. Economies of scale exist in food processing: production costs are reduced at high levels of output. The aim is to spread the fixed costs of plant and equipment over as much throughput as possible.

time utility   The utility created when a product is made available to customers when they want it. Storage, one function that provides time utility, is required to act as a buffer between day-to-day variations in supply and demand and to facilitate production scheduling.

total product   The total product marketed consists of the tangible food product, the packaging, and the intangible services.

TQM (Total Quality Management)   A method of organizing a company with specific procedures, policies, and practices that commit it to continuous quality improvement in all its activities.

trade discounts   Frequently used by manufacturers to encourage retailers to stock the product and, in many cases, to provide a special display space or favorable shelf space. Includes price discounts and "case free" offers, such as one case free with every ten purchased.

trade mark   A brand or part of a brand given legal protection of the seller's exclusive rights to use that brand name and/or brand mark.

trade promotion   Promotion by manufacturers to distributors and retailers, known as "push" marketing. Includes cooperative advertising programs where manufacturers contribute to the advertising of their products in the retailers' weekly advertisements, price discounts, and other incentives to encourage retailer support for their product.

transaction costs   In agricultural commodity marketing, the cost of searching for alternatives, costs added because of the uncertainty of exchange, and costs associated with the physical exchange.

transportation costs   All of the costs involved in moving a product from point of production to consumer. The costs include actual transport charges—truck, rail, or air, as well as the expenses of arranging and monitoring transportation activities and the cost of losses that occur during transport.

trust   Attitude developed in a relationship where parties are confident that they can predict the behavior of other parties and that the other parties will not knowingly engage in activities that are damaging to them.

type of customer and product approach   The study of marketing by type of customer—for example, a food manufacturer seeking ingredients; or by the type of product—for example, commodities, the marketing of which centers on the issues of price risk management, grades and grading systems, and pricing systems.

undifferentiated strategy   A market strategy in which a single product is aimed at the total market, assuming that individuals are the same with respect to the product.

uniform pricing   Selling at the same price in different locations irrespective of transport costs.

user market   Companies that buy a product to use in the production of their own products, including food processors, food manufacturers, food services, supermarkets, and small retailers such as butchers.

vertical channel relationships   Links between raw material suppliers, processors, and distributors at various stages of the food system.

vertical integration   The control of two or more sequential activities (production and/or marketing) in the food system by one firm.

volume   The number of purchases or sales of a commodity futures contract made during a specific period of time.

VPM (Variable Price Merchandising)   Using "specials" and other promotions to encourage store traffic and to maximize profit on the non specialed items.

wants   The particular choices (including the type of product and the specific brands) that people make to satisfy their needs.

wheel of retailing   Concept that explains the changes in retail strategies and formats over time. Change in retailing is often sparked by a new low-cost, low-price store entering the market; consumers then perceive the existing "low-cost" store as not low-cost, which gives the new low-cost retailer a chance.

wholesale club store   Retailer/wholesalers which have limited assortments of 3,500-4,000 items but up to five times the square footage of a conventional supermarket; for example, Price Costco, Sam's, or Pace.

wholesalers   In the channel of distribution, the firms which move food products between producers, manufacturers, and the final resellers—food retailers and food service companies. Wholesalers are of three types: merchant wholesalers, who take ownership, have inventories, and build assortments, brokers and agents, who do not take ownership or have a risk position, and assemblers, who deal with commodity products.

zero sum game   Losses of the losing group (or individual) in a negotiating situation equal the gains of the winning group (or individual). A zero-sum game offers no possibility of mutual benefit through cooperation.

zone pricing   Every buyer in a specific zone pays the same price.

INDEX

Pillsbury